THE MINOR
PROPHETS

Volume One

THE MINOR PROPHETS

A Commentary on Hosea, Joel, Amos

Edited by

THOMAS EDWARD MCCOMISKEY

B
Baker Academic
a division of Baker Publishing Group
Grand Rapids, Michigan

© 1992 by Thomas E. McComiskey

Published by Baker Academic
a division of Baker Publishing Group
PO Box 6287, Grand Rapids, MI 49516-6287
www.bakeracademic.com

Paperback edition published 2018
ISBN 978-1-5409-6085-6

Printed in the United States of America

The Library of Congress has cataloged the hardcover edition as follows:
The Minor Prophets: an exegetical and expository commentary / edited by Thomas Edward McComiskey.
    p. cm.
    Includes bibliographical references and index.
    Contents: v.1. Hosea, Joel, and Amos
    ISBN 978-0-8010-6285-8 (v.1)
    1. Bible. O.T. Minor Prophets—Commentaries. I. McComiskey, Thomas Edward. II. Bible.
O.T. Minor Prophets. English. New Revised Standard. 1992.
BS1560.M47 1992
224′.907—dc20   91-38388

In keeping with biblical principles of creation stewardship, Baker Publishing Group advocates the responsible use of our natural resources. As a member of the Green Press Initiative, our company uses recycled paper when possible. The text paper of this book is composed in part of post-consumer waste.

green press INITIATIVE

Contents

Abbreviations

Bibliographical

ANEP James B. Pritchard, ed. *The Ancient Near East in Pictures Relating to the Old Testament.* 2d ed. Princeton: Princeton University Press, 1969.

ANET James B. Pritchard, ed. *Ancient Near Eastern Texts Relating to the Old Testament.* 3d ed. Princeton: Princeton University Press, 1969.

BDB Francis Brown, Samuel R. Driver, and Charles A. Briggs. *A Hebrew and English Lexicon of the Old Testament.* Oxford: Clarendon, 1907; corrected printing in 1953.

BHK Rudolf Kittel, ed. *Biblia Hebraica.* 3d ed. Stuttgart: Württembergische Bibelanstalt, 1937.

BHS Karl Elliger and Wilhelm Rudolph, eds. *Biblia Hebraica Stuttgartensia.* Stuttgart: Deutsche Bibelgesellschaft, 1977.

CAD *The Assyrian Dictionary.* Chicago: Oriental Institute, University of Chicago, 1956–.

GKC Emil Kautzsch, ed. *Gesenius' Hebrew Grammar.* Trans. A. E. Cowley. 2d ed. Oxford: Clarendon, 1910.

HALAT Walter Baumgartner, et al. *Hebräisches und aramäisches Lexikon zum Alten Testament.* 3d ed. Leiden: Brill, 1967–.

Joüon Paul Joüon. *Grammaire de l'Hébreu Biblique.* 2d ed. Rome: Pontifical Biblical Institute Press, 1923.

Bible Versions

AV Authorized (King James) Version
JB Jerusalem Bible
NIV New International Version
NJB New Jerusalem Bible
NRSV New Revised Standard Version
RSV Revised Standard Version

General

LXX Septuagint
MT Masoretic Text
NT New Testament
OT Old Testament
par. parallel to

Hebrew Transliteration Scheme

Consonants			Vowels		
א	’		בָ	ā	*qāmeṣ*
ב	b		בַ	a	*pataḥ*
ג	g		בֶ	e	*sĕgôl*
ד	d		בֵ	ē	*ṣērê*
ה	h		בִ	i	short *ḥîreq*
ו	w		בִ	ī	long *ḥîreq* written defectively
ז	z		בָ	o	*qāmeṣ ḥāṭûp*
ח	ḥ		בוֹ	ô	*hôlem* written fully
ט	ṭ		בֹ	ō	*hôlem* written defectively
י	y		בוּ	û	*šûreq*
כ ך	k		בֻ	u	short *quibbûṣ*
ל	l		בֻ	ū	long *quibbûṣ* written defectively
מ ם	m		הַ	a	furtive *pataḥ*
נ ן	n		בָה	â	final *qāmeṣ hē’*
ס	s		בֶי	ê	*sĕgôl yôd* (בֶי = êy)
ע	‘		בֵי	ê	*ṣērê yôd* (בֵי = êy)
פ ף	p		בִי	î	*ḥîreq yôd* (בִי = îy)
צ ץ	ṣ		בָיו	āyw	
ק	q		בֲ	ă	*ḥāṭēp pataḥ*
ר	r		בֱ	ĕ	*ḥāṭēp sĕgôl*
שׂ	ś		בֳ	ŏ	*ḥāṭēp qāmeṣ*
שׁ	š		בְ	ĕ	vocal *šĕwā’*
ת	t		בְ	–	silent *šĕwā’*

Introduction

The corpus of biblical books we call the Minor Prophets has not enjoyed great prominence in the history of biblical interpretation. It is not difficult to understand why this is so. Where is the edification for a modern Christian in a dirge celebrating the downfall of an ancient city? How can the gloomy forecasts of captivity for Israel and Judah lift the heart today? The Minor Prophets seem to have been preoccupied with nations and events that have little relevance to today's world. How unlike the New Testament they are!

A careful study of these prophets, however, reveals that many of the themes they expound transit the Testaments. They speak of the love of God as well as his justice. Their prophecies are not all doom, but are often rich with hope. Hosea based his hope on God's compassion, while Joel envisioned a new era for the people of God. Amos spoke of the restoration of David's collapsing monarchy, and Micah foresaw the coming Ruler whose birthplace would be the insignificant town of Bethlehem. The fact that these prophets often expressed themselves in culturally and historically conditioned forms that seem foreign to us should not diminish the force of their messages. This fact should challenge us to discover how the prophets faced the foreboding circumstances of their times, and how their words illumined the dark night of human rebellion and divine justice. Anyone who turns from reading the Minor Prophets hearing only words of recrimination and judgment has not read them fairly. Within the dismal events these prophets describe lurks the hand of God, and beyond these events is the bright prospect of a kingdom inaugurated by One whom Zechariah portrays as suffering betrayal, piercing, and eventual death. The Minor Prophets are not as time-bound as we may think.

The purpose of this commentary is to clarify the messages of these spokesmen for God by bringing the reader into the structures of language in which these messages found expression. While readers who do not know Hebrew may find the Exegesis section imposing, the authors have translated the constructions so that these readers may comprehend the discussion and have access to the Hebrew text. The readers may thus observe more deeply how the author has grappled with the problems of the text. Readers of English commentaries do not always have access to this level of interpretation.

The translations in parentheses following each Hebrew construction are keyed to the Author's Translation. This translation, which appears in the left column of each translation page, is a literal rendition of the section that follows. The column on the right contains the translation of the New Revised Standard Version. The reader thus has at hand two perspectives on the sense of the text.

The Exposition section is designed to amplify the conclusions reached in the Exegesis section. The authors frequently discuss related theological and hermeneutical issues in the Exposition. The Hebrew appears in transliteration here. This alerts the reader who knows Hebrew to the constructions the author discusses without encumbering the reader who does not know Hebrew with unfamiliar Hebrew characters. It also aids the reader by facilitating pronunciation of the Hebrew constructions. The preacher will find in this section observations on the text that will stimulate ideas for using the Minor Prophets in contemporary preaching.

The Hebrew scholar, as well as the student of Hebrew, will appreciate the depth of interaction with the Hebrew text that characterizes the Exegesis section. The authors have made every effort to utilize the highest standards of scholarly exegesis, and to interact with the current literature throughout their commentaries. The helpful introductions to the commentaries cover issues that touch on various aspects of the prophecy on which each author has written.

The editor and authors present this work to the world of biblical scholarship with the hope that it will contribute to a deeper understanding of the messages of the Minor Prophets and their relevance for us today. If this commentary causes the voices of these ancient men of God to ring with greater clarity in a world that sorely needs spiritual and moral strength, the effort will have been worthwhile.

I wish to express my appreciation to the authors for their scholarly contributions, their cooperation, and patience throughout the years in which this work has been in preparation. I owe a debt of gratitude to Allan Fisher of Baker Book House for his encouragement.

Thomas Edward McComiskey
Hawthorn Woods, Illinois
1991

Hosea

Introduction

Historical Background

Hosea was an Israelite prophet of the eighth century B.C. This fact is established by the content of the prophecy, which is consonant with the historical and societal conditions of that period, and the superscription of the book (1:1).

The span of Israelite history delineated by the superscription includes the reigns of several kings of Judah. Uzziah (Azariah), the first king cited, reigned from 792/91 to 740/39, and Hezekiah, the last Judahite king to which the superscription refers, reigned from 716/15 to 687/86. Jeroboam II, the only Israelite king mentioned in the superscription (see the Exposition at 1:1), reigned from 793/92 to 753.

This extensive period witnessed several outstanding national achievements. Uzziah formed a massive standing army and spread the influence of Judah well beyond its borders (2 Chron. 26:1–15); Jotham (750–732/31) founded a number of towns (2 Chron. 27:1–9). And most remarkable of all was the religious reformation fostered by Hezekiah (2 Chron. 29:1–31:21). In the northern kingdom, Jeroboam II greatly expanded the territorial holdings of Israel (2 Kings 14:25, 28).

Yet there were dark, foreboding undercurrents. Uzziah angrily usurped the priestly function, and the light from the burning incense revealed the leprosy that marked God's displeasure (2 Chron. 26:16–21). During his regency, pagan high places continued to attract worshipers (2 Kings 15:4). The reign of Jotham witnessed the continuation of popular non-Yahwistic practices (2 Kings 15:35; 2 Chron. 27:2). In the time of Ahaz (735–716/15) the king himself encouraged the worship of Baal (2 Chron. 28:2–4), and the nation was threatened by both the Syrians and the

To my son Bruce for his devotion to scholarship, his strength of character, and his companionship through the years

Contributor:
† Thomas Edward McComiskey

Israelites. The revival under Hezekiah came at a propitious time, but it served only to slow the progress of Judah toward certain ruin. The propensity of the people to worship at pagan sanctuaries and the social decay that resulted from their departure from the Yahwistic tradition of humanitarian concern and social justice were like a dark specter lurking behind the changing national scene. This propensity was ultimately to destroy the kingdom of Judah as it had the northern kingdom. The policies of Jeroboam II in the north threatened his nation, for he followed the corrupt pattern begun by his earlier namesake, Jeroboam I (2 Kings 14:24).

At the death of Jeroboam II the northern kingdom entered a period of decline from which it would not recover. Jeroboam's successor, Zechariah, had reigned only six months (753/52) when he was assassinated by Shallum who acceded to the throne. Zechariah was the last king of Jehu's dynasty (2 Kings 14:29; 15:11). Shallum held the throne of Israel for only one month before he was assassinated by Menahem (2 Kings 15:14). Menahem reigned from 752/51 to 742/41, and was succeeded by Pekahiah who reigned from 742/41 to 740/39. Pekahiah was killed in a military coup by Pekah, one of his officers. Pekah took the throne of Israel and reigned until 732/31. The apparently stable reign of Pekah came to an abrupt end when he was assassinated by Hoshea (732–722), who virtually became a vassal of Assyria. When Tiglath-pileser III, the king of Assyria, died, he was succeeded by Shalmaneser V, and Hoshea apparently regarded this transition as an opportunity to strike for independence. He boldly withheld tribute from Assyria and attempted to establish a political alliance with Egypt (2 Kings 17:4). These courageous efforts ended in failure, however, for the Assyrians met his rebellion with decisive military action. They invaded Israel, and laid siege to the capital city of Samaria for three years. The citizens of Samaria ended their brave struggle by capitulating to the superior Assyrian forces, and Hoshea was imprisoned. Such was the ignominious end of the once proud kingdom.

As Hosea observed the troubled times in which he lived, he saw much that was disconcerting to him. He warned against the international alliances the political leaders of Israel were forging to rescue their faltering nation; he makes particular reference to the overtures made to Assyria and Egypt (Hos. 7:11).

Menahem made one of the most important efforts to curry favor with Assyria when he attempted to shore up his sagging political fortunes by forging an alliance with Tiglath-pileser as he was advancing westward. In this alliance Menahem agreed to pay heavy tribute to Assyria (2 Kings 15:19). Pekah made an alliance with Syria in an attempt to resist Assyrian efforts to advance their hegemony into Syro-Palestine (2 Kings 15:37). Hoshea's efforts to save his dying kingdom by seeking help from

Egypt actually cost Israel its national life (2 Kings 17:4), for Egypt was divided internally and could offer little help.

Israel's defection from Yahweh was not only evident to Hosea in these political intrigues, but he also saw the disregard the people had for their ancient spiritual heritage.

The ancestors of the hapless citizens of the northern kingdom had exulted in a covenant that promised national life and individual fulfilment, but that promise was for those who were faithful to the covenant's stipulations. The northern kingdom was separated from its ancient heritage by geographical boundaries and national biases, and the covenant was but a dim memory. Blindly the people removed themselves from their God to worship gods who were but an ephemeral projection of their own hopes and lusts. According to Hosea it was this syncretistic worship that, more than anything else, cost the people of Israel their national integrity.

This violation of the stipulations of the covenant was reflected in the social sphere. The burgeoning economies of the two kingdoms produced a rift between rich and poor, as an oppressing upper class brought misery to the less fortunate.

All of this, covenant violation and dependence on other national powers, demonstrated a lack of faithfulness to their God. No wonder Hosea called it fornication; no wonder his unhappy marriage is the theme of his prophecy.

Date

According to the superscription, Hosea's prophetic activity began sometime during the reigns of Uzziah, king of Judah, and Jeroboam II, king of Israel. Since Jeroboam died in 753 B.C. we may place the commencement of Hosea's ministry sometime before this. He continued to function as a prophet into the reign of Hezekiah. Thus, a date sometime after Hezekiah's accession to the throne of Judah in 716/15 B.C. rounds out the general limitations of Hosea's ministry to Israel.

Author

Hosea was a prophet to both the northern and southern kingdoms, in that he addressed both kingdoms in his prophecy. However, he directed his strongest and most urgent words to the people of Israel, the northern kingdom. The fact that Hosea's castigations of Judah are sometimes tempered with benign statements (1:7; 4:15) may reflect his optimism at the positive spiritual influences he saw from time to time in Judah. The greatest of these were the sweeping religious reforms instituted by King Hezekiah.

Little is known of Hosea, and still less of his father Beeri, but it is obvious from the book that Hosea was a man of deep moral conviction. He was a devoted Yahwist who lived in a time of national defection from the principles and institutions of Yahwism. His dedication to God was so great that he could follow God's leading even to the extent of entering a marriage that meant deep personal sacrifice and bitter sorrow.

Text

The text of Hosea is one of the most difficult in the prophetic corpus. Commentators frequently attempt to resolve the textual difficulties in this book by extensive emendation or by redactionist methodologies. These methods frequently lead only to conjecture, however, because they lack objective controls. To be sure, the Masoretic tradition (MT) is not sacred, and the consonantal text has not come through the centuries unscathed, but we may wonder if the degree to which some scholars alter the text is not extreme.

Absolute objectivity in the interpretation of literature is, of course, beyond our reach, but we must nonetheless strive for it. The objectivity we seek in Old Testament studies lies in the symbols and structures of the Hebrew language. That which strikes us as broken or awkward may have been quite acceptable to the original reader. If we do not entirely understand the language in which an ancient writer's thoughts found shape, we have no right to resort uncritically to emendation. We are obliged first to attempt to understand his language better, or to try to comprehend the author's peculiar dialect or style of expression. Failing in this, we may have to reconstruct the text.

Our study of the text of Hosea has led us to conclude that the *Vorlage* of the Septuagint is essentially that of the Masoretic Text. It becomes apparent to the reader of both traditions that the translators of the Greek version struggled with the same problems in the text of Hosea with which we moderns struggle.

The textual problems are discussed in the body of this work. The major ones occur at 1:6, 7; 2:3 [2:1]; 4:11, 16; 5:8, 11, 13; 6:5, 7; 7:4, 12; 8:13; 9:1, 13; 10:5, 10; 12:1 [11:12]; 13:2; 14:3.

Analysis

Superscription (1:1)
I. Hosea's Marriage and the Birth of His Children (1:2–2:2) [1:2–11]
  A. The Command to Marry (1:2)
  B. The Birth of Jezreel (1:3–5)
  C. The Birth of Not Pitied (1:6–7)
  D. The Birth of Not My People (1:8–9)

  E. A Statement of Hope Based on the Reversal of the Meanings of the Children's Names (2:1–2) [1:10–11]
II. The Significance of Hosea's Marriage for the Nation (2:3–25) [2:1–23]
  A. A Command to Hosea's Children to Plead with the Nation That It Give Up Its Idolatry (2:3–8) [1–6]

E. Israel's Unrestrained Disobedience to Yahweh (10:11–12)

F. Israel's Internal Corruption Will Lead to the Fall of the Monarchy (10:13–15)

XIV. **Yahweh's Love for Israel (11:1–11)**

A. Yahweh Loved Israel at the Exodus, but Israel Rebelled Against Him (11:1–4)

B. Because of Israel's Rebellion She Shall Go into Captivity (11:5–7)

C. Yahweh's Love for Israel Will Not Allow for the Absolute Destruction of the Nation (11:8–9)

D. Yahweh Will Call His People from Captivity (11:10–11)

XV. **An Oracle Against the Kingdoms of Judah and Israel (12:1–15) [11:12–12:14]**

A. Ephraim Practices Treachery but Judah Still Enjoys Fellowship with God (12:1–2) [11:12–12:1]

B. Yahweh Has a Controversy with Judah (12:3–7) [2–6]

C. Israel Is Like a Dishonest Merchant (12:8–11) [7–10]

D. Israel Is Guilty Because of Her Violation of Covenant Standards (12:12–15) [11–14]

XVI. **Hope for Ungrateful Israel (13:1–14:1) [13:1–16]**

A. Israel's Devotion to Baal Worship Will Bring Her to an End (13:1–3)

B. Israel Forgot Her God Who Brought Her out of Egypt (13:4–8)

C. Israel's Leaders Cannot Help Her (13:9–11)

D. Yahweh Will Save His Nation from Death (13:12–14)

E. The Northern Kingdom Will Fall, but There Is Hope beyond That Catastrophe (13:15–14:1) [13:15–16]

XVII. **Yahweh's Poignant Plea to Israel to Return to Him (14:2–10) [1–9]**

A. Israel Learns How She Is to Repent (14:2–4) [1–3]

B. Yahweh's Assurance of Israel's Restoration (14:5–8) [4–7]

C. Yahweh's Ways Are the Best Ways (14:9–10) [8–9]

Select Bibliography

Aejmelaeus, Anneli. "Function and Interpretation of כי in Biblical Hebrew." *Journal of Biblical Literature* 105 (1986): 193–209.

Aharoni, Yohanan. *The Land of the Bible: A Historical Geography*. Translated and edited by A. F. Rainey. Rev. ed. Philadelphia: Westminster, 1979.

Andersen, Francis I. *The Sentence in Biblical Hebrew*. The Hague: Mouton, 1974.

_____, and David Noel Freedman. *Hosea*. Anchor Bible 24. Garden City, N.Y.: Doubleday, 1980.

Bandstra, Barry L. "Is *KY* an Emphatic Particle?" Unpublished paper presented at the 1987 annual meeting of SBL in Boston, Mass., Dec. 7.

Block, Daniel I. "Israel's House: Reflections on the Use of *Byt Ysr'l* in the Old Testament in the Light of Its Ancient Near Eastern Environment." *Journal of the Evangelical Theological Society* 28 (1985): 257–75.

Buss, Martin J. *The Prophetic Word of Hosea: A Morphological Study*. Berlin: Alfred Töpelmann, 1969.

Emmerson, Grace I. "The Structure and Meaning of Hosea 8:1–3." *Vetus Testamentum* 25 (1975): 700–710.

Freedman, David Noel. "The Broken Construct Chain." *Biblica* 53 (1972): 534–36.

_____. "פשתי in Hosea 2:7." *Journal of Biblical Literature* 74 (1955): 275.

Garr, W. Randall. *Dialect Geography of Syria-Palestine, 1000–586 B.C.E.* Philadelphia: University of Pennsylvania Press, 1985.

Gesenius, Wilhelm. *Hebrew Grammar.* Edited by E. Kautzsch. Revised by A. E. Cowley. 2d ed. London: Oxford University Press, 1910.

Gevirtz, Stanley. "West-Semitic Curses and the Problem of the Origins of Hebrew Law." *Vetus Testamentum* 11 (1961): 137–58.

Gordis, Robert. *The Word and the Book: Studies in Biblical Language and Literature.* New York: Ktav, 1976.

Gordon, Cyrus H. "Hos 2:4–5 in the Light of New Semitic Inscriptions." *Zeitschrift für die Alttestamentliche Wissenschaft* 54 (1936): 277–80.

_____. *Ugaritic Textbook.* Reeditio Photomechanica. Rome: Pontifical Biblical Institute, 1967.

Harper, William R. *Amos and Hosea.* International Critical Commentary. New York: Scribner, 1905.

Harris, Zellig S. *A Grammar of the Phoenician Language.* American Oriental Series 8. New Haven: American Oriental Society, 1936.

Joüon, Paul. *Grammaire de l'hébreu biblique.* Rome: Pontifical Biblical Institute, 1923.

Mays, James Luther. *Hosea.* Old Testament Library. Philadelphia: Westminster, 1969.

McComiskey, Thomas Edward. *The Covenants of Promise: A Theology of the Old Testament Covenants.* Grand Rapids: Baker, 1985.

_____. "Idolatry." In *International Standard Bible Encyclopedia,* vol. 2, pp. 796–99. Grand Rapids: Eerdmans, 1982.

_____. "קדש." In *Theological Wordbook of the Old Testament,* vol. 2, pp. 786–89. Chicago: Moody, 1980.

Monson, James M., ed. *The Land Between: A Regional Study Guide to the Land of the Bible.* Jerusalem: James Monson, 1983.

Pritchard, James B., ed. *Ancient Near Eastern Texts Relating to the Old Testament.* 3d ed. Princeton: Princeton University Press, 1969.

Rainey, Anson F. "The Ancient Prefix Conjugation in the Light of Amarnah Canaanite." *Hebrew Studies* 27 (1986): 4–19.

Ratner, Robert J. "Gender Problems in Biblical Hebrew." Ph.D. diss., Hebrew Union College–Jewish Institute of Religion, 1983.

Rudolph, Wilhelm. *Hosea.* Kommentar zum Alten Testament 13. Gütersloh: Gütersloher Verlagshaus Gerd Mohn, 1966.

Stuart, Douglas. *Hosea–Jonah.* Word Biblical Commentary 31. Waco, Tex.: Word, 1987.

Tångberb, K. A. "A Note on *pištî* in Hosea 2:7, 11." *Vetus Testamentum* 27 (1977): 222–24.

Wolff, Hans Walter. *Hosea.* Translated by Gary Stansell. Philadelphia: Fortress, 1974.

Wood, Leon J. *Hosea.* In *Expositor's Bible Commentary,* vol. 7, pp. 161–225. Grand Rapids: Zondervan, 1985.

Superscription (1:1)

1 The word of the LORD that came to Hosea son of Beeri in the days of Uzziah, Jotham, Ahaz, and Hezekiah, kings of Judah, and in the days of Jeroboam son of Joash, king of Israel.

1 The word of the LORD that came to Hosea son of Beeri, in the days of Kings Uzziah, Jotham, Ahaz, and Hezekiah of Judah, and in the days of King Jeroboam son of Joash of Israel.

I. Hosea's Marriage and the Birth of His Children (1:2–2:2) [1:2–11]

A. The Command to Marry (1:2)

² The beginning of the LORD's speaking through Hosea. And the LORD said to Hosea, "Go, take a wife of fornications and children of fornications, because the land has committed great fornication [which has led them] away from the LORD."

² When the LORD first spoke through Hosea, the LORD said to Hosea, "Go, take for yourself a wife of whoredom and have children of whoredom, for the land commits great whoredom by forsaking the LORD."

1:1. דְּבַר־יְהוָה (the word of the LORD): In the prophetic books the term דָּבָר (word) occurs in conjunction with יְהוָה (LORD) in both the singular and plural. In the plural it denotes various divine sayings usually given over a period of time (Jer. 37:2; Ezek. 12:28; Amos 8:11; Zech. 1:6; 7:7, 12). In the singular it may denote either the word of the Lord in a general sense (Mic. 4:2; Amos 8:12) or as set forth in specific oracles (e.g., Joel 1:1; Amos 3:1; Mic. 1:1). The term is used in the latter sense in Hosea 1:1, indicating a divine origin for Hosea's prophetic oracles. אֲשֶׁר הָיָה אֶל־הוֹשֵׁעַ (that came to Hosea): הָיָה is accompanied by the preposition אֶל (to) as it is in all prophetic formulas of this type. הָיָה (came) also occurs with עַל with little or no difference in meaning in several contexts (1 Sam. 16:16; cf. v. 23; note also the interchange of אֶל and עַל in 2 Sam. 8:16; 20:23; Judg. 6:37, 39; see BDB, p. 41, for others). הָיָה with אֶל is used to describe Saul's seizure by an evil spirit (1 Sam. 16:23), and with עַל describes the act of transferring the crown of the king of Rabbah to the head of David (2 Sam. 12:30). In these cases the collocation denotes the process by which something

---

1:1. The period of history delineated by the kings cited in the superscription was a time of great economic prosperity, second only to the halcyon days of the golden age of David and Solomon. Yet there was a virulent spiritual sickness sapping the vitals of the nations of Israel and Judah. The people had violated the stipulations of the Mosaic covenant by mistreating the less fortunate and by participating in the strange syncretistic worship of the day. It is this idolatrous worship that Hosea confronted, for he saw it as the cause of Israel's certain demise. It was a time of religious confusion as Israel grew weaker and attempted to strengthen the decaying structure with international alliances.

The word of the Lord was needed in this time of declension, and it is refreshing to read at the outset of Hosea's prophecy that the divine word had entered the prophet's consciousness. The word of God had come into the sphere of human history. The gloom of this time of national and theological emergency was to be illuminated by the will of God as it was communicated to Hosea, and through him to the people.

It is difficult to understand why Jeroboam II is the only Israelite king who appears in the superscription of the prophecy. In contrast several Judean kings are cited whose combined reigns are six decades longer than the reign of Jeroboam. One should not be too quick to regard this apparent historical imbalance as evidence for a late date for the superscription. We do not possess enough evidence to pass judgment on it with confidence, and there is nothing in the prophecy of Hosea that is not in accord with conditions in the period of time delineated by the superscription.

A significant bank of material in the prophecy of Hosea is consonant with conditions in Israel following the death of Jeroboam II. This period was marred by anarchy and intrigue, for of the six Israelite kings who succeeded Jeroboam II, four were assassinated and only three managed to reign for substantial periods of time. Hoshea, the last king, was imprisoned by Shalmaneser. The northern kingdom was shaken by anarchy at the gravest time in her history.

Israelite leaders attempted to stay the mad race toward ruin by foreign alliances and political coups. The prophecy of Hosea reflects these dismal events in several graphic passages. Hosea depicts the plotting and intrigue of the time in 7:1–7 and 8:4. The factional strife and frenzied alliances that characterized this period are reflected in 5:13, 7:11, and 12:1. These verses depict, in particular, alliances with Assyria. Menahem, one of the kings of Israel in this desperate period, paid tribute to the king of Assyria, "that he might help him strengthen his grasp of the royal power" (2 Kings 15:19). The reigns of the Judean kings cited parallel this period of instability in the northern kingdom. There is no reason to doubt the accuracy of the superscription in that regard.

It is the mention of only one Israelite king, Jeroboam II, that is the problem. If possible, it is best to seek the solution to this question in the text of Hosea or in the historical period before resorting to explanations that entail the complexities of redactionist methodologies. It is important to note that Jeroboam II was the last significant king of the Jehu dynasty. His only successor in the dynastic order was Zechariah, who reigned a mere six months before he was assassinated. With the death of Zechariah, Israel's headlong plunge into oblivion began in earnest. It is possible that the superscription omits the Israelite kings who reigned after the fall of the Jehu dynasty because their legitimacy was questioned. It is clear that Hosea questions the legitimacy of a number of kings who reigned during the time in which he ministered. For example, he represents God as saying, "They set up kings, but not through me. They

external to the individual enters the sphere of that individual's experience. In Hosea 1:1 הָיָה אֶל occurs in a relative clause subordinated to דְּבַר־יְהוָה (the word of the LORD) by אֲשֶׁר (which). This structure indicates that it is Yahweh's word that enters the consciousness of Hosea and becomes a part of his prophetic experience.

2. תְּחִלַּת דִּבֶּר־יְהוָה (The beginning of the LORD's speaking): The Septuagint has λόγου (דְּבַר, word of) for the Masoretic Text's דִּבֶּר (spoke), reading the radicals דבר as a noun rather than a verb; but there is no need to emend. The use of a noun in construct with a verb is attested sufficiently in Hebrew (GKC §130d), and the Masoretic Text represents the more difficult reading which should

be preferred. When time-oriented words such as תְּחִלָּה (beginning) occur in construct with a finite verb they limit the action inherent in the verb to their time frame (אַחֲרֵי נִמְכַּר, after he is sold [Lev. 25:48]; בְּעֵת־פְּקַדְתִּים, in the time that I visit them [Jer. 6:15]). Thus the construction תְּחִלַּת דִּבֶּר denotes the beginning of the process of communication by which the word of the Lord came to Hosea. The whole phrase serves as a formula that introduces the following account of Hosea's marriage and is not subordinate to the next clause (i.e., When the Lord first spoke to Hosea, the Lord said . . .). תְּחִלָּה introduces subordinate clauses when it occurs with a preposition or an implicit prepositional idea (see Ruth 1:22; 2 Sam. 21:9–10; 2 Kings

---

set up princes, but I do not know it" (8:4). The Jehu dynasty had prophetic legitimacy (see 2 Kings 10:30), but there is no evidence that its successors did. Perhaps the mention of only one Israelite king indicates that the writer did not acknowledge the legitimacy of Zechariah's successors. Zechariah's name may not appear here because of the extreme brevity of his reign. There seems to be no reason why the writer of the superscription could not have been Hosea himself, or an editor or amanuensis who was cognizant of the prophet's viewpoint.

2. The title, "The beginning of the LORD's speaking through Hosea," lends a degree of formality to the introductory section of the book. It serves to set off the command to marry as the first divine impulsion of which the prophet was conscious. It also reflects the fact that Hosea's prophetic activity extended over a period of time and was not limited only to the immediate events of his marriage, for the command to marry occurred at the "beginning" of his prophetic ministry.

When the word of the Lord began to make its powerful influence felt within the mind of Hosea, he became conscious of the fact that God was calling him to communicate that word in prophetic activity. Other prophets had given forth the word in act as well as speech. Ezekiel made a model of Jerusalem and pretended to lay siege against it (4:1–3). Zechariah communicated the word through a symbolic act in which he made use of the person of the high priest (6:9–14). The divine impulsion urged Hosea to perform a symbolic act that must have brought revulsion and anguish. He was to marry a woman who, unlike many women in Israel, was sexually promiscuous, and perhaps was a known harlot in the community.

Hosea must have wrestled in his soul, for he was a person of deep moral sensitivity. But he yielded to the divine urging to give up the prospect of a normal married life. His unfortunate marriage thus became a powerful vehicle for the communication of God's will in a time of spiritual wantonness.

We are told that the command to marry such a woman came to Hosea when the Lord began to speak through him. Since *wayyōʾmer* (and [the LORD] said) introduces direct speech, we understand the command to marry to be the statement that initiated his prophetic experience. It does not appear to have come after the marriage as a result of Hosea's reflection on the unfortunate course it had taken. He was already conscious of his prophetic role when he gave a name of prophetic significance to his first child (1:4).

The moral problem that confronts the reader at this point is obvious. Would God command a prophet to marry an unchaste woman? The history of the interpretation of the book witnesses to the influence this problem has had. It is largely for this reason that there is such a broad spectrum of views on the prophecy.

The majority of commentators have espoused the proleptic view of Hosea's marriage. This view holds that Gomer was chaste when Hosea married her, and only after some time did her propensity to unfaithfulness manifest itself. In this view it is necessary to hold that only one group of children appears in the narratives, since Gomer had no children when Hosea took her as his wife. As a result of this, the proleptic view regards the children of 1:2 and 1:3–9 as the same. This makes it necessary to view the children of 1:2 as yet unborn, and the command to Hosea to mean that he should *have* children by Gomer—not adopt

17:25), but there is no clear linguistic signal that these conditions exist in the context of Hosea 1:2. Thus תְּחִלַּת functions as it does in Proverbs 9:10 and Ecclesiastes 10:13 to introduce an independent clause. The fact that this clause is followed by וַיֹּאמֶר (And . . . said), which also introduces an independent clause, does not determine the subordination of the clause beginning with תְּחִלַּת. The term וַיֹּאמֶר may introduce logically independent sentences as it does in Hosea 3:1. Imperfect verbs construed with *waw* introduce independent

clauses frequently in Hosea (see, e.g., 1:3, 4, 8, 9; 2:2 [1:11]). בְּהוֹשֵׁעַ (through Hosea): The preposition בְּ can connote the idea of instrument (by) as well as agency (through) when it occurs with the root דבר (speak). The agential meaning is appropriate to the preposition here because אֶל is the preposition that connotes the concept of *to* in this context (vv. 1–2). לֵךְ קַח־לְךָ אֵשֶׁת זְנוּנִים (Go, take a wife of fornications): The basic command to marry is given in the words לְקַח . . . אִשָּׁה (lit. to take a wife/woman). This is the common expression for

children already born to her. Several versions reflect this understanding of the text (RSV and NASB have; NEB get children). This is not indicated by the text, however. The command states literally, "Go take to yourself a wife of fornications, and children of fornications." The implication of this literal rendition of the command is that the prophet married an unchaste woman and, at the same time, adopted the children who were already hers because of her sexual promiscuity. Perhaps the best representation of the way in which the command is understood by adherents of the proleptic view is that of Andersen and Freedman: "The initial statement, 1:2, can only describe a reinterpretation of the first command after the marriage and family of Hosea were constituted. The original call must have been simply: 'Go take for yourself a wife and build a family with her'" (*Hosea*, p. 162).

Many arguments have been put forth in favor of the proleptic view. Andersen and Freedman state, among other things, that *zĕnûnîm* (fornications) always refers to betrothed or married women; thus we expect Gomer to have been married when she committed *zĕnûnîm* (*Hosea*, pp. 157–59). They also state that 2:7 implies that Gomer became a harlot after the children were born (p. 162). William Rainey Harper rejects the view that Hosea married an impure woman because "Hosea would scarcely have attributed such a command to Yahweh" (*Amos and Hosea*, p. 207), because *zōnâ*, the usual term for harlot, would have been used; and because marriage to an impure woman would not be consonant with the imagery of the Old Testament which depicts Israel as faithful to God at first (p. 207). He also asserts that Gomer "had in her a tendency to impurity which later manifested itself" (p. 207), but he gives no support for this. Leon J. Wood also appeals to the analogy between Gomer and Israel: "Perhaps the most convincing reason in favor of the preferred view is that it implies a significant

parallel between Hosea's marriage and God's experience with Israel" (*Hosea*, p. 166). Wood rejects the view that Gomer was unchaste when Hosea married her and observes that one would expect the word *zōnâ* (harlot) in the command of 1:2 if such were the case. The birth of the three children of 1:4–9 "directly after the indication of the command to marry Gomer makes the conclusion all but necessary that they are the children in question" (p. 165), and, "It is quite unthinkable that God would have commanded anyone—much less a religious leader—to marry such a person" (p. 165).

This examination of the proleptic view shows that a concept must be inserted into the text if it is to have credence (*have* children). This is not an invalid approach to Old Testament exegesis, for the function of ellipsis is well known to interpreters of the Old Testament. Yet one should ask if a literal rendering of the text provides a view that is exegetically cogent and consonant with other aspects of the prophecy. The following discussion will follow the text literally.

The command to Hosea was to "take a wife of fornications." "The expression *laqaḥ ʾiššâ* (take a wife) is the way Hebrew expresses the concept of legal marriage. One of the most common arguments against the view that Hosea married an unchaste woman is that, if that were the case, the text would say *qaḥ zōnâ* (take/marry a harlot), but that suggestion is questionable because *ʾiššâ* must be a part of the construction if the concept of legal marriage is in view. If the text said *qaḥ zōnâ* (take a promiscuous woman/harlot), it would have meant something other than marriage. Since *lāqaḥ* (take) is often used to describe illicit relationships (see the Exegesis), one could not be sure that legal marriage was intended by the expression. The concept of marriage to an *ʾiššâ zōnâ* (harlot) could have been expressed in a much longer expression, but this would be out of keeping with the terse second clause which is simply *yaldê*

legal marriage in the Old Testament (see, e.g., Gen. 4:19; Exod. 6:20; Lev. 21:13; 1 Sam. 25:39), although other expressions exist such as בָּעַל (to become a husband [Isa. 62:5]); יָשַׁב (give a place to dwell [Ezra 10:14; Neh. 13:23]); and נָשָׂא (take up [Ruth 1:4]). The word לָקַח (take) may connote legal marriage when it occurs without אִשָּׁה, but its meaning will almost always be made clear either by using לָקַח אִשָּׁה (take a wife) elsewhere in the context (Lev. 21:14, see v. 13; Deut. 22:14, see v. 13), by using another expression for marriage (Gen. 24:67; 34:9; Deut. 22:19), or by establishing the fact of marriage in other ways (Exod. 34:16; Deut. 20:7; 25:7–8, see v. 5). Only rarely does לָקַח (take) connote marriage when there is no apparent verbal or contextual qualification (Gen. 38:2; Exod. 2:1; 1 Chron. 2:21). On the other hand, when לָקַח (take) occurs without אִשָּׁה (wife/woman) in passages dealing with sexual relationships, it almost always connotes an illicit relationship (Gen. 20:3; 34:2; Lev. 18:17; 20:17; 2 Sam. 11:4; Ezek. 16:32), that is, the taking of a female (or a male [Ezek. 16:32])

---

zěnûnîm (children of fornications). It is difficult to conceive of a more succinct way to express legal marriage to a promiscuous woman than the words in this command. The words *laqaḥ ᵓiššâ* connote legal marriage, and the use of *ᵓiššâ* (wife) in construct with the qualifying noun *zěnûnîm* (fornications) characterizes the wife Hosea was to marry as one who engaged in illicit sexual activity (Douglas Stuart [*Hosea–Jonah*, pp. 26–27] holds that *ᵓēšet zěnûnîm* [wife of fornications] would describe any Israelite woman because they were idolators. This view reduces the force of Hosea's marriage and gives prominence to the role of the sign-children).

Andersen and Freedman argue that "in every case of *znwnym* [*zěnûnîm*] the women involved . . . were married or betrothed . . . none was a typical prostitute" (*Hosea*, p. 158). In Nahum 3:4, however, the word describes the deceitful activities of the city of Nineveh which is called in that verse a *zônâ* (prostitute). The prophecy of Nahum nowhere depicts Nineveh as a wife or widow. Andersen and Freedman also argue that *ᵓēšet zěnûnîm* describes "a wife who becomes promiscuous, not a prostitute or promiscuous woman who becomes a wife" (*Hosea*, p. 159). Characteristic genitives, however, always describe the present state of the *nomen regens*. Attributing the sense of becoming to the construct state strains its concrete function. In other cases where a verb occurs with *ᵓēšet* and a *nomen rectum* (2 Sam. 12:10; Prov. 5:18; 31:10) the construct relationship describes the state of the woman at the time of the verbal action. There is no reason why we cannot understand the words *qaḥ lěkā ᵓēšet zěnûnîm* in Hosea 1:2 to command Hosea to marry a woman who was promiscuous. We must remember that when we assign the translational equivalent *wife* to *ᵓiššāh* in the collocation *laqaḥ ᵓiššāh* we are reflecting our categories of thought. To "take a woman" is to marry. To "take a

woman of fornications" is to marry a promiscuous woman.

It is true that the words of Hosea 2:9 [7] show that Gomer became an adulteress after her marriage to Hosea. This is the implication of the word *husband* (*ᵓîš*) in that verse, but it says nothing about Gomer's behavior before or at the time of the marriage. The events of this verse are analogous to the depiction of Gomer's adulterous tryst in chapter 3.

The consonance of the marriage with the history of Israel is one of the strongest arguments for the proleptic view. If Israel was pure when God found her and took her as his bride, then the marriage of Hosea to Gomer should parallel that aspect of Israel's history, and Gomer could not have been a harlot at the time of the marriage. Three passages in Hosea appear to describe Israel as pure when Yahweh took the fledgling nation to himself (2:17 [15]; 9:10; 11:1–4). Each passage refers to the period of the exodus and Israel's subsequent defection to Baal.

The best support for the proleptic view is found in 2:17 [15] where Israel is depicted as answering "as in the days of her youth." In this context she appears as an unfaithful wife (2:9 [7]) who will again enjoy unbroken fellowship with God (2:21–22 [19–20]). The passage represents God as her husband (2:18 [16]). It seems that her unfaithfulness manifested itself after her marriage to Yahweh, because she says, "I will go back to my former husband, for it was better for me then than it is now" (2:9 [7]). Thus it appears that her youth was a time of willing response to God.

We must observe, however, that the passage says nothing about Israel's purity in the period before the defection to Baal. It says only that she responded to God when he called her out of Egypt, for the text precisely defines the "days of her youth" in 2:17 [15] by the parallel clause "as in the time that she came up from the land of Egypt." It focuses on the simple trust exhibited

for purposes of sexual gratification and not for legal marriage. Thus, if the command in Hosea 1:2 were קַח זוֹנָה (take a harlot) it would connote illicit sexual activity. It would not clearly refer to legal marriage. The idiom קַח אִשָּׁה (take a wife) is interrupted by לְךָ (to you), but the sense is not altered. The same idiom is interrupted by לוֹ (to him) in Genesis 21:21, and retains the meaning of "to marry." Also, אִשָּׁה (wife) occurs in construct form with לָקַח (take) in Leviticus 20:21 (as it does in Hos. 1:2) with the clear meaning of "marry." Thus the command to Hosea is to marry a promiscuous woman. אֵשֶׁת זְנוּנִים (lit. wife of fornications/promiscuous woman) is a genitival structure used

attributively (GKC §128p–v). It describes the אִשָּׁה (woman) Hosea is to marry. This function of the construct state (characteristic genitive or attributive genitive) occurs frequently in the Old Testament. Note the following: אִישׁ דָּמִים (man of blood: a murderer), אִישׁ דְּבָרִים (man of words: an eloquent man), and אֵשֶׁת מִדְיָנִים (a woman of contentions: a contentious woman). (See GKC §128p–v for others.) In Hosea 1:2 the construct state describes the wife Hosea is to marry as a "wife of fornications," that is, a promiscuous woman. זְנוּנִים (fornications) in usages outside Hosea describes fornication on the part of a woman, either married or unmarried (see the Exposition). וְיַלְדֵי זְנוּנִים (and children of for-

---

by the people when they followed their God out of the Egyptian bondage to the status of a nation.

This time of faithful response to God is the ideal that the prophet sets before the people. The response they showed then will again characterize their relationship to God. The prophet extracts from their history a single event to illustrate this fact. This does not mean that Hosea understood the people to be pure at the time of the exodus; it simply points to the trust they once placed in God.

Two important traditions, however, depict the people as idolatrous and thus impure in their early history. One is in Ezekiel 20:1–9. That passage tells us that the people practiced idolatry while yet in Egypt. The other is in the Sinai traditions in the account of the giving of the law. There, within the structure of the ratification and codification of the law, the people worshiped the golden calf (Exod. 32:1–10), thereby revealing an early propensity to spiritual harlotry. These two traditions support the surprising fact that when Yahweh entered into a marriage relationship with his people at Sinai, he married a people already tainted with idolatry; they were guilty of spiritual fornication.

In Hosea 9:10 the prophet depicts the delight the Lord has in the people he freed from bondage. The nation is viewed not as a female of marriageable age, but as a people; they are called the "fathers" (v. 10). Nothing is said about their purity in this passage.

In 11:1–4 Hosea pictures Israel as a male infant. God gave Israel the tender care needed by a small child. Again, there is no reference to Israel's purity; it is God's tender love for his son that Hosea emphasizes.

This consideration of the three passages in Hosea does not lead to the conclusion that the

marriage analogy is clearly present in all three. The factor common to all of them is the defection of the people to Baal. Even if we ignore the traditions noted above and base our conclusions solely on these three passages, we cannot conclude that the prophet presses the marriage analogy all the way back to the wilderness experience. Israel's rejection of God's love and her resultant defection to Baal is the emphasis of 9:10 and 11:1–4. The emphasis of 2:15 [13] is only slightly different. It is the assurance that Israel will one day be freed from her allegiance to Baal to enjoy her former devotion to Yahweh.

Jeremiah 2:2 also seems to support the purity of Israel in her national youth. The emphasis of this verse is on the devotion (ḥesed) and bridal love (ʾahăbat kĕlûlotayik) that Israel showed to God when she followed him in the wilderness. Then God said, "Israel was holy to the LORD, the first fruits of his harvest" (v. 3a, RSV). The fact that Israel was "holiness (qōdeš) to the LORD" does not necessarily mean that Israel was ethically pure. The phrase *holiness to the LORD* is defined by the parallel expression *the first fruits of his harvest* (RSV). According to the Mosaic legislation the first produce of the field went to God as his portion. Because Israel was the first fruits to God of the nations of the world, she was God's special possession and enjoyed his protection. These verses set forth one fact: Israel was set apart to God as his special possession. That is what "holiness to the LORD" means. She was separated to God, and there is no indication in these verses that Israel was intrinsically or ethically holy. Many objects used in the levitical worship were set apart as "holiness to the LORD" (see, e.g., Lev. 5:15–16; 19:24; 27:28; Josh. 6:19). Because they were inanimate, there was nothing of an intrinsic ethical

nications): If we read these words literally, they comprise the second element in a double-duty verbal structure in which קַח (take) governs both "wife of fornications" and "children of fornications." The double-duty structure is common to several Semitic languages (see GKC §117cc–ll; it is well known in Hebrew). A construction that uses לְקַח (take) in a way somewhat similar to the structure in Hosea 1:2 occurs in 1 Samuel 17:17, קַח . . . אֵיפַת הַקָּלִיא הַזֶּה וַעֲשָׂרָה לֶחֶם הַזֶּה (take . . . an ephah of this parched grain and these ten loaves). A double-duty construction with נָתַן (give) occurs in Hosea 2:17 [15]. In this type of double-duty structure the action relative to the two objects is contemporaneous with the time of the main verb. Viewed in this way the command of 1:2 requires Hosea to marry, and at the same time to adopt (לְקַח, take) children of a sexually promiscuous woman. The word לְקַח (take) denotes the process of adoption in Esther 2:7, 15. On the basis of this view זְנוּנִים (fornications) is the *nomen rectum* of a construct relationship that denotes either characteristic or source. If it is a characteristic genitive, it depicts the children as having the same propensities as their mother; they are sexually promiscuous. If it is a genitive of source, it indicates that they were born as a result of their mother's illicit relationships with her lovers. The

holiness in them. Cultic ritual transferred them from the sphere of the common to the sphere of the holy.

No clear evidence exists that Israel was pure in the wilderness period of her history. On the contrary, there is positive evidence that she had engaged in spiritual harlotry before the finalization of her union with God at Sinai. This is a startling fact, and that is why Hosea's marriage is so shocking. But against the dark background of that marriage the grace of God shines all the brighter.

According to the view set forth here, Yahweh commanded Hosea not only to marry a woman of ill-repute, but to adopt the children born to her as a result of her promiscuous relationships. This view construes the first genitive in the double-duty construction (ʾēšet zĕnûnîm, wife of fornications/a promiscuous woman) as a characteristic genitive, and the second a genitive of source. This may appear questionable. However, we should not be overly analytical in our interpretation of the genitival relationship. After all, the Hebrew language has no morphological function for indicating whether a genitive connotes source or attribute. It is satisfied with the broad genitive structure. It is we with our sophisticated concept of language who make the refinements. We must overlay the Hebrew with our linguistic models in order to make it more intelligible to our thought forms. The Hebrew ear heard only the genitive relationship.

Perhaps we are too precise, and the distinctions are artificial. It is, in the final analysis, difficult to separate source from characteristic. If the children were "children of fornications" in the sense that they were born of their mother's illicit relationships, they were still associated with promis-

cuity. The concepts of characteristic and source both apply. We must ask if the writer has defined the concept.

In Hosea 2:6–7 [4–5] we find that he has. In verse 6 [4] he uses a genitive to describe the nation. He says they are bĕnê zĕnûnîm (children of fornications). The next verse states that they are this *because* "their mother has committed fornications," that is, they were born of their mother's promiscuous acts. This is a genitive of source. Since the "children of fornications" (1:2) represent the nation, Hosea's depiction of the people of his day as having been born as a result of the nation's lust for idolatry (2:6–7 [4–5]) supports the view that yaldê zĕnûnîm (children of fornications) in 1:2 is a genitive of source, not characteristic.

If the view presented here is correct, we must posit two groups of children in the structure of the prophecy—those born to Gomer before her marriage to Hosea, and the three born to her and Hosea in legal wedlock. Several passages in the early chapters of Hosea support the concept of two groups of children. In 2:3 [1] the Hebrew says literally, "Say to your brothers, 'My people,' and to your sisters, 'Pity'" (the NRSV reads "brother" and "sister"). The word "say" is in the plural (ʾimrû). It indicates that a group of people is addressed. The only logical referent of the word is the sign-children of 1:3–9. These children were the vehicles of Hosea's prophetic message. They were commanded to convey to their brothers and sisters a message of hope based on the reversal of the significance of their names.

The plural construction of the words *brothers* and *sisters* makes it impossible to regard them as the three sign-children cited in 1:3–9. Hosea's daughter, Not Pitied, could have addressed her siblings in the plural because she had two broth-

latter function fits best with the exegetical data in the book (see the Exposition). It is the view we have adopted in this work. This view requires the two genitives to have different nuances, however, since "wife of fornications" is a characteristic genitive while "children of fornications" is a genitive of source. This is not objectionable (see the Exposition). כִּי־זָנֹה תִזְנֶה הָאָרֶץ (because the land has committed great fornication): כִּי (because) introduces the reason for the unusual marriage. It is because the אֶרֶץ (land) has been unfaithful. The word אֶרֶץ functions as a corporate designation for "people" in Hebrew. We see this in 1 Samuel 14:25, where אֶרֶץ refers to the men of Israel under the command

of Saul (all the land [אֶרֶץ, RSV people] came into the forest, see v. 29; a similar function for the word occurs in Lev. 19:29; Ezek. 14:13; Zech. 12:12). זָנֹה תִזְנֶה (committed great fornication) pairs a finite verb with an infinitive absolute. This intensifies the action of the verb (GKC §113l–r). Thus we may translate it "great fornication." מֵאַחֲרֵי (from after) is an element in the collocation זָנָה מֵאַחֲרֵי (lit. fornicate from after). זָנָה (fornicate) frequently occurs with אַחַר (after) to refer to illicit congress with objects displeasing to God, such as false deities (Exod. 34:15–16; Lev. 17:7; 20:5; Deut. 31:16), detestable things (Ezek. 20:30), the ephod of Gideon (Judg. 8:27), or one's own desires (Num.

---

ers, but the brothers could not have addressed their only sister as "sisters." If we accept the grammar at face value, we must conclude that Hosea envisions two groups of children in this passage. One, addressed by the plural word *say*, speaks to another group designated "brothers" and "sisters." This gives strong support to the view that Hosea adopted the children born to Gomer before her marriage to him. This brood of children represented the nation, as did Gomer herself (see the discussion at 2:3 [1]).

In 4:4–6 Hosea condemns the prophets and priests of his day because of the effect they had on the nation. He pictures the nation as a mother (v. 5) and children (v. 6). Since the message of this passage relates to the nation, we must see it as drawn from the analogy of Hosea's marriage. Hosea does not represent the nation by Gomer alone, but by Gomer and her children. The children here (v. 6) cannot be the sign-children, for these sign-children are separate from the nation. They speak to it. Their names have prophetic significance that relates to the nation. The literal reading of the command, "take a wife of fornications and children of fornications," is consonant with the working out of Hosea's marriage in the narrative framework of his prophecy.

In the proleptic view one must understand the words *yaldê zĕnûnîm* (children of fornications) to refer to the children born to Hosea and Gomer in legal wedlock. How could legitimate children be called "children of fornications"? Harper says they are "children born to her after marriage and begotten by another than the prophet" (*Amos and Hosea*, p. 207). But this does not take into account the fact that according to 1:3 the first child, at least, was born "to him" (*lô*). This is an indication of legitimacy. Harper observes that some

manuscripts omit this word (p. 211). Andersen and Freedman observe that "some scholars have seen in the menacing names of at least the second and third children evidence that Hosea had by now discovered that the children were not his or not certainly his. The names express his outrage, even though he keeps his family intact" (*Hosea*, p. 168). But the threatening tone of these names is directed at the nation, and reflects their status in the sight of God. It is difficult to understand the word *lô* (to him) to be anything more than a straightforward statement that Jezreel (and probably the other children as well) was Hosea's by Gomer. The "children of fornications" were the children that Hosea adopted, who were born to Gomer as a result of *zĕnûnîm*, a word that always describes the illicit activities of a fornicator.

The clause "because the land has committed great fornication [which has led them] away from the LORD" (1:2) states the reason for Hosea's marriage—it was because the people were guilty of spiritual fornication. They might have pointed the finger at Gomer and gossiped about the prophet who married her, but they were no better than she. The marriage of Hosea and Gomer was an eloquent depiction of Yahweh's marriage to his errant people.

The motif of spiritual fornication in the prophecy of Hosea goes beyond the sexual rites of Baal worship. Fornication in the spiritual sense was far broader than cultic efforts to excite the lusty Baal. It involved primarily a denial of absolute devotion and loyalty to Yahweh. We may observe this in contexts where the idea of fornication describes such things as dependence on mediums and wizards (Lev. 20:6), and the misplaced loyalty of the people in the ephod erected by Gideon in Ophrah (Judg. 8:27). In contexts

15:39). On the other hand, when the collocation includes מִן (from), as it does here (מֵאַחֲרֵי, from after), the emphasis is not on the object of misplaced desire, but on the action of turning away from God. We may observe this concept in instances where מֵאַחֲרֵי is collocated with other verbs (Num. 14:43; 32:15; Deut. 7:4; Josh. 22:16). The sense of the idiom in 1:2 is not that the people committed fornication by turning away from the Lord (RSV). The verb זָנָה (fornicate) is treated as a verb of motion with מִן (from) in this collocation and possesses an active sense. It says literally, "they fornicated away from Yahweh." It is not merely that they turned from God; rather, their spiritual fornication, demonstrated in their allegiance to the fertility cult, was the cause of their separation from God (see 9:1).

---

where it applies to pagan deities the emphasis is often on the defection from Yahweh that such worship entails rather than on the distinctly sexual nature of these cultic practices (see, e.g., Exod. 34:14–16; Lev. 20:5; Deut. 31:16; Judg. 2:17). The sin of the people of Hosea's time was their failure to give the Lord their undivided devotion, loyalty, and trust. Such fornication, since it is not limited to pagan sanctuaries, may be committed today. When Christians divide their affection between Christ on the one hand, and the flesh and the world on the other, there is spiritual fornication. The Christian is called to absolute devotion to God and Christ (Matt. 6:24). We too may feel the shock of Hosea's marriage today.

The problem that emerges from the interpretation taken here is obvious. God demanded of a prophet that he marry a woman who was known for her promiscuous behavior. We may wonder, however, if some efforts that seek to avoid this problem succeed in doing so. Do not views that regard the marriage as symbolic or allegorical merely mask the problem? If one who holds the proleptic view acknowledges that God knew of Gomer's evil propensities when he commanded Hosea to marry her, is the problem really solved?

The standard of morality in Hosea's day was the law. It prohibited marriage to a harlot only on the part of priests (Lev. 21:7). They occupied a status of special holiness within the cultus. It was not a violation of the law for a man who was not a priest to marry a harlot. We may not regard the divine command to Hosea to be a violation of the moral standard of his time. Rather, it is one of the most remarkable depictions of divine grace in the Old Testament. Hosea sacrificed a normal married life to call Israel to recognize its sin. At the same time he loved and sheltered an unfortunate woman and her more unfortunate children. Even when she reverted to her old ways after the marriage and went to live with another man, the prophet wooed her back to himself (3:1–3).

The marriage may seem questionable to us, but we must view it against the moral standards of its time. We must be careful not to stretch the principles of the law beyond their stated limit. We have no warrant for believing that because a priest could not enter such a marriage, it was wrong for others to do so. Priests were required to maintain a higher standard of holiness than any others in ancient Israel. They were forbidden to marry divorced women according to the same legal statement that prohibited their marriage to harlots (Lev. 21:7). Yet men who were not priests could marry divorced women, for the regulations relating to the remarriage of a divorced woman form an integral part of the Deuteronomic legislation (Deut. 24:1–4). One who was not a priest was not forbidden to marry a harlot.

The prophecy of Hosea is a tapestry of grace. As the prophet loved a woman whose crudeness and brazenness must have hurt him deeply, so God's grace comes to his people in their unloveliness. Our spiritual condition is never so low that God cannot woo and receive us back to himself as Hosea received Gomer.

I. Hosea's Marriage and the Birth of His Children
(1:2–2:2) [1:2–11]

B. The Birth of Jezreel (1:3–5)

3 So he went and married Gomer the daughter of Diblaim, and she conceived and bore a son to him. 4 And the LORD said to him, "Name him Jezreel, for yet a little while, and I will visit the bloodshed of Jezreel on the house of Jehu, and I will destroy the dominion of the house of Israel. 5 And it will be that on that day I will shatter the bow of Israel in the Valley of Jezreel."

3 So he went and took Gomer daughter of Diblaim, and she conceived and bore him a son.

4 And the LORD said to him, "Name him Jezreel; for in a little while I will punish the house of Jehu for the blood of Jezreel, and I will put an end to the kingdom of the house of Israel. 5 On that day I will break the bow of Israel in the valley of Jezreel."

3. וַיֵּלֶךְ וַיִּקַּח (So he went and married): The use of לָקַח (took, married) without אִשָּׁה (wife/woman) does not militate against the argument that לָקַח אִשָּׁה (take a wife) connotes legal marriage. לָקַח does appear alone with the sense of marrying, but, as we noted, it is often preceded in the context by לָקַח with אִשָּׁה, as it is here (Lev. 21:14, see v. 13; Deut. 25:7–8, see v. 5; Judg. 14:8, see v. 3; 2 Chron. 11:20, see v. 18). וַתַּהַר וַתֵּלֶד־לוֹ בֵּן (and she conceived and bore a son to him): לוֹ (to him) identifies the child as Hosea's own son (see, e.g.,

Gen. 21:3; 24:47; Judg. 8:31; 1 Chron. 2:4). Several manuscripts omit "to him" (לוֹ/αὐτῷ). This may be an effort to bring verse 3 into line with verses 6 and 8, which omit לוֹ. The evidence, however, is not strong enough to demand the deletion of לוֹ.

4. וַיֹּאמֶר יְהוָה אֵלָיו (and the LORD said to him): וַיֹּאמֶר introduces direct speech as in 1:2. There is no need to see it as an amplification of an earlier command as in some expressions of the proleptic view. קְרָא שְׁמוֹ יִזְרְעֶאל (Name him Jezreel): שֵׁם (name) with קְרָא (call) connotes to name (see, e.g.,

---

3. The prophet entered into a legal marriage with Gomer the daughter of Diblaim. We are told little about this woman. Was she a cult-prostitute (qĕdēšâ), a common harlot, or simply a loose woman? Mays argues that she was probably a cult-prostitute because "a common prostitute would satisfy the public symbolism, but not as eloquently as one whose sexual promiscuity was a matter of the very harlotry of Israel in the cult of Baal" (*Hosea*, p. 26). While this is likely, it is difficult for us to be certain. We have only the sharp command with its brief characterization of the type of woman the prophet was to marry. The emphasis is on her proclivity, not her profession.

The meaning of the name of Gomer's parent, Diblaim, is not certain, and the dual ending is difficult to explain (for a discussion of the possibilities, see Andersen and Freedman, *Hosea*, pp. 171–72). It is possible that the name was of foreign origin; if this is so, Gomer could have been a common prostitute. In ancient Israelite society harlots were chiefly foreigners. The words *zarâ* and *nakrīyâ*, which have the primary sense of foreigner or stranger, also refer to harlots (Prov. 2:16; 5:3, 20; 6:24; 7:5; 22:14). Perhaps foreign women were more likely to be prostitutes because of the strictures and attitudes of Israelite society.

The fact that the text moves from the statement of the marriage immediately to the birth of the first child is not sufficient evidence for supposing that that birth was in direct fulfilment of a command to "beget" children of fornications, as the proleptic view requires (cf. Wood, *Hosea*, p. 165). Frequently the statement that someone took a wife will be followed immediately by the observation that she bore a child (see, e.g., Gen. 30:4–5; 38:2–3; Exod. 2:1–2; 6:25). If Hosea intended to indicate that the birth of the child was in direct fulfilment of God's command, he could have stated the idea more precisely by coupling the statement that he married Gomer (*wayyiqqaḥ ʾet-*

gomer) with the familiar idiom *wayyabōʾ ʾēlehā* (and he went into her). This idiom often occurs when procreation is the goal of sexual union (see, e.g., Gen. 16:4; 29:21; 30:4). The affirmation of Hosea's obedience here attributes only one action to him, that is, his taking Gomer as his wife. This fact supports the view that there is only one action inherent in the verb *laqaḥ* (take) in the double-duty construction in 1:2 (the simultaneous "taking" of Gomer and her children), rather than two separate commands (marry Gomer, and have children by her).

The son born to Hosea and Gomer was a legitimate son of Hosea, for the child was born "to him." We do not need to assume that because the words *to him* (*lô*) are wanting in the accounts of the births of the other children that they were born to Gomer by other men. Nothing in the narrative suggests this. The concept may have carried through the entire account.

4. The names of the children were determined by God. The first child received the name *Jezreel*, which means "God sows." While the meaning of the name has symbolic significance elsewhere in the book (2:2 [1:11]; 2:24–25 [22–23]), it does not here. It represents only the geographical site known as Jezreel (or, more accurately, the events that occurred there). Naboth was murdered at Jezreel in a cruel intrigue conceived by Jezebel (1 Kings 21:8–14, see v. 1). It was at Jezreel that Jehu slew Joram, king of Israel (2 Kings 9:24, see vv. 15–17), thus bringing the Omride dynasty to an end (see 9:25–26). Jezreel was also the site of Jehu's massacre of the rest of Ahab's followers, friends, and priests (2 Kings 10:11). The Valley of Jezreel was synonymous with bloodshed.

Hosea says that it will be only a short while before the bloodshed at Jezreel will be visited on the dynasty of Jehu. The end of this dynasty came when Zechariah, the son of Jeroboam II, was assassinated by Shallum (2 Kings 15:10). Since the

Gen. 2:20; 4:17, 25; Num. 11:3; Judg. 13:24). יִזְרְעֶאל (Jezreel) has the sense of "God sows" or "may God sow." וּפָקַדְתִּי אֶת־דְּמֵי יִזְרְעֶאל עַל־בֵּית יֵהוּא (and I will visit the bloodshed of Jezreel on the house of Jehu): פָּקַד (visit) is difficult to define. It frequently describes an action that precedes the bestowal of blessing (Gen. 21:1; 50:24–25; Exod. 3:16) or the execution of judgment (Exod. 32:34; 1 Sam. 15:2; Isa. 23:17) on the part of God. Since the word may precede an act of blessing, it cannot denote the sole idea of punishment. It is best to understand it as attending to or giving heed to a person, object,

or situation before responding. This concept of mental apprehension is apparent in the frequent association of the word with זָכַר (remember; see, e.g., Jer. 14:10). There are many other nuances, but in contexts of judgment it describes an action in which God attends to the wrong he observes by intervening with appropriate action. When פָּקַד is collocated with עַל (upon) as well as a direct object and an indirect object (as it is here) in statements of judgment, the direct object is viewed as *attending* the indirect object. That is, the direct object is brought into the experience of the indirect

---

superscription places the prophetic activity of Hosea in the reign of Jeroboam II, the final days of Jehu's dynasty were not far off when Hosea made his gloomy prediction.

The expression *visit upon* (paqad ʿal) presents the interpreter with several difficulties. One of these is the sense of the word *paqad* itself. It is difficult to determine a satisfactory translational equivalent for this word because of the complexity of its range of meaning. We have suggested the verbal idea of *attend* as the closest English equivalent, although it does not capture the entire range of meaning (see the Exegesis).

This sense of *paqad* obtains in the expression *paqad ʿal*, where we may understand it to denote attend with, bring upon, visit upon, or similar concepts. We may see this clearly in Jeremiah 15:3 (see the Exegesis), where *paqad ʿal* does not denote the concept *punish for* but *punish by*. It is semantically misleading always to translate *paqad ʿal* as "punish for." It is true that this idea is a valid translational equivalent in the majority of cases, but in these instances the expression is accompanied by an object that demands requital, such as sin or other similar concepts (see Hos. 2:15 [13], where the feasts of the Baals will be brought upon [*paqad ʿal*] the nation). It is not certain that the phrase in this verse asserts that Jehu's dynasty was to be punished *for* the bloodshed at Jezreel. We observed in the Exegetical section that the sense of *attend* or *visit upon* is appropriate to all the contexts in which this collocation occurs, and we must ask of each context whether its linguistic signals call for a narrower connotation for it.

This verse is regarded by several commentators to mean that the Jehu dynasty was to be punished *for* the murders committed by Jehu. A few commentators extend that concept to the nation itself on the basis of the parallelism of the clauses; for example, Wood states, "The punishment for Jehu's sin is to be the cessation of the kingdom of

Israel as a nation" (*Hosea*, p. 171). That conclusion is tenuous, however, because nowhere else in the book are the murders at Jezreel cited as the cause of Israel's demise. It is Israel's idolatry and unwise international policies that brought about her downfall.

The clauses in parallel are critical to the interpretation of this verse:

I will visit the bloodshed of Jezreel
on the house of Jehu,
and I will destroy the dominion of
the house of Israel.

Many modern commentators understand "house of Jehu" and "dominion of the house of Israel" to be similar entities because one answers to the other in the parallel structure. Andersen and Freedman, Mays, and Wolff interpret the parallel entities to refer to the monarchy in Israel; Wood interprets the parallel elements in the other direction to refer to the nation.

Hebrew parallelism does not always require us to regard parallel elements as narrowly similar entities, however. Elements in parallel structures may share only a broad commonality. In Hosea 5:12, for example, the "moth" and "decay" are different entities; their similarity lies only in the fact that they are agents of corruption (see also 5:8a; 9:10a). The parallel elements here may find their commonality in nothing more than that they are Israelite regnal entities.

We suggest that *bet yehû* (house of Jehu) must refer only to Jehu's dynasty, and that *mamlĕkût bêt yiśraʾel* (dominion of the house of Israel) represents the dominion of the nation, not the dominion of the reigning monarchy. This view finds support in a number of ways. First, the concepts of realm and dynasty were never blurred in the Old Testament (see Daniel I. Block, *JETS* 28 [1983]: 274–75). The phrase *house of Israel* always refers to the nation, never to a dynasty. Second,

object. We may observe this in Jeremiah 15:3, where God states that four destroyers will be visited upon (פָּקַד עַל) them (the nation): "the sword to slay, the dogs to tear, and the birds of the heavens and the beasts of the earth to devour and destroy." The collocation פָּקַד עַל (visit upon) cannot denote punish *for* in this context. The nation will not be punished *for* these destroyers, but *by* them. The direct object (the four destroyers) is to come into the experience of the indirect object (the nation as the object of the preposition עַל [upon]). This sense of the idiom exists in every context where פָּקַד עַל has two objects. On the other hand, the translation "punish for" does not apply in every context. We must not assign that sense to the collocation uncritically. דְמֵי (bloodshed): the word דָּם (blood) in the plural denotes blood that has been shed (see GKC §124n). It does not possess the intrinsic sense of bloodguilt (see the Exposition). יִזְרְעֶאל (Jezreel) is the name of a large valley that is a dominant feature of the topography of Galilee. בֵּית יֵהוּא (house of Jehu): The

---

the word *mamlĕkût* (dominion) denotes the royal dominion of the entity with which it is paired in a construct relationship. It denotes the territorial dominion (Josh. 13:12, 21, 27, 30, 31) and royal authority of kings (1 Sam. 15:28; 2 Sam. 16:3; Jer. 26:1). Only in 1 Samuel 15:28 does the construct relationship connote dominion *over* Israel, rather than dominion *of* Israel, but there the structure is influenced by *mēʿal* (lit. from over). The most natural interpretation of *mamlĕkût bêt yiśrāʾel* (dominion of the house of Israel) is that it refers to the dominion of Israel as a national entity, not to the royal authority of its reigning king. Third, the explanation of the symbolic significance of Jezreel (vv. 4–5) opposes a close identification of the two entities. The application of the bloodshed at Jezreel to the house of Jehu is appropriate only to that dynasty because Jehu committed the act at Jezreel that came back to haunt his last successor. The second explanation of the significance of Jezreel (v. 5) is more appropriate to the entire nation, since it depicts the shattering of Israel's bow. The bow represents Israel's military might (Hos. 2:20 [18]). Thus Jezreel has two applications in this passage: the murders (*dĕmê*) at Jezreel will somehow repeat themselves in Jehu's dynasty to bring it to an end, and Jezreel will be the site of Israel's demise. The first reference is to the events that took place at Jezreel, the second is to Jezreel as a geographical site. These references are not identical in their significance. They point to two distinct uses of "Jezreel" in the passage.

If we understand Hosea 1:4 in this way, it states that the bloodshed at Jezreel will reappear hauntingly in Jehu's dynasty, bringing it to an end. The way in which bloodshed associated with Jezreel was visited on the Jehu dynasty has been explained variously. It is suggested here that it occurred when Zechariah, the last king in the dynasty, was assassinated by Shallum (2 Kings 15:8–12).

The Masoretic Text of 2 Kings 15:10 says that this assassination occurred "before the people" (*qabal ʿam*), but the Lucianic recension of the Septuagint reads "at Ibleam," a town in the Valley of Jezreel. While there is only one witness supporting this reading, it deserves consideration because of the difficulties in the other traditions. The Masoretic Text is anomalous because the word *qabal* (before) is found with this sense only in Aramaic, and we expect *qabal haʿam* (before *the* people). The reading is thus linguistically and syntactically questionable. The majority of recensions of the Septuagint place the consonants together to form what is apparently the name of a town (Keblaam). No such town is known to us, however, and the Septuagint omits *en* (in) from before it, witnessing to the difficulty the translators had with the reading in the Hebrew text.

The reading "at Ibleam" presents no such difficulties. We can understand it as the result of a scribe's reading *bêt* (ב) and *yôd* (י) as the two strokes of the Hebrew *qôp* (ק), the *yôd* being the vertical stroke, and the *bêt* the curved stroke. In each of the accounts in 2 Kings 15:8–30 that depict assassinations (with the exception of 15:30) the historian was careful to note the place where the assassination occurred. If we adopt the reading "Ibleam" in 15:10, the pericope (vv. 8–12) would thus fit the pattern, giving us good warrant for reading "in Ibleam." Since Ibleam was located in the Valley of Jezreel, bloodshed associated with Jezreel was visited on Jehu's dynasty. Jehu's assassination of King Joram at Jezreel ended the Omride dynasty. Now the ultimate irony was to occur; Jehu's dynasty was to be ended by bloodshed at Jezreel as well.

The word *dĕmê* (bloodshed) may appear to influence the idiom *paqad ʿal* in Hosea 1:4 in the direction of *punish for*, rather than *visit upon*. This word seems automatically to demand requital, and in a large number of contexts the translation "bloodguilt" is appropriate. But the word *damîm*

term בֵּית (house) in this expression is frequently a term for dynasty (see, e.g., 2 Sam. 3:1; 9:1; 1 Chron. 17:24; Isa. 22:22). מַמְלָכוּת (dominion of): See the discussion in the Exposition.

5. בַּיּוֹם הַהוּא (on that day): This refers to the time when Yahweh "visits upon" the dynasty of Jehu

to shatter the bow of Israel. קֶשֶׁת יִשְׂרָאֵל (bow of Israel): This is a metonymy for Israel's military might (see Jer. 51:56; Hos. 1:7; 2:20 [18]; Ps. 46:10 [9]; Zech. 9:10; 10:4), which will be destroyed in the Valley of Jezreel.

(bloodshed) does not have the intrinsic sense of bloodguilt; it always denotes bloodshed. In those instances where the translation "bloodguilt" is assigned to the word it is most frequently accompanied by prepositions such as ʿal (upon) or lĕ (to), or it occurs in collocations such as bôʾ bĕ or hayâ bĕ (come upon).

The context does not require us to view dāmîm (bloodshed) as necessarily worthy of requital (although Hosea may have personally believed it was). Jehu's bloody purge of Baal worship at Jezreel received divine approbation (2 Kings 10:30), even to the extent of affirming the continuation of his dynasty to the fourth generation. The word dāmîm (bloodshed) does not always carry with it the demand for requital, as do words for sin. Besides the several uses of dāmîm (lit. bloods) for the flow of human blood in Leviticus, it refers to bloodshed in a general sense (see Exod. 4:26; 1 Kings 2:5; Isa. 9:5 [4]; Ezek. 16:9, 22, 36; 21:37 [32]). The context always invests dāmîm (bloodshed) with a specific sense within its semantic range. Here the context does not make a moral judgment about dāmîm. Rather, it balances pāqad plus ʿal plus dāmîm with the word šābat (destroy) which connotes termination.

5. "Jezreel" here evidently refers to the Valley of Jezreel, which dominates the topography of Galilee. No historical record exists of a specific battle in this area, but because of its location and extent, it could hardly have escaped the ravages of the Assyrian invasion. Tiglath-pileser III boasted of conquering many cities in the northern and southern regions of Galilee (Pritchard,

ANET, p. 283), and it is likely that the destruction in Megiddo, Level IV, is to be attributed to him (see Y. Aharoni, *The Land of the Bible* [Philadelphia: Westminster, 1979], p. 374). The Valley of Jezreel would have witnessed the maneuvers of the opposing armies, as well as the bloody battles that brought Israel to its knees before Assyria. It is possible that it functions as a metonymy for Israel's humiliating defeat.

It is also possible that Jezreel stands for the entire northern kingdom. It is so used in 2:23–25 [21–23], where the scope of that passage does not allow for a reference only to the Valley of Jezreel (see the comments there). If the passage is understood in this way, it means that the people of the northern kingdom would suffer defeat and be taken captive in their own land, represented by this valley.

The bow of Israel is the nation's military might (see "the bow of Elam," Jer. 49:35). The Valley of Jezreel was to witness the end of Israel's faltering strength. The implications of the child Jezreel's name were staggering. His name presaged the end of Jehu's dynasty as well as the demise of the once proud nation. Twenty-five years were to elapse between the end of the dynasty of Jehu and the fall of Israel, but the portent of the child's name ultimately became a reality. Jezreel was once the scene of Gideon's stunning victory (Judg. 6:33–7:23), but the tables would turn. God was with Gideon then (Judg. 6:12), but he was not with the Israel of Hosea's day. The geographical area was the same, but that which was lacking was humble dependence on God.

I. Hosea's Marriage and the Birth of His Children (1:2–2:2) [1:2–11]

C. The Birth of Not Pitied (1:6–7)

⁶ And she became pregnant again and gave birth to a daughter. And [the LORD] said to him, "Name her Not Pitied, for I will no longer have pity on the house of Israel, but I will surely take them away. ⁷ But I will have pity on the house of Judah, and I will deliver them by the LORD their God. I will not deliver them by the bow, nor by sword, nor by war, nor by horses or horsemen."

⁶ She conceived again and bore a daughter. Then the LORD said to him, "Name her Lo-ruhamah, for I will no longer have pity on the house of Israel or forgive them. ⁷ But I will have pity on the house of Judah, and I will save them by the LORD their God; I will not save them by bow, or by sword, or by war, or by horses, or by horsemen."

6. וַתַּהַר עוֹד וַתֵּלֶד בַּת (and she became pregnant again and gave birth to a daughter): Gomer's second conception results in the birth of a daughter. Nothing in the text implies that this birth is out of wedlock. וַיֹּאמֶר לוֹ (and . . . said to him): The subject of the verb אָמַר (said) is the Lord (as in v. 4). The Syriac inserts "Lord," but there is no need to adopt this reading. The subject is stated in verse 4, and it is most natural to understand it to carry through the sequence of birth accounts. The use of לוֹ (to him) in place of אֵלָיו (unto him) as in verse 4 is difficult to explain, but appears to be nothing more than a linguistic option. The text reflects a preference for אֶל (unto), but לוֹ (to him) is used in formulas of direct address as well. קְרָא שְׁמָהּ לֹא רֻחָמָה (Name her Not Pitied): The basic connotation of the word רָחַם is mercy or pity. The concept of pity is apparent in such verses as Isaiah 9:16 [17]; 13:18; and 49:13, where it connotes the positive response of God to the less fortunate. It parallels the concept of favor in Isaiah 27:11, and in Jeremiah 6:23 it is the antithesis of cruelty; in 2 Kings 13:23 it is the positive response of God that keeps him from destroying his people. כִּי (for) introduces the reason why the child is named "Not Pitied"; it is because לֹא . . . אֲרַחֵם (lit. I will not have pity). It seems unusual for a finite verb (אֲרַחֵם) to follow אוֹסִיף. We expect an infinitive (Targum Jonathan has an infinitive here, but this may represent an effort to smooth out this difficult construction). This type of subordination of an imperfect verb to another imperfect, however, does occur (GKC §120c). "In these combinations the principal idea is very frequently represented by the subordinate member of the sentence, whilst the governing verb rather contains a mere definition of the manner of the action" (GKC §120a). Imperfect verbs occur with יָסַף (to add) in Proverbs 23:35; Isaiah 47:1; 52:1. The reason for naming the child "Not Pitied" is that God will no longer show mercy to the nation. This concept is developed further in the next clause. כִּי (but) does not connote direct causality since it does not give the reason why Yahweh will have no mercy on the nation. The function we assign to it depends, in part, on how we understand the clause it introduces. Since we understand

that clause to affirm Israel's destruction, and since כִּי introduces the apodosis of a negative sentence (כִּי לֹא אוֹסִיף), an adversative sense (but) is most appropriate. This particle frequently introduces adversative clauses after negative statements (BDB, pp. 474–75). נָשֹׂא אֶשָּׂא (I will surely take away): Some commentators and several versions understand this phrase to connote God's forgiveness. This view requires a modal sense for the infinitive absolute with the finite verb ("that I shall indeed forgive them" or "that I should forgive them at all"). While it is true that נָשָׂא frequently has the sense of forgive (as in Hos. 14:3 [2]), it is doubtful that the infinitive absolute with the finite verb clearly functions in a modal sense. No major Hebrew grammar in the twentieth century substantiates this usage. An imperfect verb alone may have this sense (GKC §107u), but it is not clear that the infinitive absolute with an imperfect verb functions to connote anything other than emphasis of the concrete verbal idea (GKC §113l–r). It is best to understand נָשֹׂא אֶשָּׂא לָהֶם as an affirmation. Another concrete translation is, "I will surely forgive them," but this contradicts the previous statement. That translation cannot be a valid representation of Hosea's thought. It is also possible that the sense of the negative in the previous clause carries over into this clause to convey the sense, "I will surely not forgive them." This is difficult, however, for if we translate כִּי as "for" in this context, we most certainly expect a stated negative. Hosea nowhere transfers negative concepts between clauses without full orthographic representation (see 2:9 [7]; 4:1, 10; 5:13; 7:9–10; 8:4, 7; 11:9; 14:4 [3]; see also our understanding of 3:3c). To posit a negative idea in the כִּי clause when one can achieve logical and grammatical sense without it is arbitrary. The translation that answers best to the syntactical and grammatical demands of the context is, "I will surely take them away." It also allows for consistency within the broad clausal structure (see the Exposition). לָהֶם (lit. with respect to them): לְ (with respect to) channels the action of the verb נָשָׂא (take away) to the indirect object הֶם (them). The preposition לְ has the same function with נָשָׂא in Jeremiah 49:29, where God

---

6. Gomer had another child by Hosea. This time a girl was born into this bittersweet marriage. She received her name from the divine impulsion that the prophet felt. It was not by his own choice that the child's name was Not Pitied. Like the previous name, *Jezreel*, the name *Not Pitied* resounded with prophetic foreboding. It would remind the

people that God had no pity on them. There was no ground for mercy.

The people in the community must have shunned and despised these children, for when they heard their names it was as though a prophet pronounced condemnation; it was as though the voice of God thundered, proclaiming the death of

says, "Their camels will be taken away [נָשָׂא] from them [לָהֶם]" (see also Gen. 18:26; 50:17; Exod. 23:21; Num. 14:19; Josh. 24:19).

7. וְאֶת־בֵּית יְהוּדָה אֲרַחֵם (But I will have pity on the house of Judah): The positive connotations of this verse determine the adversative translation of ו

(*waw*). This clause stands in stark contrast to the preceding clause. וְהוֹשַׁעְתִּים בַּיהוָה אֱלֹהֵיהֶם (and I will deliver them by the LORD their God): בְּ indicates the means of their deliverance. It is to be accomplished by Yahweh alone, not by the means cited in the last clause of the verse.

---

the nation. If God had no pity for the people, there was no positive emotion that could sway him from his determination to punish them. The nation would go into captivity, for they had broken their covenantal obligations and were in rebellion against God. This is the state of all who reject the gospel. Their act of renunciation of the grace of God is an act of overt rebellion.

God's lack of pity for the nation was to result in its extinction. He affirmed that he would "surely take them away." This interpretation of the clause *naśoʾ ʾeśśaʾ* (see the Exegesis) is supported by the antithetical structure of the two clauses that relate to Israel and Judah. The structure is as follows:

A I will no longer have pity on the house of Israel,

B but I will surely take them away.

C But I will have pity on the house of Judah,

D and I will deliver them.

Since clauses A and C of this structure are antithetical, we may expect the subordinate clauses B and D to express antithetical concepts as well. Thus, line B of the literary structure may express a concept which is the antithesis of line D. The opposite of God's deliverance of the nation is his taking them away (into captivity).

This understanding of the word *naśaʾ* (take away) also finds support in Hosea 5:14, where in a vivid metaphor the prophet pictures the way God will react to Israel's treachery. Hosea represents God like a lion to Ephraim and Judah, saying, "I will tear and . . . carry off [*naśaʾ*], and none will snatch away." Hosea's concept of the nation's destiny includes the dismal prospect that Israel is to be carried off by God.

7. In a striking antithesis Hosea represents the Lord as saying that he will have mercy on Judah. The reason for this expression of pity for the southern kingdom is not stated, only the affirmation that they will be delivered by the Lord, not by their own might. Hosea makes a similar statement in 12:1 [11:12] where, after accusing the northern kingdom of lies, he says, "Judah still wanders freely with God and is established with

the Holy One." He also says that Judah is not yet guilty (4:15), and we read that both kingdoms will eventually be restored to God's favor (2:2 [1:11]). On the other hand, Judah along with Israel is destined for judgment (5:5, 10–11, 12, 14), for both kingdoms have an ephemeral love for God (6:4). Divine judgment is certain for Judah, but not yet at hand. The die has been cast for Israel, but Judah has not yet incurred sufficient guilt for God to inflict ultimate judgment on her. The end of the northern kingdom is imminent, for it will occur in "yet a little while" (1:4).

The deliverance of Judah predicted by Hosea here (1:7) may reflect the fact that Judah was to survive the Assyrian decimations that brought the northern kingdom to final defeat. Isaiah reflected this prophetic consciousness concerning the destiny of the two kingdoms when he predicted the Assyrian invasion of 701 B.C. He said that the Assyrians would sweep away the northern kingdom and leave Judah with only the capital city of Jerusalem yet standing (7:7–9, 16–20; 8:5–8; see 1:8).

Judah's deliverance is not to be by war or the instruments of war. This affirmation is consonant with a number of prophetic statements that depict God's deliverance of his people by his strength and not by the symbols of human power in which mankind is wont to trust. Micah, another eighth-century prophet, depicted the deliverance of the remnant by God's might and not by its dependence on the vaunted objects of man's boasting and trust (5:10–15). The prophecy of Isaiah warns against trusting in chariots and horses and not in God (31:1). Amos affirms that when the divine wrath falls on Israel, "those who handle the bow shall not stand, and those who are swift of foot shall not save themselves" (2:15, NRSV). Hosea calls on Israel to return to the Lord and plead for his mercy on the basis of the fact that they will not "ride on horses" (14:4 [3]). And when he envisions Israel's restoration, he says that God will "abolish the bow, and the sword, and war from the earth" (2:20 [18]). Implements of war were symbols of human power that all too often led God's people away from a simple trust in his faithful promise to act on their behalf.

I. Hosea's Marriage and the Birth of His Children
(1:2–2:2) [1:2–11]

D. The Birth of Not My People (1:8–9)

8 And when she had weaned Not Pitied, she became pregnant and gave birth to a son. 9 And he said, "Name him Not My People, for you are not my people, and I am not yours."

8 When she had weaned Lo-ruhamah, she conceived and bore a son. 9 Then the LORD said, "Name him Lo-ammi, for you are not my people and I am not your God."

8. וַתִּגְמֹל אֶת־לֹא רֻחָמָה (And when she had weaned Not Pitied): The verb גָּמַל (wean) has the basic denotation of dealing with or dealing out to. It generally connotes to deal with in a final sense (hence the definition "deal fully" in BDB). When used of an infant, the word may mean "to wean," that is, "to deal with fully" or "to complete his nursing" (BDB, p. 168).

9. אַתֶּם (you) is plural and thus refers to the nation. לֹא עַמִּי (not my people) recalls the frequent Old Testament promise that God will take to himself a people. Here, however, that promise is negated (see the Exposition). וְאָנֹכִי לֹא־אֶהְיֶה לָכֶם (and I am not yours): The sentence seems clipped because we expect לֵאלֹהִים (God) to follow לָכֶם (to you) as in the numerous occurrences of this promise in the Old Testament (see, e.g., Exod. 6:7, וְהָיִיתִי לָכֶם לֵאלֹהִים [I shall be God to you]). However, the Hebrew makes sense as it stands. While several manuscripts and fathers reflect the read-

ing אֱלֹהֵיכֶם (your God) for אֶהְיֶה לָכֶם, there is no need to emend the Masoretic Text, for the Hebrew construction is idiomatic. The same collocation occurs in Judges 15:2 (תְּהִי־נָא לָךְ, let her become yours). In Hosea 3:3 this expression (הָיָה לְ) connotes an intimate relationship (lit. you shall not belong to another man). The clipped nature of the clause in 1:9 may reflect Hosea's writing style. We may observe the same brevity of expression in 3:3, where the words, "you shall not be involved with a man," are followed by the terse statement וְגַם־אֲנִי אֵלָיִךְ (lit. and so I to you). וְאָנֹכִי (and I) balances אַתֶּם (you) in the previous clause. אָנֹכִי (I) could have been omitted, but the resulting clause (וְלֹא־אֶהְיֶה לָכֶם) would have been flat in comparison to the previous clause with its stated pronoun (אַתֶּם, you). The use of אָנֹכִי (I) not only adds poetic ballast to the line, but lends a peculiar emphasis to the parties involved in this pronouncement of Israel's estrangement from God.

8–9. When Gomer had weaned Not Pitied, she had another child. The name of this child was even more chilling in its implications than the name *Not Pitied*. The child was called "Not My People." The ultimacy of this name showed a severing of all God's obligations to his people and spelled certain doom for the nation.

The reason for naming Hosea's son Not My People was, "For you are not my people, and I shall not be yours." This statement reflects the ancient promise first given to Abraham (Gen. 17:7–8), where the Lord would become God to his people. But in numerous other passages the promise was given in its fuller form with the addition of the affirmation, "You will be my people" (Exod. 6:7; Lev. 26:12; Jer. 24:7; 30:22; 31:33; 32:38; Ezek. 36:28; Hos. 2:25 [23]).

Here, however, the promise is denied. The denial is presented in a stark verbless clause, "For you [are] not my people" (*kî ʾattem lōʾ ʿammî*). This clause applies to Hosea's present. The context affirms Yahweh's resolve to bring Israel to an end, which means that the people are no longer his. The imperfect verb ʾ*ehyeh* (I am) in the companion clause (I am not yours) denotes incomplete action. The actions represented by the two clauses are generally contemporaneous, however, and we should not understand the imperfect verb to refer to the future. Rather, it depicts an action that

emerges from the fact stated by the noun clause. Because the people are no longer his, Yahweh will not be theirs. If Yahweh is to be faithful to his eternal promise, there will be the need for a renewal of the marriage relationship. That is why we read that Yahweh will betroth himself again to his people (2:21–22 [19–20]).

The words, *and I am not yours*, negate the second part of the promise that God will become God to his people. We may wonder why the prophet did not quote the promise more faithfully. Why did he not say, "I will not be God to you," instead of, "I will not be yours"? The use of the words "I will not be God to you" would have more closely reflected the language of the promise, but Hosea's deft alteration of those words retains their original association while imparting to them a peculiar appropriateness to the marriage relationship that underlies the book. We see a loving intimacy in the words *I am yours*, but the words *I shall not be yours* spell the end of a relationship. We have noted that the same grammatical structure (*hāyâ lĕ*) connotes this concept in Hosea 3:3. Rather than wishing simply to deny that the Lord will be God to his people, the prophet may have quoted God as saying, "I will not be yours" to reflect the denial of his loving relationship as husband to Israel.

I. Hosea's Marriage and the Birth of His Children (1:2–2:2) [1:2–11]

E. A Statement of Hope Based on the Reversal of the Meanings of the Children's Names (2:1–2) [1:10–11]

2 But the number of the people of Israel shall be as the sand of the sea which cannot be measured or counted. And it will be that in the place where it was said to them, "You are not my people," it will be said to them, "Sons of the living God." ² And the children of Judah and the children of Israel shall be gathered together, and they shall appoint for themselves one head. And they shall spring up from the earth, because great shall be the day of Jezreel.

1 ¹⁰ Yet the number of the people of Israel shall be like the sand of the sea, which can be neither measured nor numbered; and in the place where it was said to them, "You are not my people," it shall be said to them, "Children of the living God." ¹¹ The people of Judah and the people of Israel shall be gathered together, and they shall appoint for themselves one head; and they shall take possession of the land, for great shall be the day of Jezreel.

2:1 [1:10]. וְהָיָה מִסְפַּר בְּנֵי־יִשְׂרָאֵל (But the number of the people of Israel shall be): The radical shift from doom (1:9) to hope (2:1 [1:10]) requires our translating וְ as an adversative (but, yet). כְּחוֹל הַיָּם (as the sand of the sea): This expression is a frequent metaphor for great numbers (see, e.g., Gen. 22:17; 32:13 [12]; Josh. 11:4; Judg. 7:12; 1 Sam. 13:5). אֲשֶׁר לֹא־יִמַּד (which cannot be measured): The word מָדַד (measure) refers most frequently to linear measure. It can also refer to liquid (Isa. 40:12) or dry measure (Exod. 16:18; Ruth 3:15). The context of Hosea 2:1 [1:10] requires the sense of dry measure rather than linear measure for מָדַד because its object is sand. וְהָיָה בִּמְקוֹם אֲשֶׁר־יֵאָמֵר לָהֶם (And it will be that in the place where it was said to them): The niphal verb יֵאָמֵר (it was said) is the impersonal passive. The subject of the verb is unexpressed (GKC §121a), as in the case of יֵאָמֵר (it was said) in the next clause.

2:2 [1:11]. וְנִקְבְּצוּ (and . . . shall be gathered): The source of this action is unexpressed. We may understand the verb to be intransitive (1 Sam. 25:1) or to reflect the action of an unexpressed agent such as God. יַחְדָּו (together) emphasizes the unity that will result when the people are gathered. אֶחָד וְשָׂמוּ לָהֶם רֹאשׁ (and they shall appoint for themselves one head): An action subsequent to the assembling of the people is the appointment of a single leader.

2:1 [1:10]. The previous section ends with the chilling affirmation, "I shall not be yours." Deep theological questions emerge from this affirmation, chief of which is the question of the integrity of God's ancient promise to Abraham, "And I will be their God." But we must understand the words *not my people* to apply only to the status of the people in Hosea's day. The promise is eternal (Gen. 13:15; 17:7–8, 13, 19; 48:4). God affirms that though he may forsake a disobedient generation (Lev. 26:33), he will not vitiate his promise: "Yet for all that, when they are in the land of their enemies, . . . I will remember in their favor the covenant with their ancestors . . . to be their God" (Lev. 26:44–45, NRSV). God's allegiance to his covenant promise was the factor that saved his people from extermination.

That allegiance also underlies the prophet's words here, for Hosea follows the dismal account of the naming of his children with a triumphant affirmation of hope. He says that God's people will be as the sand of the sea, which recalls the imagery of the words God spoke to Abraham as his son lay bound to the altar, "I will make your offspring . . . as the sand that is on the seashore" (Gen. 22:17, NRSV).

Hosea's words here are crucial to an understanding of his theology of hope. His prophetic oracles appear to presage absolute judgment, but that was so only for his unbelieving generation. The nation's unfaithfulness to God and their trust in Assyria would be their downfall, but God would preserve a people, and out of them would spring an innumerable multitude.

This affirmation that God will increase the numbers of his people beyond counting not only assures God's loyalty to his promise and to his people, but it envisions the inclusion of countless numbers of Gentiles in the promise as well. This concept is inherent in the ancient promise itself (Gen. 12:3; 22:17–18) and is important in the theology of Paul, who finds that inclusion in the prediction of the great repopulation in Isaiah 54:1 (see Gal. 4:26–28). Because he understands the promise of repopulation to include the church, he can apply the words of Hosea's prophecy to redeemed Gentiles. The reversal of the significance of the names *Not Pitied* and *Not My People* is given meaning for the church when Paul writes, "And in the very place where it was said to them, 'You are not my people,' there they shall be called children of the living God" (Rom. 9:26, NRSV).

2:2 [1:11]. The gathering of the people of both kingdoms—Judah and Israel—under one head reflects a prophetic ideal of future unity. Ezekiel envisions an end to the rift that had engendered dissension and strife throughout the history of the divided kingdom (37:15–17). Hosea does not identify this leader, and the statements may simply be an affirmation of unity with no particular individual intended, or it may refer to Yahweh or to the messianic King. If the latter is in view, these words are similar to the reference to "the breaker" (*happореṣ*) in Micah 2:13.

The next clause explains the result of the unity that the people will achieve under the one head. The ambiguous connotation of *ʿalâ*, which has the basic sense of *go up*, makes this clause difficult to comprehend. If we assign the sense of *go up* to *ʿalâ* here and understand Jezreel to refer to the literal Valley of Jezreel, the sense of the clause is that the people will go up from the land because Jezreel, the site of their future defeat at the hands of the Assyrians, will undergo a reversal of significance and become the site of glory and triumph. However, this view is not logically coherent. Why will they go up from the land where they were victorious and which was theirs by promise?

The idiom שִׂים לְ may connote appointing to an office (Judg. 11:11), while שִׂים עַל has the sense of appointment over, hence authority over, an individual or group (Exod. 1:11). וְעָלוּ מִן־הָאָרֶץ (and they shall spring up from the earth): The connotation of עָלָה in this clause is difficult to determine. The word has a great variety of nuances, all related to the concept of ascending. The context must determine the author's intention, so we suggest that the word denotes the springing up of vegetation (see the Exposition), a connotation it has in a great number of cases (see, e.g., Gen. 41:5, 22; Deut. 29:22 [23]; Isa. 55:13). Hosea uses the word in this fashion of thorns and thistles that will spring up (יַעֲלֶה) on the nation's ruined altars (10:8). יוֹם יִזְרְעֶאל כִּי גָדוֹל (because great shall be the day of Jezreel): כִּי (because) introduces the reason why they will spring up from the earth. It is because יוֹם יִזְרְעֶאל גָּדוֹל (great shall be the day of Jezreel). Jezreel, which means "God sows," prefigures a time of sowing (or great repopulation) for the nation (see the Exposition). This statement is a verbless clause in Hebrew. In this type of noun clause, the time of the action described is determined by the context (GKC §141). In this instance the clause is future.

Where do they go? It is possible that "land" refers to Egypt, but this suggestion has similar difficulties. No linguistic signals suggest that the prophet has Egypt in mind.

Another possibility is that Jezreel is figurative. Hosea uses Jezreel figuratively in 2:24–25, where it connotes the prospect of repopulation. This figurative sense is based on the meaning of Jezreel, "God sows." This suggestion yields the sense that the people will go up from the land because God sows. But there is little coherence in this view. What, then, is the connection?

The combination of concepts that has the greatest cohesiveness is that the people will "spring up" from the earth (ʾereṣ) as vegetation because God will one day sow (Jezreel) in great abundance. Thus Jezreel, which was the site of humiliation and defeat, prefigures a time of great repopulation for Israel. The concept of increase in the number of God's people is an important prophetic theme (Isa. 54:1; Jer. 31:27; Ezek. 36:9–11). Indeed, it is the initial theme of this context (2:1 [1:10]), and is set forth again in another play on the word *Jezreel*, where Hosea says, "And I shall sow her for myself in the earth" (2:25 [23]).

This conclusion may appear to lack consonance with the preceding clause that speaks of the "one head." The appointment of a leader seems to call for a military connotation for the statement that they will go up (march up?) from the land. However, we may find support for the view set forth here in another passage where the prophet urges the people to return to Yahweh (14:2–8 [1–7]; see v. 2 [1]). When the nation returns, "His shoots will go out" (v. 7 [6]), a metaphorical depiction of the increase the restored nation will enjoy in association with their return to Yahweh and the acknowledgment of his sovereignty. Yahweh may correspond to the "one head" in 2:2 [1:11]. Thus Hosea's theology of the future envisions the refructification of the nation under Yahweh alone, for in this time of renewed growth they will renounce their idols (14:4 [3]). The view that 2:2 [1:11] is a metaphorical depiction of future national growth under the aegis of one leader is thus consonant with the theology of hope set forth in chapter 14.

The consonance between the two passages may be observed further in the statements of assurance they contain. God says that he will heal the people and love them freely (14:5 [4]), while earlier Hosea depicts their restoration to God's family (2:1 [1:10]).

This view of 2:2 [1:11] recalls the promise of offspring (see Gen. 12:2) and establishes a continuity throughout the context by the recital of cadences of the Abrahamic promise begun in 2:1 [1:10]. The view requires us to understand the use of Jezreel here as a symbol of hope, for the defeat of Israel there was not ultimate. Its dread name is actually a reaffirmation of the ancient promise to Abraham, "I will make your offspring . . . as the sand that is on the seashore" (Gen. 22:17, NRSV). Thus Hosea gives new significance to the name of the valley that witnessed the demise of the northern kingdom, but that name functions as more than an interesting literary motif in the prophecy. It is a witness to the fact that Yahweh acts in history to effect his will. The defeat of Israel was not the end, for God's ancient promise affirms a future time of prosperity for his people. Jezreel is a symbol of that great prospect.

II. The Significance of Hosea's Marriage for the Nation (2:3–25) [2:1–23]

A. A Command to Hosea's Children to Plead with the Nation That It Give Up Its Idolatry (2:3–8) [1–6]

³ Say to your brothers, "My people," and to your sisters, "Pitied."

Plead with your mother. ⁴ Plead
(for she is not my wife,
and I am not her husband)
that she put away her fornications from
before her,
and her adulteries from between her
breasts,
⁵ lest I strip her naked
and make her as on the day she was
born,
and make her like a wilderness,
and cause her to be like an arid land,
and make her die of thirst.
⁶ On her children I will have no pity,
because they are children of fornications,
⁷ for their mother has committed fornication;
the one who conceived them has
acted shamefully.
For she said, "I will go after my lovers
who give me my bread and my
water,
my wool and my flax, my oil and my
drink."
⁸ Therefore I will hedge up your path
with thornbushes,
and wall her in
so that she may not find her way.

2 Say to your brother, Ammi, and to your sister, Ruhamah.

² Plead with your mother, plead—
for she is not my wife,
and I am not her husband—
that she put away her whoring from her
face,
and her adultery from between her
breasts,
³ or I will strip her naked
and expose her as in the day she was
born,
and make her like a wilderness,
and turn her into a parched land,
and kill her with thirst.
⁴ Upon her children also I will have no
pity,
because they are children of whoredom.
⁵ For their mother has played the whore;
she who conceived them has acted
shamefully.
For she said, "I will go after my lovers;
they give me my bread and my
water,
my wool and my flax, my oil and my
drink."
⁶ Therefore I will hedge up her way with
thorns;
and I will build a wall against her,
so that she cannot find her paths.

31

2:3 [2:1]. אִמְרוּ (say): This word, construed in the plural, is addressed to a group. The closest logical referent is the three children cited in the preceding context. לַאֲחֵיכֶם (to your brothers): The New Revised Standard Version translates this and the following word (אֲחוֹתֵיכֶם [your sisters]) as singular. There is support for this reading in the Septuagint (Εἴπατε τῷ ἀδελφῷ ὑμῶν). The difficulty with the plural reading of these two words is that if the sign-children are the ones addressed, it would be impossible for the brothers to address their *sisters* (אֲחוֹתֵיכֶם), since there is only one sister, Not Pitied. However, when one allows for a group of adoptive children born to Gomer before her marriage to Hosea, the Masoretic Text makes sense. The sign-children may thus be understood as addressing their adoptive brothers and sisters. If we accept the reading of the Masoretic Text we must posit a group of children other than the three born to Hosea.

4 [2]. רִיבוּ (plead): This word is also construed in the plural and is a continuation of the address to the sign-children. כִּי (for) introduces the reason for Yahweh's pleading. It is because הִיא (she), that is, Israel, depicted as Yahweh's wife, is no longer his wife. לֹא אִשְׁתִּי וְאָנֹכִי לֹא אִישָׁהּ (not my wife, and I am not her husband): Cyrus H. Gordon (*ZAW* 54 [1936]: 277–80) suggests that these words are equivalent to the "Akkadian divorce formulae 'thou art not my wife' and 'thou art not my husband'" (p. 277). He concludes that the words of Hosea "are taken from the legal parlance in divorce proceedings" (p. 277). וְתָסֵר זְנוּנֶיהָ מִפָּנֶיהָ (that she put away her fornications from before her): וְ (that) introduces a purpose clause which is the apodosis of the sentence whose protasis is רִיבוּ (plead). It states the purpose of Yahweh's plea (Davidson, *Syntax* §65a). מִפָּנֶיהָ (from before her) has the sense of from her presence or from her experience. וְנַאֲפוּפֶיהָ (and her adulteries) indicates

---

2:3 [2:1]. The statement of hope begun in 2:1 [1:10] continues with a striking reversal of the meanings of the names of Hosea's children. The sign-children are addressed in this verse. They are instructed to speak to another group of children designated as their "brothers" and "sisters" (see the Exegesis). This passage underscores the need for seeing two groups of children in the structure of Hosea's prophecy—the adoptive children, born to Gomer before the marriage, and the children born to Hosea after his marriage to Gomer. The adoptive children represent the nation (Hos. 4:6); the sign-children communicate the prophetic message to the nation.

It is obvious that the lengthy address in 2:3–25 [2:1–23] is directed to the nation and not to Gomer personally, although the language could apply to both in many instances. However, 2:17 [15], with its reference to the exodus, makes it clear that Israel is uppermost in the prophet's mind. Since Gomer is a symbol of the nation, and Israel's sin is spiritual fornication, the language appropriately describes an unfaithful wife throughout this passage.

The reversal of the names is theologically significant. It represents the fact that Yahweh has not forgotten his ancient promise. The nation will go into captivity, but God's promise is not vitiated. Beyond the captivity is a bright future, when a new people of God with a new covenant (Jer. 31:31–34) will be born.

4 [2]. The sign-children are to plead with the nation. The verb *rîb* (plead) has a legal sense in the Old Testament. It connotes to plead a cause (1 Sam. 25:39; Pss. 35:1; 119:154; Isa. 3:13; Lam. 3:58), or to contend (Gen. 26:22; Job 9:3). The sense of "plead" is most appropriate here because an action is required by the words "that she put away her fornications from before her." These words do not appropriately follow a verb with the sense of contend. The act of pleading seeks a response, whereas contending states a grievance.

This is not a *rîb* in the classic sense, for it is not Yahweh who states the accusation. Rather, he poignantly beseeches the sign-children to fulfill their function as mediators to the nation and plead with the people. We need not expect that the children literally did this. The plea is a rhetorical device based on the prophetic function of the children's names.

The reason for the poignant plea is "for she is not my wife, and I am not her husband." The suggestion that these words represent a legal divorce formula in this passage is questionable. The view is based on Akkadian and Elephantine sources, and while it may reflect later Jewish practice with regard to divorce, it is not consonant with this context. The point is not that Yahweh has declared his relationship with Israel severed because he wants it to be so, but that the relationship has been severed by Israel's wantonness and Yahweh wants it restored. This is why he pleads with his errant wife. The passage is best

that this woman is not simply a harlot; she is guilty of adultery. Thus, the context depicts her as a wife.

5 [3]. (פֶּן־אַפְשִׁיטֶנָּה עֲרֻמָּה) (lest I strip her naked): פֶּן (lest) introduces the consequence of rejecting the pleading of Yahweh. If Israel does not forsake her idolatry she will be stripped naked. The imperfect tense (אַפְשִׁיטֶנָּה) connotes incomplete action and is thus appropriate to the hypothetical circumstance established by פֶּן (lest). כְּיוֹם הִוָּלְדָהּ (as on the day she was born): She is as a newborn infant, yet unclothed. וְשַׂמְתִּיהָ כַּמִּדְבָּר (and make her like a

wilderness): The verbs שִׂים and שִׁית connote to make or to constitute. כַּמִּדְבָּר (like a wilderness): מִדְבָּר is used figuratively of an empty, barren place (Jer. 2:31), which is its sense here. Israel was threatened with the loss of everything she had.

6 [4]. כִּי־בְנֵי זְנוּנִים הֵמָּה (because they are children of fornications): This clause gives the reason (כִּי, because) for the previous statement that God will not pity Israel's children. It is because they are children born of their mother's promiscuous activity. בְּנֵי זְנוּנִים (children of fornications) is not an

understood against the background of another prophetic tradition which depicts Yahweh as saying that the severance of his relationship with Israel was not the result of divorce, for no bill of divorce existed, but it was the result of Israel's transgression (Isa. 50:1). Israel had removed herself from her covenant obligation and from her covenant relationship to God as well.

The use of the word *adulteries* (naʾăpûp) in this context acknowledges the role of Israel as the wife of Yahweh. The poignant plea of Yahweh reflects the eternal will of God that his people give him unswerving, faithful devotion and loyalty.

5 [3]. If Israel does not return to her husband, she is to be stripped naked. Nakedness in the Old Testament symbolizes extreme want (Job 22:6; 24:7, 10; Amos 2:16) as well as shame (Mic. 1:11). The former obtains here because of the subsequent depiction of the barren wilderness. This bold metaphor indicates that Israel is to be deprived of that which is necessary to life as a nation and is to perish as a result. The words of Hosea were fulfilled when the nation was taken at sword-point into captivity by Assyria.

Then the metaphor shifts. The nation is to become *like* an arid land in that she will be stripped of all she has. But she is to be killed by thirst, something we should expect to happen *in* an arid land. The comparison is not rigid, for there is a dynamism in the metaphor that seems to reflect a greater interest on the part of the prophet in the expression of the intensity of his emotion than in precise analogical relationships. Note the similar turn in the metaphor in 14:6–8 [5–7], where the depiction of Israel as a tree changes almost imperceptibly, so that it pictures Israel as finding shade under the tree that, in the previous verse, represents Israel itself. In 7:4 the metaphor of the heated oven represents the sexual passion of the people, but in verse 6 it depicts the intensity

of their political intrigues. In 7:8 Ephraim represents not only the one who prepares the dough for baking, but the dough itself. In 10:11–12 the agricultural motifs are symbols of oppression as well as restoration. And in 13:13 Hosea pictures the pains of childbirth as coming on the child as well as the mother.

6 [4]. The nation pictured as a mother (v. 4) is now depicted as children. This characterization of the nation as both mother and children occurs also in 4:4–6. Evidently Hosea envisions corporate Israel as a mother, and the individuals who make up the nation as children. Corporate Israel had espoused the fertility cult, which was woven into the fabric of society and encouraged by the state. As a result there were generations of people who knew no other way of worship. These individuals are to receive no mercy from God, says Hosea, because they are "children of fornications."

Perhaps we cannot fully understand the reason for excluding these people from divine mercy. Was it their fault that they were children of fornications? But we must read these words against the background of the attitudes of the day. Prostitutes were social outcasts and their children bore their mother's stigma. In all probability Gomer's brood of illegitimate children were as despised as she. Hosea's readers would understand the revulsion Yahweh felt for Baal's brood of children.

We depart from the analogy when we note that these worshipers of Baal were not entirely innocent. They heard the prophets condemn them, and there still was a glimmer of the purity of Yahwism in their national heritage and religious festivals. But they went on, blindly kneeling where their parents knelt and seeking the groves their fathers sought. This section also underscores the need to posit two groups of children in the structure of the prophecy. Gomer does not stand alone as the symbol of the nation; the children born of her

33

attributive genitive, but a genitive of source, a conclusion supported by the next clause.

7 [5]. כִּי זָנְתָה אִמָּם (for their mother has committed fornication): The children are children of fornications, not because they themselves engage in fornication, but because their mother did. They were born of their mother's illicit acts, and thus are children of fornication in that sense. הוֹרָתָם הֹבִישָׁה (the one who conceived them has acted shamefully): The emphasis is again on the mother's brazen activity. The shamefulness of her activity is explained in the next clause. It is because (כִּי) she sought her living as a wanton woman, and forsook her loving relationship to her God. וּפִשְׁתִּי (and flax): It has been suggested (Wolff, *Hosea*, p. 30; Andersen and Freedman, *Hosea*, p. 232; Freedman, *JBL* 74 [1955]:275) that this word should be vocalized פִּשְׁתַּי on the analogy of the pattern of the first and third word pairs in which the first element in each pair is singular (יִ) and the second is plural (יִ). However, מַיִם (water) is intrinsically plural and cannot be spelled otherwise. The word שִׁקּוּיָי (drink) is construed in the

plural in the Masoretic Text of Psalm 102:10 [9], where it is paired with the singular לֶחֶם (bread). פֵּשֶׁת (flax) is construed in the singular in the Masoretic Text of Hosea 2:11 [9], where a plural suffix would not be consonant with the other singular suffixes. In every other instance in the Old Testament, however, this word is construed as a plural. There is no compelling reason to point this word differently from the Masoretic Text. Vocalization on the basis of rhyme or meter is tenuous (see K. A. Tångberb, *VT* 27 [1977]: 222–24).

8 [6]. לָכֵן (Therefore) introduces the logical result of the disobedience described in verse 7. שָׂךְ (hedge up): In its only other occurrence the word means to hedge up in a protective sense (Job 1:10). וְגָדַרְתִּי אֶת־גְּדֵרָה (wall her in): Literally it says, "I will wall up her wall," that is, the wall pertaining to her, the wall around her (see GKC §135m, for a discussion of this pregnant use of the pronominal suffix). The variation in the use of pronominal suffixes (דְּרְכֵּךְ [*your* way] and גְּדֵרָה [*her* wall]) is typical of Hosea, and is not infrequent in other prophetic books.

---

promiscuous behavior represent the nation as well.

The expression *children of fornications* does not necessarily imply that Gomer's children were "guilty of whoredom" (Wolff, *Hosea*, p. 34), although children of harlots in ancient Israelite society probably had little choice but to follow the profession of their mother. The children were "children of fornications" solely because their mother was a harlot. Just as children of harlots in that society suffered shame, ostracism, poverty, and disease, so all the people of Israel would pay the penalty of the nation's descent into the dark abyss of spiritual fornication.

7 [5]. The way in which ancient Israel entered her shameful life of adultery is stated in the second causal (*kî*) clause (v. 7). She resolved to pursue her lovers, whom she regarded as supplying her with food and drink. It began, perhaps, with something as innocuous as the placing of an image of Baal in a farmer's field. This is what their

Canaanite neighbors did to increase production. It is what people did in this land, and it appeared to work. Gradually the invisible Yahweh lost ground to the baals whom the people could see and handle, whose religion was concerned with the necessities of life more than rigid moral demands. It was the baals, many Israelites came to believe, who fostered their crops and blessed them with children.

8 [6]. As a result of this declension, Yahweh would block their way and wall up Israel within circumstances from which she could not extricate herself. The God of history would act, and Israel would lose her way as a nation as the captivity engulfed her. Who were the baals in comparison to the God who controlled the course of history? Where would Israel's lovers be then? This is an example of the emptiness that can come to anyone who devotes his or her life solely to meaningless pleasures and neglects the God before whom we all will one day stand.

II. The Significance of Hosea's Marriage for the Nation (2:3–25) [2:1–23]

B. Israel Resolves to Return to Yahweh (2:9–11) [7–9]

9 And she shall pursue her lovers
   and not overtake them,
and she shall look for them
   but not find [them].
Then she will say, "I will go
   back to my former husband,
   for it was better for me then than it
      is now."
10 But she did not realize
   that it was I who gave her
   the grain, and the wine, and the oil,
and who lavished on her silver
   and gold, which she used for Baal.
11 Therefore I will take back
   my grain in its time,
   and my wine in its season,
and I will take away my wool and my
      flax
   which were for covering her naked-
      ness.

7 She shall pursue her lovers,
   but not overtake them;
and she shall seek them,
   but shall not find them.
Then she shall say, "I will go
   and return to my first husband,
   for it was better with me then than
      now."
8 She did not know
   that it was I who gave her
   the grain, the wine, and the oil,
and who lavished upon her silver
   and gold that they used for Baal.
9 Therefore I will take back
   my grain in its time,
   and my wine in its season;
and I will take away my wool and my
      flax,
   which were to cover her nakedness.

9 [7]. וְרִדְּפָה אֶת־מְאַהֲבֶיהָ (And she shall pursue her lovers): רָדַף (pursue) is in the piel and may connote a more intensive action than the qal (BDB, pursue ardently). תִּמְצָא (find) does not have an object suffix (them). In this respect it does not precisely balance the preceding clause (אֹתָם, them). The presence of a suffix, coming as it would in the emphatic position in the clause, might lead us to think that the emphasis is on the lovers (find *them*). The absence of a suffix places the emphasis solely on the verbal action (see Deut. 4:29). The verb stands in stark isolation and communicates the utter futility of Israel's search for her paramours. אֵלְכָה וְאָשׁוּבָה (I will go and return): This clause is a typical example of a hendiadys in Hebrew. אִישִׁי הָרִאשׁוֹן (my former husband): This statement is curious. Did the prophet see Israel as married to Baal when she forsook him to return to Yahweh? The context suggests otherwise, for it depicts her not as a divorced wife but as an adulterous wife with many lovers. We may understand this expression as do Andersen and Freedman: "The lovers were only pseudo-husbands, surrogates for the divine husband" (*Hosea*, p. 239). מֵעָתָּה

(than it is now): מִ־ is comparative in this construction—"better than now."

10 [8]. אָנֹכִי נָתַתִּי (it was I who gave): אָנֹכִי is probably emphatic because the verb נָתַתִּי is grammatically indicated as a first-person singular. לַבַּעַל וְזָהָב עָשׂוּ (and gold which she used for Baal): While עָשָׂה ל can connote *making into*, we are not to understand the gold and silver to have been made into images of Baal. That is precluded by the fact that the word *Baal* is pointed with the article (לַבַּעַל). This structure always indicates the god himself, never an image of him. The plural form (בְּעָלִים) refers to images in Hosea (2:15 [13]; 11:2). The idiom עָשָׂה ל has the sense of making vessels for Baal (see 2 Kings 23:4; 2 Chron. 28:2), and using something for Baal (2 Chron. 24:7). The idiom עָשָׂה ל here thus connotes the idea of making gold for Baal, that is, using gold for Baal. The idiom probably includes the making of images, but its sense may not be limited to that.

11 [9]. לָכֵן אָשׁוּב וְלָקַחְתִּי (Therefore I will take back): לָכֵן introduces the result of Israel's defection. It is followed by another hendiadys (lit. I shall return and I shall take). The main verbal

---

9 [7]. The result of the hedging up of Israel's way is that she will attempt to pursue her lovers but will not be able to overtake them. Her lovers were, of course, the baals from whom she thought she derived her prosperity. Hosea does not depict Israel as a harlot who waits to receive her lovers but as an adulterous woman who shamelessly and brazenly runs after them. In this surrealistic depiction she runs here and there, but she can no longer find those whom she so easily found before.

The motive behind her resolve to return to Yahweh is all too clear: Things were better then. When the Israelites marched into captivity, feeling the sting of the lash and hearing the rude shouts of the Assyrian soldiers, her baals offered no help. Indeed, it was they who had brought her to ruin. The people might have recalled the earlier days when Baal was not so prominent and the purity of Yahwism was more obvious. Those were the better days. Her resolve to return, however, was not repentance, for Hosea depicts Yahweh as appealing to the character of a brazen woman motivated by greed. This is how he would win her back (v. 16 [14]). He would take away what she had, so that she would return to him. This is the first step in Yahweh's efforts to woo Israel. She would lose all she had in the impending invasion and exile, and true repentance would follow as

she thought about the disgrace of her former devotion to the baals.

10 [8]. Israel did not acknowledge Yahweh as the source of her material blessing. It seemed obvious to many that one should seek fertile fields and abundant harvest from the fertility god. But how wrong they were. The wealth they had accrued from Yahweh's hand was used in the service of Baal.

A Deuteronomic concept underlies the words here, for at the Feast of First Fruits Israel was to acknowledge that Yahweh was the giver of the produce of the land (Deut. 26:10–11). She could not do this in Hosea's day because she did not know it was Yahweh who had given her all she had. Her concept of deity was blurred, and she attributed the fertility of the land to Baal.

11 [9]. As a result, the prophet says, Yahweh will take back the grain, the wine, the wool, and the flax. No wine will be produced in the season of grape-gathering, nor grain when the time comes for its harvesting. The wool and flax that Yahweh gave Israel to clothe herself will no longer be available and her nakedness will be exposed to the nations. The benefits that came to her from a loving God will be no more. She will go into a foreign land and her deprivation will be seen by all.

idea is represented by the verb in the second position in the clause (וְלָקַחְתִּי), while the first verb (אָשׁוּב) functions adverbially (see GKC §120d–e). בְּעִתּוֹ (in its time) connotes in the time when it is expected or in its season (Pss. 1:3; 4:8 [7]; Jer. 5:24; 50:16). בְּמוֹעֲדוֹ (in its season): See the comments

at 2:13 [11] and 9:5. וּפִשְׁתִּי (and my flax) is not pointed יְ here and is thus construed as a singular as in the Masoretic Text of 2:7 [5]. This is another argument for the integrity of the form פִּשְׁתִּי in 2:7 [5].

II. The Significance of Hosea's Marriage for the Nation (2:3–25) [2:1–23]

C. Israel Will Pay for Her Wantonness (2:12–15) [10–13]

12 And now I will expose her lewdness
in the eyes of her
lovers, and no one will tear her from
my grasp.
13 And I will end her rejoicing,
her feasts, her new moon, and her
sabbath,
and all her feast days.
14 And I will ravage her vine and her fig
tree
of which she said,
"These are my payment
which my lovers gave to me."
And I will make them into a forest
and the beast of the field will devour
them.
15 And I will visit upon her the days of the
baals
when she burned incense to them,
and adorned herself with her ring and
her jewelry,
and went after her lovers,
and forgot me. Utterance of the
LORD.

10 Now I will uncover her shame
in the sight of her lovers,
and no one shall rescue her out of
my hand.
11 I will put an end to all her mirth,
her festivals, her new moons, her
sabbaths,
and all her appointed festivals.
12 I will lay waste her vines and her fig
trees,
of which she said,
"These are my pay,
which my lovers have given me."
I will make them a forest,
and the wild animals shall devour
them.
13 I will punish her for the festival days of
the Baals,
when she offered incense to them
and decked herself with her ring and
jewelry,
and went after her lovers,
and forgot me, says the LORD.

12 [10]. וְעַתָּה (And now) does not express immediacy in time, but in the resolve of God. אֲגַלֶּה (I will expose): The basic idea of גָּלָה is to uncover or remove. It is used in the piel of revealing one's nakedness, that is, engaging in sexual intercourse, but that cannot be its sense here. Another connotation of the word in the piel is "to reveal." It occurs in Psalm 98:2 with עֵינֵי (eyes) in a collocation similar to the one here: "In the eyes of the nations he has revealed his righteousness." The expression here connotes the fact that Israel will endure public shame. נַבְלָתָהּ (her lewdness): This word occurs only here. Its probable derivation from נָבֵל lends the word a range of meaning having to do with moral insensibility and obnoxious behavior. A companion form in Judges 19:23 (נְבָלָה) describes a wanton act. It is appropriate to understand it as lewdness (RSV, NIV) here because of the sexual connotations of the passage. לְעֵינֵי מְאַהֲבֶיהָ (in the eyes of her lovers): The lovers are witnesses to the husband's accusation. The expression (לְעֵינֵי, in the eyes of/in the sight of) frequently occurs in contexts where it connotes the activity of a witness in attesting to a previous affirmation or event (Jer. 19:10; 28:1; 32:12–13; Ezek. 20:9, 14, 22, 41). The construction בְּעֵינֵי never occurs with that sense. אִישׁ (a man): This word is used in the general sense of no one (Exod. 34:3).

13 [11]. מְשׂוֹשָׂהּ (her rejoicing) denotes rejoicing in general, but its association with the feasts cited in the companion clause indicates that the prophet applies the word to times of national rejoicing. חַגָּהּ (her feasts) is a general word for feast (Isa. 30:29; Amos 8:10; Nah. 2:1 [1:15]). חָדְשָׁהּ (her new moon) is the monthly festival. וְכֹל מוֹעֲדָהּ וְשַׁבַּתָּהּ (and her Sabbath and all her feasts): "New moon," "Sabbath," and "feast day" (מוֹעֵד) are collective singulars. They occur together frequently as a crystallized expression connoting all religious feasts (1 Chron. 23:31; 2 Chron. 2:3 [4]; 8:13; 31:3; Neh. 10:34 [33]; Ezek. 45:17).

14 [12]. וַהֲשִׁמֹּתִי (And I will ravage) is from שָׁמֵם (to devastate). גַּפְנָהּ וּתְאֵנָתָהּ (her vine and her fig tree): Like the word group above, these are collective singular nouns. "Vine and fig tree" occur elsewhere as a crystallized word pair symbolizing abundance (Jer. 5:17; Joel 2:22). These words are generally construed as feminine, but in this verse they are accompanied by a masculine pronoun (הֵמָּה) and masculine verbal suffixes. Moreover, in Hosea 10:1 גֶּפֶן (vine) is construed with a masculine participle (בּוֹקֵק). The masculine pronoun is used when its referent is two nouns of mixed gender (see Num. 12:1). It is possible that in Hosea's dialect גֶּפֶן was construed as masculine. It is not necessary to question the integrity of this verse. אֶתְנָה (payment): This word occurs only once in the Old Testament. Its verbal root (תָּנָה) does not require the connotation of engaging a harlot for money. In Hosea 8:10, for example, it expresses the idea of hiring allies among the nations. Perhaps the basic denotation of the verb is that of paying for favors. If so, the use of the noun אֶתְנָה here to refer to the gifts bestowed on an adulteress for her favors is appropriate. וְשַׂמְתִּים לְיַעַר (And I will make them into a forest): שִׂים לְ connotes to make into (Mic. 4:7). The pronominal suffix sustains the reference to the vine and fig tree which, in Hosea's analogy, will grow into a forest. וַאֲכָלָתַם חַיַּת הַשָּׂדֶה (and the beast of the field will devour them): The logical referent of the pronominal suffix in this clause is the vine and fig tree.

15 [13]. וּפָקַדְתִּי עָלֶיהָ (And I will visit on her): Yahweh will cause the days of the baals to reappear hauntingly in Israel's experience. These days will

---

12 [10]. Yahweh speaks with determination: "Now I will expose her lewdness." He had discovered Israel's wantonness, and as the offended husband he makes known to her lovers that he is aware of his wife's unfaithfulness to him. Perhaps the scene is that of a public announcement of her crime. The husband holds his wife firmly as he proclaims her wrong—so firmly that her lovers cannot wrest her from his grasp and save her from this public humiliation. Hosea represents Yahweh as saying, "No one will tear her from my grasp."

13 [11]. The joyous festivals of Israel's national and religious experience will be no more. The joy of harvest, the fellowship of friends, and the symbolic reminders of Yahweh's goodness, will cease. She will go into captivity, and for most of the people, the break with their heritage would never be repaired.

14 [12]. Not only will Israel's rejoicing end, but her prosperity as well. The vines and fig trees, which were a symbol of affluence, will become a neglected, tangled thicket in which animals move furtively and devour the wild vines and fruit until, at last, the vegetation dies.

15 [13]. The days of the baals will reappear in Israel's experience, as the nation will pay for the days of sensual religious pleasure. This is a stark reminder of the words, "Be sure your sin will find

demand requital because Israel's service to Baal was a transgression against Yahweh (see the discussion of פָּקַד עַל at 1:4). יְמֵי הַבְּעָלִים (the days of the baals): יְמֵי (days) does not necessarily refer to feast days. The word יוֹם (day), construed as a plural and occurring in construct with a substantive, denotes an extended period of time which is limited or defined by the substantive. Note "the days of your life" (Gen. 3:14), "the days of Seth" (Gen. 5:8), and "the days of Uzziah" (Zech. 14:5). In Hosea this construction refers to the days of Israel's youth (2:17 [15]) and the days of Gibeah (10:9). In 9:7 the "days" are days of punishment, while in 12:10 [9] the construction refers to the days of the appointed feasts.

Here the substantive is "the baals." In the absence of anything in the context that defines these days as feast days it is best to understand the construction to refer to the long period of Israel's pursuit of the baals. The subsequent clauses depict a wanton woman in pursuit of her lovers, so there is no need to limit this general description of Israel's pagan worship to the feast days of Baal. וְאֹתִי שָׁכְחָה (and forgot me): The terseness of this poignant statement imparts a peculiar forcefulness to it. נְאֻם־יְהוָה (utterance of the LORD): נְאֻם (utterance) is a noun form that may be based on a verbal root, but this is no longer evident. This word lends an authoritative tone to the statement it follows.

---

you out" (Num. 32:23, NRSV). Israel will not escape the wrath of a righteous God. Harvest after harvest went by, and Israel sank deeper into idolatry. No apparent punishment came from the God of history; Yahweh did not seem to care. But now the days of the baals will demand their due.

We observed in the discussion at 1:4 that the idiom *paqad ʿal* (visit upon), when it occurs with a direct object and an indirect object, implies that the direct object is brought into the experience of the indirect object. That is the case here. The direct object (the days of the baals) will be "vis-

ited upon" the nation. The fact that Yahweh will visit this period of Israel's history on the nation means that the rebellion that characterized this period will come back to haunt the nation. The long period of fertility worship, when Yahweh seemed to be far away, will suddenly appear, demanding requital.

The prophet presents Yahweh's words as those of a forsaken and broken husband: "[She] forgot me." The whole oracle concludes with words that remind us of their divine authority: "Utterance of the LORD."

II. The Significance of Hosea's Marriage for the Nation (2:3–25) [2:1–23]

D. Israel Is Restored to Her Former Status (2:16–17) [14–15]

16 Therefore, I will woo her,
 and lead her into the wilderness,
 and I will speak to her heart.
17 And from there I will give her her vineyards
 and the Valley of Achor as a door of
 hope.
And there she will answer as in the days
 of her youth,
 and as in the time that she came up
 from the land of Egypt.

14 Therefore, I will now allure her,
 and bring her into the wilderness,
 and speak tenderly to her.
15 From there I will give her her vineyards,
 and make the Valley of Achor a door
 of hope.
There she shall respond as in the days
 of her youth.
 as at the time when she came out of
 the land of Egypt.

16 [14]. לָכֵן (Therefore) generally introduces logical consequence (כֵּן + לְ, lit. to such, i.e., according to such a condition). Here, however, we do not seem to have what is logically involved in the preceding statement. We expect punishment for Israel's pursuit of the baals (v. 15 [13]), not the bestowal of divine tenderness. But לָכֵן may connote logical development as well as logical consequence. In Isaiah 26:14, for example, it connotes logical development. Isaiah states that the conquerors of the past will not rise again because they are dead. This is followed by לָכֵן, "Therefore, you have punished and destroyed them." We expect לָכֵן to introduce a concept such as, "Therefore we shall have peace." Instead we have a logical development of what is implicit in the preceding context. Here in Hosea 2:16 [14] לָכֵן does not introduce the logical consequence of the preceding verse, but the logical development of the whole passage (see the Exposition). מְפַתֶּיהָ (I will woo her): פָּתָה has the sense of to be open-minded in the sense of easily influenced. In the piel it has the sense of to make open to suggestion (Exod. 22:15 [16]), thus to woo or allure. וְדִבַּרְתִּי עַל־לִבָּהּ (I will speak to her heart): God will speak tenderly (Gen. 34:3).

17 [15]. מִשָּׁם (from there): שָׁם (there) is a locative particle. The nearest logical referent is מִדְבָּר (wilderness, v. 16). שָׁמָּה (there) often occurs after verbs of motion, but here it occurs after the verb *answer.* It points back to מִשָּׁם (from there) and carries on the directional idea in that construction.

---

16 [14]. This section begins with a "Therefore." It introduces a concept that develops logically from the preceding lengthy passage in which the Lord's pleading with Israel (2:3 [1]), his hedging up of her way (2:8 [6]), and his punishment of her wrongdoing (2:12–15 [10–13]) are all indications of his pity for his errant wife—pity that led him not to forsake her, but to woo her back to himself.

Israel in her wanton way had resolved to return to her husband (2:9 [7]), but her motive was greed, not love. She did not think with her heart but with her head. However, the Lord would speak to her heart—her deepest feelings—and she would again respond to God in simple obedience as she did in her wilderness experience.

17 [15]. The wilderness had special significance for the prophets. It was the period in Israel's history when she exhibited childlike trust in her God. It was unlike the period of the settlement when Baal worship became enmeshed in the fabric of her culture. To be sure, the wilderness period was marred by defection and failure, but viewed overall, it was a time when Israel falteringly made her way to the borders of Canaan, seeking an inheritance promised to her forefathers long ago. The most striking event in this period, however, was the exodus from Egypt. It was that event that best exemplified the nation's childlike trust in God.

We may see the prophetic concept of the wilderness period in a number of passages (Jer. 2:2; 31:2; Ezek. 20:10–38), for it is an essential element in the prophetic theology of hope. The prophets, as well as other Old Testament writers, understood the events of history to be capable of repetition, but in a far more glorious way. Hosea uses this motif frequently.

When Yahweh restores his erring wife to her previous status, he will give her vineyards "from there" (*miššam*). It is "from" the wilderness that the vineyards will be given. The word *from* (*min*) causes us to look beyond the wilderness. It is from there and beyond. The people are viewed as having entered the land, while the wilderness depicts the state of childlike obedience. Because of that obedience they will receive the tokens of divine providence. We have observed that vineyards represent prosperity.

The Valley of Achor ("Valley of Trouble") seems to have no great geographical significance, although it is significant historically. This valley was the site of Achan's execution and burial (Josh. 7:26). We may understand Hosea's use of this place in the same way we understood his reversal of the meaning of Jezreel (1:11, see the Exposition); the Valley of Trouble will become a door of hope.

Israel will answer "there" (*šama*). The word *there* points back to the place of Israel's obedience. The prophet's perspective moves from the land (the place of her vineyards) back to the wilderness. He pictures the exodus, the epitome of Israel's trust in her God. There will be a repetition of the exodus, a repetition of the simple trust that Israel placed in God when he led her from the land of Egypt.

II. The Significance of Hosea's Marriage for the Nation (2:3–25) [2:1–23]

E. The Blessings of Israel's Restoration (2:18–22) [16–20]

18 And it will be in that day, utterance of the LORD, that you will call me "My husband" and no longer will you call me "My Baal." 19 For I will remove the names of the baals from her mouth, and they will no longer be remembered by their name. 20 And I will make a covenant for them in that day with the beast of the field, and with the bird of the heavens, and the creatures that creep on the ground. And I will abolish the bow, and the sword, and war from the earth, and I will cause them to lie down in security.

21 And I will betroth you to me forever. And I will betroth you to me in righteousness, and in justice, and in lovingkindness, and in mercy. 22 And I will betroth you to me in faithfulness, and you will know the LORD.

16 On that day, says the LORD, you will call me, "My husband," and no longer will you call me, "My Baal." 17 For I will remove the names of the Baals from her mouth, and they shall be mentioned by name no more. 18 I will make for you a covenant on that day with the wild animals, the birds of the air, and the creeping things of the ground; and I will abolish the bow, the sword, and war from the land; and I will make you lie down in safety. 19 And I will take you for my wife forever; I will take you for my wife in righteousness and in justice, in steadfast love, and in mercy. 20 I will take you for my wife in faithfulness; and you shall know the LORD.

18 [16]. בַּיּוֹם־הַהוּא (in that day): That day is the day of Israel's renewal of obedience. תִּקְרְאִי אִישִׁי (you will call me "My husband"): אִישׁ (husband) is in contrast to the mode of address in the following clause. וְלֹא־תִקְרְאִי־לִי עוֹד בַּעְלִי (and no longer will you call me "My Baal"): The word בַּעַל is an alternate form for "husband" (Exod. 21:3, 22; Deut. 22:22; Joel 1:8).

19 [17]. שְׁמוֹת הַבְּעָלִים (names of the baals): In all probability the plural (שְׁמוֹת, names) refers to the various appellations ascribed to this god (see the Exposition). The Septuagint levels out the pronouns in this section to the third person, but there is no need to depart from the Masoretic Text. Interchange of persons is well attested in nonbiblical Semitic materials (see the Exposition). מִפִּיהָ (from her mouth): The people of God will no longer speak the name of Baal. יִזָּכְרוּ עוֹד בִּשְׁמָם וְלֹא־ (and they will no longer be remembered by

their name): This thought parallels the preceding, for if the name *Baal* will not be uttered at all in religious litanies, oaths, or common speech, it will be forgotten through lack of usage. The word שֵׁם (name) is in the singular. It reflects the common name *Baal*, fractioned though it was by the shrines scattered throughout the land.

20 [18]. וְכָרַתִּי לָהֶם בְּרִית (I will make a covenant for them; כָּרַת . . . בְּרִית, lit. cut a covenant): This is the common expression for "make a covenant." לָהֶם (for them): לְ has the sense of *for* here. The covenant is to be made with (עִם) the animal world on behalf of (לְ) the people. בַּיּוֹם הַהוּא (in that day): This takes up the reference to "that" day in 2:18 [16] and should be interpreted by it. The expression refers to the time of Israel's restoration set forth in the preceding context.

21 [19]. וְאֵרַשְׂתִּיךְ (And I will betroth you to me): אָרַשׂ (betroth) does not designate a practice simi-

---

18 [16]. The words *in that day* refer to the time when Yahweh restores his erring wife to himself. Hosea refers to this day several times in the prophecy (3:5; 11:10–11; 14:5–8 [4–7]). In this day the people will change the words they use to address God. The concept of name-changing, which we have observed in the narrative to this point, is not limited to the names of the children. Even Israel's mode of address to God will change, for when Yahweh restores Israel to proper marital status with himself, she will not address him as "My baal" but as "My husband" (אִישִׁי). The word *ba'al* was a term for husband (Deut. 24:4), but because of its association with Israel's syncretistic worship it will no longer be a part of the vocabulary of the nation. They will not even use the word in the sense of husband.

19 [17]. Israel will no longer use the word *ba'al* because it will have been expunged from the language. This is the meaning of the affirmation that God will remove the names of the baals from the lips of the people. The use of the plural (names) probably points to the several names for Baal that we may observe in the Ugaritic epic material. We find there such designations for him as *aliyn b'l*, *rkb 'rpt*, *b'l spn*, *bn dgn*, and *zbl b'l*.

The gender indicators in the preceding verse are feminine. This is appropriate because Israel is depicted there as a wife who addresses her husband. Here the word *mouth* has a feminine singular suffix (*piha*), but the verb *yizzakrû* (remember) is construed as a masculine plural. This interchange of referents does not warrant emendation, for we see this pronominal oscillation else-

where in Hosea. It occurs also in ancient Near Eastern treaty materials and such nontreaty literature as the *Funerary Inscription of Aqbar*, *Tabnit*, the *Eshumunazar Inscription*, and the *Byblos Inscription*. See the comment of Stanley Gevirtz, *VT* 11 (1961): 157.

The text states that it is the *names* of the baals, not the baals themselves, that Yahweh will remove. The name attached to a deity gives a sense of reality to the deity, even though that reality exists only in the mind. One can speak about the deity and attribute causation to it because the name gives it a sense of logical existence. The Israelites were commanded to wipe out the names of pagan deities when they entered the land (Deut. 12:3). This was tantamount to destroying the religion that the images represented.

20 [18]. In this time of restoration Yahweh will make a covenant with the animal world. This use of the word *covenant* cannot involve mutual agreement. The word *bĕrît* (covenant) sometimes designates a unilateral stricture imposed on unresponsive entities (see Jer. 33:20; Zech. 11:10). Carnivores and other harmful creatures will do no harm in this time of peace because God will impose severe restrictions on them and effect a change in their natures. Not only will this be true, but the abolishment of war and its cruel weapons will lead to an environment in which the people will be able to sleep without fear.

21–22 [19–20]. When Yahweh allures Israel into the wilderness, he will betroth her to himself, and a new marriage will take place. This will be necessary not because Yahweh had divorced Israel,

lar to modern engagement. It was the finalization of the commitment to marry; only cohabitation remained after betrothal (Deut. 20:7). It was not a tentative commitment (2 Sam. 3:14). In fact, a "betrothed virgin" is called a "neighbor's wife" (Deut. 22:23–24); in the eyes of the law she was legally a wife. The finality of the betrothal of Yahweh to his people is seen in the word לְעוֹלָם (forever). בְּ (in) forms a collocation with אָרַשׂ (betroth) that denotes the sphere of the action of the verb. Yahweh's efforts to woo Israel will be in the sphere of, and thus limited and defined by, the following attributes. צֶדֶק (righteousness) has the basic idea of conformity to a standard. In Deuteronomy it refers to the standards of truth judges were to observe (1:16; 16:18, 20) and to a correct standard of measure (25:15). Along with its companion word צְדָקָה it designates righteousness, which is conformity to God's standards. מִשְׁפָּט (justice) has a wide range of nuances. Here, however, the words which accompany it impart to it a positive ethical sense. It is "judgment" or

"justice" in the sense of proper execution of the law's requirements—thus, true religion. Hosea uses the word in this sense in 12:7 [6]. חֶסֶד (lovingkindness): See the comments at 4:1 and 6:4.

22 [20]. אֱמוּנָה (faithfulness) is based on the word אָמַן which has the basic sense of giving firm support. It is used of the supporting posts of a door (2 Kings 18:16) and of a nurse who carries a child (Num. 11:12). The word אֱמוּנָה reflects the idea of firmness as well. It describes the steadiness with which Aaron and Hur supported the arms of Moses (Exod. 17:12) and refers to the stability of the times in which a people may live (Isa. 33:6). The sense of firmness is not lacking in the uses of the word in an ethical sense. We may observe the idea of steadfastness in the many instances in which the context requires the sense of faithfulness, as well as in contexts that require ideas akin to sincerity or good faith (Prov. 12:22; Isa. 59:4; Jer. 5:1, 3; 7:28; 9:2 [3]). וְיָדַעַתְּ אֶת־יהוה (and you will know the LORD): See the Exposition and the discussion at 5:4.

---

but because she had severed her relationship to God by her disobedience to the old covenant. Because of her spiritual adultery, she deserved to be cast off forever, but her lover will initiate a new marriage covenant with her. This covenant, unlike the old, will never end; it is eternal (*lĕʿôlām*). In order for the new marriage contract to be inviolable there must exist not only unbroken fidelity on the part of Yahweh to his commitment of love, but a change of heart in his beloved, whose evil propensities had severed the earlier relationship.

We are not surprised then to find that the betrothal will be within the sphere of ethical concepts Hosea lists here. These words have their own distinctive nuances, but it is doubtful that we should press them. Together they describe a betrothal relationship that is based on the concept of covenant loyalty.

We observed in the Exegetical section that the preposition *bĕ* (in) describes the limitations of the action inherent in the verb *ʾāraś* (betroth). This idiom indicates that Israel's new relationship to God will be in the sphere of righteousness, justice, lovingkindness, mercy, and faithfulness. Her betrothal will be bound and sealed by these sym-

bols of covenant obedience. The new relationship will not be "in" lust or "in" greed as was her relationship with the baals.

Because this new relationship will be characterized by these expressions of loving obedience, the blessing of the covenant will be secured because its conditions will have been met. Obedience on the part of God's people will be facilitated by Yahweh's sovereign act of love. The words of Hosea foresee the new covenant of which Jeremiah would speak (31:31–34). As a result of this loving act of betrothal, the people will know God. They will enter into an intimate relationship with him; they will understand his ways and enjoy his fellowship.

The concept of the restored wife of Yahweh is not to be identified only with national Israel. It also includes the church. This is an important factor in the theology of Paul. He quotes two passages from the prophecy of Hosea in support of Gentile inclusion in promise (Rom. 9:25–26; see 2:1 [1:10]). The prospect of security associated with the promise of the land in the Old Testament becomes the promise of landedness in Christ in the New Testament (Heb. 3–4).

II. The Significance of Hosea's Marriage for the Nation (2:3–25) [2:1–23]

F. The Effect Israel's Restoration Will Have on the Universe (2:23–25) [21–23]

23 And in that day it will be that I shall respond, utterance of the LORD,
I shall respond to the heavens,
and they shall respond to the earth,
24 and the earth shall respond to the grain, the wine, and the oil;
and they shall respond to Jezreel.
25 And I shall sow her for myself in the earth,
and I shall have pity on Not Pitied,
and I shall say to Not My People, "You are my people,"
and he will say, "My God."

21 On that day I will answer, says the LORD,
I will answer the heavens
and they shall answer the earth;
22 and the earth shall answer the grain, the wine, and the oil,
and they shall answer Jezreel;
23 and I will sow him for myself in the land.
And I will have pity on Lo-ruhamah,
and I will say to Lo-ammi, "You are my people";
and he shall say, "You are my God."

23 [21]. בַּיּוֹם הַהוּא (And in that day) continues the reference to the time of Yahweh's restoration of his people that we observed in 2:18 [16]. אֶעֱנֶה (I shall respond): עָנָה (respond) most frequently connotes response to another in conversation. In some instances, however, it connotes response to a situation or condition that is explicit or implicit in the context (Ps. 20:2 [1]; Isa. 41:17; 49:8; Hos. 14:9 [8]). The same root has the sense of sing, but the previous use of עָנָה in the sense of respond in 2:17 [15] and the lack of any linguistic or contextual signal demanding the idea of singing makes that connotation unlikely in this context. The sequence of verbs in this and the following verse does not follow the usual pattern of the imperfect followed by perfects consecutive. Hosea's use of the imperfects in this fashion isolates each verbal idea and lends a note of deliberateness to it. As a result, the force of the sequence of ideas is not dulled as it might have been had *waw* connected the verbal units in this section. וְהֵם יַעֲנוּ (and they

shall respond): We need not understand this phrase, which occurs twice in this section, to have the children as its subject (Andersen and Freedman, *Hosea*, p. 287). In none of its occurrences in this context are Hosea's children the nearest logical referent of the verb עָנָה (respond to). In the case of the two plural uses of the verb (vv. 23–24) the nearest referent of the first is the heavens and of the second, grain, wine, and oil. In the case of the singular use of the word (v. 24) the nearest logical referent is the earth.

24 [22]. הַדָּגָן . . . הַיִּצְהָר (the grain . . . the oil) were critical to Israel's economy. This crystallized expression denotes agricultural produce in general (Deut. 12:17; 14:23; 2 Chron. 32:28). In Deuteronomy it denotes the material blessing that will result from obedience to the law (7:13; 11:14); disobedience will result in the loss of these products (Deut. 28:51). Jeremiah uses this expression to depict eschatological blessing (Jer. 31:12). Hosea

---

23 [21]. The name *Jezreel* will have significance, not only for Yahweh's restored wife—the people with whom he will be reunited (2:2 [1:11])—but for the universe as well. The depiction of the event that Hosea envisions here is filled with grandeur. It is a highly metaphorical account that is almost surreal. The scene depicts Yahweh answering (ʿanâ) the heavens, which is followed by a chain of responses through various natural phenomena that culminates with Jezreel.

The word ʿanâ (answer/respond) does not have the usual connotation of answer (verbal response) in this statement. There is nothing in the context to which Yahweh must reply verbally when he initiates the chain of responses. It is best to understand the word in its sense of response to a condition or situation. If we understand ʿanâ (respond) simply as a surrogate for "say," we find no verbal communication that it introduces.

We find several contexts in which ʿanâ (answer/respond) does not follow a previous question. In Psalm 20 the word occurs twice (vv. 2, 7 [1, 6]), referring to God's response to the needs of his people apart from any stated reference to prayer on their part. In Isaiah 41:17 the word refers to God's response to the poor and needy, and in 49:8 it is in parallel with the word ʿazar (help). In Hosea 14:9 [8] Yahweh says to Israel, "It is I who answer and look after you" (NRSV), with no reference to a question or a plea for help on the part of Israel in that context.

The fact that Yahweh answers the heavens implies some reason for intervention on his part. We may find the reason in Hosea's theology; he makes several statements affirming that the universe will be restored. God states that a change will occur in the animal world that will give security to his people (2:20 [18]). Hosea sets forth the theological principle that the disobedience of the nation had caused the land to mourn and the people and animals to languish (4:1–3). He writes that as a result of their spiritual harlotry, "threshing floor and winevat shall not feed them, and the new wine shall fail her" (9:2). The sin of the people had a profoundly negative effect on the security and fecundity of the land, but here in 2:23–25 [21–23] Hosea affirms that God will respond to that condition.

The chain begins with Yahweh's response to the heavens; the heavens take up the response and answer the need of the earth for rain. Fecundity will be assured in the days of restoration.

24 [22]. The rejuvenated earth meets the needs of its produce represented by grain, wine, and oil. Then, in the final statements, the produce of the land responds to Jezreel.

We cannot understand "Jezreel" to refer only to the Valley of Jezreel. That interpretation is too narrow for the cosmic scope of Hosea's depiction and is not consonant with the theological concepts we observed above. Jezreel represents a need to which Yahweh must respond. That valley functions as a metonymy for the disaster Israel expe-

uses the expression in a general sense in 2:10 [8]; here it has the same sense.

25 [23]. וּזְרַעְתִּיהָ לִי (And I shall sow her for myself): זָרַע (sow) is the verbal root underlying the previous word *Jezreel*. It occurs here in an obvious play on words. The feminine suffix הָ refers to the nation (see the Exposition). בָּאָרֶץ (in the earth): אֶרֶץ may connote either land or earth in Hebrew. It is best to translate it "earth" in this context. Hosea makes no clear statement elsewhere about a return to the land, and the previous use of אֶרֶץ in

2:24 [22] clearly refers to the earth. The imagery of sowing is consonant with the translation "earth" as well. If the interpretation of וְעָלוּ מִן־הָאָרֶץ (they shall spring up from the earth) in 2:2 [1:11] is correct, Hosea again depicts the repopulation of the people of God in terms of vegetation that grows up from the earth. וְהוּא (and he) finds its referent in the preceding word אַתָּה (you), which refers to the child Not My People. It is that child who responds with the words, "My God!"

---

rienced there. Hosea refers to that disaster (1:5), claiming that Yahweh will "break the bow of Israel in the valley of Jezreel." Israel's population was decimated and the land ravished in that humiliating defeat at the hands of the Assyrians. When Yahweh responds to the need represented by Jezreel, he will greatly multiply God's people and supply them with spiritual bounties represented by grain, wine, and oil. A nation perished at Jezreel, but Yahweh's sovereign response to the demise of the nation will cause a new nation to arise. This will be a nation of far greater numbers of people than ancient Israel boasted. We know from several Old Testament passages that this repopulation included the Gentiles (e.g., Gen. 12:3). The following words, "I shall sow her for myself in the earth," are an apt depiction of the scope of this great repopulation.

25 [23]. The refructification of the earth is an obvious polemic against the Baal cult. It is Yahweh, not Baal, who will revive the forces of nature to restore the prosperity of his people. Israel attributed her abundance to Baal (2:7 [5]), but the experience of Jezreel will forcibly impress on her that it is really Yahweh who supplies her needs. In our relationship with God material loss sometimes leads to rich spiritual gain.

The word *sow* in this dramatic description of Yahweh sowing his people in the earth is the word on which Jezreel (God sows) is based. The use of the word *sow* in this fashion is a play on words in which Hosea applies the meaning of the name to his theology of hope. This word-play reverses the awful significance that Jezreel has in the prophecy and affirms God's continuing fidelity to

his promise to make Abraham's offspring as numerous as the sands of the sea. The feminine suffix (sow *her*) indicates that Hosea continues to think of Israel as Yahweh's betrothed.

The promise of an increase in agricultural productivity does not apply literally to the people under the new covenant. They are a spiritual people (1 Pet. 2:5) who do not live within the borders of Canaan. It is best to see the promise of refructification as a symbol of the glory and blessings that belong to the body of redeemed Jews and Gentiles today.

The name *Jezreel* in Hosea 2:23–25 [21–23] functions as a rhetorical link between the promise of renewed blessing for God's people and the motif of name-reversal that follows. The response of God to his people will result in his becoming their God once again. The names of the children "Not Pitied" and "Not My People" will lose their significance, just as the foreboding implications of the name *Jezreel* will change to a symbol of glory for the people of God.

The reversal of the significance of the names in this verse marks a monumental moment in salvation history, for the element of the promise from which all the other elements spring is reaffirmed by the dramatic change of names. That element is the statement that Yahweh will be their God and they shall be his people (see, e.g., Lev. 26:12). It is reaffirmed when God says, "You are my people" (v. 25 [23]), and Hosea's son ("Not My People") responds with the words, "My God." As the child speaks these words, he depicts the coming of a new era of grace in God's dealings with his people.

III. Hosea Reclaims His Wayward Wife (3:1–5)

A. Gomer Purchased Back from Her Paramour (3:1–2)

3 And the LORD said to me, "Again go love a woman who is loved by a paramour, and who is an adulteress; as the LORD loves the people of Israel, though they turn to other gods and love raisin cakes." ² So I bought her for myself for fifteen pieces of silver, and a homer and a lethech of barley.

3 The LORD said to me again, "Go, love a woman who has a lover and is an adulteress, just as the LORD loves the people of Israel, though they turn to other gods and love raisin cakes."

² So I bought her for fifteen shekels of silver and a homer of barley and a measure of wine.

3:1. עוֹד (Again): This particle connotes continuance of action. It may occupy various positions in a clause depending on emphasis. The question of its position in this sentence is a perplexing one. Syntax and usage allow for its placement with either clause. It may occur at the end of a clause that begins with the *waw*-consecutive (as in Gen. 46:29; Exod. 4:6). Thus, it could be a member of the first clause here which begins with וַיֹּאמֶר (And . . . said). This placement of עוֹד (again) would give the first clause the sense of, And the LORD said to me again. However, עוֹד (again) is not out of place as the initial element of the second clause (1 Kings 22:44 [43]; Isa. 5:25; 10:32; Mic. 6:10). The verbal idea of this clause is expressed in the command formula, "Go . . . love." In this sharpened form of command the first verb initiates the action while

the second defines it. There are many combinations of this crystallized mode of expression in the Old Testament (such as, "go . . . take"; "arise . . . go"). This command formula admits an adverbial modifier before it as in Exodus 5:18, where the formula לְכוּ עִבְדוּ (go work) is preceded by עַתָּה (now). עוֹד (again) precedes an imperative verb in Zechariah 1:17; 11:15. If עוֹד (again) appeared after לֵךְ (go) to form the command, "Go again love a woman," no doubt as to its placement would remain, but the command formula is apparently never broken by anything stronger than נָא which frequently occurs with imperatives. A writer may not have had the syntactical right to place עוֹד in that position. On the other hand, if the writer intended עוֹד (again) to go with the first clause he had an option open to him that would have made

---

3:1. This chapter begins with a command to Hosea to love a woman. We have construed the word *again* (ʿôd) with the second clause (see the Exegesis). This construction gives the clause the sense of *again go love a woman*. The translation "Again go" may seem to imply that Hosea was commanded to marry a woman other than Gomer. This is unlikely. The indefinite ʾiššâ (woman) may be "indeterminateness for the sake of amplification" (GKC §125c). The suffix on ʾekkĕreha (v. 2) supports the idea that the woman of this chapter is Gomer. It would be imprecise and grammatically anomalous to command marriage to an unidentified adulteress and subsequently refer to that woman by the feminine suffix (her). We expect a reference to the identity of the woman before the feminine suffix. Hosea follows the original command in 1:2, which is also indefinite, with a direct reference to Gomer, the daughter of Diblaim (v. 3). Only then does he go on to use the third-person referents.

The narrative structure also supports the suggestion that Gomer is the woman of chapter 3. The initial narrative (1:1–2:2 [1:1–11]) depicts Hosea's yet untroubled marriage to Gomer and the births of their three children. The second major narrative—the application of the marriage motif to the experience of the nation (2:3–25 [2:1–23])—goes beyond the relatively stable relationship pictured in the previous narrative. In this latter passage the relationship between Yahweh and Israel is a stormy one. Yahweh is pictured as beseeching the sign-children to plead with Israel, his wife, to give up her promiscuous activities. She is accused of adultery (2:4 [2]). There has been

a severance of the relationship because of unfaithfulness on the part of Israel, and she has many lovers who provide her with food and drink.

We have seen none of these things so far in Hosea's experience with Gomer. We may wonder if the prophet has gone beyond the scope of his marriage to depict the nation as even more promiscuous than Gomer. If the narrative of 1:1–2:2 [1:1–11] depicts the totality of Hosea's relationship with Gomer, however, we have little basis in fact for the analogy to the nation set forth in 2:3–25 [2:1–23]. But in 3:1–5 we learn about the actual experiences that underlie the previous description of the adulterous nation. Gomer had a lover (3:1; see 2:9 [7]), she was an adulteress (3:1; see 2:4 [2]), and she was reclaimed by her husband (3:3; see 2:16 [14]).

Hosea's devotion to God was tested again, for Gomer left him for a lover. Hosea may have felt some relief at this, but God was not through with his prophet. The analogy was not yet complete, and God was yet to act in greater grace on behalf of his people, for Hosea's sacrificial love would reflect that grace in concrete terms. Hosea was to take Gomer back and continue to love her by showing tender care to this brazen woman.

The Septuagint describes the woman of 3:1 as a "lover of evil," probably reading ʾohebet roaʿ, but the Masoretic tradition requires the translation "loved by a paramour." The latter reading is superior because we learn from verse 2 that Hosea "bought" his wife. If we did not have the reference to the paramour here we would not know from whom he bought her; "so I bought her for myself" would stand in clumsy isolation with no

this clear. He could have placed that particle after וַיֹּאמֶר (And . . . said). This may seem awkward because it precedes the subject of the clause, as well as its indirect object. But the particle appears in this position in Exodus 3:15. The avoidance of this option by the author here shifts the weight of evidence in the direction of the inclusion of עוֹד (again) in the second clause. עוֹד (again) indicates the resumption of an interrupted action. אִשָּׁה (a woman) is indeterminate and may be understood in the sense of "such a woman" (GKC §125c). The sense would thus be "such a woman as Gomer," that is, Gomer herself. אֲהֻבַת רֵעַ (loved by a paramour): The Septuagint reads "a lover of evil" (see the Exposition). רֵעַ (paramour) is a companion. In this case the context calls for the sense of *lover*. וּמְנָאָפֶת (and an adulteress) identifies the woman of this context as a married woman. The וְ (and) more narrowly defines the woman of the preceding clause. Not only is she "loved by a paramour," but she is also (וְ) an adulteress. כְּאַהֲבַת (as [the LORD] loves): The intended analogy is introduced by כְּ (as). The previous action is analogous to Yahweh's love for Israel. וְהֵם (though they) introduces a concessive clause. This is a classic example of concession introduced by a *waw*-copulative preceding a transitive participle (GKC §141e). אֲחֵרִים (other) designates gods other than Yahweh. It occurs frequently in Deuteronomy. וְאֹהֲבֵי (and love): It is not likely that this refers to the deities of the previous clause, for the

writer could have expressed this idea by a relative clause. The וְ is a simple copulative that sustains the concessive idea of the preceding clause.

2. בְּ . . . וָאֶכְּרֶהָ (so I bought her . . . for): Orthographically the verb וָאֶכְּרֶהָ may be from כָּרָה (buy) or נָכַר (regard). Many scholars prefer the latter and translate the word "purchase." This is not a well attested connotation of that verb, however. This view is frequently supported by appeal to 1 Samuel 23:7, where נָכַר seems to have the sense of selling or delivering over, but this is tenuous. The Septuagint translates the word "sell" in that context, but may have read מָכַר (sell). The evidence for this view is weak. There is no reason why this form (וָאֶכְּרֶהָ) cannot represent the more contextually appropriate root כָּרָה (buy). We may understand the *dagesh* not as an indicator of assimilated *nun*, but as *dagesh forte dirimens*. This *dagesh* makes the *shĕwa* more audible (GKC §20h). We normally expect a silent *shĕwa* under the consonant כ (*kap*) in this verb but *dagesh forte dirimens* apparently overrides that rule (note the imperfect verb in 1 Sam. 28:10, the perfect in Judg. 20:32, and the imperative in Ps. 141:3). The placement of *dagesh forte dirimens* is not determined solely by the consonant in which it occurs, but also by the following consonant. This *dagesh* frequently precedes the consonant ר (*rêš*) as it does here (e.g., see 1 Sam. 28:10; Job 9:18; 17:2; Ps. 141:3; Prov. 4:13; Amos 5:21). There is no compelling reason to reject the reading כָּרָה (buy).

---

contextual support. Also the reference to the paramour sustains a better parallel to the third line of the verse, which refers to the people's turning to other gods. The clausal patterns in verse 1 compare Hosea's love for his erring wife to the Lord's love for his people ("Again go love a woman / as the LORD loves the people of Israel"). The fact that the Lord loved a people who forsook him for other lovers answers to Gomer's defection to another man and complements the assertion that the Lord loves the people "though they turn to other gods." The description of the woman of verse 1 as an adulteress fits more comfortably with a reference to a paramour as well.

It is difficult to know how raisin cakes functioned in the worship of the time. Perhaps they

were eaten by the people in their observations of Baal worship, in which case they would parallel the gifts Israel received from her lovers (see 2:7 [5]). The grammar does not sustain the notion that it was the idols who loved these cakes (see the Exegesis).

2. Hosea bought this woman back from her paramour for fifteen pieces of silver and a homer and lethech of barley. While the fifteen shekels of silver approximate the value of a slave (Exod. 21:32), there is probably no significance to this. The precise notation of the amount and the inclusion of food along with the currency probably represent no more than the end result of a transaction that probably involved much haggling on the part of Hosea and Gomer's lover.

III. Hosea Reclaims His Wayward Wife (3:1–5)

B. The Significance of Gomer's Reclamation for
the Nation (3:3–5)

[3] And I said to her, "You are to dwell as mine for many days. You shall not be promiscuous, and you shall not be involved with a man, and so I shall be to you. [4] For the people of Israel will dwell many days without a king, and without a prince, and without sacrifice, and without pillar, and without ephod and teraphim. [5] Afterward the people of Israel will come back, and seek the LORD their God, and David their king; and they shall turn in fear to the LORD and to his goodness in the latter days."

[3] And I said to her, "You must remain as mine for many days; you shall not play the whore, you shall not have intercourse with a man, nor I with you." [4] For the Israelites shall remain many days without king or prince, without sacrifice or pillar, without ephod or teraphim. [5] Afterward the Israelites shall return and seek the LORD their God, and David their king; they shall come in awe to the LORD and to his goodness in the latter days.

3. יָמִים רַבִּים (many days) denotes a long but indefinite period of time. תֵּשְׁבִי לִי (You are to dwell as mine): לְ is possessive and cannot connote dwell or stay *with*. The idiom for that idea is יָשַׁב construed with עִם (Gen. 22:5; 27:44; 29:19; 1 Sam. 22:4) or אֵת (Josh. 15:63; Judg. 19:4). וְלֹא תִהְיִי לְאִישׁ (you shall not be involved with a man): The idiom הָיָה לְ (belong to) may connote the idea of marriage (Judg. 15:2, let her be yours). In Hosea 1:9 the idiom with לֹא (not) denotes the dissolution of the marriage relationship between Yahweh and Israel. Here, however, the influence of the context warrants the more general sense of involvement with another man. וְגַם־אֲנִי אֵלָיִךְ (and so I shall be to you): גַּם (so, also) connotes correspondence or addition. The words אֲנִי אֵלָיִךְ (lit. I to you) seem clipped. We expect the verb הָיָה (be), but there is little doubt that these words represent the same idea as in the previous clause. The word גַּם (also) establishes a logical correlation between the two clauses. It makes little difference that the clause is clipped. The literal statement, "you shall not belong to another man, and also I to you," is clear enough. The action of the second clause is the same as the first; both depict romantic involvement. This concise mode of expression is typical of Hosea's style. It is unlikely that the negation of the first clause extends to the second. The words *and also I to you* may stand as a declarative statement in this clausal structure, affirming in a positive way what the previous clause expresses negatively.

4. כִּי יָמִים רַבִּים (For . . . many days): This phrase, which also appears in verse 3, ties together the concepts of verses 3 and 4. מַצֵּבָה (pillar) refers either to a memorial (see, e.g., Gen. 28:18, 22; 31:13; Exod. 24:4; Isa. 19:19) or to an image of a pagan deity (see, e.g., Exod. 23:24; Lev. 26:1; Deut. 7:5; 1 Kings 14:23). It is never used to connote a Yahwistic religious symbol. אֵפוֹד (ephod) was one of the vestments worn by the high priests in their ministrations at various cultic functions. תְּרָפִים (teraphim) are images; they are generally understood to be household gods. תְּרָפִים is not construed with אֵין (no) as are the other constituents of this

---

3. This verse begins the second of two sections in this chapter. In 3:1–2 Hosea was commanded to take back his adulterous wife; this act was an analogy of God's love for Israel in spite of her idolatry. This section is introduced by the words *wayyōʾmer YHWH ʾelay* (and the LORD said to me). The second section beginning here is introduced by *waʾōmar ʾeleha* (and I said to her). It depicts the working out of the divine command in the actual circumstances of Hosea's relationship with his wife.

Hosea instructed Gomer to dwell with him for an indefinite period designated "many days." During this time she was to remain loyal to him. He said, "You are to dwell as mine." She was his not only by right of marriage but also by right of purchase. She was to cease her promiscuous conduct and no longer engage in sexual activity with other men.

This proscription is set forth further in a biclausal construction at the end of this verse, in which the second clause imposes a restriction on the prophet. The subject of the first clause is Gomer (*you* shall not be involved), and the indirect object is "a man." The subject of the second clause is Hosea (I), and the indirect object is Gomer (you). Just as Gomer was no longer to have intimate relations with other men, so Hosea was not to have an intimate relationship with Gomer. They would live together; he would provide for her, but they would not live as man and wife.

4. The meaning of all this for Israel is given in the *kî* (for) clause that begins here. The analogy between the marriage and Israel is made clear by the repetition of the words *yamîm rabbîm* (many days). Just as Gomer was to dwell for "many days" without full wifely privileges, so Israel is to have a similar experience. The restrictions placed on Gomer prohibited her illicit escapades and robbed her of her husband's full expression of love. So with Israel. She would continue as a nation, but without a monarchy, without the constituents of her spiritual harlotry, and without the levitical worship that established her intimacy with Yahweh.

These elements of worship are set forth in a symmetrical pattern that we state literally, "no king and no prince." Without a king there could be no centralization of divine government for the nation. The symmetry continues with an intermixture of Yahwistic and pagan symbols of worship—"no sacrifice and no pillar." Without sacrifices Israel's relationship to Yahweh would suffer because no means of atonement would be available to the people. Israel would not engage in idolatry either, for she no longer would utilize pagan *maṣṣebōt* (pillars) in her worship. Finally, she would no longer have ephod (a levitical vestment) and teraphim (pagan gods). We wonder why the

sequence. It is thus closely associated with אֵפוֹד (ephod). This word pair occurs in several places in Judges (17:5; 18:14, 17, 18, 20).

5. וּבִקְשׁוּ (and seek): The word בָּקַשׁ has the sense of seeking to gain or regain a person or thing. In some instances the connotation is that of seeking to attain something that is the object of one's desire (Num. 16:10; Deut. 13:11 [10]; 2 Sam. 4:8; Ps. 54:5 [3]; Prov. 14:6). When one seeks God, it is to make him the object of one's allegiance and desire (Deut. 4:29; 1 Chron. 16:11; Ps. 27:8). One seeks God by turning to him to do his will and observe his requirements (2 Chron. 11:16; 15:15; Zeph. 2:3), and by turning to him in prayer (Jer. 29:13, see v. 12; Dan. 9:3). One fails to seek God by continuing to disregard His will (Isa. 65:1, see vv. 2–7; Zeph. 1:6). Hosea reflects the same nuances in his prophecy: Israel did not return to

the Lord or seek him (7:10). Because of the people's disregard for Yahweh's will, they will not be able to seek him successfully (5:6). וּפָחֲדוּ אֶל (turn in fear to): This collocation occurs on only two other occasions in the Old Testament. In Jeremiah 36:16 the words פָּחֲדוּ אִישׁ אֶל־רֵעֵהוּ may be translated, "they turned one *to* another in fear." The same idea obtains in Micah 7:17, but with reference to God. טוּבוֹ (his goodness): While this word may connote the goodness of God which is intrinsic to his nature (Ps. 25:6 [7]), it most frequently connotes concrete manifestations of that goodness (Neh. 9:25, 35; Pss. 27:13; 31:20 [19]; Isa. 1:19; Jer. 31:12, 14; Zech. 9:17). בְּאַחֲרִית הַיָּמִים (in the latter days) does not always have an eschatological perspective. It always denotes a period of time that, from the writer's standpoint, is in the indefinite future (Gen. 49:1; Deut. 31:29).

---

prophet intertwined these elements of Yahwistic worship with the hated symbols of paganism. Perhaps he wanted to portray their syncretistic religion for what it was—paganism through and through. Whether this is so, the point of the passage is clear. At some time beyond the threatening events that lay before her Israel would renounce her idolatry just as Gomer let go of her lovers. And just as Gomer's relationship with Hosea lost its intimacy, so the loss of sacrifice and ephod, symbols of Israel's access to God, would affect Israel's intimacy with Yahweh. Today the people of Israel have no king, they do not practice idolatry, and they no longer observe the levitical institution of sacrifices. The prophet had no basis on which to prognosticate these things in the day in which he lived. It is a remarkable prediction. The fact that the prophet refers to kings and princes before the symmetrical portrayal of Israel's syncretistic worship is significant. In this way he portrays the two aspects of Israel's disobedience to God: her political leaders, who made unwise alliances, and her paganized Yahwism. This passage is a vivid literary depiction of Israel's internal sickness.

5. A time is coming, however, when this condition will end. It is introduced by the vague term *afterward* (ʾaḥar). Israel will come back to Yah-

weh and to David her king. The designation *David* applies to the messianic King in several places in the Prophets (Jer. 30:9; Ezek. 34:23, 24). In that time idols of wood and stone will no longer be the objects of their search, but they will seek Yahweh and his King. They will give their allegiance to the Lord and to the one who will come in the spirit and power of David to establish and secure the eschatological reign of God. The people will turn in fear to Yahweh and his goodness. They will come trembling to their husband and to the benefits that he will bestow. They sought the welfare of the baals, but that proved to be ephemeral. They will return to Yahweh's "goodness."

In 2:9 [7] we learned that Israel will resolve to return to Yahweh, but only because things were better when she belonged to him. The motive was selfish. Now we find that when she is restored to Yahweh she will come in fear to him and his benefits, not in a spirit of brazen arrogance. This will take place in the latter days. Hosea gives us no eschatological events by which we may determine the time of the restoration of his people to Yahweh and to his King. It is enough for him to assure us that it will occur.

IV. Yahweh's Controversy with His People (4:1–10)

A. The Pronouncement of the Controversy (4:1–3)

4 Hear the word of the LORD, O people of Israel,

> for the LORD has a controversy
> with the inhabitants of the land,
> because there is no truth, and no lov-
>> ingkindness,
>> and no knowledge of God in the
>> land.

2 [There is] oath-taking, and deceit, and
> murder,
>> and theft, and committing adultery.
>> They erupt [in violence;]
>> and murder touches murder.

3 Therefore the land mourns
>> and everyone who lives in it lan-
>> guishes.
> They will be taken away along with the
>> beast of the field,
>> and the bird of the air,
>> and even the fish of the sea.

4 Hear the word of the LORD, O people of Israel;

> for the LORD has an indictment
>> against the inhabitants of the
>> land.
> There is no faithfulness or loyalty,
>> and no knowledge of God in the
>> land.

2 Swearing, lying, and murder,
>> and stealing and adultery break out;
>> bloodshed follows bloodshed.

3 Therefore the land mourns,
>> and all who live in it languish;
> together with the wild animals
>> and the birds of the air,
>> even the fish of the sea are perishing.

4:1. כִּי רִיב לַיהוָה (for the LORD has a controversy): כִּי introduces the reason for the command to hear (שִׁמְעוּ) in the preceding clause. לְ is the *lamed* of possession. The basic denotation of רִיב (controversy) is a dispute (see Gen. 13:7; 2 Sam. 22:44). It occurs frequently in contexts of litigation (see, e.g., Exod. 23:2, 3, 6; Deut. 21:5; 25:1). The prophets sometimes represent Yahweh as having a dispute (רִיב) with his people or with the nations (Jer. 25:31; Hos. 12:3 [2]; Mic. 6:2). The second כִּי (because) introduces another causal clause giving the reason for the statement in the preceding כִּי (for) clause. The reason for the controversy is that there is אֵין־אֱמֶת וְאֵין־חֶסֶד (no truth and no lovingkindness) in the land. The word אֱמֶת is the Hebrew word closest to our concept of truth. While אֱמֶת and חֶסֶד frequently occur as a word pair (Exod. 34:6; 2 Sam. 15:20; Pss. 40:12 [11]; 85:11 [10]; 89:15 [14]; Prov. 3:3; 14:22) it is unlikely that they function here with the broadly shared meaning we expect in word pairs. Each has its own negative particle and sets off אֵין־חֶסֶד (no lovingkindness) in the same way it sets off אֵין־דַעַת (no knowledge), which is a separate element in the binary structure. אֱמֶת connotes truth as a moral attribute (honesty and trustworthiness in word and deed), while חֶסֶד (lovingkindness) relates to the quality of mutual concern that should bind people together. The words אֱמֶת and חֶסֶד are shaped by the following series of negative concepts in which false swearing (oath-taking) and deceit head the list. These two concepts more narrowly define אֱמֶת (truth) as a lack of honesty in social relationships. The antitheses to חֶסֶד (lovingkindness) are murder, theft, and adultery. This indicates that the emphasis of חֶסֶד (lovingkindness) in this context is specifically that of social concern. The absence of חֶסֶד among the people of Hosea's day has led to a rending of the social fabric and threatens the existence of the nation. דַעַת אֱלֹהִים (knowledge of God) is not theoretical knowledge, but the understanding of God's ways and moral requirements (Hos. 4:1; 6:6).

4:1. At this point we leave the account of Hosea's marriage and begin a new section, which extends to the end of the book and contains oracles of doom and hope. Even in this section, however, we are never far from Hosea's marriage, for it is always in the background and is the catalyst for his message to his people. We see it in the references to the nation as mother and children, as well as in the numerous allusions to spiritual harlotry and adultery.

Hosea's marriage pictures sin not as disobedience to the demands of an austere God, but as an affront to love. It is ingratitude to God, who has loved us in our unloveliness and who has delivered us from the sordidness of life without him.

The people are to hear Yahweh's word because he has a dispute with them. The *rîb* (or disputation form) in the Prophets is not static in its structure. It can be as spare in its formulation as in Jeremiah 25:31 or as complex as in Micah 6:2–16. The *rîb* here contains four elements: the announcement of the *rîb* (4:1), the people addressed (4:1), the reason for the *rîb* (4:1b–2), and the punishment given in response to the wrong they had done (4:3).

The reason for Yahweh's dispute with his people is their violation of the ethical standards crystallized in the terms *truth, lovingkindness,* and *knowledge of God.* Any civilization is threatened when it neglects honesty and concern for others. Israel the more, because her national security and prosperity depended on obedience to her sovereign Lord.

We have concluded (see the Exegesis) that *ʾĕmet* (truth) and *ḥesed* (lovingkindness) are separate entities in Hosea's gloomy observation about his nation, and that *ʾĕmet* is appropriate to the first two offenses in the litany of wrongdoing (oath-taking and deceit) in verse 2. The second word (*ḥesed*), a word that frequently describes aspects of covenant loyalty, would then govern the remaining offenses. This conclusion gains support from the fact that the Mosaic covenant specifically cites these wrongs (murder [*rāṣōaḥ*], Deut. 5:17; theft [*gānōb*], Exod. 20:15; Deut. 5:17 [19]; adultery [*nāʾōp*], Exod. 20:14; Deut. 5:17 [18]), but not the first two. It appears that Hosea has aspects of loyalty to the Mosaic covenant in mind in the words that *ḥesed* governs.

The knowledge of God, of which Hosea speaks in this verse, is not theological knowledge only, but knowledge of Yahweh's directive will. The nation is to be destroyed for lack of this knowledge (4:6). The fact that the knowledge of God is in parallel with *ḥesed* (lovingkindness) in 6:6 indicates that knowledge of God involves an understanding of the ethical sphere in which God's people must live if they are to experience Yahweh's love and bounty. Even today, disobedience to the ethic of the new covenant, which is expressed in the New Testament, can hinder the blessing of God on his people.

2. אָלֹה (oath-taking) is not wrong in itself (1 Kings 8:31–32), but the association of the word with כָּחֵשׁ (lying) indicates that the prophet has false swearing in mind. He uses the word אָלֹה in a similar sense (אָלוֹת שָׁוְא, false oaths) in 10:4. פָּרָצוּ (erupt [in violence]): The Septuagint construes the concepts in the preceding catalog of wrongs as the compound subject of this verb (χέω, pour out). This yields the sense, "Cursing . . . burst forth (abound)," but this is questionable. These concepts are all infinitives absolute and their use as the subject of a finite verb is comparatively rare and confined mainly to poetry. The verb פָּרָץ (erupt) can stand as an independent clause with the people (בְּנֵי יִשְׂרָאֵל, v. 1) as the subject. It functions this way in Micah 2:13, where it forms an isolated clause, the subject of which is stated in verse 12. The infinitives are antitheses to the qualities cited in the previous line, for they tell us what qualities the nation really possesses. We may introduce the line with "there is" in our translation, as in Hosea 9:8, where the construction מַשְׂטֵמָה בְּבֵית אֱלֹהָיו has the sense of, *"There is* hatred in the house of God." The introduction of a substantive in this way needs no grammatical indication. פָּרָץ (erupt) has a variety of nuances, all reflecting the idea of bursting forth. It connotes rapid population growth (Gen. 28:14; 30:30; Exod. 1:12), bursting forth from the womb

(Gen. 38:29), the defeat of hostile forces (2 Sam. 5:20; 1 Chron. 13:11; 14:11; 15:13), breaking down an object (Isa. 5:5), increasing in number (Job 1:10), and forceful urging (2 Sam. 13:25; 2 Kings 5:23). The hostile sense of the verb is limited to divine activity. However, a noun form of this root (פָּרִיץ) describes a violent person (Ezek. 18:10) and occurs in association with bloodshed. The verse states, "If he begets a violent son [פָּרִיץ] who is a shedder of blood. . . ." The context of Hosea 4:2 lends a sense of violence to the verb פָּרָץ (erupt), for it is followed by the words דָּמִים בְּדָמִים נָגָעוּ (murder touches murder). This expression indicates that acts of bloodshed occurred in rapid succession.

3. עַל־כֵּן (Therefore) introduces the logical result of the disobedience of the people. It is expressed in the words תֶּאֱבַל הָאָרֶץ (the land mourns). While אֶרֶץ may refer to people (1 Sam. 14:25; 2 Sam. 15:23), it does not here. The feminine singular suffix on בָּהּ (in it) and the locative preposition בְּ (in) preclude that possibility. It is not the people who mourn, but the land. Hosea personifies the land to depict the fact that it will suffer the devastating results of the people's sin. בְּחַיַּת . . . . יֵאָסֵפוּ (along with the beast . . . they be taken away): This sentence is difficult, but if we understand אָסַף to be collocated with the three prepositions בְּ, we achieve good

---

2. The catalog of sins is imposing. Oath-taking was false and insincere; people made sworn oaths they did not intend to keep; the society was rampant with killing and theft; adultery was practiced extensively; eruptions of violence took lives with startling frequency. Hosea depicts the frequent killings in the expression *murder touches murder.* Killings occurred in such rapid succession that the intervals between them seemed nonexistent. Perhaps this refers to the frequent assassinations of kings in this time (see the Introduction). No wonder God has a controversy with his people!

The absence of the concepts of truth, lovingkindness, and the knowledge of God (v. 1) is reflected in specific moral wrongs (see the Exegesis). All these wrongs relate directly or indirectly to the Decalogue, the normative expression of Yahweh's will for the nation (see Jer. 7:9). The violation of God's law caused the nation to sink into decadence. They had opened the door to the curses of the covenant foreseen by Moses (Deut. 28).

3. It is not surprising then to hear Hosea say that the "land mourns," for several of the covenant curses involve the land (Deut. 28:16, 17, 30, 33, 38–42). God had said that the fecundity of the land depended on obedience to the covenantal stipulations (Deut. 11:13–17). Amos sets forth the same principle when he asserts that natural catastrophes are a divine discipline to bring the people back to God (4:6–11). Jeremiah attributes the lack of spring rain to the fact that the people have played the harlot (3:2–3). We must be careful today about attributing natural disasters and national calamities to God's judging hand. Under the new covenant, the counterpart of landedness is the believer's position in Christ (Heb. 3–4). The primary application of Hosea's words today is to the negative effect that sin will have on that relationship. But we must not lose sight of the fact that when perversion and violence are rampant in a society, that society will suffer, if not in the produce of the land, certainly in the vitality of its national life.

sense. בְּ commonly indicates accompaniment, and while אָסַף בְּ is not a clearly attested collocation (but see Neh. 9:1) the use of בְּ with אָסַף here can hardly connote anything other than *be gathered along with*. Thus the subject of יֵאָסֵפוּ is the inhabitants of the land (יוֹשֵׁב) who are to be taken away along with the animals, birds, and fish.

Not only is the land to suffer but its inhabitants as well. This reflects the divine warning (above) in which God pronounces judgment on the people of the land, "And you will perish quickly off the good land that the LORD is giving you" (Deut. 11:17, NRSV).

The results of Israel's idolatry would be devastating: The people were to be taken away from the land. To demonstrate this more forcefully, Hosea states that they will be taken away along with the animal life of the land. Their country is to be decimated.

IV. Yahweh's Controversy with His People (4:1–10)

B. The Nation Will Fall (4:4–6)

4 Surely, let no man contend,
  and let no one dispute,
    for your people are like those who
    dispute with priests.
5 For you will stumble by day,
  and even the prophet will stumble
    with you by night,
  and I will destroy your mother.
6 My people are destroyed for lack of
    knowledge.
  Since you have rejected knowledge,
  I will reject you from being a priest
    to me.
And [because] you have rejected the law
    of your God,
  I also will reject your children.

4 Yet let no one contend,
  and let none accuse,
    for with you is my contention, O
    priest.
5 You shall stumble by day;
  the prophet also shall stumble with
    you by night,
  and I will destroy your mother.
6 My people are destroyed for lack of
    knowledge;
  because you have rejected knowl-
    edge,
  I reject you from being a priest to me.
And since you have forgotten the law of
    your God,
  I also will forget your children.

4. אַךְ (Surely) may function as an asseverative (surely) or restrictive (yet, howbeit) particle. The restrictive force seems inappropriate here, since the command to refrain from disputing does not clearly contrast with the preceding section. On the other hand, the asseverative function of אַךְ may appear too abrupt. But the pericopes of chapters 4–14 are not marked by consistent logical flow. They find their unity in their relationships with the overarching themes of the book rather than in logical conceptual connections. Thus the translation "surely" is appropriate to the command of verse 4. אִישׁ (no one) functions in this negative clause as it does in the negative clause of 2:12 [10] to mean *no one*, literally, *no man*. אַל־יָרֵב (let [no one] contend): אַל with a jussive verb expresses prohibition (GKC §109c). וְאַל־יוֹכַח אִישׁ (and let no one dispute): The parallel relationship of the verb יָכַח (dispute) with רִיב (contend) limits

the nuance of יָכַח to legal disputation or defense as in Job 13:15. וְעַמְּךָ (for your people): The masculine suffix on עַם (people) may refer directly to the nation or to the man (אִישׁ) of the previous clause. While אִישׁ must be translated "no one" in that clause, it does not necessarily lose its personal or individual connotation. We may understand אִישׁ to refer to an unspecified, hypothetical person who represents the nation (note Exod. 34:3). כִּמְרִיבֵי כֹהֵן (as those who dispute with priests): The literal translation of this verbal form is "disputers of priests" (as in לֹקְחֵי חִטִּים [takers of wheat], 2 Sam. 4:6; נֹתְנֵי לַחְמִי [givers of my bread/who give me my bread], Hos. 2:7 [5]; and מַסִּיגֵי גְּבוּל [movers of boundaries], Hos. 5:10).

5. וְכָשַׁלְתָּ (For you will stumble): Note the discussion of the suffix on עַמְּךָ (*your* people) in verse 4. הַיּוֹם . . . לָיְלָה (by day . . . by night) are accusatives of time (see Ps. 1:2).

---

4. The dramatic disputation between Yahweh and his people continues in this section, but there is no reply from the people. They cannot answer, for the voice of the Lord is heard ringing, "Surely, let no man contend." All response, all opposition to his complaint, is silenced. Israel is represented in this scene as a man (ʾîš). That is why the suffixes are in the second-person masculine singular, for it is the nation, envisioned as the adversary in the dispute, that the Lord addresses—and silences. We see no need to identify the protagonists in this dispute as Yahweh and a hypothetical priest (Andersen and Freedman, Gordis, Wolff) if we translate the accusation as, "Your people are like those who dispute with priests."

In all likelihood this accusation reflects a Deuteronomic concept in which the people were warned to comply with the decisions of the priests and judges in all legal disputes (Deut. 17:8–13). Anyone who did not was put to death (v. 12). Hosea asserts that the people of his day are like those who do not humbly accept the decisions of their spiritual leaders. The people have a hard and rebellious spirit and are prone to protest their innocence. They rationalize and deny the list of wrongs set forth in Yahweh's *rîb* (4:1–3).

5. Because of their unwillingness to hear the dispute of the Lord, they will stumble and eventually fall as a nation. This is an evident reference to the coming captivity. In the dark times of confusion when they need a prophet of God, the prophet as well as the people will stumble in their

bewilderment. The nation, along with its institution of prophecy, will collapse.

Hosea represents the nation here as a mother. Once again Gomer appears hauntingly in the tapestry of the nation's destiny. We have observed that the mother represents corporate Israel, while the children represent individuals in the nation (Hos. 1:2 and 2:6 [4] of the Exposition). Isaiah uses the same analogy when he addresses the nation as children, and asks, "Where is your mother's bill of divorce?" (Isa. 50:1; see 49:22, 25). The occurrence of the word *mother* here challenges the prevalent view that Yahweh's protagonist in the dispute is a priest. Why should this hypothetical priest's mother be included in the accusation? The reference to the "mother" of a specific cultic figure living in Hosea's time is out of keeping with the general tenor of the passage, unless one severely emends the text. The statement that Yahweh will destroy the mother is balanced by the words, "My people are destroyed for lack of knowledge" (v. 6a). The repetition of the word *destroy* (*dāmâ*) makes it likely that the same object of destruction is in view in both clauses, that is, the people. The analogy of a mother for the nation is most appropriate for this book and occurs in 2:4 [2], 7 [5]. Throughout this context the pairing of similar concepts occurs with unusual regularity (contend/dispute; stumble/stumble; destroy/destroy; reject/reject). The balancing of "mother" and "people" in this structure thus supports the view that the mother corresponds

6. נִדְמוּ (are destroyed) is a niphal (passive) verb and continues the action set forth actively by the same root in the previous verse (דָּמִיתִי, I will destroy). כִּי (since/because) does not introduce the reason for the statement in the previous clause. Rather, it indicates causation within the clause it governs: "Because [Since] you have rejected knowledge, I will reject you." It is apparent that this is so because the subsequent clause ("I will reject you") would stand in awkward isolation if the כִּי (since) clause were the apodosis of the preceding clause. Also, the two clauses introduced by כִּי (since) are connected by several elements that lend conceptual balance to them, that is, the repetition of the verb מָאַס (reject) and the use of the second person. The preceding clause refers to

Israel in the third person (see the discussion at 5:3). וְאֶמְאָסְאךָ (I will reject you): The א that follows the final radical of this verb is difficult to identify grammatically. It may be the vestige of an early voluntative or emphatic form. In all probability it is a scribal error induced by the preceding מ which also precedes א and is somewhat similar in form to ס. מִכַּהֵן לִי (from being a priest to me): כָּהַן in the piel denotes the act of serving as a priest (see, e.g., Exod. 28:1; Lev. 7:35; Num. 3:3). וַתִּשְׁכַּח . . . אֶשְׁכַּח (And . . . you have rejected . . . I will reject): This structure balances two affirmative statements. The second clause states the result or consequence of the first, and is based on the reality of the state described in the first clause.

to the nation, not to the mother of a hypothetical priest.

6. The reason for the destruction of the nation is its lack of knowledge. We have observed that knowledge in Hosea may connote comprehension of God's requirements for blessing—knowledge of his ways and his nature. The hypothetical figure who represents the nation (see v. 4) is told that because the people have rejected knowledge, God will reject them from being a priest. Again the promise is in view, for when the Mosaic covenant was ratified at Sinai, God said, "You shall be for me a priestly kingdom" (Exod. 19:6, NRSV, lit. kingdom of priests). Hosea announces that another aspect of the promise is to be denied to the people.

Hosea does not quote these words exactly as they appear in Exodus 19:6, where it says *wĕʾattem tihyû-lî mamleket kōhănîm* (and you shall be to me a kingdom of priests). The verb *hāyâ* (to be) is omitted in Hosea's statements, but this is typical of his style. We observed in 1:9 another statement of the promise that was worded in a more cursory form than its original statement.

Since the nation has forgotten the law, its national constitution and guarantee of security, God will forget its children. Gomer's brood of children (adopted by Hosea) appear before us again and represent the nation. Culpable or not, all individuals in this rebellious nation are to suffer the same fate.

IV. Yahweh's Controversy with His People (4:1–10)

C. Priest and People Will Suffer the Same Fate (4:7–10)

7 The more they increased,
  the more they sinned against me:
  I will exchange their glory for shame.
8 My people feed on sin,
  and each one sets his desire on their
    iniquity.
9 But it will be that, as with the people,
  so with the priest.
  For I will visit his ways upon him
  and return his deeds to him.
10 They shall eat and not be satisfied,
  they shall commit fornication, but
    not increase,
  because they have given up their regard
    for the LORD.

7 The more they increased,
  the more they sinned against me;
  they changed their glory into shame.
8 They feed on the sin of my people;
  they are greedy for their iniquity.
9 And it shall be like people, like priest;
  I will punish them for their ways,
  and repay them for their deeds.
10 They shall eat, but not be satisfied;
  they shall play the whore, but not
    multiply;
  because they have forsaken the LORD
    to devote themselves to [whoredom.]

7. כֵּן . . . כְּ (lit. as . . . so) is the most common form of comparison (lit. according to their increase, so they sinned against me). כְּבוֹדָם (their glory): There is no compelling contextual reason for understanding כָּבוֹד (glory) to designate Yahweh. Since the destruction of the nation is in view throughout this section, glory applies most appropriately to the national prominence and economic prosperity the nation achieved during the eighth century B.C. This is confirmed by the fact that כָּבוֹד (glory) parallels כְּרֻבָּם (lit. their increase), which refers to the increase in the nation's prosperity. אָמִיר (I will exchange): Note the sense of *exchange* for this word in Leviticus 27:10, 33; Ezekiel 48:14.

8. חַטַּאת (sin) may denote sin as well as the sin offering (see, e.g., Lev. 7:37; 2 Kings 12:17 [16]). יֹאכֵלוּ (they eat): The subject is the people, as in the preceding context (see the Exposition for a discussion of the view that the subject is corrupt priests). עֲוֹנָם (their iniquity) combines the concepts of iniquity and guilt, as well as punishment for sin. וְאֶל־עֲוֹנָם יִשְׂאוּ (lit. on their iniquity they set):

נָשָׂא with אֶל and the adjunct נֶפֶשׁ form a collocation having the sense of setting one's desire on an object (Deut. 24:15; Prov. 19:18; Ps. 86:4). The indirect object of the verb נָשָׂא (lift up) here is עֲוֹנָם (their iniquity). נַפְשׁוֹ (his desire) has a masculine singular suffix which functions as a collective or distributive as in Deuteronomy 21:10: "When you go forth to war against your enemies, and the LORD your God gives them [lit. gives him: נְתָנוֹ] into your hands" (RSV). Isaiah 2:8 says, עָשׂוּ אֶצְבְּעֹתָיו לַאֲשֶׁר (lit. to that which they have made with *his* own fingers). We have reflected the idea of this distributive function here in Hosea 4:8 in the words "each one sets *his* desire" (see the Author's Translation).

9. וּפָקַדְתִּי עָלָיו דְּרָכָיו (lit. and I will visit upon him his ways): The evil ways of the nation will appear again, demanding requital and punishment. The fact that פָּקַד עַל (visit upon) does not simply mean "punish for," but possesses the sense of causing something to reappear in one's experience (see Hos. 1:4), is clear from the parallel expression וּמַעֲלָלָיו אָשִׁיב לוֹ (and return his deeds to him). דְּרָכָיו (his

---

7. As the nation increased, so did its sin, according to Hosea. This is a typical eighth-century prophetic concept. As the rich grew richer, the underprivileged classes suffered the more. As the prosperity of the nation increased, so did the complacency of the people. The welfare of the nation was probably attributed to the baals by many of Hosea's fellow citizens; idolatry then became even more entrenched in Israelite society.

As a result of their violation of the covenant standard, God declares that he will exchange their national glory for shame. They are to fall from the heights of economic prosperity to a position of subservience, as they bow to their captors and leave their homes for the humiliation of the captivity.

8. Those who hold the priesthood is in view in this passage translate the word *ḥaṭṭaʾt* (sin) as "sin offering." This is a viable translation of the word, and its association with "eat" (ʾakal) makes this a tempting option, for the priests ate portions of certain sacrifices (Lev. 24:9). The parallel clause, however, militates against this view, for its reference to making iniquity the object of one's desire calls for a similar idea in the first clause. We may express that idea by translating the first clause, "My people feed on sin" (see the Author's Translation). Sin was their sustenance, the object of their delight and satisfaction. The two clauses set forth the fact that the people subsisted on and

delighted in things that were in actuality sin. This may refer to their economic prosperity (v. 7), which was ill-gotten and symbolized their rebellion against God.

9. The words *it will be* frequently introduce statements of doom in the prophetic books. The clause that follows these words portends trouble for the priests as well as for the people. If the priests are in view in the passage to this point, we wonder why Hosea says, "As with the people, so with the priest." If this statement marks a transition in which he moves from an indictment of the priests to include the people, we should expect to read, "As with priest, so with people." As it stands, this statement leads us to expect the priests to be included in Hosea's prediction of judgment only at this point.

We need not think that the material that follows this transitional statement applies exclusively to the priests, for the language is too broad for that. The statement "they shall commit fornication, but not increase" (v. 10) is most appropriate to the nation and Hosea simply includes the priests along with the people.

It is possible that the masculine singular suffixal referents in verse 9b refer to a hypothetical priest because they follow the reference to the priest in verse 9a, but we cannot be sure. Hosea's use of gender is too flexible to allow for certainty in this regard. He uses singular referents in verses

ways): The Old Testament frequently uses the word דֶּרֶךְ (way) to refer to ethical deeds and behavior (see, e.g., 1 Kings 2:4; Prov. 10:9; Jer. 3:21). It is clear that this is its use here because the parallel word מַעֲלָלָיו (their deeds) determines its nuance.

10. הִזְנוּ (they shall commit fornication) is construed in the hiphil. The usages of the hiphil form of this verb outside Hosea (Exod. 34:16; Lev. 19:29; 2 Chron. 21:11, 13) reflect a causative sense (*cause to commit fornication*). Hosea, however, uses the hiphil of this word in a simple active sense (*commit fornication*) as in 4:18 and 5:3. עָזְבוּ לִשְׁמֹר (they have given up their regard): This use of שָׁמַר without an object is rare, but we may understand it as a pregnant expression as in Jeremiah 3:5, where it also occurs alone.

4–6 and refers to the nation in the masculine singular frequently in the book. He reverts to plural referents in verse 10 with no observable transition in his thought. The singular referents do not give strong support to the possibility that a priest stands before us in this verse.

The ways of the people will be visited upon them (see 1:4). It is clear from this usage of the collocation *paqad ʿal* (visit upon) that it does not have only the narrow sense of punish *for*. The parallel clause *return his deeds to him* invests *pāqad ʿal* with the sense of bringing something into the experience of someone (or something) else (see the Exegesis at 1:4). In this case the people's ways (the direct object) are to be brought into the experience of the people (the indirect object). Because their deeds and their ways are intrinsically evil, a fact Hosea sets forth at the beginning of this indictment (v. 7), their return is not innocuous. Their ways will come back to haunt them; their deeds will demand their due. That is the way of sin.

10. The people "shall eat and not be satisfied." This use of "eat" (ʾakal) does not require us to posit a priest here. If one holds to the view that a priest is in view in the previous section, the use of "eat" may seem to demand that conclusion (see v. 8). But the reference is just as appropriate for the people. The sense is that the people will continue to feed on sin (v. 8) but they will never find satisfaction. They will also continue their fornication, but they will not achieve the great population growth that Yahweh promised his people. These practices are not the way to national health and prosperity, because they are not based on regard for the Lord.

In all probability the *rîb* ends with this statement. The following material appears to be isolated from the preceding context by its peculiar literary structure. The concluding words of the *rîb* are at once poignant and condemning: "They have given up their regard for the Lord."

V. An Oracle Based on a Proverb (4:11–14)

¹¹ Fornication, and wine, and new wine
  take away the understanding.
¹² . . . My nation inquires of its wood,
    and its sticks of wood make pro-
      nouncements to it,
  for a spirit of fornication leads [it] astray,
    and they have gone off from their
      God, committing fornication.
¹³ On the summits of mountains they sac-
    rifice,
    and on the hills they burn incense,
  under oak, and poplar, and terebinth,
    because its shade is suitable.
  Therefore, your daughters commit for-
    nication,
    and your daughters-in-law adultery.
¹⁴ I will not visit upon your daughters the
    fact that they commit fornication,
    nor your daughters-in-law that they
      commit adultery,
  for the men themselves go off with har-
    lots,
    and sacrifice with cult prosti-
      tutes. . . .
  And a people without understanding
    will come to ruin.

¹¹ . . .
  Wine and new wine
    take away the understanding.
¹² My people consult a piece of wood,
    and their divining rod gives them
      oracles.
  For a spirit of whoredom has led them
    astray,
    and they have played the whore, for-
      saking their God.
¹³ They sacrifice on the tops of the moun-
    tains,
    and make offerings upon the hills,
  under oak, poplar, and terebinth,
    because their shade is good.

  Therefore your daughters play the
    whore,
    and your daughters-in-law commit
      adultery.
¹⁴ I will not punish your daughters when
    they play the whore,
    nor your daughters-in-law when they
      commit adultery;
  for the men themselves go aside with
    whores,
    and sacrifice with temple prostitutes;
  thus a people without understanding
    comes to ruin.

11. זְנוּת (fornication) is always used in a metaphorical sense of unfaithfulness to God in either the national sphere (Ezek. 23:27) or the religious sphere (Num. 14:33; Jer. 3:2, 9). Most commentators construe this word with the preceding clause to read עָזְבוּ לִשְׁמֹר זְנוּת (lit. they have forsaken [the LORD] to cherish fornication). The Septuagint, however, places πορνείαν (זְנוּת, fornication) with the following clause. The consonantal text also favors the placement of זְנוּת with the following clause because the word יַיִן (wine) has a ו (waw) attached to it. This construction would be awkward at the head of this sentence (see the Exposition). תִּירוֹשׁ (new wine) generally refers to fresh wine. It refers to the juice of the grape (Isa. 65:8; Prov. 3:10), and Micah 6:15 states that תִּירוֹשׁ produces יַיִן (wine). While תִּירוֹשׁ generally refers to new wine (Hos. 9:2) and יַיִן to fermented wine, one is a satisfactory poetic complement of the other because of their close association. It is also possible that תִּירוֹשׁ has a semantic range broad enough to include fermented wine (Judg. 9:13). לֵב (understanding) may connote, among other things, the cognitive or emotional nature of mankind (see, e.g., Gen. 6:5; Exod. 7:23; 2 Sam. 18:3; 2 Kings 5:26).

12. עַמִּי (My nation) is grammatically construed as a singular as in 4:14. בְּעֵצוֹ יִשְׁאָל (inquires of its wood): שָׁאַל בְּ connotes to inquire of someone or something (see Judg. 1:1). וּמַקְלוֹ (and its stick of wood): מַקֵּל is a piece of wood that may have various functions. Jacob fashioned such a branch for breeding purposes (Gen. 30:37); Jeremiah uses the word for the branch of an almond tree (1:11); and in 1 Samuel 17:40 it refers to a walking staff. יַגִּיד (make pronouncements): נָגַד denotes the idea of declaring. It is used here in an oracular sense, for it describes the pronouncements of that which was conceived to be a deity. כִּי (for) introduces the reason for the incredible fact that a nation consults its timber for guidance. רוּחַ זְנוּנִים הִתְעָה (a spirit of fornication leads [it] astray): רוּחַ has a broad semantic range. It often connotes that aspect of mankind, imperceptible in itself, which manifests itself in attitude and action (Exod. 6:9; 1 Chron. 5:26; Jer. 51:11). It refers here to the disposition of the Israelites that led them to forsake the holiness of Yahweh for the fertility cult of Baal. הִתְעָה (leads [it] astray) is used in the hiphil in the sense of causing to wander. It applies to a bridle (Isa. 30:28) and to shepherds and princes who lead others astray (Jer. 50:6; Isa. 19:13). The fact that the people were led astray by something within

---

11. This section forms an interesting literary pattern, for it appears to be based on a popular or prophetic proverb. The proverb is, "Wine and new wine take away the understanding, and a people without understanding will come to ruin." The proverb is not intact, for it appears that the writer detached the second line from the first to form a prologue and epilogue to this section (see vv. 11 and 14).

We have suggested (see the Exegesis) that Hosea modifies the proverb by the inclusion of zĕnût (fornication) in the first line. This alters its symmetry and the awkwardness that results is not typical of many of the proverbial sayings in the Wisdom material. If, however, there were no reference to fornication in the introductory statement, the proverb would have little significance for the context to which it is affixed. We find nothing about wine in this section; its topic is spiritual fornication. The disruption of the meter in this fashion introduces a jarring note and a jarring concept. It points out to the nation that there is something other than wine that dulls the mind; it is their enthrallment with idolatry.

12. The words of the prophet here are a vivid illustration of the previous statement. They show us how the people's spiritual fornication has dulled their minds. The nation, he says, inquires of its timber, and its sticks of wood speak its oracles. Frequent references in the Prophets attest to the fact that pagan idols were made of wood as well as stone (Isa. 37:19; 40:20; 45:20; Jer. 2:27; 3:9). Isaiah also wonders at the dullness of the minds of those who burn part of a piece of wood for heat, another piece for cooking, and what is left they fashion into an image before which they fall in worship (44:19). Not only did this fact show the spiritual dullness of the people, but it reflected a rejection of the prophetic institution which was the repository of divine truth in Yahwism (Deut. 18:9–22).

The reason for this plunge into the abyss of idolatry is the fact that the people have been led astray by a propensity to religious fornication which Hosea terms "a spirit of fornication." He knew of this all too well, for he had spent a period of time separated from his wife, who was all the while in another man's company. He realized then that the tendency to promiscuity, which had led

them, that is, a propensity to religious fornication, reflects the directive idea of the hiphil. מֵתַחַת אֱלֹהֵיהֶם (from their God) connotes, literally, from under their God, from under his sphere of authority (note the sense of this expression in Ps. 18:48 [47]). The word תַּחַת is used of a woman who is under the authority of her husband (Num. 5:19, 20, 29). Ezekiel 23:5 is important in this regard: "Oholah committed fornication while she was mine" (תַּחְתָּי, under me). On the use of מִן (from) with זָנָה (fornicate), see the discussion at 1:2.

13. כִּי טוֹב צִלָּהּ (because its shade is suitable): The reason for the people's observance of fertility worship under oak, poplar, and terebinth is given here. The singular feminine suffix *it* probably reflects Hosea's envisioning the trees as a grove rather than individually. The feminine suffix is used in this fashion when the gender of a concept cannot be determined (GKC §145k). עַל־כֵּן (Therefore) introduces the result of the foregoing statement—their daughters and daughters-in-law engage in

the pernicious cult that represents gross unfaithfulness to their God.

14. לֹא־אֶפְקוֹד עַל (I will not visit upon): The direct object of the idiom פָּקַד עַל (visit upon) is the object clause introduced by כִּי (that). See the discussion in the Exposition on this verse and at 1:4. כִּי תִזְנֶינָה (the fact that they commit fornication): כִּי (the fact that) cannot be causal here, for the sense would then be, "I will not visit upon your daughters, *the reason being* that they commit fornication." This is not an explanation for the withholding of divine punishment and is a non sequitur. Rather, כִּי introduces an object clause (GKC §157a–b) with the sense, "I will not visit upon your daughters *that* [the fact that] they commit fornication." The reason for the withholding of divine judgment from the female population is given in the next כִּי (for) clause. כִּי־הֵם עִם־הַזֹּנוֹת יְפָרֵדוּ (for the men themselves go off with harlots): הֵם (the men) is a masculine pronoun; hence it refers to the male population. פָּרַד

Gomer into her sordid ways, had not left her. So too with Israel; the national psyche reflected the same bent toward idolatry, not only in the wilderness when their marriage contract with Yahweh was ratified (Exod. 32:1–10), but also as far back as the period of Egyptian servitude (Ezek. 23:27).

The clause parallel to the statement concerning their spirit of fornication states, "They have gone off from their God, committing fornication." Literally it says that they have committed fornication *out from under* their God, that is, away from the sphere of subjection to God. This is also what Gomer did when she took up with a lover (3:1–2). We must not limit Israel's fornication only to the sexual acts involved in the fertility cult, for her fornication was primarily her consort with idols. Jeremiah said of his people that they committed adultery "with stone and tree" (3:9, NRSV).

13. This verse depicts Israel's fornication in terms appropriate to the nature cult. The people sought out the hills and woodlands, finding them suitable for the kind of worship in which they engaged. The high places, or pagan shrines that were vestiges of earlier Canaanite religion, came into use again. They may have been altars placed in groves of trees where the sacrifices were roasted and eaten. The "suitable" shade of which the prophet speaks may reflect a note of sarcasm. It was suitable because of another aspect of the cultic worship following the sacrifice, and which was intended to excite the lusty Baal, that is, the sexual rites that involved the sacred prostitutes.

The next clause begins with a "therefore." It states the logical result of the previous observation. Their daughters and daughters-in-law are fornicators and adulteresses. This would normally have been an insult, but the spiritual blindness of the people prevents them from seeing what they have become.

14. We expect a statement of judgment on these women who prostitute themselves in the name of religion, but it is strangely withheld. Yahweh will not punish them for their acts. Hosea again expresses the concept of punishment in the idiom *paqad ʿal*. We observed in the discussion at 1:4 that when this collocation occurs with two objects, the direct object is viewed as coming into the experience of the indirect object. In this context the indirect objects of the preposition *ʿal* are "daughters" and "daughters-in-law." The direct object is the object clause introduced by *kî*. The negative clause in which *paqad ʿal* occurs states that Yahweh will not "visit upon" the female population the fact that they commit fornication, that is, this fact will not come back to them to demand requital. These women will be spared punishment for their participation in the fertility cult.

The next line tells us why the women are spared. It is because the men consort with cult prostitutes. The women are not to blame, because the men foster and encourage such worship. Perhaps men recruited young women for these religious orgies and so sustained the greater guilt.

has the basic sense of *to divide* or *separate*. It pictures the men as separating from others to consort with cult prostitutes in offering sacrifices

(note the parallel clause). יִלְבֵט (will come to ruin) occurs only here and in Proverbs 10:8, 10. Its Arabic cognate connotes *to strike the ground*.

The remaining line of the proverb introducing this section stands in stark conceptual isolation from the context. This fact forces us back to the first line of the proverb in which (if we have understood it correctly) Hosea warns that fornication, as well as wine, dulls the mind. We have seen in our imagination the practices of which he speaks. His vivid style has caused us to see the blue smoke of the sacrifices hovering over the groves, and we have heard the brazen laughter of the cult prostitutes. Now it all fades, and we hear that a people whose minds have been made dull and insensitive by such practices will come to ruin.

VI. A General Denunciation of Israel (4:15–19)

15 Though you commit fornication, Israel,
    let not Judah incur guilt.
Do not go to Gilgal,
    and do not go up to Beth-aven,
    and do not swear, "As the LORD
    lives,"
16 for Israel is stubborn,
    like a stubborn heifer.
Now, the LORD will pasture them
    like sheep in a broad expanse.

17 Ephraim is joined to idols.
    Let him alone!
18 Their drink is gone. They give them-
    selves up to fornication.
Her shields love shame.
19 A wind has enveloped her in its wings,
    and they will be ashamed of their
    sacrifice.

15 Though you play the whore, O Israel,
    do not let Judah become guilty.
Do not enter into Gilgal,
    or go up to Beth-aven,
    and do not swear, "As the LORD
    lives."
16 Like a stubborn heifer,
    Israel is stubborn;
can the LORD now feed them
    like a lamb in a broad pasture?

17 Ephraim is joined to idols—
    let him alone.
18 When their drinking is ended, they
    indulge in sexual orgies;
    they love lewdness more than their
    glory.
19 A wind has wrapped them in its wings,
    and they shall be ashamed because
    of their altars.

15. אִם־זֹנֶה אַתָּה (though you commit fornication) is a concessive clause introduced by אִם with a participle in the protasis. The apodosis, governed by a jussive with the negative אַל, expresses the prohibition of a concept, that is, Judah's guilt. יֶאְשַׁם (incur guilt): אָשַׁם has both the sense of committing wrong and being held liable for wrong (guilty).

The context calls for the latter sense. Though Israel persists in its fornication, Judah is not to be charged with guilt. וְאַל־תָּבֹאוּ (and do not go) introduces a series of jussives with אַל connoting negative command. The verbs in this sequence are construed in the plural while the verb in the first clause is singular. This transition in number in the addresses to Israel may indicate that Hosea

---

15. This section begins with a statement of bitter irony. We may broadly paraphrase it, "You may act like a whore Israel, but let not Judah incur the guilt you have incurred." Irony pervades the entire section, and we must grasp that irony if we are to understand Hosea's words.

Hosea stands before the northern kingdom in this address, but in his mind he stands before a brazen woman, hardened by her promiscuous sexual activity. What he says would bring a flush even to her cheeks, for he compares her to another woman and expresses the wish that Israel will not contaminate her. The other woman is Israel's hated sister Judah. How small Israel would have felt when she learned how the prophet viewed her—as someone apart, someone who would spread her guilt, someone to avoid.

If we understand it in this way, there is no need to view the reference to Judah as a later Judahite redaction. The reference to Judah fits the context well if we view it as irony. Even if we cannot prove that some Judahites strayed over their northern border to worship at the cult centers cited by Hosea, it is of no consequence. The prophet addresses his words only to Israel. As Mays observes, "The exhortation to Judah not to visit Israel's favourite shrines is simply bitter condemnation of their cult meant for the ears of those who did worship in them" (*Hosea*, p. 77).

The religious sanctuaries of Gilgal and Bethel (Beth-aven) played a prominent role in Israel's observance of the fertility cult. Beth-aven means "House of Evil," and the prophet scornfully applies this appellation to the town of Bethel as a pun on its name. Jeremiah (48:13) and Amos (5:5) also put Bethel in a bad light, and Gilgal also figures in the fabric of Amos's prophecy (4:4; 5:5). Jeroboam I established Bethel as the main sanctuary of the northern kingdom where the cult of the golden calves found expression (1 Kings 12:25–33). Amos may have provided the basis for the unusual nickname for Bethel, for he uses the term *'awen* in connection with that city (5:5). Hosea's command not to frequent these places is a prohibition against the observance of the worship carried on at those sites.

Not only are the people warned to avoid the cult centers, but they are commanded not to swear, "As the LORD lives." No clear evidence exists that this formula was uttered in the liturgy of the worship carried on at these sites. It is a common oath-form in the Old Testament. It is placed on the lips of Yahweh (Ezek. 5:11; 34:8; Zeph. 2:9) and uttered frequently by the people (Judg. 8:19; 1 Kings 1:29; Jer. 4:2; 5:2; 16:14, 15). Its purpose was not to affirm primarily the existence of God, but to lend credence to an affirmation. Its sense is that as surely as the god of the oath lives, so surely will the sworn intent be carried out. David swore to Bathsheba, "As the LORD lives . . . as I swore to you . . . so will I do this day" (1 Kings 1:29–30, NRSV). This oath should not be seen as a cultic affirmation of the existence of Yahweh, for the succession of *waw*-clauses in which the oath occurs need be nothing more than a grouping of those aspects of Israelite society that were particularly galling to the prophet. These elements were tangible displays of the religious defection of the people, that is, their overt participation in the orgiastic worship at the cult sites, and their spurious and insincere oaths. Indeed, Hosea places oath-taking at the head of the list of wrongs in his society (4:2), being evidence of the lack of knowledge of God in the land.

It is true that the prophet Amos castigates those who swore in the name of deities associated with cult centers (8:14), but there is nothing to indicate that anything more is intended here than a reference to the oath-taking common to ordinary life and business. If we understand the oath in this way, Hosea's command to the two kingdoms is that they end their participation in the state religion and mend the social wrongs in their society. Jeremiah refers to the same oath, but with no indication of its association with cultic litany. He says, "And if you swear, 'As the LORD lives!' in truth, in justice, and in uprightness, then nations shall be blessed by him, and by him they shall boast" (Jer. 4:2, NRSV). The

thinks of Israel as a harlot when he uses the singular verb, and as a people when he uses the plural. חַי־יְהוָה (as the Lord lives) is a frequently occurring oath in the Old Testament (see, e.g., Isa. 49:18; Jer. 38:16; Ezek. 35:6; 33:11; Zeph. 2:9).

16. כִּי (for) does not introduce direct causation. It makes little sense to say that Israel is not to swear "As the Lord lives" because she is stubborn. כִּי introduces proximate cause as it does in many instances (see Isa. 28:10–11, where the כִּי in v. 11 introduces the proximate cause for the statement in v. 10). The implied reason for the prohibition against the aspects of worship in Hosea 4:15 is that Israel's stubbornness has led to her abandonment by God (see the Exposition). סֹרְרָה (stubborn): סָרַר describes stubborn refusal to submit to authority, hence occasionally rebellion (Isa. 1:23;

30:1; Jer. 5:23; Hos. 9:15). בַּמֶּרְחָב (in a broad expanse) indicates basically a wide area. It does not have the intrinsic meaning of pasture (Hab. 1:6), but the presence of רָעָה (graze, pasture) calls for that sense in this context.

17. חָבוּר (joined) refers to the coupling and compaction of objects (Exod. 26:3), as well as to the making of personal alliances (2 Chron. 20:35). It indicates here that the people are joined to idols as their confederates. עֲצַבִּים (idols) is from the verb עָצַב (shape, fashion, BDB, p. 781). The noun based on this verb conveys the fact that an idol is something fashioned. The word occurs only once in the singular (Jer. 22:28). Its use in the plural would call to mind the many images and amulets existing throughout the northern kingdom. הַנַּח־לוֹ (Let him alone!): נוּחַ in the hiphil forms a collocation

---

point is that if the people dealt with one another in honesty and sincerity, covenant blessing would be restored to them.

16. The reason for Hosea's prohibitions is given in a causal (*kî*) clause that expresses proximate causation (see the Exegesis). The sense of this and the following clause is that Israel's stubbornness had led to her abandonment by Yahweh (see the subsequent interpretation of the metaphor of sheep in a broad expanse). We may paraphrase the complex clausal structure in this way: "Do not worship at Gilgal and Bethel, and do not swear, 'As the Lord lives,' *because* [*kî*] it will do no good. Your stubbornness has led the Lord to abandon you as sheep in a vast wilderness." The negative jussives may seem to imply that the judgment might have been averted, but such a conclusion is tenuous. It was inevitable, and Hosea's marriage already foreshadowed the period of Israel's severance from her God.

The causal clause sets forth the prophet's assessment of Israel; she is like a stubborn heifer, a balky cow that will not go where the herdsman directs. The following word *now* implies resolution on the part of the speaker: *Now* the Lord will tend them like sheep in a broad expanse of land. This sounds comforting, for the reference to sheep brings to mind helpless animals under a shepherd's care. The broad expanse of territory, moreover, would seem to speak of freedom from danger and restrictions. The word *merḥab* (broad expanse) has this sense in a number of contexts (2 Sam. 22:20; Pss. 31:9 [8]; 118:5), but something appears wrong with its usage here. The context leads us to expect judgment, not comfort, and the sheep are out in

the broad ranges with no mention of a sheepfold. We begin to suspect that Yahweh has led the people to this lonely place not to care for them, but to abandon them. The subsequent words, "Let him alone!" (v. 17), confirm our suspicion.

This view gains support from the following construction of the clauses:

A Israel is stubborn, like a stubborn heifer.
B Now, the Lord will pasture them like sheep in a broad expanse.
C Ephraim is joined to idols.
D Let him alone! Their drink is gone.

Clauses A and C are conceptually parallel; they accuse Israel of wrong. Clause D influences B in this structure. Since clause D depicts Israel's abandonment (as well as the resultant end of her revelries), we may understand B in the way we have suggested.

17. Yahweh abandons Israel because she is confederate with idols. This is one of Hosea's strongest statements about Israel's relationship to the fertility cult, for it pictures Israel bound together with idols in an inextricable relationship. The confederation with Yahweh in the bond of the covenant has dissolved.

The words "Let him alone!" are not spoken arbitrarily. Israel's stubborn refusal to turn to God (see v. 16) and her allegiance to idols make it clear that Yahweh can do nothing with them. In Hosea's metaphor Yahweh leads his people like sheep, brings them to a broad expanse, and leaves them without a shepherd among the hostile nations of the world. The analogy effectively

with לְ, having the sense of *let alone* (Exod. 32:10; 2 Sam. 16:11; 2 Kings 23:18).

18. סָר סָבְאָם (their drink is gone) is a difficult construction. The Septuagint reads ᾑρέτισεν Χαναναίους (he [Ephraim] has chosen the Canaanites). Evidently the Septuagint construes סָבְאָם as a participle (Canaanites = carousers). Wolff suggests "When their carousing is past" (*Hosea*, pp. 72–73), while Andersen and Freedman translate it "He has turned aside from their drunkenness" (*Hosea*, p. 344). The emendation suggested in BHS (סֹד סֹבְאִים, a crowd of drunkards) is appropriate to the context, but its lack of manuscript evidence renders it conjectural. It is possible that סָר represents dittography induced by the first two consonants of the next word, but dittography before the word that influences it is somewhat unusual. The difficult reading should be preferred. Since the consonantal text is our most important control, we should work within its framework before altering the text or positing emendations. The Masoretic Text pointing of סָבְאָם renders the meaning, "Their *strong drink*." סָר may be read as a third-person singular of סוּר (depart). Martin J. Buss (*Prophetic Word of Hosea*, p. 12) derives סָר from סָרַר (rebellious): "*Rebellious* (?) is their drinking-party." But סָר (rebellious) always applies directly to people in the Old Testament. Wood (*Hosea*, p. 188) understands the word סָר to refer to the depletion of the wine imbibed during the orgiastic worship described in this context ("finished their drinks"). However, we may wonder if סוּר has the sense of depletion. There is an ultimacy about this word that goes beyond the idea of temporarily running out of material: "The bitterness of death *is gone*"

(1 Sam. 15:32), "the LORD has *turned away from you*" (1 Sam. 28:16), "*turn away from evil*" (Prov. 3:7), and "the feasting of those who stretch themselves *shall pass away*" (Amos 6:7). This last verse is particularly instructive because of its similarity to Hosea 4:18. Wolff (*Hosea*, p. 91) follows Van Gelderen and translates it: "When their beer, i.e., their drinking, is past, then they commit fornication, etc." But the word סור indicates *departing* in the qal and does not appear to allow for the translation "is past." There is an option that retains the sense of finality in this word, however. We may understand the word to state that their drink is gone because it will no longer be available to them; their drinking will cease (as in Amos 6:7). אָהֲבוּ הֵבוּ (love): The current discussion of this obscure structure centers on whether we should read it as one word or two. Several recent scholars (i.e., Mays, *Hosea*, p. 76; Wolff, *Hosea*, p. 73) explain it as a misreading of אָהֹב אָהֲבוּ (loving they love). One of the suggestions of Andersen and Freedman is that it is a reduplicative stem after the analogy of נַאֲפוּפֶיהָ (adulteries) in 2:4 [2]. It is possible, but conjectural, that הֵב (love) was an alloform for אָהַב (love) in Hosea's dialect. We cannot rule out dittography as a possibility either. If the consonants in the orthography have not suffered in transmission and represent the original words of the writer, we may understand the two words in the Masoretic Text as a single reduplicative verbal form of אָהַב (love) similar to the *pĕʿalʿal* stem (אֲהַבוּהֲבוּ). The *šureq* on אָהֲבוּ may represent *plene* writing of an original *u* vowel as in נַאֲפוּפֶיהָ (see above). A *u* vowel written *plene* appears in the same position in a reduplicated (*paʿlēl*) verbal form

---

depicts the abandonment the people felt when they went into captivity.

18. We construe the next clause, "Their drink is gone," with the previous one. The shepherd says, "Let him alone! Their drink is gone." These clipped sentences are not connected syntactically. It is not necessary to conclude that the people were left alone because their drink was gone. The first statement orders their abandonment, while the second describes their condition. The word *drink* stands for that which contributed to the people's drunken orgiastic worship at the high places, a symbol of their debauchery. We may understand it to say, "Her debauchery is over." Israel was to be left alone in the wilderness, her shameful revels at an end. This motif of the shepherd may be another example of irony in this passage, for the pastoral motif shifts to become a

statement of doom. Irony was one of the sharpest weapons the prophets had.

Hosea's next statement is an emphatic assertion. It states literally, "fornicating, they fornicate." He moves from the statement of future doom back to the reality of the moment. This statement, along with Hosea's subsequent indictment of their "shields," balances clauses A and C in the structure noted above. Since the following clause, "A wind has enveloped her," presages judgment, these clauses follow the same pattern. We may include them in the structure as clauses E and F.

Israel's leaders (depicted as shields) love shame (see the Exegesis). This statement balances the previous clause and reflects its intensity. "Shame" refers to their fornication. The context, with its emphasis on debauchery, colors the word

in Psalm 88:17 [16] (צַמְּתוּתֻנִי). The reduplication may have imparted intensity to the action of the verb. מָגִנֶּיהָ הֵבוּ (her shields) functions as the subject of אָהֲבוּ. The word *shields* may refer to leaders (Pss. 89:19 [18]; 47:10 [9]).

19. צָרַר (caught up) denotes *to bind* or *compress* (see Exod. 12:34; 1 Sam. 25:29). בִּכְנָפֶיהָ (in its wings): כָּנָף is associated with the wind in 2 Samuel 22:11.

---

fornication with the sense of sexual fornication, not fornication in the sense of international alliances.

19. The word *wind* (*rûaḥ*) in Hosea's metaphor is the same word that describes the spirit of harlotry controlling the people of Hosea's society (v. 12). But here wind has no contextual connection with the psychological forces at work in the nation. Rather, it depicts the people, caught up in the currents of forces over which they have no control. The divine will and the machinations of national leaders will carry the nation onward until they stand as displaced persons, cast out of home and country. They will look back to those revels and recall the acrid odor of burning sacrifices offered to the forces of nature, and they will be ashamed. Jeremiah summons his generation to a similar response through a voice calling the people to acknowledge that the hills and the orgies on the mountains are a delusion, with the high point being, "Let us lie down in our shame, and let our dishonor cover us" (3:21–25, NRSV).

VII. An Oracle Addressed to Various Levels of Israelite Society (5:1–15)

A. The People and Their Leaders Have Gone Too Far (5:1–4)

5 Hear this, O priests!
　Give attention, O house of Israel!
　Listen, O house of the king!
　　For the judgment pertains to you;
　for you have been a snare at Mizpah,
　and a net spread on Tabor,
² and through slaughter they sink ever
　　deeper into acts of rebellion,
　but I am chastisement to all of them.

³ I know Ephraim,
　and Israel is not hid from me.
Because now that you, Ephraim, have
　　committed fornication,
　Israel is defiled;
⁴ their deeds do not permit them
　to return to their God,
because a spirit of fornications is in
　their midst,
　　and they do not know the LORD.

5 Hear this, O priests!
　Give heed, O house of Israel!
　Listen, O house of the king!
　　For the judgment pertains to you;
　for you have been a snare at Mizpah,
　and a net spread upon Tabor,
² and a pit dug deep in Shittim;
　but I will punish all of them.

³ I know Ephraim,
　and Israel is not hidden from me;
　for now, O Ephraim, you have played
　　the whore;
　Israel is defiled.
⁴ Their deeds do not permit them
　to return to their God.
For the spirit of whoredom is within
　them,
　　and they do not know the LORD.

5:1. שִׁמְעוּ־זֹאת הַכֹּהֲנִים (Hear this, O priests): This section begins with a summons to the priests to hear the prophet's words. זֹאת (this) does not refer to a particular entity to which one can assign gender; thus it is in the feminine abstract. הַקְשִׁיבוּ (Give attention) along with the following verb, הַאֲזִינוּ (listen), are common words for the command *to hear*, and often occur in various parallel combinations. There is no evident difference of meaning between them. בֵּית יִשְׂרָאֵל (house of Israel) and בֵּית הַמֶּלֶךְ (house of the king) are not necessarily synonymous because they occur in this sequence of three entities. They are simply poetic complements that represent aspects of Israel's political and religious leadership (see 1:4). Hosea would not have regarded הַכֹּהֲנִים (priests) and בֵּית הַמֶּלֶךְ (house of the king) as identical elements. כִּי (for) introduces the reason why they must listen. לָכֶם הַמִּשְׁפָּט כִּי (For the judgment pertains to you): "You" refers to the nation viewed corporately, as well as through its leaders. מִשְׁפָּט (judgment) has a broad translational range: statutes, justice, legal decision, fashion or manner, lawful, true religion, legal right, and punishment. Since this context sets forth a clear statement of the way God will respond to the people's sin (vv. 5–7), we understand the word in the sense of punishment. The second כִּי (for) introduces the reason for the judgment announced in the previous clause. פַּח (snare) is a trap for birds. The word frequently occurs in a metaphorical sense to picture efforts made to bring about someone's downfall (Ps. 140:6 [5]; Jer. 18:22), dangers that lurk in the way of the godly

(Prov. 22:5), the exigencies of life (Job 22:10), and other similar human experiences. לְמִצְפָּה (at Mizpah): Since מִצְפָּה is always definite in the Masoretic Text, the lack of the article here is curious. A possible explanation for this construction is that the word does not refer to any of the geographical sites named Mizpah, but to a tower or height. Against this is the qāmeṣ in the second syllable. We expect a sĕgôl in this case (see 2 Chron. 20:24). The reference in the parallel clause to the hill called Tabor favors a geographical referent for מִצְפָּה. Since there is no apparent evidence that bird snares were set on towers and since an unvocalized text would not reflect the determination of this word, it is best to understand Mizpah as a place. In all probability the reference is to Mizpah of Gilead, a lofty mountain to the east of the Jordan. רֶשֶׁת (a net) was also used for catching birds (Prov. 1:17). תָּבוֹר (Tabor) is a mountain in the Valley of Jezreel. The preposition עַל (on) shows that the writer has a mountain in mind, not the area near Bethel called Tabor (1 Sam. 10:3).

2. וְשַׁחֲטָה (and through slaughter) is unattested elsewhere. If it has not undergone alteration in the process of transmission, or is not a biform of שַׁחַת (pit), we may understand the word only as a feminine noun from the verb שָׁחַט which connotes *to slaughter*. The suggestion that the word connotes *pit* is attractive in view of the accompanying verb עָמַק in the hiphil (lit. they dig); however, this sense is unattested. The Masoretic Text makes sense if וְשַׁחֲטָה is understood as an accusative of

---

5:1. This oracle is addressed to the priests, the people (the house of Israel), and the house of the king. The house of the king refers to the reigning monarch (as in Isa. 7:2, where "house of David" is construed in the singular and connotes King Ahaz). The oracle announces judgment on the entire nation, including its leaders. The reason for the judgment is set forth in a complex of four clauses beginning, "For you have been a snare at Mizpah." The word *net* in the following clause balances *snare* in the parallelism and thus limits its range. We are to think of a snare made of netting into which a bird could easily fly and become trapped. Hosea pictures the snare as stretched on a lofty height.

No contextual warrant exists for limiting "you have been a snare" only to the reigning king. This verse includes the entire nation as well as its leaders. As birds become entangled in the meshing of a net and are killed and eaten, so the structure of

Israelite society is a fabric of intrigue and assassination in which blood flows freely in factional strife. We catch glimpses of the interweaving of political factions in Hosea's society as we read his scathing denunciations. He says of the priests, "As robbers lie in wait for someone, so the priests are banded together; they murder on the road to Shechem, they commit a monstrous crime (6:9, NRSV); he implicates the people in the same crimes when he states, "All of them are hot as an oven, and they devour their rulers. All their kings have fallen; none of them calls upon me" (7:7, NRSV). This is a vivid reflection of the period following the death of Jeroboam II, when anyone who took the throne was in danger of losing his life.

2. The third clause carries on the same thought. The slaughter that characterized this dismal period of Israelite history was not an isolated phenomenon, for like so many societal trends it had worsened. The nation found itself sinking ever

means (through slaughter). שֵׁטִים (acts of rebellion) is from שׂוט (to swerve or fall away). It also is unattested elsewhere. A biform (סֵטִים) of the word occurs in Psalm 101:3. Most commentators understand סֵטִים in that context as a reference to individuals (NRSV those who fall away). It seems more consistent, however, to translate the word as "acts of rebellion." This is in keeping with the other elements listed in the first four verses, which are moral concepts rather than direct descriptions of people. הֶעְמִיקוּ (they sink ever deeper): עָמַק connotes *to make deep* in the hiphil. It occurs in Hosea 9:9 with the sense of sinking deep into corruption. We understand it here in the sense that the people made rebellious acts deeper. This is after the analogy of Isaiah 31:6: "They have deepened [their] apostasy." מוּסָר (chastisement) combines elements of instruction and punishment in its range of meaning (note the Ugaritic *ysr*, to chasten, instruct; Gordon, *UT*, p. 412). While the primary concept of the word here is punishment, the subsequent context sets forth a benign and instructive result of Yahweh's judgment: "Come, let us return to the LORD; for he has torn, that he may heal us; he has stricken, and he will bind us up" (Hos. 6:1). אֲנִי מוּסָר (I am chastisement) is an

unusual construction; we expect a participle, but the noun clause makes good sense. The word occurs in a somewhat similar sense in Ezekiel 5:15: "And it shall be [NRSV you shall be] . . . chastisement [*mûsār*] . . . to the nations . . . when I bring judgment on you." In the noun clause the substantive in the predicate (מוּסָר) may receive a degree of emphasis (GKC §141c).

3. כִּי עַתָּה (Because now that): כִּי should not be construed with the preceding clause because of the lack of an obvious causative connection with it. Rather, the causation is internal to the clauses introduced by כִּי. Ephraim's fornication was the cause of Israel's defilement (see the Author's Translation). הִזְנֵיתָ (you . . . have committed fornication) is in the hiphil (see the Exegesis at 4:10), and is a second masculine singular referring to Ephraim. There is no need to follow the conjecture (זָנִיתָ) of BHS. נִטְמָא (is defiled): Defilement could result from sexual wrongs (Lev. 18:24; Num. 5:13–31) as it does in this case.

4. לֹא יִתְּנוּ ([their deeds] do not permit): נָתַן (give) may be translated "permit" (Gen. 20:6; Exod. 3:19; Num. 20:21) when construed with לְ plus an infinitive. כִּי (because) states the reason for their inability to return to God: it is because of a spirit of fornication (see 4:12).

deeper into a morass of rebellion. In the mind of the prophet, the structure of his society was interwoven from top to bottom with intrigue. Kings were assassinated, the priests were corrupt, and the people lusted for blood and lawlessness.

Yahweh speaks in the final clause and says, "I am chastisement." This unusual expression is a verbless clause that defines the essence of the subject. The Lord himself will be the punishment; Yahweh—with his attributes, his power, and his authority—will step into the realm of history bringing chastisement to the nation. The word *mûsar* (chastisement) includes an element of discipline or instruction. We may see the instructional side of Yahweh's attributes expressed in the events surrounding the ratification of the law. Moses said, "Consider the discipline of the LORD your God, his greatness, his mighty hand and his outstretched arm" (Deut. 11:2, RSV). We may see it also where Yahweh says he has dealt Israel "the punishment [*mûsār*] of a merciless foe" (Jer. 30:14, NRSV), but he concludes, "In the latter days you will understand this" (30:24, NRSV).

3. Hosea goes on to say that the people of Israel are not hidden from Yahweh's view. No one can hide from the Sovereign of the universe. The

nation's devotion to idolatry had defiled them, and there was no longer the possibility of repentance. This sorry state came about as a result of the mind-set of the people to which Hosea points—the spirit of fornication (4:12).

Ephraim is in tandem with Israel in the parallel structure of the first line of this verse, but in the second line there is a distinction between the two entities. Ephraim is blamed for Israel's defilement. See the discussion at verse 5 (below).

4. Earlier we heard Yahweh say, "I know Ephraim" (v. 3); here the prophet says that the people do not know the Lord. This apparent word-play on the word *know* underscores the negative side of knowledge in its relation to God. Yahweh's knowledge of Ephraim is not positive, for he knows Israel's evil penchant for idolatry. The people do not know God, for they do not have a loving, intimate relationship with God (4:1). Knowing God involves understanding his ways and his character; it involves comprehension of his righteous demands and the benign effect that these demands can have (see 2:21–22 [19–20]; 4:1; 6:6). Israel knew Baal better than she knew Yahweh.

VII. An Oracle Addressed to Various Levels of Israelite Society (5:1–15)

B. Both Judah and Israel Will Be Judged for Their Unfaithfulness to Yahweh (5:5–7)

5 And the pride of Israel testifies to his
    face,
    and Israel and Ephraim will stumble
      in their guilt.
    Judah will also stumble with them.
6 They will come with their sheep and
    cattle
    to seek the LORD,
  but they will not find [him];
    he has withdrawn from them.
7 They have been unfaithful to the LORD,
    for they have had alien children.
    Now, the new moon will devour
      their tracts of land.

5 Israel's pride testifies against him;
    Ephraim stumbles in his guilt;
    Judah also stumbles with them.
6 With their flocks and herds they shall
    go
    to seek the LORD,
  but they will not find him;
    he has withdrawn from them.
7 They have dealt faithlessly with the
    LORD;
    for they have borne illegitimate chil-
    dren.
    Now the new moon shall devour
      them along with their fields.

5. וְעָנָה בְּ (And . . . testifies): The idiom עָנָה בְּ occurs in several legal contexts in the sense of bringing damaging testimony against another party (1 Sam. 12:3; 2 Sam. 1:16). The וְ seems awkward after the preceding clause, but we may understand it to introduce the consequence of the previous statement. גְאוֹן־יִשְׂרָאֵל (the pride of Israel): גָאוֹן when used of nations refers to that for which they are known and of which they may be proud (Ps. 47:5 [4]; Isa. 13:19; 16:6; Jer. 13:9). וְאֶפְרַיִם וְיִשְׂרָאֵל (and Israel and Ephraim): The coupling of apparently identical entities in this construction seems redundant. Many commentators delete יִשְׂרָאֵל because of its apparent superfluity and the consistent pattern of alternating names. The Septuagint, however, witnesses to the integrity of the two names, and the rest of the clause answers grammatically to a plural subject (see the Exposition). יִכָּשְׁלוּ בַּעֲוֹנָם (will stumble in their guilt): The writer again prefigures the fall of the nation in the word כָּשַׁל (stumble). The fact that the verb is in the niphal has no exegetical significance. This verb prefers the niphal for the imperfect. The

heinous sins of which Israel was guilty were the sphere (בְּ) in which she fell. She will perish in her sin with no deliverance; the die has been cast.

6. בְּצֹאנָם וּבִבְקָרָם (with their sheep and cattle): בְּ with הָלַךְ (come) denotes accompaniment. "Sheep and cattle" includes the broad spectrum of farm animals. לְבַקֵּשׁ (to seek): The לְ introduces the purpose for the action inherent in הָלַךְ (come). חָלַץ (withdrawn) is used on occasion of taking off a shoe (Deut. 25:9–10; Isa. 20:2). In general it connotes the loosing of a bond.

7. בָּגָדוּ (they have been unfaithful): Besides its frequent references to Israel's treatment of Yahweh, this term describes the unfaithfulness of a wife (Jer. 3:20), the deceitfulness of Job's friends (Job 6:15), and dishonesty in one's dealings with a slave (Exod. 21:8). It is clear that the concept of unfaithfulness in marriage is the primary nuance here because of the following clause. זָרִים יָלָדוּ כִּי־בָנִים (for they have had alien children): כִּי (for) introduces the reason for the conclusion. Israel's children are not Yahweh's children, but were born of other men. זָרִים refers in this context to some-

---

5. The litigious atmosphere of the passage (see 5:1) continues as we hear the witness speak. The witness is the pride of Israel that testifies to his face. No contextual warrant exists for understanding the "pride of Israel" to be Yahweh. It is best understood as the magnificence of the nation—its history, wealth, territory, and institutions—of which she was so proud, but which were in a state of decay. Hosea uses the expression *pride of Israel* in this way in 7:10, where he pictures the nation in a state of weakness and decline (7:8–10). Aliens were devouring the nation's strength, yet the people paid no heed; that which was the object of their vaunted pride was in a state of decay, but they did not observe it.

Here the object of Israel's pride stands as an accusing witness before her. It is clothed in tatters; it is frail and dying. It testifies of the truth of Yahweh's words expressed by the prophet. The nation is already falling. Its kings are being assassinated; its government is unstable. Israel must find its support in pagan nations. The weakened state of the nation presages its eventual fall.

The Masoretic Text reads, "Israel and Ephraim will stumble." The statement seems awkward, since throughout the prophecy both names designate the northern kingdom, but there is no need to emend. The syntax of this clause witnesses to a distinction between Israel and Ephraim that we may observe elsewhere in the book. Earlier Hosea

states, "Because now that you, Ephraim, have committed fornication, Israel is defiled" (5:3). It is as though the sin of the major tribe of Israel has infected the whole kingdom. God's desire to restore Israel is impeded by the sin of Ephraim, which finds the focus of its expression in Samaria, its capital (7:1). The prophet singles Ephraim out from Israel, saying, "When Ephraim spoke, there was trembling; he was lifted up in Israel; but he incurred guilt through Baal and died" (13:1). These statements differentiating Ephraim from Israel evidently reflect the influence Ephraim, Israel's most prominent tribe, had on the nation.

The prophet also envisions the fall of Judah here. The defection from Yahwism was not as extreme in the southern kingdom at this time as it was in Israel, but the same trends were there. Hosea knows it is only a matter of time.

6. One day it will be too late. The people will realize the false promises of the baals. They will learn what their sin has cost them and will seek to return to their God, but he will have severed his relationship with them. They will come with their herds of animals for sacrifice, but they will have no God to respond to them.

7. Hosea observes the unfaithfulness to Yahweh in the generation of his day, which did not know the purity of Yahwism. They knew only the tainted Yahwism of the northern kingdom. This, as far as they knew, was their religious heritage,

one of another family (Lev. 22:12; Deut. 25:5; 1 Kings 3:18). חֹדֶשׁ (new moon): The first day of the month was set aside in Israelite tradition as a holy day similar to the Sabbath, with which it is frequently associated. Specific sacrifices were mandated for the new moon (Num. 28:11–15). The prophets sometimes spoke disparagingly of this festival (as well as other feasts) because of the prevailing tendency to observe it as an end in itself without concern for an ethical response to God (Isa. 1:13–17). חֶלְקֵיהֶם (their tracts of land): The basic idea of the verb underlying this noun is *to divide*. The noun denotes a share or portion. It seems to have no direct reference to the land as the object of divine promise. In all likelihood it refers to the fields from which the produce necessary for the sacrifices of the new moon was harvested, and by extension to the land itself.

---

and Hosea regards this generation of people as children born out of wedlock. Their father was not Yahweh, but Baal, the god of fertility.

As a result of this unfaithfulness, the new moon will devour their tracts of land. Their defection from pure Yahwism to a corrupted religious externalism, symbolized by the Festival of the New Moon, will bring about the downfall of the nation. Their life as a nation was in their allegiance to their covenants, but they had forsaken these instruments of divine grace for rites that were devoid of life.

VII. An Oracle Addressed to Various Levels of Israelite Society (5:1–15)

C. The Final Doom of Israel (5:8–12)

8 Blow the trumpet in Gibeah,
 the horn in Ramah!
Raise an alarm, Beth-aven!
 [They pursue] after you, Benjamin!
9 Ephraim shall become a desolation
 in the day of punishment.
Among the tribes of Israel
 I declare what is certain.
10 The princes of Judah have become
 like those who alter a boundary line;
on them I will pour out my fury like
  water.
11 Ephraim is oppressed, crushed in judgment,
 because he determined to go after
  nonsense.
12 And I was like a moth to Ephraim,
 and like decay to the house of Judah.

8 Blow the horn in Gibeah,
 the trumpet in Ramah.
Sound the alarm at Beth-aven;
 look behind you, Benjamin!
9 Ephraim shall become a desolation
 in the day of punishment;
among the tribes of Israel
 I declare what is sure.
10 The princes of Judah have become
 like those who remove the landmark;
on them I will pour out
 my wrath like water.
11 Ephraim is oppressed, crushed in judgment,
 because he was determined to go
  after vanity.
12 Therefore I am like maggots to Ephraim,
 and like rottenness to the house of
  Judah.

8. תִּקְעוּ (blow) is in the plural. The reference is probably to hypothetical watchmen in the towns of Gibeah and Ramah. The basic sense of the word is to *thrust* or *strike*. With reference to a horn it depicts the act of thrusting air through the instrument to produce sound, thus to blow or blast. שׁוֹפָר (trumpet): This is a ram's horn that, when blown, produced a limited range of notes. Its sharp, sonorous quality made it useful for various functions. Besides its use in religious observances (Lev. 25:9; 2 Sam. 6:15), it was used to sound a summons to battle (Judg. 3:27; 6:34; 1 Sam. 13:3) and as a signal in battle (2 Sam. 2:28; Job 39:25; Amos 2:2). The שׁוֹפָר was also used to warn of impending danger (Jer. 6:17; Ezek. 33:3, 5, 6; Joel 2:1; Amos 3:6). The context of Hosea 5:8–9 calls for the last connotation because of the reference to the "day of punishment" (v. 9). The חֲצֹצְרָה (horn) was a long slender instrument that was used similarly to the שׁוֹפָר. Its use also included the sounding of an alarm in battle (Num. 10:9; 31:6; 2 Chron. 13:12, 14). הָרִיעוּ (Raise an alarm): It is not certain that the words of the first line influence this verse so as to limit the connotation of

הָרִיעוּ to sounding an alarm with a trumpet. The major linguistic force at work in determining the semantic limits of this word is the influence of the parallel clause in the sentence, not the clauses of the broad poetic structure. These clauses may determine the general atmosphere of the passage, but not necessarily the narrow limits of the words within associated clauses. The companion clause (after you, Benjamin!) is a verbal warning; thus הָרִיעוּ may have the general sense of shouting an alarm. בֵּית אָוֶן (Beth-aven) does not have a locative preposition as do the place-names in the first verse. It is not necessary, however, to posit the word as an adverbial accusative and translate it "at Beth-aven" (Gilgal). Since the companion clause is addressed directly to Benjamin, we may understand this clause as a direct address to Beth-aven. אַחֲרֶיךָ (after you) is unaccompanied by a verb and seems awkward. The Septuagint reads ἐξέστη (is amazed), but this offers little help. The reading of the Masoretic Text makes sense if we understand אַחֲרֶיךָ as a pregnant expression (GKC §119gg) in which the verbal idea is implicit (see the Author's Translation and the Exposition). For

---

8. This section begins with a rhetorical command to sound an alarm. In ancient times a trumpet blast often signaled the approach of the enemy. Amos reflects the fear that such an alarm would have caused in a community (3:6). The address of the command is in the plural, and in all probability we are to think of several watchmen in each city who sound the alarm as the enemy approaches.

Efforts to date this section have generally proved unsatisfying. It seems best to regard it as a statement anticipating the final doom of the northern kingdom. The language of this section has an ultimacy about it which seems to preclude events earlier than the final downfall of the nation.

Gibeah and Ramah are most certainly the towns of those names located in the territory of Benjamin because of the occurrence of "Benjamin" in the parallel clause. Bethel (Beth-aven; see 4:15) was also located in Benjamin. If there is any significance to the order in which the towns appear in this verse, we may picture the invader advancing northward through Benjamin to Ephraim, where the final onslaught was to occur, for the next verse says that Ephraim will be reduced to a ruin. It is not clear, however, that such an invasion from the south ever took place. In all probability we are to see no directional sig-

nificance in the order in which the names of these towns are given in the clausal structure. Hosea stated earlier (1:5) that the Valley of Jezreel was to be the site of Israel's demise. Perhaps we are to understand these towns, which were located at the southern edge of Israel and had their roots in Benjamin, to indicate that the invading armies would advance to the border of Judah.

The expression *ʾaḥăreka binyamîn*, which we have translated "[They pursue] after you, Benjamin," is a difficult construction. If we understand it as a pregnant expression (see the Exegesis), however, it makes sense. We must determine the verbal idea omitted by the writer. Several verbal concepts are associated with *ʾaḥar* that fit this context, such as, to pursue after and to draw the sword after. We are to see some sort of hostile military action in the construction. Perhaps the idea of pursuing is best. This view is consonant with the reference to the alarm in the previous context. The approach of an army involved the initiation of hostilities, and the people of the area, formerly occupied by the Benjamites, learned from this statement that they, like their neighbors to the north, would bear the brunt of the assault. The desultory nature of the expression may be intended to convey the excited cry of a soldier in the heat of battle, warning a fellow soldier that the enemy is upon him.

a fuller discussion of the incomplete sentence, see the Exposition at 8:1.

9. לִשַׁמָּה תִהְיֶה (shall become a ruin): הָיָה לְ has the sense of *become* (see BDB, p. 512). שַׁמָּה (desolation) differs from its companion noun שְׁמָמָה in that the former word emphasizes the reaction of horror caused by a desolation, while the latter describes the ruin itself. תּוֹכֵחָה (punishment) sometimes indicates correction or reproof, but not in every context. This nuance may be present when the verb occurs in parallelism with מוּסָר (Prov. 3:11) or עֵצָה (Prov. 1:25), words that connote discipline and counsel. In Ezekiel 5:15 the word occurs within a context where only punishment is set forth. The context in which this word is found in Hosea also presents little warrant for understanding the word in any way other than punishment. נֶאֱמָנָה (what is certain): אָמַן has as its basic sense the idea of firmness. It is used of pillars that support a door (2 Kings 18:16) and a nurse who holds a child (2 Sam. 4:4). In the niphal it may have the sense of being made firm, that is, confirmed or certain.

10. כְּמַסִּיגֵי גְּבוּל (like those who alter a boundary line): The hiphil of נָסַג may describe the action of altering something by changing its position. It describes the changing of a boundary line in several contexts (Deut. 19:14; 27:17; Prov. 22:28; 23:10). עֶבְרָתִי (my fury) is based on the verbal concept of passing over or overflowing. The noun represents overflowing fury.

11. עָשׁוּק . . . רְצוּץ (oppressed . . . crushed) are qal passive participles. The passive expresses the idea of external action brought upon the subject, but the source of the action is not expressed. מִשְׁפָּט (judgment) may have the benign meaning of justice in several contexts (Mic. 6:8), but the associative concepts here require the negative meaning of judgment. כִּי (because) introduces the reason for the judgment and oppression of the previous clause. הוֹאִיל (determined) stresses the volitional response of an individual to a circumstance requiring the exercise of choice or decision. Hence it frequently has the idea of determination (Josh. 17:12; Judg. 1:27). צָו (nonsense) has been understood in various ways. Andersen and Freedman (*Hosea*, p. 409) suggest "filth" (from the root צוֹא). The Revised Standard Version translates it "vanity" (note Heb. שָׁוְא, vanity). These are attractive suggestions. The word צָו is attested in Isaiah, however, and we should consider its use there before turning to emendation. It occurs in Isaiah 28:10, 13, where it is generally associated with the idea of command (RSV precept; NIV do). It is probably best, however, to

---

9. The onslaught prefigured by Hosea is to result in Ephraim's becoming desolate. This is to occur in "the day of punishment," a reference to the ultimate reaction of God to the sin of the northern tribes. We should probably understand the words "I declare" (*hōdaʿtî*) in this verse to be spoken by Yahweh, not Hosea, since it is Yahweh who says, "I will pour out my fury," in the next verse.

The declaration is made among the "tribes of Israel" (*šibṭê yiśraʾel*), a concept reminiscent of the tribal convocation in Deuteronomy (chaps. 27–31). There Moses summoned the tribes and warned them of the dire consequences of disobedience to the covenant stipulations set forth in the preceding chapters. This dismal prospect included their becoming a "ruin" (*šammâ*, Deut. 28:37), which is the same word Hosea uses here.

10. The proscription against moving a boundary line is also Deuteronomic (Deut. 19:14; 27:17). It is difficult to understand why, out of all the Deuteronomic proscriptions, the writer chose this one. We look in vain for boundary disputes or border raids in Hosea's day that might fit this accusation. The expression, however, is basically an analogy: "They are *like* those who alter a boundary line." The reference is probably to the deceitfulness that could lead to such violations of human rights. Like those who surreptitiously moved boundary markers for their own advantage, the princes of Judah violated canons of human rights to advance their causes.

11. The prophet turns his attention back to Israel (Ephraim) and pictures the judgment of God that already hangs heavily over the nation. The reason for the oppression of the time was that the people had determined to go after nonsense. The construction of the last clause (go after) reflects a similar crystallized expression having to do with following idols. The word *ṣaw* (nonsense) is difficult to understand. The view taken here is that its use in Isaiah 28:10, 13, determines its function as a nonsense syllable (see the Exegesis). Perhaps the reiteration of meaningless sounds depicted the way one would speak to an infant in the first stages of teaching it to speak. Isaiah uses this syllable (as well as *qaw*) to describe the incomprehensibility of the Assyrian tongue. It seems best to see *ṣaw* as a nonsense syllable familiar to the people of the time, which Hosea uses to depict the emptiness and meaninglessness of that to which

understand its use there simply as a nonsense syllable with no intrinsic meaning. Its derivation from צָוָה (command) is not at all certain. In Isaiah 28:10, it may refer to the nonsense syllables that one may use in rapid succession when speaking playfully to an infant. This suggestion gains support from verse 13, where the word occurs in a context dealing with the incomprehensibility of the Assyrian language (v. 11). הוֹאִיל (he determined) is followed by a finite verb (הָלַךְ), not an infinitive, but there is no need to emend הָלַךְ to an infinitive. The verb יְאַל precedes finite verbs elsewhere (Deut. 1:5; see Josh. 7:7; Judg. 19:6; 2 Sam. 7:29; 2 Kings 6:3). הָלַךְ אַחֲרֵי (go after) is frequently used for following after false gods (see, e.g., Deut. 4:3; 6:14; 8:19; Jer. 2:23). Hosea uses the expression of following the Lord in 11:10.

12. וַאֲנִי כָעָשׁ (And I was like a moth) is a noun clause. The context determines the time to which a noun clause refers (GKC §141f). Since passive participles refer mainly to the past (Davidson, *Syntax* §100c) the participles in verse 11a almost certainly describe a situation that began in the past and which continues into the present ("Ephraim is oppressed . . ."). The noun clause is connected by וְ to that context and continues the thought. Thus, we have translated it "I *was* like a moth." עָשׁ (moth) is from the verb עָשֵׁשׁ which means "to waste." עָשׁ always denotes the moth as a means of destruction (Job 13:28; Ps. 39:12 [11]; Isa. 50:9; 51:8). רָקָב (decay) is a general word for rottenness.

---

the people had devoted themselves—idolatry and lack of concern for social values.

12. God himself is a means of corruption to the nation. The metaphor is a shocking one. Yahweh himself has become like an agent of putrefaction working within the nation to promote decay and ultimate destruction. The direct involvement of God in the nation's downfall is reminiscent of the words, "I am chastisement to all of them" (5:2).

VII. An Oracle Addressed to Various Levels of Israelite Society (5:1–15)

D. Israel's Dependence on Assyria Will Lead to Her Downfall (5:13–15)

13 And Ephraim saw his sickness,
   and Judah his wound,
and Ephraim went to Assyria,
   and sent to the king of Yareb.
But he was not able to heal you
   or cure you of your wound.
14 For I am like a lion to Ephraim,
   and like a young lion to the house of Judah.
   I, I will tear and go away,
      I will carry off, and none will snatch away.
15 I will go and return to my place
   until they have borne their guilt.
      Then they will seek my face,
      in their distress they will seek eagerly for me.

13 When Ephraim saw his sickness,
   and Judah his wound,
then Ephraim went to Assyria,
   and sent to the great king.
But he is not able to cure you
   or heal your wound.
14 For I will be like a lion to Ephraim,
   and like a young lion to the house of Judah.
   I myself will tear and go away;
      I will carry off, and no one shall rescue.
15 I will return again to my place
   until they acknowledge their guilt
      and seek my face.
      In their distress they will beg my favor:

13. חֳלִיוֹ (his sickness): The range of meaning for this word includes sickness in general (Deut. 7:15; Isa. 38:9) and, more specifically, wound. It is balanced by מָזוֹר, which connotes a wound in need of care (Jer. 30:13). The picture is of a debilitating laceration. מֶלֶךְ יָרֵב (the king of Yareb): יָרֵב (Yareb) is pointed in the Masoretic Text as a jussive of רִיב (let him contend). The Septuagint does not translate here and reads Ἰαρείμ. The absence of the article before מֶלֶךְ in the Masoretic Text renders that word definite and requires the translation "the king of. . . ." The consonants can be reordered to read מַלְכִּי רַב (my king is great), after the analogy of several Hebrew proper names, but this offers little help. The text may reflect the reading מֶלֶךְ רַב (a great king), which one could construe as a translation of the Assyrian titular name šarru rabû (great king). The ' is difficult to explain, however, unless it represents the nominative or oblique indicators of Akkadian nouns. It is difficult to explain why this vestige appears in a translation. Another possibility is that the ' represents an anaptyctic vowel affixed to מֶלֶךְ (spelled *malk* or *milk* in earlier Hebrew) to relieve the succession of three unvocalized consonants (*l, k, r*) in the words *malk rab* (see Douglas Stuart, *Hosea–Jonah*, p. 99). Zellig S. Harris (*Grammar*, pp. 33–34), however, cites only examples of anaptyxis in Phoenician that occurs between the second and third root radicals. W. Randall Garr (*Geography*, pp. 45–47) points to examples of anaptyxis only in Phoenician and Aramaic in Syria–Palestine in the eighth and seventh centuries B.C. The least complex reading, and the one that best reflects the Masoretic Text, is "the king of Yareb." In all probability יָרֵב is not to be understood as the proper name of a king because we would then expect the article before מֶלֶךְ as in אָמוֹן הַמֶּלֶךְ (King Amon, 2 Kings 21:24). See the discussion in the Exposition. יִגְהֶה מִכֶּם (cure you of): גָּהָה has the sense of being freed from, after the analogy of the Aramaic cognate.

---

13. The prophet says that Israel finally became aware of her sickness. The people began to realize that their political and social conditions were rapidly deteriorating. Instead of turning back to their God, however, they turned to Assyria for help. It is impossible to identify the historical event Hosea has in mind. In all probability it was Menahem's efforts to curry Assyrian favor by giving tribute to Tiglath-pileser III (2 Kings 15:19–20). Menahem raised the tribute by imposing a burdensome tax on landowners. It appears that he believed that Assyrian support would strengthen his weak hold on the throne.

Regardless of the particular event described by Hosea, the narrative records Israel's fatal error in trusting in human methods rather than in divinely established standards. Suffering internally and near collapse, the nation sought help from a potential enemy.

This striking irony is set forth in the reference to "the King of Yareb." While this reference to Yareb is impossible to understand with certainty, we have noted that the Hebrew grammar limits the possibilities. If we seek to reflect the Masoretic Text we have few choices outside of reading "the King of Yareb."

It is doubtful that *yareb* refers to Egypt (although that country is paired with Assyria in Hos. 7:11; 9:3; 11:5) because of the singular pronoun *hû* (he, it) in the next line. If two countries were intended, then we would not expect a singular pronoun in the second line. It is quite possible that the text has suffered in transmission, and that the original text stated something similar to "the great king" (Akk. *šarru rabû*). On the other hand *yareb* may represent the authentic reading. No place of this name is known, however, and it is possible that we have a play on words here that masks the actual meaning of Yareb.

The phrase *melek yareb* (king of Yareb) is the poetic complement of Assyria in this sentence, and *yārēb* may have been a prophetic denominative for Assyria. We have noted (see the Exegesis) that the grammar of the clause and the Masoretic vocalization allow our reading Yareb as a jussive of *rîb* (to contend). Thus, the translation "let him contend" is suitable. Perhaps we are to understand the word *Yareb* to have prophetic significance as did the names of Hosea's three children. The name would thus be somewhat analogous to Jeshurun, a denominative for Israel (Deut. 32:15; 33:5, 26; Isa. 44:2). If Yareb had prophetic significance, it could have conveyed Hosea's conviction that Assyria would prove to be Israel's conqueror. Since the name means "contend" or "let him contend," each time it was read in the prophecy or heard in Hosea's sermons, it would remind the people that Assyria would ultimately contend with them as a nation. In this way Yareb functioned as did Jezreel to remind the people that judgment was inevitable. It was ironic that Israel appealed for help to a nation that would one day be her captor.

85

14. כִּי (For) introduces the reason for the Assyrian king's inability to heal Israel; it is because the sovereign God inflicts the wounds like a powerful beast of the jungle. אֲנִי אֲנִי (I, I) draws attention to the fact that Yahweh has caused Israel's sickness.

15. יֶאְשְׁמוּ (they have borne their guilt): אָשַׁם may have the sense of bearing guilt as it does in two instances in Hosea (10:2; 14:1). יְשַׁחֲרֻנְנִי (they will seek eagerly for me): Note the instances of שָׁחַר meaning "to seek eagerly" (Job 24:5; Prov. 1:28).

---

14. Israel's desperate appeal to Assyria will not bring about the healing of her factious strife, however. The reason for this, according to Hosea, is that it was Yahweh, her God, who inflicted the wounds. Like a ferocious lion from which no one would dare try to snatch its prey, Yahweh was tearing the nation apart. Not even the mighty nation of Assyria could heal such wounds or oppose such a God.

15. The prophet represents Yahweh as rending the nation as a carcass and then returning as a lion to its lair. Yahweh would wait until the people had borne their guilt. God had not abandoned his people nor had he forsaken his promise to Abraham, but they would pay for their sin in political turmoil and ultimate captivity as a nation.

When they have borne their guilt they will seek the Lord in their distress. We do not have enough data in the context to determine whether this restoration refers to the return after the exile or an eschatological restoration. In all probability it refers to the restoration of the people of God under the aegis of the Messiah (Hos. 3:5).

VIII. A Plea for Repentance (6:1–11a)

A. Yahweh Will Respond to the People's Repentance (6:1–3)

6 Come, and let us return to the LORD
>   for he has torn, but he will heal us:
>>   he smites, but he will bind us up.
> ² After two days he will restore us to
>   health;
>>   on the third day he will cause us to
>>   arise
>   that we may live before him.
> ³ Let us know—let us press on to know
>   the LORD.
>>   His going forth is as certain as the
>>   dawn,
> and he will come to us as does the rain,
>   as the latter rains water the earth.

6 "Come, let us return to the LORD;
>   for it is he who has torn, and he will
>   heal us;
>>   he has struck down, and he will bind
>>   us up.
> ² After two days he will revive us;
>>   on the third day he will raise us up,
>>   that we may live before him.
> ³ Let us know, let us press on to know
>   the LORD;
>>   his appearing is as sure as the dawn;
> he will come to us like the showers,
>>   like the spring rains that water the
>>   earth."

6:1. לְכוּ וְנָשׁוּבָה (Come, and let us return): In this structure, the cohortative following an imperative expresses intention (GKC §108d). כִּי (for) states the reason for the call to return to Yahweh; it is because he will heal the hurt he has caused. הוּא (he): The use of this pronoun here underscores the fact that the one they are to resort to for help is the one who has afflicted them. יָךְ (he smites) is not construed with וְ, but this is not syntactically anomalous. The clause it initiates forms a literary parallel with the previous clause in which the pronoun הוּא (he) extends its influence to this clause. In 9:1 the particle כִּי governs two verbal clauses in which the second is not construed with וְ. The clipped nature of the clauses unconstrued with וְ is an effective device that sets off each clause in a pleasing literary balance. חָבַשׁ (he will bind . . . up) has the general sense of to bind. In several passages it connotes the application of bandages to a wound (Isa. 61:1; Ezek. 30:21).

2. יְחַיֵּנוּ (he will restore us to health) is the hiphil of חָיָה (to be alive); hence it has a causative function. While it has the general sense of letting live

or giving life to, the context, with its motifs of wounding and healing, calls for the connotation of restoring to health (see 2 Kings 5:7; Isa. 38:16). מִיָּמִים בַּיּוֹם הַשְּׁלִשִׁי (After two days . . . on the third day): מִן (After) marks "the period immediately succeeding the limit" (BDB, p. 581). מִיָּמִים (After two days) thus points to the chronological unit that follows it, that is, "the third day." The period of three days represents a short while. יְקִמֵנוּ (he will cause us to arise) has nothing to do with resurrection. The context and the parallel verb יְחַיֵּנוּ (he will restore us to health) imply the reestablishment of the nation in its former stability and vigor. וְנִחְיֶה לְפָנָיו (that we may live before him): וְ introduces a result clause stating the consequence of God's raising them up as it were from a sickbed; they will live before him, that is, they will enjoy the blessings of life lived in God's presence, a living relationship to Yahweh involving his loving, watchful care and provision.

3. וְנֵדְעָה נִרְדְּפָה לָדַעַת (let us know—let us press on to know): נִרְדְּפָה is literally "let us pursue." It sets the knowledge of God as the object of the peo-

---

6:1. In this section we hear a clarion call to the people to repent. The prospect of God's bestowing his favor on the people seems to lack consonance with the darker side of the prophet's message, which we have observed in 2:6 [4], 8 [6], 13 [11]; 4:5, 6; 5:4. But even within these gloomy statements there are rays of hope (2:4 [2], 16 [14], 23–25 [21–23]). These expressions of hope are mainly sovereign declarations of God, however, with few references to the need for national and individual repentance. But here we find a clear call to the people to turn back to God.

The Septuagint has the word *legontes* (saying) at the head of this section, thus construing it as a statement of the resolve of the people (5:15), not the prophet's call to them. The New Revised Standard Version follows the Septuagint, also making the words a statement of the people. This construction, however, is unnecessary since the prophecy of Hosea is marked by abrupt transitions, and we have already encountered a similar plea in 2:4 [2]. We see many examples of abrupt changes of style (see, e.g., 11:8–9, see v. 7; 12:8, see v. 9; 13:14, see v. 13; 14:1 [13:16], see 14:2 [14:1]). We may also note the similar plea for repentance in 14:2 [1].

The call to repentance is based on the fact that Yahweh, who tore the nation as a lion rends its prey, is willing also to heal the people and bind up the wounds he inflicted. This prospect envi-

sions an end to the rebellion against God that led Israel to her downfall. The postexilic community realized the truth of the prophet's statement, if only for a limited time. It is a universal truth that when a spiritually dead people turn in humility to God, he will respond in mercy (see 2 Chron. 7:14).

2. Hosea assures the people that God will respond to their repentance in a short time. He designates this brief period "after two days" and says that the nation will arise on the "third day." We find here no hint of a cultic belief in the dying-rising God, for the nation is depicted in this context as being ill and not dead. The point is that when the people respond in sincerity to God, his response to them will be quick; they will have to wait only a short time for relief. The rising of the nation refers to their restoration to national stability.

Their repentance will lead to their living before God. Life is the viability of the relationship of the nation to the promised inheritance. Its antithesis, death, represents the cessation of a vital relationship with God and the promises made to Abraham and his descendants. We may find this concept of "life" in several places (Deut. 8:1; 16:20; 30:18; Amos 5:14).

3. The prophet pleads further with the people. We may render his words literally, "Then let us know, let us pursue to know the LORD." The

ple's fervent pursuit. כְּשַׁחַר נָכוֹן (as certain as the dawn): כּוּן in the niphal connotes that which is established, hence certain (Deut. 17:4). It establishes the fact that God's "going forth" is as certain as the sun's rising each day. מוֹצָאוֹ (His going forth): This noun (based on the root יָצָא [go out]) denotes the act of going forth. In Numbers 33:2 it connotes a departure, and in 2 Samuel 3:25 it refers to going about one's everyday activities. It is clear from the parallel clause here (come to us) that the word refers to Yahweh's going forth into history to effect his sovereign will. That clause, like its companion clause in the structure, appeals to the phenomena of nature and sets forth the certainty of Yahweh's coming to aid his people. גֶּשֶׁם (rain) is a general word for rain. מַלְקוֹשׁ (latter rain) is the spring rain. יוֹרֶה may be read as a noun (early rain) or a participle (waters). We have chosen the latter translation, because when יוֹרֶה functions as a noun, it is usually in the crystallized expression יוֹרֶה וּמַלְקוֹשׁ (early rain and latter rain, Deut. 11:14). Also יָרָה appears as a verb in Hosea 10:12.

---

statement is intense. The people are to make the knowledge of God the object of their pursuit. We have observed that knowing God entails a knowledge of his ways, his purposes, his loving requirements, and his promises (4:1).

Hosea is certain that God will come to the aid of his repentant people, for Yahweh's "going forth" is as sure as the dawning of the day. The people should have recognized this fact, for the early history of Israel demonstrated Yahweh's loving response to an obedient people. But the people of Hosea's day had strayed so far from their historic roots, and had become so enmeshed in the fertility cults, that they had come to view Yahweh as they viewed the pagan gods. He was to be placated by the observation of religious externals; he was no longer the God of the covenant to them. That covenant affirmed the certainty of Yahweh's willingness to enter the arena of time and history to work on behalf of his people. Moses declared that if the people repented, "then the LORD your God will restore your fortunes and have compassion on you, gathering you again from all the peoples among whom the LORD your God has scattered you" (Deut. 30:3, NRSV). Like the rising of the sun and the regularity of the seasons, so surely will Yahweh respond to his people should they return to him.

The plea for repentance seems anomalous against the background of Hosea's statements concerning Israel's incurable sickness. However, it affirms that God will always turn in love to his people when they come to him in brokenness of spirit. Hosea knew the captivity was certain, because he realized that a spirit of harlotry had seized the people and they would not turn to God. But God's faithfulness had not diminished, nor his willingness to demonstrate his love.

VIII. A Plea for Repentance (6:1–11a)

B. The Ephemeral Love of Judah and Israel (6:4–6)

4 What shall I do with you, Ephraim?
　What shall I do with you, Judah?
For your love is like a morning cloud,
　and like the dew which leaves early.
5 Therefore I have hewn by the prophets,
　I have slain them by the words of my
　　mouth,
　and my judgment goes forth as the
　　light.
6 For I delight in lovingkindness and not
　　sacrifice,
　and the knowledge of God rather
　　than burnt offerings.

4 What shall I do with you, O Ephraim?
　What shall I do with you, O Judah?
Your love is like a morning cloud,
　like the dew that goes away early.
5 Therefore I have hewn them by the
　　prophets,
　I have killed them by the words of
　　my mouth,
　and my judgment goes forth as the
　　light.
6 For I desire steadfast love and not sacri-
　　fice,
　the knowledge of God rather than
　　burnt offerings.

4. מָה אֶעֱשֶׂה (What shall I do . . .?) is uttered in frustration. Hosea goes on to show the futility of Yahweh's efforts to come to the aid of his people. וְחַסְדְּכֶם (For your love): See the discussion of this word at 4:1. When used of people, חֶסֶד refers to the demonstration of lovingkindness that flows from a sense of one's obligation to God. כַּעֲנַן (like a . . . cloud): עָנָן (cloud) also has a transitory sense in 13:3, where it refers to the passing away of the nation. מַשְׁכִּים (early): שָׁכַם connotes *to start early*. It frequently has the idea of starting early on a journey (see, e.g., Judg. 19:9). We may translate this clause literally, "as dew, starting early, goes away." הֹלֵךְ (goes away) modifies מַשְׁכִּים (lit. starting early) not חֶסֶד (love) after the analogy of the identical expression in 13:3 where the singular הֹלֵךְ (goes away) is in grammatical agreement with טַל (dew), but not "they," which is the subject of the plural verb יִהְיוּ (they will be). The verb שָׁכַם (rise early) is linked closely to another verb (as it is here) in Psalm 127:2. In Genesis 19:2 it is linked with הָלַךְ in the expression *rise early and go on your way*. The absence of the article on the participle מַשְׁכִּים is significant. If it were definite, it would indicate that הֹלֵךְ modifies חֶסֶד ("your love

. . . like the dew, the early rising [dew], goes away"). The clause is a relative clause in which the relative particle is unexpressed (see the Author's Translation). This construction occurs with a participle, as it does here, in Isaiah 10:24 and Jeremiah 31:25.

5. עַל־כֵּן (Therefore) introduces what Yahweh did to overcome the negative results of their ephemeral love. חָצַבְתִּי בַּנְּבִיאִים (I have hewn by the prophets): This collocation (חָצַב בְּ) has the sense of hewing with an instrument (see Isa. 10:15). The prophets were instruments by which God hewed the nation. The prophets cannot be false prophets whom God hewed down. The sense of the collocation חָצַב בְּ (hew by) does not permit this, nor does its companion element in the structure, הֲרַגְתִּים בְּאִמְרֵי־פִי (I have slain them by the words of my mouth), which contains the instrumental element בְּאִמְרֵי (by the words of). וּמִשְׁפָּטֶיךָ אוֹר יֵצֵא (my judgment goes forth as the light): The Masoretic Text reads, "your judgments go forth as light." This reading is questionable, however, because of the lack of agreement in number between the plural subject and the singular verb (יֵצֵא, goes forth). It is true that precise syntactical

---

4. The transition is typically abrupt. We have listened to the prophet's plaintive call for repentance, but suddenly we hear the words of Yahweh. The frustration reflected here is obvious: "What shall I do with you, Ephraim? What shall I do with you, Judah?" The next clause sets forth his frustration in a vivid metaphor that expresses the ephemeral nature of the people's love; it is like a morning cloud and early dew that pass away almost imperceptibly. How can the Lord deal with the people on the basis of the covenant when their loyalty to the covenant is so evanescent? No wonder the words "What shall I do with you?" open this section.

Hosea uses personification to depict the covenant loyalty for which Yahweh longed. He describes the dew as rising early and going away. He appeals to natural phenomena in the metaphorical language of the previous verse, but there the phenomena establish the certainty of God's response. Here the phenomena of nature symbolize Israel's ephemeral love. This is typical of Hosea's lack of consistency in his use of metaphorical statement.

Hosea cites both Israel and Judah in his accusation. Israel's sister nation to the south was not as far along in the course to disaster as was Israel, but Judah suffered from the same lack of knowl-

edge of God that had affected Israel. The love of both nations for God was evanescent.

5. Because of this lack of covenant loyalty on the part of the people, Yahweh hewed them by the prophets. There is no clear instance of the word *hew* (ḥaṣab) meaning to hack in the sense of doing physical harm to a person. In Isaiah 51:9 it depicts Yahweh's assault on the mythical Rahab, but chiefly it connotes the idea of fashioning by cutting or digging. It describes, for example, the digging of wells (Deut. 6:11) and fashioning of pillars (Prov. 9:1) and stones (1 Kings 5:29 [15]; 2 Chron. 26:10). This may seem to imply that Yahweh's use of the prophets according to Hosea was to shape the nation to conform to his will. But this is not in keeping with the parallel concept *slay* (ḥarag). The words of Yahweh's mouth are paired with the prophets in the parallel structure. The conceptual relationship of these poetic complements is Yahweh's communication of his will through the prophets. Thus the word of God that came to the nation through the ministry of the prophets slew the nation. There is no reason why the word ḥaṣab (hew), determined as it is by ḥarag (slay), could not have signified the devastating effect the prophetic word had on the people. The use of this word in Isaiah 51:9 shows it did have the active sense of slay.

agreement is not a mark of Hosea's style, but there are few instances in the book where a plural subject occurs with a singular verb. Compound subjects may take a singular verb (as in 4:11) and plural subjects occur with singular passive verbs (see 8:4; 10:14), but these conditions do not exist here. We may achieve a more appropriate reading by shifting כְּ to אוֹר (light). The י on מִשְׁפָּט (judgment) may be construed with the Septuagint, Targum Jonathan, and Syriac Peshitta as the first-person singular suffix (*my* judgment). Andersen and

Freedman observe that this reading is consonant with first-person statements in the sentence (*Hosea*, p. 429).

6. כִּי (For) gives the reason for the display of divine judgment. It is the lack of חֶסֶד (lovingkindness). חָפַצְתִּי (I delight in) is used of Shechem's delight in Jacob's daughter (Gen. 34:19), the Lord's delight in his people (Num. 14:8), and a man's feeling for his wife (Deut. 21:14). The word is broader in meaning than simple desire. The sense is that of wanting something

---

We may wonder how the utterances of prophetic figures such as Elijah, Micaiah, Amos, and others slew the nation. It seems that the nation fell because of unwise national policies, corrupt officials, and, above all, by its departure from the pure Yahwistic traditions. But God's word is a sword (Heb. 4:12) that has devastating force. The prophets slew the nation in the sense that its destruction did not come about apart from the intelligible communication of the divine will through them. No Israelite could say that the demise of the nation was due only to the fortuitous course of national events or the caprices of foreign kings. The prophets declared the coming of Assyrian and Babylonian bondage, the demise of capitals, and the destinies of kings. The nation was destroyed by means of the prophetic word in that the destructive force of divine power found shape, reality, and effectiveness in the voices of Israel's men of God. All this was done as a response to Israel's failure to respond with sincerity to the covenant obligations to which they had prescribed their allegiance. From Sinai onward Israel's *ḥesed* (lovingkindness) was weak and ephemeral.

Throughout the long history of Israel Yahweh's judgments went forth as the light, and continued to do so. That is the force of the imperfect verb *yēṣēʾ* (go forth). If the reference to light continues the sequence of metaphors derived from nature, it is possible that Hosea meant to say that God's judgment was as certain as the light of each day. In this case the metaphors move from the expression of certainty (v. 3), to evanescence (v. 4), and back to certainty (v. 5). However, we cannot be sure of this. In all probability the metaphor depicts the brilliance and pervasiveness of light, that is, Yahweh's meting out of justice had been so brilliantly displayed throughout Israel's history as to be like light in its clarity. The judgments of which the prophets warned came as the prophets said

they would. The people should have observed and heeded them.

6. Why did Yahweh's judgment fall on his people? Why such a cruel stroke? The prophet answers these questions in the words, "For I delight in lovingkindness rather than sacrifice." The people had failed to fulfill the heart of the law, which was to love God totally and their fellow man as well. Their devotion to God was misspent on harlots and gods of stone; they forgot the rock from which they had been hewn. As in earlier times, a prophet came forward to speak words of God that hewed the nation like a sword. It was Hosea whose prophetic message exposed Israel's miserable status before Yahweh, her husband.

We need not think that the prophets viewed sacrifices as a hated Canaanite intrusion that had no role to play in Israel's covenant obligations. In the eighth century sacrifice was a perverted expression of religious externalism that masked the ethical response God wanted to receive from his people. Samuel's question about sacrifice (1 Sam. 15:22–23) seems to denigrate that levitical institution, yet it was asked by one who officiated at many sacrifices (1 Sam. 9:13). If the prophets considered the sacrifices a despicable practice, we wonder why they were not more direct in their approach. Their use of the rhetorical question and indirect allusion seems more an appeal for the balancing of obedience with the ritual of sacrifice than outright condemnation of levitical sacrifices.

Yet Hosea's words here do not seem to reflect this view of sacrifice. The first clause of his statement, "For I delight in lovingkindness and not sacrifice," is brutally forthright. While it is possible to translate the construction *mēʿōlōt* (rather than) as "more than," allowing for a favorable attitude by God toward sacrifice, the translation "rather than" appears to reflect more accurately the view of sacrifice that Hosea holds. Wherever he states an opinion about sacrifice it is a nega-

which is the object of delight. מֵעֹלוֹת (rather than burnt offerings): We have opted for the translation "rather than burnt offerings" instead of "more than burnt offerings." The partitive function of מִן (from) allows for the basic sense of *away from*

when it is construed with a noun. We may observe this sense in Micah 3:6, for example: "Therefore it shall be night to you, without [מִן] vision, and darkness to you, without [מִן] revelation" (NRSV). See the Exposition.

---

tive one (4:19; 8:13; 9:4); but it is the sacrifices of the nation's syncretistic cult that he condemns. The people offered sacrifices in the wrong spirit and in ignorance of God's requirements. If Hosea has in mind here the sacrifices of the cultic worship he condemns throughout the prophecy, the translation "rather than burnt offerings" is an appropriate one.

Once again Hosea speaks of the knowledge of God, an important theme in this book. The people

knew the ways of the fertility cults; they consorted with harlots and observed rituals, but they did not know the ways of the God who wanted purity and brokenness of heart. The knowledge of God is influenced in the parallel structure by *ḥesed* (lovingkindness). Thus knowledge of God is more than factual knowledge; it is knowledge of Yahweh's just requirements; it involves a loving response to the God of the covenant.

VIII. A Plea for Repentance (6:1–11a)

C. Israel Has Broken the Covenant (6:7–11a)

7 But they, like Adam, have broken the covenant;
    there they dealt treacherously with me.
8 Gilead is a city of evildoers,
    trodden with blood.
9 As members of marauding bands lie in wait,
    so do gangs of priests.
  They commit murder on the way to Shechem
    for they commit shameful crimes.
10 In the house of Israel, I have seen a horrible thing;
    Ephraim's fornication is there—Israel is defiled.
11a For you also, Judah, a harvest is appointed.

7 But at Adam they transgressed the covenant;
    there they dealt faithlessly with me.
8 Gilead is a city of evildoers,
    tracked with blood.
9 As robbers lie in wait for someone,
    so the priests are banded together;
  they murder on the road to Shechem,
    they commit a monstrous crime.
10 In the house of Israel I have seen a horrible thing;
    Ephraim's whoredom is there, Israel is defiled.

11 For you also, O Judah, a harvest is appointed.

7. כְּאָדָם (like Adam) is frequently emended to read בְּאָדָם (in Adam or at Adam), referring to a town of that name where some breach of the covenant is supposed to have occurred. The emendation is influenced by the locative שָׁם (there) and the sequence of place-names in the passage. The Septuagint understands אָדָם as "man" (אדם) and reads, "But they are like a man transgressing a covenant." This is not in keeping with the consonantal text as we have it, because the verb is plural and thus not in agreement with the singular subject. Andersen and Freedman retain the כְּ, translating the construction "as in/at Adam" (*Hosea*, p. 39) with reference to a geographical site. They appeal to 2:5 for an analogical structure (כְּמִדְבָּר), but this structure need not be translated as "in" (see the discussion at 2:5). We have chosen to understand אָדָם to refer to the first man (see the Exposition). עָבְרוּ (have broken): עָבַר has the basic denotation of passing over. With reference to a covenant, it means to pass beyond the stric-

tures established by that covenant or to break it. בְּרִית (covenant) has as its underlying thrust a relationship involving obligation. Mutual agreement is not essential to the idea of covenant (Jer. 33:20; Hos. 2:20; [18]). The intent of a covenant may be effected unilaterally (Gen. 9:9; Jer. 33:20; Hos. 2:20 [18]) or bilaterally (Gen. 21:27, 32; 26:28–29; 1 Kings 5:26 [12]). שָׁם (there) is an adverbial particle which occurs most frequently in a concretely locative sense. In Psalm 14:5, however, it occurs in a nongeographical sense, pointing to the state of transgression which evildoers are in (v. 4) when divine judgment comes upon them. Here it has a similar function, for it points to the state of those who are in violation of the Mosaic covenant. בָּגְדוּ (dealt treacherously) has the sense of treachery in Isaiah 24:16 and Job 6:15.

8. אָוֶן (evil) is a general word for wrongdoing. Because the crimes described here are social in nature, it seems not to have the primary sense of idolatry in this context. BDB defines עֲקֻבָּה (trod-

---

7. This section begins with a *waw* and thus is almost certainly syntactically connected to the preceding sentence which represents Yahweh as preferring lovingkindness to sacrifice. Since the context speaks of some failure to comply with Yahweh's will, the *waw* should be translated adversatively.

In the view taken here the people have transgressed the covenant as did Adam. The suggestion that the word *Adam* represents the town of that name seems attractive in view of the place-names in the succeeding verses (Gilead and Shechem), but two names hardly establish a dominant sequence. Indeed, Hosea's use of place-names is so varied as to render such a conclusion tenuous. If we examine his use of place-names (other than the names of the northern and southern kingdoms), we find that he frequently pairs them in parallelism (4:15; 5:1–2; 9:6; 10:7–8). But in 5:8 he arranges four names in sequence; in 10:5 we find two names that are not parallel; in 10:9 the same place-name occurs twice; and in 9:9, 10, 15 there is one place-name in each verse. The occurrence of Gilead and Shechem (6:8–9) does not require us to view Adam as a geographical site. The verb tenses (v. 7) point to the past, while the grammatical structures (vv. 8–9) point to contemporary situations. If Adam is understood as a geographical site, we should expect that some act of corporate disobedience took place there that had tainted the people's relationship to God and which lived on in their national memory. In all

probability this would have taken place in Israel's earlier history, but the town of Adam seems not to have figured prominently in that period.

If we understand "Adam" to refer to the first man, the application of the analogy to the whole nation becomes clear. As Adam violated covenant strictures imposed on him, so the people of Hosea's day had violated the covenant made with them at Sinai. The strictures placed on the man Adam fall into the category of *běrît* (covenant), even though the term *běrît* (covenant) does not appear in the context that describes the nature of Adam's probation (Gen. 2:17). The basic concept of covenant is that of a relationship that involves obligation (Thomas E. McComiskey, *Covenants of Promise*, p. 63). Covenants were implemented in various ways, and mutuality of agreement was not always necessary to them; the concepts of relationship and obligation were. Both are present in the account in Genesis 2:17. The people of Hosea's day were like Adam in that they violated a covenant as did he. The perfect tenses (v. 7) construe the covenant violation of which the people were guilty as an established fact.

8. Gilead refers mainly to Transjordanian Israel in the Old Testament. Only Hosea 6:8, Judges 10:17, and 12:7 imply that there was a town of that name. The passages cited, however, are somewhat vague and it is possible that in Hosea 6:8 Gilead represents the territory of Israel beyond the Jordan. If so, it functions, as does the name *Ephraim* in Hosea, as a part for the whole. The

den) as "follow at the heel" (p. 784). It is used in Hosea 12:4 [3] of Jacob supplanting his brother. The word has the sense of supplanting or overreaching (see Gen. 27:36; Jer. 9:3 [4]). In each instance in the qal it has a hostile sense. It is best to see עֲקֻבָּה as a denominative of עָקֵב (BDB, heel or footprint) after the pattern of a passive adjective. This gives it the sense of trodden or tracked (RSV). עָקֵב denotes a footprint in Psalms 56:7 [6] and 89:52 [51]. מִדָּם (with blood): מִן indicates the source of the action described by the adjective (i.e., *from blood*).

9. וּכְחַכֵּי (lie in wait) fits the pattern of the piel infinitive construct of חָכָה with י in place of the normal ה. This change occurs occasionally with ô and ê (GKC §23l). Since the infinitive construct functions to set forth verbal action in the abstract, we must translate כְּחַכֵּי as "like the lying in wait of." The subject of the action of the infinitive (דִּים אִישׁ גְּדוּ, members of marauding bands) is in the genitive (GKC §115e): like the lying in wait of . . . marauding bands. It is unlikely that this construction connotes "as marauders lie in wait *for* a man." This translation makes גְּדוּדִים (marauders) the subject of the infinitive and thus separates it from the infinitive. The subject of the action of an infinitive, however, almost always immediately follows the infinitive (GKC §115e). כְּ (as) centers the simile on the action of lying in wait, not on אִישׁ (a man). אִישׁ is taken here as a collective noun (members; GKC §123b). This is in keeping with the companion word in the poetic structure (חֶבֶר), which has the sense of gang/s. חֶבֶר כֹּהֲנִים (so do gangs of priests): The comparative כְּ carries

over to the second half of the clause and thus achieves comparison by parataxis. חֶבֶר (gangs) is regarded as a collective. דֶּרֶךְ (on the way to) is not in the place we expect it to be in this structure. The more normal order is דֶּרֶךְ שְׁכְמָה with דֶּרֶךְ (way) in the construct state. It is possible to regard both דֶּרֶךְ (way) and שְׁכְמָה (Shechem) as adverbial accusatives and to translate them literally, "in the way, they murder, to Shechem," but this is awkward. It is clear that the words דֶּרֶךְ and שְׁכְמָה belong together. In all probability this is a construct relationship interrupted by a verb (see the discussion of this phenomenon in the Exposition at 14:3). כִּי (for) seems not to be causative. Many scholars identify it as asseverative (indeed, surely). This seems appropriate since it balances two clauses of similar content. This function of כִּי is not well substantiated, however, and a degree of causality is usually apparent in כִּי clauses when they follow the main clause (see the discussions of proximate causation at 4:16; 7:1). If the כִּי is not asseverative, the clause it introduces states the reason why they murder on the way to Shechem. It is because they are wont to commit shameful crimes. The fact that עָשׂוּ (they commit) is in the perfect tense may be significant. It indicates completed action, and thus may function as a characteristic perfect. We may paraphrase it, "It is an established fact that they commit shameful crimes; that is the reason for their committing murder on the way to Shechem." יְרַצֵּחוּ (they commit murder) never connotes the act of killing in a figurative sense. זִמָּה (shameful crimes) is a strong word for sin that describes acts of perversion (Lev.

---

designation *city* (*qiryat*) may be metaphorical here because the imagery used is appropriate to a town.

Gilead is accused of being a city of evildoers. The reference is a general one, for it is impossible to discover what particular crime Hosea may have had in mind. He pictures Gilead as a town covered with bloody footprints, however, and this implies the crime of murder. Perhaps a political assassination occurred there, or other bloody crimes that stood out in the prophet's memory. Gilead was not a town with footprints of mud and dust in its streets, but a town whose roads were tracked with blood.

9. The priests also were guilty of murder. Those who should have led Israel to a loving relationship with God were caught up in the cruel political intrigues of the time. It is difficult to determine why the "way to Shechem" is mentioned by Hosea. Shechem seems to have had no partic-

ular religious or political significance at this time. However, it is not Shechem itself that is significant; it is the *way* to Shechem that Hosea cites. Shechem lay at a juncture in the road that led from Samaria to the cult site of Bethel. It seems that the priests of the time were more concerned with the advancement of their political interests than their religious responsibilities, and stooped to assassination to secure their influence and power. Perhaps such assassinations had occurred on the road to Bethel. Whatever the crime, its nature was so heinous to Hosea that he calls it a "shame" (*zimmâ*, shameful crimes) and likens the priests who committed the crimes to a band of highwaymen. These references to the bloodguilt of Gilead and the priests of Israel may be difficult to identify historically, but the prophet has given us enough of a description to enable us to feel the revulsion he felt at the lack of respect for human

18:17; 20:14), adultery (Job 31:11), and idolatry (Jer. 13:27; Ezek. 16:27). It also refers to wickedness in general with no implications of sexual wrongdoing (Prov. 10:23; 21:27). Its use here appears to have no sexual connotations. Rather, its function appears to be that of setting the bloody crimes of the priests in the darkest of terms.

10. שַׁעֲרִירִיָּה (horrible thing): This unusual word is best explained as a reduplicated formation from the root שָׁעַר. Several forms of this word occur in Jeremiah in contexts relating to disgusting things. The word שַׁעֲרוּרָה occurs in association with שַׁמָּה (horror, Jer. 5:30), and refers to the incredible wickedness of the false prophets (23:14). The form שַׁעֲרֻרִת occurs in a context that deals with the fact that the Israelites had forgotten God (18:13), and שֹׁעָרִים is used of rotten figs (29:17). The *qěrē* emends the word in Hosea 6:10 to read שַׁעֲרוּרִיָּה, which is more in line with the pronunciation of the somewhat similar forms in Jeremiah. The weight added to the word by the additional consonants here may have lent intensity to it. The feminine ending (יָּה) on the word here may indicate that it is a biform of שַׁעֲרִית in which the final ת was rejected in favor of the feminine ending ה ָ. In feminine nouns terminating in י ִ, the ending

becomes יָּה, the form we have here (GKC §80c). שָׁם (there) resumes the reference of בֵּית יִשְׂרָאֵל (house of Israel) in the preceding clause. זְנוּת (fornication): See the comments at 4:11. לְאֶפְרַיִם (Ephraim's): לְ here is possessive. נִטְמָא (is defiled) connotes ritual uncleanness under the law. Uncleanness was reversed only by the regulations in the law governing the procedures for ritual cleansing. Such defilement excluded an individual from worship or religious service. Defilement could result from sexual wrongs (see 5:3). The association of the word טָמֵא (defile) with זְנוּת (fornication) shows that is the case here. Because Israel was defiled, she was excluded from the benefits of the covenant. She could expect only its curses.

11a. גַּם (also) includes Judah in the same fate as Israel. שָׁת (is appointed) is best understood as having a passive connotation (as in Job 38:11). This is after the analogy of the impersonal third person. Note one of many instances of the impersonal third person in Genesis 11:9 ("one calls its name" or "its name is called"). קָצִיר (harvest) is used of judgment (as it is here and in Isa. 18:5; Jer. 51:33).

life that pervaded the social structure of Israel and that had brought it to such unspeakable depths of shame.

10. Not only does Hosea accuse the northern kingdom of bloodshed in this section, but of fornication as well. This is another of the horrors he saw in Israel. This passage (vv. 9–10) reflects the combination of social decay and religious corruption that led to the nation's downfall. Hosea repeats the observation that Israel had defiled itself through its unfaithfulness to God (5:3).

11a. Hosea goes on to pronounce judgment against the southern kingdom as well: "For you also, Judah, a harvest is appointed." This line appears to be intrusive and some interpreters assign it to a later Judean redactor. One reason for this is that the words appear to lack coherence with the preceding context, for the fact that Judah will *also* be subjected to a harvest leads us to expect a pronouncement of similar judgment on Israel in the immediately preceding statement. But there is none. We must go back to verse 5 for it, but the judgment depicted there is on Israel as well as Judah, not Israel alone. The statement of judgment here cannot refer back to verse 5, for the words *also, Judah* would be redundant and desultory.

If the statement here is ascribed to a redactor, it is difficult to see what is achieved, for the problems of meaning and coherence remain. They are simply placed at another's doorstep, and that with little or no evidence. It is best to ask whether the author could have made this statement at this particular place, and if it finds consonance with authorial material elsewhere.

The prospect of judgment for Judah is certainly a concept authentic to Hosea, unless we want to deny to him all references to Judah. This is somewhat difficult to do, for it leads to a rending of the fabric of the book. The reference to Judah in 1:7 is not a typical gloss and clearly reflects an eighth-century prophetic concept of divine judgment and destruction (Mic. 5:10–15; see Hos. 2:20 [18]; 10:13–14). Both Judah and Israel are united grammatically in 2:2 [1:11], 4:15, and 5:5–6. And if the references to Judah in the poetic parallels were to be denied to the original form of the book, the result in some cases would be flat statements lacking poetic ballast (5:12–13; 6:4; 8:14).

While it is true that the Ephraim material in 6:7–10 does not speak of judgment, the idea may be inherent in that context. Several passages in Hosea accuse the people of sin, and while the resulting judgment is not stated in concrete terminology, it is clearly inherent in the accusation (see 8:10).

We know that the reference to the sexual crimes of the male population (4:14b) has within it the concomitant idea of punishment, because of the negative reference in verse 14a. Although verse 14b contains no direct reference to punishment, the withholding of judgment from the female population (v. 14a) implies that the male population will be punished.

The words "though you commit fornication, Israel" (4:15a) presuppose inherent guilt, even though it is not specifically mentioned. This is revealed by the next clause, "Let not Judah incur guilt."

Judgment is also lurking in the accusations of 7:1 that describe the evil deeds of Samaria, for the passage goes on to say that "they do not say in their hearts [that] I remember all their evil. Now their deeds have surrounded them, they are before me" (7:2). God's cognizance of their sin involved more than simple apprehension of their deeds; it involved certain judgment. We find little difference between act and consequence in Old Testament religious thought. We may observe this, for example, in two words for sin (*ḥaṭaʾ* and *ʿawōn*) which possess a broad range of meaning covering not only the concrete act of sin but its penalty as well. BDB defines *ʿawōn* as "iniquity, guilt, or punishment of iniquity" (p. 730), and we read, "But if you do not do this, behold, you have sinned [*ḥaṭaʾtem*] against the LORD; and be sure your sin [*ḥaṭṭaʾtĕkem*] will find you out" (Num. 32:23, NRSV).

We find a similar phenomenon in Amos, where the masculine suffix *nû* (him/it) on *ʾăšîbennû* (I will [not] turn *it* back) must refer to a threatened judgment where no specific judgment is cited (1:3, 6, 9, 11, 13; 2:1, 4, 6). Amos also states, "Therefore thus I will do to you, O Israel; because I will do this to you" (4:12, NRSV), but we do not know what Yahweh will do; the punishment is only implicit in the statement.

It is not difficult to see the presence of impending divine judgment in Hosea 6:7–10. As the prophet describes the covenant faithlessness of the people (v. 7), their bloodguilt (v. 8), the murderous deeds of the priests (v. 9), and their sexual defilement (v. 10), consciousness of the certainty of judgment is as much a part of the narrative as the description of the sins included in the shameful catalog. The reference to the harvest for Judah, rather than being an intrusive element in the narrative, may thus reflect an underlying theme of judgment which may not be immediately apparent to us, but which the prophet and the people would have clearly understood.

The harvest motif may find consonance with the preceding context, for Hosea's judgment motifs are frequently conceptually appropriate to the crimes to which they relate. In 13:3 the judgment is stated in terms that depict natural phenomena (as in 6:11) and follows a reference to an aspect of fertility worship ("Men kiss calves!" [13:2]). In 9:11–14 the judgment on human procreation follows a reference to the worship of Baal, the god of human and natural fertility (v. 10).

The use of the motif of harvest (6:11a) immediately following the reference to Israel's fornication (*zĕnût*) may betray the full range of content that the prophet gives to Israel's spiritual harlotry. To him Israel's unfaithfulness involved consort with the forces of nature symbolized by Baal, one of the chief gods of the nature cults. The word *zĕnût* (fornication) appears from 4:12 to have involved strong nature motifs in the mind of Hosea, where it occurs in a context describing nature worship as well as certain natural phenomena (vv. 12–14). If this same content obtains in the word in 6:10, the use of the harvest motif would have provided an appropriate depiction of judgment for what was essentially the sin of unfaithfulness to Yahweh committed by consort with the forces and phenomena of nature. The people will one day reap the results of their betrayal of Yahweh in a harvest of judgment.

IX. Israel's International Alliances Will Lead to Her Destruction (6:11b–7:16)

A. Yahweh Will Expose the Treachery of Israel's Dependence on Assyria (6:11b–7:3)

11b When I restore the fortunes of my people,
7 when I heal Israel;
  then the guilt of Ephraim will be revealed,
  and the evil deeds of Samaria;
  for they practice deceit,
    and a thief comes,
    and a band [of robbers] plunders outside.
2 Yet they do not say in their heart
  [that] I remember all their evil.
  Now their deeds have surrounded them,
    they are before me.
3 They make the king happy with their evil,
    and the princes with their lies.

When I would restore the fortunes of my people,
7 when I would heal Israel,
  the corruption of Ephraim is revealed,
    and the wicked deeds of Samaria;
  for they deal falsely,
    the thief breaks in,
    and the bandits raid outside.
2 But they do not consider
    that I remember all their wickedness.
  Now their deeds surround them,
    they are before my face.
3 By their wickedness they make the king glad,
    and the officials by their treachery.

11b. בְּשׁוּבִי (When I restore) is translated by the New Revised Standard Version, "When I would restore." It is doubtful, however, that the infinitive construed with בְּ ever has a modal sense (would). The infinitive construct with בְּ may refer to the future (when I shall), as it does in the similar expression in Zephaniah 3:20 ("'I will make you honored and praised among all the people of the earth, when I restore your fortunes [בְּשׁוּבִי אֶת־שְׁבוּתֵיכֶם] before your eyes,' says the LORD"). The construction frequently occurs in the clause-initial position; thus our construing it as beginning a new sentence presents no problem (see, e.g., Judg. 8:9; Pss. 9:4 [3]; 14:7; 126:1). שְׁבוּת (fortunes) is from שָׁבָה (take captive). In most of its occurrences שְׁבוּת may be translated "captivity," but it does not always connote captivity in a foreign land. It also refers to captivity to circumstances. Therefore the idiom שׁוּב שְׁבוּת has the primary sense of restoring the fortunes of. The return from exile is only one of the blessings subsumed under this idiom (Deut. 30:3), and in Job 42:10 שְׁבוּת refers to the renewed fortunes of Job. In Jeremiah 33:11 the idiom cannot have a primary reference to the exile, because it is accompanied by כְּבָרִאשֹׁנָה (as at the first). The translation "I will restore the captivity . . . as at the first," is indefensible because there was not a previous restoration from captivity. The collocation must refer here to the prosperity and stability of earlier times. All the uses

of this expression in Jeremiah have this sense (see also Pss. 14:7; 53:7 [6]; 85:2 [1]; 126:4). We may observe this connotation of the collocation also in Ezekiel 16:53, Joel 4:1 [3:1], and Amos 9:14 (see the Exposition).

7:1. כְּרָפְאִי (when I heal): The temporal sense of כְּ is determined by the temporality of בְּשׁוּבִי in the preceding parallel clause (6:11b). וְנִגְלָה (then . . . will be revealed) expresses the action consequent to Yahweh's restoration and healing of his people. עָוֹן (guilt) has a broad semantic range including concepts of overt sin, guilt for sin, and punishment for sin. וְרָעוֹת (and the evil deeds): The plural indicates sinful acts; it cannot have the sense of sin in the abstract. The focus is thus on sinful deeds. Because it is a poetic complement to עָוֹן, it further characterizes that concept by describing the concrete expression of their guilt in terms of wicked deeds. כִּי (for) introduces a causal clause, but it does not give a direct reason why Israel's sin will be revealed. It is best understood as expressing proximate cause (see the discussion at 4:16). The reason that God will expose their sin when he determines to heal them is that their sin exists: "They practice deceit." Before the festering wound can be lanced, it must be brought out into the open. שָׁקֶר (deceit) frequently has the sense of deception (see, e.g., Jer. 6:13; Exod. 20:16). וְגַנָּב יָבוֹא (a thief comes): The imperfect tense of יָבוֹא (comes) expresses action that takes place over

---

11b. A lengthy Ephraim oracle begins here and probably extends to 8:14, for a new oracle appears to begin at 9:1. This Ephraim oracle is almost completely denunciatory; except for 6:11b, it contains not one statement of hope.

The perspective changes for a moment here as we find the prophet looking ahead to the restoration of his people. It is the time when God will heal them; however, this healing will not be without pain, for it will take place only when Israel's sin has been revealed (7:1).

We observed in the Exegesis that the expression *restore the fortunes of* does not have a primary reference to the exile in many of its occurrences. Hosea may have had the return from the exile in mind, but the emphasis is not on that event in this passage. It is on restoration and healing, but the restoration of the people's fortunes will not occur apart from the manifestation of their wickedness.

7:1. Hosea says nothing about the need for repentance for national healing, but it would be

inconceivable that the exposure of the people's sin would lead to restoration without their asking for forgiveness. In 14:2–4 [1–3] Hosea pleads with the people to repent based on the exposure of their sins, for Hosea directs them to admit that their idolatry and their dependence on a foreign power are wrong. The statement of 6:11b–7:1 is thus an affirmation that God will restore his people, but not as long as their sin remains an impediment. He will expose their sin first, and this will lead to their healing.

The perspective suddenly reverts to the present and we are reminded once more of the sordid condition of the nation. Hosea says, "They practice deceit." This cursory statement affirms the need for the exposure of the people's sin. It points to that which stands in the way of their national healing. The people had only to look to the deviousness that marked their society to know why they were a dying nation.

The references to the thief who steals into the house and marauders who threaten harm in the

a period of time. They have been and are being robbed by thieves. The balancing of יָבוֹא (comes) with בַּחוּץ . . . פָּשַׁט (plunders . . . outside) may indicate that an antithetical relationship exists between the two entities, that is, a thief comes (in), and a band (of robbers) plunders outside. Thus the threat to the people was both external and internal.

2. וּבַל (not) is a negative particle used mainly in poetic and prophetic speech. לִלְבָבָם (in their hearts): לֵב refers to the seat of human cognition. The prophet could have omitted לֵב (heart) from his statement because the words *they do not say* alone would have adequately reflected the thought processes that underlie verbal communication. Speech is, after all, the expression of thought. The inclusion of לֵב (heart) in the expression places the emphasis on the inner processes of thought. The idea is that the people observed the turmoil in their midst, but failed to make the logical connection between that turmoil and the fact that God's hand was heavy upon them because of their sin. זָכַרְתִּי (I remember) has Yahweh as subject. It sustains the first-person references to Yahweh begun in 6:11b. The verb זָכַר (remember) may involve action along with its sense of recollection. We may observe the sense of appropriate and obligatory action in this word in Genesis 9:15, Numbers 15:39, 1 Samuel 25:31, and Jeremiah 14:10. The fact that זָכַר (remember) is in the perfect tense, in contrast to its companion verb in the structure (יֹאמְרוּ, say) which is in the imperfect, may lay stress on the action of remembering as a complete or established aspect of God's character. עַתָּה (now) brings forward the present perspective of the circumstances set forth in the previ-

ous line. סְבָבוּם (have surrounded them) has a hostile sense, as it has in many passages (see, e.g., Josh. 6:7; Judg. 16:2). It does not imply simply that the people's sins were so numerous as to surround them on all sides. When we consider that Hosea made much of the fact that sin demands requital (see 1:4), it is not difficult to posit a hostile sense for the word here. The word עַתָּה (now), which initiates this clause, frequently introduces judgment-sayings in Hosea (2:12 [10]; 5:7; 8:13; 10:2; 13:2). The fact that the people's deeds are before God (פָּנַי) means that he is aware of them and that divine judgment is imminent. Hosea pictures the nation's sin as an enemy about to attack from all sides. The situation is hopeless. נֶגֶד פָּנָי (before me) underscores the affirmation of the parallel line which says that God remembers sin. But its relationship to the preceding clause in the second line is of greater importance because it continues the thought expressed in that clause (Now their deeds have surrounded them). The relationship of these clauses affirms that Yahweh's cognizance of their wrongdoing had invested their evil deeds with a hostile force.

3. בְּרָעָתָם (with their evil): רָעָה (evil) occurs here for the second time in the brief compass of this passage. In its first occurrence (v. 2a) it served as the object of זָכַר (remember) and referred to the wicked deeds God would judge. Here their wicked deeds, worthy of divine judgment, are represented as delighting the king. The absence of the article on מֶלֶךְ (king) may denote kings in general, not a particular king. Rather than encouraging moral behavior and compliance with covenant standards, the kings encouraged intrigue, assassinations, and social wrong. These things delighted them

---

streets are representations of the situation of the nation. They may refer to the tribute imposed by the Assyrians who were like plunderers. Israelite officials had to impose heavy taxes on the people to satisfy the demands of the Assyrian king; thus the nation was in a state of turmoil.

2. As economic conditions worsened, the people did not appear to consider the fact that God remembers sin. Since God's remembering involves appropriate action (see the Exegesis), Hosea's words mean that the people seemed to be unaware of the fact that the dismal economic situation was the result of God's awareness of their wrongdoing. They had gone to Assyria for help, and now they were suffering. They had forsaken Yahweh, and he had not forgotten that.

This observation is followed by a vivid illustration of the fact that sin demands requital. The prophet personifies their wicked deeds, picturing them as an army that had surrounded the nation. Their deeds were like enemy troops who had gained a stranglehold on them. Their continued lawless acts were leading them to certain ruin.

3. The officials delighted in these wrongs, however. If Hosea had in mind Menahem's alliance with Assyria to strengthen his weak hold on the throne, we can understand how the king might have been delighted with such a coup. Hosea, however, would have viewed it as an act of treachery. Any deed done to advance the king's interests—wrong or not—would have made the king happy.

because they advanced their interests. To what depths the nation had fallen! The kings who should have been faithful guardians of the purity of the nation's Yahwistic heritage not only failed to punish its wrongdoing but took delight in it. וּבְכַחֲשֵׁיהֶם (with their lies): בְּ (with) sustains the instrumental mode of בְּ in the previous clause. כַחֲשֵׁיהֶם (their lies) further defines the "evil" of the previous clause as deceit. Evidently the government structure of the time was permeated by deceit and intrigue. שָׂרִים (princes) need not be understood as an exact synonym for מֶלֶךְ, since poetic parallelism may involve the balancing of entities that are alike only in the broadest relational sense. We may observe a distinction between king and prince in 7:5.

IX. Israel's International Alliances Will Lead to Her Destruction (6:11b–7:16)

B. Israel's Corrupt Leaders (7:4–7)

4 They are all adulterers;
  like a burning oven are they.
 The baker has left off stirring [the fire]
  from the kneading of the dough until
  it is leavened.
5 On the day of our king the leaders
  became sick with the heat of wine;
  he drew his hand with scorners.
6 For they bring their heart[s] like an oven
  into their treachery.
 All night long their baker sleeps;
  in the morning it burns like a blazing fire.
7 All of them are hot as an oven,
  and consume their judges;
 all their kings have fallen,
  yet not one of them calls to me.

4 They are all adulterers;
  they are like a heated oven,
 whose baker does not need to stir the
  fire,
  from the kneading of the dough until
  it is leavened.
5 On the day of our king the officials
  became sick with the heat of wine;
  he stretched out his hand with
  mockers.
6 For they are kindled like an oven, their
  heart burns within them;
  all night their anger smolders;
  in the morning it blazes like a flam-
  ing fire.
7 All of them are hot as an oven,
  and they devour their rulers.
 All their kings have fallen;
  none of them calls upon me.

4. כֻּלָּם (They are all) continues the plural subject of verses 1–3, which is the people. תַּנּוּר (oven) denotes a small oven frequently used for baking bread. בֹּעֵרָה (heated) is a feminine participle according to the arrangement of the consonants in the Masoretic Text, but תַּנּוּר is masculine. This lack of agreement in gender is unusual even for Hosea. It is doubtful that it represents the original text. In all probability, the ה on בֹּעֵרָה should be read with the following מ to form the pronoun הֵם (they). This reordering of the consonants yields a reading that is both logical and syntactical, "Like a heated oven are they." The construction of the consonants in the Masoretic Text reads, "Like an oven heated by [מִן] the baker." Not only does the lack of agreement in gender between "heated" and "oven" militate against this, but also the fact that the presence of a baker in the line describing the heat of their sexual passion is superfluous; a burning oven is enough to depict their adulteries. The fact that the pronoun הֵם (they) comes at the end of

the clause in this reconstruction is not objectionable. Personal pronouns frequently occur at the end of a clause (see, e.g., Gen. 24:34; Lev. 18:15; 1 Sam. 23:22; 1 Kings 22:32). יִשְׁבּוֹת מֵעִיר (has left off stirring): We understand מֵעִיר as a hiphil participle of עוּר with the sense of rouse or stir up (BDB, p. 735). The verb occurs with several objects such as love (Song of Sol. 2:7) and the dawn (Ps. 57:9 [8]). The implication is that the baker began to tend the fire, but for some reason he neglected his task. The imperfect tense of יִשְׁבּוֹת (left off), with its sense of incomplete action, is appropriate to the time clause that follows: עַד . . . מֵ, *from the kneading of the dough until it is leavened*. The imperfect tense indicates that the baker's neglect extended through the time period thus described.

5. יוֹם (on the day) is an adverbial accusative that denotes some aspect of time (on). חֲמָת (heat of): In other contexts this word connotes fever, as well as the metaphorical idea of burning rage. In this context it must refer to the flush of wine. מִיָּין

---

4. The recital of the sins of the people continues in this section with the accusation, "They are all adulterers." It is clear from the opening lines of the oracle that all the people (note "Israel" and "Ephraim" in 7:1) are in view, not only the leaders in Israelite society.

Hosea cites the sins of deceit and political intrigue in the previous section of this oracle (vv. 1, 3). Here he brands the people adulterers (see 4:2). When he uses the word *adultery*, Hosea may have in mind either marital unfaithfulness, or unfaithfulness to Yahweh as expressed in Israel's international alliances. In all likelihood it is the former, for he never uses the figure of adultery elsewhere to depict the political treachery of the nation. It always represents adultery in the strict moral sense. It is possible that Hosea blends adultery and drunkenness in this bold portrait of debauchery in order to express the deep disgust he feels for all the classes of people in his society who are inflamed by lust and drink.

The adulterous passion of the people is described by the prophet as an oven for baking bread. In his analogy the oven has been heated, but something has gone awry; the baker has left off stirring the fire. Perhaps he became tired and fell asleep. The baker neglects to stir the fire "from the kneading of the dough until it is leavened." In all probability dough was kneaded in the evening and left to rise during the night to be ready for baking in the morning. The baker in Hosea's analogy did not tend the fire as he should

have, and so in the morning the fire was a blaze rather than a bed of hot coals. It was unsuitable for baking. The picture is an appropriate description of the inflamed passions of the people that led them into such disregard for the sanctity of marriage.

5. The reference to the "day of our king" is obscure. The construct relationship basically expresses possession, and thus points to some day that related to the king. It is difficult to be more precise. Perhaps Hosea had the king's investiture in mind, or some other day of royal celebration. More appropriate to the context, however, is the possibility that this was the day when the king successfully completed negotiations with Assyria. The king may have been Menahem (see the Introduction). Or the expression may refer to King Hoshea's efforts to effect an alliance with Egypt (see the Exposition at 7:11–12). It makes little difference which interpretation is correct, for the significant thing is what happened on that day.

On that day the nobles were so sated with wine that they became ill. Isaiah had witnessed a similar circumstance when he said, "The priest and the prophet reel with strong drink. . . . All tables are covered with filthy vomit; no place is clean" (28:7–8, NRSV). The destiny of the nation was in the hands of such as these; leaders who were doing nothing about the headlong dash to ruin. They made no apparent effort to reverse the tide of evil and revelled in the same wickedness that characterized the people. The word *sar* (leader) need not

(with . . . wine): מִן (with, lit. from) indicates the source of the sickness. מָשַׁךְ (drew) does not represent an extending of the hand which would be expressed by שָׁלַח (Gen. 22:10; 48:14; Exod. 9:15); rather, it reflects the action of drawing as in the drawing of a bow (1 Kings 22:34) or drawing someone to one's self (Jer. 31:3). The preposition אֶת (with) indicates that מָשַׁךְ (drew) has an associative connotation in this context. There appears to be such a usage of the word in Psalm 28:3. While the Revised Standard Version translates the verb מָשַׁךְ in that verse as "take off" (*"Take* me not *off* with the wicked"), it is not clear that it ever has the meaning "take away." In contexts where there is a clear directional perspective the action of the word appears always to be directed *toward* the initiator of the action, not *away*. It seems best to translate the verb in Psalm 28:3 "do not *draw me into*" or "do not *associate me with* the wicked." If so, the verb מָשַׁךְ here may have the sense, "he drew in his hand with scorners," that is, he associated his hand (the physical symbol of strength and ability) with scorners. He joined with those who were wicked. Because מָשַׁךְ is singular, it finds its referent, not in the plural שָׂרִים (princes), but in מֶלֶךְ (king) in the first line. לֹצְצִים (scorners) is a *poʿlel* participle of לִיץ (scorn). It describes an individual whose heart is hardened against godliness and who is incapable of learning from rebuke (Prov. 9:8; 15:12).

6. כִּי (For) introduces the reason, not for the king's drawing his hand, but for the fact that those

with whom he associated were scorners. It is because they engaged in treachery. קֵרְבוּ (they bring) is construed as a piel in the Masoretic Text; thus it has the sense of bringing near rather than drawing near. Its subject is שָׂרִים, the princes, who are also designated לֹצְצִים (scorners). It is this latter word that is the closest logical referent of the plural inflection of קֵרְבוּ (they bring). אָרְבָּם (their treachery) occurs only here and in Jeremiah 9:7 [8]. It is from אָרַב (to lie in wait) and denotes an ambush. In Jeremiah 9:7 it connotes treachery. The context of Hosea 7:6 calls for a similar sense. יָשֵׁן (sleeps) is an adjective from יָשֵׁן (to sleep). Many commentators understand the word in the sense of *smolder* and repoint אֹפֵהֶם (their baker) to read אַפְּהֶם (their anger). This yields the sense of *their anger smolders*, but this form of אַף always appears as אַפָּם and יָשֵׁן never occurs elsewhere with reference to a smoldering fire. Hosea associates a baker with an oven earlier in the context (v. 4), and his use of oven (תַּנּוּר) again here makes the reference to a baker quite consonant with the flow of thought in the passage. He implies that the baker in his analogy fell asleep during the night (v. 4). בֹּקֶר (in the morning), like the preceding הַלַּיְלָה (night), is an accusative of time. Hosea construes the first word of the pair (לַיְלָה) with an article. This is the same pattern as in 4:5 לַיְלָה . . . הַיּוֹם). הוּא (it) refers to the oven (תַּנּוּר) of the previous context because it is described as burning (בֹּעֵר) like a blazing fire.

---

refer only to the nobility, for it is used of the leaders of Israel (Num. 21:18) and appears not to have lost that sense in the later literature (Ezra 8:24; 1 Chron. 27:22; see also Isa. 23:8). The whole national leadership is in view.

The prophet then turns to speak of the king: "He drew his hand with scorners." The ribaldry of that regal occasion was born of hardened hearts and careless minds. What a picture of the responsibility of leadership. When religious leaders are no different from the masses, there can be no hope of spiritual power or divine blessing. A nation with a foolish leader may survive because of wise counselors, but when a head of state throws in his lot with fools, the prospect is a dismal one. We are reminded of Rehoboam whose willingness to accept the foolhardy advice of his peers led to the division of the nation (2 Chron. 10:1–16).

6. Hosea explains that they are scorners because they bring their hearts like an oven into their

treachery. The heart (*lēb*) is the seat of thought and motivation (see the comment at 2:16 [14]; 4:11). As they applied the processes of thought to their political intrigues, the people applied minds that were like an oven—not normal minds, but minds fired by passion and strong drink. Their deliberations were not reasoned and impassioned, but were fevered by plotting that gave little thought to the means by which their ends were to be achieved.

Hosea's metaphor of the oven has undergone a slight twist here (see the Exposition at 2:5). We have found this to be typical of his literary style. In the first part of the section the oven represented the heat of sexual passion (v. 4). Here it is the intensity of political intrigue that is before us. Jeremiah provides insight into the meaning of a burning heart when he says, "If I say, 'I will not mention him . . . then within me there is something like a burning fire shut up in my bones; I

7. כֻּלָּם (all of them): It is best to understand the plural suffix to refer to the people, not only to the princes. Even though שָׂרִים (princes) is the closest logical referent, the subject changes almost imperceptibly in this context. Those to whom כֻּלָּם (all of them) refers are distinguished from the kings and judicial leaders in the subsequent context. שֹׁפְטֵיהֶם (their judges) need not be limited only to judicial officials in this context. The word שֹׁפֵט (judge) is used of kings as well. It occurs in parallel with

מֶלֶךְ (king) in Hosea 13:10. Here the application of the same general fate to both the judges (whom the people devoured) and the kings (who have fallen) supports their identity. אֵין (none) is a particle of nonexistence. קְרָא . . . אֵלַי (calls to me): קְרָא has the sense of calling for help in a number of passages (see, e.g., Prov. 21:13; Isa. 58:9). God is represented as speaking as at the beginning of the oracle (6:11b/7:1).

am weary with holding it in, and I cannot" (20:9, NRSV). Jeremiah was a prophet and could not keep silent. He had to speak about God, for his prophetic consciousness was like a fire within him that he could not hold in for long. Such was the burning intensity of the hearts of the national and religious leadership of the nation of Israel. But it was an impassioned desire for wrong that they could not contain, not a consciousness of the divine will as with Jeremiah.

The metaphor of the oven continues in the next sentence. Hosea gave the analogy of a careless baker earlier (v. 4); now the baker reappears, and we find that he was asleep after all. Indeed, our metaphorical baker had slept the night away while the fire blazed higher. In this deft and colorful way Hosea brings us back to the central theme of this section—the intensity with which the people engaged in wrongdoing. The reality of the metaphor is that the fire in the hearts of the people was out of control, flames leaping upward around the imaginary oven, so that bread could not be baked in so hot an oven. The leaders approached their political machinations with hearts fired in a similar way.

7. The prophet concludes this section by citing the oven for the last time as he pictures how the people's heated passion manifested itself. It was in the fact that they "consume their judges." The

subject (kullām), "All of them," is the same form (kullām) as in verse 4, where the people were in view (see the Exegesis). We find no need to see it as a reference only to the leaders here (v. 7), for what is said is true of all the people. Indeed, the word leaders (šōpĕtêhem) is the object of the verb consume; thus we have returned to a denunciation of the society as a whole.

The heated passion, depicted as an oven, characterized the people as well as their wine-sodden leaders. It had its manifestation in the crimes of political anarchy that had led to the instability of the post-Jeroboam era. The last thirty years of Israel's history are a vivid testimony to the truthfulness of Hosea's depiction of his society. Four of the six kings during that period were assassinated. The fact that Hosea calls the fallen kings judges (šōpĕtîm) underscores the enormity and stupidity of the actions of the people. They murdered their counselors—wicked though they were—and left themselves like a ship without a rudder.

Incredulity marks the mood of Hosea's closing statement. As he surveys the three decades in which the kings had fallen, he marvels that no one views the situation for the desperate plight it is. They do not call on God for help. Prayer is absent and the nation is headed for a certain doom.

IX. Israel's International Alliances Will Lead to Her Destruction (6:11b–7:16)

C. Israel's Unwise Political Alliances Are Responsible for Her Declining Strength (7:8–10)

8 Ephraim: he mixes himself with the
    nations;
  Ephraim has become a cake not
    turned.
9 Foreigners have consumed his strength,
  but he does not know it.
  Also, grey hair is sprinkled on him,
  but he does not know it.
10 And the pride of Israel answers to his
    face;
  yet they have not returned to the
    LORD their God,
  nor have they sought him in all this.

8 Ephraim mixes himself with the
    peoples;
  Ephraim is a cake not turned.
9 Foreigners devour his strength,
  but he does not know it;
  gray hairs are sprinkled upon him,
  but he does not know it.
10 Israel's pride testifies against him;
    yet they do not return to the LORD
    their God,
  or seek him, for all this.

8. עַמִּים (nations) frequently refers to the nations that surrounded Israel, many of whom were Israel's enemies. הוּא (he) is probably a ballast element, not an intensive. But even so, it calls a degree of attention to itself by virtue of its weight in the line. It refers the reader back to Ephraim. יִתְבּוֹלָל (mixes himself) is a reflexive form of בָּלַל which, when construed with בְּ, as in בָעַמִּים (with the nations), means "to mix with" (Exod. 29:40; Lev. 2:4, 5; 7:10). It occurs most frequently with שֶׁמֶן (oil). הָיָה (has become) reflects a degree of completion or certainty because it is in the perfect tense. Ephraim has already become an unturned cake. עֻגָה (cake) is in all probability from a root meaning "circular." The word is general in nature, connoting various types of breads (Gen. 18:6; 1 Kings 19:6; Ezek. 4:12). הֲפוּכָה (turned): הָפַךְ connotes *to turn* or *overturn* (BDB, p. 245). Here the sense is to turn the flat bread over in order to bake it on both sides.

9. כֹּחַ (strength) most frequently implies physical strength and depicts the might of nations in several contexts (see, e.g., Josh. 17:17; Nah. 2:2 [1]; Hab. 1:11). וְהוּא (but he): We must translate וְ (but) adversatively because of the contrasting concepts in the line. הוּא (he) answers to the הוּא (he) above (v. 8) and adds an element of symmetry to the lines. גַּם (Also) indicates that the writer added a concept to the previous one. Not only is Ephraim losing his strength, but grey hairs (שֵׂיבָה) are sprinkled on his head. Andersen and Freedman suggest that the word designates "not grey human hair, but the hairs of mold on food." The reasons for this include the fact that זָרַק (sprinkle) "is used mainly for blood. It cannot be applied to hair in the same sense," and the suggested translation completes the imagery of food begun in verse 8, where Israel is depicted as a cake (*Hosea*, p. 467). There is no reason, however, why Hosea could not have pictured grey hairs as scattered on the

---

8. Hosea makes effective use of illustrations from the commonplace. We have observed how he gave vent to the way he felt about the people's sin by using the analogy of the oven. We felt the heat of their passion in the simile. In this way he was like Jesus who also appealed to common aspects of life to enhance his teaching.

The lengthy Ephraim oracle continues with another domestic allusion. Like the allusion to the oven, this one has to do with the preparation of food, but there is no contextual warrant for assuming that the oven motif extends to this section. The picture seems to be that of preparing dough for baking bread, and Israel is now likened to that dough. In the process Ephraim mixes himself with the foreign nations. We see no baker in this depiction, for Ephraim is both the dough and the one who prepares it. This is not a precise use of metaphorical elements, but typical of Hosea's use of them.

While it may not be true to life, the metaphor is true to the conditions as they existed then. No one but Ephraim itself was to blame for the national calamity brought on by alliances with the surrounding nations. This admixture with an impure nation rendered the end product impure. Assyria's intrusion into the national life of Israel would ultimately lead the nation to lose its internal cohesiveness. Assyrian political interference and military domination were incompatible with the national unity that their constitution could have provided had they simply trusted in their

God. But the plural *nations* leads us to go beyond Assyria. We must think also of Egypt and the political machinations that involved that country (see the comments at 7:11). While the next section (7:11–13) places the emphasis on international alliances, it is possible that Hosea has in mind the intrusions of Canaanite religion and culture as well.

The second metaphor depicts Ephraim as an unturned loaf. Because it has not been turned it is scorched on one side. This figure is not a prediction of what will yet occur, for the nation was already partially burned by its relations with Assyria and Egypt. The verb tenses in this passage support that, as well as the emphasis on the fact that the people were not aware that their calamities witnessed to their current state of apostasy from God ("he does not know it").

9. This metaphor finds its explanation in this verse: "Foreigners have consumed his strength." This was evident in the unstable conditions of the monarchy. The feverish efforts of the officials of Israel to shore up their tottering nation with the help of Assyria proved unwise. Assyria demanded and received a massive amount of tribute for her trouble, draining Israel's coffers dry.

The fourth line of the quatrain, "Also grey hair is sprinkled on him," is conceptually parallel to the preceding line, "Foreigners have consumed his strength." The particle *gam* (also) adds a note of emphasis to the word *śēbâ* (grey hair). The strength of Ephraim was declining as with the approach of

head even though the word is not otherwise used of hair. It is used of substances other than blood, such as dust and coals (Ezek. 10:2), and Isaiah uses the word to depict the scattering of seed (28:25). The reference to greying hair is an appropriate complement to the imagery of the companion clause which describes another characteristic of old age, that is, diminution of strength, and which is closer in the context than the reference to cake (v. 8). It is clear that faltering strength and greying hair are related images because they occur in clauses united by the common words לֹא יָדָע (but he does not know it) and are thus conceptually parallel. The major problem with the word זָרְקָה (is sprinkled) is that it is never elsewhere intransitive. Perhaps this is why the Septuagint reads ἐξήνθησαν (burst forth), probably reflecting זָרְחָה (come forth). We do not know enough about the states of Hebrew verbs to say with certainty that זָרַק (sprinkle) could not have

functioned intransitively (see GKC §117v, y). Note the intransitive use of לְבֵשׁ (to clothe) in Psalm 109:29 (be clothed).

10. וְעָנָה גְאוֹן־יִשְׂרָאֵל בְּפָנָיו (And the pride of Israel answers to his face): See the comments at 5:5. וְלֹא (yet . . . not): The context requires a concessive idea in English. בִקְשֻׁהוּ (sought him): בִּקֵּשׁ (seek) represents an important theological theme in the Old Testament. One of the most helpful descriptions of the concept involves turning to God with the whole heart and soul (Deut. 4:29); the word is complemented by שׁוּב (return, v. 30). Here בִּקֵּשׁ is also in parallel with שׁוּב (returned). בְּכָל־זֹאת (in all this): בְּ introduces the sphere of activity described by בִּקֵּשׁ (seek); it is "all this." זֹאת (this) is construed as a feminine because of the impossibility of determining a gender for the series of circumstances set forth in this context. The feminine gender frequently indicates abstract concepts.

---

old age, but he did not perceive it; death was approaching, but he was not aware of it.

10. There was a witness to the slow but sure decline of the nation, a witness to which it should have paid attention. It was "the pride of Israel." Even though the people did not perceive the approaching end, the "pride of Israel" testified to them of that fact. The expression *the pride of Israel* occurs also in 5:5, where it refers to Israel's national glory. How it had suffered since the days of Jeroboam II! The social corruption and national decay of this period of Israelite history had brought them low. Should it continue without a return to their God, it would lead them to ruin,

but they did not perceive that. Perhaps the decline was so slow as to be almost imperceptible.

The people did not do that which would stop their headlong plunge to destruction. They did not return to Yahweh or seek him in these dismal circumstances. "Seeking" and "returning" are not synonyms, but they have overlapping meanings. We see a directional perspective in seeking, just as there is in returning. The prophet calls on the people to return to God, to seek his favor and covenant blessings, and to do so with sincere purpose of heart. If they sought to learn his ways, they would find him.

IX. Israel's International Alliances Will Lead to Her Destruction (6:11b–7:16)

D. Israel's International Policies Will Cause Her Destruction (7:11–13)

11 And Ephraim has become like a simple dove,
  lacking sense—
  they have called to Egypt, they have gone to Assyria.
12 As they go I will spread my net over them;
  I will bring them down like birds of the heavens,
  I will chastise them when a report [comes] to their community.
13 Woe to them, for they have fled from me!
  Destruction to them, for they have rebelled against me!
 I would redeem them,
  but they speak lies against me.

11 Ephraim has become like a dove,
  silly and without sense;
  they call upon Egypt, they go to Assyria.
12 As they go, I will cast my net over them;
  I will bring them down like birds of the air;
  I will discipline them according to the report made to their assembly.
13 Woe to them, for they have strayed from me!
  Destruction to them, for they have rebelled against me!
 I would redeem them,
  but they speak lies against me.

11. פוֹתָה (simple) has as its rudimentary concept the idea of openness. The root פתה may connote a state of open-mindedness in which one is easily influenced or deceived (see 2:16 [14]). The word *naive* is an appropriate translation in some contexts. Note the use of the noun פֶּתִי (simple, Prov. 14:15). לֵב (sense) has the connotation we observed earlier (see 4:11), that is, the processes of thought or the seat of the intelligence. מִצְרַיִם (Egypt) and אַשּׁוּר (Assyria) are not construed with prepositions. They are thus accusatives of direction (to). קָרָאוּ (they call) has as its subject Ephraim, which is construed in the plural in this clause. This abrupt change of number (see v. 11a) is typical of Hosea's style.

12. יֵלֵכוּ (they go) is an imperfect verb that communicates the sense of durative action established by כַּאֲשֶׁר (as). The sense is, "In the course of their going [to these nations] I will spread over them my net." אֲיִסִרֵם (I will chastise them) is an unusual form. The vocalization points to an uncontracted

hiphil form of יָסַר (chastise). We expect אֲיִסִרֵם because י regularly forms the diphthong יִ after short *a* (GKC §24f). The form here represents the pointing before contraction. Note the similarly uncontracted hiphil form of יְיַשְׁרוּ (in Proverbs 4:25. The causative sense sometimes required by the hiphil is a problem in Hosea 7:12. However, it is possible that the hiphil has a sense similar to the piel, as with יָשַׁר and אָבַד (see GKC §53c). If that is the case, the form here reflects the sense of *to chastise*. כְּשֵׁמַע (when a report [comes]): שֵׁמַע connotes tidings (Gen. 29:13), a report (Exod. 23:1), and, by extension, fame or reputation (Num. 14:15). לַעֲדָתָם (to their community): In most of its occurrences in the Old Testament עֵדָה (community) refers to the assembly of Israelites. This specific use of the term diminished sharply during the period of the united monarchy. Common to all the occurrences of the word is the concept of community. Besides the numerous references to the community of Israelites, it also designates a

---

11. As Hosea views Israel's desperate efforts to establish international alliances, an analogy comes to mind. The nation is like a dove that flutters erratically here and there with no apparent course of flight. This is an apt description of the national affairs of the time. We observed Menahem's efforts to curry favor with the Assyrian king (2 Kings 15:19–20) by paying him tribute. When Menahem's son Pekahiah was assassinated after only two years on the throne, his successor, Pekah, reversed national policy and entered into an alliance with Syria against Judah (2 Kings 16:5; cf. Isa. 7:1–6). As a result he suffered the loss of much of his kingdom (2 Kings 15:29). Hoshea succeeded Pekah and reversed the previous policy by paying tribute to the king of Assyria (2 Kings 17:3). Later, however, Hoshea stopped the payment of tribute in an intrigue that involved the king of Egypt (2 Kings 17:4). But Egypt proved to be a weak ally, for when the king of Assyria discovered the treachery he came against Israel, took Samaria, and imprisoned Hoshea. No help came from Egypt, and what remained of the once proud kingdom of Israel was lost forever (2 Kings 17:5–6). The flitting of Israel between the two powers was senseless. The nation's leaders made alliances and then broke them, and what Hosea predicts in the next verse became a stark reality.

12. The words *as they go* pick up on the verb *gone* in the preceding clause (*halak*). The sense is that while the people are in the course of their political intrigues God will bring them down like

birds trapped in a net. The history of the time witnesses to the accuracy of Hosea's words. It was while the nation was in the course of its political maneuverings that Assyria brought them down like a bird suddenly arrested in its flight by a trapper's net. The figure of the net, of course, refers to the captivity.

Hosea views the captivity as a chastisement, an experience from which the people might learn. It was a hard lesson, for as they spent the weary years in captivity, they would come to understand why it had all happened. Zechariah, a postexilic prophet, reflects that realization when he says of the people, "But they refused to listen, and turned a stubborn shoulder, and stopped their ears . . . and I scattered them with a whirlwind among all the nations that they had not known" (7:11, 14, NRSV).

We have understood Hosea to say that the chastisement would take place when a report comes to their community. The pronominal suffix *am* (their) indicates that Hosea stands aloof from his community; he views it from outside. Thus, the "report" does not refer to tidings that came to the ancient congregation in the wilderness. Hosea would have used the crystallized expression *hā'edâ* (the congregation), and would not have disassociated himself from his forebears. Indeed, the obedience of the people in that period was to him a spiritual ideal (2:17 [15]).

The reference to the report is in the third line of this series of clauses describing Israel's demise;

swarm of bees (Judg. 14:8) and a company of godless people (Job 15:34). The use of the suffix ם‎ (their) limits the application of the word עֵדָה‎ to the community of Hosea's day and injects a strong note of sarcasm into his words, because it disassociates that community from the true congregation of Israel (*their* community, not *the* community). When the word עֵדָה‎ (community) has a suffix, the indication is that the writer is speaking of a group from which he disassociates himself (note the references to the company of Korah; see, e.g., Num. 16:5, "He said to Korah and all *his* company," 6, 16). The words כְּשֵׁמַע לַעֲדָתָם‎ are difficult, but a somewhat analogous statement in Isaiah 23:5 supports the translation, "When a report [comes] to their community." It says לְמִצְרָיִם‎ כַּאֲשֶׁר־שֵׁמַע‎ (when the report comes to Egypt). It is obvious that this is an elliptical expression in which the לְ‎ points to an implicit verbal idea (comes). While this clause begins with כַּאֲשֶׁר‎ and the clause here begins with כְּ‎, there is no difference in sense because כְּ‎ shares a temporal function with כַּאֲשֶׁר‎ (Davidson, *Syntax* §145a). The clause here is also elliptical. The presence of לְ‎ in this clause directs the action of the implicit verbal idea (comes) to עֵדָתָם‎ (their community).

13. נָדְדוּ‎ (they have fled): נָדַד‎ has the basic sense of movement; other nuances are added to the word by contextual requirements or associative prepositions. For example, the word refers to the movement of a bird's wing (Isa. 10:14), with no directional connotation. When the word is associated with מִן‎ (from), however, the nuance *away from* is added to the word. The nature or intensity of this movement is determined by the context. Thus we must translate it "flee" in contexts where some reason for flight is present (as in Ps. 31:12 [11]; Isa. 10:31; 21:15, "they have fled from the sword"). In Nahum 3:17 it must be translated "fly away" because its subject is locusts. It describes the fruitless wandering of the wicked in search of food (Job 15:23), and the straying of a bird from its nest (Prov. 27:8). In the context of Hosea 7:13 it is accompanied by מִן‎ (from/away from), and is parallel to the verb פָּשַׁע‎ (rebel). This parallel concept adds a force to the word that the concept of straying does not satisfy. Thus we have the word *flee* in our translation to express the idea of rebellious departure from God (see the discussion of this verb at 9:17). שֹׁד‎ (Destruction) in the Prophets denotes the ruin that may come on a nation (Isa. 13:6; 16:4; 22:4; Jer. 48:3; Amos 5:9). It complements אוֹי‎ (woe) in that it more clearly

---

the chastisement in the third line sustains the references to the impending calamity in the first two lines, and, if we have understood it correctly, adds another element. It associates the calamity with an event, that is, a report that will come to their community. Because of the parallel structure of these three lines, we may understand the allusion to the report to be contemporaneous with the captivity, prefigured by the reference to the entrapment of the birds. While the report is difficult to place historically, there was a report that came to the officials of Israel that was contemporaneous with the events that led and contributed to Israel's collapse.

According to 2 Kings 17:4, King Hoshea attempted to avoid paying tribute to Assyria by effecting an alliance with Egypt. He sent messengers to the king of Egypt and in all probability they returned from that country with a positive report. It is likely that the tribute was withheld because of assurances from Egypt that they would support Israel against Assyria. It was this desperate maneuver that led to Israel's downfall, for we read that "in the ninth year of Hoshea the king of Assyria . . . carried the Israelites away to Assyria"

(2 Kings 17:6, NRSV). The nation fell like a trapped bird during the time when it flitted senselessly among the nations.

13. These events prompt Hosea to proclaim woe to the nation. The woe, defined more precisely by its poetic complement *destruction* (šōd), is to come on the nation because they have fled from God. In the same line the verbs *nādĕdû* (they have fled) and *pašĕʿû* (they have rebelled) are poetic complements partially overlapping in meaning. This enables us to determine the focus of the prophet's thought: the wicked deeds of the people were a manifestation of an overt and willful separation from Yahweh. They had proved to be a rebellious tributary to Assyria, but far worse was their rebellion against the Lord.

Like a glimmer of light in the gloom of this hour in Israelite history are the words, "I would redeem them." But the light is immediately snuffed out in the next clause, "But they speak lies against me." The lies that the people speak against Yahweh are not defined. It is not difficult to imagine what they were, however. The metaphorical description of Israel's relationships with her lovers in 2:7–15 [2:5–13] depicts Israel as

depicts what the "woe" will be. פָּשְׁעוּ בִי (they have rebelled against me) is a collocation that connotes any kind of rebellion. In its secular sense it refers to national rebellion (2 Kings 1:1; 3:5, 7). אֶפְדֵּם (I would redeem them) does not necessarily refer to redemption from the bondage in Egypt because the verb פָּדָה (redeem) is not construed with וְ and thus is not clearly a preterite. The pronoun אָנֹכִי is construed with וְ, however. Thus the וְ carries forward the action of the narrative to the pronoun אָנֹכִי (I), not to the verb. It introduces the next logical thought in the narrative sequence. The pronouncement of impending destruction in the previous statements might have raised the question

of God's role in all this. This clause speaks to that question. The pronoun construed with וְ brings God into the picture. He is pictured as saying אֶפְדֵּם (I would redeem them). It was Yahweh's intent to save his people from the doom that lurked in the shadows of national events; but the next clause renders that intent futile. וְהֵמָּה (but they) introduces a concept that contrasts with the benign atmosphere of the preceding clause. We must therefore translate the וְ as an adversative particle. The previous clause is best translated as an optative (I would redeem them) because the latter clause states an impediment to the intention expressed in אֶפְדֵּם.

---

stating erroneously that her lovers, not Yahweh, gave her the food on which she subsisted (vv. 7, 14 [5, 12]). Perhaps this is what the people were saying in the dark days before the end. As a brazen woman who leaves her husband for the love of another covers her wrong by saying of her hus-

band that he could not provide for her, so Israel may have said of Yahweh that he was not able to help her or provide for her in her dismal circumstances. Whatever the people said, corrupted as they were by pagan concepts, was wrong.

IX. Israel's International Alliances Will Lead to Her Destruction (6:11b–7:16)

E. Because Israel Has Rebelled Against Yahweh She Shall Go into Captivity (7:14–16)

14 And they do not cry out to me from
   their hearts,
   but they wail on their beds;
they cut themselves for the sake of grain
   and wine—
   they depart against me.
15 But I am the one who trained them—I
   strengthened their arms,
   but they devised evil against me.
16 They do not return upward;
   they are like an untrustworthy bow.
Their princes shall fall by the sword
   because of the indignation of their
   lips.
This will be their derision in the land
   of Egypt.

14 They do not cry to me from the heart,
   but they wail upon their beds;
they gash themselves for grain and
   wine;
   they rebel against me.
15 It was I who trained and strengthened
   their arms,
   yet they plot evil against me.
16 They turn to that which does not profit;
   they have become like a defective
   bow;
their officials shall fall by the sword
   because of the rage of their tongue.
So much for their babbling in the land
   of Egypt.

14. זָעֲקוּ אֵלַי (they do not cry out to me): זָעַק has the basic sense of crying out. The particular nuance of the word is determined by context and adjunctive prepositions. The collocation here is זָעַק אֶל, which directs the action of the verb toward an object. The context, with its gloomy recital of destruction and its depiction of Israel's resistance to Yahweh, makes it clear that the idiom connotes *to cry out for help*. בְּלִבָּם (from their hearts) is literally, "in their heart." They do not cry out to God within the sphere of reason and emotion. If their cry were directed by reason it would reflect a correct appraisal of their desperate situation and would be a sincere petition for help. כִּי (but) is best translated as an adversative because it follows a negative clause (BDB, pp. 474–75). See the discussion at 1:6. However, the explicative function (because) of this particle is not entirely lacking. We may paraphrase it like this, "They do not cry out to me *because* they howl on their beds." יְיֵלִילוּ (they wail): In each of its occurrences יָלַל connotes *to wail in anguish*.

The parallel element, *cry out from their hearts*, underscores that connotation. יִתְגּוֹרָרוּ (they cut themselves) is pointed as a *hithpôlēl* of גּוּר (sojourn) or a *hithpôlēl* of גָּרַר (drag). The former possibility is unlikely since this word never occurs with עַל, and the use of the word with "grain" and "wine" is difficult. The second possibility makes no sense in the context. A number of Hebrew manuscripts and the Septuagint witness to a word connoting *cut*. It is likely that the word גָּדַד (cut) originally stood in this verse. The letters ד and ר are easily confused, and this reading makes sense in the context. The preposition עַל would then have the sense of *for the sake of*. יָסוּרוּ בִי (they depart against me) is another difficult collocation in this complex pericope. It is surprising that this verb of motion is not construed with a more compatible preposition such as מִן (from), but the concept of motion away from is inherent in the verb, and the preposition may add a sense of hostility to the people's departure from God.

---

14. The people did not cry out to the Lord in their desperate plight. They did cry out, but not to their God; rather, they wailed on their beds. The reason for their wailing is obscure, but perhaps the next clause offers some help. If we are correct in understanding it to say, "They cut themselves for the sake of grain and wine," then some rite of the fertility cult is in view. The prophets of Baal in their contest with Elijah on Mount Carmel lacerated themselves in order to entreat Baal to intervene (1 Kings 18:28). If self-mutilation was an aspect of the worship of the nature deities in Hosea's day, then the words of this passage are most appropriate. The picture comes to mind of someone who, to insure an abundant harvest, seeks to placate the gods of nature by gashing the flesh and writhing in pain on his bed. This sort of crying out had replaced the heartfelt cry of prayer.

This observation of a pagan fertility rite was evidence of the fact that the people had turned from God. "They depart against me" is not idiomatic in English, but reflects the sense of the Hebrew construction. Their pagan worship was a violation of the commandment, "You shall not make for yourself an idol . . . ; you shall not bow down to them or worship them" (Exod. 20:4–5, NRSV). The state cult of the northern kingdom represented more than a departure from God; it was also a rebellion against him. It stood in violation of his will for his people. The idiom *depart*

against deftly describes their religious observances.

The accusation "they depart against me" refers not only to the pagan practices of the nation, but to their political alliances as well. It is part of the larger context in which the flow of thought moves from their alliances with Assyria and Egypt to the description of pagan self-laceration. The observation that they cut themselves describes what the people did in their national upheaval; they tried to placate God by lacerating themselves. The previous clause states what they failed to do; they did not cry out to God from their hearts. This sequence of clauses lays emphasis on the response of the nation to its plight. When governments with whom they had entered into alliance proved to be untrustworthy, the people responded as pagans. Their political policies and their religious practices were a rebellion against God. Isaiah reflects the same spirit in an oracle against those who had made a league with Egypt:

> "Woe to the rebellious
>   children," says the LORD,
> "who carry out a plan, but
>   not mine;
> and who make a league, but
>   not of my spirit,
> that they may add
>   sin to sin." (30:1, RSV)

15. וַאֲנִי (But I) functions here as does the same form in verse 13b to draw attention to the speaker who is Yahweh. יִסַּרְתִּי (trained): יָסַר has the basic sense of discipline. Since it describes a function related to strengthening the arm (חִזַּקְתִּי, strengthened), the translation "trained" is most suitable. יְחַשֵּׁבוּ (they devised): חָשַׁב connotes *to think*, and in the piel (the form in this verse), *to devise*.

16. יָשׁוּבוּ לֹא עָל (They do not return upward): This unusual expression also occurs in 11:7 (see the discussion there). In all its occurrences in the qal in Hosea שׁוּב (return) has the sense of returning to a place previously occupied. עָל (upward): In three of its uses outside of Hosea this word modifies "heavens." In 2 Samuel 23:1 it describes David's exalted position. Andersen and Freedman understand לֹא עָל as a negative divine name ("Not-ʿAl") in which עָל derives from ʿelyon (*Hosea*, p. 477). This is highly speculative, however. Wolff translates it, "They turn themselves, (but) not (to me)" (*Hosea*, p. 108), but this con-

struction does not reflect the full meaning of the word שׁוּב (return) as noted above. There is no one to whom the people could have returned other than Yahweh. The connotation of שׁוּב also militates against the popular emendation of לֹא עָל to לְבַּעַל (to Baal) since the people could not have returned to Baal. In Hosea 11:7 a similar expression (אֶל־עַל) parallels a clause in which the verb is רוּם (be high). This points to some sense of upward direction for the idiom, as do the uses of עָל outside of Hosea. The parallel clause here, depicting a faulty bow, sets forth the concept of inaccurate direction; this lends support to the view that the expression connotes misdirected action. רְמִיָּה (untrustworthy) has the sense of deceit in all its occurrences. A bow is deceptive when it is not true. Such a bow cannot be trusted to direct the arrow toward the target. The same expression occurs in Psalm 78:57, "they twisted like a deceitful bow" (RSV). מִזַּעְמָם (because of the indignation): מִן indicates the source of or reason

---

15. Hosea goes on to represent Yahweh as stating what he had done for Israel—he had trained and strengthened her arms. This type of poignant statement may be found in several prophetic oracles (Amos 2:9–11; Mic. 6:4–5). The training and strengthening of the arm probably refer to the use of the bow, emphasizing that it was God who had led Israel and who had given the people strength to overcome their foes. He could do this even in the face of the threat from the mighty nation of Assyria. But the people chose to depend on loose alliances and fragile treaties to shore up their shaky kingdom. The people failed to remember the past; the exodus was forgotten and the conquest had become a dim memory. When we forget God's past benefits, there is nothing to hold on to in the times when he seems not to be there.

Even though God had helped them achieve a measure of national strength in the past, the people had become ungrateful and devised evil against him. The reference is evidently to the alliances they sought to cement, probably the alliance with Egypt. Hosea would have considered this as rebellion against God because it reflected a lack of dependence on him. Isaiah considers the league with Egypt as sin: "That they may add sin to sin" (Isa. 30:1).

16. The statement *they do not return upward* is difficult. Several alternatives to the view taken here may be seen. One is to understand the clause to say, "They do not return on high." This translation sustains the reference to the fallen bird

(v. 12), but the parallel clause which refers to a deceitful bow militates against it. The emendation *turn to Baal* is also tenuous, because *šûb* has the sense of *return* not *turn* to in Hosea. The translation adopted here has a number of considerations in its favor, including the usage of ʿal (upward) in the more definitive context in 11:7, and the inappropriateness of the verb *šûb* (return) to the defection to Baal (see the Exegesis).

Another important consideration is the conceptual balance that this translation achieves. The subsequent clause, which refers to the deceitful bow, depicts a weapon that is not true; the arrows miss their mark. So it was with Israel; she did not follow a path toward higher things. The people did not return to the high privilege and national blessing promised to them on condition of obedience to the stipulations of the covenant. They shunned the things of God and spoke of them in lying terms. They had sunk to the very bottom, and they would not return upward. This is the lot of all who forsake God, the very opposite of Paul's attitude: "I press on toward the goal for the prize of the upward call of God in Christ Jesus" (Phil. 3:14, RSV).

The national leaders are singled out because of their complicity in the political intrigues that spelled doom for the nation. In their weak efforts to support the collapsing government structure they were to be slain. Assyria would stamp its erstwhile protectorate out of existence forever, and the schemes of Israel's leaders would fail.

for the fall of the nation depicted in the verb יִפְּלוּ (shall fall) that heads this clause. זַעַם denotes indignation. It occurs in combination with two other words for indignation in Psalm 78:49. In Isaiah 30:27 it occurs in association with lips (as in Hos. 7:16), but with reference to God. When used in connection with lips, it connotes the expression of anger. The reference in Hosea 7:16 is thus to the angry words of the princes which were evidently directed against God. לַעְגָּם (their derision) occurs seven times in the Old Testament, each time in a context which requires the idea of scorn.

It was used of Job's allegedly scornful words about God (Job 34:7), and in Psalm 44:14 [13] it describes the state of those who are the object of taunting and mockery. This concept is evident in Ezekiel 23:32, where it occurs in association with "laughed at." זוֹ (this) refers to what has gone before in the context, since there is nothing in the subsequent context to which it may refer. This usage is contrary to the general function of the demonstrative pronoun זֶה from which it is derived; this particular form of the pronoun occurs only here and in Psalm 132:12.

The reason for the fall of Israel's leaders was their "indignation." The word za'am is used almost exclusively of divine wrath in the Old Testament, but in Jeremiah 15:17 it refers to Jeremiah's own anger. While it is God who caused that anger, it was not God's anger, for God does not call it my anger. It was anger that God caused to well up within the prophet Jeremiah, showing this word to be a possible depiction of the anger of Israel's political leaders. This indignation was "on their lips." It found expression in angry words against God.

This expression of anger is not the primary reason for the fall of the nation, for it fell because of its defection from God. It is the collapse of the government in power at that time (designated "their princes") that Hosea has in mind, one that dealt in treachery and which eventually suffered for that. The nation fell along with its government, for it was too weak to sustain the blow. Hosea says only that those who seek help from Egypt and Assyria will find that these intrigues—well-meaning as they might be—will be the cause of their demise.

When at last they go into captivity (metaphorically depicted as a return to Egypt) the collapse of the nation will be a source of taunting on the part of their captors. The use of Egypt to depict the impending Assyrian captivity is part of the larger philosophy of history that permeates the thought of many Old Testament writers. To them history could and would be repeated. This principle was set forth earlier when God declared that if the people did not obey his law, they would be taken back in ships to Egypt (Deut. 28:68). Hosea makes use of this motif in several places in his prophecy, for to him Egypt stands for the place of captivity. It is not literal Egypt, for he knows full well Israel would go to Assyria (11:11). History is about to repeat itself as the people again become captives in a foreign land.

X. The Enemy Will Take Israel into Captivity (8:1–14)

A. The Enemy Approaches (8:1–3)

8 The horn to your mouth!
   [The enemy swoops] like an eagle over
      the house of the LORD,
   because they have broken my covenant,
     and they have rebelled against my
     law.
2 To me they cry out,
    "O God of Israel, we know you."
3 Israel has rejected the good;
    the enemy shall pursue him.

8 Set the trumpet to your lips!
   One like a vulture is over the house of
     the LORD,
   because they have broken my covenant,
     and transgressed my law.
2 Israel cries to me,
    "My God, we—Israel—know you!"
3 Israel has spurned the good;
    the enemy shall pursue him.

8:1. חִכְּךָ (your mouth) does not denote the lips as such, but the area of the mouth. In Job 6:30 it is used in parallel with לָשׁוֹן (tongue) to connote the sense of taste. In Job 20:13 it refers to the oral cavity, the place where food is held. In Job 33:2 it is the cavity where the tongue "speaks." It also connotes the roof of the mouth (Lam. 4:4) and is a metaphor for speech (Job 31:30). It occurs in parallel with שָׂפָה (lip) in Proverbs 5:3 and 8:7. שֹׁפָר (horn) is written defectively here (as it is in Josh. 6:20; 2 Sam. 15:10; 18:16; 20:1, 22; Job 39:25). There is no need to see this form of the word as contributing to the complexity of the passage. כַּנֶּשֶׁר (like an eagle) introduces a verbless clause.

In all probability this clause forms an elliptical expression (see the Exposition). נֶשֶׁר (eagle) was probably a general designation for large birds of prey. In most of its occurrences in the Old Testament it refers to the eagle with its speed of flight (Jer. 4:13), its ability to soar at great heights (Prov. 23:5; Jer. 49:16), and its strength (Exod. 19:4). The vulture may be in view in Micah 1:16, but not necessarily so. It seems best to understand the word to refer to an eagle here. יַעַן (because) implies cause in this instance. יַעַן usually takes the clause-initial position in an independent clause, but there are several instances in which it introduces a subordinate clause, as it does here (see 1 Kings 21:20,

---

8:1. The relationship of the first two clauses of this verse is problematical, and the second of the two clauses seems broken. Numerous suggestions have been made for solving the questions posed by them. The first clause, like the second, has no verb; it stands before us with only the barest essentials for communicating the thought. It breathes urgency and haste. The ram's horn (*šōpār*) is ordered to the mouth. It is to sound an alarm, for the enemy approaches.

The desultory nature of these clauses may convey the emotion the prophet feels. We find a verbless clause in 5:8b in a context much like this one. The trumpet is ordered to be sounded at the beginning of that verse. Then we hear the words, literally, "After you, Benjamin!" This clipped means of expression may reflect an urgent warning shouted in the heat of battle. The same atmosphere obtains in the command here.

The horn is ordered to the mouth, not the lips; but the shophar was blown with the lips. We observed in the Exegesis that the word *ḥēk* (mouth) occurs in parallel with *śāpâ* (lips) on several occasions and is not confined to the oral cavity. We use the word *mouth* to refer to the lips as well. The figure may be a crude one, but it is appropriate to the atmosphere of the passage.

The second clause says literally "as an eagle over [or on] the house of the LORD." The desultory nature of the clause does not require emendation (but see the interesting suggestion of Grace Emmerson, *VT* 25 [1975]: 700–710), because we may understand it as an elliptical expression similar to the one noted above (5:8b), which called for a verbal action appropriate to the constituent elements of the clause, "[They pursue] after you, Benjamin!" The elements of the clause in 8:1 require a verbal action suitable to an eagle over (or on)

the house of the Lord. The concept of swooping fits these requirements and is consistent with the urgent atmosphere of the preceding clause. The alarm sounds because the enemy swoops on Israel. The concept of a vulture soaring over the house is also possible (RSV), but it seems to lack consonance with its companion clause in that the lazy soaring of a vulture and its patient waiting for the death of its prey do not reflect the imminent approach of the enemy which the blast of a trumpet signals.

Elliptical or incomplete sentences such as this are not uncommon in Hebrew and occur most frequently in excited speech. In these constructions the predicate is often suppressed (see Judg. 7:20; 1 Kings 22:36). For further discussion of the incomplete sentence, see GKC §147.

The house of the Lord does not represent the temple. The plural subject of the verb *ʿābĕrû* (they have broken) assumes a previous reference to the people. In 9:8 the house of God is the nation; in 9:15 the prophet represents God as saying that he will expel the people from his house. The context of that verse (see the Exposition at 9:15) shows that he will expel them from the sphere of familial love.

The reason for the approach of the enemy according to this verse is that God's people have broken Yahweh's covenant. The word *bĕrît* (covenant) answers to *tôrâ* (law) in the poetic structure and represents the divine standards that form the heart of the Mosaic covenant. This breaking of the covenant was considered by God as rebellion (*pāšaʿ*). See the comment on *pāšaʿ* at 7:13.

The idea that an enemy would come upon them because of covenant violation is Deuteronomic. If the people neglected to obey God's commandments (Deut. 28:15) they would fall before their

"I found you, because"). עָבְרוּ (they have broken): See the comment at 6:7.

2. לִי (to me) represents Yahweh as speaking, similar to the previous line (as designated by the first-person suffixes). יִזְעָקוּ (they cry out) also occurs in 7:14, where it refers to a cry for help to God. Here the people cry out, not for help, but in protest, pleading their relationship to God. אֱלֹהַי (God of): The Masoretic Text reads "My God" (יְ). This is a difficult reading. We expect אֱלֹהֵינוּ (our God) because the subject of יָדַע (know) is plural. The Septuagint omits "Israel." The vocalization of the Masoretic Text requires us to understand יִשְׂרָאֵל (Israel) to be in apposition to "we" (the subject of יָדַע [know]) rather than to the referent of the suffix (see below). The translation "O God" of Israel requires only a slight alteration of the vocalization (אֱלֹהַי to אֱלֹהֵי). In the Pentateuch the name אֱלֹהִים denotes a general concept of God. Yahweh (יְהוָה) portrays a more personal aspect of God's character. After Exodus 3 the name אֱלֹהִים (Elohim) occurs less as a proper name and more as an appellative: *the God of* or *your God*. This function of the word connotes God as the deity of a people, as in "the LORD your God."

The name *Elohim* refers to many aspects of God, including his transcendence and sovereignty. In Hosea 8:2, however, there is probably little theological content in the appellative. It is the form of address the people used for God. It means nothing more than that Yahweh was their God. יְדַעֲנוּךָ (we know you) presents a striking contrast to earlier statements in which Hosea said the people did not know the Lord (5:4), but would know him in the restoration (2:22 [20]). יִשְׂרָאֵל (Israel) may be either the *nomen rectum* of a broken construct chain separated by the verb (see 6:9 and 14:3 [2]), or an element in apposition to the subject of the verb. The former yields the sense of "O God of Israel, we know you"; the sense of the latter is, "My God! We, Israel, know you." We have opted for the former (which requires a vocalic alteration of *patah* to *sere*) for the reasons that follow. As noted above, the pointing of the Masoretic Text creates a disagreement between the person and number of "my God" and "we know you." If we repoint אֱלֹהַי as אֱלֹהֵי, this apparent disparity is eliminated and the construction יִשְׂרָאֵל אֱלֹהֵי is then in apposition to the object suffix (ךָ) on יְדַעֲנוּךָ (we know you) (note the

---

enemies (v. 25). The consequences of disobedience are stated in similar terms, "Therefore you shall serve your enemies whom the LORD will send against you" (v. 48, NRSV). An elliptical expression parallel to the simile of the eagle in Hosea 8:1 states, "The LORD will bring a nation . . . from the end of the earth" (v. 49, NRSV). The statement goes on to say, *kaʾăšer yidʾeh hannāšer* (lit. As the eagle flies). It is elliptical because we are not told precisely what aspect of flight was intended, probably emphasizing the swiftness of the eagle's flight (so RSV As swift as the eagle flies).

Hosea may have had (and in all probability did have) this passage in mind in writing this oracle, even to the extent of reflecting the simile of the eagle in the same terse mode of expression as Deuteronomy 28:49. While the clausal relationships present us with difficulty, the reading of the Masoretic Text is not unintelligible. When we read the verse against the background of the classical Deuteronomic literature, it is both syntactical and literary.

2. This verse provides insight into the syncretistic worship of the state cult. The people practiced idolatrous forms of worship, but continued to call out to Yahweh, the God of Israel. This is the supreme irony. The previous statement affirms their violation of the covenant, which was

the basis of their relationship to Yahweh, but they still owned him as their God. The ancient promise that God gave to Abraham had as one of its elements the prospect of a relationship between God and the nation expressed in the words, "I will be their God" (Gen. 17:8). That promise continued throughout the era of law; it was not vitiated by it (Gal. 3:17–18). The law served to maintain the relationship of the people to the promise. The promise granted the inheritance; the law provided the means of obedience by which the people might continue to experience its blessing. If that law was broken, the bilateral structure would collapse and the nation would lose its inheritance. The promise would continue in force, but the disobedient people would fail to receive its benefits. When they cried, "My God!" they were not aware of the stark reality that they had severed their relationship with God by their rebellion against him. The cold, hard fact was that he was not their God, and they were not his people. The symmetrical relationship crystallizes within itself eons of redemptive history (vv. 1b, 2a).

The cry of the people continues with the protestation, "O God of Israel, we know you" (see the Exegesis for a substantiation of this translation). They thought they knew God, but their knowledge was based only on history and tradition. It

somewhat similar instance of permutation in Jer. 31:2, הָלוֹךְ לְהַרְגִּיעוֹ יִשְׂרָאֵל, "Let me go to give *him* rest, *Israel*"). The subject of the suffix is the substantive *Israel*. Hosea follows this pattern elsewhere (note: אֵיךְ אֶתֶּנְךָ אֶפְרַיִם, "How can I give *you* up, O *Ephraim!*" in 11:8). It is thus unlikely that יִשְׂרָאֵל (Israel) is in apposition to the subject of the verb (we). If, however, we regard the structure as a broken construct chain (O God of Israel) there is an agreement between the second masculine singular suffix (which refers to God) and the one it addresses, that is, "the God of Israel."

3. זָנַח (has rejected) is used in the psalms to express God's apparent rejection of his people (Pss. 44:10 [9]; 74:1) or of the psalmist himself (43:2). We may observe an element of movement away from in the word in its usage with מִן (from) in Lamentations 3:17 (lit. you have rejected me from peace). In 2 Chronicles 11:14 Jeroboam rejected the Levites from (מִן) the priesthood. When construed with מִן, "cast off" is an appropriate equivalent; without מִן the idea is to spurn or reject. The latter sense obtains here. טוֹב (the good) has a broad range of meaning in Hebrew. In this context, however, it has Deuteronomic overtones (see the Exposition). אוֹיֵב (enemy) is a participle of אָיַב (to be hostile to). This root occurs in Ugaritic in parallel with *šn'*, "to hate" (*UT*, pp. 35–36).

---

reminds us of the words of the Jews of Jesus' day, "We are descendants of Abraham" (John 8:33, NRSV). The concept of knowing God was a covenantal one. A marriage relationship had been established between Yahweh and his people, but like Hosea's marriage had suffered because of the infidelity of the nation (see 2:4 [2]). The people who said they knew Yahweh were the same people who stole off to the gloomy groves where the laughter of prostitutes echoed. They performed acts of religious devotion to idols of stone; they gave their allegiance to grain and wine, and still expected God to act on their behalf. They did not know the ways of Yahweh. They knew better the ways of Baal.

3. The cadences of the great speeches of Deuteronomy had grown dim in the minds of the people, but not in Hosea's mind. We hear their echoes again in the words of this section. He says that Israel has spurned the "good" (*ṭôb*). This word signifies more than simply the opposite of evil. It represents what Yahweh wanted to do for his people if they obeyed the covenant. We hear this word used several times in the sequel to the blessings and curses in the Book of Deuteronomy: "The LORD your God will make you prosperous in every work of your hand . . . in the fruit of your land for *good*"; "The LORD will again rejoice over you for *good*"; "I have set before you this day life and *good*" (30:9, 15). The concept of good represents the positive response of God to the obedience of his people. Sincere obedience to the law affected every aspect of individual and national life, from the fertility of the fields to the security and prosperity of the people as a national entity. The consort of the people with Baal had cost them dearly. They had lost the "good," but they had lost more, for good was paired with life (Deut. 30:15). In rejecting the good they rejected life; they were to die as a nation.

The Book of Deuteronomy foresaw the result of the people's disobedience. If they were not obedient, they would fall at the hands of their enemies (see Deut. 28:25, 31, 48, 53, 55, 57, 68). This section also speaks of the enemies who "pursued" (*radap*) them (30:7), the same idiom that we find in Hosea 8:3. Whether the people were aware of these Deuteronomic themes did not greatly matter, for they were given new life by Hosea. Their truthfulness was confirmed; their dark portents were about to materialize as the specter of Assyrian power glided ever closer.

X. The Enemy Will Take Israel into Captivity (8:1–14)

B. The Frantic Efforts of the People to Defend Themselves (8:4–6)

4 They set up kings, but not through me.
  They set up princes, but I do not
  know it.
 [From] their silver and their gold they
  make idols
   for themselves, so that it may be
   destroyed.
5 He has spurned your calf, O Samaria;
  my anger has become hot against
  them.
 How long will they continue unable to
  be innocent?
6 For [it is] from Israel,
  and—this thing—a workman made it;
   and it is not God,
 for the calf of Samaria
  will become splinters.

4 They made kings, but not through me;
  they set up princes, but without my
  knowledge.
 With their silver and gold they made
  idols
   for their own destruction.
5 Your calf is rejected, O Samaria.
  My anger burns against them.
 How long will they be incapable of
  innocence?
6 For it is from Israel,
 an artisan made it;
   it is not God.
 The calf of Samaria
  shall be broken to pieces.

4. הֵם (they) refers back to the subject of verse 3, Israel. The interchange of number in the references to Israel in verses 3–4 (v. 3, him; v. 4, they) is typical of Hosea's style. הִמְלִיכוּ (they set up kings) is in the hiphil and reflects the causative sense of that conjugation. וְלֹא מִמֶּנִּי (but not through me): מִן (through) denotes the concept of source; thus Yahweh is not (לֹא) the source of their king-making. יָדָעְתִּי (I do not know it) amplifies its poetic complement (מִמֶּנִּי, from me) by showing that the kings are not from Yahweh because he has not been consulted; he does not even know what they are doing (note "know" in 7:9). The statement is an example of irony. כַּסְפָּם (their silver) is an adverbial accusative (as is זְהָבָם). We must supply the idea of *from* or *of.* Silver and gold were the materials from which the people made their idols (see 13:2). This grammatical construction is an accusative of material. Note Genesis 2:7 where עָפָר (dust) functions as such an accusative. עֲצַבִּים (idols): The emphasis of the verb

עָצַב (make, fashion) is particularly appropriate in this context (see the comment at 4:17). לְמַעַן (so that) has the sense of purpose. The people made idols *in order that* the idols might be destroyed; but the people were not aware that they were making their idols for that end. This statement reflects the prophet's perspective. יִכָּרֵת (it may be destroyed) is in the singular, while its referent (עֲצַבִּים, idols) is plural. This is another example of the lack of precision in Hosea's representation of grammatical person and number. The verb denotes *be cut off,* which may imply separation from or absolute termination. Whatever the object, it will come to an end according to the sense of this word. This applies to enemies (Mic. 5:8 [9]), the wicked (Prov. 2:22), and the name of the dead (Ruth 4:10). The statement is filled with irony; the people used precious metals to make objects that would ultimately disappear from their experience.

---

4. The reference to Israel's pursuit by the enemy (v. 3) is followed by a description of the frenzied political situation of the time: "They set up kings," but the kings they made lacked the authority of divine appointment because they were not from God (*mimmennî*, through me). It is as though the people attempted to defend themselves against the enemy's pursuit by seeking political leaders who they thought could deal effectively with the Assyrian government. The last king of Israel to receive the authority of divine approbation was Zechariah, whose death brought Jehu's dynasty to an end.

The people also made princes. It is likely that the verb *to make princes* refers to the government officials (nobles) of Hosea's time rather than kings. We need not understand the verbal concept to be semantically identical to "make kings" in the preceding clause. Hosea makes a distinction between the king and the princes (7:5), and parallelism does not demand our understanding poetic complements as exact synonyms. In Hosea 1:4, for example, "house of Jehu" is the poetic complement of "house of Israel," yet we know that the Old Testament writers maintained a distinction between the concepts of "realm" and "dynasty." The two entities there are complementary only in that they are both regnal concepts. The same situation may obtain here as the parallelism may exist only in the fact that both verbal concepts refer to officials of the government. The fact that Yahweh did not know that they were appointing officials indicates

that he was not consulted. The government acted solely on the basis of expediency and political motivation without any recourse to God.

Several events in Israel's history warned about the institution of the monarchy. Jotham spoke a fable about the bramble (Judg. 9:7–21), and Samuel gave a warning to the people that ended with the words, "In that day you will cry out because of your king" (1 Sam. 8:18, see vv. 9–18, NRSV). In Hosea's day the monarchy could not deliver the nation from certain doom. The kings were, after all, only weak human beings, and the people had put their trust in a faltering system. If they had sought divine guidance in the choice of their leaders, perhaps Yahweh would have worked through the institution of the monarchy to redeem the nation.

An abrupt change of thought appears in the middle of this verse. The depiction moves from the frantic appointment of kings and princes to the making of idols. But we must remember that the section began with the blast of a trumpet warning of the approach of an enemy. The making of idols was probably the response of the people to the threat that faced them. This is how Isaiah describes the frenzied efforts of the nations to meet the approach of the forces of Cyrus (41:5–7). The making of idols that Hosea refers to shows how Israel had rejected the good (8:3). They rejected the covenant of Moses that prohibited the use of idols in worship (Exod. 20:3–6, 23). Idol worship was apparently common in the syncretistic worship of Hosea's day (4:17; 13:2; 14:9 [8]).

5. זָנַח (He has spurned) is a third-person perfect according to the Masoretic Text. The subject of the poetic complement (חֲרָה) is God (אַפִּי, *my anger*), and thus God is the subject of זָנַח (he has spurned). The change from the third person to first person in the clausal structure is stylistic. Hosea does this frequently, so there is no need to emend. We find the second-person to third-person change in 2:8 [6] and 14:9 [8], the third feminine singular to third-person plural in 2:19–20 [17–18] and 4:19. And a verb whose subject is Yahweh (represented as הוּא) occurs in 10:2 with no previous introduction of the tetragrammaton. This last construction is somewhat similar to the use of זָנַח (he has spurned) here. עֶגְלֵךְ (your calf) is construed with a second feminine singular suffix, but its counterpart in the poetic structure (בָּם) is a third masculine plural and refers to the people who worshiped the calf. Evidently Hosea views Samaria as a corporate entity in the first clause, but in the second clause he envisions the people (see the Exposition for the significance of עֵגֶל [calf]). חֲרָה (has become hot) always occurs with reference to anger or intense emotion in Hebrew, but cognate languages establish its basic relationship to burning. אַף (anger) is literally "nose" or "face" (cf. Assyrian *appu*, face). It occurs most frequently with the sense of anger in the Old Testament and may refer to the redness of the face in anger. בָּם (against them) indicates the direction of the action of חֲרָה. The preposition בְּ is used in a hostile sense. עַד־מָתַי (how long): The two elements which make up this collocation are עַד (unto) and מָתַי (when); thus the sense of *unto when* or *how long*. יוּכְלוּ (will they continue unable): The imperfect tense is compatible with עַד־מָתַי (over how long a period of time?), because that tense denotes incomplete action. נִקָּיֹן (to be innocent): The root of this word (נָקָה) probably has the basic sense of emptying out. The derivation מְנַקִּיָּה (sacrificial bowl, BDB, p. 667) supports this concept, as does the Akkadian *naqû* (make a libation). The cognate verb in Syriac has a

Because they had broken the covenant in this way, they could not expect "good" at Yahweh's hand.

Whatever their reason for fashioning idols of gold and silver, it was all futile, for their images were to be cut off. This occurred when the nation fell and the people were removed into captivity. When Isaiah depicts the frantic efforts of the nations to withstand the onslaught of Cyrus by multiplying idols (41:5–24) he, like Hosea, points out the futility of idol worship (v. 24).

5. No historical reference may be found to a calf-idol in Samaria, and Hosea places the calf in Bethel (Beth-aven; see 10:5). The account of the origin of the cult of the golden calf states that two calves were made at the behest of Jeroboam and were placed respectively in Bethel and Dan (1 Kings 12:25–33). While it is possible that there was a golden calf in the capital city of Samaria, it is more likely that "Samaria" here represents the whole northern kingdom (see, e.g., 1 Kings 13:32; 16:24; 2 Kings 17:24, 28; Jer. 23:13; 31:5). We find several examples of this type of metonymy in Hosea. The king of Israel is called "Samaria's king" (10:7); and the numerous uses of "Ephraim" referring to the northern kingdom also represent this metonymy.

In all probability the cult of the golden calf did not represent an absolute defection from the Yahwistic religion. When this same cultic practice emerged early in Hebrew history (Exod. 32:1–6) the intent was not to construct an image to a false god, for the worship of the people was directed to Yahweh (v. 5). In several ancient cultures the god was represented as standing on the back of an animal. The golden calf was evidently an expression of the spiritual presence of Yahweh.

The Ugaritic epic material represents Canaanite deities theriomorphically, yet there is a stele from Ras Shamra that pictures the god El (called the "bull" in the epic material) as a human. The animal motif probably served to associate the deity with properties of an animal that were appropriate to the deity, such as strength or procreative ability (McComiskey, "Idolatry," *ISBE*, 2:796–97).

Hosea depicts Yahweh as spurning the calf worship of the northern kingdom (v. 5a). While the cult of the calf involved an acknowledgment of Yahweh, it was dangerous because of its syncretistic nature. It was an expression of rebellion against God because the Sinai covenant forbade the use of idols in worship. Any physical representation of God is dangerous because of the impossibility of representing in material substance the One who is spirit (Isa. 40:18–20, 25–26; 46:5–7). Such efforts will lead to erroneous representations of him, and the depiction of God in any form can lead to a fractioning of the concept of deity, particularly when the image takes on geographical distinctives. This appears to have happened to Baal whose attributes became localized at various shrines.

The heat of the prophet's emotion is apparent in the syntax. We observed (see the Exegesis) the changes of person in this verse. In the Masoretic

similar meaning. The word is used in Isaiah 3:26 of a city emptied of people and goods, while in Zechariah 5:3 it refers to a city emptied of liars. It is not difficult to understand how the word came to have the sense of being free from punishment, hence innocent as in Numbers 5:31, where it occurs with מִן (from) and עָוֹן (iniquity). This usage underscores the sense of freedom *from*. The word in Hosea 8:5 is נִקָּיוֹן, a noun form. It is used in Amos 4:6 of cleanness of teeth (i.e., lacking food); in Genesis 20:5 the word refers to hands free of intent of malice, thus innocent. The sense of Hosea's question is: How long will they be unable to be free [of guilt]?

6. כִּי מִיִּשְׂרָאֵל (for . . . from Israel) is another difficult expression. There are, however, several important grammatical accompaniments to this expression that give support to the translation "for [it is] from Israel," referring to the "calf of Samaria" (v. 5). First, the וְ (and) introducing the following clause (וְהוּא, and this thing) in verse 6b

points to a continuation of the thought of the preceding clause (GKC §136a). It is clear from the clause in which it occurs that הוּא (this thing) refers to an idol made by a workman. Thus the grammatical indicators point to an implicit reference to idols in the clause in verse 6a. Second, the כִּי (for) in the clause in verse 6a indicates a logical connection with the preceding context, the major theme of which is idol worship. Third, מִן (from) in verse 6a indicates the presence of some concept related to the ideas of separation or movement away from. This is the basic sense of מִן. The nearest referent to מִן is the calf in verse 5a. If we regard the clause in verse 6a as an elliptical expression that requires the sense of the unexpressed copula (is), the clause becomes a logical component of the broader context: for *it* (the calf-idol of v. 5) is *from* Israel, that is, it had its origin with men, not God. Fourth, the particles וְ and כִּי weave the clauses of verses 5–6 together into one logical section that begins and ends with

---

Text, Yahweh is referred to by the first verb, "He has spurned" (*zanaḥ*), but is represented as speaking in the words *my anger* (*ʾappî*). Also, the calf is the object of the first verb, but the people are the objects of God's anger in the parallel clause (note how the reference to the people is sustained by the next clause). This latter change of person is significant. Both the calf and the people were the objects of God's scorn; both were objects of divine judgment.

The question, "How long will they continue unable to be innocent?" is rhetorical. We cannot be wholly certain who the questioner is. Yahweh speaks in the preceding clause ("my anger"), but Hosea is imprecise in the use of person indicators. The question may express his own anguish, for both sorrow and anger find expression in this and in the preceding clause. The question expresses frustration over the inability of the Israelites to live free of the deeds of rebellion that severed their relationship with Yahweh.

6. The discussion in the Exegesis demonstrated the difficulty of determining how the word *for* (*kî*) relates to the preceding statements. If the translation "[it is] from Israel" is correct, we must look in the preceding context for a singular referent, of which it could be said that it finds its origin in Israel. This means that we must bypass the previous clause because it contains no such referent. In verse 5a we find an appropriate referent in the calf. In all probability, then, the rhetor-

ical question in the previous clause is an ejaculatory utterance of Hosea's that sustains no direct logical connection to the flow of the passage. The *kî* (for) relates to the words of the first line of verse 5. The sense of this structuring of the clauses (vv. 5–6) is that Yahweh spurns the calf and is angry at the people because the calf had its origin in Israel. It was made by artisans; it was not from God.

The reference to the origin of the cult of the golden calf is consonant with Israel's early history. While this cult apparently had its origin shortly after the exodus (Exod. 32:1–6), it resurfaced in Israel when Jeroboam I established a state cult that was distinctly Israelite and which would provide the people with religious centers away from Jerusalem. This Israelite expression of the cult was undoubtedly different from its earlier expression in the wilderness, particularly because of its Canaanite entanglements. Thus it was from Israel, not from God.

To further substantiate the statement Hosea says that a workman made the calf, therefore it is not God. We see an emphasis on the suffixes in this statement. A literal translation is, "And *it*, an artisan made it, and *it* is not God." We note a bit of the scorn we observed in the verb that begins verse 5 (*zanaḥ*, spurned): This thing—why a workman made it! This thing is not God!

The proof that the calf was not God is that it will be broken into splinters. The calf of Samaria

a reference to the calf of Samaria. The calf is the theme of the entire section, and thus it is in all likelihood the theme of the clause in verse 6a as well. The relationship of the two clauses (vv. 5b and 6a) in parallel structure is a problem, but the כִּי (for) indicates some sort of logical connection, probably a causal one. It may set forth the reason for (כִּי) their lack of innocence, that is, the calf of Samaria is not God. As long as they worshiped the product of human hands, they were not free from guilt. It is also possible that the question in verse 5b functions as a parenthetical rhetorical question. In this case the clause in verse 6a sets forth the reason for God's anger against the calf and the people in verse 5a. וְהוּא (and it), as we sug-

gested above, refers to the עֵגֶל (calf) implicit in the verbless clause of verse 6a. חָרָשׁ (workman) connotes an artisan. The term occurs in several contexts with specific reference to idol-makers (see, e.g., Isa. 45:16; Jer. 24:1; 29:2). עָשָׂהוּ (made it): The suffix on this verb, in combination with the pronouns הוּא (this thing/it) that begin and end the line, insistently draw our attention to the hated calf of Samaria. כִּי (for) gives logical substantiation to the prophet's previous statement. The calf is not God because it will become שְׁבָבִים (splinters). This word occurs only here. Several cognates support the sense of *splinter* (Arabic, cut; Aramaic, splinter).

---

will suffer destruction when Assyria rolls over the nation. So much for its god.

The statement *it is not God* is structurally parallel to the problematical clause "*For [it is] from Israel.*" This lends support to the view that the clause states something about the human origin of the calf, that is, it was from Israel.

X. The Enemy Will Take Israel into Captivity (8:1–14)

C. Israel Will Eventually Suffer at the Hand of Assyria, the Nation with Which She Has Entered into an Alliance (8:7–10)

7 Because they sow the wind,
   they will harvest a gale.
The standing grain has no head,
   it produces no meal.
If it were to produce,
   strangers would devour it.
8 Israel is devoured;
   now they are among the nations
   as a vessel about which there is noth-
      ing that gives pleasure.
9 For they have gone up to Assyria,
   a wild donkey isolated unto itself.
Ephraim has hired lovers.
10 Though they hire among the nations,
   now will I gather them,
and they will begin in a little while [to
      suffer]
   because of the burden of the king of
      princes.

7 For they sow the wind,
   and they shall reap the whirlwind.
The standing grain has no heads,
   it shall yield no meal;
if it were to yield,
   foreigners would devour it.
8 Israel is swallowed up;
   now they are among the nations
   as a useless vessel.
9 For they have gone up to Assyria,
   a wild ass wandering alone;
   Ephraim has bargained for lovers.
10 Though they bargain with the nations,
   I will now gather them up.
They shall soon writhe
   under the burden of kings and
      princes.

7. כִּי (Because) does not sustain an apparent causal relationship with the previous clause. It is best to understand it to indicate causality within the sentence it introduces. The וְ at the head of the second clause introduces the apodosis of the causal sentence as in 4:6 and 10:13–14: Because they have sown the wind, the prophet says, they will reap a gale. This metaphor does not mean only that they will reap what they have sown; it means that their deeds will come back upon them with such force as to overwhelm them. The expression "sow . . . reap" (see 2 Cor. 9:6; Gal. 6:7) occurs in many forms in the Old Testament. It refers metaphorically to the sowing of some object or concept that will reappear in later experience. Here it means simply that what began as a seemingly innocent venture became the cause of Israel's demise. We need not read the statement "sow in the wind, reap *in* a gale" (see Andersen and Freedman, *Hosea*, p. 481). When Hosea uses the expression "sow . . . reap" to mean something other than sow an object he expresses the preposition orthographically (see 10:12). סוּפָתָה (gale) does not connote only a whirlwind, although that is probably in the range of meaning (Isa. 5:28); it is a general word for a strong wind storm (Job 21:18; 27:20; Isa. 29:6). קָמָה (standing grain) is from קוּם (stand) and refers to grain standing in the field. The sickle may be put to it according to Deuteronomy 16:9, and Deuteronomy 23:26 [25] indicates that ears may be plucked from it. אֵין־לוֹ (has no): אֵין negates the element it precedes. If the order of

the words in this clause is the usual one, the clause reads literally, "The standing grain, not to it a shoot," that is, there are no heads on the grain. This interpretation requires that לוֹ (to it), which has a masculine suffix, modify a feminine noun (קָמָה), but this is not necessarily antithetical to the interpretation. While it is possible that the text has suffered in transmission, it is also possible that the masculine suffix reflects grammatical imprecision. Numerous examples of irregularities in the representation of agreement in gender exist in the Old Testament (GKC §110k; §135o; §144a; §145p, t, u; for a systematic study of this phenomenon, see Robert J. Ratner, "Gender Problems in Biblical Hebrew" [Ph.D. diss., Hebrew Union College–Jewish Institute of Religion, 1983]), and we have observed Hosea's lack of grammatical precision in a number of places. צֶמַח (head) is a shoot or sprout. In the case of grain it probably refers to the head that contains the kernels. בְּלִי (no) negates the verb יַעֲשֶׂה (makes/produces). It is rare for this particle to negate a finite verb, but it has this function elsewhere (Gen. 31:20; Isa. 14:6; 32:10). It negates the verb עָשָׂה (produce) in Hosea 9:16. קֶמַח (meal) probably refers to the kernels from which meal is made, since it is the poetic complement of צֶמַח (head). אוּלַי (If it were) in combination with the incomplete action of the imperfect verb (יַעֲשֶׂה) determines a hypothetical mood for the clause (if perhaps). יִבְלָעֻהוּ (devour it) is used of someone being swallowed by a monster (Jer. 51:34), and it depicts the act of being swal-

---

7. This verse contains two statements that utilize phenomena of nature to express the impending destruction of the nation. It is difficult to determine whether these sayings attribute Israel's demise to the cult of the golden calf or to her unwise international policies. If we are correct in understanding the *kî* (because) to have no connection with the preceding pericope, then verse 7 introduces a new logical unit. Since this unit goes on to speak of Israel's alliance with Assyria, it seems best to refer the two statements to Israel's efforts to curry favor with Assyria.

These efforts, which seemed politically expedient at the time, are likened to a wind by Hosea, a wind that is to become a gale that will sweep the nation away. The gale represents the force of Assyria's military might, as the winds of international diplomacy became a gale of oppression. This is another example of Hosea's theology of divine retribution. Just as the bloodshed at Jezreel came back to haunt Jehu's dynasty (1:4–5) and the

days of the baals returned bringing divine retribution (2:15 [13]), so the political machinations of the northern kingdom eventually brought divine requital because they were acts of rebellion against Yahweh.

In the second saying the words *head* and *meal* rhyme in Hebrew (ṣemaḥ/qemaḥ). It is possible to translate the expression as a condition, "If the grain has no kernels, it will produce no meal," but the final clause, "If it were to yield, strangers would devour it," shows that the prophet wishes to express a greater degree of finality than that. It is best to understand these statements as setting forth the utter devastation about to come on the nation. Perhaps we are to picture the wind of Hosea's first saying as sweeping across the fields of grain of the second saying. Perhaps not; the sayings may be unrelated. At any rate, the second saying affirms the desperate plight of the nation. It is like grain that cannot produce meal; even if it

lowed by the deep (Ps. 69:16 [15]). The picture in Hosea 8:7 is that of foreigners swallowing the produce of the field.

8. נִבְלָע (is devoured) is the passive (niphal) of the preceding verb. עַתָּה (now) in combination with the perfect verb הָיוּ (they are) sets forth the action of the verb הָיוּ (they are) as an established fact. The poetic complement נִבְלָע, which is also in the perfect tense, and the context, which continues the theme of Israel's political alliance with Assyria (v. 9), also establish the action of this context as present, not future. כְּלִי (vessel) is a general word that connotes the equipment or containers necessary to some activity or occupation. It refers to the weapons of a soldier (Judg. 18:16) and to a receptacle (Gen. 43:11). Nothing in the context indicates the particular nuance of the word here. We may understand it as an article of some kind that no longer gives satisfaction.

9. כִּי (For) gives the reason for the statement in the preceding clause that they are like a worthless article among the nations. This is because they have gone up to Assyria. פֶּרֶא (a wild donkey) has a metaphorical use in several contexts (see, e.g., Job 6:5; 11:12; Jer. 2:24). We gain little help,

however, from those passages for understanding the usage of the word in Hosea 8:9 (see the Exposition). בּוֹדֵד (isolated) is used elsewhere in the Old Testament of a lovebird on a housetop (Ps. 102:8 [7]) and of a straggler isolated from the ranks of marching soldiers (Isa. 14:31). The verb does not denote going alone, but being alone. לוֹ (unto itself) strengthens the concept of isolation. הִתְנוּ (has hired) is in the hiphil in verse 9 and the qal in verse 10. Since this verb (תָּנָה) occurs only in these two places, it is difficult to determine the distinction in meaning between the stems. Perhaps we should understand the hiphil in the sense of causing to hire, that is, sending representatives to the nations to effect alliances. The only noun form of this verb is אֶתְנָה (payment to a harlot, Hos. 2:14 [12]). If the verb shares this connotation with the noun its use with אֲהָבִים (lovers) is appropriate.

10. גַּם (Though) with כִּי expresses a hypothetical or imagined situation (BDB, yea though, p. 169; see also Ps. 23:4; Isa. 1:15; Hos. 9:16). עַתָּה (now) with the imperfect verb אֲקַבְּצֵם (will I gather) expresses the determination of God to begin accomplishing the action expressed in the verb.

---

could, the grain would be devoured by foreigners. The nation of Israel will be left with nothing.

8. The word *devoured* reappears in this verse and applies to Israel. It is as though the destruction envisioned in the hypothetical statement above has become a certainty. The ultimacy reflected in the final statement is now a reality. Assyria already had a stranglehold on the northern kingdom; Israel was as good as dead.

"Now" is chronological, not emphatic. Israel was among the nations even as Hosea spoke. The prophet represents Yahweh as saying that the nation was like a once precious article in which one has lost interest. The nation had forsaken him to seek help from Assyria, and so he no longer views it as his peculiar treasure. There may be an echo of Exodus 19:5 in this poignant statement. In that passage we find the promise that if the nation will be obedient, they will be Yahweh's own possession among all the nations. In Hosea's day they were disobedient and had become like an object that God had discarded. They had lost the distinctiveness that Yahweh longed for. Jeremiah uses a similar figure in his prophecy (22:28), and in the new covenant Christians are also called a distinctive people (1 Pet. 2:9–10).

9. The next clause amplifies the preceding statement. Israel is among the nations because she her-

self determined to enter the sphere of the nations. She went to Assyria. Hosea goes on to picture Israel as a lone donkey. The metaphor does not fit well either with the preceding or following statements. It is a simple description of an isolated, senseless donkey. It does not communicate; it looks at the world with dull eyes. To Hosea Israel was the same; they had isolated themselves from God. Their spiritual dullness was like the stupidity of a donkey.

The theme of spiritual adultery reappears at this point, for the nation is pictured as paying for lovers. Once again Hosea's marriage provides the catalyst for his message. However, her unfaithfulness is not idolatry in this context; it is her unlawful congress with Assyria. The allusion to hiring lovers can refer only to the massive tribute Israel had to pay to curry Assyrian favors.

10. Because of their unfaithfulness Yahweh will "gather them." The people are to be gathered for punishment. We have suggested that the clause is elliptical (see the Exegesis): In a short while they [will suffer] because of the burden of the king of princes. We have suggested similar ellipses in Hosea (see, e.g., 5:8; 8:1 [where the verbal idea associated with *nešer* (eagle) is missing in the Masoretic Text]; 9:3 [food], 4, 6).

קָבַץ (gather) presages judgment in 9:6 and blessing in 2:2 (1:11). Its sense here depends in large measure on the interpretation of the next clause. וַיָּחֵלּוּ (and they will begin): The Septuagint reads κοπάσουσιν (cease), apparently reflecting the verb חָדַל. Mays (*Hosea*, p. 114) follows Wolff and W. Rudolph in vocalizing the word וְיָחִילוּ (writhe). Andersen and Freedman translate it "contorted in pain" (*Hosea*, p. 501). These suggestions differ from the Masoretic Text in that they posit the verbal root as חוּל (writhe), rather than חָלַל (begin) in the hiphil. The ' we expect in the suggested form, however, is absent. While it is possible that ' passed from the consonantal text during the history of its transmission, the Masoretic Text is intelligible if we construe the clause as an elliptical expression. It would thus be necessary to incorporate an appropriate verbal idea into the clause (as in 10:6). This idea, which would normally be expressed by the infinitive with ל, must reflect the atmosphere of the passage and be consonant with the syntactical structures. The מִן (because) on מִמַּשָּׂא (because of the burden) points to some implicit action that occurs because of the burden of the Assyrian king. This can be only the suffering they were to endure as a result of their unwise policies. The absence of a specific verbal indication of suffering is reminiscent of the similar mode of expression in Amos (see the Exposition at 6:11a for the passages). The word מְעַט may connote *in a little while* as in 1:4. The sense would thus be that in just a little while they will begin to suffer because of the burden of Assyria (see the Exposition for a fuller discussion of this suggestion). The gathering of the nation (קָבַץ) is thus for the purpose of punishment. מִמַּשָּׂא (because of the burden): מִן indicates source. The Septuagint apparently read מִמְּשֹׁחַ (from anointing) kings and princes.

If we understand Hosea 8:10 in this way, there is no need to emend on the basis of the Septuagint's "cease from anointing king and princes" (Author's Translation). The expression *king of princes* (*melek śarîm*) in the Masoretic Text is an evident reference to the king of Assyria. According to Isaiah the Assyrian king boasted, "Are not my commanders all kings?" (10:8, NRSV). Perhaps this tradition is behind Hosea's words. The "burden" of Assyria crushed the nation when the Assyrian king led his forces into Israel and deported its people.

X. The Enemy Will Take Israel into Captivity (8:1–14)

D. Israel's Mosaic Institutions Will Do Her No Good: The Nation Will Perish (8:11–14)

11 Because Ephraim has multiplied altars
　　for sinning,
　　they have become to him altars for
　　sinning.
12 If I were to write for him ten thousand
　　[precepts of] my law,
　　they would be regarded as a strange
　　thing.
13 The sacrifices of my love-things (?) they
　　sacrifice—
　　the flesh [they sacrifice] and eat—
　　but the LORD does not have delight
　　in them.
Now he will remember their iniquity
　　and punish their sins:
　　they shall return to Egypt.
14 For Israel has forgotten his maker,
　　and has built palaces;
and Judah has multiplied fortified cities:
　　but I will send fire on his cities
　　and it will devour her strongholds!

11 When Ephraim multiplied altars to expi-
　　ate sin,
　　they became to him altars for sin-
　　ning.
12 Though I write for him the multitude
　　of my instructions,
　　they are regarded as a strange thing.
13 Though they offer choice sacrifices,
　　though they eat flesh,
　　the LORD does not accept them.
Now he will remember their iniquity,
　　and punish their sins;
　　they shall return to Egypt.
14 Israel has forgotten his Maker,
　　and built palaces;
and Judah has multiplied fortified cities;
　　but I will send a fire upon his cities,
　　and it shall devour his strongholds.

131

11. כִּי (Because) does not relate logically to the preceding sentence. In all probability it introduces a causal clause subordinate to the clause that follows (see the Exposition). לַחֲטֹא (for sinning) is pointed as an infinitive. Because לְ is affixed, it denotes purpose. In the eyes of the prophet, the Israelites worshiped for the purpose of sinning. לוֹ (to him): The nearest logical referent for this preposition is Ephraim.

12. אֶכְתּוֹב (If I were to write) is an imperfect form. *Qĕrē* reads אֶכְתָּב, but does not alter the tense. It makes little sense in the context to translate this verb as future (I shall write). The Torah already existed in Hosea's day; he refers to it in 4:6 and 8:1 and a promise from God to write tens of thousands more laws is not a realistic concept. The use of the hyperbolic "tens of thousands" suggests a hypothetical sense for the verb, "If I were to write." The condition is thus expressed by the juxtaposition of clauses (Josh. 22:18; see Davidson, *Syntax* §132, Rem 2; GKC §159b, for other examples). רֻבֵּי (tens of thousands) was pointed by the Masoretes as a construct plural of רֹב (multitudes). However, this noun is never elsewhere construed in the plural. The consonantal text reads רִבּוֹ (ten thousand). If we regard the construction as elliptical and read it as "[precepts] of my law" (see BDB, p. 914), however, the conso-

---

11. As Hosea made his way through the cities and countryside of his nation, he observed numerous altars. He did not view them as objects of devotion to Yahweh, but for the purpose of sinning. The word *sinning* (*ḥaṭōʾ*) denotes to miss a mark (see Judg. 20:16; Prov. 19:2). It frequently occurs in parallel with other words for sin, where the basic sense is not apparent. In Hosea the word seems always to have the idea of overt sin (see, e.g., the pairing of *ḥeṭʾ* and *ʿawōn* in 12:9 [8]).

The prophet's statement about these altars is enigmatic. Why did he say that altars made for the purpose of sinning would become altars for the purpose of sinning? Evidently the word *sinning* is used in different senses. The solution to this problem depends, in part, on the way we understand the particle (*kî*) that introduces the clause.

The function of the *kî* (because) is problematical. It has no logical connection to the preceding context, and asseveration (indeed) is unlikely because the proper grammatical conditions are lacking (GKC §159ee). Wolff (*Hosea*, pp. 135, 144) suggests this is deictic *kî* (indeed). However, this function of *kî* awaits fuller attestation. Several of the examples cited by Wolff express causation if in a somewhat less direct sense than other instances of causal *kî* (see the discussion of *kî* denoting proximate cause at 4:16). The simplest solution is to regard *kî* as denoting causation (or circumstance) within the clauses it introduces: "Because Ephraim has multiplied altars for sinning, they have become to him altars for sinning" (see the discussions at 4:6 and 5:3).

This translation seems incongruous, but the apparent redundancy diminishes when we note that the verb in the first clause is *hirbâ* (multi-

plied). The people did not simply *make* altars for sinning; they *multiplied* them. This multiplication of altars was a violation of Deuteronomic law in which the concept of the central sanctuary is set forth (Deut. 12). This law required the Israelites to worship only at the site where the Lord chose to put his name (vv. 5, 11). This passage may have been in Hosea's mind as he wrote the words of 8:11–13, because references to offering sacrifices and eating them appear in both passages (Deut. 12:6–7; see Hos. 8:13). If this is so, the sense of the clauses here may be that the altars the people multiplied for sinning (i.e., for pagan worship) became altars for sinning in another sense, that is, their increase in number was a violation of another Deuteronomic proscription besides the prohibition against idolatry, that is, the law of the central sanctuary. The more the people increased their pagan altars, the more they compounded their sin.

12. We find a note of incredulity in the prophet's next statement, where he represents God as saying that if he should write the law again and again, ten thousand times, it would still be unfamiliar to the people. Like the wild donkey (8:9), their minds were dull; they could not comprehend God's will as it was expressed in their own Torah. This reference to the law may indicate that the Deuteronomic law is in view here. If Yahweh were to write his laws by the tens of thousands, the people would continue to be insensitive to the fact that their multiplication of pagan altars was morally wrong and an affront to their God.

How ironic it was that they continued to offer sacrifices that broadly followed levitical guidelines. They ate the flesh of the sacrifices (v. 13a) as required for the communal offerings (Lev. 7:19–21;

nantal text does not require alteration. נֶחְשָׁבוּ (they would be regarded) is a niphal (passive) of חָשַׁב (think), hence, regarded.

13. הַבְהָבַי (my love-things) adds to the difficulties of an already perplexing passage. It may be a reduplicative noun, either from יָהַב (give) or אָהַב (love). It would thus be similar in form to the reduplicated noun צֶאֱצָא (offspring) which is from יָצָא (go out; see BDB, p. 425, for instances of this noun). We suggest that it is from אָהַב (love) after the analogy of the similarly contracted form of אָהַב (הֵבוּ) occurring in 4:18 (see the Exposition). These modified forms may be dialectical. The first-person suffix logically refers to Yahweh who is the subject of the preceding sentence. בָּשָׂר וַיֹּאכֵלוּ (the flesh [they sacrifice] and eat): This view of הַבְהָבַי (love-things) requires us to construe בָּשָׂר (flesh) as the object of וַיֹּאכֵלוּ (and eat), but this results in an apparent syntactical anomaly. We expect to find the *waw*-affix on בָּשָׂר (flesh), not on אָכַל (eat), or we expect some syntactical indication that בָּשָׂר (flesh) is the direct object of אָכַל (eat). In all likelihood the dynamics of Hebrew poetry are at work here, and we must posit an implicit verbal idea in the second clause that complements the verbal action of the first clause. The verb in the first clause is יִזְבָּחוּ (sacrifice). The resultant translation is, "The flesh [they sacrifice] and eat." Note,

for example, the implicit verbal idea in the second line of the couplet in Hosea 5:8a:

> Blow the trumpet in Gibeah,
> the horn in Ramah.

The writer may have omitted the word because of the ballast added to the line by the words לֹא רָצָם יְהוָה (the LORD does not have delight in them). It is also possible that this structure is a *casus pendens*, "The sacrifices of my love-things—they sacrifice flesh and eat it." רָצָם (delight in them): רָצָה may take as its object either the person making the sacrifice (Jer. 14:12; Ezek. 20:40) or the sacrifice itself (Amos 5:22; Mic. 6:7). It is not likely that the suffix (them) on רָצָה finds its referent in זְבָחַי (sacrifices) in the previous clause. זְבָחַי (sacrifices) is removed from the suffix by a formidable distance, and suffixal relationships generally do not transect clauses that are logical units. The referent closest to the suffix is the subject of the verb וַיֹּאכֵלוּ (and they eat) which is the people. Thus Yahweh rejected the people who offered sacrifices to him. The implication is that they offered them in the wrong spirit. עַתָּה (now) determines the commencement of the action described by יִזְכֹּר (remember). The sense is that Yahweh has now begun to remember their sin. It is the logical complement of the verb רָצָה (have delight in) which is in the perfect tense, denoting completed

---

19:5–8), and they offered sacrifices that Yahweh called his own (Hos. 8:13a). Because their syncretistic worship destroyed the uniqueness of Yahweh it had nothing in it to commend itself. Even its levitical vestiges were unacceptable to him.

13. The word translated "love-things" is understood here as a noun form of the verb *ʾahab* (love). Its exact sense eludes us, for it does not appear elsewhere in the Old Testament. The word *love* occurs several times in Deuteronomy in connection with legal statutes, however, and since Deuteronomic concepts emerge throughout this section, it may be well to seek the solution to the problem in that book.

Moses commanded the people to obey the statutes of the Deuteronomic law because of God's love for their forefathers (4:40, 37). These statutes included numerous directives for sacrifice (12:6–7, 27; 15:19–23; 16:1–8; 17:1; 18:3; 27:6–8). The demonstration of God's love was dependent on obedience to the divine ordinances (7:13). On the other hand, the statutes were also a medium for expressing love to God (10:12–13;

11:1, 13; 30:20). The sacrifices, as part of the Deuteronomic corpus of laws, related to the expression of love on the part of God and the people. Perhaps the association of the sacrificial ordinances with the expression of love is what Hosea has in mind. They ate the flesh of the sacrifices as the law required (Deut. 12:7), but Yahweh did not delight in them. The suffix (them) on *raṣâ* (delight) refers to the people, not the sacrifices. The offering represented the heart attitude of the people. Hosea's words are reminiscent of Genesis 4:4, where the Lord regarded Abel *and his offering.*

When a sin is practiced with persistence, there comes a point at which its pleasure fades and its malevolent character becomes apparent. The people had come to this point in Hosea's day, for Yahweh had remembered their sin (see the comment at 7:2) and he would attend to their iniquity. Sin was to reveal its terrible reality. Like a cruel tyrant it would drive them into captivity, metaphorically represented by the Egyptian bondage (see the comment at 7:16).

action. We may paraphrase it: to this point Yahweh has had no delight in their sacrifices; now he will begin to punish them. Since Yahweh's remembering sin involves his taking action against it (see the comment at 7:2), he has now determined to punish their iniquity. This is confirmed by the parallel concept. וְיִפְקֹד (and punish): The discussion at 1:4 led to the conclusion that this verb has the sense of *attend*. Yahweh will attend to their sin, for now he will remember it and act in a way appropriate to their disobedience. הֵמָּה (they) refers to the people. מִצְרַיִם (to Egypt) is an adverbial accusative that denotes place.

14. עֹשֵׂהוּ (his maker): עָשָׂה (make) in the creation accounts denotes primarily the fashioning of an object, whereas the companion word בָּרָא (create)

emphasizes the newness of the created object (see Isa. 41:20; 48:6–7; and בְּרִיאָה in Num. 16:30). The emphasis of the word is not on the initiation of Israel as a nation among the nations of the world, but on the fact that God established and formed the nation. הֵיכָלוֹת (palaces) may refer either to temples or palaces. It is the counterpart of אַרְמְנוֹת (strongholds) in the parallel structure (אַרְמוֹן, הֵיכָל, עִיר/עִיר). The word אַרְמוֹן generally denotes a fortified building (Ps. 48:4 [3]; Isa. 34:13) or a fortified section of a building (1 Kings 16:18; 2 Kings 15:25). It also refers to large residences (Jer. 9:20 [21]). The relationship of הֵיכָלוֹת (palaces) with אַרְמְנוֹת (strongholds) in the poetic structure of Hosea 8:14 does not point to הֵיכָל as a temple, but as a palace or some other type of large building.

---

14. This section closes with the dismal observation that Israel had forgotten its Maker. It was Yahweh who had brought them into existence as a nation and whose loving hand had fashioned them into a people, but they had forgotten him. The Prophecy of Isaiah sets forth a theology of God as Maker that may enhance our understanding of Hosea's statement. A time is coming when men will regard their Maker, not the works of their hands (Isa. 17:7–8); as Maker of the universe, his power is apparent (51:12–13); and Israel's Maker is also her husband (54:5).

The first of these theological concepts is reflected in this verse. The people had forsaken their proper role in the universe. They stood admiring the magnificent works of their hands—palaces, strongholds, and cities—but they failed to see the insignificance of these things. They had forgotten that it is God who is in control; their vaunted palaces were about to be destroyed.

Many scholars consider verse 14 to be a later redactive intrusion for several reasons: It begins

with a *waw*-consecutive verb; Judah is cited along with Israel; Yahweh is called Israel's Maker, a concept found in Deutero-Isaiah (see above); and the last clause is reminiscent of the refrain in Amos 1:4, 7, 10, 12, 14; 2:2, 5.

While it is true that the *waw*-consecutive verb appears not to have a logical connection with the preceding clause, it is not unlike other consecutive verbs in Hosea (see, e.g., 5:5, 13; 6:3; 7:10). The pairing of Israel and Judah is Hosean (1:6–7; 2:2 [1:11]; 4:15; 5:5, 12, 13, 14; 6:4; 10:11; 12:1 [11:12]). We need not question the integrity of the unit on this account. The theological concept of God as Maker is attested in the eighth century (Isa. 17:7). The verdict formula (v. 14b) may have belonged to a bank of prophetic material shared by Hosea and Amos. The variation in the gender of the suffixes is typical of Hosea and argues for the authenticity of the section. There is no compelling reason for doubting Hosean authorship of this whole pericope.

XI. Results of the Captivity (9:1–6)

A. The People Will No Longer Enjoy the Produce of
the Land (9:1–3)

9 Do not rejoice, O Israel,
    with great exultation as [do] the nations,
    for you have gone off from your God,
      committing fornication;
      you have loved the payment a harlot
      receives
      on every threshing floor of grain.
2 Threshing floor and winevat shall not
      feed them,
    and new wine shall fail her.
3 They shall not remain in the land of the
    Lord;
    but Ephraim shall return to Egypt,
    and they shall eat unclean [food] in
    Assyria.

9 Do not rejoice, O Israel!
    Do not exult as other nations do;
    for you have played the whore, depart-
      ing from your God.
    You have loved a prostitute's pay
    on all threshing floors.
2 Threshing floor and winevat shall not
      feed them,
    and the new wine shall fail them.
3 They shall not remain in the land of the
    Lord;
    but Ephraim shall return to Egypt,
    and in Assyria they shall eat unclean
    food.

9:1. אַל־תִּשְׂמַח (Do not rejoice) is a negative clause expressing prohibition. אֶל־גִּיל (with great exultation) is emended by several commentators to אַל־תָּגֵל (do not exult) after BHS. The Septuagint reads μηδὲ εὐφραίνου (neither exult). These readings understand אל as the negative particle אַל rather than the preposition אֶל (unto). The suggested emendation requires an alteration of the consonantal text as well as of the Masoretic pointing, for גִּיל must be read as the imperfect תָּגֵל if it is to be construed with אַל. The emendation is unnecessary, however, since the noun גִּיל occurs with the poetic form of אֶל (אֱלֵי) in Job 3:22, where it heightens the idea of rejoicing, reading literally,

"who rejoice unto [אֱלֵי] rejoicing" (NRSV who rejoice exceedingly). כָּעַמִּים (as [do] the nations): Since the atmosphere of this passage is the harvest, the reference is probably to the rejoicing of all peoples at the time of harvest (see the Exposition). כִּי (for) introduces the reason why they are not to rejoice; it is because זָנִיתָ מֵעַל אֱלֹהֶיךָ (you have gone off from your God, committing fornication). The clause reads literally, "You have committed fornication from beside your God." זָנָה (commit fornication) is treated as a verb of motion construed with מִן (from). Thus the spiritual fornication of the people had moved them away from God. מֵעַל (from) has the sense of *from beside* in

---

9:1. This section begins with a command to Israel to refrain from rejoicing like the other nations. The nature of the rejoicing is not clearly stated, but it is likely that Hosea has in mind the rejoicing at harvest which was common to all agricultural nations. There is a logical progression of thought in the pericope that unites the concept of the rejoicing of nations with the bounties of the field cited in the subsequent clauses. We may observe this progression in the following descriptive reconstruction of the clausal structure:

A The command not to rejoice like the nations.
B The reason for (*kî*) the command: Israel's spiritual fornication depicted as selling sexual favors on the threshing floors.
C The declaration that the threshing floor, winevat, and new wine will fail them.
D The declaration that they shall eat unclean food in Assyria.

Sections A and B are related syntactically by the particle *kî* (for). Section B thus follows logically from section A by stating the reason for the prohibition in A. Section B is related to section C by the reference to the threshing floor. The logical connection is that the threshing floor, which is the place where Israel shamelessly displayed her wantonness, will no longer provide for her. Section C is related to D by the motif of food; she will lack food in her own land, and will eat unclean food in Assyria. This passage is thus a logical unit in which there is a progression of thought through the clauses. The command to refrain from rejoicing does not have a primary relationship to the preceding context, but to the concepts that follow. We must look to them for a referent to Hosea's command.

The only element in the pericope that answers logically to the concept of rejoicing is the motif of agricultural produce expressed in the terms *threshing floor, winevat,* and *new wine.* These aspects of the harvest, symbols of the perennial joy of agricultural peoples when their fields have produced in abundance, will not be a source of joy to Israel because they will fail her (v. 2). Israel will not rejoice at harvest-time like other nations, because the fertility cult, which seemed to offer the promise of great bounty, will be seen for what it really is—the cause for Israel's expulsion from her land. Their threshing floors and winevats will no longer feed the people because their disloyalty to Yahweh will lead them to captivity in a distant country, far from the scenes of their earlier harvest celebrations.

The reason why Israel is not to rejoice like the nations is introduced by the words, "You have gone off from your God, committing fornication." The suffix (your) on "God" (*ʾĕlohĕka*) may imply that Hosea draws a distinction between Israel's God and the gods of the nations. The sense of the implication in this case is that the nations rejoice in their agricultural produce, but Israel will not rejoice in hers; she has forsaken her God, and may no longer expect him to provide for her.

The sordid depiction of Israel as a prostitute consorting with her lovers on the threshing floor vividly portrays the shame with which Hosea views his nation's devotion to the fertility cult. The people of Israel expressed their gratitude for the harvest not to Yahweh, but to idols and pillars that were symbols of a deity other than their God. The unusual expression, *zānîtā mēʿal ʾĕlohĕka,* which states literally, "you have fornicated from beside your God," underscores the fact that it was Israel's idolatry that led to her separa-

numerous occurrences in the Old Testament (see, e.g., Gen. 17:22; Num. 16:26; Judg. 3:19). אֱלֹהֶיךָ (your God): The prophet does not say "from God," but "from *your* God" (ךָ) (see the Exposition). This may indicate that he wants to make an implicit distinction between the gods of the nations (עַמִּים) and Israel's God. אֶתְנָן (the payment a harlot receives), occurring only here, is best understood as a nominal form from תָּנָה (hire). The verbal form of this word occurs in 8:10 with the sense of hiring allies; in 8:9 תָּנָה has the sense of payment for sexual favors, for its object is "lovers." Here in 9:1 אֶתְנָן is paired with זָנִיתָ (committing fornication) which imparts the sense of payment for amorous favors. עַל (on) introduces the location of Israel's acceptance of payment—on גָּרְנוֹת דָּגָן (threshing floors), literally, "threshing floors of grain."

2. גֹּרֶן וָיֶקֶב (Threshing floor and winevat) are collective nouns. Their verb (יִרְעֵם) is in the singular and thus does not follow the usual rules of agreement between a compound subject and its predicate (see GKC §146d). בָּהּ (her) has the feminine

singular suffix while the preceding suffix (יִרְעֵם) is masculine plural. The variations in gender are typical of Hosea. The feminine suffix may indicate that in this clause Hosea envisions Israel as a harlot or an unfaithful wife.

3. אֶרֶץ יְהוָה (land of the LORD) is a construct relationship that denotes possession. טָמֵא (unclean food) refers to uncleanness in general, rather than simply unclean food. However, the association of this word with the verb אָכַל (eat) in the following clause indicates that Hosea has unclean food in mind. The verbs in the last two clauses of this verse are positioned chiastically: שָׁב (return) is in the clause-initial position, while יֹאכֵלוּ (eat) is in the final position in its clause. Francis I. Andersen (*The Sentence in Biblical Hebrew* [The Hague: Mouton, 1974], p. 67) states that this construction represents two views of a single event. This clausal construction thus indicates that Hosea views the return to Egypt (i.e., the captivity) and the eating of unclean food as two facets of one event, that is, the exile.

---

tion from God. Her devotion to the syncretistic deity of the fertility cult was not devotion to the God whose voice thundered on Sinai, "You shall have no other gods before me" (Exod. 20:3).

The payment Israel received for her sexual favors was elucidated earlier (2:7 [5]). There we are told that Israel thought it was her lovers who supported her with bread and water, wool and flax, oil and drink. She consorted with the baals believing that in return she would receive the necessities of life. When Hosea represents Yahweh as asserting that it was really he who provided for Israel (2:10 [8]), the prophet uses two of the words in 9:1–3, that is, "grain" (*dagan*) and "new wine" (*tîrôš*). Like Gomer who left her husband, Hosea, to take up with a paramour (chap. 3), Israel had left Yahweh. Throughout the period of separation she mistakenly believed it was her lovers who kept her. But they did not, for the lovers received her favors for nothing. It was her husband, Yahweh, who continued to provide for her, even as she flaunted his love in the embrace of the baals.

She did this "on every threshing floor of grain," perhaps the many threshing floors in the northern kingdom. In all probability there was scarcely a floor where there was not some representation of the fertility religion or some act of devotion dedicated to the deification of nature.

2. Hosea's understanding of sin, as involving both deed and punishment, comes to the fore in

this verse. The threshing floor and winevat, symbols to Hosea of Israel's defection to Baal, will no longer feed the people and the new wine will fail them. The scenes and symbols of their religious orgies will become catalysts for judgment. Israel had all the trappings of religion in the nature cult—the joyous celebrations, the warmth of comradery, the false comfort of believing they had placated the deity, the conviction that they were serving God. They had everything but the heart of true religion: unfeigned faith and humble obedience to God.

3. The people will no longer enjoy harvests in the land, because they will not remain in "the LORD's land." The concept of "the land of the LORD" is not amplified in the Pentateuch, although Deuteronomy frequently speaks of the land as a gift from Yahweh, and God states, "The land shall not be sold in perpetuity, for the land is mine" (Lev. 25:23, NRSV). The expression *the LORD's land* is an aspect of the prophet's polemic against the fertility cult. It was not Baal who provided the bounty of the land, for the land belonged to Yahweh.

Hosea has already couched the dismal prospect of the impending captivity in terms of a recurrence of the Egyptian bondage (7:16; 8:13), but now we learn for the first time the literal intention of the metaphor—the bondage will be in Assyria. Egypt serves as a motif of bondage in

Hosea's philosophy of history. Basic to this philosophy is the belief that the God who acted in the past is the God who will act in the future.

In Assyrian bondage not only will the produce of Canaan's fields be unavailable to the people, but they will eat unclean food. This concept of clean and unclean food was an important aspect of the levitical legislation. Ritual defilement resulted from the failure to observe food laws. The major reason for the laws of cleanness and uncleanness (Lev. 11–16) was that the people were to be holy (Lev. 11:44–45). The concept of holiness involved the maintenance of a distinction between the sacred and the profane. Not only would the eating of unclean foods violate their tradition, but it would affirm that their distinctive relationship with their God had been severed.

XI. Results of the Captivity (9:1–6)

B. The People Will No Longer Observe Levitical Rituals (9:4–6)

4 They shall not pour out wine to the LORD,
> and their sacrifices shall not please him.
> Like the bread of mourners [shall their bread be] to them,
>> all who eat of it shall defile themselves:
> for their bread [will be used] for their own desires;
>> it will not come into the house of the LORD.

5 What will you do on the day of the appointed festival,
> and on the day of the feast of the LORD?

6 For behold, they shall depart from desolation,
> but Egypt shall gather them,
> Memphis shall bury them.
> Nettles shall possess their precious things of silver,
>> thorns [shall be] in their tents.

4 They shall not pour drink offerings of wine to the LORD,
> and their sacrifices shall not please him.
> Such sacrifices shall be like mourners' bread;
>> all who eat of it shall be defiled;
> for their bread shall be for their hunger only;
>> it shall not come to the house of the LORD.

5 What will you do on the day of appointed festival,
> and on the day of the festival of the LORD?

6 For even if they escape destruction,
> Egypt shall gather them,
> Memphis shall bury them.
> Nettles shall possess their precious things of silver;
>> thorns shall be in their tents.

4. לֹא־יִסְּכוּ (They shall not pour out): נָסַךְ has the basic sense of pouring out and is used metaphorically with עַל for the pouring out of a spirit of deep sleep (Isa. 29:10); it also signifies the pouring out of molten metal (Isa. 40:19). In other occurrences in the qal stem נָסַךְ refers to the pouring out of libations (Exod. 30:9; Isa. 30:1). לַיהוָה (to the LORD) confirms the action of נָסַךְ in this context as the pouring out of a libation. יֶעֶרְבוּ (shall not please) is pointed by several modern commentators as hiphil (cause to enter or bring) after the analogy of the cognate verb (ʿrb) in Ugaritic. While this pointing of the verb achieves a better parallel with the first clause (pour out libations/bring sacrifices) it is doubtful that the word had this meaning in Hebrew. The verb ʿrb occurs in line 159 of the krt epic (Gordon, *UT*, p. 251) in a context dealing with sacrifice, but is not in parallel with the word dbḥ (sacrifice). Rather, the words imr dbḥ (lamb of sacrifice) find their parallel in lla (a lamb) in the next line. In all likelihood the verb ʿrb connotes *to enter* in this context, but does not relate to sacrifices. This gains support from the fact that it is followed by bẓl ḥmt (into the shade of a tent). The word עָרֵב (please) occurs in Jeremiah 6:20 in parallel with לְרָצוֹן (lit. for acceptance) with reference to sacrifice. There is no reason for understanding it otherwise here, for Hebrew poetic parallelism does not require the balancing of precisely similar concepts. Indeed, several of the clausal structures in 9:1–6 reflect a balancing of concepts which are not precise parallels. The evidence does not require a departure from the Masoretic Text (shall not please). כְּלֶחֶם (Like the bread of) requires the insertion of an idea if the clause is to be complete. The clause states literally, "Like bread of mourners to them." The concept required is "their bread": "Like the bread of mourners [shall *their bread* be] to them." This gains support from the fact that the comparison is incomplete as it stands, and the suffix (it) on אֹכְלָיו (who eat of it) requires a more concrete referent than that given by לֶחֶם (bread) in the comparison "as the bread of." We expect the suffix to refer to bread actually eaten, not bread that serves only as a comparison. אוֹנִים (mourners): The word אָוֶן connotes trouble or sorrow. We have assigned the more specific connotation of mourning to the word here after the analogy of its use in Deuteronomy 26:14 (see the Exposition). אֹכְלָיו (who eat of it): See the comment above. יִטַּמָּאוּ (shall defile themselves), like the use of טָמֵא in verse 3, refers to food that is ceremonially unclean (see the Exposition). כִּי (for) explains the reason for the previous statement. They will defile themselves because their bread is לְנַפְשָׁם (for their own desires; lit. for themselves). When נֶפֶשׁ is construed with לְ and a pronominal suffix it may reflect "for one's desire." This collocation occurs in Deuteronomy 21:14 (וְשִׁלַּחְתָּהּ לְנַפְשָׁהּ), lit. You shall send her *where*

---

4. Another result of the expulsion of the people from the land is that they will no longer be able to offer animal sacrifices and libations of wine to the Lord. Libations of wine were not common in the levitical sacrifices, but did accompany some of them (Exod. 29:40; Lev. 23:13; Num. 15:1–10). It is best to understand the offerings that Hosea cites here as elements of levitical worship rather than rites of the fertility cult, because they were presented "to the LORD." The references to the expulsion of the people from "the land of the LORD" (v. 3a) and the levitical concept of uncleanness (tâmēʾ, v. 3c) point to aspects of the nation's Yahwistic heritage. The captivity would bring to an end the sacrifices that served to establish the relationship of the people with their God.

In the captivity their bread would be like mourners' bread, defiling those who eat it. The allusion is probably to Deuteronomy 26:12–15, the account of the triennial tithe. The worshiper was to affirm that he had not eaten of the tithe of his produce while he was mourning (bĕʾōnî, v. 14). Evidently food eaten on the occasion of mourn-

ing was ritually unclean, and one who ate it would suffer defilement. The word ʾawen (mourning) signifies primarily sorrow or distress. The subsequent clauses support the idea of ritual uncleanness while in a state of mourning for the dead.

The reason for the defilement is that the bread will not come into the Lord's house; the people will use it only to satisfy their hunger and not in the sacred rituals. Hosea seems to have departed from the Deuteronomic account of the triennial tithe in his reference to the "house of the LORD" (v. 4c). Moses does not state that the tithe was to be brought into the central sanctuary, for the expression "before the LORD" (Deut. 26:13) may signify prayer in general, and the tithe was gathered throughout the land for feeding the Levites and underprivileged (v. 12, see Deut. 14:28–29). Rather Hosea appears to refer to the general uses of bread in the levitical sacrifices (Lev. 23:17–18; 24:5–7) offered at the tabernacle. We have observed a similar lack of precision in Hosea's analogies in other passages.

she wills), Psalm 78:18 (the food they craved), Ecclesiastes 6:2, and Jeremiah 34:16. It also occurs with the preposition כְּ (see Deut. 23:25 [24], as many as you wish). The idiom here may thus be translated literally, "Their bread is used for their own desires."

5. לְיוֹם מוֹעֵד (on the day of the appointed festival): מוֹעֵד (appointed) applies to feasts, held at specific times, which were occasions for holy convocations (Lev. 23). חַג (feast) is the term for a number of celebrative festivals, but refers primarily to the feasts of Passover, Unleavened Bread, Weeks, and Booths. Of the feasts termed מוֹעֵד in Leviticus 23, the feasts of Unleavened Bread (v. 6) and Booths (v. 34) were also designated חַג (feast). The Feast of Booths is called חַג־יהוה (the feast of the LORD, v. 39). This expression also occurs here. The Feast of Weeks was also designated חַג in Exodus 34:22. There appears to be no reason to regard the words מוֹעֵד (appointed festival) and חַג (feast) as anything more than functional synonyms. The use of מוֹעֵד (appointed festival) earlier (Hos. 2:13 [11]) does not necessarily indicate that Hosea makes a distinction between the two words, for the word מוֹעֵד (appointed festival) may function there as a general term for the joyous festivals cited in the preceding clause.

6. כִּי (For) gives the reason for the statement couched in the terms of the rhetorical question in verse 5 by connoting proximate causation (see the discussion at 4:16). They will be able to do nothing on the days of the feasts (9:5), because (v. 6) they will have gone into captivity. The implication is that they will be far from the temple where their convocations were held. In the captivity their joyous festivals will be no more. הִנֵּה (behold) is an emphatic particle that strengthens the following assertion. הָלְכוּ (they shall depart) is in the perfect tense. This tense, which connotes completed action, indicates Hosea's view of the captivity as an accomplished fact. מִשֹּׁד (from desolation) states the point from which they will depart. שֹׁד (desolation) is a general word for destruction connoting the violence of the wicked (Ps. 12:6 [5]; Prov. 21:7; 24:2) and the destruction of the Lord (Isa. 13:6; 22:4; Hos. 7:13). It is an apt term for the impending destruction of the nation. The Revised Standard Version emends שֹׁד to Assyria, but this is unnecessary. Egypt is not in parallel with שֹׁד in this context but with Memphis, and the word שֹׁד was used a significant num-

---

Bread will not be brought into the house of the Lord because the temple will not be accessible to the people in the captivity. Their bread will have only one function—to be eaten. The people will not use it in the joyous rituals at the temple any longer: they will use it only for their own needs and desires (*lěnapšam*).

5. The rhetorical question that comprises this verse implies that the people will be able to do nothing when the various feast days arrive. They will be far from the temple and will no longer observe their holy days. It is possible that Hosea had the Feast of Booths in mind as he wrote this section. When Jeroboam I became king of Israel he designated the eighth month as the month for observing that feast (1 Kings 12:25–32) instead of the seventh month as prescribed in the Mosaic legislation (Lev. 23:34; see 1 Kings 8:2). It is more likely, however, that Hosea refers to the entire calendar of appointed feasts. The word *day* may be collective, including all the feasts. The context gives no reason for seeing a specific reference to the observance of this feast in the northern kingdom. Since all the religious rites in 9:1–6 can be shown to be levitical, there is no need to see allusions to the fertility cult in the context. The central theme of the entire section is the loss of the people's inheritance because of their inability to observe the law's requirements. A veiled reference to a calendar dispute would add little to the prophet's argument.

6. The people would be able to do nothing on those holy occasions because they will not be in their land. They would leave destruction behind them with only the prospect of burial in a strange land before them. Their kingdom with its religious shrines and sacred rituals would become a desolation.

When the prophet says that Egypt will gather the people, he uses "Egypt" metaphorically (see 11:5). They will be gathered into another national bondage, and there they will be buried. While there their expensive possessions and their dwelling places will be overgrown with weeds. We have here a startling testimony to the truth of the words of Deuteronomy 28:36–46.

We need not understand "their precious things of silver" as a reference to idols. Nothing in the context points to that. Hosea says they will "depart from desolation," and the picture of their possessions overgrown with weeds vividly depicts his assertion.

141

ber of times by the eighth-century prophets. The emendation has no textual support. תְּקַבְּצֵם (shall gather them): See the discussion at 8:10. לְכַסְפָּם מַחְמַד (their precious things of silver) literally means "the precious thing[s] belonging to their silver." קִמּוֹשׂ (nettles) occurs in parallel with חֲרֻלִּים (a kind of weed) in Proverbs 24:31 and in association with חוֹחַ (bramble) in Isaiah 34:13. In both instances קִמּוֹשׂ (nettles) is a sign of desolation. יִירָשֵׁם (shall possess) depicts the nettles as taking over the valuables left behind by the captives. חוֹחַ (thorns) is also a sign of desolation (Job 31:40; Isa. 34:13). בְּאָהֳלֵיהֶם (in their tents): בְּ is locative. The construction requires the insertion of a verbal idea appropriate to the preposition בְּ, that is, "Thorns *shall be* in their tents."

XII. The Captivity Is a Recompense for Israel's Sin (9:7–17)

A. The Captivity Is a Recompense for the Sinful Attitude of the People toward the Prophets (9:7–9)

7 The days of reckoning have come,
 the days of recompense have come;
 Israel shall know [it].
The prophet is a fool,
 mad is the man of the Spirit,
because of the enormity of your iniquity
 and the intense hatred.
8 The prophet is the watchman of
 Ephraim along with my God;
yet the snare of a fowler is on all his
 ways,
  there is hatred in the house of his
  God.
9 They have deeply corrupted, as in the
 days of Gibeah.
He will remember their iniquity,
 he will attend to their sin.

7 The days of punishment have come,
 the days of recompense have come;
 Israel cries,
"The prophet is a fool,
 the man of the spirit is mad!"
Because of your great iniquity,
 your hostility is great.
8 The prophet is a sentinel for my God
 over Ephraim,
yet a fowler's snare is on all his ways,
 and hostility in the house of his God.
9 They have deeply corrupted themselves
 as in the days of Gibeah;
he will remember their iniquity,
 he will punish their sins.

7. בָּאוּ (have come) is in the perfect tense denoting completed action. It describes the action of the verb as certain in the mind of the writer while still future in actuality. הַפְּקֻדָּה (reckoning): The verbal form (פָּקַד) that underlies the noun פְּקֻדָּה (reckoning) does not have the inherent denotation of punishment. The verb פָּקַד often precedes the bestowal of blessing (see, e.g., Gen. 21:1; 50:24; 1 Sam. 2:21; Jer. 29:10) or the execution of judgment (Exod. 32:34; Isa. 26:14; 27:1; Jer. 6:15; Hos. 8:13) on the part of God. In the majority of cases the word *attend*, with such concomitant ideas as give heed to, look after, care for, visit, accompany, or pay attention to, is a satisfactory English translation. The frequent occurrence of פָּקַד in parallel with זָכַר (remember) underscores the concept of mental apprehension inherent in פָּקַד (see the discussion at 1:4). פְּקֻדָּה shares the rich nuancing of the verb פָּקַד, for we may translate it by such concepts as oversight (Num. 3:32), visit (Num. 16:29), office (2 Chron. 23:18), reckoning (1 Chron. 23:11), overseers (Isa. 60:17), and punishment (Jer. 11:23). The noun פְּקֻדָּה thus represents basically an attending to, in the sense of taking account of or giving heed to. We have chosen the translation "reckoning" for פְּקֻדָּה because it best reflects the mental apprehension in the word along with its implications of punishment. There is no associative word that informs us of what is attended to or given heed to, but it is clearly the sin of the people which will finally bring divine retribution. הַשִּׁלֻּם (recompense) is parallel to פְּקֻדָּה (punishment) and further delineates the sense we are to see in פְּקֻדָּה. The word שִׁלֻּם occurs on only two other occa-

sions; in Isaiah 34:8 it is in parallel with נָקָם (take vengeance), and in Micah 7:3 it connotes a bribe. The concept of recompense is common to both contexts, for vengeance is recompense for a wrong while a bribe is recompense for favorable consideration. The nuance of פְּקֻדָּה, thus delineated by שִׁלֻּם, is of an attending to Israel for the purpose of demanding requital for her deeds. יֵדְעוּ יִשְׂרָאֵל (Israel shall know [it]) is complicated by the absence of an object for יֵדְעוּ (know). Another possible translation is, "They [the days of recompense] will know Israel." That is, Israel will come into the sphere of the days of recompense and thus experience judgment (cf. the use of יָדַע in Isa. 53:3). But the writer could have indicated this sense unequivocally by the use of the sign of the direct object before "Israel." The word יָדַע (know) occurs in several other contexts in Hosea without orthographic representation of the direct object (7:9a, b; 8:4). In these instances (all negative clauses) the object is implicit in the preceding clause. For example, Hosea 7:9 states, "Foreigners have consumed his strength, but he does not know *it.*" In all probability the clause here is another such expression in which we must supply an object derived from the previous clause. This clause, along with its companion clause (v. 7a), depicts impending punishment. Thus, if this approach to the problem is valid, Hosea intends to say that Israel will know (or experience) punishment when the "days of recompense" come upon her. אֱוִיל (a fool) has a moral connotation in the Wisdom material where it signifies one separate from godly wisdom. Here, however, its com-

---

7. The perfect tense verbs here create an atmosphere of dread certainty—The days have come! These days, an evident reference to the captivity, are days of recompense. The prophet represents Yahweh as saying that the captivity was a payment for the sin of the nation. One of the primary themes of this prophecy is the stark truth that sin demands requital, and Israel was soon to know that by experience. The present respite from national calamity was not to last forever.

The subsequent statements present an intensely personal view of the way Hosea perceives his reception by the people. They regarded the prophets as fools and madmen. Hosea's hearers apparently regarded the pronouncement of impending retribution in the parallel clauses here as insane babbling. Other prophets received the same treatment; the prophet who anointed Jehu king was called a "mad" fellow (2 Kings 9:11), and

prophets were called madmen in Judah (Jer. 29:26). Jesus spoke of the persecution of prophets (Matt. 5:12) as an analogy to the treatment his disciples might expect. He said a prophet would not receive honor in his own house or country (Matt. 13:57). The world does not treat well those who expose its wrongdoing.

The basis for this negative attitude was the enormity of the people's sin. Israel is addressed in the second person in this statement (ʿăwōněkā, your sin), while in the previous clause they were spoken about in the third person plural (yēdĕʿû, they will know). Hosea's address to the people is as personal and direct as their characterization of him.

This negative attitude toward the prophets had two aspects: iniquity and hatred. The prophets exposed iniquity and proclaimed retribution for it; if the people would not acknowledge that the

panion word מְשֻׁגָּע (mad) indicates that אֱוִיל (fool) has the sense of mental incompetency, for מְשֻׁגָּע always refers to madness in the Old Testament (Deut. 28:34; 1 Sam. 21:15–16 [14–15]). It is also applied disparagingly to God's prophets (2 Kings 9:11; Jer. 29:26). אִישׁ הָרוּחַ (the man of the Spirit) is parallel with נָבִיא (prophet) and is a surrogate for it. The expression *man of the Spirit* does not occur elsewhere as a designation for a prophet, but it is not an inappropriate designation. Prophets were frequently associated with the Spirit of God in the Old Testament (see the Exposition). עַל (because of) denotes *upon*. This sense has a causal connotation in numerous contexts where it indicates the basis on which something was done (see Gen. 20:3, "You are a dead man because of [עַל] the woman whom you have taken"). The clause introduced by עַל here thus contains the reason for asserting in the previous clause that the prophets are mad. מַשְׂטֵמָה (hatred) occurs only in Hosea 9:7–8, but its sense is clear. The verb that underlies this noun (שָׂטַם) denotes strong animosity (Gen. 27:41; 49:23; 50:15).

8. צֹפֶה (watchman) connotes watchmen in the ordinary sense in numerous passages (see, e.g., 1 Sam. 14:16; 2 Sam. 13:34; 18:24), but it also refers metaphorically to the prophets (Jer. 6:17; Ezek. 3:17; 33:7; Mic. 7:4). This clause defines it by the word נָבִיא (prophet). עִם (with) is emended by the Revised Standard Version (see also BHS) to

עַם (people). The clause is syntactical as it stands, however, and the reading עִם (with) is consonant with Hosea's theology. This reading asserts that the prophets were associated with God (עִם, with), and that God watched over Ephraim as did the prophets ("the prophet is the watchman of Israel along with my God"). We find both concepts in this prophecy, for Hosea views the prophets as working in concert with God (6:5; 12:10, 13), and he depicts God as observing Israel (5:3; 6:10). פַּח (snare) is a trap for birds (Prov. 7:23). It frequently occurs as a metaphorical depiction of calamity or plotting evil (Ps. 91:3; Jer. 48:43). דְּרָכָיו (his ways): The nearest logical referent to the masculine suffix (his) is נָבִיא (prophet) in the preceding clause. דֶּרֶךְ (way), among its other nuances, connotes activities that are characteristic of a person. Hosea speaks of the ways of the people (4:9; 12:3 [2]) and the ways of God (14:10 [9]). The ways of the prophet are the activities associated with Israelite prophetism. בְּבֵית אֱלֹהָיו (in the house of his God): The suffix (his) finds its logical referent in נָבִיא (prophet). The term *house of God* is not a designation of the temple in this context. Prophetic activity was rarely associated with the temple, and Hosea uses the term in other ways. While the temple is in view in the expression *house of the LORD* (9:4), Hosea uses "house" with reference to God in 9:15 to depict metaphorically the separa-

---

prophetic accusations were true, there was little else for them to do but pronounce the prophets mad. The other aspect, hatred, also applies to the prophets, for they painted a gloomy picture of Israel's future which would not curry the favor of the people. The word of God was choked off because the people hated Yahweh's messengers and considered their pronouncements senseless babbling.

The phrase *man of the Spirit* is an apt designation for the prophets because they were associated with the term *rûaḥ* (spirit) throughout the Old Testament (Num. 11:25, 29; 24:2; 1 Sam. 10:6–8; 19:23; 1 Kings 22:24; 2 Kings 2:9). The prophet Micah says he is filled with the Spirit (3:8), and Ezekiel makes numerous references to the Spirit in association with his prophetic ministry (see, e.g., 2:2; 3:24; 11:5). He also speaks of the false prophets who follow their own spirits and not Yahweh's Spirit (13:3). Thus we capitalize Spirit here.

8. The positive statement concerning the prophets in this verse counters the popular view of them reflected in Hosea's previous statement. The prophets were watchmen in that they observed the behavior of the nation and judged it against the covenantal standards. The word *ṣapa* (watch) often describes the activity of watchmen. As watchmen listen for every night sound and observe every shadow, so the prophets observed Israel.

The prophets watched over Israel for her own good, and they did this in association with God. We may observe several places in the prophecy where Hosea pictures the prophets as spokesmen for God. He says that God punished the people by the prophets (6:5), spoke through the prophets (12:11 [10]), and even brought them out of Egypt by a prophet (12:14 [13]). God watched over Israel through his prophets.

Yet a snare was on all their ways. The prophets were unable to convict the nation of its sin and stay it in its headlong dash to ruin. The sinful atti-

tion of the people from the family of Yahweh, that is, from their covenantal heritage.

9. הֶעְמִיקוּ (deeply) is literally "they have made deep." In tandem with שִׁחֵתוּ (they have corrupted) it connotes corrupting deeply. This verb usually has a stated object, but not always. In Exodus 32:7 it occurs without an object in the phrase שִׁחֵת עַמְּךָ

כִּי (for your people have corrupted). The structure here, which states no object, is thus syntactical. We must insert some object, such as "themselves." יִזְכּוֹר (he will remember): See the comment at 7:2. יִפְקוֹד (he will attend): See the comments at 1:4 and 9:7.

---

tude of the people hindered the prophets' work. There was hatred in God's house, and Israel was like a family torn apart by strife.

9. Hosea likens the deep corruption of the people to the "days of Gibeah." The reference is evidently to the heinous crime which is recorded in Judges 19. The rape, murder, and subsequent dismemberment of the concubine in this account probably never faded from Israel's corporate memory, for, "Such a thing has never happened or been seen from the day that the people of Israel came up out of the land of Egypt until this day" (Judg.

19:30, RSV). To Hosea the corrupt behavior of the men who so cruelly violated the Levite's concubine is an appropriate analogy for the depth of the corruption of the people in his day.

God will remember their sin and he will attend to it. In the Book of Judges the account of the concubine's awful death (chap. 19) precedes the account of the retribution that came to Gibeah as various tribes took military action against it (chap. 20). Perhaps this was in Hosea's mind as well as he concluded this section with the affirmation of divine retribution.

XII. The Captivity Is a Recompense for Israel's Sin (9:7–17)

B. The Captivity Is a Recompense for the People's Defection to Baal (9:10–14)

10 Like grapes in the wilderness,
   I found Israel.
Like first fruit on a fig tree
   in its first [season]
   I saw your fathers.
[But] they went to Baal-peor
      and consecrated themselves to shame,
      and they became detestable things
      like the thing they loved.
11 Ephraim—their glory will fly away like a bird;
      [they shall be bereft] of birth, womb, and conception.
12 Indeed, if they bring up their children,
      I will bereave them of every one,
   for woe to them
      when I depart from them!
13 Ephraim—just as I have chosen [judgment] for Tyre, planted in [its] place,
      so [I have chosen for] Ephraim to lead forth its sons to the murderer.
14 Give them O LORD—
      what shall you give?
   Give them a womb that miscarries,
      and breasts that are dry.

10 Like grapes in the wilderness,
   I found Israel.
Like the first fruit on the fig tree,
   in its first season,
   I saw your ancestors.
But they came to Baal-peor,
      and consecrated themselves to a thing of shame,
      and became detestable like the thing they loved.
11 Ephraim's glory shall fly away like a bird—
      no birth, no pregnancy, no conception!
12 Even if they bring up children,
      I will bereave them until no one is left.
   Woe to them indeed
      when I depart from them!
13 Once I saw Ephraim as a young palm planted in a lovely meadow,
      but now Ephraim must lead out his children for slaughter.
14 Give them, O LORD—
      what will you give?
   Give them a miscarrying womb
      and dry breasts.

147

10. כַּעֲנָבִים בַּמִּדְבָּר (Like grapes in the wilderness) is an unusual expression, since grapes would not likely be found in a wilderness. However, the analogy heightens the emotion of the statement. For if a traveler in the wilderness who was in need of refreshment did find grapes there, they would be the more deeply appreciated. מָצָאתִי (I found) connotes the sense of pleasant discovery established by the preceding simile. יִשְׂרָאֵל (Israel) is in parallel with אֲבוֹתֵיכֶם (your fathers) and thus represents Israel in its early history. בְּכוּרָה (first fruit) always refers to early figs which were a delicacy (Isa. 28:4; Jer. 24:2; Mic. 7:1). בְּרֵאשִׁיתָהּ (in its first [season]): The referent of the feminine suffix הָ can be either בְּכוּרָה (first fruit) or תְּאֵנָה (fig tree). Since the root בָּכַר and its derivatives denote youngness, it is unlikely that the referent is בְּכוּרָה (first fruit). This connection would create a redundancy. We are not told what "first" signifies with reference to a fig tree, but it could hardly be anything other than the fig tree's first season. הֵמָּה

(they) finds its nearest logical referent in אֲבוֹתֵיכֶם (your fathers). וַיִּנָּזְרוּ (and consecrated themselves): נָזַר (consecrate) used with לְ (to) has the sense of *separation to*. This collocation occurs in Numbers 6:2, 6:5, and 6:12, where it depicts the consecration of the Nazirites to Yahweh. בֹּשֶׁת (shame): The Revised Standard Version emends to "*Baal*," and this is also suggested by BHS. The Septuagint, however, reflects the Masoretic Text (αἰσχύνην, sense of shame). There is no need to emend because בֹּשֶׁת (shame) occurs in apposition to Baal in Jeremiah 11:13, and other writers substitute בֹּשֶׁת (shame) for Baal in proper names. Note, for example, אִישׁ בֹּשֶׁת (man of shame) in 2 Samuel 2:8. שִׁקּוּצִים (detestable things): The various forms of the root שׁקץ have in common the idea of detest or detestable (see Akkadian *šikṣu*, impurity). שִׁקּוּץ (detestable thing) is used in Nahum 3:6 of filth cast at someone and in Deuteronomy 29:16 [17] it refers to idols. It also reflects the detestation of the Israelites for pagan gods in several passages

---

10. The gloomy, foreboding atmosphere of verses 1–9 changes now to one of pathos. The words here are at once tender and loving. The simile of the grapes and figs is a literary vehicle for Hosea's theology of divine love. This section depicts Israel's sin, not as rebellion against a code of laws, but as departure from a loving relationship with Yahweh to a sordid alliance with Baal.

The choice of grapes in Hosea's analogy suggests the delight that Yahweh had in Israel in their early experience together. There is nothing about Israel's purity in the simile. Rather, it describes the emotive context in which the verb *maṣaʾtî* (I found) is set. The emotion is entirely on the side of Yahweh. Like a hot, weary traveler who finds grapes in the wilderness, or who discovers the most delectable figs, so Yahweh found Israel and took delight in her.

The reference to their "fathers," with its emphasis on the pristine days of the nation, indicates that there was a time when Yahweh delighted in his people. This was no longer true in Hosea's time. The turning point appears in the last clause of the verse where we read that the people went to Baal Peor.

The baal of Peor was a representation of the fertility god Baal who was worshiped at Peor in the Moabite mountains. The account of the original defection to this baal is recorded in Numbers 25:1–18. We read that the Israelites bowed down to the gods of Moab (v. 2). The statement that "the people began to play the harlot with the

daughters of Moab" (v. 1, RSV) may allude to the sexual rites associated with the fertility cults. The result of this defection was a plague in which 24,000 Israelites died (v. 9). The spirit of Peor never left Israel. In Hosea's time it continued to manifest itself in the cult of the northern kingdom. In the religious defection at Peor the people "consecrated themselves to shame." Hosea does not use the hated name of Baal, but the surrogate *bošet* (shame). This characterization of the defection at Peor communicates Hosea's detestation of the name *Baal* and underscores the abominable nature of the people's apostasy from God.

Israel's obedience to God in the earliest phase of the wilderness experience represents an ideal to Hosea. He envisions the wilderness as the site of Israel's restoration (2:16 [14]), and he alludes to the wilderness period ("from the land of Egypt") as the time when Yahweh "knew" Israel (13:4–5). Yahweh's delight in the nation changed to detestation because of the people's participation in the fertility worship. The people had become "detestable things" just like the hated elements of the cult they had come to love. The grammatical construction of this statement is important because it asserts that the people had taken on the very character of the cult in which they took part. Like the fertility cult they had become the objects of Yahweh's detestation.

The fertility cults did not consist only of idols and shrines; they involved worshipers as well. These worshipers participated in acts that Yah-

(e.g., 1 Kings 11:5). The sense of the statement here is that Israel has become as detestable as the pagan worship in which she participated. אֲהֵבָם (the thing they love) occurs in the singular only here. In this structure it can refer only to their false worship.

11. אֶפְרַיִם כָעוֹף (Ephraim . . . like a bird): This construction allows for two translations: "Ephraim is like a bird, their glory will fly away," or, "Ephraim—like a bird their glory will fly away." The first possibility seems illogical since it is Ephraim that is likened to a bird, but it is Ephraim's glory that will fly away. This translation, however, is in keeping with Hosea's imprecision in the use of metaphor (see 2:5 [3] of the Exposition). The second possible translation is consonant with several constructions in which Hosea cites the name *Ephraim* before going on to speak about the nation (*casus pendens* or "topic and comment"). We may observe this in 9:13 (see the Author's Translation), as well as in 7:8a (see 14:9 [8]). While the sense is similar in each of the two translations, the latter is preferable due to its close affinity with the observable stylistic phenomena of Hosea's use of "Ephraim" in the examples given above, and in the one that follows in verse 13. כְּבוֹדָם (their glory) is defined by the neg-

ative clause that follows as the population growth the nation had experienced. מִלֵּדָה (of birth): מִן is difficult to construe with the verb *fly*, because the clause governed by that verb is a complete sentence. If we posit an ellipsis here, however, the clause makes good sense. We must thus insert a verbal idea appropriate to the separative connotation of מִן (from). Pregnant expressions with מִן are not uncommon in the Old Testament (see GKC §119x, y, ff). Note the somewhat similar construction in Isaiah 38:17, where we must supply the idea of deliverance: "You have loved my life [and delivered me] from [מִן] the pit of destruction." In pregnant expressions such as this, the preposition often depends on a verbal idea that is unexpressed but implicit in the governing verb (see GKC §119ee). In Hosea 9:11 we must read the sense of separation reflected in the verb *fly away* into the ellipsis (see the Author's Translation).

12. כִּי אִם (Indeed, if): Since these particles introduce a clause which goes beyond the concept of the previous clause, we must translate them as "Even though" or "Indeed if." The latter translation is supported by Exodus 22:22 [23], "Indeed, if [or *when*] he cries out to me." בְּנֵיהֶם (their children) are any children that may be born in this hypothetical situation. וְשִׁכַּלְתִּים (I will bereave

weh could not condone. Thus those who participated in these cults were as much the objects of Yahweh's displeasure as the idols themselves. The worshipers were "detestable things" as were the idols. The same is true today, for those who reject God to worship at the shrines of self-indulgence, illicit sex, prurient self-interest, violence, and other such ideologies are in God's eyes objects of the same displeasure he has for the ways they have chosen. The detestation of Yahweh was not limited only to the events that took place earlier at Peor. Israel was guilty of the same wrongdoing in Hosea's day. This guilt was the basis of the prophet's pronouncement in the next verse.

11. The glory of Ephraim is her people, but that glory will fly away. This idea of loss continues in the next clause where it is the loss of the population that is set forth in the imagery of "birth," "womb," and "conception." The parallelism of the two clauses establishes the fact that the "glory" of the first clause answers to the reference to population growth in the second. Israel was to suffer the loss of future generations. We have supplied the verb *bereft* to express that concept in the proposed ellipsis (see the Author's Transla-

tion and the Exegesis). The growth of the nation in the eighth century was an aspect of its glory, but this glory was to fly away when the people went at sword point into Assyria.

12. The affirmation that even if children were born and reared, they too would die seems unnecessary after the preceding statement which asserts so strongly that the growth of the nation will cease. It appears, however, to be a hypothetical device used to strengthen the force of the preceding assertion (cf. 9:16). Zechariah uses the same device to affirm the removal of the false prophets from Israel in the restoration (13:2), for in the subsequent clauses he sets up a hypothetical situation to underscore the ultimacy of the affirmation. He says, "If any prophets appear again, their fathers and mothers who bore them . . . shall pierce them through when they prophesy" (v. 3, NRSV). Hosea's hypothetical statement also adds a greater sense of ultimacy to his pronouncement concerning the gloomy future of Israel.

This forecast of depopulation, like so many of Hosea's statements, reflects the curses of Deuteronomy, one of which says, "And as the LORD delighted in doing good to you and *multi-*

them) introduces a result clause. If, somehow, children should be born, in spite of the negative affirmation of the previous clause, the people will be bereft of even those children. מֵאָדָם (every one) is literally "from a man." It connotes separation away *from a man*, that is, not a single individual will be left. כִּי (for) gives the reason for the great depopulation of the nation. It is because of the woe to come on the nation when God departs from them. גַּם (untranslated) adds force to the assertion. בְּשׂוּרִי (when I depart) is temporal, a common function of the infinitive construct with בְּ. מֵהֶם (from them): סוּר is separative. It channels the action of the verb שׂוּר (depart) to its object הֶם (them).

13. אֶפְרַיִם (Ephraim) is spoken about, not addressed, as the subsequent clauses indicate. The function in which an apparently syntactically independent noun appears at the head of a section containing an observation about the noun is designated "topic and comment" by modern linguists

(see v. 12). That function may obtain here, in which case the conjectural emendation in BHS is unnecessary. In this linguistic function the writer cites a topic, then comments on it. Here, Ephraim reappears (from 9:11) and the author gives us new information (the comment). This function serves to focus on what is predicated about the subject rather than on the subject itself. כַּאֲשֶׁר (just as) introduces a comparison, its most common function. רָאִיתִי לְצוֹר (I have chosen for Tyre) is a collocation that means "to choose for." In 1 Samuel 16:1 רָאָה (see) is in the first person in this collocation (רָאִיתִי בְּבָנָיו לִי מֶלֶךְ), lit. I have seen for myself a king among his sons, that is, I have chosen a king, 1 Sam. 16:1, see also v. 17). It is in the third person in אֱלֹהִים יִרְאֶה־לּוֹ הַשֶּׂה (God will choose for himself a lamb, Gen. 22:8). While in Genesis 22:8 and 1 Samuel 16:1 the inflection of רָאָה (see) agrees with the suffix construed with לְ and functions in a reflexive sense (*I have seen for myself*), 1 Samuel 16:17 shows that the colloca-

---

plying you, so the LORD will delight in bringing ruin upon you and destroying you" (28:63). When Hosea says that there will be no "birth," "womb," or "conception," he affirms the end of the nation's blessing and the beginning of its downfall. God will no longer multiply the nation.

The chilling statement that woe will come to the people when Yahweh departs from them may reflect an element of the Abrahamic promise to which Hosea alluded earlier (1:9). The promise that the Lord would be God to his people (Gen. 17:7–8), which the name *Not My People* temporarily vitiated (Hos. 1:9), could not be realized if Yahweh abdicated his position as God of his people. Woe will come to the nation because God's sovereign hand would no longer protect and guide them, and they would become a prey to the nations.

13. The clausal structure of this verse presents one of the greatest difficulties in the Prophecy of Hosea. Most commentators have not regarded *raʾîtî lĕ* (I have chosen) as a collocation, but recognition of this function contributes substantially to a translation that is both logical and syntactical.

Our study of this collocation (see the Exegesis) has shown that in its few occurrences it is construed with both a direct object and an indirect object. The proposal that the direct object is implicit in Hosea's use of this expression, and should be understood as a concept expressing judgment (see the Author's Translation and the Exegesis) gains support from Hosea's frequent ellipses,

as well as from the second clause in the comparative structure which sets forth the prospect of the slaughter of Ephraim's sons. Since the particle *kaʾăšer* often compares similar concepts, we may expect some unexpressed reference to judgment in the first clause.

The allusion to Tyre in the Masoretic Text seems anomalous. That city appears nowhere else in this context. Yet the future destruction of Tyre was an important concept in the corpus of eighth-century prophetic material. Both Isaiah and Amos predicted its downfall (Isa. 23:1–18; Amos 1:9–10). Hosea may have appealed to a common bank of prophetic material for this judgment-saying about Tyre.

The Septuagint achieves poetic balance in its translation, "Ephraim, as I saw, has given their children for a prey [thēran]; and Ephraim . . . to bring out his children to slaughter" (Author's Translation). The word *thēran* evidently reflects the Hebrew *ṣayid* ("hunting, game," BDB, p. 844), not the Masoretic Text's *ṣōr* (Tyre). The Septuagint translation posits an ellipsis in Hosea's enigmatic words.

The Hebrew consonantal text is represented substantially in the Septuagint. We may see this not only in the ellipsis in the second clause, but also in the words *has given their children* in the first clause. The word *given* (*parestēsan*) may indicate that the translators read the first three letters of *šĕtûlâ* (planted) as *šatû* ("they gave" or "placed") from *šît*. The remaining *lâ* may have

tion does not demand agreement of person ("choose for me a man"). If we understand the idiom to mean "choose for," then Tyre (in Hos. 9:13) functions as the indirect object (as do the suffixes with לְ in the citations above). We may thus translate the construction, "I have chosen *for* Tyre," and understand the object as some unexpressed judgment (see the Exposition). שְׁתוּלָה (planted) is feminine and may find its referent in either Tyre or Ephraim. The former is the more likely, because, with only one possible exception (5:9), Ephraim is masculine in Hosea. It is masculine in the immediate context (note the suffix: *his* sons), and the participle שְׁתוּלָה (planted) is closest to Tyre in the clause. נָוֶה has as its basic sense the concept of place. The word is richly nuanced by the contexts in which it occurs. It was used of the place where the ark of the covenant was situated (2 Sam. 15:25); it refers to human dwellings (Prov. 3:33; 21:20; 24:15; Job 5:3; 18:15), and metaphorically to righteousness (Jer. 31:23), as well as to the

place where animals are pastured or kept secure (see, e.g., 2 Sam. 7:8; Isa. 65:10; Jer. 33:12). It refers to a city (Isa. 27:10; 33:20), as well as to the abode of God (Jer. 25:30). In Hosea 9:13 the word is nuanced by שְׁתוּלָה (planted), which brings the sense of firmly established. The sense thus seems to be that Tyre was firmly established in its place. וְאֶפְרַיִם (so . . . Ephraim): וְ introduces the apodosis of the comparative clause introduced by כַּאֲשֶׁר, as it does in, "As [כַּאֲשֶׁר] the LORD commanded Moses, so Aaron placed it [וַיַּנִּיחֵהוּ] before the testimony" (Exod. 16:34, RSV). לְהוֹצִיא (to lead forth) is understood here as a purpose clause, dependent on the verbal idea of the protasis, which is unexpressed in the apodosis (see the Exposition). הֹרֵג (the murderer) when used substantivally refers to murderers (Jer. 4:31) and one who kills with the sword (Ezek. 21:16 [11]). The verb הָרַג has several nuances. It is used mainly of killing people, often in a violent sense; it is used sometimes of killing animals (Lev. 20:15; Isa. 22:13), but never for sac-

---

had a directive or reflexive function which they left unexpressed. The words *their children* represent the *bĕnāweh* (in [its] place) of the Masoretic Text which the Septuagint evidently read as the consonants *bnyh* (lit. her sons; LXX their children).

The Septuagint translation presents several minor problems, however. If the *lā* of *šĕtūlā* (planted) was present in the Hebrew text which was before the translators, its function in that text cannot be explained, and if *bnyh* is read "her sons" rather than "in a place," then the writer assigned both masculine and feminine genders to Ephraim within the same verse (see the masculine suffix, on *bānayw* in line 2). While Hosea's use of gender indicators is not precise, he does not elsewhere assign different genders to Ephraim in such a narrow compass. We can understand the consonantal text as represented in the Masoretic Text, however, without syntactical anomalies.

There may be a conceptual consonance between the Masoretic Text here and the Tyre material in Isaiah and Amos. The concept of Tyre being "planted" or firmly established in its place may reflect the fact that Tyre was a stronghold (Isa. 23:14). And Yahweh's choosing (*rāʾîtî lĕ*) for judgment reflects the words of Amos 1:9–10 where, along with other nations, God had destined Tyre for destruction. In Isaiah's oracle against Tyre it is Yahweh who purposed Tyre's downfall (23:8–9); so it is here.

The inclusion of Ephraim along with Tyre in this pronouncement of doom is a powerful statement of the depths to which Israel had fallen. They were no different from their pagan neighbor Tyre, and were to suffer a punishment similar to Tyre's. This underscores the statement above, "Woe to them when I depart from them!" (v. 12). The nation had lost its covenant privilege.

Amos did something similar in his prophecy. In the prophetic oracles in 1:3–2:16 God grouped Israel and Judah with several pagan nations and pronounced doom on all of them. Later he erased the distinction between Israel and the nations when he said, "Are you not like the Ethiopians to me, O people of Israel?" (9:7, NRSV). Jesus spoke of the importance of his followers maintaining their distinctiveness in the world when he said, "You are the salt of the earth; but if the salt has lost its taste, how can its saltiness be restored?" (Matt. 5:13, NRSV).

The judgment on Ephraim is that they will lead out their sons to the murderer. Both Israel and Tyre fell before the Assyrian onslaught. Judah's headlong dash to ruin was stayed for a while, however, mainly because of the religious reforms under King Hezekiah.

The purpose clause *lĕhôṣîʾ* (to lead forth) stands starkly isolated. Some commentators understand the *lamed* to be asseverative (indeed) rather than an indicator of purpose (Andersen and Freedman, "indeed brought"). This suggestion, however, does not sustain the conceptual balance we expect in

rifice; it is used of judicial execution (Deut. 13:10 [9]); it is used of divine punishment (Hos. 6:5; Amos 4:10). On the basis of the sense of the participle and the lack of any distinctive requirements of the context, the word here may be a metonymy for the Assyrians.

14. מַה־תִּתֵּן (what shall you give?) interrupts the two imperatives תֵּן־לָהֶם (give to them) in this structure. The prophet pauses in his prayer to

search for the appropriate divine response to the threat of verse 11 that Israel would suffer an end to its population growth. רֶחֶם מַשְׁכִּיל (a womb that miscarries): מַשְׁכִּיל is the hiphil of שָׁכֹל. In the qal the sense is to be bereaved (Gen. 43:14). The causative sense of the hiphil requires the idea of a womb that has been bereft of a child, a miscarrying womb rather than a barren womb that cannot conceive.

a comparison clause in parallel structure. The isolation of this construction is relieved if we posit a concomitant verbal idea in the clause. We find numerous instances in the poetry of the Old Testament where a verbal concept that occurs in the first line of a binary structure is implicit in the second line as well. For example, we read, "As a door turns on its hinges, so [turns/does] a lazy person on his bed" (Prov. 26:14). Hosea states, "Blow the trumpet in Gibeah, [blow] the horn in Ramah" (5:8). If the proposal that rāʾîtî lĕ connotes "I have chosen for" is correct, the dynamics of parallelism support the inclusion of that idea before the infinitive lĕhôṣî (to lead forth). The sense is that Yahweh chose Ephraim to lead its sons to slaughter, just as he chose Tyre for the same destiny.

14. The concluding statement of this section is a prayer in which the prophet asks God to give

the nation "a womb that miscarries, and breasts that are dry." It is a well-considered prayer, for Hosea pauses before stating his petition to ask, "What shall you give?" The request is curious. We might have expected him to pray that God would extend mercy to them, but God could not show mercy to the nation until their guilt was expunged. He might have prayed that God would give them more time, but their spirit of harlotry was evident as far back as the events at Peor. Probably Hosea paused in his prayer because he knew that judgment was inevitable and it was difficult to know how to pray. The petition he uttered was not judgmental, but merciful. He prayed that they would not produce offspring, for the fate of their children was to be led out to a murderer. It was all he could pray.

XII. The Captivity Is a Recompense for Israel's Sin (9:7–17)

C. The Captivity Is a Recompense for Israel's Syncretistic Religion (9:15–17)

15 All their evil is in Gilgal,
  for there I began to hate them.
Because of the wickedness of their deeds
  I will expel them from my house.
I will not love them anymore;
  all their princes are rebels.

16 Ephraim is smitten:
  their root is dried up;
  they will produce no fruit.
Even if they produce offspring,
  I will slay the precious things of their
  womb.
17 My God casts them off because they
  have not listened,
  and they shall become wanderers
  among the nations.

15 Every evil of theirs began at Gilgal;
  there I came to hate them.
Because of the wickedness of their deeds
  I will drive them out of my house.
I will love them no more;
  all their officials are rebels.

16 Ephraim is stricken,
  their root is dried up,
  they shall bear no fruit.
Even though they give birth,
  I will kill the cherished offspring of
  their womb.
17 Because they have not listened to him,
  my God will reject them;
  they shall become wanderers among
  the nations.

15. כָּל־רָעָתָם (All their evil) indicates that the focus of Israel's evil is בַּגִּלְגָּל (in Gilgal). Gilgal was a cult-site in Hosea's time (see the Exposition). כִּי (for) seems not to function in its usual causative sense here (see the Exposition). שָׁם (there) is a locative adverb which answers to Gilgal in the parallelism. It demonstrates that the paramount concept of the preceding clause is the function of Gilgal as the place where Israel's sin is focused. The emphasis of the two clauses is thus not on the whole of Israel's sin (כָּל, all), but on its localization in Gilgal. שְׂנֵאתִים (I began to hate them): שָׂנֵא has a sphere of meaning that ranges from an attitude of extreme detestation to the milder attitude of simply loving a person or object less than another. In Genesis 29:31 the Lord saw that Leah was hated (שְׂנוּאָה), but verse 30 refines that statement by noting that Jacob "loved Rachel more than Leah." Here, however, the hatred is intense. עַל (Because) functions causally here as in 9:7.

---

15. The previous section (vv. 10–14) began with a tender expression of Yahweh's love. This section (vv. 15–17) begins with an affirmation of his hatred. The previous section looked back to the wilderness; this section looks back to Gilgal. Hosea views God as acting in history; thus historical events and the geographical sites where they occurred become vehicles of divine truth. The events of the exodus from Egypt spoke volumes about God, as did the events that took place in the wilderness and at Gilgal. To Hosea God's response to the people at those places forever remains as crystallized truth about the nature of God.

The prophet points an accusing finger at the town of Gilgal: "There," he says, "is all their evil." Gilgal was prominent in Israelite history in a number of instances. In Israel's early history it was the place where the people made Saul the first king of the united kingdom (1 Sam. 11:14–15); in Hosea's time it was one of the cult sites of the northern kingdom.

It is possible that Hosea castigates Gilgal because it was the place where the monarchy began. It is clear from his prophecy that Hosea had little time for the kings and princes of his day. He saw them as worthy of judgment (5:1, 10) and unwise (7:5). In 13:10–11 he delivers his strongest denunciation of the monarchy. He quotes God as saying, "I give you kings in my anger" (v. 11). This negative view of the monarchy reminds us of the prophetic tradition recorded in 1 Samuel 8:4–18 where the people's request for a king was met by Yahweh's words to Samuel, "They have not rejected you, but they have rejected me from being king over them" (v. 7, NRSV).

However, it is unlikely that this is the reason for Hosea's reference to Gilgal. It is true that the word *anger* (ʾap) depicts the attitude of God in giving them kings (13:11), and the word *hate* (śanēʾ) here describes God's anger at what occurred in Gilgal, but that does not establish a connection between the two passages. The reference to Yahweh's giving and taking kings in his anger (13:11) could well have described the instability of the monarchy that followed the death of Jeroboam II. The question "Where is your king?" (13:10) applies to the contemporary situation. We need not understand 13:10–11 to be a denunciation of the monarchy as an institution; that passage is best understood as a denunciation of the kings of Hosea's day, whose legitimacy he denies (8:4).

Hosea never elsewhere regards the institutional monarchy as the reason for God's judgment of the nation, yet here he states that the evil of Gilgal not only led to Yahweh's hatred of the people but to his punishment of them as well. Also, the poetic structure of the first two lines emphasizes Israel's wrongdoing as the cause of her misfortune; Hosea does not blame the monarchy for that (see below). We must look for another reason for Hosea's allusion to Gilgal.

Hosea refers to the town of Gilgal on two other occasions. In 4:15 he emphasizes its function as a contemporary cult site; and in 12:12 [11] he speaks of the altars and sacrifices that were aspects of the worship carried on there. Thus in the mind of the prophet, Gilgal represents the syncretistic religion of his day. Hosea never attributes Israel's downfall to anything other than her unfaithfulness to God. That is why he could say of his nation, "*All* their evil is in Gilgal," and that is why this prophecy has as its central motif Hosea's unhappy marriage to Gomer.

Hosea explains his denunciation of Gilgal in a *kî* clause in which he says, "For there I began to hate them." The function of *kî* in relating the two clauses of this line presents a serious difficulty. We understand it as a causal particle (for/because): All their evil is in Gilgal, *for* I hated them there. But this need not imply that the source of the moral wrong of the nation was God's hatred rather than a lack of moral concern on the part of the people. The causal function for *kî* would be no problem if *raʿâ* had the sense of evil as calamity (see BDB, p. 949) not moral evil. We may para-

מִבֵּיתִי (from my house) has a sense broader than the land. It is a separation from the covenant privilege that belonged to the nation because of its familial relationship with Yahweh (see the Exposition). אֲגָרְשֵׁם (I will expel them): גָּרַשׁ has several nuances in the qal, one of which is to divorce a wife (Lev. 21:7). In the piel (the stem used in Hos. 9:15) it is stronger. It is used, in part, of driving out nations from the land (Exod. 23:28, 31; Num. 22:11), of expulsion from the Lord's heritage (1 Sam. 26:19), and of expulsion from the priesthood (1 Kings 2:27). It connotes more than divorce in the piel. We are to understand Hosea here to say that the people were to be driven out from the household of God. לֹא אוֹסֵף (not . . . anymore) is literally "I will not add." We may translate it "again" in non-negative clauses, but in negative clauses "any more" is adequate. אֲהֲבָתָם (love them) connotes not only the emotional aspect of love, but the visible expression of love as well. God's

phrase this possibility, "The impending calamity springs from your cultic worship at Gilgal, *because* it is your participation in the cult that leads me to hate you."

There are several problems with this, however. Hosea never elsewhere uses *ra'â* in the sense of calamity, but always of moral evil (7:1, 2, 3, 15; 10:15), and the parallelism of *ra'â* with its companion word in the next line (*roa'*), a word that almost always connotes moral wrong (note, "wickedness of their deeds"), supports the same nuance for *ra'â* (evil) in the first line.

If we understand *ra'â* to connote moral evil, a pattern emerges in this structure of clauses. The first clause in each line affirms the moral wrong of the people. Since the second clause of the second line affirms the result of Yahweh's negative attitude toward the people (I will expel them from my house), the parallel clause in line 1 may also function as an affirmation of that attitude. In poetic language *kî* sometimes denotes proximate causation (see the discussion at 4:16), that is, it gives the reason for a thought that is not stated but implied in the preceding statement. If that is the case here, *kî* introduces the reason for a concept implicit in the wickedness of Gilgal. Since a basic concept of Hosea's theology is that sin demands requital, the concept left unstated may be that of Gilgal's destruction. This understanding of the statement about Gilgal brings it into closer relationship with its parallel line which states a specific punishment.

Since we cannot limit Yahweh's hatred of the cult of the northern kingdom to one event or a narrow period of time, we understand the perfect tense of *śĕnē'tîm* (hated) as inchoative: Yahweh *began* to hate them in Gilgal. This is the function of the perfect tense in which the effects of facts established earlier continue to the present (GKC §106g).

Gilgal may function as a metonymy for the entire cult because it was apparently one of its most important centers (Hos. 4:15; 12:12 [11]). The

words *for there I began to hate them* thus affirm Yahweh's hatred of the cultic practices carried on at Gilgal and establish the basis for the parallel clause in which the writer depicts him as expelling the people from his house.

The house of the Lord denotes the sphere of familial love and privilege. This is underscored by the next clause that states that Yahweh no longer loves the nation. Expulsion from covenant privilege involves more than losing the land; it also involves separation from God's love and the tangible acts by which that love finds expression.

Hosea does not limit the results of Israel's idolatry only to their loss of the land. In 1:9 he echoes another element of the promise to Abraham—the affirmation that the Lord would be God to his people. This promise, as well as the promise of the land, was vitiated when God said, "I will not love them anymore."

The ultimacy of this statement seems to lack consonance with the statements of hope in the prophecy (2:1–2 [1:10–11]; 2:3 [1]; 2:16–25 [14–23]; 6:2; 11:8–11; 12:10 [9]; 13:14; 14:5–8 [4–7]), but this is not a major difficulty. Rather, it serves to give greater clarity to Hosea's message. Hosea's generation would not receive the promised inheritance because of their defection from God. They would go into captivity, but beyond the long years of estrangement from God Hosea envisions a restoration of God's people in which he will interpose his love and give them abundant blessing (11:8–9; 14:5–8 [4–7]). Hosea depicts this aspect of God's gracious activity on behalf of his people in 3:1–5 where he talks about the restoration of his unfaithful wife.

The people would remain in the land only so long as they kept the terms of the Mosaic covenant. This is clear from Deuteronomy, where disobedience to the law would bring on the nation all the curses listed in 28:15–68. But God also makes it clear that the curses were not ultimate, for he would not forsake his eternal promise: "When they are in the land of their enemies, I will

withdrawal of love means the withdrawal of his demonstrations of love (cf. Gen. 37:4; Isa. 48:14). In Hosea 3:1 the command, "Go love a woman," signifies far more than the mere emotion of love. It means to demonstrate love in the act of restoring the erring woman to fellowship, and in 11:1 God's love for Israel was manifested in the exodus from Egypt. סֹרְרִים (rebels): סָרַר is not used in the Old Testament of the rebellion of nations. The emphasis is on stubbornness, hence the frequent translation of "rebellion" for the root סָרַר. It is used of a rebellious son (Deut. 21:18, 20), a stubborn generation (Ps. 78:8), and a stubborn heifer (Hos. 4:16).

16. הֻכָּה (is smitten) is used in Jonah 4:7 of a worm smiting a plant. This sustains the metaphor

established in the following words of Hosea 9:16, where Ephraim's root (שֹׁרֶשׁ) is dried up. בְּלִי (not) is read בַּל in the *qĕrē*. However, it does not seem necessary to emend to בַּל. Hosea uses בְּלִי to negate the same verb (עָשָׂה) in 8:7 (see the comments there). גַּם (Even) denotes addition, thus "moreover" is an adequate translation in many instances. With כִּי (if), however, a conditional concept is added to the argument, setting forth a hypothetical situation that lends support to it; thus "even if" reflects the Hebrew sense of the two particles in the context. כִּי (if) functions as a conditional particle (i.e., with the sense of supposing that . . . in case that [GKC §159l]). וְהֵמַתִּי (I will slay) is the causative stem of the verb *to die*, hence *to kill*. מַחֲמַדֵּי (precious things) occurs here

---

not spurn them, or abhor them so as to destroy them utterly and break my covenant with them . . . but I will remember in their favor the covenant with their ancestors, whom I brought out of the land of Egypt in the sight of the nations, to be their God: I am the LORD" (Lev. 26:44–45, NRSV).

In Paul's theology the restored people of Hosea's prophecy include redeemed Gentiles. He refers to Hosea 2:25 [23] and 2:1 [1:10] to support that (Rom. 9:25–26). This concept is consonant with a broad corpus of teaching in the Old Testament that includes Gentiles in the promise. Thus under the new covenant the people of God who stand as inheritors of the promise are redeemed Jews and Gentiles, for whom the dividing wall of hostility has been broken down (Eph. 2:14).

The statement that their princes are rebels is conceptually related to the previous clause that denies God's love to the people. The relationship is not obvious, but probably we are to understand that the leaders of the nation were, to a large extent, responsible for the change in Yahweh's attitude. They were the cause of the nation's rebellion against God. The alliteration in Hosea's characterization of the princes is striking: *śārêhem sōrĕrîm* (their princes are rebels).

The emphasis of the word *rebel* is on the princes' stubbornness. They were unwilling to adhere to Yahweh's demands. Their unbending attitude was reflected in the nation as well.

16. The denial of Yahweh's love and the stubborn rebellion of the princes led to the death of the nation. Hosea pictures this fact in a metaphor in which he likens the nation to a tree stricken by blight or harmful insects. The root of the

nation had withered; it would produce no more fruit.

The fruit in the metaphor represents future population growth, for Hosea goes on to say that even if they should produce children, those children would die. This reaffirmation of an already absolute assertion is similar to his statement earlier (see the comments on 9:12). One of the curses of Deuteronomy was on the offspring of the future generations: the fruit of the rebels' bodies will be cursed (28:18) and their children taken from them (vv. 32, 41).

The glory of the northern kingdom in the eighth century was its great population and economic prosperity. The diminution of the population meant that Israel's glory would flee (see v. 11). When Hosea says that even if they should have children the children would be slain, he may be reflecting Moses' closing song in which he said that one of the results of Israel's disobedience would be that the sword will destroy "the young man and woman alike, nursing child and old gray head" (Deut. 32:25, NRSV).

It would be straining Hosea's metaphor of the stricken nation to understand him to say that the Israelites in the Assyrian captivity would bear no children. He foresaw a restoration from the captivity (11:11) and a rebirth of the nation (14:5–8 [4–7]). Rather, the metaphor depicts the end of the nation as they knew it. The corrupt society of Hosea's day was to come to an end, never to be restored. The glory that had contributed to its false pride and its rebellion against God would perish.

Hosea, however, envisions a restoration of God's people when the population will again

in connection with בֶּטֶן (womb) designating the children, yet unborn, who were precious to the people, but who would be included in the hypothetical destruction depicted by the prophet.

17. The reason for the casting off (יִמְאָסֵם) of the people is introduced by כִּי (because). They are cast off because they have not listened (שָׁמַע) to God. "God" is construed with a first-person suffix (*my* God). It is as though God is no longer the God of the people, while remaining Hosea's God. שָׁמַע (listened) has the added sense of *obey* in many contexts, just as *listen to* has in English. Adam listened to (שָׁמַע) the voice of his wife (Gen. 3:17) and Israel's disobedience is represented as not listening to (שָׁמַע) the voice of God (Ps. 81:12 [11]). Thus because they were disobedient to Hosea's God,

his God will cast them off. לוֹ (to him) finds its nearest logical referent in אֱלֹהַי (my God). נֹדְדִים (wanderers): נָדַד has a broad range of meaning (see the Exegesis at 7:13). The contextual requirements here point to the sense of *wander* for this verb. The people are cast-offs (יִ֫מְאָסֵם, casts them off), and the context makes no reference to a threat from which they must flee. The preposition בְּ (among) channels the action of the verb to a particular sphere (גּוֹיִם, the nations). The idea of movement away is not present in the context as it would be if the writer had used מִן (from). Thus "flee" is not consonant with the contextual requirements. We must understand the word to connote the sense of wandering among the nations.

---

increase. He says in the metaphor of the tree in 14:5–8[4–7] that its shoots will spread out, an evident reference to increased propagation. We observed the same concept in 2:1–2 [1:10–11]. Isaiah uses the figure of an increase in population in his description of Israel as a barren woman who would give birth to a multitude of children (54:1), a figure that Paul applies to the church (Gal. 4:27–28). And when Jeremiah envisions the restored community, he says that God will sow "the house of Israel and the house of Judah with the seed of humans and the seed of animals" (31:27, NRSV). This metaphor depicts the numerical growth of people and animals; it asserts that the people of God will enjoy renewed blessing and glory in the restored community that inherits the promise.

17. According to Hosea the reason for the demise of the nation was their failure to obey God: "They have not listened." This assertion, like so much that we have seen in Hosea's

prophecy, is Deuteronomic in background. In fact, this section of the prophecy (9:15–17) appears to be a crystallization of Deuteronomy 28:62–64. That passage affirms the diminution of the population should they fail to obey God: "Although once you were as numerous as stars in heaven, you shall be left few in number" (v. 62, NRSV). This was the thrust of Hosea's reference to the stricken tree and the slaughter of the children. The passage bases the decimation of the nation on their failure to obey the Lord. Both passages use the word *šamaʿ* (hear) to express the called-for obedience (Deut. 28:62; Hos. 9:17).

The concept of wandering among the nations occurs in Deuteronomy as well: "The LORD will scatter you among all peoples, from one end of the earth to the other" (v. 64, NRSV). Hosea had the unhappy task of announcing to his people that the curses of Deuteronomy were soon to overtake them.

XIII. Internal Corruption of Israel (10:1–15)

A. Israel's Idolatry Increased in Proportion to Its Affluence (10:1–3)

10 Israel is a luxuriant vine,
   it established fruit for itself.
The more its fruit increased,
   the more it increased the altars;
the more its country improved,
   the more they improved pillars.
² Their heart is smooth,
   now they shall bear punishment.
He will break down their altars;
   [he] will destroy their pillars.
³ For now they shall say,
   "We have no king,
for we do not fear the LORD,
   and the king—what could he do for
     us?"

10 Israel is a luxuriant vine
   that yields its fruit.
The more his fruit increased
   the more altars he built;
as his country improved,
   he improved his pillars.
² Their heart is false;
   now they must bear their guilt.
The LORD will break down their altars,
   and destroy their pillars.
³ For now they will say:
   "We have no king,
for we do not fear the LORD,
   and a king—what could he do for
     us?"

10:1. גֶּפֶן (vine) is construed here in the masculine as indicated by בֹּקֵק (luxuriant), which is masculine, and also by the masculine construction of לֹו (for itself), which refers back to גֶּפֶן (vine). This is the only place in the Old Testament where גֶּפֶן is masculine. This may be a dialectical peculiarity of Hosea's, but more likely it is an indication that the nation of Israel was more in his mind than was the metaphorical vine. בֹּקֵק (luxuriant): The basic sense of the root בָּקַק is *to empty*. It refers to destructive forces that will empty the land of Babylon (Jer. 51:2); it refers to plunderers (Nah. 2:3 [2]); בָּקַק connotes counsel that is made void (emptied, Jer. 19:7). This word does not occur elsewhere with reference to a vine. We may not conclude, however, that because it has the sense of empty that it depicts a vine devoid of fruit and foliage. On the contrary, we are told in the next line that it produces fruit. We must understand this word metaphorically in the sense of emptying, spilling forth, overflowing, luxuriant. יְשַׁוֶּה (it established): There are two roots שָׁוָה in Hebrew. One has the sense of *to smooth* in the piel; the other, which occurs only in the piel, denotes *to set* or *place* (see 2 Sam. 22:34; Ps. 16:8). Neither of these senses appears to be appropriate to Hosea's analogy of the vine. The Septuagint reads εὐθηνῶν (thrive, flourish), but this seems to be a paraphrase. The denotation *to smooth* does not fit the imagery of the vine, so we must work from the other root, *to set*. In each instance where שָׁוָה (established) has the sense of placing or putting the translation "fix" or "establish" is also appropriate. The psalmist *fixed* the Lord before him (Ps. 16:8); the Lord *fixed* the psalmist's feet like a deer's feet (Ps. 18:34 [33]). Hosea evidently does not want to express the idea of producing fruit in this metaphor. He expresses that idea in 8:7 and 9:16 by using the verb עָשָׂה (do, make) with an appropriate object. The sense of the idiom in 10:1 is to fix or establish fruit on the vine's branches. לֹו (for itself/for himself) has a reflexive function that underscores the fact that the nation did this with its own interests in view. כְּרֹב (the more . . . increased) sets up a comparison between the noun רֹב (increased) and the statement concerning the altars. The Hebrew says literally, "According to the abundance of its fruit it increased altars." We have translated רֹב (abundance) as a verb for sake of clarity. לְפִרְיֹו (its fruit): לְ has a possessive function that unites the noun *abundance* and the word *fruit*. הִרְבָּה (it increased) is in the third person. Its subject is obviously Israel, because the object is altars. Hosea has moved beyond the figure of the vine to speak of the reality behind it. לְ occurs frequently with verbs in the hiphil to designate the object of the verb. כְּטֹוב (the more . . . improved) introduces a comparative clause that says literally, "As good [came] to his land, they caused altars to be good." The idea of the com-

---

10:1. The analogy of a vine occurs in several places in the Bible. We recall Isaiah's use of that metaphor (chap. 5) and the familiar use of the same figure by Jesus (John 15). In each of these metaphors the emphasis is on the fruit. Jesus spoke of the necessity of bearing fruit, and Isaiah pictured Israel as a vine that bore fruit not fit for eating. Hosea uses the analogy to picture the fruits of the affluent society of his time.

There is no moral judgment made on this fruit by Hosea. Affluence is not wrong in itself, for Moses predicted blessing on the fruit of the body and field should the people be obedient (Deut. 28:4, 11), and he noted that great wealth was to go hand-in-hand with obedience: "You will lend to many nations, but you will not borrow" (v. 12, NRSV).

Hosea's deep concern is that as the nation became more affluent in the eighth century, it became more idolatrous. Instead of expressing their gratitude to God in greater dedication to the principles of Yahwism and an ever-deepening response of the heart to Yahweh, the people expressed their devotion at pagan shrines and sought further affluence from the images of Baal. The nation was like a luxuriant vine in that the people enjoyed great economic prosperity. The fruit represents the visible evidence of their national welfare.

The vine had established this fruit for itself. This statement does not appear to be an appropriate metaphor, for the word *šawâ* (fix) does not occur elsewhere to describe the production of fruit. But we must remember that the fruit in Hosea's imagery stands for the symbols of Israel's wealth and power. It appears that the nation, not the vine, is uppermost in his mind when he speaks of the fruit. He does not set forth his metaphor by first speaking of the characteristics of a vine and then going on to present the lesson borne by the analogy. He mixes these elements almost immediately. We know from the masculine suffixes that it was the nation that had fixed for itself these symbols of affluence. Hosea may

parative structure is that, to the extent the land enjoyed prosperity, altars were improved. טוֹב (good) has the sense of economic and political welfare because it describes the nation. The word has this sense in Deuteronomy 26:11, where it occurs in the account of the triennial tithe, "And you shall rejoice in all the good [טוֹב] which the LORD your God has given to you" (RSV, see also Deut. 30:9). הֵיטִיבוּ (they improved) is the hiphil (causative) of יָטַב (be good). When used with an object, the verb means to do good to the object in a way appropriate to the parameters of the context. It has the sense of making the lamps of the temple good (i.e., trimming them, Exod. 30:7). It is also used of adorning the head (2 Kings 9:30). The sense of the statement in Hosea 10:1 is that as conditions in the country improved, the people were more diligent in keeping up the altars and improving them. מַצֵּבוֹת (pillars) does not always connote objects of pagan worship. It refers to a memorial (2 Sam. 18:18), a grave marker (Gen. 35:20), tribal representations (Exod. 24:4), and a sign attesting the validity of an agreement (Gen. 31:45). In pagan worship these largely unshaped pillars were closely associated with the deities. The fact that the word is indefinite (pillars, not *the* pillars or *their* pillars) is significant. The indefiniteness of the noun places emphasis on pillars as an entity, not specific pillars. The people did not use their wealth for the improvement of the lot of the poor, but to improve pillars. The irony is evident.

2. חָלַק (smooth) occurs mainly in a figurative sense in the Old Testament, but the literal connotation appears in the hiphil with the sense of smoothing metal with a hammer (Isa. 41:7). Figuratively it connotes smooth speech (Ps. 55:22 [21]) that masks the true intent of the heart, hence, deceptive speech. The adjectival form (חָלָק) conveys the same concept in several instances. It describes deceptive speech (Prov. 5:3), and it occurs in parallel with לְשׁוֹן־שֶׁקֶר (a lying tongue, Prov. 26:28). חָלָק (smooth) is used in Ezekiel 12:24 to denote a flattering prophecy. When applied to לִבָּם (their heart), which refers to the seat of cogitation, it indicates that the people were false and deceptive at the very core of the mental processes which direct thought and determine action. עַתָּה (now) indicates the imminency of the action of the following verb. יֶאְשָׁמוּ (they shall bear punishment): אָשַׁם may connote committing an offense as well as being guilty of an offense. It is similar to other words for sin that include within their range of meaning both the act of disobedience and the incurring of guilt or punishment (see the comments at 1:4). The context determines how the reader should understand the sense. This verb is in the imperfect tense, which indicates incomplete action. Since עַתָּה (now) indicates the starting point of the continuing action of the verb, its verbal action is inceptive. אָשַׁם (bear punishment) thus cannot have the primary sense of committing sin, because that was already true of the people and the perfect tense would better express that idea. The sense of punishment for sin is more appropriate to the future perspective of the verbal action (imperfect tense) and to the subsequent context which depicts divine judgment on the cult cen-

---

have wished to reflect the fact that the people thought their new-found wealth and national prestige were permanent institutions that they had established for themselves.

Under the new covenant, material wealth is not an indication of divine blessing. It was so under the old covenant because the inheritance of the people included the physical territory of Canaan as well as the status of nationhood. It followed naturally that the disposition of the inheritance and the experience of the people within the boundaries of the land involved physical blessing. Under the new covenant, however, the people of God are a spiritual people (1 Pet. 2:5) who belong to a kingdom that is not limited to geographical boundaries (John 18:36). The inheritance of believers is in heavenly places (Eph. 2:4–7) and their blessings are spiritual blessings (Eph. 1:3).

2. As Hosea observed the growing affluence of his nation it seemed to him that pagan altars were multiplying in proportion to the increase in the nation's wealth. He observed also that the pillars at the pagan shrines became more ornate as the nation became richer. There was only one conclusion that he could reach: Because the nation was deceitful at its very heart, it was ripe for punishment.

Hosea focuses the impending display of divine wrath on the visible symbols of the cult, its altars and pillars, the very things to which the people gave attention in the midst of their luxury. God will literally "break the neck" of their altars. If he intended to convey the full sense of this verb, he might have meant it in a way similar to our "break the back of," which connotes an absolute end to something, such as the military power of a nation.

ters (v. 2b). הוּא (He) logically refers to God, although the last reference to God occurs in 9:17 (My God). יַעֲרֹף (break down) is the verbal affinity of the noun עֹרֶף (neck) and occurs elsewhere only with the sense of breaking the neck of an animal. There is no reason, however, why Hosea could not have used the word in an expanded sense to express more forcefully and creatively the fact that the altars were to be broken down. Micah uses the word נָשַׁךְ (bite) in a similar way (3:5). Apart from its secondary connotation of paying interest, this verb connotes the biting of a serpent. Micah appears to use the word in the sense of biting to describe the way the greedy false prophets of his day voraciously accepted the bribes given to them for their prophetic activity. His use of the word in this way thus imparts a peculiar force to the narrative. Perhaps Hosea uses עֹרֶף in the same way. There is a finality about breaking the neck of an animal, which Hosea might have wished to transfer to the destruction of Israel's altars. The use of the word in parallel with שָׁדַד (destroy) underscores the ultimacy of the destruction of the altars and pillars.

3. כִּי (For) does not introduce direct causation. It bears a causal relationship to the preceding con-

text, but only in the broadest sense. It introduces a circumstance caused by the preceding depiction of doom—because the nation will be destroyed, they will have no king. עַתָּה (now) is used on several other occasions by Hosea to introduce impending judgment (5:7; 8:10, 13). יֹאמְרוּ (they shall say) has the same referent as the plural suffixes of the preceding clauses, that is, the people. אֵין (no) is a particle of nonexistence. לָנוּ (we have) is literally "to us." The לְ is possessive. כִּי (for) is causative and introduces the reason for their not having a king. It is because they do not fear the Lord. יָרֵאנוּ (we . . . fear) continues the words of the people. It is imperfect and thus connotes continuing action. See the Exposition for a discussion of the significance of this word. וְ (and) on הַמֶּלֶךְ (the king) is conjunctive, establishing a logical relationship between its clause and the series of clauses that precede it. הַמֶּלֶךְ (the king) is definite. Several functions are possible for the article: it may designate a specific king, it may connote a class, or it may indicate that a person or thing spoken of earlier has become more definite to the mind of the speaker (see GKC §126). The context must determine its function (see the Exposition).

---

3. We have understood the *kî* that introduces this verse to have a general causal connection to the preceding clause (see the Exegesis). The repetition of the word *now* is resumptive; it takes up the thought of ʿattâ (now) in verse 2, and is in apposition with it. The thought is, "Now they shall bear punishment . . . now they shall say, 'We have no king.'" This appositional function places both actions governed by ʿattâ (now) in the same time period. The first action is the nation's punishment, which will begin when the altars and pillars are demolished. The second action is the acknowledgment of the people that they have no king. The destruction of the symbols of their syncretistic worship will be contemporaneous with the abolishment of the monarchy. This happened when Assyria conquered the northern kingdom.

The observation that they have no king is followed by another *kî* (for) clause in which the people state the reason for this situation: "For we do not fear the LORD." In the turmoil surrounding the collapse of the monarchy the people will acknowledge that they have been unfaithful to their God, and that their failure to fear him is the cause of their national distress. This acknowledgment will come too late, however. Their hearts were so deceptive and their eyes so blind that it

took the loss of everything they owned and cherished to bring them to acknowledge that their national stability and welfare depended on their relationship to God.

The word *yārēʾ* (fear) represents a complex concept in Hebrew. Awe is a factor in fear (Ps. 33:8); it involves turning from evil (Job 28:28; Prov. 8:13). Humble obedience (Jer. 26:19) and deep and genuine piety (Gen. 22:12) are also factors. Fear in the strict sense of the word is involved as well (Exod. 20:20). In short, fear involves turning from evil to a relationship with God that involves submission, awe, and fear of offending him.

The people will also acknowledge that their trust in a king failed them in the long run. Hosea represents the people as saying, "And the king—what could he do for us?" The article on *melek* (king) is best explained as indicating that the word was definite in the thought of the narrator or speaker(s); in this case the people (see *bassēper* in 1 Sam. 10:25; *hayyôm* in 2 Kings 4:8). The people living at the time of the fall of the monarchy would naturally have the last reigning king in mind as they evaluated the worth of a king. The thought seems to be, "We have no king now. But what could the king have done to save us anyway?"

161

Another possible interpretation of the statement of the people is that it was uttered in sarcasm before the actual collapse of the monarchy. As the people viewed the increasing weakness and instability of their monarchical system it may have seemed that they had no king. But this is unlikely.

We observed in the Exegetical section that Hosea uses 'attâ (now) to introduce impending judgment. The words "now they shall say, 'we have no king,'" coupled with their acknowledgment that they do not fear the Lord, are more a statement of painful regret than of biting irony.

XIII. Internal Corruption of Israel (10:1–15)

B. Israel's Society Was Riddled with Dishonesty
and Deceit (10:4–6)

4 They speak empty words,
    taking false oaths, making covenants,
so justice springs up like bitter weeds
    in the furrows of the field.
5 The inhabitants of Samaria will be
    afraid
    for the calves of Beth-aven,
for its people will mourn for it,
    its priests [will mourn] for it as well.
    They shall tremble over its glory,
    because it has departed from it.
6 Moreover, it will be carried to Assyria,
    a tribute to the king of Yareb.
Shame will seize Ephraim,
    and Israel shall be ashamed of its
    counsel.

4 They utter mere words;
    with empty oaths they make cov-
    enants;
so litigation springs up like poisonous
    weeds
    in the furrows of the field.
5 The inhabitants of Samaria tremble
    for the calf of Beth-aven.
Its people shall mourn for it,
    and its idolatrous priests shall wail
    over it,
    over its glory that has departed from
    it.
6 The thing itself shall be carried to
    Assyria
    as tribute to the great king.
Ephraim shall be put to shame,
    and Israel shall be ashamed of his
    idol.

4. דִּבְּרוּ (They speak): In all likelihood the subject of this verb is the people, not the king. It is possible to construe מֶלֶךְ (king) as the subject of this verb. Hosea could have shifted from the singular to the plural to express the corporate concept of monarchy (he was not always precise in his grammatical expression), and what is said in the next line about oaths and covenants applies appropriately to the responsibilities of kings. The plural constructions of the verbs in the contexts immediately preceding and following this verse, however, clearly represent the people. The words אָלָה (oath) and בְּרִית (covenant) do not apply specifically to the monarchy in Hosea, but to the nation (see the Exposition). Hosea's observation, "They speak empty words," is consonant with his accusation against the people, "Their heart is smooth" (v. 2). דְּבָרִים (empty words) completes a collocation (speak words) that apparently means to speak *only* words, hence words devoid of substance, "empty words." The same expression occurs in Isaiah 58:13 (lit. speaking a word) which the Revised Standard Version translates "talking idly." אָלוֹת (taking . . . oaths) is pointed either as the plural of the noun אָלָה (oath) or the infinitive absolute of אָלָה (to swear or curse). The Revised Standard Version understands it in the former sense (with empty oaths they make covenants). The problem is difficult, but it seems best to regard אָלוֹת as an infinitive absolute by analogy with the following infinitive absolute כָּרֹת (making). If it is construed as an infinitive absolute, the unusual spelling (normally אָלֹה) may be phonetically analogous to כָּרֹת. We may observe this phenomenon

in Psalm 32:1, in the unusual spelling of the participle נְשׂוּי (lifted), which is analogous to כְּסוּי (covered). כָּרֹת (making) describes an action (making covenants) which is not intrinsically wrong, yet the other actions in the line (speaking empty words and taking false oaths) are morally wrong. We can understand this structure best if we regard כָּרֹת בְּרִית (making covenants) as a *casus adverbialis*, a grammatical function in which the infinitive absolute defines more precisely the manner in which the action of the main verb is performed (see GKC §113i). That is, the verbal actions of speaking empty words and taking false oaths are more precisely defined by the infinitive absolute (כָּרֹת) as part of the process of making covenants. When the people of Hosea's day took on the obligations of a covenantal agreement, it was apparently not uncommon for them to do so by making meaningless affirmations and swearing oaths they did not intend to keep. וּפָרַח (so . . . springs up): Except for its metaphorical usages, this verb describes the sprouting or budding of vegetation. In Hosea it refers to the blossoming of a lily (14:6 [5]), and a vine (14:8 [7]). רֹאשׁ (bitter weeds) has the basic sense of bitterness when used of vegetation, but it also connotes the idea of poisonous. In several passages it is associated with the venom of a serpent. The word occurs in association with לַעֲנָה (wormwood), a bitter but not necessarily poisonous plant in Deuteronomy 29:17 [18] (see also Jer. 9:14 [15]; 23:15; Lam. 3:19; Amos 6:12). In Deuteronomy 32:32 it occurs in parallel with the noun מְרֹרָה (bitter thing), and in Psalm 69:22 [21] it is in parallel with חֹמֶץ (vinegar). In Jeremiah 8:14

---

4. The impending judgment on Israel receives further amplification in this section where the calf of Bethel is the focus of Hosea's denunciation. It will be taken to Assyria as tribute to the Assyrian king (v. 6).

The passage begins with the basis for the judgment. The people spoke "empty words" when they took oaths and entered into covenants. We understand this accusation to be directed to the nation, not to the king alone (see the Exegesis). It is thus in keeping with the description of the people's dissimulation (v. 2) and continues the series of accusations that emerges from Hosea's figure of the vine (v. 1). Hosea accuses the people of insincerely taking oaths (4:2) and it is "Ephraim" who makes a *bĕrît* (covenant) with Assyria (12:2 [1]). The accusation of 4:2 is in a litany of societal wrongs of which the people were guilty. There seems to be no indication in the prophecy that

Israel's dishonesty in the matter of covenants extended to the international sphere. The political alliances with Assyria were probably quite sincere efforts to shore up the tottering national structure. There is no indication in 12:2 [1] that Israel's pact (*bĕrît*) with Assyria was necessarily devious. Hosea condemns only the fact that it had been made.

With the society riddled with dishonesty and deceit, we are not surprised to read that "justice springs up like bitter weeds." The word *mišpāṭ* (justice) denotes the crystallization of the law's ethic and intent. In Hosea's metaphor he pictures justice as bitter, noxious weeds growing in the furrows where grain should have grown. These weeds, repulsive to the taste, represent perverted justice. True justice would have been like grain nourishing and sustaining the nation; the per-

the context may require the concept of poisonous water because of the references to death. The context of Hosea 10:4, however, does not appear to require the sense of poisonous, although the Hebrew may have associated the concepts of bitter and poisonous. מִשְׁפָּט (justice): In Hosea this word has the connotation of justice (2:21 [19]; 12:7 [6]) as well as judgment (5:1, 11). The former sense is more likely here because it is consonant with the previous clause in which the words have ethical content. If Hosea intends the word to refer to the impending judgment, his picture of weeds growing unchecked in a field hardly represents that concept. The captivity was a cataclysmic event (see 7:12) that the slow growth of weeds would not properly represent. In verse 5 he speaks of the departure of the glory of Samaria's calf, an evident reference to the captivity. If we understand מִשְׁפָּט to refer to judgment (divine punishment) current in Hosea's society as a result of the prevalence of the evils cited in the first line of this verse, there is no logical connection between that and the cataclysmic judgment about which we read in the subsequent context. It is best to understand the word to refer to the bitter results of the lack of social justice and equity that resulted from the specious affirmations common in the legal transactions of Hosea's day. מִשְׁפָּט (justice) is not limited only to kings or other judicial officials in the Prophets. When used in the sense of right or justice, the prophets most frequently apply it to the people.

5. לְעֶגְלוֹת (calves) is a feminine plural, while its syntactical referents in the next line are masculine singular. The Septuagint construes the word in the singular. When used of calves as objects of worship the word never elsewhere occurs as a feminine (see 8:6). If this is not a dialectical peculiarity of Hosea's, the feminine construction of the word may point to a syntactical function for the feminine plural. The feminine frequently expresses abstract concepts in Hebrew (GKC §122q). The plural also relates to the expression of abstract concepts (GKC §124a, d–f). It may express the concept of combining elements in a particular thing (Davidson, *Syntax* §16b). It also functions as a plural of eminence or majesty. In the former usage of the plural, the plural nouns are unusual traits and are rarely concrete. Since עֶגְלוֹת (calves) is not a trait or attribute but a concrete noun, it is likely that it falls into the latter category in which the idea of the singular is intensified by the plural (see Davidson, *Syntax* §16c; GKC §124g–i). It is unlikely that Hosea would have sincerely attributed majesty to Bethel's calf, but he could have done so sarcastically. בֵּית אָוֶן (Beth-aven) is a surrogate for Bethel (see 4:15). יָגוּרוּ (will be afraid) could also be read "will dwell" or "sojourn," and is so understood by the Septuagint, which reads παροικήσουσιν (dwell near). But this translation makes little sense in the context, and the collocation (לְעֶגְלוֹת) גּוּר לְ does not occur in the Old Testament with this sense. It is best to understand the root to be גוּר in the sense of dread or awe. When used with מִן (from/of), the expression has the sense of to be afraid of. The use of לְ must indicate the idea of fear *for.* This is substantiated by the context, which indicates that some cata-

verted execution of the law in Hosea's day could bring only harm to the nation.

Hosea's warning to his people has relevance today. If those at the highest levels of government deceive the people and promise to carry out policies they do not intend to implement, the foundations of democratic rule are weakened, for the people have no firm basis on which to make political decisions. Deceit is as dangerous an element in government affairs today as when Hosea denounced it.

5. We must not lose sight of the fact that the larger context has to do with Israel's affluence and her devotion to the elements of pagan worship. These themes are inherent in the metaphor of the luxuriant vine (v. 1). They continue throughout the pericope as here Hosea singles out the central element of Israel's syncretistic worship—the calf. Hosea uses the metaphor of the vine as the basis

for his depiction of Israel's falseness of heart (v. 2). This lack of integrity found its expression not only in their deviant worship, but also in their personal affairs; their word could not be trusted. Hosea could include the reference to their empty words along with the account of the demise of Bethel's calf, because they were both expressions of the spiritual sickness that the nation suffered even as it continued to prosper economically.

Because the calf was a focus of their deceit, it was to become the object of God's wrath. We see an element of sarcasm in the word *calf,* for Hosea puts it in the plural. If this is the plural of majesty, he may have intended to say, "This *great* calf will be taken to Assyria." Then the devotees of the calf would tremble in fear because of the calf of Bethel. The irony of the people fearing for the fate of a calf to which they attributed deity and power

clysm will overtake the calf worship of Israel. שֹׁכֵן (inhabitants) is an adjective which, in this context, describes one who lives in Samaria, hence an inhabitant (see Isa. 33:24). It likely does not connote the calves as resident in Samaria, for the writer could have expressed that thought unequivocably by affixing לְ to שֹׁכֵן (inhabitants) to carry forward the dative sense. It is unusual for Hosea to make a change of subject without indicating it in some fashion. If שֹׁכֵן (inhabitants) refers to the calves there is no subject stated for the verb יָגוּרוּ (they fear). There is, however, if we construe שֹׁכֵן (inhabitants) as the subject of the verb. The poetic complement of שֹׁכֵן (inhabitants) is עַם (people) in the second line. This supports the view that the people are the subject of the plural verb יָגוּרוּ (be afraid). כִּי (for) does not appear to introduce a causal relationship between the clauses. Mourning for the calf of Bethel is not a cause or reason for the fear spoken about in the first clause. Scholars frequently explain כִּי here as asseverative (yes). While כִּי has this function in oath formulas or conditional clauses, its function in ordinary clauses may encompass a broader range of causality than that to which the Western mind is accustomed. For example, כִּי may introduce the reason for a thought that is implicit, not expressed, in the previous clause. The fact that the worshipers of the calves will mourn (אָבַל) for them strongly implies that the calves will come to an end. This is a sufficient (if indirect) reason for the statement of the previous clause that the people of Samaria will fear for the calf. עָלָיו (for it): The suffix (ו) is masculine singular, but its referent עֶגְלוֹת (calves) is feminine plural. This appears to support the view that שֹׁכֵן (inhabitants) refers to the calves, not the inhabitants of Samaria. שֹׁכֵן is, after all, a singular adjective, but the interchange of grammatical indicators is common in Hosea. For example, in 8:4 the singular verb יִכָּרֵת (it may be destroyed) has as its subject the plural noun עֲצַבִּים (idols). In 11:4 the grammatical indicators which find their

referent in Israel shift from plural to singular in the last instance (אֵלָיו, him). If we are correct in concluding that the plural construction of עֶגְלוֹת (calves) in the first line is the plural of majesty, the singular grammatical constructions in the second line may indicate that Hosea views the calf as a single entity when he refers to it in the intensive plural (plural of majesty). Note the similar phenomenon in 1 Samuel 19:16, where the noun תְּרָפִים (gods) governs a singular suffix (מְרַאֲשֹׁתָיו). עַמּוֹ (its people), that is, its (the calf's) devotees: The word עַם denotes followers (Gen. 14:16; 32:8; Judg. 3:18; 8:5; 2 Sam. 15:17; Jer. 41:13–14). וּכְמָרָיו (its priests) is not the usual word for priest (כֹּהֵן), but designates only idolatrous priests. It occurs only two other times in the Old Testament (2 Kings 23:5; Zeph. 1:4). יָגִילוּ (they shall tremble) finds its logical referent in כְּמָרָיו (its priests). It commonly has the sense of rejoice, but that cannot be so here. We must understand the word to have the sense of tremble, a connotation it has in Psalm 2:11 (but see the conjectural emendation in BHS). כִּי (because) introduces the reason for the trembling and mourning of the previous statements. גָּלָה (it has departed): It is best to understand the subject of this verb to be כְּבוֹדוֹ (its glory) which has departed from the calf, rather than understanding it to be the calf itself which has departed from the people. The suffix on מִמֶּנּוּ (from it) requires a third masculine singular referent. It is possible that Hosea sees the referent of the singular suffix as "the people" viewed collectively, but this is unlikely. The people are represented only in the plural construction of the verb יָגִילוּ (they shall tremble), not in pronominal representation. Suffixes most frequently refer to substantives that are given concrete representation. The masculine singular suffix most naturally refers to the singular כְּבוֹד (glory), which also is masculine. גָּלָה is the word that heads the clause, and has the basic sense of depart, but frequently has the sense of going into exile (see, e.g., Isa. 5:13; Jer. 52:27; Amos 6:7; Mic. 1:16). The perfect tense denotes

---

is apparent. Hosea disparages Bethel by calling it "house of evil," as he did earlier (4:15; 5:8).

Hosea eloquently depicts the fear and sorrow of the devotees of the calf. His description goes to the heart of pagan religion and exposes it for what it is. Reliance on symbols of religion as a means of achieving access to the deity they represented would no longer be accessible if those symbols were destroyed. Traditional Yahwism taught the pure spirituality of God and forbade the use of any

type of visible representation of him (Exod. 20:4–6). Hosea's words remind us of the superstitious dependence on the ark of the covenant (1 Sam. 4:3–11) which Jeremiah roundly denounced centuries later (7:12).

The people will mourn the departure of the calf's glory. They had elevated the shaped mass of metal to the level of deity. When Assyrian soldiers carried the lifeless image away from Samaria, the people no longer saw glory in what had been

completed action—the captivity is certain although it has not occurred in actuality. There is an apparent play on words in the use of יָגִילוּ (tremble) and גָּלָה (depart).

6. גַּם (Moreover) is a connective particle that denotes addition; it connects its clause with the preceding and adds further clarification. It tells us that not only will the calf's glory depart, but also (גַּם) the calf itself (see below). אוֹתוֹ (it): The masculine suffix on the sign of the direct object sustains the reference to the calf in the suffix of מִמֶּנּוּ (from it) in the previous verse, which is the nearest logical referent. The focus shifts from the removal of the calf's glory to the removal of the calf itself. The suffix cannot refer to the noun כָּבוֹד (glory) because of the impossibility of presenting such an intangible thing in tribute to a king. מֶלֶךְ יָרֵב (the king of Yareb): See the comments at 5:13. בָּשְׁנָה (Shame) occurs only here. The form of the word is analogous to a feminine noun form of a root בָּשָׁן. However, such a word is unattested. Since the companion concept in the parallel structure is "be ashamed" (יֵבוֹשׁ), we may understand the word to be a form of בּוֹשׁ (be ashamed). The ending נָה, however, cannot be satisfactorily explained. It may be dialectical. Andersen and Freedman (*Hosea*, p. 557) explain it as possibly of "Hosean coinage," and point to אֶתְנָה in 2:14 (12), which also occurs only in Hosea. מֵעֲצָתוֹ (its counsel): עֵצָה has the basic sense of advice. It is unlikely that the suffix refers to the calf, since עֵצָה (counsel) is never used of a pagan deity, and we do not know that counsel was ever sought from the calf. The word has several nuances in the Old Testament; it connotes the counsel that shapes national policies (Deut. 32:28; Jer. 19:7), personal advice (2 Sam. 15:31; 1 Kings 12:8), and a philosophy of life that one may urge on others (Ps. 1:1; Prov. 1:30). Basically it denotes advice which is intended to be followed. We may observe this sense to one degree or another in all its occurrences. Since the subject of the two parallel clauses is Israel, the suffix on עֵצָה (counsel) most naturally refers to the nation (designated "Ephraim" in the first clause). The nature of Israel's shame is thus more narrowly defined in the parallel clause as shame for her counsel, that is, the unwise national policies that the nation followed. These policies led ultimately to its downfall. בּוֹשׁ . . . מִן is a collocation meaning "to be ashamed of" (Zech. 13:4).

---

the object of their revels and religious devotion. There was no glory in a symbol of deity that foreigners could take captive to their land.

6. That land was Assyria. The very land with which they sought alliance was to become the land that received their calf as tribute. Again we encounter the title *Yareb* for Assyria. Perhaps there is a note of irony in the two contexts in which this appellation occurs. The name may signify "contend" (or let him contend). Earlier Hosea said the people sought help from the king of this country that would eventually contend with them (5:13). Here Hosea may picture the way in which Assyria would contend—by taking them and their calf into captivity.

It is when the calf is carried off that shame will seize them. It is ironic that shame did not seize the people when they consorted with the brazen cult prostitutes, or violated the purity of their traditions, or lied and cheated for profit. It was only when they saw the end result of their folly that they were ashamed. They had learned too late. Their international policies and their worship of the forces of nature had led them to ultimate shame and degradation.

XIII. Internal Corruption of Israel (10:1–15)

C. Israel's Idolatry Will Lead to the Demise of Her King (10:7–8)

7 Samaria—her king shall be brought to
an end
like a splinter on the surface of the
water,
8 and the high places of Awen—the sin of
Israel—
shall be destroyed.
Thorns and thistles shall spring up on
their altars;
and they shall cry to the mountains,
"Cover us,"
and to the hills, "Fall on us."

7 Samaria's king shall perish
like a chip on the face of the waters.
8 The high places of Aven, the sin of
Israel,
shall be destroyed.
Thorn and thistle shall grow up
on their altars.
They shall say to the mountains, Cover
us,
and to the hills, Fall on us.

7. נִדְמֶה (shall be brought to an end) is pointed as a participle in the Masoretic Text, but this form seems to be an anomaly among the finite verbs in this section. The consonants permit our constructing the verb also as a third masculine singular perfect and this is probably the better reading. The sense of the clause is that Samaria will be cut off with reference to her king, or, as we have translated it, "Samaria—her king shall be cut off." Hosea uses the same construction in 9:11: "Ephraim—their glory will fly away like a bird" (see the comments there). It pronounces judgment on Samaria, but focuses specifically on the ruler. This depicts Samaria's collapse in terms of the cessation of the monarchy. The masculine gender of the verb seems inappropriate for שֹׁמְרוֹן (Samaria), which is identified as a feminine noun by the feminine suffix on מַלְכָּהּ (its king). But the masculine is the preferred gender for compound nouns (GKC §145o). If we understand this verb as a perfect, it differs from the sequence of the imperfect verbs in this context. But this is adequately explained by Davidson: "the imagination suddenly conceives the act as accomplished, and interjects a perf. amidst a number of imperfs." (*Syntax* §41b). The word דָּמָה has the sense of *to cease.* Thus we are to think in terms of the cessation of the monarchy. There is no hint of conflict or assassination in the word. קֶצֶף (splinter) occurs only here. A form קְצָפָה occurs in Joel 1:7, however, where it describes the splintering of a tree; thus "splinter" or "chip" is an appropriate translation.

8. וְנִשְׁמְדוּ (and . . . shall be destroyed): שָׁמַד carries the sense of severe (and sometimes permanent) destruction. It refers mainly to the destruction of persons and so its use here is appropriate to Israel's king (or the monarchy as an entity). בָּמוֹת (high places): בָּמָה (of which בָּמוֹת is the feminine plural) has the basic sense of height. It connotes pagan sanctuaries (Jer. 7:31; Ezek. 20:29), a place of security (Deut. 32:13; Hab. 3:19), and the place of military advantage (Deut. 33:29; Ezek. 36:2). There is no question about its meaning here. Hosea predicts the destruction of the pagan centers of worship. אָוֶן (Aven) is the surrogate for Bethel that Hosea uses in 4:15 and 5:8. Here in 10:8 it occurs without בֵּית (house). Even though אָוֶן (evil) stands alone, it still recalls the derogatory name given to the city by Hosea. The omission of בֵּית here lends a starkness to the word, which underscores its connotation of evil.

---

7. Not only would the calf of Bethel come to an end, but the monarchy as well. Hosea pictures the dissolution of the monarchy in a metaphor based on aspects of nature. This type of analogy is typical of Hosea. We see in our minds a splinter of wood carried along on the undulating surface of a stream. The splinter cannot resist the force of the water's flow; it is totally at the mercy of the stream. The current carries it along until it is out of sight. So will the monarchy of Israel disappear from history, helplessly carried off by the military forces of a foreign power.

This analogy recalls the words of the prophet where the people bemoaned the loss of their king (10:3). The themes of the motif of the luxuriant vine evidently continue throughout the section. We learn here more about the loss of their king. We do not need to regard the word *melek* (king) to be "a title for the bull image" (vv. 5–6, see Mays, *Hosea,* p. 142). While this suggestion establishes a positive continuity with verse 6, references to pagan worship and the monarchy are intertwined throughout the sermon on the vine. Hosea refers to pagan altars and pillars (vv. 1–2), he depicts the national mourning over the collapse of the monarchy (v. 3), and he reverts back to the pagan worship as he depicts the fate of the image of the bull (v. 8). The reference to the king (v. 7) is thus not out of keeping with the pattern of the oracle of the vine.

8. The prediction of the destruction of the high places in this verse continues the pattern of alternating references to the king and to the cult. In his denunciation of Israel's pagan worship Hosea moves from the image of the calf that occupied a prominent place in Bethel to the high places scattered throughout the countryside. A high place was a pagan shrine that generally consisted of an altar on an elevated site, usually within or near a grove of trees. A pillar representing Baal probably dominated most of these sites. The destruction of these symbols of the fertility cult presaged the end of the cult in Israel. The nation was to fall along with the pagan ideology that led to its demise.

These symbols of Israel's devotion to the cult were not to endure only temporary damage, for weeds would grow over the scattered stones that once formed the pagan altars. In years to come the places where pagan shrines once stood would be only weed-grown patches, and the pillars that represented Baal would be eroded by time and hid-

חַטַּאת (the sin of): Hosea designates the high places of wickedness as "Israel's sin." It is as though he focuses all Israel's guilt, misfortune, and wrongdoing on the hated fertility cult. וְדַרְדַּר קוֹץ (thorns and thistles) occur together also in Genesis 3:18, where they depict an aspect of the curse that God pronounced on the earth. Perhaps Hosea has this in mind when he describes Israel's

devastation, but in all likelihood he intends only to convey a picture of ruined altars overgrown with weeds. וְאָמְרוּ (and they shall cry): אָמַר denotes the verbal expression of thought (say) with no inherent emotive nuances. The desperate plight of the people who ask the hills to crush them, however, warrants a stronger translation (cry).

---

den by thorns and thistles. This is the lot of all ideologies that are not anchored in the eternal God.

Hosea refers specifically to the high places of Awen, that is, Bethel. He focuses his attention on the center of Israel's idolatry. The word *bamôt* (high places) probably included the shrine of the calf, as well as the sanctuaries and shrines that

may have existed outside the city and on its streets.

When this cataclysm occurs, the people will cry to the mountains and the hills to fall on them and crush them. This vivid motif depicts the wish of the people to escape the events of the coming captivity by perishing and thus ending their suffering (see also Luke 23:30; Rev. 6:16).

XIII. Internal Corruption of Israel (10:1-15)

D. The Spirit of "Gibeah" Continues in Israel
(10:9-10)

9 From the days of Gibeah you have
sinned, O Israel;
there they have remained.
War against the sons of violence did
not overtake them in Gibeah.
10 In my desire I will chastise them,
and nations shall be gathered against
them
when they bind [them] before their
two eyes.

9 Since the days of Gibeah you have
sinned, O Israel;
there they have continued.
Shall not war overtake them in
Gibeah?
10 I will come against the wayward people
to punish them;
and nations shall be gathered against
them
when they are punished for their
double iniquity.

9. מִימֵי (from the days of): מִן establishes the time period of the action of the main verb (חָטָאתָ) as beginning with Israel's experiences at Gibeah. שָׁם (there) is a locative adverb that resumes the earlier geographical reference to Gibeah. עָמְדוּ (they have remained): עָמַד has the basic sense of standing, but its association with a particular locale (Gibeah) requires the nuance of stopping or remaining. The word has this sense in several passages (Gen. 45:9; Josh. 10:19; 1 Sam. 9:27; 20:38; 2 Sam. 2:28). לֹא־תַשִּׂיגֵם (did not . . . overtake them) presents a serious problem. The hiphil of נָשַׂג has the clear sense of overtake, but the negative particle לֹא (not) introduces a clause that may be either a negative statement or a rhetorical question. Did Hosea say, "War did [or will] not overtake them," or, "Will not war overtake them"? Hebrew grammar does not greatly help us with this problem because questions are not always introduced by the interrogative ה (GKC §150a). Usually some element of emphasis or a particu-

lar ordering of words will indicate a question in the absence of interrogative indicators, but no such indicator exists in this context. It is best to understand such statements as affirmations unless the context demands otherwise. עַל (against) occurs elsewhere with מִלְחָמָה (war), but exclusively in idiomatic expressions (e.g., קוּם עַל [rise against]; כָּבֵד עַל [press hard against]). These idioms show, however, that עַל is appropriately understood in the sense of *against* when used with מִלְחָמָה. עַלְוָה (violence) is in all probability from the root עָוֶל, the letters ו and ל having undergone transposition. A root עלי that would make sense in this context is otherwise unknown. עַוְלָה (violence) occurs with בֵּן (son) on four other occasions (2 Sam. 3:34; 7:10; 1 Chron. 17:9; Ps. 89:23 [22]). In each of these instances the emphasis is on violence.

10. בְּאַוָּתִי (In my desire) is pointed in the Masoretic Text as the noun form אַוָּה (desire), but there are other options. One is that it is a form of

---

9. Hosea's reference to Gibeah in this context recalls his earlier reference to that city (9:9). We concluded there that Hosea had not forgotten Gibeah's awful crime (see the discussion at 9:9). It continued to symbolize the wicked spirit of his people. His use of the expression *From the days of Gibeah* extends the period over which that spirit was manifested from the time of Gibeah's heinous crime to Hosea's day.

The prophet underscores this contention with the words, "There they have remained." The locative particle *šam* (there) can refer only to Gibeah because it is the only geographical element in the context. Hosea's assertion that they have stopped or stayed at Gibeah indicates that the people never removed themselves from the spirit of Gibeah. It is as though they never advanced beyond the moral boundaries of what Gibeah had come to represent.

The following statement, introduced by the negative *lo'*, confronts us with one of the most difficult exegetical problems in this passage (see the Exegesis). We have chosen to regard the statement as an affirmation that war did not overtake the people in Gibeah. We have no clear indication that we must understand the statement as a question, and it makes sense if we read it as a statement of fact. Against this view, however, is the fact of a military action against the Benjamites by a tribal confederation shocked by the events that had taken place at Gibeah (Judg. 20). But we must remember that at this point in the context Hosea

has moved from the reference to the town of Gibeah to his use of that town as a symbol of moral depravity. In that sense war had not yet come to Gibeah. The spirit of moral turpitude that characterized the people throughout Israel's long history had not yet come to final judgment. The tribal confederation had indeed judged Gibeah's sin, but the spirit of Gibeah that continued in Hosea's day had not yet come under judgment.

In our view the war which had not yet come was to be against "the sons of violence," an expression that probably sustains the Gibeah motif. The crime against the concubine which occurred there (Judg. 19) was perpetrated by violent men. The wrongs of Hosea's day may not have been similar to the crime at Gibeah, but as we observed, that crime is used by Hosea as an analogy for the corruption in his society.

10. Justice will come, and it will be in accord with the divine desire. The words *in my desire* indicate that the ultimate punishment of Israel's spirit of wickedness will be by God, as and when he chooses. The spirit of Gibeah went unpunished for a long time, but the punishment was about to come as determined by God's sovereign choice. The judgment of God is often slow according to our measure of time, but it is certain.

The nature of the judgment is strangely reminiscent of the tribal retaliation against Gibeah (Judg. 20). Just as armies came against the Benjamites then, so they will come against Israel in the future. But the armies will be armies of

the verb אָתָה (come) which appears only in poetic material (Ugaritic 'tw), but the consonantal tradition does not support that reading unless one posits metathesis. Another option is to read אַוִּתִי (which is pointed as a noun in the Masoretic Text) as an infinitive construct. This yields the sense *when I desire*, but this seems unnecessary. The construction is grammatical as it stands. Note the occurrences of the expression *in my anger* (see, e.g., Isa. 63:6; Jer. 33:5; Ezek. 22:20; 43:8; Hos. 13:11) to denote the sphere in which the action of the main verb takes place. The וְ on אֶסֳרֵם is *waw*-apodosis. The construction here indicates that the action of the main verb (אֶסֳרֵם, I will chastise) takes place within the sphere of the divine will. וְאֶסֳרֵם (I will chastise them) forms an independent clause according to the interpretation given above. The וְ, however, does not present a problem for this view since the same construction occurs in 11:1, where the independent clause (וָאֹהֲבֵהוּ) following the dependent clause (נַעַר יִשְׂרָאֵל).

כִּי) also begins with וְ. אֶסֳרֵם may be parsed as a *qal* imperfect first-person singular from יָסַר (chastise) with the י assimilated to the second radical (GKC §71). וְאֻסְּפוּ (and . . . shall be gathered): The passive (pual) formation of this verb indicates an external force at work on the nations to bring them against Israel. Taken in conjunction with the construction בְּאַוָּתִי (in my desire), which expresses the control of divine sovereignty over these events, we may assume the external force to be God. עֲלֵיהֶם (against them): The suffix sustains the reference to the people of Israel that we find throughout (see v. 9). בְּאָסְרָם (when they bind [them]) is literally "in their binding." The third-person suffix now reverts to the nearest plural referent, that is, עַמִּים (nations). It is the nations who bind. No object is expressed grammatically, but in this context it can be none other than Israel who is the object of all the threats in this passage. לִשְׁתֵּי (before . . . two): When used with עַיִן (eye) לְ may indicate the idea of before the eyes of, that is, in the sight of.

---

nations. Israel's punishment was to take place in the international arena.

According to this view, Hosea represents Yahweh as saying, "When they bind [them] before their two eyes." We have chosen to reject the emendation of "their two iniquities" because "their two eyes" is a legitimate reading. While it is true that the word *eyes* is never elsewhere construed as a plural, its dual nature is determined by the numeral 2 in this statement. Paired body parts are not always construed in the dual (note *zĕroʿ ôt*, arms). The word *kĕlayôt* (kidneys) is always construed in the plural and, when necessary, qualified by the numeral (see, e.g., Exod. 29:13; Lev. 3:4). We have found that Hosea's Hebrew does not always follow orthographical and grammatical norms (see comments at 4:18 and 8:13). Perhaps this singular construction was a dialectical or Hosean peculiarity of speech. The expression *before their two eyes* conveys the sense of before their very eyes.

One of the difficulties with this view is that it requires that Israel be at once the recipient and witness of the action of the verb *ʾasar* (bind)—Israel will be bound before its own eyes. This difficulty is relieved, however, when we recall Hosea's lack of precision in his literary devices. In the metaphor of 14:6–8 [5–7], for example, he pictures Israel as a flourishing tree (vv. 6–7 [5–6]) but also enjoying the shade of that same tree (v. 8 [7]).

Those who adopt the emendation *iniquities* (ʿawōn) have made several suggestions as to what Israel's two iniquities or double guilt may signify. Keil suggests the two transgressions are Israel's apostasy from God and from the house of David (*Minor Prophets*, 1:133; see Wood, *Hosea*, p. 210). Mays suggests that it could refer to "the sum of the incidents in Judg 19–21 and, Saul. . . . But Hosea may see 'then' and 'now,' the original deed and its subsequent continuation, as two phases which double the iniquity" (*Hosea*, p. 144). Andersen and Freedman suggest several possibilities: the two iniquities could be two idols like "sin" and "shame," but point out that Jeremiah 2:13 suggests otherwise (*Hosea*, p. 566). The two iniquities could also reflect "the episode at Gibeah and the war between the tribes and Benjamin." Another suggestion is "the episode and the consequent refusal to surrender the criminals" (*Hosea*, p. 566). Wolff suggests (*Hosea*, p. 185) that "Gibeah's former sin is doubled by Gibeah's present guilt ('There they remained' v. 9)."

The suggestion of Keil is based on 3:5 where it says that Israel will return to the Lord and to David their king. But this statement is a positive affirmation of Israel's restoration. There is no implication of apostasy in the passage. Nowhere does Hosea state that Israel's defection from the Davidic house was wrong. Mays' suggestion is in keeping with the context, but it is doubtful that we should observe two phases of disobedience in Israel's history. Hosea describes the entire period

173

We find Jacob laying the rods לְעֵינֵי הַצֹּאן (before the eyes of) the flock (Gen. 30:41; see also Gen. 47:19; Lev. 26:45; Deut. 4:6). עֵינֹתָם (their eyes) is frequently emended by scholars to עָוֹן (iniquity), largely on the basis that עַיִן (eye) is always construed in the dual. While the emendation involves only ו and י, these are letters that copyists could easily have confused. It presents certain difficulties. One of these is the need to identify "two iniquities" of Israel. On the other hand, the numeral שְׁתֵּי (two) is quite compatible with "eyes." In spite of the anomalous plural for עַיִן (eye), the consonantal text reads "before their two eyes" (see the Exposition).

---

as continuing from the days of Gibeah. The treatment given this problem by Andersen and Freedman underscores its difficulty. The suggestion that the war between the tribes and Benjamin is one of the iniquities lacks support. In all probability it was a just retaliation. The other suggestion, like the first, is dependent on an interpretation that places the whole context in the past. The expression bĕʾawwātî (in my desire) is translated by Andersen and Freedman, "When I came" (*Hosea*, p. 560). Such a perspective may be warranted, but this translation is uncertain. Wolff also bifurcates the continuum of Israel's sin established by the words *from the days of* (*Hosea*, p. 185).

The translation "before their two eyes" conveys the sense that the threatened cataclysm of war will erupt within their midst. They will watch as fellow citizens are bound and taken as their land is invaded by a conquering nation. This view finds support later when the prophet refers again to this war of retribution. Hosea says that "a tumult" will arise against his people, and their fortresses will be destroyed, and the tumult would be similar to Shalman's destruction when mothers were "dashed in pieces with their children" (v. 14, see v. 15). It is not difficult to picture Israelites in the midst of this tumult watching in fear as these things took place before their two eyes, that is, in their very sight.

XIII. Internal Corruption of Israel (10:1–15)

E. Israel's Unrestrained Disobedience to Yahweh (10:11–12)

¹¹ And Ephraim is a trained heifer
    that loves to thresh,
    but I will disregard the beauty of her
      neck:
I will harness Ephraim;
    Judah will plow;
    Jacob will harrow by himself.
¹² Sow for yourselves in accordance with
    righteousness;
    reap according to covenant loyalty;
    plow for yourselves unbroken soil,
for it is time to seek the Lord
    until he comes and rains righteous-
    ness upon you.

¹¹ Ephraim was a trained heifer
    that loved to thresh,
    and I spared her fair neck;
    but I will make Ephraim break the
      ground;
    Judah must plow;
    Jacob must harrow for himself.
¹² Sow for yourselves righteousness;
    reap steadfast love;
    break up your fallow ground;
for it is time to seek the Lord,
    that he may come and rain righ-
    teousness upon you.

11. וְאֶפְרַיִם (And Ephraim): וְ connects this verse with the preceding one and thus sustains the reference to punishment. עֶגְלָה מְלֻמָּדָה (trained heifer): The pual (passive) of לָמַד (learn) connotes being taught or trained. It refers to trained singers (1 Chron. 25:7) and trained soldiers (Song of Sol. 3:8). This is a heifer that has learned and is thus a trained heifer. אֹהַבְתִּי (that loves): The ending (תִּי) affixed to this participle is in all probability an obsolete case ending which lends special emphasis to the construct state (see GKC §90k–m). A similar construction occurs in Zechariah 11:17 (הָעֹאן עֹזְבִי, who deserts the flock). Relative clauses (that loves) are not always introduced by אֲשֶׁר (which, that) but may omit that particle when the antecedent is expressed (see Davidson, *Syntax* §143). Because participles may function as nouns, they occur frequently in the construct state (GKC §116g). A preposition may appear between the construct state and its genitive, as is the case here (לָדוּשׁ). This function does not alter the sense of the construct relationship (see GKC §90l). לָדוּשׁ (to thresh): דוּשׁ has the sense of treading or crushing, and secondarily threshing (the use of the word in Judg. 8:7 as "flail" may be a metaphorical representation of the act of threshing). It is clear from Isaiah 25:10 that the word does not always connote the process of threshing, for in that passage it describes the treading of straw in a dung-pit. In Job 39:15 it depicts the act of treading by an animal. In Micah 4:13 it depicts the act of threshing grain under the hooves of an animal. We cannot regard the reference to Israel's threshing in verse 11a as a reference to her servitude in captivity, for that idea is not consonant with the fact that she "loves to thresh." Verse 11a is a noun clause with a present perspective describing Israel in the period before the yoke of exile was placed on her; thus we translate it in the present tense. וַאֲנִי (but I): The subsequent interpretation of this passage requires an adversative function for וְ (but). אֲנִי (I) can refer only to Yahweh in this context. עָבַרְתִּי עַל (disregard) presents a serious difficulty to the interpreter. The collocation עָבַר עַל frequently has the sense of crossing over or passing before. However, this would make little sense in the context. It cannot connote the act of passing a yoke over the neck of Israel because that idea is expressed by עָבַר in the hiphil. It is in the qal in this context. The idiom has another sense more appropriate to the context, however. It is the idea of passing over in the sense of disregarding. There are only two clearly attested occurrences of the collocation with this sense in the Old Testament (Prov. 19:11; Mic. 7:18), but that does not invalidate the assignment of that connotation to it here. Meaning is not determined by statistical frequency. The context plays a vital role in delineating and defining the connotations of its constituent elements. In Proverbs 19:11 the idiom occurs with פֶּשַׁע

---

11. Hosea again appeals to the analogy of a heifer to describe Israel. He had used that figure to depict Israel's stubbornness (4:16), but here that analogy is the vehicle for a different concept. It is a grim portrayal of Israel's impending captivity.

Evidently this heifer did not thresh by drawing a cart (Isa. 28:28) or a threshing sledge (Isa. 41:15) but by trampling the stalks of grain. Micah describes this method of threshing by depicting restored Israel as an animal on a threshing floor, treading on the nations with hooves of iron and bronze (4:12–13). Hosea in his analogy says that the heifer loved to do that for which it had been trained. We get the picture of a sleek young animal bounding about on a threshing floor strewn with grain. The animal is unyoked and its unleashed energy is used for threshing.

The purpose of the analogy is to depict Israel in the long period before the exile. She was like a playful, unbridled heifer that enjoyed its freedom from the drudgery of hauling heavy loads. Like the heifer in Hosea's analogy she had not experienced the strictures of divine law; the nation exulted in the unrestrained liberty of the nature cult. Hosea uses the analogy of the threshing floor elsewhere to represent the sphere of Israel's wanton unfaithfulness to Yahweh (9:1); here it has the same significance. It is the sphere of unbridled devotion to the syncretistic national religion of the northern kingdom.

The days of unrestrained disobedience to Yahweh will come to an end, however. He will disregard the fact that the sleek neck of this metaphorical animal has never borne a yoke. Israel will drag the plow and the harrow through the stubborn clods, and she will do it by herself. She will be like an animal straining at the yoke without the help of another animal as she endures the oppressive yoke of exile. She will have none to help or intervene, not even her God.

The inclusion of Judah in the pronouncement of doom seems anomalous. Mays notes, "'Judah' is the work of a Judean redactor who probably substituted it for the name 'Israel'" (*Hosea*, p. 145).

(offense): "it is their glory to overlook [עָבַר] an offense" (NRSV). If we understand the idiom in this way here, the sense of the statement is that Yahweh will disregard the sleek beauty of the animal's neck, yet untouched by a yoke or harness. He will place on Israel the galling yoke of exile. אַרְכִּיב (I will harness) is the hiphil of רָכַב (to ride). In the hiphil it connotes causing to ride or plow, hence harnessing or fitting for plowing. יַחֲרוֹשׁ (I will plow): חָרַשׁ connotes the sense of cutting or engraving, and in many instances plowing. יְשַׂדֶּד־לוֹ (will harrow by himself): Since שָׂדַד לְ is not an attested collocation, we must understand לוֹ as an independent entity in this sentence (by himself). It is difficult to determine whether לוֹ has the sense of by himself or for himself. We have opted for the former because of the anomaly of a yoked animal plowing for its own benefit. It seems best to understand לוֹ to depict Israel as an animal plowing alone. This analogy fits the prospect of the nation, separated from her God, yoked by the bondage of exile.

12. זִרְעוּ לָכֶם (Sow for yourselves): The plural number of the verb indicates that the picture of an animal has receded into the background as the prophet turns his attention to the people. לִצְדָקָה (righteousness) is a general term for righteousness.

Its distinctive sense in a given context is determined by the linguistic signals in the context, such as parallel words, contextual influences, and other similar elements. In this instance the context colors the word by חֶסֶד (covenant loyalty), which occurs often in the Prophets denoting the ethical bond between Yahweh and his people which was determined and described by the Mosaic covenant. The לְ (לִצְדָקָה) has the sense of *with reference to*. The people are to guide their actions in life by righteousness. It does not function as the sign of the direct object here (although it could in late Hebrew [Davidson, *Syntax* §73, Rem. 7; GKC §117n]), because the element that answers to it in the clausal structure is לְפִי (according to). לְפִי frequently occurs with the same sense as כְּפִי (in proportion to; see, e.g., Exod. 16:16, 18 [לְפִי], and v. 21 [כְּפִי]; see BDB, p. 805). נִיר connotes unbroken or virgin soil (see Jer. 4:3). וְ (for) connects the subsequent clause to the preceding series of imperative statements, and introduces the reason for those statements. דָּרַשׁ (to seek), when used of the Lord, has the sense of searching out and acknowledging God's will and direction, often in a particular circumstance (see Gen. 25:22; Exod. 18:15; 2 Kings 22:13; 1 Chron. 16:11; Pss. 22:27 [26]; 24:6; Amos 5:4). עַד־יָבוֹא

However, the names *Judah* and *Israel* are intertwined in other pericopes in Hosea in which the inclusion of Judah is essential to the integrity of the passage. In 5:12 the line that includes Judah is necessary to the parallel structure. In 8:14 the poetic structure supports the integrity of the line that contains the reference to Judah because the subsequent lines resume the reference to the great structures cited in the first two lines. The word *cities* (ʿārîm) in the third line answers to that word in the second line, and the word *strongholds* (ʾarmĕnôt) in the fourth line answers to *palaces* (hêkalôt) in the first. There is no reason why Hosea could not have observed the same ominous signs of social and religious decay in Judah that presaged doom for the northern kingdom.

12. Hosea holds no hope for his nation, for destruction is sure. But that fact does not deter him from showing Israel the way out of her misery. It is to "sow in accordance with righteousness" and "covenant loyalty." This admonition went unheeded by the people and thus served to condemn them the more, since they knew the cure for their nation's illness but refused to accept it. The prophetic message seems to have hardened

hearts more than it softened them (see Isa. 6:10–12; Ezek. 3:4–7). The word of God condemns as it enlightens.

The agricultural motifs in verses 11 and 12 differ in their significance. Plowing and harrowing are symbols of Israel's impending oppression (v. 11), but the agricultural figures of sowing, reaping, and breaking up fallow soil represent the path to Israel's restoration (v. 12). This lack of literary restraint is a characteristic of Hosea's writing style (see the comments at 2:5 [3]).

The words sĕdaqa (righteousness) and hesed (covenant loyalty) convey the idea of the moral response to God that was necessary for maintaining the relationship of the people to the inheritance promised in the Abrahamic covenant. Renewed allegiance to the standards of the Mosaic covenant would restore the people to covenant privilege and blessing. Only when that allegiance was restored would the promise of a land to Abraham's descendants continue to be a reality.

The path to restoration for the nation involved several steps. They were to sow according to righteousness, that is, they were to live in accordance with the standards of Yahwism. If they were obe-

(until he comes): Since the action predicated by עֹד is yet future, the imperfect tense of the verb (יָבוֹא), with its emphasis on incomplete action, is appropriate to Hosea's statement. וְיֹרֶה (and rains): יָרָה has the basic sense of direction. When this is done with motion, it may be translated "throw" or "shoot," while in other cases "teach" is appropriate. The noun form יוֹרֶה (early rain) shows that the basic verbal idea is compatible with the idea of rain. Perhaps the sense is to throw or direct water. The connotation of the verb here seems to be that of "throw water" (BDB, p. 435), that is, to rain something upon an object. In this case, that which

rains is צֶדֶק (righteousness). See the comments at 2:21 [19]. In its secular occurrences the word צֶדֶק has the sense of justice or fairness. It is used of accurate weights for weighing and dispensing food (Lev. 19:36) and of equity in the legal process (Deut. 16:18). In the ethical sphere it frequently connotes personal righteousness (see, e.g., Job 6:29; Pss. 7:9 [8]; 15:2; 17:15). When it applies to God, the word indicates the standard of fairness and equity that is essential to the divine character and which shapes and determines the nature of God's activity in the arena of human events (Pss. 9:5 [4], 9 [8]; 35:24; 96:13; Isa. 11:4–5; 42:21).

---

dient to these standards they would reap in accordance with covenant loyalty. Up to this time they had reaped in accordance with their disobedience to Yahweh. Instead of sowing righteousness, they had sown rebellion and had reaped national disaster. But if they were to observe the covenant stipulations, they would reap what covenant loyalty and righteousness produced—divine blessing. The prophet also calls on the people to make a new start, saying, "Plow for yourselves unbroken soil." This command to break up new ground meant that they were to renounce the old ways and open new fields. If they began anew, they were assured of God's favor.

Hosea concludes by saying, "It is time to seek the LORD." The people were to turn to Yahweh in prayer and obedience. This process of seeking was to continue until the Lord intervened and showered righteousness on them. Perhaps Hosea believed it was the time to seek the Lord because

of the impending disaster. But in all likelihood he would have said this even when his nation had only begun to flirt with the fertility gods. But whatever the circumstances, the principle still is this: "Behold, now is the acceptable time" (2 Cor. 6:2, RSV).

The last element in this series of agricultural motifs is that which is the ultimate necessity for an abundant harvest—rain. Yahweh will rain righteousness on the people. The word for righteousness here is ṣedeq, not ṣĕdaqâ (as earlier). God would respond to their spiritual renewal by dealing with them in fairness and equity; he would act in conformity to his covenantal obligations and restore them to covenant privilege. By showering them with righteousness he would deliver them from their precarious state and restore the stability and prosperity that was his original intention for them.

XIII. Internal Corruption of Israel (10:1–15)

F. Israel's Internal Corruption Will Lead to the Fall
of the Monarchy (10:13–15)

13 You have plowed evil,
  you have reaped wickedness,
  you have eaten the fruit of lying.
Because you have trusted in your way,
  in the multitude of your mighty
  men,
14 therefore a tumult will arise against
  your people,
  and all your strongholds shall be
  destroyed
as Shalman destroyed Beth-arbel on the
  day of battle;
  mothers were dashed in pieces with
  their children.
15 Thus Bethel will do to you
  because of the evil of your evil.
In the dawn the king of Israel
  shall be utterly cut off.

13 You have plowed wickedness,
  you have reaped injustice,
  you have eaten the fruit of lies.
Because you have trusted in your power
  and in the multitude of your warriors,
14 therefore the tumult of war shall rise
  against your people,
  and all your fortresses shall be
  destroyed,
as Shalman destroyed Beth-arbel on the
  day of battle
  when mothers were dashed in pieces
  with their children.
15 Thus it shall be done to you, O Bethel,
  because of your great wickedness.
At dawn the king of Israel
  shall be utterly cut off.

13. חֲרַשְׁתֶּם־רֶשַׁע (You have plowed evil, that is, you have prepared the soil of evil [see Job 4:8]): עַוְלָתָה (wickedness) is a double feminine form (see GKC §90g). It is often translated "injustice," but in most of its occurrences it has the general sense of wickedness. אֲכַלְתֶּם פְּרִי (you have eaten the fruit of): פְּרִי (fruit) is used metaphorically of the effect or consequences of one's previous actions (Jer. 21:14; 32:19). It is used with אָכַל (eat) in a negative sense in Proverbs 1:31 and in a positive sense in Isaiah 3:10. כַחַשׁ (lying) refers to the princes of Israel in Hosea 7:3. כִּי (Because): It is difficult to determine whether this particle belongs with the previous clauses or the subsequent ones. If we take it with the preceding clauses, it presents the reason why the people have reaped the consequences of their actions—they trusted in their misguided way and in their leaders. If we construe it with the following clauses, it gives the logical basis for the impending tumult of war predicted in verse 14 (see the Author's Translation). While the two concepts are similar and the rules of syntax permit both, the logical flow of the passage appears to call for the latter option. The first two lines of verse 13 set forth a present reality—the people had sown evil and wickedness. This was their way. The last line of verse 13 is resumptive. We may paraphrase it, "Because you have trusted in this your way, you will reap the consequences of your actions in a future calamity—a tumult

will arise against you." This view also finds support in the change of number in the two segments. In the initial clauses of verse 13 the constructions are plural, while the כִּי clause as well as the subsequent clause is construed in the singular. This indicates a break in the flow of thought and grammatically divorces the כִּי clause from the previous clauses while establishing a conceptual relationship between the כִּי clause and its companion clause in verse 14a. It is also more likely that וְ (וְקָאם) in verse 14 introduces a subordinate clause related to the previous clause than an independent clause. בָּטַחְתָּ (you have trusted): בָּטַח has the sense of placing confidence in a person or object. It is used of God (2 Kings 18:5, 22; Ps. 22:5 [4]), persons (Judg. 20:36; Prov. 31:11), concepts (2 Kings 18:19; Pss. 13:6 [5]; 52:10 [8]), and objects (Job 6:20; Ps. 119:42). Rarely does it occur without a stated object (Job 11:18; Prov. 28:1), and in these instances it has the sense of confidence. בְּדַרְכְּךָ (in your way): דֶּרֶךְ (way) occurs frequently with the metaphorical sense of manner of behavior (see, e.g., Gen. 6:12; Exod. 33:13; Prov. 3:6; Isa. 10:24; Ezek. 3:18; 20:30). Hosea uses the word with that sense in 4:9; 9:8; 12:3 [2]; and 14:10 [9]. Here it is the manner of behavior of the nation reflected in their course of action. גִּבּוֹרֶיךָ (your mighty men): גִּבּוֹר represents a strong or valiant man and it often refers to warriors (Judg. 6:12).

---

13. Through the years of Israel's existence as a nation she had prepared the soil for the fruit she was now reaping. She was soon to learn that the wages of sin is death (Rom. 6:23). Israel would perish as a nation. To Hosea this event was a certainty, so he could speak of it in verbal tenses that depicted it as a present reality: "You have plowed evil, you have reaped wickedness."

The impending calamity—the exile—is presented in somber language in this pericope. Throughout the history of his nation Hosea observed the subtle departure of the people from the standards of their national constitution, the Mosaic law. He observed the lying and deceit that characterized national affairs. With his prophetic foresight he envisioned the end result of this history of offenses against Yahweh. But one did not have to be a prophet to know what lay beyond, for the warning was clear: "If you do not diligently observe all the words of this law . . . the LORD will scatter you among all peoples, from one end of the earth to the other" (Deut. 28:58, 64, NRSV). These words had been drowned out by the noise of

the religious revels, for the people had forsaken the purity of Yahwism to sow the seeds of national and social decay.

Hosea bases the certainty of Israel's demise on their "way" and their trust in their "mighty men." The pairing of these terms in the syntactical structure indicates that they were overlapping concepts in the mind of Hosea. The "way" of the people was to trust in their "mighty men." This is supported by the lack of waw (and) between the two relevant clauses (see the Author's Translation) which establishes an appositional relationship between them.

We do not find anything elsewhere in Hosea about the people's trust in their military might. But other eighth-century prophets alluded to this misplaced confidence. The people in Amos's day boasted that they had taken Karnaim in their own strength (Amos 6:13); Micah said that when God restored his people he would cut off their horses and chariots (5:10); and Isaiah said of the nation that "their land is filled with horses, and there is no end to their chariots" (2:7, NRSV).

14. וְקָאם (therefore . . . will arise): וְ (therefore) introduces the resultative segment of the causal structure introduced by כִּי (see Gen. 29:33). קָאם (will arise) is a qal perfect of קוּם (rise). The א serves as a vowel letter (GKC §23g; §72p), as it frequently does in Aramaic. שָׁאוֹן (tumult) connotes a great noise. The context determines its referent. In Amos 2:2, for example, it is the tumult of war, as it is here. בְּ (against) completes the collocation קוּם בְּ (rise against). שַׁלְמָן (Shalman): The identification of this figure is uncertain. For current interpretations, see Andersen and Freedman (*Hosea*, pp. 570, 571). בֵּית אַרְבֵאל (Beth-arbel): The Septuagint records several traditions for the Masoretic Text's אַרְבֵאל (Ιεροβααλ, AQ^c; Ιεροβοαμ, BQ*; Ιεροβοαλ, C; αρβεηλ, L). The reading Ιεροβααλ probably represents an effort to tie Hosea's allusion into the account where Abimelech slew his brothers (sons of Jerubbaal, Judg. 9:5), but there is nothing in Judges 9:5 that explains the presence of Shalman in Hosea 10:14. The reading Ιεροβοαμ is historically questionable. עַל (with) functions to connect entities that are alike (with the sense of *together with* as in Exodus 35:22 הָאֲנָשִׁים עַל־הַנָּשִׁים, both men and women).

15. כָּכָה (Thus) is somewhat more emphatic than the adverbial particle כֹּה. It may be translated literally "in accordance with this." It serves to apply the previous analogy to the reality of Israel's circumstances. עָשָׂה (will do) must have a

future reference because the tumult predicted in verse 14 and the cutting off of Israel's king (v. 15) are future events. לָכֶם (to you) is plural, in contrast to the singular constructions in the previous lines. Like the change in number observed in verse 13, the shift to the plural reveals a definite but almost imperceptible development in the flow of thought in the passage. This phenomenon indicates that the narrative flow has moved from the description of Shalman's cruel hostilities to the logical conclusion of Hosea's allusion to that cruel battle. בֵּית־אֵל (Bethel): The Septuagint reads, "house of Israel," but there is no need to emend. Taken as it stands, the Masoretic Text blames Bethel for Israel's impending captivity and even makes it an active agent in that event. This is not anomalous to Hosea's concept of Bethel's role in Israel's difficulties (see the Exposition). מִפְּנֵי (because of) frequently expresses cause (Gen. 6:13). רָעַת רָעַתְכֶם (the evil of your evil) is a periphrastic expression that connotes the superlative (GKC §133i). Note, for example, שִׁיר הַשִּׁירִים (Song of Songs) in Song of Solomon 1:1. This construction in Hosea 10:15 describes the people's evil as great (NRSV your great wickedness). בַּשַּׁחַר (In the dawn) may continue the motif of the crime at Gibeah (see the Exposition). נִדְמֹה נִדְמָה (shall be utterly cut off) is an intensive form with an infinitive absolute that connotes an absolute cutting off of Israel's king.

---

14. The tumult that Hosea envisions is the tumult of war—the cries of battle, the wailing of women carried off as spoils of war, the screaming of children. This prediction was realized in the battles that accompanied the invasion of Israel by the Assyrians. Hosea likens that invasion to Shalman's conquest of Beth-arbel. Neither Shalman nor Beth-arbel is known to us. Some commentators suggest that Shalman is a shortened form of Shalmaneser, others that it represents Salamann, an official of Moab. It seems best to regard this allusion as an event that we cannot identify with certainty, similar to the historical allusions in Amos, several of which are difficult to attest historically (1:3–2:16). Shalman's cruel attack must have lived on in the minds of Hosea's contemporaries. It would have made little sense for him to allude to it otherwise. The unpleasant associations it stirred up were an appropriate analogy for the cruelty Israel was to endure.

15. The fact that Bethel will do this to Israel seems an anomaly. Why did he not say that

Assyria would bring about the fall of Israel's monarchy? The Revised Standard Version follows the Septuagint in reading "O house of Israel" for "Bethel," but does not follow the Septuagint in making God the active agent of the destruction ("thus I shall do to you"). It is difficult to make a judgment here, but we should give more weight to the more difficult reading. A glance at the Septuagint traditions shows that the translators struggled with this passage just as we do. We need not emend here, however, for Hosea's prophetic philosophy allowed for an active role for Bethel in Israel's demise.

Bethel's role as a cult center made it a focal point for the fertility religion that Hosea despised. Since the basic concept of Hosea's prophetic philosophy was that Israel would collapse because of her allegiance to the baals, it is not difficult to understand how Bethel could be a causal factor in that collapse. In the mind of Hosea Bethel embodied the evil of the fertility cult. His derogatory designation of Bethel (house of God) as Beth-aven (house of evil) was no mere literary device; it reflected his view of Bethel as the crystallization of Israel's rebellion against God.

Earlier Hosea associated Bethel with the exile itself (10:5). Its calves, as the focal point of God's wrath, would be carried to Assyria. Amos did something similar when he said, "Gilgal shall surely go into exile, and Bethel shall come to nothing" (5:5, NRSV). Bethel could be an instrument of Israel's demise because it was the symbol of her rebellion against Yahweh, and thus an active force in her downfall.

The reference to the dawn may recall the motif of the slaughter of the concubine (Judg. 19) which seems to be intertwined throughout this section. It was at dawn (Judg. 19:26) that the awful crime came to light. More likely, however, is the possibility that Shalman's attack took place at dawn, or that the dawn was considered the most advantageous time for military action. Whatever the motif means, it serves to underscore the fact that Israel's monarchy would be cut off.

XIV. Yahweh's Love for Israel (11:1–11)

A. Yahweh Loved Israel at the Exodus, but Israel
Rebelled Against Him (11:1–4)

11 When Israel was a child, I loved him,
and out of Egypt I called my son.
² The more they called to them,
the more they went from them;
they kept sacrificing to the baals
and burning incense to idols.

³ Yet it was I who attentively watched
over Ephraim,
he took them up in his arms;
but they did not know that I healed
them.
⁴ With cords of a man I led them:
with bonds of love,
and I became to them as those who ease
the yoke on their jaws,
and I fed him gently.

11 When Israel was a child, I loved him,
and out of Egypt I called my son.
² The more I called them,
the more they went from me;
they kept sacrificing to the Baals,
and offering incense to idols.

³ Yet it was I who taught Ephraim to
walk,
I took them up in my arms;
but they did not know that I healed
them.
⁴ I led them with cords of human kindness,
with bands of love.
I was to them like those
who lift infants to their cheeks.
I bent down to them and fed them.

11:1. כִּי (When) introduces a temporal clause (GKC §164d) that brings us back in time to Israel's early history. There is no logical causation apparent in the function of כִּי. נַעַר (child) designates no specific age; in Exodus 2:6 it refers to an infant of three months (see 2:2). וָאֹהֲבֵהוּ (I loved him): ו introduces the apodosis of the temporal clause and transfers the preceding concept of temporality to it (when . . . then). אֹהֲבֵהוּ (I loved) is in the perfect tense. The concept of completed action connoted by this tense focuses the divine love specifically on the period of time delineated by the protasis of the temporal clause, that is, the period of Israel's national infancy when she was delivered from Egyptian bondage. This limited application of the verb אֹהֲבֵהוּ (I loved) is evident also in the temporality of the following clause (out of Egypt).

קָרָא לְ (call) has several senses. It frequently has the connotation of summoning (Gen. 46:33) as it does here. The preposition מִן designates Egypt as the location from which the action of the verb קָרָא (call) took place.

2. קָרְאוּ (The more they called) introduces a clause of comparison. This is indicated by כֵּן in the apodosis. Comparison clauses may omit כַּאֲשֶׁר (as) in the protasis (Davidson, *Syntax* §151). The comparison is between the actions of the two verbs, literally, "As they called to them, so they went from them." The plural subject of קָרְאוּ is discussed in the Exposition. יְזַבֵּחוּ (they kept sacrificing) is imperfect. The incomplete action of this tense extends the action of the verb over the period of Israel's apostasy delineated in the previous comparison clause. פְּסִלִים (idols) is a noun

---

11:1. The atmosphere changes here. We leave behind the tumult of war and the slaughter of innocents to move back through time to the halcyon period of Israel's early history. It was a time marked by the greatest event in her national experience—the exodus from Egypt. Hosea pictures Israel in this period as an infant, dependent on an adult for care and training. The analogy is one of deep tenderness. The picture of divine love in this section is almost unparalleled in the Old Testament as Yahweh is pictured as a loving father and Israel as his infant son.

The love of which Hosea speaks found expression in the exodus, an event that was foundational to Israel's understanding of God. It finds frequent expression in the Old Testament (see the Exposition at 7:16). Like other events, the exodus was often invested by Old Testament writers with a significance that extended beyond its original implications. Hosea, for example, uses the Egyptian bondage as a motif for the impending Assyrian captivity (7:16; 8:13; 9:3, 6; 11:5), and he gives the exodus broad significance when he applies it to Israel's future restoration (2:17 [15]; 11:11; 12:10 [9]; 13:4). Matthew seems to use a similar approach to historical events when he expands the allusion to the exodus in Hosea 11:1 to apply to the safe departure of Jesus from his temporary refuge in Egypt (Matt. 2:15).

2. According to the comparative structure with which this verse begins, Yahweh's call to his people to come out of Egypt did not represent the only time he called. He called them on later occasions as well, but the more he called, the more they went away from him. Like a loving father who beckons

to his child because he wants to express his love to the child, Yahweh beckoned to Israel, but Israel was an uncaring son who ran insolently from him.

The repeated calls that followed the initial call to Israel to leave Egypt are expressed in the plural (*they* called). It is possible that this is an indefinite plural which is to be translated as a passive: "The more they were called." This view has the advantage of avoiding the abrupt change of subject that results if a plural subject is assigned to the verb *qārəʾû* (they called). Yahweh would thus be the subject of the verb *qārāʾ* in its two occurrences here. However, this suggestion is unlikely because the plural subject is retained throughout the construction; the suffix on *mippənêhem* (from them) is also plural. It is hardly likely that this suffix ("the more they went from *them*") refers to Yahweh.

The best solution to the problem is to posit a plural subject that has a close conceptual connection to Yahweh, who is the subject of the first verb *qārāʾ*. The most appropriate subject is the prophets. We observed in the discussion at 9:8 (see also 6:15) that the prophets sustained a close relationship to Yahweh according to Hosea's theology. God spoke through the prophets (12:11 [10]) and brought Israel out of Egypt by a prophet (12:14 [13]). Throughout Israel's history the prophets called to her, urging her to turn to God, but the people all too often spurned the prophets' call. When the nation rejected the prophets, they rejected Yahweh himself.

Hosea says that while Yahweh continually called to Israel, the people kept sacrificing to the baals. This statement emphasizes God's longsuf-

form of the verb פָּסַל which connotes to hew or to carve into a specific shape. The noun form פְּסִיל refers in most of its occurrences to carved images.

3. וְאָנֹכִי (Yet it was I): וְ establishes a syntactical juncture that we must translate into English as an adversative (but, yet). It marks the logical change in the flow of the context between Israel's unfaithfulness to Yahweh and Yahweh's love for Israel in spite of her defection. In all probability the orthographic representation of אָנֹכִי (I) places the emphasis on that pronoun (it was I). תִּרְגַּלְתִּי (attentively watched) is a difficult form. It is in the perfect tense, but the quadriliteral form is unusual (GKC §30p). The root רָגַל underlies the word, and the ת may be a grammatical adjunctive. The verb רָגַל has the sense of going about as an explorer or spying (BDB, p. 920). The form תִּרְגַּלְתִּיה fits the pattern of a tD verb, that is, a piel verb with a ת (t) affix. This form may appear as a verbal noun in Ugaritic (Gordon, *UT*, p. 81). The piel form of the verb רָגַל (reconnoiter, spy) complemented by the reflexive ת (t) may connote an idea akin to moving one's self about for the purpose of careful observation of an object, thus, being attentive. לְ channels the action of the verb to the object אֶפְרַיִם (Ephraim). We have reflected this in the word *over* (see the Author's Translation). קָחָם (he took them) does not require emendation. לְקַח undergoes a similar aphaeresis of the ל in Ezekiel 17:5 (GKC §19i). The interchange of persons in the two clauses of this line is typical of Hosea. We may observe the same interchange in other speeches attributed to Yahweh (5:4 [see vv. 2–3]; 8:12–13; 9:16–17; 11:11 [see v. 10]; 12:1 [11:12]). וְלֹא (but . . . not): וְ functions as an adversative indi-

cator in this context in which the writer describes Israel as ignorant of God's benign activity on her behalf.

4. בְּחַבְלֵי (with cords of): בְּ is instrumental. חֶבֶל (cord), apart from secondary senses (a measuring line; a band of people), denotes a rope or line that one could use to pull (Isa. 5:18) or bind (Job 36:8) an object. אָדָם (a man): The construct relationship (cords of a man) frequently connotes a characteristic (note, אֵשֶׁת חַיִל, a virtuous woman). Thus we may translate the expression literally "human cords" (see the Exposition). The same sense obtains in the following construct relationship (בַּעֲבֹתוֹת אַהֲבָה, with bonds of love), where the bonds are characterized by love (love cords), not harshness. כִּמְרִימֵי (as those who ease): כְּ (as) relates the action of וָאֶהְיֶה (and I became) to מְרִימֵי in a comparative mode. מְרִימֵי can be translated literally "as lifters of [yoke]." The plural denotes a general classification. מְרִימֵי does not have the sense of *remove* in this context. The fact that the accompanying preposition is עַל (on), not מִן (from), is significant in that regard. The yoke is not lifted *from* (מִן) the jaw, but it is lifted *on* the jaw. Thus it is shifted in location; it was eased on the animal's jaw. וְאַט (gently) is understood as a hiphil verb by several commentators (Andersen and Freedman [*Hosea*, p. 582], "heeded"; Wolff, [*Hosea*, p. 191], "bent down"; Mays [*Hosea*, p. 150], "bent down"). Wolff observes that אַט cannot be an adjective because the adjective אַט always follows the verb. However, there is only one other instance of the word in the form אַט (not לְאַט) associated with a verb (1 Kings 21:27), but there the verb is *waw*-consecutive which allows

fering nature. He did not snuff out the people for one or two instances of insolent behavior. Yahweh is the persistent lover, but Israel persisted in her rejection of his love. The years, indeed the centuries, rolled on, but ultimately God's patience ran out and the end came.

3. In a statement reminiscent of 2:10 [8] Hosea implies that the people did not know that it was Yahweh who had shown them the attentive loving care that had brought them from slavery to nationhood. Once again there is an abrupt change of person in Hosea's excited speech. He first represents Yahweh as speaking, "It was I who attentively watched over Ephraim." Then it is as though the prophet speaks to the people about God, "He took them up in his arms."

The people, however, were not cognizant of the fact that it was Yahweh who restored them when

they were threatened with extinction and who healed them in national crises. The people gave their thanks for these favors to the fertility gods. In gloomy groves and before pagan altars they worshiped the baals. They spurned the God who had brought them out of Egypt.

4. Yahweh was not a cruel master; he did not treat Israel as a recalcitrant beast of burden. Rather, he led her with "cords of a man," that is, with cords suitable for humans, not beasts; the bonds were bonds of love, not cruel, painful strictures. Yahweh is not like those who treat their beasts of burden in an uncaring way, but like those who ease the yoke on an animal when they see it causing pain. He fed them and cared for them in gentleness. The picture is a poignant one that expresses God's love in terms familiar to the people.

no constituent grammatical element to precede it. The evidence is not conclusive. The adjective לְאַט heads a clause in 2 Samuel 18:5 as אַט does here. There is fluidity in the placement of the adjective in Hebrew. On the other hand, the concept of gentleness is consonant with the caring atmosphere of the preceding clause. If the idea intended by Hosea were, "*I bent down* to him to feed him" (see the translations of אַט above), he could have expressed it better by the placement of ו or לְ before the appropriate form of אָכַל (feed). אֵלָיו (him) reverts to the singular. Perhaps Hosea thinks of Israel as a child here as he does in verse 1 where the constructions are singular. The abrupt change of number is similar to the change of person noted in verse 3.

XIV. Yahweh's Love for Israel (11:1–11)

B. Because of Israel's Rebellion She Shall Go into Captivity (11:5–7)

5 [He] shall not return to the land of
    Egypt,
  but Assyria it shall be his king,
  because they have refused to return.
6 The sword shall sweep against his cities
    and consume his gate bolts,
    and devour because of their schemes.
7 My people are bent on turning from me;
    they call him upward,
    but together he does not rise.

5 They shall return to the land of Egypt,
    and Assyria shall be their king,
    because they have refused to return
      to me.
6 The sword rages in their cities,
    it consumes their oracle-priests,
    and devours because of their
      schemes.
7 My people are bent on turning away
      from me.
    To the Most High they call,
    but he does not raise them up at all.

5. לֹא (not) seems anomalous in view of the statements in Hosea that affirm a return to Egypt (the metaphorical depiction of Assyria). Several commentators emend to לוֹ (to him), or posit an asseverative לֹא with the sense of *surely*. Andersen and Freedman prefer the latter (*Hosea*, pp. 584, 585); Wolff leaves the question open (*Hosea*, pp. 191, 192); Mays reads לוֹ (to him) and places it at the end of verse 4 (*Hosea*, p. 150). The problem is a difficult one, but the statement in the Masoretic Text makes sense, particularly in view of the presence of הוּא (it) in the apodosis. This pronoun is probably emphatic because it does not function as the sole orthographic representation of the subject. The subject (Assyria) appears at the head of the clause. If לֹא (not) is read, הוּא relieves the resultant anomaly. We may paraphrase it, "He will not return to the land of Egypt, rather *it is* [הוּא] Assyria that will [really] be his king." This is the last time Hosea will use Egypt as a motif for the impending Assyrian captivity; perhaps the prophet wants to make the awful reality of his analogy unmistakably clear at this point. כִּי (because) introduces the reason why the people will be ruled by a foreign king. It is because they refused to return. לָשׁוּב (to return): The infinitive שׁוּב (return) is not modified with a suffix, but evidently means to return to the Lord.

6. וְחָלָה (shall sweep): The word חָלָה (חוּל) denotes writhing or whirling. It is descriptive here of a

sword wielded in the hand of a warrior. בַּדָּיו (his gate bolts) is a general word for extended parts of a person (limbs, Job 18:13) or an object (handles, Exod. 25:13). In this case it represents the bars or bolts by which one locks a gate. וְאָכְלָה (and devour), like כִּלְתָה (consume) and חָלָה (sweep), is feminine. This indicates that the feminine חֶרֶב (sword) is the subject of all three verbs. אָכְלָה (devour) is not construed with a suffix. While the translator may supply one, the prophet may have intended to isolate the action of the verb from an object in order to lay emphasis on the act of destruction. The next clause contains the reason for the impending destruction. מִמֹּעֲצוֹתֵיהֶם (because of their schemes): מִן often has a causal force because of its sense of motion from a source. מֹעֲצוֹתֵיהֶם (their schemes) refers to considered, purposeful conduct, generally in opposition to God (although see Prov. 22:20). The word occurs in parallel with "their own ways" (Prov. 1:31), and in association with "the stubbornness of their wicked hearts" (Jer. 7:24). Here the word reflects the deliberate choices and actions of the nation that led it on its present course.

7. וְעַמִּי (My people): וְ seems to have no function other than the light, narrative connective sense shared by the other instances of וְ in the section beginning at verse 4. תְּלוּאִים (are bent) has the basic sense of hang in the *qĕrē* of 2 Samuel 21:12. This connotation seems to fit the use of this difficult

---

5. The references to a return to Egypt scattered throughout the foregoing material in Hosea receive unmistakable clarity in the opening words of this verse. Their meaning was never far from us in the early contexts, but they were clothed in metaphor. Here the metaphor is dropped, and the motif stands starkly before us. It is not really Egypt that will rule over the people; it is Assyria. The people will return to the humiliating bondage they endured in the days of their infancy as a nation. All this calamity was coming because the people refused to return to Yahweh. One wonders how the sordid worship of the baals, with its prospect of national decay, found more allegiance than the purity of Yahwism with its promise of national prosperity. The fallen human heart cannot see beauty in holiness, but finds pleasure in that which ultimately may bring ruin.

6. The result of the people's refusal to return to their God is to be destruction by military force. The sword, wielded by strong warriors, will twist through the streets of their cities; the bars of their

gates, whose imposing size must have created feelings of security, will be consumed by this military might. The reason for this calamity is their "schemes." The prophet has said much to this point about the route the nation followed: social decay (4:2), defection from Yahwism (4:12), and unwise foreign policies (8:9–10). These foreign policies in particular were schemes designed to avert the certainty of national disaster, but they would all fail.

Hosea has already referred to these unwise international policies, for he had said that the alliances with Egypt and Assyria would lead to destruction (7:11–13). Their schemes to keep their heads above water in the sea of international political intrigue were futile efforts.

7. We understand the words *my people* to be the words of Yahweh, not Hosea, because the first-person suffix on *mĕšûbatî* (turning from me) complements the first-person suffix *my* in this structure. Yahweh still called his people his own, for he could not let them go. This glimpse into the

word in Deuteronomy 28:66, where it is said that the lives of the people will hang in the balance. If "hang" is the sense of the word, its function in Hosea 11:7 may be to state that the people are suspended on one thing from which they cannot deviate, that is, apostasy from God. מְשׁוּבָתִי (turning from me) is literally "my turning" with reference to (לְ) Yahweh. This is not a subjective structure, since there is no way we can attribute the act of turning away to Yahweh. Rather, the function is that of an objective formation, which directs the action to the person designated by the suffix. In Genesis 16:5, for example, Sarah is represented as saying to Abraham, literally, "My wrong [חֲמָסִי] be

upon you." The sense is, "May the wrong *done to me* be upon you." We may understand this difficult expression here similarly. "My apostasy" is thus "apostasy from me." אֶל־עַל (upward): See the discussion at 7:16. יִקְרָאֻהוּ (they call him) has a plural subject as it does in 11:2, where we identified the subject as the prophets. יַחַד (together) connotes the sense of unitedness. It occurs in the clause-initial position before a verb on several occasions (Deut. 33:5; Job 3:18; Ps. 41:8 [7]; Mic. 2:12). The sense is that the people as a whole refused to heed the prophets' call to aspire to that which was higher and more noble than apostasy from God.

---

heart of God is the prelude to the outpouring of emotion in the next verse: "How can I give you up, O Ephraim!"

Yahweh's people, however, were bent on turning from God (v. 7); they were set in their ways.

The prophets had called them to rise up out of their rebellion, but while the nation experienced some periods of revival in its history, the overall moral direction of the people was downward.

XIV. Yahweh's Love for Israel (11:1–11)

C. Yahweh's Love for Israel Will Not Allow for the Absolute Destruction of the Nation (11:8–9)

⁸ How can I give you up, O Ephraim!
   How can I deliver you over, O Israel!
How can I treat you like Admah!
   How can I make you like Zeboiim!
My heart overturns within me,
   all my feelings of compassion grow warm.
⁹ I will not execute my burning anger,
   I will not again destroy Ephraim;
for I am God and not man,
   the Holy One in your midst,
   and I will not come into any city.

⁸ How can I give you up, Ephraim?
   How can I hand you over, O Israel?
How can I make you like Admah?
   How can I treat you like Zeboiim?
My heart recoils within me;
   my compassion grows warm and tender.
⁹ I will not execute my fierce anger;
   I will not again destroy Ephraim;
for I am God and no mortal,
   the Holy One in your midst,
   and I will not come in wrath.

8. אֵיךְ (How) is more an exclamation than an interrogative here. אֶתֶּנְךָ (can I give you up): נָתַן has the basic sense of give in Hebrew, but here it is colored by the context and the companion verb מָגֵן (deliver over) with the sense of giving up or relinquishing to another. אֲמַגֶּנְךָ (can I deliver you over): This verb, which occurs only two other times in the Old Testament (Gen. 14:20; Prov. 4:9), has the connotation of giving or placing (Prov. 4:9). In Genesis 14:20, however, the context requires the sense of delivering enemies into one's hand. The same contextual force acts on מָגֵן here to give it the sense of giving up or giving over to another. אֶתֶּנְךָ (can I treat you) is accompanied by כְּ to form an idiomatic expression. The verb נָתַן (give) frequently has a sense similar to שִׂים, its companion word in this structure. This sense is to place or put. In this context, "make" is an appropriate translation. The word נָתַן has this sense in Isaiah 3:4, for example, "And I will make [וְנָתַתִּי] boys their princes" (NRSV). נֶהְפַּךְ (overturns): הָפַךְ has the sense of turn. Several contexts call for the sense of overturn or overthrow. This sense obtains particularly in contexts that depict the conquest of a city or country (Gen. 19:25; Deut. 29:22 [23]; Jon. 3:4). In contexts where לֵב (heart) indicates the presence of psychological overtones, the word often denotes a change of heart. In 1 Samuel 10:9 Saul's attitude changed, and in Exo-

dus 14:5 the heart of Pharaoh was changed. In Lamentations 1:20 הָפַךְ לֵב occurs in a context where it is parallel to expressions that denote great emotional turmoil. Context determines which sense we are to see in the word (see the Exposition). עָלַי (within me): Note the uses of עַל where the sense of within is required (see 1 Sam. 25:36; Jer. 8:18). לִבִּי (my heart) frequently denotes the mind as the center of cogitation and emotion (see, e.g., Gen. 45:26; Judg. 16:15; 1 Sam. 2:1; Neh. 2:2). יַחַד (all) occurs in the clause-initial position here (as it does in v. 7). The word connotes the union of various entities. Here it is the compassion of God, grammatically construed in the plural, that is governed by יַחַד. נִכְמְרוּ (grow warm) occurs only four times in the Old Testament, always in the niphal. In Genesis 43:30 and 1 Kings 3:26 it describes the welling up of compassion; in Lamentations 5:10 it describes the heat of the skin of people suffering from famine (זַלְעָפוֹת, intense heat). Here it denotes the intense welling up or kindling of the warmth of compassion within God. נִחוּמָי (my feelings of compassion): In Isaiah 57:18 this noun occurs with the sense of comfort. There is a strong element of compassion, however, in the verbal root נָחַם. This element may be inherent in Hosea's use of נִחוּם in this context.

9. לֹא אֶעֱשֶׂה חֲרוֹן אַפִּי (I will not execute my burning anger): The same expression occurs in

---

8. The drastic change of emotion that takes place between this verse and the previous context is one of the most significant aspects of Hosea's prophetic message. We feel Yahweh's deep emotions welling up within his heart. He looks at his erring child and is overwhelmed by love; he knows that what his rebellious son has done is worthy of expulsion from his house, but he cannot reject him forever. The punishment will not be ultimate. We see the grace of God here as we have not yet seen it in the whole prophecy. Yahweh will not give up his people.

The destruction of Admah and Zeboiim took place when their sister cities, Sodom and Gomorrah, were also destroyed. The overthrow of these cities became a symbol of absolute destruction (Deut. 29:23; Isa. 1:9; 13:19–20; Jer. 50:39–40; Zeph. 2:9; 2 Pet. 2:6; see Matt. 10:15; Rom. 9:29). Yahweh's love did not nullify the impending captivity according to this context; it did, however, negate the possibility that he would cast off his people forever and thus abrogate his promise (see 2:1 [1:10]). The people would go into captivity, but

God would not vitiate the promise of the land (see Gen. 12:7).

The parallel structure of the two clauses in the third line does not strongly support the possibility that the words *my heart overturns within me* connote the idea of a change of heart. This concept is appropriate to several contexts (see the Exegesis), but the companion clause delineates another emphasis. The words *all my feelings of compassion grow warm* speak primarily of the welling up of emotion, not of a definitive change of action. Viewed in this way, the use of *hapak* here is similar to Lamentations 1:20 where the word connotes the turmoil of deep, wrenching feelings.

The intensity of emotion is underscored by the word *yahad* (together). This appears as "all" in the Author's Translation. It pictures all the emotions of tenderness and love in Yahweh as burning within his heart.

9. The statement that Yahweh will not execute his burning anger is influenced by its companion clause in the parallel structure, "I will not again destroy Ephraim." The emphasis is on the fact

1 Samuel 28:18. לֹא אָשׁוּב (I will not again): שׁוּב (return) frequently functions as an auxiliary verb with the sense of *again* when followed by another verb (as in Gen. 26:18, "Isaac dug again the wells of water," NRSV). כִּי (for) introduces the reason why God will not destroy Ephraim in his anger. אֵל (God) has the same general range of connotation as Elohim. Its usage differs from that of Elohim in some respects, however. It is used in theophoric names, for example, and in statements where deity is contrasted with humanity, as here (see also Num. 23:19; Isa. 31:3; Ezek. 28:2). בְּקִרְבְּךָ (in your midst): God's presence in the midst of his people denotes his active intervention on their behalf (Exod. 8:18 [22]; 17:7; 34:9; Num. 14:14). If he is not in the midst of the people, they may not expect success (Num. 14:42; Deut. 1:42; 31:17). His presence also means that he watches the people (Deut. 6:15) and punishes them if he observes that which is unholy among them (Deut. 23:15 [14]). קָדוֹשׁ (the Holy One) connotes that which is distinct from the common or profane. Thus God is free from all moral imperfections and human frailties (Lev. 19:2; Isa. 17:7; 30:11). וְלֹא אָבוֹא בְּעִיר (and I will not come into any city) is a difficult clause. Mays reads "*lĕbāʿēr*" (*Hosea*, p. 151); Andersen and Freedman regard לֹא as asseverative and translate, "I . . . will certainly come into the midst of your city" (*Hosea*, p. 575). Wolff reads עִיר as "excitement" (see BDB, p. 735) and translates, "And I will not become enraged" (*Hosea*, p. 193). The suggestion of Mays requires the translation, "I will not come to consume" (*Hosea*, p. 151). It posits בָּעַר (consume) as the verb and thus assumes an alteration in the consonants. This is conjectural. The suggestion that לֹא is asseverative (see the comments at v. 5) is a valid one (see Wolff, *Hosea*, p. 178; Gordis, *Studies*, p. 178), but uncertainties surround the use of לֹא in this way, and one should not appeal to it uncritically. Andersen and Freedman regard the entire verse as a sentence of doom, but this is not consonant with the emo-

---

that God will not destroy his people a second time. Yahweh's refusal to execute his wrath must mean that he will not execute it to its fullest intensity. It does not deny his intent to send his people into captivity. The following verses depict a return from captivity, and several passages in the subsequent chapters affirm that as well. They will go into captivity, but he will not again return to vent his yet unquenched anger and destroy them forever. Such an action would vitiate the ancient promise given to Abraham (Gen. 12:1–7; see Lev. 26:44).

The reason that Yahweh will not give up his people is that he is God, not man. This contrast between the divine and human is not one of power, but of moral purity. This verse describes Yahweh as the Holy One; it is thus similar to Numbers 23:19 which states that God is not like man in that God does not lie.

This thought is carried forward in the reference to Yahweh as the Holy One. The implications of the parallel clauses are profound. Because Yahweh is holy he cannot condone evil; that would involve a blurring of the distinction between the holy and the profane (see Lev. 10:10; Num. 16:37–38; Ezek. 22:26). This means that Yahweh had to remove himself from the wickedness that existed in Israel. Yet he had made a promise to Israel to which his holy nature bound him. Hosea does not explain this apparent dilemma theologically. The sublime solution of Christianity set forth in a cross raised on a lonely hill seems to have remained beyond Hosea's horizon. It is enough to know that the love of God that Hosea depicts in deep emotive terminology was the motivation for the cross. In this way Hosea's portrayal of divine love spans the centuries.

The fact that Yahweh was the Holy One *in their midst* implies his active presence among them. Yahweh's presence with his people assured success in various ventures (Exod. 17:7; 34:9; Num. 14:14); his absence meant failure (Num. 14:42; Deut. 1:42; 31:17). His proximity to the people enabled him to observe them (Deut. 6:15) and to punish them if he saw unholiness among them (Deut. 23:15 [14]). Thus, as the Holy One in the midst of his people, his holiness was a factor that defined and motivated the nature of his activity among them. He had promised them a marvelous inheritance; his holiness demanded he fulfill his promise.

The words *and I will not come into any city* are connected to the preceding clause by *waw* and extend its thought. The juxtaposition of the affirmation of holiness in the preceding context, and the assurance that Yahweh will not enter a city implies an absence of hostile intent on the part of God. The word *ʿîr* (city) occurs in 13:10 and refers to that which the king must defend, for cities were objects of hostile military action. The word *ʿîr* (city) is indeterminate in the Masoretic Text, as in the Septuagint. In light of the previous reference to Yahweh's presence within the nation this is an acceptable pointing. Yahweh will

tional upheaval in the heart of Yahweh that verse 8 describes. If we understand the expression בְּעִיר אָבוֹא (come into any city) to have a hostile military connotation, it is consonant with the immediate context and with the references to cities in verses 6 and 8 (see the Exposition). The וְ that begins this clause serves as a light connective between this clause and the preceding one. It thus indicates a conceptual connection between them.

---

enter *none* of their cities to destroy them. He is actively present among them (see the Exegesis), but his holiness precludes his treating any of Israel's cities like Admah and Zeboiim. He will not stamp out the rebellious nation as a human conqueror would, because he is God and not man. The indeterminate status of a noun may indicate "indeterminateness for the sake of amplification" (GKC §125c); thus we translate "any city."

XIV. Yahweh's Love for Israel (11:1–11)

D. Yahweh Will Call His People from Captivity
(11:10–11)

10 They shall go after the LORD,
 he will roar like a lion;
 for, he will roar,
  and his children shall come trembling from the sea.
11 They shall come trembling like birds out of Egypt,
  and like doves from the land of Assyria;
  and I will return them to their homes; utterance of the LORD.

10 They shall go after the LORD,
 who roars like a lion;
 when he roars,
  his children shall come trembling from the west.
11 They shall come trembling like birds from Egypt,
  and like doves from the land of Assyria;
  and I will return them to their homes, says the LORD.

10. יֵלְכוּ (they shall go) finds its referent in the people, represented by Ephraim (v. 9). The abrupt change of person is typical of Hosea. This interchange of person may denote logical sections. כִּי (for) does not introduce direct causation, but is explicative in function. BDB states that כִּי has this function of "justifying a statement by unfolding the particulars wh[ich] establish or exemplify it" (p. 473; note Isa. 1:30; 13:10). Here the clause introduced by כִּי repeats the previous concept of Yahweh's roaring and further explicates the statement of the previous clause that "they shall go after the LORD." They will do this by coming from the west at the summons of Yahweh. הוּא (he) probably func-

tions as poetic ballast here rather than as an indicator of emphasis because the clause would be unnecessarily flat and abrupt without it. וְיֶחֶרְדוּ (and . . . shall come trembling): חָרַד means only "to tremble." The concept of motion (*come* trembling) must be supplied because of the influence of מִן (from) on the idiom מִיָּם (from the sea). יָם (sea) designates the coastlands and islands of the Mediterranean. Since this body of water lay to the west of Israel, יָם became a surrogate for the west (see, e.g., Josh. 5:1; Isa. 11:14).

11. יֶחֶרְדוּ (They shall come trembling) occurs with מִן. It is the same as the collocation in verse 10.

---

10. The hope of a future restoration is set forth in terms of a vivid metaphor which depicts Yahweh roaring like a lion. The terrifying sound causes his people to follow him as they tremble in fear at his voice. His children will come trembling from the west. We must observe that a dispersion has taken place according to this statement; the captivity has become a reality. So this section continues the theme of hope that looks beyond the captivity to a future restoration of the people to their land (see v. 9). We must not lose sight of the fact that the prospect of a bright future for the people of God is based on Yahweh's faithfulness to his promise.

The motif of Yahweh's roaring occurs several times in the Prophets. It presages divine judgment on the nations (Jer. 25:30; Amos 1:2); it summons his people from dispersion among the nations.

11. Hosea pairs Egypt and Assyria again here as he did in 9:3. The reference to the return of the people to their homes recalls the ancient promise of a land for God's people (Gen. 12:7). This statement affirms God's loyalty to his promise. It applies to Christians as well because our landedness is in Christ (Heb. 3–4).

XV. An Oracle Against the Kingdoms of Judah and Israel (12:1–15) [11:12–12:14]

A. Ephraim Practices Treachery but Judah Still Enjoys Fellowship with God (12:1–2) [11:12–12:1]

12 Ephraim has surrounded me with lies,
and the house of Israel with deceit;
but Judah still wanders freely with God
and is established with the Holy
One.
2 Ephraim grazes on the wind
and pursues the east wind all day
long;
he multiplies deceit and violence.
They make an agreement with
Assyria
and oil is carried to Egypt.

12 Ephraim has surrounded me with lies,
and the house of Israel with deceit;
but Judah still walks with God,
and is faithful to the Holy One.

12 Ephraim herds the wind,
and pursues the east wind all day
long;
they multiply falsehood and violence;
they make a treaty with Assyria,
and oil is carried to Egypt.

12:1 [11:12]. סְבָבֻנִי (has surrounded me): This is the only place where בְּ occurs with סָבַב when that verb has the sense of *surround*, but the collocation can scarcely connote anything other than *surround with*. וּבְמִרְמָה (and . . . with deceit): The basic connotation of מִרְמָה is deceit. It describes false or deceptive balances (Hos. 12:8 [7]; Amos 8:5; Mic. 6:11) and deceptive speech (Gen. 34:13). When it depicts deceit in the sense of betrayal of a trust, "treachery" is an apt translational equivalent. The context must delineate the nuance intended by the writer (see the Exposition). וִיהוּדָה (but Judah): We understand this statement about Judah to be positive in contrast to the negative treatment of Israel in the foregoing statement; thus וְ is understood to have an adversative function. The originality of יְהוּדָה (Judah) in this pericope is questioned by some, but Judah is contrasted with Israel elsewhere in the prophecy (see the comments at 1:7). The Septuagint witnesses to the presence of Judah in the Hebrew consonantal text, but pairs it with Israel (οἶκος Ἰσραὴλ καὶ Ἰούδα, house of Israel and Judah). This arrangement is questionable. The pairing of the two houses is not expressed in this fashion (house of Israel and Judah) in the later Old Testament literature. It is expressed in the more expansive collocation, "house of Israel and house of Judah" (Jer. 2:4; 5:11; 11:10, 17; 13:11; 31:27, 31; 33:14; Zech. 8:13). Only in 2 Samuel 12:8 does the collocation appear as "house of Israel and of Judah," but this expression describes the united monarchy and is appropriate to the status of the two houses before the rupture of the nation. Since there is no contextual warrant for supposing that Hosea had the ideal of the united kingdom in mind when he wrote this section, we must conclude that the Hebrew usage is against the clausal structure of the Septuagint. Also, the Septuagint requires the awkward balancing of "Ephraim" with "house of Israel and Judah." The presence of οἶκος (house) in the Septuagint witnesses to the presence of the singular בֵּית (house) in the Hebrew consonantal text. רָד (wanders freely) is enigmatic. It is pointed as a third-person perfect or a participle of רוּד (wander, roam). It cannot be an aphaeresized form of יָרַד (go down), for that verbal idea makes no sense in the context. The Septuagint reads רָד as יָד and joins it to the following עַם to yield the read-

---

12:1 [11:12]. The prophet pictures Yahweh surrounded by lies. As he stood in the midst of Israel (see 11:9), Yahweh saw deceit and evasion of truth wherever he turned. He could not allow such behavior to tarnish his holiness, so we are not surprised to read the somber pronouncement of doom that follows in the next pericope.

Judah's situation was different from Israel's, however, for her relationship with God was still secure. Yet we learn from other references to Judah in Hosea that her fate was sealed too (5:5, 10, 12, 14; 6:11; 8:14; 10:11; 12:3 [2]). She was not to fall at the same time as her sister nation to the north; she was to be spared for a while (1:7). She had not yet incurred the guilt that Israel had brought on herself (4:15).

The words of the prophet in the second line of this verse are obscure. We have suggested that the Masoretic Text is logically and grammatically superior to that of the Septuagint; it depicts Judah as still walking freely with God. Her relationship to him was still unencumbered by the evils that were soon to lead to Israel's demise. Perhaps the security of Judah's association with God was due to the fact that the Holy One in their midst (11:9) could continue to abide for a while in Judah. The superscription to the prophecy places a portion of Hosea's ministry in the time of Hezekiah, whose sweeping religious reforms stayed God's hand, if only for a while.

Several commentators understand *qĕdôšîm* (the Holy One) to refer to holy gods (Andersen and Freedman, *Hosea*, pp. 593, 603; see Mays, *Hosea*, p. 160), that is, deities of the Canaanite pantheon. One reason for this is that a positive statement about Judah's relationship to God is contrary to verse 3, which pronounces judgment on Judah. Against this view is the fact that *qĕdôšîm* (the Holy One) never clearly refers to pagan deities, but to saints (Ps. 16:3) and angels (Job 5:1; Zech. 14:5); *qĕdôšîm* also refers to God (Prov. 9:10; 30:3), apparently as a plural of majesty (GKC §124g–i). It is unlikely that *ʾēl* (God) refers to El, the chief god of the Canaanite pantheon. His influence seems to have diminished before the lusty Baal, who, after all, was the god favored by the adherents of the fertility cult. Both *ʾēl* and *qādôš* refer to Yahweh in 11:9. The statement about Judah here is consonant with similar statements elsewhere (see the discussion at 10:11) and the fact that it precedes a statement condemning Judah is typical of Amos's style (Hos. 4:15; see 5:5).

The divine names *ʾēl* (God) and *qādôš* (the Holy One) have the sense of divine "otherness" (11:9); God is not man and he exists in the sphere of the holy. At this time Judah still enjoyed access to the holy God. It is difficult to imagine why she

ing יְדָעָם ([God] knows them). The עתה (now) in the Septuagint evidently represents the עֹד that stands in the consonantal text. Perhaps they read it as עַד (until) or, less likely, as עַתָּה (now). If the original reading were יְדָעָם (he knows them), as the Septuagint suggests, we expect some grammatical indication of contrast before עֹד ([but] now God knows them). Since this is not reflected in the Hebrew, the accuracy of the Septuagint's rendering is questionable. The Masoretic Text is difficult, but not grammatically untenable. In Jeremiah 2:31 the word רוד refers to freedom from Yahweh. We may paraphrase it, "We roam freely; we will not come any longer to you [Yahweh]." The sense of wandering freely may obtain in the use of this verb in Judges 11:37 as well. The action of the verb in Hosea 12:1 is limited by the preposition עִם (with) to the sphere of association with God. It is thus possible to understand the construction in the Masoretic Text to depict Judah as wandering freely within that relationship. Thus Judah's relationship to Yahweh was not fettered by lying and deceit to the extent that Israel's was. This view gains support from the companion clause which describes Judah's relationship to Yahweh as established and secure. אֵל (God): See the Exegesis at 11:9. וְעִם (and . . . with) serves to carry the sense of association established by עִם (with) in the previous clause into this clause. קְדוֹשִׁים (the Holy One) does not connote holy ones because it is balanced by אֵל (God) in the parallel clause. This plural form of קָדוֹשׁ (holy) is used of God in Proverbs 9:10 and 30:3.

The plural is either intensive or the plural of majesty. נֶאֱמָן (is established): אָמַן has the basic sense of firmness or security in the qal (see the discussion at 5:9). In the niphal the sense of *established* is often appropriate. We may understand the parallel clauses to depict Judah's relationship with God to continue intact because it was unhindered by treachery and deceit.

12:2 [12:1]. רֹעֶה has the sense of feeding or grazing (BDB, p. 944) when used intransitively (see Isa. 44:20). רוּחַ (wind) connotes here that which is empty or worthless (see, e.g., Job 7:7; 15:2; Eccles. 1:14; Isa. 41:29). קָדִים (east wind) probably serves only as a poetic complement to רוּחַ (wind). There is no need to press its meaning further than that. שֹׁד (violence) occurs frequently in the Prophets as social wrong (see, e.g., Jer. 6:7; 20:8; Amos 3:10). Hosea uses the word in the more general sense of the violence that is to befall his nation (7:13), but the context of 12:2 [1] requires the connotation of social wrong. בְּרִית (an agreement) is discussed at 2:20 [18] and 6:7. The reference here is reminiscent of Hosea's words in 5:13 and 7:11. It reflects the political turmoil of the time when the nation's leaders attempted to shore up the sagging national structure by appealing for help to Assyria. The nation forsook the aid of their God to seek help from a potential enemy. The word בְּרִית (an agreement) thus reflects the national alliances that characterized Israel's dealings with her more powerful neighbors. יִכְרֹתוּ (make): See 2:20 [18].

---

forsook her relationship with Yahweh to follow the path of her sister nation.

12:2 [12:1]. Hosea uses pastoral imagery to depict the futility of Israel's national policies. We see in his metaphor an animal that rejects vegetation to graze on the wind; it tries to satisfy its hunger by running to snap at the breezes. The stupidity of this activity is heightened by the fact that this hypothetical animal does this "all day long" (kol-hayyôm). It is possible that this pastoral imagery appears in the previous verse as well, where the verb rād (wanders freely) may picture a flock with ('im) its shepherd (God).

The reference to Israel's multiplication of deceit and violence brings the hypothetical analogy into the sphere of reality. This concept receives further amplification in the next clause which connects to the previous clause by *waw*. Hosea associates the lying and violence with Israel's international policies, which included an alliance with Assyria and traffic with Egypt. This was all futile, and these efforts would not save Israel. It was like eating the wind—no good could come of that. The political events reflected here may be those recorded in 2 Kings 17:1–6.

XV. An Oracle Against the Kingdoms of Judah and Israel (12:1-15) [11:12-12:14]

B. Yahweh Has a Controversy with Judah (12:3-7) [2-6]

3 And the LORD has a controversy with Judah,
   and will visit upon Jacob in accordance with his ways:
   according to his deeds he will cause to return to him.
4 In the womb he supplanted his brother,
   and in the strength of his manhood he strove with God.
5 And he strove with an angel and prevailed,
   he wept and supplicated him.
At Bethel he found him,
   and there he spoke to him.
6 The LORD, the God of hosts—
   the LORD is his name.
7 And you, turn to your God,
   observe lovingkindness and justice,
   and wait continually for your God.

2 The LORD has an indictment against Judah,
   and will punish Jacob according to his ways,
   and repay him according to his deeds.
3 In the womb he tried to supplant his brother,
   and in his manhood he strove with God.
4 He strove with the angel and prevailed,
   he wept and sought his favor;
he met him at Bethel,
   and there he spoke with him.
5 The LORD the God of hosts,
   the LORD is his name!
6 But as for you, return to your God,
   hold fast to love and justice,
   and wait continually for your God.

3 [2]. וְרִיב (And . . . a controversy): וְ (And) connects the subsequent Judah-material to the foregoing context (see the Exposition). רִיב (a controversy) is discussed at 4:1. לַיהוָה (the LORD has) expresses possession (GKC §129a). וְלִפְקֹד (and will visit): The infinitive construct with לְ, preceded by וְ, depends on the idea expressed in the previous construction (GKC §114p). In Exodus 32:29, for example, וְלָתֵת (and to give) depends on the idea of the previous statement, "Fill your hand this day for Yahweh . . . and [that] to give [וְלָתֵת] you a blessing this day." The construction וְלִפְקֹד (and will visit) states the intent of the רִיב introduced in the previous clause, "The LORD has a רִיב, *and that is* to visit . . ." פָּקַד (see 1:4 for the discussion of the collocation פָּקַד עַל [visit upon]). כִּדְרָכָיו (in accordance with his ways): This expression differs from the somewhat similar expression in 4:9 in that דְּרָכָיו (his ways) is the object of פָּקַד עַל there, whereas here it is construed with the preposition כְּ (according to) and there is no stated object. This does not nullify the conclusions reached in the discussion at 1:4 concerning the reciprocal nature of the collocation, for the parallel clause here יָשִׁיב לוֹ (he will cause to return to him) shows that reciprocity is involved, but the context does not state the object of the reciprocal action. The use of the expression here is similar to its function in those instances where there is only one object (see 1:4 in the Exegesis). In Isaiah 10:12, for example, only the indirect object appears. It says, "I will visit upon (פָּקַד עַל) the fruit of the pride of heart of the king of Assyria, and upon the glory of the loftiness of his eyes." It is obvious that we cannot understand the collocation to connote the sense of *punishing for* in this case, because the nouns cited are objects of punishment, not bases of punishment. In these instances the center seems to shift from the object of the visitation to the one who does the punishing. כִּדְרָכָיו (in accordance with his ways) provides the measure of the punishment. The divine visitation will be in accordance with the ways that characterized the nation. We observed some of these "ways" in 12:1 [11:12]. כְּמַעֲלָלָיו (according to his deeds) is broadly defined by the parallel דְּרָכָיו (his ways) as those actions that characterize an individual or a nation (see, e.g., Deut. 28:20; Jer. 4:4; Hos. 4:9; 5:4; 7:2; 9:15; Mic. 7:13; Zech. 1:4). יָשִׁיב לוֹ (he will cause to return to him), like its companion verbal collocation (פָּקַד עַל), has no stated object (see the Exposition).

4 [3]. עָקַב (he supplanted) is related to עָקֵב (heel).

---

3 [2]. This section begins with the chilling announcement that Yahweh has an indictment against Judah as well. The *rîb* (legal controversy) form was discussed earlier (see 4:1). The same elements exist in the *rîb* form here, but they are compressed into one verse. We find here the announcement of the *rîb*, the people addressed, the reason for the *rîb* (Judah's ways and deeds), and the affirmation of punishment. It is unlikely that this last element of the *rîb* extends beyond verse 7 because of the positive statement of hope in the next section (v. 10 [9]), an element anomalous to the nature of the *rîb*. The *rîb* form in this context differs from the *rîb* that begins in 4:1 in that it contains a lengthy recital of three events from the life of Jacob, which shows that the *rîb* was not a static formulation.

The events in Jacob's life serve as a basis for the plea to the people of Judah (v. 7 [6]). It is as though Hosea recalls these events in order to provide an emotional basis for his plea. He holds before the people the memory of their ancestor who prevailed with God; could they not also prevail with God?

The fact that the *rîb* is addressed to Judah seems anomalous in view of our interpretation of 12:1 [11:12] which views Judah's relationship to God in a positive way. Yet we observed in the discussion that Judah was not exempt from the divine wrath. Her relationship with God was secure at this time, but the prophet was painfully aware of the fact that the sister nation had the same illness. Israel was closer to death than Judah. Perhaps this is the reason for Hosea's tender supplication to Judah to return to God; the sickness was not yet terminal.

The intent of the *rîb* is stated in the structure of an infinitive with *lĕ*, "to visit upon" (*paqad ʿal*). We are not told what will be visited upon Judah, for the direct object is not stated. It is clear from the parallel expression *yāšîb lô* (he will cause to return to him) that no particular object was intended because we are not told what was to be returned to Judah. Evidently the expression "according to his deeds he will cause to return to him" means that Yahweh will requite the people of Judah according to the wrongs they have done. Thus *paqad ʿal* (visit upon) must have a similar sense by virtue of its position in the clausal structure. It too connotes *to requite* in this context. The nature of the requital is left vague and uncertain because the punishment is not stated.

4 [3]. The first aspect of Jacob's life about which we read occurred at his birth when he grasped his

In Genesis 27:36 it occurs in a definitive context where it clearly has the sense of supplanting, for Esau cited two ways in which Jacob had superseded him. In Jeremiah 9:3 [4] it denotes devious treatment on the part of a brother. The implication is that one brother seeks to supplant another. In Job 37:4 the sense is obscure, but it seems to indicate that God does not supplant the lightning (i.e., leave it behind or restrain it). וּבְאוֹנוֹ (and in the strength of his manhood): The word אוֹן has the basic sense of strength. It is applied to God (Isa. 40:26), and to Behemoth (Job 40:16). It also refers to humans (Isa. 40:29), and in several contexts it describes the vigor of early manhood (Gen. 49:3; Deut. 21:17). Since this word is paired with בְּבֶטֶן (in the womb), it is likely that it shares with

that construction the function of designating a period of time in Jacob's life. Thus we paraphrase it, "In the strength of his manhood." שָׂרָה (he strove) occurs only here and in Genesis 32:29 [28]. Its meaning in Genesis 32 is clear; it describes Jacob's striving with the supernatural figure at the Jabbok.

5 [4]. וַיִּתְחַנֶּן (and supplicated): In the qal חָנַן connotes showing favor. In the hithpael (the form of the word here) it has the sense of seeking favor (Gen. 42:21). לוֹ (him): לְ with חָנַן transfers the action of the verb to the person who is the object of the supplication (Esther 4:8; 8:3; Job 19:16). בֵּית־אֵל (Bethel) is an accusative of place—at Bethel (GKC §118d–g).

---

brother's heel (Gen. 25:26). Hosea uses the word ʿaqab to describe this. Perhaps the word had a broader sense in Hosea's time, such as grasp the heel or follow at the heel, but the few occurrences of this word preclude our knowing that. The evidence we have points to the meaning of supplant. If this is the sense of the word here, then Hosea views the grasping of Esau's heel as in some way related to the act of supplanting Esau. Perhaps Hosea understands this as a foreshadowing of Jacob's later acts of supersession (Gen. 27:36) or as an act of supersession in itself. At any rate, this unusual event, coupled with Jacob's striving with God in his manhood, underscores an aspect of Jacob's character that was important to Hosea's illustration. Jacob was a man who sought to overcome. Whether it was God or his brother, Jacob was persistent in the pursuit of his goals. Hosea does not comment on the ethical dimension of Jacob's efforts to dominate; he instead emphasizes that aspect of the character of Judah's ancient ancestor.

With one bold sweep of his brush Hosea portrays Jacob's character as the same in his later years as it was foreshadowed at his birth. From his birth to his early manhood Jacob strove to overcome.

5 [4]. The second aspect of Jacob's life cited in this context is his encounter with the mysterious figure at the Jabbok (Gen. 32:22–32). The statement that Jacob strove with God (Hos. 12:4 [3]) is refined here to state that he strove with an angel. We need not understand this theophany as an actual appearance of God, nor a preincarnate appearance of Christ. The manifestation of the divine presence was in an angel. There is no question that the angel of the Lord in the Old Testa-

ment is identified with God in many contexts (Gen. 16:13, see v. 9; Judg. 6:14, see v. 11; 13:21–22) as he is here, but the angel is often distinguished from God (Exod. 23:23; 32:34; 2 Sam. 24:16; Zech. 1:12). It is best to understand the angel of the Lord as a self-manifestation of God in a way that would communicate certain aspects of God's character peculiar to the existing circumstances. The appearance of the angel of the Lord depicted, for example, God's immanence and concern.

The clauses in the subsequent context present a problem because Hosea is not consistent in stating the subjects of the key verbs in the clausal arrangement. Who prevailed in the encounter? Who found whom? We have arranged the clauses in a way that seems to be both logical and symmetrical:

A In the womb he supplanted his brother,
B and in the strength of his manhood he strove with God.
C And he strove with an angel and prevailed,
D he wept and supplicated him.

It seems best to place the last clause with the foregoing material rather than with the subsequent clause. It was certainly Jacob, not the angel, who "wept and supplicated." This statement fits with the foregoing clauses that describe the actual encounter. Since the next clause, "at Bethel he found him," refers to another event in Jacob's life, we may not include it in this sequence of clauses. We find no mention of Jacob's weeping in the account in Genesis; perhaps this is an independent tradition or an embellishment. The description of Jacob weeping and beseeching the angel offsets the impression of brashness and arrogance

201

6 [5]. וַיהוָה אֱלֹהֵי הַצְּבָאוֹת (The LORD, the God of hosts): וְ is epexegetical—"even the LORD." צְבָאוֹת denotes armies. This title may have been attributed to Yahweh as a result of the appearance to Joshua of an angel called "the commander of the host of the LORD" (Josh. 5:13–15). The "hosts" appear to be the hosts of heaven who intervene with Yahweh in the affairs of history (Isa. 13:4). זִכְרוֹ (his name) signifies a remembrance. It is a noun form of זָכַר (remember) and occurs in parallel with שֵׁם (name) in a number of passages.

7 [6]. וְאַתָּה (And you) is understood by some commentators to introduce a direct address by God to Jacob (see the Exposition). However, we may find several direct addresses to Israel earlier in Hosea (see 11:8). חֶסֶד (lovingkindness) connotes the covenant loyalty that the Mosaic covenant called for. It reflects an attitude of love to God that prompts obedience to his will and love to one's fellow man. It is a condition for the reception of covenant blessing and maintenance of

covenant privilege (see 4:1; 6:4). וּמִשְׁפָּט (and justice) is colored by its companion word (חֶסֶד) to have a benign sense (see the comments at 2:21 [19]). שָׁמֹר (observe): Basic to the semantic range of this word is the concept of giving careful attention. It is used in the sense of giving attention to the commands of God (see, e.g., Lev. 8:35; Deut. 4:6). In Genesis 30:31 it connotes keeping something secure. The former sense is overwhelmingly represented in the Old Testament. The command in Hosea 12:7 is to be careful to do that which is entailed in מִשְׁפָּט (justice) and חֶסֶד (lovingkindness). The idea of *doing* these covenantal obligations is not grammatically anomalous. The verb עָשָׂה (do) is used with חֶסֶד (Jer. 9:23 [24]; Zech. 7:9) and שָׁמַר occurs with חֶסֶד in several contexts (Deut. 7:9; 1 Kings 8:23; 2 Chron. 6:14; Neh. 1:5; 9:32). These passages contain the crystallized expression *keep covenant and lovingkindness* (חֶסֶד) and refer to God. The implication is that God gives careful attention to his covenant obligation. Here the peo-

---

that Hosea's description of Jacob thus far may have created. Jacob prevailed in his struggle not only by persistence, but by tearful pleading as well.

The next event from Jacob's life that Hosea cites is his encounter with God at Bethel. The name *Bethel* is in the clause-initial position and thus receives emphasis. Bethel receives further emphasis from the adverb *šam* (there), which finds its referent in Bethel and is also in the clause-initial position. Hosea shifts our attention from the Jabbok to Bethel in this clause. We were reminded of Jacob's encounter with the angel; now Bethel is before us. That place was the scene of another encounter.

The subjects of the verbs in this clause are not stated. It is best to see God as the subject of *yĕdabbɛr* (he spoke), however, because there is no record in the account in Genesis 28:10–22 of Jacob speaking to God, and Genesis 35:15 emphasizes the fact that God spoke to Jacob at Bethel. This view posits God as the subject of *yimṣāʾɛnnû* (he met him) as well. This also finds support in the Jacob cycle (Gen. 35:1, 6, 7), where God is shown as the one who initiated the encounter with Jacob; it is God who found him and spoke to him according to the Genesis narratives.

6 [5]. The divine title *Yahweh God of hosts* confirms the conclusion that the subject of the preceding verbs is God. The epexegetical *waw* sets this title in apposition to the previous clause. We learn from the title that the one who found Jacob

and spoke to him is none other than Yahweh. In the appellation *God of hosts*, the word *hosts* likely refers to the angelic beings Jacob observed in his dream (Gen. 28:12).

This dramatic title receives a peculiar dignity in the way it is set in apposition to the preceding context, for it comprises an entire clause. The next clause repeats the name *Yahweh* and it too is set in apposition to the title. This positioning of the name *Yahweh* gives it peculiar emphasis and force: Yahweh, God of hosts; Yahweh is his name! This structure recalls the awesome significance of the name *Yahweh*. It provides a profoundly theological basis for the appeal to the people that follows.

7 [6]. We see no need to understand the words *and you* to be the words of God to Jacob at Bethel. This is the prophet's plea to his people. We should expect it to follow immediately after the word *yĕdabbɛr* (he spoke/said) if it were a direct quotation, and there is nothing like these words in the Jacob cycle. Hosea addresses Judah in the second-person singular in 6:4 and 11. It is a pointed address to Judah that brings the illustrations from Jacob's life home to her with tender yet telling force.

Hosea tells Judah to turn to God, keep covenant loyalty, and continually wait for God. This admonition follows the portrait of Jacob's persistent efforts to gain divine favor. Hosea's words reflect both the attitude of the ancient patriarch and the contemporary situation. Jacob enjoyed an unusual

ple are called to do the same. וְקַוֵּה (and wait . . . for) always refers to God with the sense of waiting for him to act. Those who wait for God will never be frustrated (Ps. 25:3). God will act in his own time to effect his purpose (Ps. 37:9). Those who wait for God to act in his time will have renewed strength when at last he comes to the aid of his people (Isa. 40:31). The Lord is good to those who wait for him (Lam. 3:25).

---

relationship with God, and Hosea instructs the people to renew their relationship to God by turning back to him. They could do this by renewing their loyalty to the covenant stipulations. They were to be like Jacob in that they were to wait persistently for God to act. He would act if they would return to him.

XV. An Oracle Against the Kingdoms of Judah and Israel (12:1–15) [11:12–12:14]

C. Israel Is Like a Dishonest Merchant (12:8–11) [7–10]

8 A merchant—in his hand are deceptive scales—
   he loves to extort.
9 And Ephraim says, "How rich I am!
   I have gained wealth for myself.
All my possessions
   do not incur guilt for me
   which is sin."
10 But I am the LORD your God,
   from the land of Egypt,
I will again cause you to dwell in tents
   as in the days of the appointed feast.

11 And I spoke to the prophets;
   and it was I who multiplied visions
   and, by the hand of the prophets,
   gave parables.

7 A trader, in whose hands are false balances,
   he loves to oppress.
8 Ephraim has said, "Ah, I am rich,
   I have gained wealth for myself;
in all of my gain
   no offense has been found in me
   that would be sin."
9 I am the LORD your God
   from the land of Egypt;
I will make you live in tents again,
   as in the days of the appointed festival.

10 I spoke to the prophets;
   it was I who multiplied visions,
   and through the prophets I will bring destruction.

8 [7]. כְּנַעַן (A merchant) also denotes "Canaan" in Hebrew. Because the Canaanites were known as traders, the word took on the secondary sense of merchant (Ezek. 16:29; 17:4; Zeph. 1:11). מֹאזְנֵי (scales) were comprised of a bar from which hung two balanced surfaces. Weights (generally stones) were used to determine the value of the money to be weighed. Cheating could occur if the balance was improperly suspended or the weights altered. מִרְמָה (deceptive): See the discussion of this word at 12:1 [11:12]. לַעֲשֹׁק (to extort) has the sense of oppression in a number of contexts, but in contexts that deal with possessions or gain the word has to do with obtaining something by force or intimidation (Ps. 62:11 [10]; Jer. 22:17; Ezek. 22:12), that is, extortion. The reference to deceitful scales in the companion clause here energizes לַעֲשֹׁק with the sense of extortion by the use of illegal power.

9 [8]. אַךְ עָשַׁרְתִּי (How rich I am!): אַךְ is an asseverative that communicates an idea closely akin to *surely*. We have attempted to capture this sense with the paraphrase. מָצָאתִי (I have gained) has the basic sense of finding, but, as in English, the word may connote the gain of something (Gen. 6:8; 18:3; Prov. 3:13; 18:22; Isa. 10:10). The context calls for the sense of monetary gain here. יְגִיעַי (my possessions) is related to the verb יָגַע which has as one of its nuances the sense of toil. The noun

יְגִיעַ reflects that nuance in its reference to wealth or possessions which are the product of toil (see Deut. 28:33; Isa. 45:14; 55:2; Jer. 3:24). יִמְצְאוּ (incur) is construed in the plural. The nearest plural referent is יְגִיעַי (my possessions). מָצָא (incur), as in the previous occurrence of this word, has the sense of finding or gaining. Because its object is עָוֹן (guilt), we translate it "incur." אֲשֶׁר (which) functions in relative clauses to define the substantive on which it depends (GKC §138a). Thus עָוֹן (guilt) is defined in the relative clause as חֵטְא (sin). חֵטְא (sin) is a denominative of the verb חָטָא (to sin), which in its secular usage designates the idea of missing a mark (Judg. 20:16). It is likely that the word does not retain that distinctive sense in all the contexts where it refers to sin, because various forms of the root חָטָא occur in parallel with other words for sin. If any verbal or nominal forms do retain this sense, the idea is that of falling short of God's standards. The idea that this clause describes is that Ephraim, which is depicted as a merchant, boldly asserts that his wealth has not incurred guilt. The word חֵטְא (sin), in the relative clause introduced by אֲשֶׁר, depicts Ephraim as protesting that his wrongdoing should not receive the harsh designation of sin.

10 [9]. וְאָנֹכִי (But I) is in the place of emphasis in the clause. וְ (and) joins this clause to the preceding context. מֵאֶרֶץ (from the land): מִן (from) extends

---

8 [7]. This portion of Hosea's message is based on the analogy of a merchant, a forceful one that has no syntactical connection to the preceding context. Suddenly a hypothetical merchant appears in Hosea's speech. It is difficult to determine whether Hosea's use of the term *Canaan* for this merchant is meant to convey the negative associations that this term had for the Hebrews. It is enough to know that the merchant was dishonest.

This merchant totals the payment he receives for his goods with deceptive scales. The altered scales work to his benefit, of course, but this merchant is not just a cheat; he loves to extort as well. He is not beyond the use of force and intimidation to gain wealth.

9 [8]. The merchant in the analogy represents Ephraim (Israel), who boasts of his great wealth. The comparison between this rich man and Israel aptly described the northern kingdom in Hosea's day. Israel had become wealthy in the eighth century, but according to the prophetic perspective, her gain was ill-gotten. The economic prosperity

of the eighth century was hers, not because of her ethical response to the benign regulations of the covenant, but because of the deception and extortion she practiced. The poor were cheated and oppressed. Amos also depicted the wealthy classes of his day as engaging in deception and oppression, longing on one occasion for the end of the Sabbath, "that we may . . . practice deceit with false balances, buying the poor for silver and the needy for a pair of sandals" (8:5–6, NRSV).

This merchant, who depicts Israel, boasted that he had incurred no guilt in the course of becoming wealthy. We observed in the discussion at 1:4 that Hebrew words for sin often include the concept of punishment. To incur guilt could also mean to suffer punishment for that guilt. It is difficult to determine with certainty what this boastful statement intends, but in all likelihood it is that Israel's deceptive practices had brought her no punishment.

10 [9]. The words of this verse are an enigma. We wonder why the analogy of the merchant is followed by the benign assurance that Yahweh is

the state of Yahweh's relationship to his people over the span of time from the exodus to the time of Hosea. מוֹעֵד (appointed feast): See the comments at 2:11 [9] and 9:5.

11 [10]. וְדִבַּרְתִּי (And I spoke): וְ (and) functions, as does the preceding וְ, as a light connective that combines its clause with the preceding clause. Thus verses 8–11 [7–10] form a complete logical

---

their God and they will again dwell in tents. It is difficult to conclude that this is an isolated saying because the *waw* connects it conceptually to the foregoing analogy.

The statement that Yahweh is their God from the land of Egypt associates the name *Yahweh* with the events of the exodus. It recalls the peculiar significance imparted to the name by those events (Exod. 3:13–15). The word *from (min)* indicates that Yahweh had remained unchanged. He is still the God of the exodus. This fact is underscored in the next clause where Hosea depicts him as acting again as he did in the exodus; he will make the people live in tents.

This statement recalls the Feast of Booths, which commemorated the conditions under which the people lived after their flight from Egypt (Lev. 23:39–43). We have no clear explanation in the Old Testament of the significance of the booths. Did they recall the mean conditions in which that early generation lived, or did they symbolize Yahweh's provision for them? In all probability both concepts lay behind this solemn celebration.

Hosea does not say that they will again dwell in tents as in the days of the wilderness wanderings, but "as in the days of the appointed feast." He draws his analogy, not from Israel's earliest history, but from the accounts of the Feast of Booths (Lev. 23:39–43; Deut. 16:9–12). That feast was to be a time of rejoicing (Lev. 23:40; Deut. 16:11), so the prospect of their living in tents again was not necessarily a dismal one.

The statement here seems to contain two intentions. The nation which, like a dishonest merchant, gained its status through deceptive practices, would be reduced to living in greatly reduced circumstances, and God would sweep away the symbols of the nation's grandeur. At the same time, however, this impoverishment would be a tender act of God on Israel's behalf, for he would provide for their spiritual needs. The wilderness period is a symbol to Hosea of the childlike trust that the people had when they followed Yahweh from Egypt through the wilderness. It serves as an analogy for the conditions that would lead to Israel's restoration to fellowship with Yahweh. This is similar to the prophet representing God as saying, "I will now allure her,

and bring her into the wilderness, and speak tenderly to her. . . . There she shall respond as in the days of her youth" (Hos. 2:16–17 [14–15], NRSV).

This idea is not unique to Hosea. Other prophets proclaimed that Israel's hope of restoration lay in the loss of her objects of misplaced trust. Micah states that God will remove the instruments of war and the symbols of idolatrous worship from Israel when he intervenes in history on her behalf (5:10–15). Kings were not to multiply horses (Deut. 17:16). Isaiah condemns his nation because it is filled with gold and horses (2:7). Zechariah says that in the restoration God will cut off the chariot and the war horse from his people (9:10). Hosea says that Israel, the wealthy merchant, will be reduced to poverty, but we may view this humiliation as a loving act of God by which he will restore their need for dependence on him.

11 [10]. The next clause is conceptually dependent on the previous clause as the *waw* indicates. It appears to reflect the significance of *min* (from) in verse 10 [9] which extends Yahweh's divine authority over the whole of Israel's history as a nation. Throughout that history God sent prophets to speak to the people. This statement, like the previous one, also appears to have a double perspective. God's provision of prophets was a gracious act (see Amos 2:11), but it was a negative factor in their experience as well, for their disobedience to the prophets served to condemn them.

The allusion to the prophets may correspond to the second part of Hosea's illustration of the merchant just as the allusion to their living in tents answers to the first part. The two aspects of the illustration are the merchant's great wealth and his boast of innocence. The statement that Israel will be reduced in circumstances answers to the first aspect; the protestation of innocence parallels the statement about the prophets. The presence of the prophets belied Israel's protestations of innocence, because prophetic activity was always in response to disobedience. The prophetic communication of divine revelation was for the purpose of calling Israel back to God. Hosea's analogy of the merchant is itself one of the similitudes of which Hosea speaks here (as was his marriage),

unit. וְאָנֹכִי (it was I) is emphatic. It directs attention back to the speaker who is described by the title "the LORD your God" (v. 10 [9]). חָזוֹן (visions) is collective. It refers to the numerous visions of the prophets. The word is from חָזָה, which occurs mainly in poetic language. The verb frequently occurs in the Prophets to denote the mode of reception of the revelatory material (see, e.g., Isa. 1:1; Lam. 2:14). The noun form חָזוֹן connotes the material they received and emphasizes the mode of reception. Since the prophets did not always visually observe what God revealed, perhaps "per-

ception" is a more encompassing translation of the word. הִרְבֵּיתִי (multiplied) in the hiphil denotes to make many or much (Hos. 2:10 [8]; 8:11; 10:1). The word refers here to the numerous visions received by the prophets over the course of Israel's history from the time of the exodus. וּבְיַד (by the hand of) expresses the concept of agency. It frequently applies to the prophets (see, e.g., Exod. 9:35; 2 Kings 9:36; Neh. 8:14). אֲדַמֶּה (gave parables) has the active sense of *liken* or *compare* in the piel. When it applies to the prophets, it refers to the giving of prophetic messages based on analogy and comparison.

---

and it is a scathing denunciation of Israel's lust for gain.

The intertwining of condemnation and restoration in the motifs of this section is reminiscent of the statement of divine love in 11:8–9. God's

love prevented the absolute dissolution of the nation and established the basis on which statements of doom could blend with affirmations of hope.

XV. An Oracle Against the Kingdoms of Judah and Israel (12:1–15) [11:12–12:14]

D. Israel Is Guilty Because of Her Violation of Covenant Standards (12:12–15) [11–14]

12 Since Gilead is wickedness,
  surely, they shall come to nought.
 In Gilgal they sacrifice bulls;
  even their altars shall be like heaps
  of stones
 on the furrows of the field.
13 And Jacob fled to the fields of Aram,
  and Israel worked for a wife,
  and for a wife he kept [flocks].
14 And by a prophet the LORD brought
  Israel up from Egypt
 and by a prophet he was guarded.
15 Ephraim has caused bitter anger;
  and his bloodguilt he will leave upon
  him,
  and his Lord will turn his reproaches
  back upon him.

11 In Gilead there is iniquity,
  they shall surely come to nothing.
 In Gilgal they sacrifice bulls,
  so their altars shall be like stone
  heaps
 on the furrows of the field.
12 Jacob fled to the land of Aram,
  there Israel served for a wife,
  and for a wife he guarded sheep.
13 By a prophet the LORD brought Israel up
  from Egypt,
  and by a prophet he was guarded.
14 Ephraim has given bitter offense,
  so his Lord will bring his crimes
  down on him
  and pay him back for his insults.

12 [11]. אִם (Since): Noun clauses with אִם express true contingency but with varying degrees of possibility. The condition may be unrealized (as in Exod. 7:27 [8:2]; Judg. 4:8) or realized (as in Josh. 17:15; 2 Kings 1:10). The context determines the degree of possibility in the construction. Here the condition is realized. Gilgal is wicked. Hosea makes that clear in 6:8. We have chosen to translate אִם "since." It is unlikely that אִם (since/if) extends its force beyond the apodosis to the following clause making it conditional as well ([if] in Gilgal . . .). In the instances in which that type of conceptual transfer occurs the tense of each verb in the protasis, as well as the subject of each verb, generally remains the same (Prov. 9:12; Job 10:15; 16:6; 22:23 [cited in GKC §159ff]). Here, however, not only is there a change of subject (Gilead/they [the people of Gilgal]), but the protasis of the first sentence is a noun clause, while the protasis of the second is a verbal clause. אָוֶן (wickedness) has a broad semantic range that includes ideas as varied as wickedness, trouble, sorrow, and idolatry. The word appears in 6:8, where it refers to social crimes committed at Gilead. The use of אָוֶן here probably does not go beyond that. Even though the next sentence may contain a reference to pagan sacrifice, there is not enough material in the immediate context to establish that אָוֶן (wickedness) has connotations of idolatry. In all probability it assumes and builds on the fact established in 6:8 that social crimes were rife in the town of Gilead. The juxtaposed sentences thus present two facets of Israel's wickedness: social wrong and pagan worship. אָוֶן (wickedness) functions here as the predicate of a noun clause (see Hos. 5:2 as another example; GKC §141b). אַךְ (surely) is an asseverative which lays emphasis on its associative concept. שָׁוְא (nought) expresses the idea of emptiness. Job 7:3 speaks of months of emptiness, and Isaiah 1:13 warns against meaningless sacrifices. It is construed here with הָיָה, which yields the sense either of they are nothing or they shall come to nought. While the latter concept would probably be expressed by הָיָה לְ (become), הָיָה apart from לְ may also connote the sense of *become* (see BDB, p. 226). הָיוּ (shall be) is in the perfect tense and denotes certitude (Davidson, *Syntax* §130, Rem. 4, see §41). In this regard its sense complements the asseverative אַךְ that heads its clause. The

---

12 [11]. The conditional clause that opens this section allows for no alternatives. It assumes that Gilead is intrinsically wicked. We have translated it, "Since Gilead is wickedness" (see the Exegesis). We concluded in the Exegetical section that there is no urgent contextual warrant for understanding "wickedness" (ʾawen) to have a primary reference to the wickedness of idolatry. It appears to refer to the social wrongs for which Gilead was noted. Because of this wickedness, they shall come to nought. This interpretation of šawʾ hayû (see the Exegesis) finds support in the balance of clauses. The reference to Gilgal's wrongdoing in the "B" line is balanced by Gilead's wickedness in the "A" line, and the dismal picture of destruction in the second clause of the "B" line determines a similar prospect for its companion clause in the "A" line. Thus the words šawʾ hayû must convey a sense of impending destruction. This supports the translation "they shall come to nought," not "they are nothing." This was the point of the analogy of the merchant. The nation boasted of the wealth it had gained by wicked practices, but it was soon to suffer a reduction in its circumstances. Its gain was to come to nought.

Gilgal is accused of sacrificing bulls. While this was not wrong in itself, it is probably a reference to sacrifice in the cult of Baal. This practice would lead to the destruction of their altars according to the next clause. Thus we must view sacrifice here as an act worthy of punishment. Hosea uses the word zābaḥ (sacrifice) with reference to pagan sacrifice in most of its occurrences (4:13, 14; 11:2; 13:2).

The words *Gilead is wickedness* are ungrammatical in English. Wickedness is not an adjective. However, a noun can occur with a substantive in Hebrew to impart a degree of emphasis to it. We observed this earlier in "I am chastisement" (see the Exegesis at 5:2).

The punishment for Gilgal is the destruction of its altars. The particle *gam* (even) identifies the altars on which they sacrifice bulls as the altars that will suffer destruction. Hosea moves our attention from these blood-stained altars to heaps of stones standing on the furrows of a field. The field has been plowed. Apparently as the plowman worked his field, he paused from time to time to clear away the stones. He threw them on the furrows in heaps, perhaps to be carried away later. It is an apt picture of the destruction of the pagan altars that will become shapeless piles of rubble.

The cities of Gilead and Gilgal represent the whole nation. The destruction of Gilgal's altars occurred when the northern kingdom fell. This is

clausal relationships are determinative here (see the Exposition). זָבֵחוּ (they sacrifice) is perfect and communicates the idea that this type of sacrifice is characteristic of the people. גַּם (even) serves to lay emphasis on מִזְבְּחוֹתָם (their altars). גַּלִּים (stone heaps) is related to the verb גָּלַל (to roll). It denotes that which is rolled together, such as waves of the sea (Jer. 5:22) or heaps of stones (Isa. 25:2). Since these "heaps" are on "the furrows" of the fields, we are to think of stone-heaps.

13 [12]. וַיִּבְרַח (And . . . fled): Aside from the obscure sense of passing through (Exod. 36:33), the word בָּרַח connotes the idea of hurried flight, often from a threatening situation (see, e.g., Exod. 14:5; 2 Sam. 13:34; Jer. 26:21), as in the descrip-

tion of Jacob's flight to Haran (Gen. 27:43). בְּ . . . וַיַּעֲבֹד (worked for) is a collocation that denotes working for a price. It occurs in the account of Jacob working for a wife (Gen. 29:18, 20). The sense of the collocation is extended to the second occurrence of אִשָּׁה (wife) by the repetition of the preposition בְּ. שָׁמַר (kept) can refer only to Jacob's keeping or tending animals since it is parallel to וַיַּעֲבֹד (and . . . worked) in the clausal structure. שָׁמַר (kept) occurs in 1 Samuel 17:20 with the sense of keeping flocks. In Genesis 30:31 it stands without a stated object as it does here.

14 [13]. וּבְנָבִיא (And by a prophet): בְּ is instrumental. וְ continues the flow of the narrative. We are not to posit a definite logical break here.

---

another example of Hosea's frequent use of metonymy. These two towns represent the two facets of Israel's guilt: Gilead represents her social wrongs and Gilgal her idolatry.

13 [12]. The reference to Jacob is typical of Hosea's abrupt style. It apparently has a connection to the preceding verse because of the *waw* that introduces its clause, but that connection is difficult to determine. It is like the previous reference to Jacob (12:4 [3]) which occurs with somewhat similar abruptness.

The key to understanding the juxtaposition of clauses here is the word *flee* (*baraḥ*). It is an emotive word and never occurs with the simple sense of go. The statement that Jacob *fled* into Aram recalls the threat that his brother Esau posed to his life. It revives memories of Jacob's arrogant duplicity. His wrongdoing led to his flight and eventual lengthy servitude for his wife. The difficulty Jacob endured in Aram is underscored by the reference to his tending flocks. Jacob himself observed the hardship of this period of servitude (Gen. 31:40–41).

The abrupt allusion to Jacob evidently illustrates in some way the previous references to Israel's wrongdoing. The way it does this is obscure, but we may find a clue in the statement that concludes this section. In verse 15 [14] it says of Ephraim that the "Lord will turn his reproaches back upon him." This is what happened to Jacob. The reproach he cast on his brother came back on Jacob's head when he had to flee to Aram, where he endured a lengthy period of humiliating servitude. This is why the word *fled* is crucial to understanding the allusion to Jacob (see the Exegesis). It is not simply a vague reference to an

aspect of Jacob's life; it recalls the wrong that caused him to flee.

14 [13]. The allusion to a prophet here is even more difficult to understand than the reference to Jacob. The prophet is obviously Moses. He led the people out of Egypt, and the law he gave guarded them as a nation. But why did Hosea bring Moses into this oracle? We have here an allusion to a Deuteronomic concept recorded in Deuteronomy 26:5–11, beginning with, "A wandering Aramean was my ancestor" (v. 5, NRSV). This reference to Jacob apparently was a creedal statement to be uttered in the land at the time of the harvest. The subsequent context (vv. 6–11) refers not only to Jacob's sojourn in Aram, but to his emigration to Egypt, the oppression, and the subsequent deliverance of the people from Egyptian bondage to nationhood. In this statement the people were to acknowledge their humble origins and confess that it was only by the power of God that they were a nation.

Ephraim, however, provoked God to bitter anger. Instead of humbly acknowledging that Yahweh was the source of its national status and its prosperity, the people attributed their economic wealth to Baal (2:7 [5], 14 [12]) and, like the merchant in Hosea's analogy, they boasted, "I have gained wealth for myself."

The allusion to Moses and the previous reference to Jacob would recall to the minds of the people two figures who played prominent roles in their history. Jacob represented the early period when they were an oppressed tribal people. Moses, who stands here in spirit, represented the period of Israel's establishment as a nation. All in all, the two historical allusions condemned Israel and served as a basis for the words of judgment that

15 [14]. הִכְעִיס (has caused . . . anger) in the qal is "to be angry." In the hiphil the causative sense of provoking to anger comes to the fore. תַּמְרוּרִים (bitter) is literally "bitterness." It functions as an adverbial accusative (GKC §118q) that describes the nature of Ephraim's provocation. וְדָמָיו (and his bloodguilt): דָם (blood) in the plural frequently connotes bloodshed. Like a number of Hebrew words, especially words for sin, דָּמִים has a connotation broader than its intrinsic sense when it comes over in translation. The word refers to bloodshed, but in certain contexts we must translate the word with the sense of bloodguilt. That is not to say that this sense was native to the word, but that its use in certain contexts favors English terms that convey the sense of bloodguilt. For example, in Exodus 22:1 [2], God states that if a thief is killed while in the act of breaking in, there will be no bloodshed for (לְ) him, that is, no blood will be shed for his blood. By extension this means that there will be no bloodguilt in the matter (see Ezek. 18:13). The word occurs several times in legal contexts apart from the crime of murder (see, e.g., Lev. 20:9, 11, 13). In Leviticus 20:9 one who curses his father or mother is to be put to death; his bloodshed is upon him. It is evident that bloodshed signifies the death of the individual; if bloodshed is upon him, then his death has been

determined by the nature of his crime. The translation "bloodguilt" is appropriate for the various Hebrew expressions in which bloodshed (death) is legally decreed for an individual. יִטּוֹשׁ (he will leave) has as its subject אֲדֹנָיו (his Lord). נָטַשׁ (leave) does not occur elsewhere with דָּמִים (bloodshed) in the sense discussed above. Evidently the sense is that the bloodguilt of Ephraim will not be removed. חֶרְפָּתוֹ (his reproaches): חֶרְפָּה has the specific connotation of casting blame or scorn. Job protested that his heart did not reproach him for any of his days (27:6). The wisdom teacher did not want to incur reproach (blame) from others (Prov. 27:11). The reproaches here are reproaches initiated by Ephraim because they are to be turned back upon him. They answer to the bitter provocation in the first line of this verse. אֲדֹנָיו (his Lord): The root ʾdn occurs in Ugaritic with the connotations lord and father (Gordon, *UT*, p. 352). In each occurrence in the Old Testament the sense of authority or superiority may be observed. The Masoretic Text points this word in its various occurrences with two plural suffix endings. אֲדֹנָי and אֲדֹנָי. Probably the plural endings denote the plural of majesty and the variation in the vocalization distinguishes the uses of אֲדֹן where the name has a sacred character from those uses that refer to human beings.

---

follow. Moses is not mentioned by name here, but this oblique reference to him as "a prophet" may be purposeful. We observed in 12:11 [10] that the presence of the prophets in Israel was an indication of the need of the people to return to God (see 9:8). The use of the name *Moses* might have conjured up images of the greatness of this man and the grandeur of the period in Israelite history that he represented. Hosea does not want the people to recall only the glory of the exodus and the giving of the law. He wants them to know that Gilead was wicked (12:12 [11]). He does not want them to forget that when they became a nation there was a prophet among them who cried out against their wickedness.

15 [14]. The nation had provoked its Lord to bitter wrath. As a result they were guilty of a crime

punishable by death; bloodguilt was upon them. Hosea appears to have studiously avoided the name *Yahweh* here; he uses *ʾădonay* instead. This name depicts Yahweh as a superior. As *ʾădonay* he must render judgment, and when he does, he will determine to leave bloodguilt on the nation. The scorn they have cast on God will come back on them, just as Jacob's reproaches came back to him.

The punishment seems ultimate. But we must bear in mind that Hosea never absolved Israel of her responsibility for her sin. Hosea's hope looks beyond this doomed generation. God will not forget his promise (1:10), for his people will yet be like the sands of the sea, and will truly be God's people (Rom. 9:25–26).

XVI. Hope for Ungrateful Israel (13:1–14:1) [13:1–16]

A. Israel's Devotion to Baal Worship Will Bring Her to an End (13:1–3)

13 When Ephraim spoke there was trembling;
　　he was lifted up in Israel;
　　but he incurred guilt through Baal
　　　　and died.
² And now they continue to sin,
　　and make for themselves a molten
　　　　image:
　　idols from their silver according to their
　　　　skill—
　　all the work of craftsmen.
　　To them they say, "My sacrifice";
　　men kiss calves!
³ Therefore they shall be like the morning
　　　　mist,
　　or like the dew that goes away early,
　　like chaff that blows away from the
　　　　threshing floor,
　　and like smoke from a vent.

13 When Ephraim spoke, there was trembling;
　　he was exalted in Israel;
　　but he incurred guilt through Baal
　　　　and died.
² And now they keep on sinning
　　and make a cast image for themselves,
　　idols of silver made according to their
　　　　understanding,
　　all of them the work of artisans.
　　"Sacrifice to these," they say.
　　People are kissing calves!
³ Therefore they shall be like the morning mist
　　or like the dew that goes away early,
　　like chaff that swirls from the threshing floor
　　or like smoke from a window.

13:1. כְּדַבֵּר (When . . . spoke): כְּ may be translated temporally (when), since the action of the verb it influences (דַּבֵּר) compares with the action of רְתֵת (trembling), literally, "As Ephraim spoke, there was trembling." This is tantamount to saying, "When Ephraim spoke." רְתֵת (there was trembling) occurs only here. The root in Aramaic has the sense of trembling, and that sense complements the concept of exaltation in the next clause. נָשָׂא (was lifted up) is intransitive in this context, as with several verbs in the qal (see GKC §117v–w). There are several instances in the Masoretic Text that require an intransitive sense for נָשָׂא (Ps. 89:10 [9]; Nah. 1:5; Hab. 1:3). וַיֶּאְשַׁם (but he incurred guilt): אָשֵׁם may have the sense of committing wrong or incurring guilt (see at 4:15; 5:15; 10:2). Since the result was death (וַיָּמֹת), אָשֵׁם has the sense of incurring guilt worthy of death. The guilt was incurred בַּבַּעַל (through Baal). The practice of Baal worship was the means by which Ephraim became guilty of a crime punishable by death. וַיָּמֹת (and died): See the Exposition and Exegesis (v. 2).

2. וְעַתָּה (And now) points to the time of Hosea. This places the action of the previous verb (וַיָּמֹת) in the past, or at least traces the beginning of its consequences to the past. Israel had died as a nation, yet it continued to do the things that had led to its demise. יוֹסִפוּ (they continue) is literally, "They add to." It connotes the idea of doing more and more (see, e.g., Gen. 8:21; Amos 7:8). מַסֵּכָה (molten images) is from the verb נָסַךְ (to pour out). The word מַסֵּכָה (molten images) describes images of cast metal. כִּתְבוּנָם (according to their skill): We expect this form to be represented orthographically as תְּבוּנָתָם. There is no need to regard it as an otherwise unattested masculine form of the word, however. More than likely this is an instance in which we find a rare, or dialectical form in the Masoretic Text (GKC §91e). The Septuagint reads εἰκόνα (fashion) perhaps reading תַּבְנִית (pattern). BHS follows the Septuagint in suggesting the emendation כְּתַבְנִית, but the major alteration of the consonants required for this suggestion renders it conjectural. While the versional evidence favors a

---

13:1. In the premonarchic period the tribe of Ephraim rose slowly to a place of prominence among the other tribes. It was the chief tribe of the western encampment in the wilderness (Num. 2:18–24). The tribe grew to greater prominence in the civil strife that led to the establishment of Israel as an independent kingdom, for Jeroboam I, the leader of the secession, was from the tribe of Ephraim. We may observe the importance of this tribe in Hosea's day in the frequency with which he designates the northern kingdom *Ephraim.*

Hosea alludes to Ephraim's prominence among the tribes in the opening words of this section. This proud tribe, which represents the whole of the northern kingdom here, had encountered the worship of Baal and died. The pleasures of the fertility cult and its lack of stern moral proscriptions must have attracted the people of Israel, but in reality these pleasures proved to be the poison that brought about Ephraim's death.

The concepts of "life" and "death" in the Torah are behind Hosea's words here. "Life" denotes the viability of the relationship of the nation (or an individual) to the promised inheritance; "death" denotes the cessation of a viable relationship to the inheritance. Stated simply, the disobedience of the people would eventually lead to the cessation of Israel as a nation. This is national death (Deut. 30:18–19).

2. According to verse 1, the nation has already died. This fact is underscored by the word *now* in

this verse. In the time of Hosea ("now") the people continued in their wanton ways, and even though the nation had died, they went on drinking the poison that had killed them. The analogy is not precise, but this is typical of Hosea's figures of speech (see the discussion at 2:5 [3]).

The word *sin* (ḥāṭōʾ) in the first line is further clarified by the reference to making idols in the companion clause. The sin of the people was idolatry. The people crafted images of silver in accordance with their skill.

These images must have been beautifully made. They were not shapeless representations fashioned of unyielding stone, but glistening idols of artistic beauty. They were not homemade images of roughly carved wood, for all of them were made by craftsmen. There may be a deep attraction in the things that Yahweh's law opposes, but pleasure and beauty are not always truth. Indeed, they can mask death. Spiritual life and beauty are found in obedience to the will of God.

We have opted for the Masoretic Text's *tĕbûnāh* (skill) rather than *tabnît* (fashion/model) which requires a considerable alteration of the consonants. The latter option yields the following clausal pattern:

A And now they continue to sin,

B and they make for themselves a molten image

word with the sense of idol or fashion, the parallelism supports the concept of *according to their skill* (see the Exposition). תְּבוּנָה (understanding) refers to wisdom in a general sense in a number of passages (1 Kings 5:9 [4:29]; Job 12:12; 32:11; Ps. 49:4 [3]), but it takes on the sense of skill or ability (i.e., the power of intellect) in a number of other passages. This may explain its frequent use in Proverbs and elsewhere (see, e.g., Exod. 31:3; 35:31; 36:1; 1 Kings 7:14; Job 26:12; Pss. 78:72; 136:5; 147:5; Isa. 40:28; Jer. 10:12). The semantic range of this word does not easily allow for the sense of religious understanding; rather it is intelligence in the sense of ability. What the people made with their hands was according to and limited by their human skills. לָהֶם (to them): The pronominal references in this line present a problem. Much depends on how we interpret the whole line. We understand לָהֶם (to them) to refer to עֲצַבִּים (idols), which is the principal substantive in the previous line, and the nearest logical referent. הֵם (they) answers best to the third plural subject of the previous lines (*they* continue to sin; *they* make images; *their* silver; *their* ability), which is the people. This finds support in the fact that the people

אָדָם, men) are the subject of the companion verb יִשָּׁקוּן (kiss). It is unlikely that עֲצַבִּים is the subject of אֹמְרִים (say); idols are never represented in the Old Testament as speaking (see Ps. 115:5). זִבְחֵי (Masoretic Text, sacrifices of) makes little sense as the content of the speech introduced by אֹמְרִים (say). If this word is repointed זִבְחִי (my sacrifice), however, it may represent a formula of presentation (see the Exposition). אֹמְרִים (say) probably does not have the sense of speak (to them they speak), since speech in the abstract sense is denoted by דִּבֶּר (Job 2:13; Amos 5:10). אָדָם (men): We have understood this noun as a collective and thus appropriate to the plural verb יִשָּׁקוּן (kiss, see Davidson, *Syntax* §17 and the example in Gen. 41:57).

3. לָכֵן (therefore) introduces the logical result of the idolatry of the nation. מַשְׁכִּים (early): See 6:4 for this word and for a discussion of the imagery of the mist and dew. יְסֹעֵר (is blown) is the *pōʿēl* of סָעַר (to storm) and depicts the vigorous swirling of wind. מֵאֲרֻבָּה (from a vent): אֲרֻבָּה is not a window in the strict sense, but a latticed aperture (Isa. 60:8). In other instances it denotes metaphorical sluices in the sky from which the rain falls (Isa. 24:18).

    C from their silver according to the fashion
       of idols,
    D the work of craftsmen, all of it.

The result is an awkward B-C structure that is clumsy even for Hosea. More in line with his poetic style is the pattern:

    A And now they continue to sin,
    B and they make for themselves a molten
       image;
    C idols from their silver according to their
       skill,
    D all the work of craftsmen.

It is difficult to determine syntactically with which line *mikkaspām* (from their silver) goes, but since Hosea has already told us that the people made idols (ʿăsabbîm) from silver (8:4), it is likely it belongs in the same line with that word.

The last line is obscure. The translation we suggested in the Exegesis is but another attempt to make sense of an almost unintelligible sentence. Perhaps the text is corrupt or perhaps Hosea omitted a concept now completely lost to us. The suggestion in the Exegesis requires repointing the Masoretic Text, but while this tradition is our best interpretive control, it is not sacred.

This translation depicts the people of Ephraim as saying to their images, "My sacrifice." Perhaps this statement was all or part of a liturgical formula uttered at the presentation of sacrifices. Hosea may allude to a similar formula in 14:4 [3], "We shall say no more, 'our God' to the work of our hands." The absurdity of the act is evident. They spoke to the works of their own hands; instead of offering sacrifices to the Creator, they presented them to their own artistic creations (see Isa. 44:12–17). The absurdity of their worship is also the theme of the following clause: the people kissed calves. Thus this view achieves a conceptual balance between the clauses. On the basis of this interpretation the *lahem* (to them) that begins the third line refers to the idols which were addressed by the words, "My sacrifice." The *hem* (they), which is the subject of *ʾōmĕrîm* (say), refers to the people. It is not the idols who speak.

3. The terrible result of all this is Ephraim's demise as a nation. The people will disappear like vapor, without a trace. Gone will be the once proud nation. Like chaff that swirls in eddies from the threshing floor, and like smoke from an aperture in a house, they will vanish. The contrast between the strong nation (v. 1), and the representation of the nation as weak and evanescent (v. 3) is apparent.

XVI. Hope for Ungrateful Israel (13:1–14:1) [13:1–16]

B. Israel Forgot Her God Who Brought Her out of
Egypt (13:4–8)

4 Yet I am the LORD your God
   from the land of Egypt;
and you know no God but me,
   and besides me there is no deliverer.
5 It was I who knew you in the wilderness,
   in the land of drought.
6 Because of their pasturage, they became
   full;
   they were full and their heart was
   lifted up;
   therefore they forgot me.
7 So I will become to them like a lion,
   like a leopard along the way I will lie
   in wait.
8 I will confront them like a bear robbed
   [of her cubs],
   I will rip open their chest
and I shall devour them there like a
   lion:
   the wild beast will rend them.

4 Yet I have been the LORD your God
   ever since the land of Egypt;
you know no God but me,
   and besides me there is no savior.
5 It was I who fed you in the wilderness,
   in the land of drought.
6 When I fed them, they were satisfied;
   they were satisfied, and their heart
   was proud;
   therefore they forgot me.
7 So I will become like a lion to them,
   like a leopard I will lurk beside the
   way.
8 I will fall upon them like a bear robbed
   of her cubs,
   and will tear open the covering of
   their heart;
there I will devour them like a lion,
   as a wild animal would mangle
   them.

4. וְאָנֹכִי (Yet I) seems not to be emphatic because the lack of inflected elements in the clause requires the personal pronoun. We have translated the וְ as "yet" because of the contrast between the benign description of Yahweh here and the depiction of his judgment in verse 3. מֵאֶרֶץ מִצְרָיִם (from the land of Egypt): See the comment at 12:10 [9]. וֵאלֹהִים (and . . . God) is used in a general sense of the nation's God. It has a similar meaning in the first clause. In the Pentateuch אֱלֹהִים usually connotes a general concept of God. It depicts God as a transcendent being, and, in that way, it is different from the name *Yahweh* (the LORD) which depicts the attributes of God in a more palpable and personal way. Because of this connotation אֱלֹהִים may refer to false gods or depict the general sense of deity. When used of the true God, it is grammatically construed in the singular. זוּלָתִי (besides me) connotes removal; thus "except" or "besides" is an appropriate translation in certain instances. תֵדָע (know) is in the imperfect tense, with the sense that Israel does not *now* know any God besides Yahweh. וּמוֹשִׁיעַ (and . . . deliverer): יָשַׁע in the hiphil has the basic sense of deliver; it does not always connote salvation in a redemptive sense (see, e.g., Deut. 20:4; Judg. 2:18; Ps. 3:8 [7]). The context here requires the word to refer to God as a deliverer of the nation. אַיִן (no) connotes nonexistence. בִּלְתִּי (but me): Etymologically this word is related to בָּלָה, which means "to become

old and worn out" (BDB, p. 115). It is unlikely, however, that the native Hebrew speaker always understood this derivation. From this come various negatives that share the related sense of *without*. The negative בְּלָתִי (בֶּלֶת) has several specific functions. When it follows another negative (as it does here), it may be translated "except" (Num. 32:11–12). The first-person suffix renders the sense as *except me*.

5. אֲנִי (It was I) probably reflects emphasis because of the inflected verb it modifies. Sometimes the separate pronoun is necessary in a context because the subject to which it refers occurs several clauses earlier and the pronoun must be stated to indicate the resumption of the subject. That is not the case here, however, because the referent of the pronoun is in the suffixes of the immediately preceding line. There is no syntactical need for the separate pronoun other than emphasis. We thus translate it, "It was I." תַּלְאֻבוֹת (drought) occurs only here. Cognate languages (Arabic and Aramaic) support the sense of aridity or drought. The plural form is intensive.

6. כְּמַרְעִיתָם (Because of their pasturage): כְּ (lit. as) functions as a comparative. It likens the action of the verb to its noun (lit. in accordance with their pasturage they became full). Their pasturage was abundant and so they ate to the full. וַיִּשְׂבְּעוּ (they became full) is an imperfect with a וְ. We retain the sense of the imperfect, however, "They

---

4. It is not uncommon for the prophets to represent Yahweh as appealing to his mighty acts on behalf of his erring people (see Amos 2:9–11). Here he reminds the people that he is the God of the exodus (see 12:10 [9]). The personal name *Yahweh*, with its warm connotations, is coupled with Elohim to connote the sense of Yahweh, the God of the Israelites.

The construction of this clause extends Yahweh's authority over the period of time from the exodus to Hosea's day (see the discussion at 12:9). We can thus understand the use of the imperfect *tedaʿ* (you know) to complement this idea. The statement that they know no God other than Yahweh seems strange in the light of their experience with the cult of Baal, especially since the word *know* is used of the worship of false deities (see, e.g., Deut. 13:3 [2]). This difficult statement must be understood in relation to the companion clause where Yahweh calls himself a deliverer. Over the course of their history the Israelites knew no other god to be a deliverer like Yahweh. The people may

have attributed their success to Baal (2:7 [5]), but it was Yahweh who was their national Savior.

5. The words *I knew you in the wilderness* recall the halcyon days of Israel's early experience with Yahweh. These words bring us back to the period of history designated by "from the land of Egypt" (v. 4). The emphatic use of the pronoun, "It was I," serves to further differentiate Yahweh from the baals. It was not Baal who knew them in that early period; it was Yahweh who led them out from Egypt (11:1). It was he, not Baal, who loved these people in their wilderness experience (9:10), for in that land of drought he helped them.

As with other passages of this type in the prophecy, there is nothing said about Israel's purity. This verse describes a sovereign act of God, with the emphasis on Yahweh's knowing and delivering his people. It does not say that he knew them because they were pure, or because there was anything in them worth loving.

6. It was their prosperity that led them away from Yahweh. Hosea says that the people became

became full." שָׂבְעוּ (they were full) is a perfect and connotes completed action. Thus, when the act of becoming satisfied became a reality, they went on to lift up their hearts. וַיָּרָם (and . . . was lifted up) is a qal (lit. was high). This expression occurs with לֵב (heart) with the same function in Deuteronomy 8:14. Evidently Hosea depends heavily on this passage in this context (see the Exposition). לֵב (heart), besides its reference to the physical organ, also connotes the emotional and cognitive nature of mankind (see, e.g., 1 Sam. 2:1; 1 Chron. 16:10; Job 15:12). עַל־כֵּן (therefore) introduces us to the result of their pride—they forgot God (*me*).

7. וָאֱהִי (So I will become): וְ (so) connects this doom statement to the preceding accusation; therefore "so" is an appropriate translation. וָאֱהִי (I will become), even though the *wayyiqtol* form, probably retains the future sense of the imperfect by virtue of the companion verb אָשׁוּר (I will lie in wait) and the future perspective of the entire pericope (vv. 7–8); thus the activity of God is pending (see GKC §111n). The function of the *waw*-consecutive is primarily to connote temporal succession or logical consequence. Thus we translate

the construction וָאֱהִי "So I will become." Yahweh's becoming a lion to the people is the logical consequence of their forgetting him (v. 6). שָׁחַל (lion) occurs mainly in poetry. אָשׁוּר (I will lie in wait) has the basic sense of observe or behold. It depicts the intent watching of a trap by a hunter (Jer. 5:26). Here it depicts not simply lying in wait, but the intent staring of an animal waiting for its prey.

8. אֶפְגְּשֵׁם (I will confront them) has the sense of encounter, not primarily of attack (Exod. 4:24; 2 Sam. 2:13). It occurs in Proverbs 17:12 in a similar context. שָׁכוּל (robbed [of her cubs]) is simply "robbed"; we must supply the evident object. סְגוֹר לִבָּם (their chest) is literally "enclosure of the heart." The noun סְגוֹר denotes either the pericardium (BDB) or the chest. The former seems too precise and clinical for Hosea's bold imagery. שָׁם (there) has no stated referent in the context. It seems to be a vague reference to the place where the hypothetical animal that depicts Yahweh's punishment devours its prey (see the discussion of שָׁם at 6:7). כְּלָבִיא (like a lion): כְּ does not extend its influence to the next clause making it comparative as well (see v. 7). The different inflections of the verbs

---

full "because of their pasturage." The pasturage answers to their economic prosperity in Hosea's analogy. They were sated with riches and they forgot their humble beginnings and the One who tenderly delivered them.

This section (vv. 4–6) is closely connected with Deuteronomy 8:11–20. The consonance between the two passages is linguistic as well as conceptual. The word for being full, *sabaʿ* (v. 6), occurs in Deuteronomy 8:10, 12 (eat and be full); *rûm lēb* (v. 6) occurs in Deuteronomy 8:14 of the lifting up of the heart; *midbar* (wilderness, v. 5) occurs in Deuteronomy 8:15, 16; *ʾereṣ miṣrayim* (land of Egypt, v. 4) appears in Deuteronomy 8:14; the concept of forgetting God (*šakaḥ*, v. 6) is found in Deuteronomy 8:14; and the idea of Yahweh knowing the people from the beginning (v. 5) occurs in Deuteronomy 9:24. The message is clear: the very things that Deuteronomy (chaps. 8–9) warned against had become a reality in Hosea's day.

7. The judgment to befall the nation is typical of Hosea's vivid, emotionally charged metaphors. The God who tenderly cared for his people in their early days will become like a voracious carnivore. The reason for the change in God's nature is not arbitrariness on his part, but the treachery of the Israelites. They had removed themselves from the basis of covenant blessing which was covenant

loyalty. The curses of Deuteronomy were a loving warning to them, but when they became a reality, how different God seemed to them.

8. Israel's encounter with God will be like meeting an angry bear that towers above its prey, ripping open its victim's chest. Israel will be devoured as though by a wild beast.

Hosea identifies Yahweh with the animals as a simile (see 5:14), but his motif of the ferocious beast is somewhat different from the levitical traditions where literal beasts are represented as the instruments of destruction (Lev. 26:22). Jeremiah uses the same motif (5:6), and in his passage, as well as here, the punishment was ultimate. Hosea's generation would be left a pitiful carcass.

We must not allow the sounds of the angry beasts, however, to drown out the words of 2:1 [1:10]: "But the number of the people of Israel shall be as the sand of the sea." Out of the carnage will arise a new people, "and they shall spring up from the earth, because great shall be the day of Jezreel" (2:2 [1:11]). Nor must we forget the analogy on which the prophecy is based—Hosea's marriage. After the long period of Israel's estrangement, she will return to God (3:4–5) just as Gomer returned to Hosea (3:1–2). Paul identifies this restored nation with the church (Rom. 9:22–26; cf. Hos. 2:1 [1:10]).

prohibit that. Other syntactical indications of the extension of comparison are lacking as well (Davidson, *Syntax* §151). Perhaps this is a bold metaphor that depicts Yahweh as a destroying beast of the field.

More than likely, however, it takes up the metaphor of 2:14 [12] that states that wild beasts will destroy the nation, depicted there as a forest. תְּבַקְּעֵם (would rend them) thus has a modal sense (would).

XVI. Hope for Ungrateful Israel (13:1–14:1) [13:1–16]
C. Israel's Leaders Cannot Help Her (13:9–11)

9 It has destroyed you, O Israel,
    that [you are] against me, your help.
10 Where is your king—where?
    And [where is] your deliverer in all
      your cities—
  and your judges of whom you said,
    "Give me a king and princes"?
11 I give you kings in my anger,
    and take [them] away in my wrath.

9 I will destroy you, O Israel;
    who can help you?
10 Where now is your king, that he may
      save you?
  Where in all your cities are your
      rulers,
  of whom you said,
    "Give me a king and rulers"?
11 I gave you a king in my anger,
    and I took him away in my wrath.

9. שִׁחֶתְךָ (It has destroyed you) is pointed as a third masculine singular piel perfect in the Masoretic Text. The range of meaning of this word in the piel includes the concepts of ruin or corruption. The Septuagint reads τῇ διαφθορᾷ (in your destruction). כִּי (that): The function one assigns to this particle depends, in a large part, on one's conclusions about the clausal structure of this section (see the Exposition). בִּי (against me): The preposition בְּ is basically locative in function, denoting such ideas as inclusion, proximity, and accompaniment. The concept of proximity allows for its frequent usage with verbs of hostility in the sense of against. בְעֶזְרֶךָ (in your might): בְּ is understood here as a *beth essentiae*. This function of בְּ designates a substantive as standing in the predicate position in a clause and denotes the substantive as that of which the subject of the clause consists or in which its essential nature is expressed (GKC §119i). We may observe this function with עֵזֶר (help, Exod. 18:4, כִּי־אֱלֹהֵי אָבִי בְּעֶזְרִי,

because the God of my father *is* my help). See the Exposition for a discussion of the sense of this clause.

10. אֱהִי (Where) occurs here and in verse 14. It is unlikely that this form represents the first-person imperfect of הָיָה (I would be [your king]). This rendering is logically incompatible with אֵפוֹא (where). It is best to understand אֱהִי (where) as an alternate (or dialectical?) form of אַיֵּה (where). It is heightened by אֵפוֹא, another word for where. וְשֹׁפְטֶיךָ (and your judges): שָׁפַט does not always have a primary judicial sense. It frequently applies to kings or government officials (Isa. 16:5; 33:22; 40:23; Amos 2:3; Mic. 4:14 [5:1]; see Hos. 7:7). אֲשֶׁר (of whom) unites the king, deliverer, and judges in the first line as the object of the request for a king. It underscores the fact that the word שֹׁפְטִים (judges) applies to kings or officials of the government. לִי (to me) is singular. In the narration of the nation's original request for a king (1 Sam. 8:4–9) the analogous pronoun is plural (vv. 5–6). Hosea

9. The initial word of this verse, *šiḥetka* (It has destroyed you), is pointed as a third-person singular in the Masoretic Text. It is possible to repoint it *šiḥattîka* (I have destroyed/will destroy you), but this does not seem necessary. We have assigned an indefinite subject to the verb *šiḥetka*. (This is not uncommon in Hebrew and is discussed in GKC §144b.) Note the following similar expression: "And it was told (*wayyuggad*) to Solomon *that* (*kî*) Shimei had gone" (1 Kings 2:41). The expression also occurs with an active verb: "It pleased . . . the Lord *that* Solomon had asked for this" (1 Kings 3:10). If we understand the clausal structure in this way, the particle *kî* (that) which begins the second half of the clause introduces an object clause.

Several commentators who emend *šiḥetka* to *šiḥattîka* understand the *kî* that introduces the second clause to be adversative: "*But* in me is your help." The sentence would thus present an anomaly to the people, for the one who destroyed them is actually their helper. This fits with the subsequent context which shows that their kings could not help them. This view requires a slight emendation, however, for the *bĕ* on 'ezrā (help) must represent dittography (see the preceding *beth* [*bî*]).

A number of solutions have been suggested: "(I) will destroy you, O Israel. (Who will help you?)" is offered by Wolff (*Hosea*, p. 221). Mays translates, "I destroy you, O Israel! Who then is your helper?" (*Hosea*, p. 176). These suggestions require

emending *bî* to *mî* (who). Andersen and Freedman translate, "I will destroy you, Israel, for (you rebelled) against me, against your helper" (*Hosea*, p. 625). Keil reads, "O Israel, it hurls thee to destruction, that thou (art) against me, thy help" (*Minor Prophets*, p. 157).

It does not seem necessary to emend this sentence as in the first two renderings. As we observed, everything is grammatical. The translation of Andersen and Freedman reflects the Masoretic Text and, at the same time, is consonant with Hosea's style, who uses numerous ellipses in his book. If the *bĕ* on 'ezrā (helper) is regarded as a *beth essentiae* (see the Exegesis), it thus describes an essential attribute of Yahweh, who is the subject of the first-person suffix on *bî*. The preposition *bĕ* (*bî*, against me) often occurs with verbs of hostility with the sense of *against*. If we supply any such idea (be against/rebel against) we are probably not far from Hosea's intention.

10. The question "Where is your king?" reflects the unstable conditions of the monarchy in the time of Hosea. The king at this time, if they had one, was too weak or too preoccupied with international ventures to help his nation. It is clear that Hosea is thinking about the king's inability to help, for he pairs "king" with "deliverer" in the parallel structure, and thus invests the word with this nuance.

The reference to the people's demand for a king in the second line may reflect the secession under Jeroboam I, when the people of the northern king-

studiously keeps all the references to Israel in the first-person singular in this section, whereas in the two preceding verses they are plural. This device serves to give internal consistency to the pericopes and often denotes logical junctures.

11. אֶתֶּן (I give): It is tempting to regard this verb as past tense (I *gave* you kings in my anger) since it follows the reference to the establishment of the monarchy and introduces a statement appropriate to King Saul's accession and downfall. It is best, however, to regard it as a general statement (I give), because the previous context deals not only with the institution of the monarchy, but with the general failure of the monarchy ([where is] your deliverer?). The reference to the institution of the monarchy is in a subordinate clause (v. 10b). It is not the main thought of the context. The central idea of this section is that the monarchy is unable to deliver the nation. Hosea can ask, "Where is your king?" because Yahweh gives kings and takes them away. מֶלֶךְ (kings) is regarded as a collective, literally, "I give you a king . . . and I take [him] away." בְּאַפִּי (in my anger) and its companion word עֶבְרָה (wrath) are general words for anger. They give no clue as to the specific historical situation to which the context relates.

---

dom established an independent monarchy. But more than likely it refers to Israel's initial request for a king (1 Sam. 8:4–9). It is there that we find words that come closest to Hosea's words *tĕnâ-lî melek* (Give me a king), when the people said, *tĕnâ-lanû melek* (Give us a king, 1 Sam. 8:6).

The question, "Where is your king?" is more than rhetorical. It echoes a philosophy. Trust in a king to deliver them was no substitute for Yahweh's aid, for the people's request for a king was regarded as tantamount to a rejection of Yahweh (1 Sam. 8:7).

11. "I give you kings in my anger, and take [them] away in my wrath" is a powerful prophetic statement, asserting that the unstable conditions of the monarchy in Hosea's day were but another aspect of Yahweh's displeasure with the northern kingdom.

The request of their forebears for a king proved to be what Samuel said it would be (1 Sam. 8:9–18). The monarchy had turned to dust in their hands. The nation and its kings would soon be no more.

XVI. Hope for Ungrateful Israel (13:1–14:1) [13:1–16]

D. Yahweh Will Save His Nation from Death (13:12–14)

12 The guilt of Ephraim is bound up,
   his sin is stored up.
13 The pangs of a woman in childbirth
      come upon him,
   but he is a senseless son
 in that when it is time he does not pre-
      sent himself
   at the mouth of the womb.
14 From the power of Sheol I shall ransom
      them,
   from death I shall redeem them.
 Where are your plagues, O death?
   Where is your destruction, O Sheol?
   Relenting is hidden from my eyes.

12 Ephraim's iniquity is bound up;
   his sin is kept in store.
13 The pangs of childbirth come for him,
   but he is an unwise son;
 for at the proper time he does not pre-
      sent himself
   at the mouth of the womb.

14 Shall I ransom them from the power of
      Sheol?
   Shall I redeem them from Death?
 O Death, where are your plagues?
   O Sheol, where is your destruction?
   Compassion is hidden from my eyes.

12. צָרוּר (bound up): צָרַר has the sense of making something compact by some action such as wrapping and compressing. It refers to kneading bowls wrapped in mantles (Exod. 12:34). Hosea uses the word of wind that had enveloped the people in its wings (4:19). Here the sense is influenced by צְפוּנָה (stored up). We must think of Ephraim's guilt as having been sealed, all of it carefully kept in store. The word applies to Isaiah's prophetic words which are sealed for future fulfilment (Isa. 8:16). צְפוּנָה (stored up) has the basic sense of hiding (Exod. 2:2; Josh. 2:4). It also occurs with the sense of carefully preserving an object (Job 21:19; Prov. 7:1).

13. יוֹלֵדָה (a woman in childbirth) is a feminine participle that denotes a woman in childbirth, not the act of childbirth per se. לוֹ (upon him) sustains the reference to Ephraim in the preceding verse, since no other masculine subject appears here. The sense is that the pangs of childbirth have come on Ephraim. הוּא (but he): We have given an adversative sense to this clause because the circumstance it depicts is contrary to what we expect in a normal birth. הוּא (he) answers to the suffix on לוֹ (upon him). In combination with בֵּן (son), הוּא (he) signals a change in Hosea's thinking. Ephraim suffers the pangs of childbirth in the previous clause, but in this clause Ephraim (הוּא) is the infant at the point of birth. This may be another example of Hosea's lack of precision in the use of metaphor (see the Exposition at 2:5 [2:3]), or an indication that he views the nation as both a mother and a child (see the Exposition at 4:5–6). לֹא חָכָם (senseless, lit. not wise): חָכָם does

not have a specialized sense here (as it does in the wisdom material). It is to be understood as in Deuteronomy 32:6 where it is in apposition with נָבָל (foolish). It occurs there with reference to Israel and is probably the basis of Hosea's depiction of Israel here. כִּי (in that) introduces a causal clause that tells us why the child is senseless. עֵת (when it is time) is an adverbial accusative. יַעֲמֹד (he does not present himself): עָמַד has the sense of presenting oneself before when it occurs with לִפְנֵי (before; see, e.g., Gen. 43:15; Exod. 9:10). Here, however, the associated preposition is בְּ. The sense is thus *at* or *in* (as in Dan. 1:4, not in front of as with לִפְנֵי). בְּמִשְׁבַּר בָּנִים (at the mouth of the womb) is literally "at the point or breach of children," that is, the point at which children emerge from the womb at birth. Note the use of מַשְׁבֵּר in 2 Kings 19:3 (בָּנִים עַד־מַשְׁבֵּר, children have come to the point of birth).

14. מִיַּד (From the power): יַד (lit. hand)—it is doubtful that this construction introduces a question, "From the power of Sheol shall I ransom them?" There is no grammatical indication that we have a question here, and numerous examples exist in Hosea of clauses constructed of a preposition and an imperfect verb that are indicative clauses (see, e.g., Hos. 5:10; 7:4, 12, 14, 15). In fact no other such clause in Hosea is interrogative. שְׁאוֹל (Sheol) represents the grave. It is not clearly the place of departed spirits in the Old Testament. Isaiah 14:9 is commonly used to support this idea, but Isaiah may be making a metaphorical reference to the leaders of the earth who have gone to the grave. The use of שְׁאוֹל in parallel with מָוֶת

---

12. Hosea pictures Ephraim's guilt as bound up like a bundle and stored away. The ultimacy of this affirmation is typical of Hosea's doomsayings. Also typical is the use of vivid analogy to underscore the intensity of his feelings (12:1 [11:12], 8 [7], 12 [11]; 13:3, 7–8). The analogy here is that of an abnormal birth.

13. Hosea pictures the nation as a woman in travail. There is no need to see an analogy between the birth pangs and the desperate plight of the nation in Hosea's day. The point of the metaphor is Israel's stupidity, not its national condition. The time of birth has come, but Israel does not present itself at the mouth of the womb. The foolishness of Ephraim can be only a negative factor, something that deprives the nation of good. Thus the birth represents deliverance, the opportunity to be born to a new national life. But Israel is like a foolish child who refuses to be born to a

new relationship with God. This analogy recalls the offer of national and individual life in the law. Life in the law was not eternal life, but life as a nation. As long as the people were obedient to the covenantal stipulations, they maintained a viable relationship to the promised inheritance and would not perish as a nation (Lev. 18:5; Deut. 30:16–18; see also Deut. 4:1; 5:33; 8:1; 16:20; Rom. 10:5–13).

14. Several commentators regard the first line as a compound question, "Shall I ransom them"/"Shall I redeem them?" (see Mays, *Hosea*, p. 178; Wolff, *Hosea*, p. 221). We have understood these words as an assertion (I shall ransom them). It seems too abrupt a change to move from the certainty of doom (vv. 12–13) to a strong assurance of deliverance (v. 14), but this is not untypical of Hosea. The theological framework for this motif appears in 11:8–9, where an affirmation of

(death) shows that Hosea has only the concept of the cessation of life in mind. אֶפְדֵּם (I shall ransom them): The basic sense of the word פָּדָה is to effect the transfer of ownership of a person or object to another. This can be done by purchase (Lev. 27:27) or by force (Deut. 9:26). The companion verb אֶגְאָלֵם (I shall redeem them) shares the same general sense, but sometimes emphasizes the role of a kinsman in effecting redemption (Lev. 25:25, 48; Ruth 3:13). This emphasis, however, is not clearly present in all instances (Exod. 6:6; 15:13; Jer. 31:11; Mic. 4:10). The juxtaposition of these two words in Hosea 13:14 emphasizes the deliverance of God's people from death. The distinctive nuances of the words have moved into the background. אֱהִי (Where) may also represent a first-person imperfect of הָיָה (should I?/I would/I will) as with later Greek versions and the Vulgate. This form of הָיָה never occurs in the Old Testament apart from a waw-affix, however (see, e.g., Judg. 18:4; Ezek. 11:16; Job 30:9; see Hos. 13:7). It is best to understand אֱהִי as "where." Perhaps it was a word peculiar to Hosea's dialect. As in verse 10, the expected answer is, "Nowhere." דְּבָרֶיךָ (your plagues): Wolff (Hosea, p. 221, after KB) reads "thorns." The word pair דֶּבֶר and קֶטֶב occurs in Psalm 91:6 in a sense that gives greater support to the traditional translations "plagues" and

"destruction" because it is more likely that pestilence would be depicted as "walking" than thorns. The word קֶטֶב is described in the same context as "wasting" (יָשׁוּד), an idea that does not strongly complement "sting" (see Wolff, Hosea, p. 221). "Death" and "Sheol" form a striking chiasm in this context. נֹחַם (relenting) with this pointing occurs only here. We must look to the verb to delineate the semantic limitations of this word. The verb נָחַם appears to have the primary sense of changing one's mind. This concept is appropriate to all the contexts where the word appears. In the piel the word has the sense of effecting a change. The change is always in the direction of comfort in the piel. In no context where the word is used of God in the niphal does compassion effect the change in God. Compassion is not the primary sense of the word. God may be changed in the direction of pity (moved to) as in Judges 2:18, but compassion need not always effect the change. In Jeremiah 4:28 the word is in apposition with אָשׁוּב (turn back) with no emotive connotations in the clausal structure. In Exodus 13:17 it connotes a change of heart motivated by fear. Thus we must be careful not to read too much into נֹחַם in Hosea 13:14. The sense of compassion may not be required for the word, whereas the idea of relenting is necessary in all its occurrences.

---

doom (v. 7) was followed by the description of Yahweh's burning love (see 12:8–9).

It is doubtful that questions were intended by Hosea. We cited reasons for this in the Exegetical section. There is no need to regard the statement as anything more than an effective juxtaposition of concepts. The placing of an affirmation of deliverance immediately after a denunciation serves to intensify the promise of redemption. It gives it a greater emotional value because it is not a theological treatise, but an expression of the heart of God (11:8–9) that will not allow him to exterminate his people (see Lev. 26:44).

The following questions are thus appropriate to the context. Hosea can metaphorically face the specter of national death and triumphantly ask, "Where are your plagues?" There are none. And Sheol has no destructive power. The people of God will not lose their existence as a result of the captivity; they will not perish from history. Hosea's generation will perish, but beyond that looms a bright prospect, the prospect of thousands upon thousands of redeemed Jews and Gentiles who

will form a new people of God (Jer. 31:31, 34; Rom. 9:25–26). Paul transfers the triumph of Hosea's questions from the nation to the concept of resurrection (1 Cor. 15:54–55).

The last clause (relenting is hidden from my eyes) presents several problems. Not only is the sense of noḥam (relenting) obscure, but the relationship of this clause to its context is uncertain. Does it conclude the former pericope or introduce a new one? Wolff adopts the latter view (Hosea, p. 222), while most commentators take it with the foregoing material. To a great extent one's understanding of the atmosphere of the previous section is determinative.

The discussion in the Exegesis led to the conclusion that the idea of relent lies at the heart of this word. We can be sure of nothing else. If we assign that sense to the word here, the statement affirms the impossibility of God changing his mind with regard to the affirmations of hope in the preceding lines. The concept of hiding from the eyes also appears in Amos 9:3.

XVI. Hope for Ungrateful Israel (13:1–14:1) [13:1–16]

E. The Northern Kingdom Will Fall, but There Is Hope beyond That Catastrophe (13:15–14:1) [13:15–16]

¹⁵ For he—a son of brothers—shall be fruitful.
> The east wind shall come, the wind of the LORD,
> rising up from the wilderness; and his spring will dry up,
and his fountain become dry;
> it shall plunder the treasure;
> [remove] every precious thing.

14 Samaria will bear guilt
> because she has rebelled against her God:
by the sword they shall fall;
> their children will be dashed to pieces,
> and his pregnant women ripped open.

¹⁵ Although he may flourish among rushes,
> the east wind shall come, a blast from the LORD,
> rising from the wilderness;
and his fountain shall dry up,
> his spring shall be parched.
It shall strip his treasury
> of every precious thing.
¹⁶ Samaria shall bear her guilt,
> because she has rebelled against her God;
they shall fall by the sword,
> their little ones shall be dashed in pieces,
> and their pregnant women ripped open.

15. כִּי (for): We understand this particle to balance the last clause of verse 14 in the clausal structure by introducing the reason why God will not relent of his promise to redeem his people from death. It is because Ephraim is a בֵּן אַחִים (a son of brothers). Scholars have emended this unusual statement in various ways (Wolff, *Hosea*, p. 222, "among [the reeds]"; Mays, *Hosea*, p. 179, "midst rushes"). Both translations read אָחוּ (reeds) for אָח (brother). It is possible, however, that the expression reflects the account of Jacob's blessing of Ephraim (Gen. 48, see the Exposition). In this view הוּא (he) is not emphatic, but resumes the subject (Ephraim) stated at the head of the pericope (v. 12). יַפְרִיא (shall be fruitful) is almost certainly a hiphil of פָּרָה (be fruitful) spelled with א to form a play on words with Ephraim. According to Joseph this name connoted the concept of fruitfulness (Gen. 41:52). יָבוֹא (shall come) is not connected with the preceding context by וְ. It is thus likely that it begins a new logical section. רוּחַ יְהוָה (the wind of the LORD) is a genitive of source and indicates that the east wind was sent by Yahweh. הוּא (it) resumes the reference to קָדִים (east wind)

---

15. The connotation of the root *nhm* (relent) has led us to conclude that the final clause of verse 14 is a positive statement. Many commentators understand the *ki* which opens this verse to introduce a concessive clause similar to the translation of the Revised Standard Version: "Though he may flourish." This makes for an unusually long apodosis, however, and the fact that the resultant apodosis is not introduced by *waw* is suspicious. If, however, we regard the *ki* clause as the apodosis of a compound clause introduced by *noham*, the result is syntactical and logical: "Relenting is hidden from my eyes, for he—a son of brothers—will be fruitful." The sense of this clausal arrangement is that it is impossible for God to relent of his determination to redeem the people from national extermination because it is Ephraim's destiny to be fruitful.

The expression *a son of brothers* is perplexing. But it may reflect a significant event in the life of young Ephraim, the progenitor of the tribe that bore his name. We read that Jacob elevated his grandsons, Ephraim and Manasseh, to the status of sons (Gen. 48:5). By virtue of this legal transaction Ephraim became a direct inheritor of the Abrahamic promise through Jacob. The specific aspect of the ancient promise that Jacob cited was the offspring promise, "Let them grow into a multitude" (Gen. 48:16, RSV).

According to Jacob's blessing (vv. 15–16) the two sons were to grow into a multitude, but Ephraim was to be the greater (v. 19). If Hosea has this event in mind, he also has the promise in mind. We have found elsewhere that he cannot speak of the absolute cessation of God's people. On several occasions, when Hosea's language of judgment approaches ultimacy, either the promise or God's love intervenes to stay God's hand (1:10, see v. 9; 2:16 [14], see v. 15 [13]; 6:1–3, see 5:14; 11:1, see 10:15; 14:5 [4]). Perhaps Yahweh could not relent because of the eternality of the offspring promise, a promise that envisioned a new people of God. Ephraim learned from Jacob that he would bear fruit. God's promise could not fail. Hosea has already told us that "the number of the people of Israel shall be as the sand of the sea" (2:1 [1:10]). This determination made it impossible for God to change his mind.

Scholars have explained the difficult expression *son of brothers* variously. Several (Andersen and Freedman; Wolff; Mays) read *bn* as a form of *bên* (between) with the sense of *among*. But that particle does not appear elsewhere in Hosea in a shortened form.

Perhaps the expression is a term that Hosea uses to describe Ephraim's elevation to the status of an adoptive son of Jacob. This event may have involved the legal institutions of adoption and fratriarchy, which flourished in certain cultures in ancient Mesopotamia. Fratriarchy involved the elevation of a young man to the status of "brother" and afforded him certain legal rights. Ephraim's adoption by Jacob granted him fratriarchal rights equivalent to those of Jacob's natural sons Reuben and Simeon (Gen. 48:5).

Did Ephraim's elevation to the position of legal son of his grandfather Jacob also elevate Joseph, the natural son of Jacob, to a legal position of "brothership" in which he could be regarded as the legal brother of Jacob? If it did, then Ephraim was the son of brothers in a legal sense. The ancient practices of fratriarchy and adoption may not have allowed for an elevation in the status of Joseph, but the expression *son of brothers* may represent Hosea's description of what he observed in the ancient traditions about Jacob.

It seems strange to read in the next line that a wind will come from the Lord and remove the sources of their national fecundity. The transition is too abrupt. But we have found this abrupt transition from doom to hope and from accusation to assurance elsewhere in Hosea (11:7–8, 11–12;

which is masculine. אוֹצָר (treasure) is not treasury (Neh. 10:39 [38]) but the treasure itself (Josh. 6:19; Isa. 2:7) because it is parallel to כְּלִי (every precious thing).

14:1 [13:16]. תֶּאְשַׁם (bear guilt) has the sense of

be guilty (as in 10:2). This is determined by the following clause which sets forth the accusation that Samaria has rebelled against God. כִּי (because) gives the basis for the guilt. It is Samaria's rebellion.

12:9–10 [8–9]; 13:13–14). The explanation for the abruptness is Hosea's understanding of the people of God. Ephraim will surely go into captivity, but beyond that bitter prospect Hosea sees a new people, the people of the promise.

The treasure of which Hosea speaks was evidently Israel's national treasure—the precious vessels of the nation—and was the symbol of the nation's prosperity. The name *Ephraim* means "flourish," and indeed the nation had flourished, but Yahweh would remove the fruits of its prosperity.

14:1 [13:16]. Hosea directs this segment of the

oracle against Samaria, the capital of the northern kingdom. The capital represented the nation itself, and was the source of Israel's international intrigue. The state cult was, if not regulated, at least condoned by the officials in Samaria.

Hosea depicts a dark destiny for Samaria: It will fall by the sword. The picture is gruesome, but other prophets used similar imagery to describe judgment (Isa. 13:6; Amos 1:13; Nah. 3:10). These vivid depictions never fail to create revulsion within us, but they remind us of the result of rebellion against God. We read of the fulfilment of Hosea's prediction in 2 Kings 17:5.

XVII. Yahweh's Poignant Plea to Israel to Return to Him (14:2–10) [1–9]

A. Israel Learns How She Is to Repent (14:2–4) [1–3]

2 Return, O Israel, to the LORD, your God,
　　for you have stumbled in your guilt.
3 Take with you words,
　　and return to the LORD.
Say to him:
　　"Forgive all guilt,
and accept that which is good,
　　and we shall offer
　　our lips as bulls.
4 Assyria will not deliver us,
　　we shall not ride on horses,
and we shall say no more 'Our God'
　　to the work of our hands.
[You are] the one by whom the orphan
　　is shown compassion."

14 Return, O Israel, to the LORD your God,
　　for you have stumbled because of
　　　your iniquity.
2 Take words with you
　　and return to the LORD;
say to him,
　　"Take away all guilt;
accept that which is good,
　　and we will offer
　　the fruit of our lips.
3 Assyria shall not save us;
　　we will not ride upon horses;
we will say no more, 'Our God,'
　　to the work of our hands.
In you the orphan finds mercy."

14:2 [14:1]. שׁוּבָה (Return) with עַד (up to) is stronger than the more frequent שׁוּב אֶל (return unto), which stresses direction. שׁוּב אֶל has the sense of directing the heart toward God, while עַד שׁוּב emphasizes the extent of the action of the verb (up to, as far as). In this context, שׁוּב עַד connotes true repentance. אֱלֹהֶיךָ (your God): See the comments at 13:4. כִּי (for) introduces the reason why they are to return. כָּשַׁלְתָּ (you have stumbled) is in the perfect tense and denotes a concrete condition. It does not appear to have the sense of stumbling and falling. The people are about to fall, but there is a way for the nation to avoid absolute downfall. This is stated in verse 3 [2]. בַּעֲוֹנֶךָ (in your guilt): See 5:5.

3 [2]. קְחוּ (Take) is plural in contrast to the singular constructions of the preceding verse. We observed earlier that this device of changing number and person may mark logical divisions in Hosea. דְּבָרִים (words): The content of the words they are to speak is stated following אִמְרוּ (say) in the next line. וְשׁוּבוּ (and return): וְ sets the two clauses in apposition to one another; the taking and returning are part of one action. שׁוּב (return) is construed with אֶל (unto) with the emphasis on the direction of the verb. The sense is, "Turn your hearts toward him [the LORD]" (see v. 2 [1]). עָוֹן כָּל־תִּשָּׂא ("Forgive all guilt"): In this unusual expression (lit. all forgive guilt) the construct relationship is broken by the verb (תִּשָּׂא). The construct chain is broken in a number of instances in the Old Testament (see GKC §128c; although most are explained as corruptions). Construct relationships with כָּל are interrupted elsewhere as in 2 Samuel 1:9 where עוֹד is interjected (see the Exposition). וְקַח (and accept): וְ connects this clause to the preceding one and represents the clause it governs as continuing the words the people are to say. טוֹב (that which is good) stands for that which is worthy of divine acceptance. וּנְשַׁלְּמָה (and we shall offer) is from שָׁלַם, which has as one of its nuances *repay*. Instead of offering bulls (פָּרִים) to

---

2 [1]. As we move toward the conclusion of Hosea's prophecy, the thundering voice of the prophet becomes a tender whisper as he pleads lovingly with Israel. Hosea must have pleaded in the same way with Gomer when he bought her from her paramour (chap. 3). He had besought her to return with him to their home and establish a new relationship. Now Hosea calls on Israel to leave her lovers and come to God in repentance.

Hosea calls his people not only to turn toward God, but to make him the termination of their return. This is complete repentance. They are to reenter the sphere of Yahweh's dominion. The words *the LORD, your God* are significant. The people had left the sphere of Yahweh's love and had consorted with idols. Now Hosea calls them to come back to their God that they might enjoy his favor.

The nation had stumbled and had begun a headlong dash to ruin, but there was still time. Even though Hosea had predicted the certainty of the captivity at every turn in his prophecy, the possibility of repentance was always there. God's love had not come to an end. The offer of grace that stands before us was a sincere offer, but the hearts of the people were now too dull to receive it (see Isa. 6:9–11).

3 [2]. The dullness of their minds is reflected in the way Hosea directs their repentance; he puts the words into their mouths. It is as though he was with Gomer again when her heart was hardened by lust and greed. Such a person would have to be reached in the most basic way, the way one would deal with a child. Hosea begins, "Take with you words." The people are encouraged to express their resolve to return to God in statements that include the whole range of their guilt.

We understand the first statement in Hosea's litany of repentance to say "forgive all guilt." This unusual construction (lit. all forgive guilt) seems awkward, but there is no need to emend. Broken construct chains appear elsewhere in Hosea (see the discussion at 6:9 and 8:2). If we are correct in identifying the structure *ʾĕlōhay yĕdaʿănûkā yiśrāʾēl* (God of Israel, we know you) as a construct relationship (8:2), we find it similar to the construct chain here in that it too is broken by a verb.

The second statement they are to utter is, "accept that which is good." It is unlikely that this clause has the sense of receive graciously (see, e.g., NASB). Forgiving guilt and accepting good are two sides of one coin. It was not enough for their sin to be expunged; God looked for obedience as well. Obedience to the law was the means by which the people could continue to enjoy national blessing. According to the law "life" was a viable relationship to God sustained by obedience. This is a concept reflected in Deuteronomy, where the people were encouraged to do good that it might go well with them (6:18), and where "good" is paired with *yāšar* (right), imparting to the word *good* the sense of that which is pleasing to God (12:28).

God, Hosea encourages the repentant nation to repay God's gracious acceptance of them with their lips. פָּרִים (bulls) is frequently emended to פְּרִי (fruit) after the analogy of the Septuagint, which reads καρπὸν χειλέων ἡμῶν (fruit of our lips). If the translators had before them the consonants represented in the Masoretic Text, they apparently arranged them to read פְּרִי מִשְּׂפָתֵינוּ (lit. fruit from our lips). Against this arrangement is the fact that פְּרִי never occurs with מִן to communicate the sense of fruit of. This sense is always set forth by the construct relationship (see, e.g., Hos. 10:13). On the other hand, if we allow פָּרִים (bulls) to stand we may explain its function in this clause as an adverbial accusative (as bulls). We may observe similar functions in Deuteronomy 2:19 ([for] a possession); 1 Samuel 2:18 ([as] a boy); 2:33 ([as] men); and Isaiah 21:8 ([as] a lion).

4 [3]. עַל־סוּס (on horses): סוּס (horse) is a collective noun. וְלֹא (and . . . no) connects its clause to the preceding one and introduces the last of the series of statements that Hosea encourages the nation to make to God. לְמַעֲשֵׂה (to the work): מַעֲשֵׂה

has as its primary sense *that which is made*. Here it refers to idols (as it does in Ps. 115:4; Isa. 2:8). אֲשֶׁר ([you are] the one): It is doubtful that we should assign the sense of for to אֲשֶׁר in this clause (NIV). אֲשֶׁר does not clearly have this sense (BDB, pp. 81–84). The accompanying preposition בְּךָ (lit. in you) serves to define the person indicated by אֲשֶׁר. The sense of the construction is thus "you who" because the preposition בְּ is inflected by a second-person indicator. There are enough examples of this function of אֲשֶׁר in the Old Testament (Job 37:17; Pss. 71:19, 20; 139:15; 144:12; Isa. 49:23; Jer. 31:32) to show that it is not necessary to hold that the אֲשֶׁר clause is awkward here, and, thus, is a later addition. אֲשֶׁר resumes the address to God begun at the head of this series of statements. בְּךָ (by whom): בְּ is instrumental. The phrase אֲשֶׁר־בְּךָ reads literally "who by you." יְרֻחַם (is shown compassion): רָחַם is used mainly of God. In the pual it denotes the reception of mercy bestowed by an external force; in this case it is God who bestows compassion.

There was not much good that Yahweh could accept, but the next clause here allows for that lack. The repentant people would offer as sacrifices that which God really wanted, their lips. It was their words, the expression of repentance, that they were to speak under the prophet's guidance. This was more acceptable to God than the carcasses of bulls burned in the worship of pagan deities. Without this heartfelt response to God even the levitical sacrifices would not please him (see 1 Sam. 15:22–23; Ps. 51:18–19 [16–17]; Mic. 6:6–8).

4 [3]. The affirmation that Assyria will not deliver them strikes at the heart of their misplaced loyalty. It was an admission that their trust in Assyrian power was treachery against Yahweh. Paired with this is the reference to trust in horses. This includes everything of a military nature that could be the objects of trust (see 10:13).

We expect their statement of repentance to include the crime to which Hosea gives the most attention—their idolatry. We find this evil in the last line. The people will no longer say "Our God" to their idols. These words may be a formula uti-

lized in the worship of idols (see the discussion at 13:2). This reference to idols reflects the absurdity of idol worship, for idols are the work of human hands (13:2).

It is Yahweh who shows compassion to the orphan. No matter how artistic their idols, the people could find no love in the cold, staring images they had crafted. The reference to the orphan recalls similar references in Deuteronomy. The law sought to bring solace and provision to the orphan (see, e.g., Deut. 10:18; 14:29; 16:11; 24:19), for it mirrored Yahweh's love for the fatherless. Hosea appeals to this divine attribute here, but he applies it to his people. They are like the orphans depicted in the law.

Several commentators have noted the striking similarities between this section and the second birth narrative in 1:6–7. Andersen and Freedman argue that the linguistic similarities between the two sections show the authenticity of chapter 14 (*Hosea*, p. 646). We have argued for the authenticity of the last clause of this section (see the Exegesis).

XVII. Yahweh's Poignant Plea to Israel to Return to Him (14:2–10) [1–9]

B. Yahweh's Assurance of Israel's Restoration (14:5–8) [4–7]

5 I will heal their waywardness;
   I will love them freely,
     for my anger has turned away from
     him.
6 I will be as dew to Israel;
   he shall blossom like the lily,
   he shall strike his roots like [the
     trees of] Lebanon.
7 His shoots will go out;
    and its splendor will be like the olive
    tree,
    and its fragrance like [the trees of]
    Lebanon.
8 They shall return and dwell in its shade,
   they shall cause the grain to flourish,
and they will blossom as the vine.
   Its renown [will be] as [that of] the
   wine of Lebanon.

4 I will heal their disloyalty;
   I will love them freely,
     for my anger has turned from them.
5 I will be like the dew to Israel;
   he shall blossom like the lily,
   he shall strike root like the forests of
    Lebanon.
6 His shoots shall spread out;
   his beauty shall be like the olive tree,
   and his fragrance like that of
    Lebanon.
7 They shall again live beneath my
   shadow,
   they shall flourish as a garden;
they shall blossom like the vine,
   their fragrance shall be like the wine
   of Lebanon.

5 [4]. אֶרְפָּא (I will heal) identifies the apostasy of the nation as an illness. מְשׁוּבָתָם (their waywardness) signifies turning away from God (see 11:7). It is the object of the verb רָפָא (heal). כִּי (for) explains why God can love them and heal their apostasy; it is because his wrath has turned from them. מִמֶּנּוּ (from him) has a masculine singular suffix and thus does not refer to מְשׁוּבָתָם (waywardness), which is feminine (turned from their waywardness). Hosea is flexible in his grammatical indication of number, but not as flexible with regard to gender. The transition from the plural suffix (ם) to the singular suffix (נוּ) is not unusual. Hosea has moved from the plural to the singular

---

5 [4]. The statement of repentance is followed by the words of Yahweh. Hosea represents him as assuring the people that he will heal their waywardness and freely love them. The people thought they could find the cure for their nation's sickness by going to Assyria, but Assyria could not heal them (5:13). Hosea pleaded with the people to return to Yahweh for healing (6:1). He said that healing could not come to the nation until they brought their guilt out into the open and acknowledged it (7:1). Yahweh could not heal his people as long as sin remained an impediment.

If the people had heeded the prophet and uttered words of repentance in sincerity, their national healing would have begun. Hosea did not call them to change their ways, but to acknowledge their waywardness. Hosea viewed their waywardness as a sickness. It was evident in their misplaced trust in national alliances, military might, and pagan idols. The simple acknowledgment of their shameful guilt would have removed the impediment that prevented Yahweh from loving them freely. The words of Hosea are a treatise on spiritual healing that is as relevant today as it was in his day.

The basis on which Yahweh can heal the nation is stated in a *kî* (for) clause. It is because Yahweh's anger has turned from Israel (see the Exegesis). The verb *šab* (turned away) is in the perfect tense. It denotes an accomplished fact. We wonder how the prophet could represent Yahweh as making this statement. The Book of Hosea is so full of pronouncements of judgment. Has God's resolve to judge his people given way to his overwhelming love for them? Will he prevent the Assyrians from taking the nation captive?

We must remember that the *kî* (for) clause sets forth the basis on which Yahweh will heal and love the nation. It has nothing to do with the impending judgment. We see a somewhat similar concept set forth in Hosea 11:8–9. This passage, which is probably the heart of Hosea's prophecy, establishes the theological basis for Yahweh's assertion here that his anger has turned from the people. The familiar statement in 11:8–9 depicts Yahweh's love as the overwhelming emotion that governs his determination not to execute his fierce anger against his people and destroy them.

This loving affirmation (11:8–9) follows one of the most explicit judgment sayings in the book (11:5–7). Hosea identifies Assyria as the captor nation (v. 5). He states the reason for the captivity in no uncertain terms ("they have refused to return"), and depicts the horror of the Assyrian invasion in vivid language ("The sword shall sweep against his cities" [v.6]). And he concludes the judgment saying with this depiction of the people: "Together he does not rise" (v. 7).

We know from this passage that the compassion that welled up in Yahweh's heart did not stay his hand of judgment. The captivity occurred. Hosea made it clear that his theology of hope did not include the defeat of the Assyrians at the borders of Israel. This might have occurred if the nation had repented, but Hosea held out little hope of that.

Hosea's theology of hope looked beyond the exile. His magnificent depiction of divine love (11:8–9) did not vitiate Yahweh's resolve to judge his people's sin. Yahweh's emotion of love does not make him a placid deity who views evil as an annoying human aberration. He must punish all rebellion against his holy nature.

We know that Hosea looked beyond the gloomy prospect of the exile to find hope for his people because he envisioned them as returning to God from captivity. In the words that immediately follow the tender assurances that Yahweh's love will not allow him to execute his fierce anger (11:8–9), we find what his love will do. Yahweh will call his children from their captivity in Assyria and return them to their homes (11:10–11). His love did not eliminate the fact that his people would go into captivity; rather it prevented him from utterly wiping them out. It gave a hope beyond the captivity and affirmed Yahweh's fidelity to his eternal promise to Abraham.

We may understand Hosea's words here in a similar way. They do not vitiate the captivity that Hosea predicted. They look to the distant future and paint the picture of a people restored to God's loving care. They flourish like a tree, and their

in several clauses in which the nation is the subject (see, e.g., 10:9; 11:6; 14:1b [13:16b]).

6 [5]. טַל (dew) does not denote that which is ephemeral as it does in 6:4 and 13:3. Rather it describes Yahweh's benign treatment of Israel. יִפְרַח (he shall blossom) finds its referent in יִשְׂרָאֵל (Israel). וְיַךְ (he shall strike): נָכָה refers to the act of striking. In this context it probably describes a root thrusting itself into the ground. Note the concept of thrust for this word in 1 Samuel 2:14. כַּלְּבָנוֹן (like Lebanon): It is not clear that "Lebanon" when it occurs alone ever stands for the trees of Lebanon. This is probably another elliptical expression (see the Author's Translation).

7 [6]. יֵלְכוּ (will go out) is governed by the following word. יֹנְקוֹתָיו (his shoots) is from יָנַק (to suck). It denotes a sucker or a shoot. The suffix *his* sustains the earlier reference to Israel. There is no need to transfer the suffixal referents here and in the following clauses to the tree. The flourishing tree is an analogy for Israel. לוֹ (its) is possessive. כַּלְּבָנוֹן (like Lebanon): see above.

8 [7]. יָשֻׁבוּ (They shall return): The subject changes from the singular to the plural and is somewhat obscure. The subject may be either יֹשְׁבֵי (dwellers of?) or Israel viewed in the plural. The latter is preferable because the former option requires that those who are already dwelling in its shadow will return. This is anomalous to the intent of this section. יֹשְׁבֵי (and dwell; lit. dwellers of) is understood to have a verbal sense here, which stated literally is, "They shall return, dwellers in its shade." We may paraphrase it, "They shall return dwelling [or, and dwell] in its shade." This usage of the participle is not uncommon. In Genesis 3:5 the construct participle functions in a similar fashion. It follows a finite verb and has a distinct verbal sense: "you will be like God *knowing*" (lit. knowers of good and evil; see נֹתְנֵי לַחְמִי, those who give me my bread [Hos. 2:7 (5)]). The construct relationship is interrupted here by a preposition as it is in Isaiah 9:1 [2] (יֹשְׁבֵי בְּאֶרֶץ). This function appears to give greater precision to the construct relationship by more clearly denoting the sphere of the action. יְחַיּוּ (they shall cause

---

renown is like the wine of Lebanon. The statement that Yahweh's anger has turned from his people indicates the reversal of his will to destroy them as he did the cities of the plain (11:8).

6 [5]. The removal of Yahweh's anger will allow him to be like nourishing dew to the nation. They would flourish like a lily. They would become a mighty nation in their own right with their roots struck deeply into the earth. We may observe what happened because of their refusal to return to God. Assyria proved to be their nemesis; the object of their trust became the cause of their demise.

7 [6]. Hosea's depiction of the restored nation moves about freely within the realm of nature. The nation will be like a lily nourished by morning dew (v. 6 [5]), and like a garden as renowned as Lebanon's wine (v. 8 [7]). But it is the analogy of the tree that receives prominence.

In verse 6 [5] we learn that its tap root will pierce deeply into the rocky soil. This depicts the strength and security of the nation. It will be as majestic as the olive tree, and will have the fragrance of Lebanon's cedars. Such will be the position of Israel among the nations. This is true of God's people today, for the church finds its strength not in political power, but in a humble walk with God. It will spread abroad its fragrance in the world when its adherents live as did their Master.

8 [7]. A shift in the metaphor occurs in this verse. The tree, which referred to Israel to this point, now represents the source of shelter for the people. It no longer stands for the nation (see the Exposition at 2:5 [3]). The return of the people takes place beyond the captivity. In this, it is similar to other prophetic oracles (Isa. 11:6–9; Amos 9:13–15). It includes the great day envisioned by the prophets when the Gentiles would enjoy the privilege of divine election along with Jews (see Rom. 11:17–24). A prophetic ideal is reflected in Hosea's words—it is the prospect of God's people producing crops in abundance: "They shall cause the grain to flourish." Jeremiah also reflects this ideal when he speaks of the people of the new covenant as farmers, and those who follow as the flock (Jer. 31:24).

This pastoral motif may have sprung from a belief that the urbanization of society brought with it certain evils. Hosea accused Judah of building fortified cities and predicted their destruction (8:14). This concept of trust in fortified cities and other symbols of military might is condemned in the litany of repentance in 14:3–4 [2–3]. This vision of an agricultural people, freed from the evils of urban civilization and international intrigues, recalls the halcyon days of the exodus from Egypt when the people trustingly followed their God.

. . . to flourish): חָיָה in the piel denotes the impartation of life. There are several nuances to this concept: allowing one to live (Exod. 1:17; Josh. 9:15); giving life to man at creation (Job 33:4); and renewing life (Ps. 85:7 [6]). While the use of the word here in Hosea is unusual, it evidently refers to the ability of the restored people to produce grain. זִכְרוֹ (Its renown) has a third-person singular suffix which logically connects this word to the tree in Hosea's imagery, not the people who are the subject of the preceding plural verb (וְיִפְרְחוּ). The word זֵכֶר has the concrete sense of memorial or renown (see 12:6 [5]). The change of subject reflected in the singular suffix indicates that זִכְרוֹ belongs with the second clause in the structure. We must supply a verbal idea (will be). כְּיֵין (as [that of] the wine): The כְּ compares the renown of the tree with the renown of Lebanon's wine. לְבָנוֹן (Lebanon) here refers not to the trees of Lebanon, but to the country itself.

The flourishing of grain recalls the cosmic drama of 2:23–25 [21–23] in which the earth will undergo vast changes. That section rings with sovereign authority. It is not a blessing that hinges on the people's repentance.

This section concludes with another example of the way the restored people will flourish if they turn to God. They will be like a garden that was as well known as the wine of Lebanon. Lebanon is not known for its wine in the Old Testament, but it must have been a very fertile area. Streams spilling from the mountain ranges produced fertile valleys suitable for the production of grapes. All this could have been true of Israel, but they turned their backs on Hosea's poignant plea to turn to God.

XVII. Yahweh's Poignant Plea to Israel to Return to Him (14:2–10) [1–9]

C. Yahweh's Ways Are the Best Ways (14:9–10) [8–9]

9 O Ephraim, what have I ever had to do with idols?
    I am the one who answers [him] and watches over him.
  I am like a luxuriant cypress:
    in me your fruit is found.
10 Who is wise, then let him discern these things;
    who is discerning, then let him know them;
  for the ways of the LORD are right,
    and the righteous walk in them,
    but the rebellious stumble in them.

8 O Ephraim, what have I to do with idols?
    It is I who answer and look after you.
  I am like an evergreen cypress;
    your faithfulness comes from me.
9 Those who are wise understand these things;
    those who are discerning know them.
  For the ways of the LORD are right,
    and the upright walk in them,
    but transgressors stumble in them.

9 [8]. מַה־לִּי (what have I): The collocation מָה לְ has the literal sense of *what is there to . . . ?* With the first-person suffix (as here) we may translate it, "What is there to me?" It occurs frequently as a formula of repudiation (מַה־לִּי וָלָךְ, What have I to do with you?). When an indirect object with לְ follows this collocation as it does here (לָעֲצַבִּים, with idols) the sense of the לְ is *with reference to.* We may see this in Jeremiah 2:18 where the words מַה־לָּךְ לְדֶרֶךְ מִצְרַיִם state literally, "What is there to you *with reference* to the way to Egypt?" That is, "What do you gain by going to Egypt?" We may translate it here literally, "What is it to me with reference to idols?" It is a repudiation of idols with reference to God. עוֹד (ever): This word's sense of still or yet is difficult to translate. It has a sense of continuance in the past or continuance in the present (still). We may translate the entire question, "What have I *still* to do with idols?" Since the idiom is a formula of repudiation, we may reflect the ideas of continuance (עוֹד) and repudiation by translating it, "What have I *ever* had to do with idols?" Yahweh never had, and still (עוֹד) has nothing to do with pagan images. אֲנִי (I am the one

who): Because אֲנִי refers to God in contrast to idols and because it precedes an inflected verb, it is emphatic. עָנִיתִי (answers [him]): See the discussion at 2:23 [21], where the word describes Yahweh's response to a need. Here it depicts his response to the needs of his people. וַאֲשׁוּרֶנּוּ (and watches over him): The verb שׁוּר (watch) occurs in 13:7, where it describes the intent stare of an animal lying in wait for its prey. The basic idea of the word is to behold. Its association with עָנָה (answer, respond), however, influences the word in the direction of watchful care. אֲנִי (I) is not emphatic but serves to indicate that the subject of the preceding clause continues into the clause it introduces. נִמְצָא . . . מִמֶּנִּי (in me . . . is found) is literally, "from me." מִן (from) indicates the source of the action of the verb מָצָא (find).

10 [9]. חָכָם (wise) is related to the concept of skill in many contexts; it connotes more than native intelligence. It is wisdom that acts on the basis of knowledge to benefit the individual. וְיָבֵן (that he may discern): The imperfect with וְ indicates the logical or temporal consequence. Here the consequence of being wise is discernment of

---

9 [8]. The question with which this section begins called the attention of the people of the northern kingdom to the long span of history over which Yahweh had manifested himself. Never did he have anything to do with idols. His law began with the command, "You shall have no other gods before me" (Exod. 20:3). The Deuteronomic expression of the law warned against the worship of idols (Deut. 29:16–28). The prophets of the eighth century viewed idolatry as a destructive influence at work within the social fabric of Israel.

Israel's God never worked through the mediation of idols. It was he himself who responded to the needs of his people and who intently watched over them. The word we have translated "watch over" is *ʾăšûrennû.* Without the suffix it appears in transliteration as *ʾāšûr* which sounds suspiciously like the Hebrew word for Assyria (*ʾaššûr*). Did Hosea want to overlay the name of Assyria with Yahweh's affirmation that it was he, not Assyria, who watched over Israel? Is this the reason he chose a word that does not have the primary meaning of watch in the sense of care? We cannot be sure, but if this is his intent, it echoes the philosophy that Assyria is not able to cure or heal them (5:13).

"I am the one," said Yahweh, "who answers [him]." We found at 2:23 [21] that this word (*ʿānâ,* answer) sometimes refers to response to a need.

Over the course of Israel's history it was Yahweh who responded to them. When they were a helpless infant, alone in desert wastes, he responded to their need. It was he who brought them to national prominence. Could they not see that their idols were helpless to save them from their desperate national plight?

Hosea continues his appeal to the phenomena of nature by picturing Yahweh as a luxuriant evergreen tree. Trees of this type are not known to bear fruit, but that is not the point. It is in Yahweh that their fruit is to be found. The metaphor of the tree serves only to represent productiveness.

The reference to fruit (*pĕrî*) recalls the name *Ephraim,* which means fruitful (perhaps *doubly fruitful*). In the discussion at 13:15 we suggested that Ephraim's fruitfulness was the result of the ancient promise made first to Abraham and later reiterated to Jacob. It was the promise of numerous offspring that finds emphasis there. Fruitfulness can be found only in Yahweh. It was he who granted them the blessing first granted to their ancient patriarch.

10 [9]. The prophecy ends with a wisdom-saying. There is no reason to doubt its integrity. It rounds off the book nicely and contains a number of linguistic and conceptual affinities with the body of the book. The word *ḥakam* (wise) appears

Hosea's words (אֵלֶּה, these things). נָבוֹן (is discerning) is the niphal form of the preceding verb בִּין (וְיָבֵן). In the niphal the sense is to be intelligent or to have understanding. כִּי (for) does not introduce direct causality because it follows the series of two questions. Rather, it denotes proximate cause, giving the reason for what is implicit in the questions, that is, it is wise to understand the words of Hosea. The implication is that it is wise to walk in Yahweh's ways, because those ways are right and have no impediments for the righteous. יְשָׁרִים (are right) is used in a secular sense of straight paths (Jer. 31:9), and of that which is right in an individual's estimation (Deut. 12:8; Judg. 17:6; 21:25; 2 Sam. 19:7 [6]). Its ethical sense occurs in its association with words such as "good" (Deut. 6:18) and "just" (Deut. 32:4). In 1 Samuel 29:6 it represents honesty (perhaps lack

of deviousness). דַּרְכֵי יְהוָה (ways of the LORD) is a concept that occurs several times in Deuteronomy. It is associated in each instance with concepts that refer to a loving, ethical response to God (Deut. 10:12; 11:22; 19:9; 26:17; 28:9; 30:16). The ways of the Lord are those aspects of God's governance of man that he has prescribed for His glory and for man's good. צַדִּקִים (the righteous): See the discussion of the root meaning of this word at 2:21 [19]. יֵלְכוּ (walk) is imperfect and connotes continuous action. The righteous continually walk in God's ways. וּפֹשְׁעִים (but the rebellious): The root פָּשַׁע describes rebellion in its various forms (see the discussion at 7:13). יִכָּשְׁלוּ (will stumble) appears to have a sense of ultimacy about it (stumble and fall), as it does in 4:5 and 5:5. בָּם (in them) refers, as does the previous usage of בָּם, to the ways of the Lord.

---

in 13:13 with the sense it has here, and the concepts of rebellion and stumbling occur throughout the book. Without the words of verse 10 the book would have ended abruptly.

This saying is an appeal to all the readers of the book. Those who have skill in understanding will discern the message of Hosea. That message is that the Lord's ways are right. From the picture of Gomer in her pitiful condition, to the depiction of Yahweh as a stately tree we have seen this fact set forth. Ephraim's ways will lead to death; Yahweh's ways will bring life. This fact, like so many concepts we have observed in Hosea, is Deuteronomic. In Deuteronomy 30:19–20 two ways were set before the people: life and death, blessing and curse. Ephraim had rejected the good and had chosen to die.

The ways of God are free of obstacles for the righteous. The upright realize the benefits of God's laws and proscriptions, and they know that

his ways are wise. What God has instituted is for our good. We find satisfaction and nobility in a life that is lived humbly before God. Those who rebel against God's yoke will stumble over his commands; they will find his strictures too hard to bear. Hosea vividly describes the heart of the rebellious in 7:13–16.

Hosea's marriage was bittersweet, but so was Yahweh's relationship with his people. They stumbled in the way and fell. They rationalized their adherence to their syncretistic religion and defended their national policies as necessary to their survival. All the while they moved closer to extinction. The key to survival and eventual exaltation as a people was simple, yet profound. They had only to take with them words (14:3 [2]) and acknowledge their wrongdoing. If their hearts were broken, their relationship to God would be mended.

Joel

Introduction

Author

The Book of Joel is attributed (1:1) to an otherwise unknown Joel son of Pethuel (LXX: Bethuel). Though another dozen persons mentioned in the Old Testament are named Joel, the prophet cannot with confidence be associated with any of these individuals, nor is his father otherwise known. The fact that no other information is included in the superscription may imply that Joel was well known to his contemporaries and that further qualification was unnecessary (see the Exposition of 1:1). The prophet presumably lived in the environs of Jerusalem, which provide the setting for the book. Because of his familiarity with the temple and his concern with worship there, some have identified him as a cultic or temple prophet (Kapelrud, *Joel Studies*; Ahlström, *Joel and the Temple Cult*). This identification is problematic since the precise relationship of the prophets with the temple is one of the most debated issues in Old Testament study. If by "temple prophet" one intends a cultic official whose maintenance was also drawn from temple revenues, there are insufficient data to warrant identifying Joel in this way, and such an identification is doubtful for the other prophets mentioned in the Bible. Some prophets were also priests (e.g., Ezekiel, Zechariah), but they are not prophets by virtue of their priestly office. Prophetic office is not hereditary. If one intends to indicate no more than a prophet whose ministry routinely brought him into the environs of the temple, however, this appellation could apply to Joel and a great number of others.

Insofar as authorial intent remains an important key to the meaning of any text, the Book of Joel will then unavoidably be problematic. Since we know little about the individual himself,

For Joel Bryan Dillard
Jonathan Bruce Dillard
Joshua Albrecht Dillard,
with praise from their parents to their heavenly Father, because he has fulfilled his promise to our children (Acts 2:39) and has poured out his Spirit on our sons (Joel 2:29)

Contributor:
† Raymond Bryan Dillard

we are forced to turn to the sociological, religious, political, and cultural milieu in which he lived in the hopes that it may provide some additional control over the intent of the book. For this reason the date of the book becomes an important question.

Date

But here too we encounter a thicket of seemingly insoluble questions. The book itself contains no direct testimony regarding its historical setting, as is common in the superscription of other prophetic books (e.g., Isa. 1:1; Jer. 1:1–3; Zeph. 1:1), nor does it mention personages otherwise known that would permit inferences regarding the historical setting. There is little external evidence for its date, so we must turn to the internal evidence from the book itself to answer the question of date. The following internal evidence constitutes the primary data for inferring a historical setting.

Most would agree that the book was written sometime after the outbreak of a locust plague (chap. 1). However, such outbreaks were probably common; even if we had some source reporting the history of such outbreaks, we would probably not be able to date the one reported in the book.

The book presumes the existence and routine operation of the temple (1:9, 13–16; 2:15–17); for this reason a date between 586 and 516 B.C., the period during which the temple was in ruins, can be eliminated with confidence.

A number of other nations are mentioned, primarily as enemies on whom the Lord will take vengeance (Phoenicians, Philistines, Egypt, Edom, the Greeks, and Sabeans—see the Exposition of 4:4–8, 19 [3:4–8, 19]). However, these are largely traditional enemies of Israel. Greek trade in the Levant is known from Assyriological sources as early as the eighth century B.C. (4:6 [3:6]). Though the Sabeans dominated trade routes to the east in the fifth century B.C. (4:8 [3:8]), they were also active in trade in the Solomonic period (1 Kings 10 par. 2 Chron. 9). What is striking in this regard is less the names that are mentioned than those that are not. One cannot help but notice the absence of any reference to the Assyrians or Babylonians, those powers whose actions had the greatest impact on Israel and Judah. Though it is of course an argument from silence, it suggests that the book was written prior to the hegemony of Assyria along the Mediterranean coast (mid-eighth century B.C.) or after the fall of Babylon (late sixth century B.C.).

The book presumes a situation in which the leadership of the community is in the hands of elders and priests (1:2, 13; 2:16); there is no mention of kings or royal officials. Though once again it is an argument from silence, the leadership of the nation suggests a period either without a monarchy (postexilic period) or one in which the monarchy had a limited role (such as during the minority of Joash in the late ninth century B.C.—2 Kings 11–12 par. 2 Chron. 23–24).

There is also no mention of the northern kingdom. The designation of Judah as "Israel" (2:27; 4:2, 16 [3:2, 16]) most naturally presumes a time when the northern tribes had been carried into exile (722 B.C.); the description of Judah as "Israel" is more commonly found in postexilic books.

There are numerous agreements in phraseology and concepts between Joel and other prophetic books. This can be explained in several ways: (1) Joel may have made extensive use of earlier prophetic literature; (2) his prophecy had a decided impact on those who followed and cited his work; (3) Joel often employed a common stock of prophetic idioms and was not really dependent on other compositions; or (4) each citation must be evaluated on its own merits to determine whether Joel used or was used by others. This question has been the subject of extensive debate (a number of the parallels are noted in the commentary). By and large those who have investigated these possible citations have concluded that Joel was dependent on the earlier texts (see Lattimore, "Date of Joel," pp. 88–99; Gray, "Parallel Passages in Joel").

The theological concepts in the book may also provide evidence for the date of its composition. God did not reveal himself to Israel all at once, but instead gradually unfolded the nature of his relationship to Israel over a period of time through the prophets. In many instances one can trace the way in which particular themes, motifs, or images were successively used and modified through time so that the development of a particular concept can be arranged in a chronological order. Joel's portrayal of the nations assembled for battle against the Lord (4:9–17 [3:9–17]) is found primarily in late materials (Ezek. 38–39; Zech. 12:1–5; 14:1–7; cf. Isa. 66:18). The description of a fountain flowing from the temple (4:18 [3:18]) is also found in Ezekiel 47:1–12 and Zechariah 14:8. While these examples are drawn from the later stages in the growth of biblical literature, it is at least possible that they depended on earlier materials; once again it is difficult to make confident assertions regarding the date of Joel from this evidence.

The references to the wall of the city (2:7, 9) have been taken as implying that the date of the book was after the completion of the city wall by Nehemiah. This line of argument has no value for date (see the Exegesis of 2:9).

References to the dispersion of the Jews into surrounding lands (4:1–2 [3:1–2]) may also suggest a postexilic date, though such scattering was by no means limited to the actions of the Babylonians (Zech. 2:1–4 [1:18–21]). Population relocation was a routine policy of the Assyrians; according to Assyriological sources, Sennacherib had already subjected Judah to a major deportation, so that references to a diaspora need not refer to the Babylonian captivity alone (see Stohlmann, "Judaean Exile after 701 B.C.E.").

Arguments from style and date of language are largely inconclusive. While many linguistic features of Joel are held in common with late biblical books, we lack sufficient data to determine whether these features were later innovations in the development of Hebrew or simply coincidence. While arguments from language can have a corroborative role for other arguments, we lack a sufficient corpus to use them with confidence. Many linguistic features that have been identified as late have been disputed by Kapelrud (*Joel Studies*, pp. 86–87, 111–12) and Ahlström (*Joel and the Temple Cult*, pp. 1–22).

The position of Joel in the Hebrew canon between the eighth-century prophecies of Hosea and Amos has been taken by many as indicative of date; however, in the Septuagint Joel is found after Micah. Its position between Hosea and Amos is probably the result of the similarities between Amos 1:2 and 9:13 and Joel 4:16, 18 [3:16, 18] and the fact that both Amos and Joel mention Tyre, the Philistines, and Edom (Allen, *Joel*, p. 21).

Though once again an argument from silence, it is worth noting the absence of any polemic against syncretized worship or the worship of foreign deities, indictments so characteristic of preexilic prophecy. Even if idolatry had been briefly suppressed at the time of Joash, one would at least expect some references to it in Joel's preaching, especially since the book is taken up with issues of rainfall and fertility—areas of concern in fertility cults and the particular area of Baal's expertise as a storm deity. Kapelrud (*Joel Studies*) did attempt to read Joel's concern with fertility against the backdrop of Canaanite fertility religion, but by and large his efforts have not proved convincing.

This survey of the major lines of evidence cited for establishing the date of Joel is inconclusive, though it is fair to say that it tilts toward a date in the postexilic period. In the history of scholarship a wide variety of dates has been proposed for the book. Here is a representative list of some of the dates proposed by various scholars (see the more detailed discussion in Prinsloo, *Theology of the Book of Joel*, pp. 5–8; and Allen, *Joel*, pp. 19–24).

9th century, time of Joash: K. A. Credner, G. C. Aalders, E. J. Young, M. Bič
late 7th century: A. S. Kapelrud, C. A. Keller, K. Koch
early 6th century: W. Rudolph
late 6th to mid-5th century: W. F. Albright, J. M. Myers, B. Reicke, G. Ahlström, L. Allen

late 5th to mid-4th century: A. Weiser, H. W. Wolff, J. A. Bewer,
F. R. Stephenson
early 3d century: M. Treves
as late as 2d century: B. Duhm

Most recently D. Stuart (*Hosea–Jonah*, p. 226) has associated the
impetus for the book with invasions of Judah by the Assyrians
or Babylonians in 701, 598, or 588.

In spite of Delitzsch's judgment (*Old Testament History of
Redemption*, p. 113) that the "bringing down of Joel into the post
exilic age by Duhm, Merx, Stade, and others, is one of the most
rotten fruits of the modern criticism," the position argued by
Ahlström, Myers, and Allen appears to this writer to represent
the best handling of the evidence.

Literary Structure

The fact that the Book of Joel so resists attempts to date it
may in part reflect another important characteristic of the book.
Several features suggest that the Book of Joel as a whole is either
a liturgical text intended for repeated use on occasions of national
lament or at least a historical example of one such lament.

Some psalms appear to have been composed for such occasions, and a few narratives also provide examples of the practice. In times of natural disaster or military threat, (1) the people
were often summoned to a fast at a sanctuary (Joel 1:13–14;
2:15–17; cf. 2 Chron. 20:3–4; 1 Kings 21:9–12; Isa. 22:12; Ezra
8:21; Jer. 36:8–10; 49:3–6; Jon. 3:7–8), where (2) they would present their complaint to God in prayer and remind him of his
past mercies (Joel 1:2–12, 15–20; 2:1–11; cf. 2 Chron. 20:5–13;
Pss. 12:2–5 [1–4]; 60:3–7 [1–5]; 85:2–8 [1–7]), and (3) receive an
answer of weal or woe from God (Joel 2:12–4:21 [3:21]; cf. 2
Chron. 20:14–17; Pss. 12:6–9 [5–8]; 60:8–14 [6–12]; 85:9–14 [8–13];
see Dillard, *2 Chronicles*, pp. 154–55; Ogden, "Prophetic Oracles and Joel 4").

If the Book of Joel was intended to serve as part of a liturgy at
the temple, the difficulty in dating the book is all the more easily
understood. Repeated liturgical use would call for a composition
that could be used on many different occasions, whether natural or military disaster threatened. Specific historical references
would narrow the range of events to which the text could be
applied or for which it could be used liturgically. Note also how
the text is "dehistoricized" in reference to the confession of sin:
though the text calls for repentance (1:13–14; 2:12–14), no particular sin is mentioned as causing the plight of the people. The
less specific a liturgical text is, the wider the range of its appli-
cability. This feature of the book may help explain not only why

it is so difficult to date, but also how it achieves the kind of time-lessness that makes it such powerful literature in our own day. Chary (*Les prophètes et le culte*, pp. 209–12), on the other hand, argues that the book was composed with reference to a single historical event and without any reference to possible repeated use.

The Unity of the Book

Up until the early part of this century the unity of the Book of Joel remained essentially unchallenged. However, early in the twentieth century B. Duhm advanced the argument that the book consisted of the work of at least two different individuals. A pre-exilic prophet delivered oracles concerning a local locust out-break; his utterances comprise the bulk of 1:1–2:27. A later apoc-alypticist assigned to the Maccabean period incorporated this earlier prophet's work into his own utterances regarding the day of the Lord; Duhm attributed 3:1–4:21 [2:28–3:21], 1:15, 2:1–2, 2:10–11 to this later figure. Duhm was followed in his assess-ment by J. A. Bewer and T. H. Robinson, both with minor modi-fications regarding the passages assigned to the later prophet.

More recent scholars (Allen, Chary, Kapelrud, Keller, Myers, Rudolph, Stuart, Thompson, Weiser, Wolff) have tended to view the book as the composition of a single author, though possibly including smaller redactional additions (see the Exposition of 4:4–8 [3:4–8]). The most influential argument in favor of the essential unity of the book derives from the form-critical appre-ciation of the literary structure of the book as a lament. Those passages identified as interpolations from a later writer into chap-ters 1–2 are viewed as integrally related to their context. From the perspective argued in this volume, 2:1–11 is already escha-tologically oriented rather than simply a description of a histor-ical locust outbreak, and assigning all eschatological passages in the book to the later apocalypticist would leave only chapter 1 as the utterances of the original preexilic prophet; at this point the unity of chapters 1–2 is most easily understood as the work of a single author.

Analysis

Select Bibliography

Ahlström, Gösta W. "*Hammōreh liṣdāqāh* in Joel 2:23." In *Congress Volume: Rome 1968*, pp. 25–36. Supplements to Vetus Testamentum 17. Leiden: Brill, 1969. Reprinted in Ahlström, *Joel and the Temple Cult of Jerusalem*, pp. 98–110. Supplements to Vetus Testamentum 21. Leiden: Brill, 1971.

———. *Joel and the Temple Cult of Jerusalem.* Supplements to Vetus Testamentum 21. Leiden: Brill, 1971.

Allen, Leslie C. *The Books of Joel, Obadiah, Jonah and Micah.* New International Commentary on the Old Testament. Grand Rapids: Eerdmans, 1976.

Bach, Robert. *Die Aufforderungen zur Flucht und zum Kampf im alttestamentlichen Prophetenspruch.* Wissenschaftliche Monographien zum Alten und Neuen Testament 9. Neukirchen: Neukirchener Verlag, 1962.

Baron, Stanley. *The Desert Locust.* New York: Scribner, 1972.

Baumgartner, Walter. "Joel 1 und 2." In *Beiträge zur Alttestamentlichen Wissenschaft: Karl Budde zum siebzigsten Geburtstag*, pp. 10–19. Edited by Karl Marti. Beiheft zur Zeitschrift für die Alttestamentliche Wissenschaft 34. Giessen: Töpelmann, 1920.

Bennett, L. V. "Development of a Locust Plague." *Nature* 256 (1975): 486–87.

Bewer, Julius A. *A Critical and Exegetical Commentary on Obadiah and Joel.* International Critical Commentary. Edinburgh: T. & T. Clark/New York: Scribner, 1911.

Bič, Miloš. *Das Buch Joel.* Berlin: Evangelische Verlagsanstalt, 1960.

Bourke, J. "Le Jour de Yahvé dans Joël." *Revue Biblique* 66 (1959): 5–31, 191–212.

Borowski, Oded. *Agriculture in Iron Age Israel.* Winona Lake, Ind.: Eisenbrauns, 1987.

Bracke, John M. "*Šûb š^ebût:* A Reappraisal." *Zeitschrift für die Alttestamentliche Wissenschaft* 97 (1985): 233–44.

Budde, Karl. "Der Umschwung in Joel 2." *Orientalische Literaturzeitung* 22 (1919): 104–10.

———. "'Der von Norden' in Joel 2:20." *Orientalische Literaturzeitung* 22 (1919): 1–5.

Buis, Pierre. "Étude biblique (de la Semaine de la Pentecôte) (Joel 3:1–5, Acts 2:14–40): Le don de l'Esprit Saint et la prophétie de Joel." *Assemblées du Seigneur* 52 (1965): 16–28.

———. "Joel announce l'effusion de l'Esprit." *Spiritus* 2 (1961): 145–52.

Calvin, John. *Commentaries on the Twelve Minor Prophets.* Vol. 2: *Joel, Amos, Obadiah.* Translated by John Owen. Edinburgh: Calvin Translation Society, 1846. Reprint, Grand Rapids: Eerdmans, 1950.

Cannon, William W. "The Day of the Lord in Joel." *Church Quarterly Review* 103 (1926): 32–63.

Carroll, Robert P. "Eschatological Delay in the Prophetic Tradition?" *Zeitschrift für die Alttestamentliche Wissenschaft* 94 (1982): 47–58.

Chary, Théophane. *Les prophètes et le culte à partir de l'exil autour du Second Temple: L'idéal cultuel des prophètes exiliens et postexiliens.* Bibliothèque de Théologie 3/3. Tournai: Desclée, 1955.

Childs, Brevard S. "The Enemy from the North and the Chaos Tradition." *Journal of Biblical Literature* 78 (1959): 187–98.

Cole, R. Alan. "Joel." In *The New Bible Commentary Revised,* pp. 716–25. Edited by Donald Guthrie, J. Alec Motyer, Alan M. Stibbs, and Donald J. Wiseman. 3d ed. London: Inter-Varsity/Grand Rapids: Eerdmans, 1970.

Cooper, David L. "The Message of Joel." *Biblical Research Monthly* 47 (1982): 21–23.

Couve de Murville, M. N. L. "Joel." In *A New Catholic Commentary on Holy Scriptures,* pp. 689–92. Edited by Reginald C. Fuller, Leonard Johnston, and Conleth Kearns. London: Nelson, 1969.

Craigie, Peter C. *Twelve Prophets,* vol. 1. Daily Study Bible. Philadelphia: Westminster/Edinburgh: Saint Andrew, 1984.

Dahood, Mitchell. "The Four Cardinal Points in Psalm 75:7 and Joel 2:20." *Biblica* 52 (1971): 397.

———. "Hebrew *tamrûrîm* and *tîmarôt.*" *Orientalia* 46 (1977): 385.

———. "Hebrew-Ugaritic Lexicography IX." *Biblica* 52 (1971): 337–56.

———. *Ugaritic-Hebrew Philology: Marginal Notes on Recent Publications.* Biblica et Orientalia 17. Rome: Pontifical Biblical Institute, 1965.

———. "Joël—de Pinksterprofeet." *Verbum* 25 (1958): 197–205.

Delitzsch, Franz. *Old Testament History of Redemption.* Translated by Samuel I. Curtiss. New York: Scribner/Edinburgh: T. & T. Clark, 1881.

Dennefeld, Ludwig. "Joël." In *Dictionnaire de Théologie Catholique,* vol. 8, cols. 1489–95. Edited by Alfred Vacant, Eugène Mangenot, and Émile Amann. Paris: Letouzey & Ané, 1925.

———. "Les Problèmes du livre de Joël." *Revue des Sciences Religieuses* 4 (1924): 555–75; 5 (1925): 35–57, 591–608; 6 (1926): 26–49. Reprinted as *Les Problèmes du livre de Joël.* Paris: Geuthner, 1926.

Dillard, Raymond B. *2 Chronicles.* Word Biblical Commentary 15. Waco, Tex.: Word, 1987.

Dressler, H. H. P. "Ugaritic *uzr* and Joel 1:13." *Ugarit-Forschungen* 7 (1975): 221–25.

Ellul, Danielle. "Introduction au livre du Joël." *Études Théologiques et Religieuses* 54 (1979): 426–37.

Evans, Craig A. "The Prophetic Setting of the Pentecost Sermon." *Zeitschrift für die Neutestamentliche Wissenschaft* 74 (1983): 148–50.

Fishelson, Lev. *Fauna Palestina: Insecta.* Vol. 3: *Orthoptera, Acridoidea.* Jerusalem: Israel Academy of Sciences and Humanities, 1985.

Frankfort, Thérèse. "Le כִּי de Joël 1:12." *Vetus Testamentum* 10 (1960): 445–48.

Freund, Y. "Multitudes, Multitudes in the Valley of Decision." *Beth Miqraʾ* 21 (1975/76): 271–77, 315 [Hebrew].

Gamberoni, Johann. "Die Geistbegabung im Alten Testament, besonders nach Joel 3:1–5." In *Die Gabe Gottes,* pp. 9–32. Edited by Paul Nordhues and Heinrich Petri. Paderborn: Bonifacius, 1974.

Gelin, Albert. "L'Annonce de la Pentecôte (Joël 3:1–5)." *Bible et Vie Chrétienne* 27 (1959): 15–19.

Görg, Manfred. "Eine formelhafte Metaphor bei Joel und Nahum." *Biblische Notizen* 6 (1978): 12–14.

Graham, J. N. "Vinedressers and Plowmen: 2 Kings 25:12 and Jeremiah 52:16." *Biblical Archaeologist* 47 (1984): 55–58.

Gray, George Buchanan. "The Parallel Passages in 'Joel' in Their Bearing on the Question of Date." *Expositor,* 4th ser., 8 (1893): 208–25.

Haupt, Paul. "The Valley of the Gorge." *American Journal of Philology* 43 (1922): 240–41.

Hitzig, Ferdinand. *Die zwölf kleinen Propheten*. 4th ed. Kurzgefasstes exegetisches Handbuch zum Alten Testament 1. Leipzig: Hirzel, 1881.

Hobson, Richard, Jr., and John Lawton. "New Battle in an Ancient War." *Aramco World Magazine* 38/3 (May–June 1987): 6–13.

Holladay, William L. *The Root Šûbh in the Old Testament, with Particular Reference to Its Usages in Covenantal Contexts*. Leiden: Brill, 1958.

Hosch, Harold. "The Concept of Prophetic Time in the Book of Joel." *Journal of the Evangelical Theological Society* 15 (1972): 31–38.

Hubbell, T. H. "Locust." In *Encyclopedia Britannica*, 1963 ed., 14: 282–83.

Jacob, Edmond; Carl-A. Keller; and Samuel Amsler. *Osée, Joël, Abdias, Jonas, Amos*. Commentaire de l'Ancien Testament 11a. Neuchâtel: Delachaux & Niestlé, 1965.

Jeremias, Gert. *Der Lehrer der Gerechtigkeit*. Studien zur Umwelt des Neuen Testaments 2. Göttingen: Vandenhoeck & Ruprecht, 1963.

Jones, Douglas R. *Isaiah 56–66 and Joel: Introduction and Commentary*. Torch Bible Commentaries. London: SCM, 1964.

Joüon, Paul. *Grammaire de l'hébreu biblique*. Rome: Pontifical Biblical Institute, 1923.

Kapelrud, Arvid S. *Joel Studies*. Uppsala Universitets Årsskrift 1948:4. Uppsala: Lundequist/Leipzig: Harrassowitz, 1948.

Karp, Laenu. "A Comparative Analysis of Stylistic Embellishment in the Speeches of Hosea and Joel." *Society of Biblical Literature: Proceedings* 1974: 55–67.

Katzenstein, H. Jacob. *The History of Tyre: From the Beginning of the Second Millennium B.C.E. until the Fall of the Neo-Babylonian Empire in 538 B.C.E.* Jerusalem: Schocken Institute for Jewish Research, 1973.

Kedar-Kopfstein, Benjamin. "The Hebrew Text of Joel as Reflected in the Vulgate." *Textus* 9 (1981): 16–35.

Keimer, Ludwig. "Pendeloques en forme d'insectes faisant partie de colliers égyptiens." *Annales de Service des Antiquités de l'Égypte* 32 (1932): 129–50; 33 (1933): 97–130; 37 (1937): 143–64.

Keller, Carl-A. See Jacob, Edmond; Carl-A. Keller; and Samuel Amsler.

Kennedy, J. Hardee. "Joel." In *The Broadman Bible Commentary*, vol. 7, pp. 61–80. Edited by Clifton J. Allen. Nashville: Broadman, 1972.

Kerrigan, Alexander. "The 'Sensus Plenior' of Joel 3:1–5 in Acts 2:14–36." In *Sacra Pagina: Miscellanea Biblica, Congressus*

Internationalis Catholici de Re Biblica, vol. 2, pp. 295–313. Edited by Joseph Coppens, Albert Descamps, and Édouard Massaux. Bibliotheca Ephemeridum Theologicarum Lovaniensium 13. Gembloux: Duculot/Paris: Lecoffre/Gabalda, 1959.

Kessler, John A. "The Shaking of the Nations: An Eschatological View." *Journal of the Evangelical Theological Society* 30 (1987): 159–66.

Keulenaer, J. "Poenae Phoeniciis et Philistaeis denuntiatae apud Joel 3:4–8." *Verbum Domini* 18 (1938): 268–71.

Kline, Meredith G. *Images of the Spirit.* Grand Rapids: Baker, 1980.

Kutsch, Ernst. "Heuschreckenplage und Tag Jahwes in Joel 1 und 2." *Theologische Zeitschrift* 18 (1962): 81–94.

―――. "Die Wurzel עצר im Hebräischen." *Vetus Testamentum* 2 (1952): 57–69.

Lattimore, Ralph E. "The Date of Joel." Th.D. thesis, Southern Baptist Theological Seminary, 1951.

Leibel, Daniel. "יַעְבְּטוּן." *Lešonénu* 24 (1959/60): 253.

―――. "יעבטון—יערבון." *Lešonénu* 29 (1965/66): 222–25.

―――. "עבר בשלח." *Tarbiz* 33 (1963/64): 225–27.

Lewis, Jack P. "Joel." In *The NIV Study Bible,* pp. 1338–44. Edited by Kenneth Barker. Grand Rapids: Zondervan, 1985.

Lewy, Hildegard. "Miscellanea Nuziana." *Orientalia* 28 (1959): 1–25.

Loewenstamm, Samuel E. "ובעד השלח יִפֹּלוּ." *Lešonénu* 26 (1961/62): 62.

―――. "יַעְבְּטוּן = יְעַוְּתוּן‬?" *Lešonénu* 24 (1959/60): 107–8.

Loisy, Alfred. "Notes sur l'origine du livre de Joel." In *Actes du Congrès International d'Histoire des Religions tenu à Paris en octobre 1923,* vol. 2, pp. 35–44. Paris: Champion, 1925.

Luria, Ben Zion. "And a Fountain Shall Come Forth from the House of the Lord." *Dor leDor* 10 (1981): 48–58 [Hebrew].

―――. "משמר בלנה." *Beth Miqra'* 15 (1965): 3–15 [Hebrew].

Mallon, Elias D. "A Stylistic Analysis of Joel 1:10–12." *Catholic Biblical Quarterly* 45 (1983): 537–48.

Manns, Frédéric. *Le Symbole eau-esprit dans le Judaïsme ancien.* Studium Biblicum Franciscanum Analecta 19. Jerusalem: Franciscan, 1983.

Mariès, Louis. "À ropos de récentes études sur Joël." *Recherches de Science Religieuse* 37 (1950): 121–24.

Mariottinni, Claude F. "Joel 3:10 [H 4:10]: 'Beat Your Plowshares into Swords.'" *Perspectives in Religious Studies* 14 (1987): 125–30.

Michel, Albert. *Le Maître de justice d'après les documents de la Mer Morte, la littérature apocryphe et rabbinique.* Avignon: Maison Aubanel, 1954.

Milik, Józef T. "Notes d'épigraphie et de topographie palestiniennes." *Revue Biblique* 66 (1959): 550–75.

Miller, Patrick D., Jr. "The Divine Council and the Prophetic Call to War." *Vetus Testamentum* 18 (1968): 100–107.

Myers, Jacob M. "Some Considerations Bearing on the Date of Joel." *Zeitschrift für die Alttestamentliche Wissenschaft* 74 (1962): 177–95.

Nestle, Eberhard. "Miscellen I: Joel 1:17." *Zeitschrift für die Alttestamentliche Wissenschaft* 20 (1900): 164–65.

Oca, E. C. dell'. "El Valle de Josafat: Nombre simbólico o topográfico?" *Revista Bíblica* (Rafael Calzada, Argentina) 28 (1966): 169–70.

Ogden, Graham S. "Joel 4 and Prophetic Responses to National Laments." *Journal for the Study of the Old Testament* 26 (1983): 97–106.

———. "Prophetic Oracles against Foreign Nations and Psalms of Communal Lament: The Relationship of Psalm 137 to Jeremiah 49:7–22 and Obadiah." *Journal for the Study of the Old Testament* 24 (1982): 89–97.

Pearson, William L. *The Prophecy of Joel: Its Unity, Its Aim and the Age of Its Composition.* Leipzig: Stauffer, 1885.

Plath, Margarete. "Joel 1:15–20." *Zeitschrift für die Alttestamentliche Wissenschaft* 47 (1929): 159–60.

Price, Walter K. *The Prophet Joel and the Day of the Lord.* Chicago: Moody, 1976.

Prinsloo, Willem S. "Die boek Joël: Verleentheid of geleentheid?" *Nederduitse Gereformeerde Teologiese Tydskrif* 24 (1983): 255–63.

———. *The Theology of the Book of Joel.* Beiheft zur Zeitschrift für die Alttestamentliche Wissenschaft 163. Berlin: de Gruyter, 1985.

Rabinowitz, Isaac. "The Guides of Righteousness." *Vetus Testamentum* 8 (1958): 391–404.

Rad, Gerhard von. "The Origin of the Concept of the Day of Yahweh." *Journal of Semitic Studies* 4 (1959): 97–108.

Rainey, Anson F. "Wine from the Royal Vineyards." *Bulletin of the American Schools of Oriental Research* 245 (1982): 57–62.

Reicke, Bo. "Joel und seine Zeit." In *Wort—Gebot—Glaube: Beiträge zur Theologie des Alten Testaments: Walther Eichrodt zum 80. Geburtstag,* pp. 133–41. Edited by Hans J. Stoebe, Johann J. Stamm, and Ernst Jenni. Abhandlungen zur Theologie des Alten und Neuen Testaments 59. Zurich: Zwingli, 1970.

Romerowski, Sylvain. *Les Livres de Joël et d'Abdias.* Commentaire Evangélique de la Bible. Vaux-sur-Seine: Edifac, 1989.

Roth, Cecil. "The Teacher of Righteousness and the Prophecy of Joel." *Vetus Testamentum* 13 (1963): 91–95.

Rudolph, Wilhelm. "Ein Beitrag zum hebräischen Lexikon aus dem Joelbuch." In *Hebräische Wortforschung: Festschrift zum*

80. Geburtstag von Walter Baumgartner, pp. 244–50. Edited by Benedikt Hartmann et al. Supplements to Vetus Testamentum 16. Leiden: Brill, 1967.

————. *Joel, Amos, Obadja, Jona*. Kommentar zum Alten Testament 13/2. Gütersloh: Mohn, 1971.

————. "Wann wirkte Joel?" In *Das Ferne und Nahe Wort: Festschrift Leonhard Rost*, pp. 193–98. Edited by Fritz Maass. Beiheft zur Zeitschrift für die Alttestamentliche Wissenschaft 105. Berlin: Töpelmann, 1967.

Schmalor, Josef. *Das Buch des Propheten Joel übersetzt und erklärt*. Alttestamentliche Abhandlungen 7/4. Münster im Westphalia: Aschendorff, 1922.

Schüngel, Paul H. "Noch einmal zu פארור קבצו Jo[el] 2:6 und Nah[um] 2:11." *Biblische Notizen* 7 (1978): 29–31.

Segal, Judah B. *The Hebrew Passover from the Earliest Times to A.D. 70*. London Oriental Series 12. London: Oxford University Press, 1963.

Sellers, Ovid R. "A Possible Old Testament Reference to the Teacher of Righteousness." *Israel Exploration Journal* 5 (1955): 93–95.

————. "Stages of Locust in Joel." *American Journal of Semitic Languages and Literatures* 52 (1935–36): 81–85.

Selms, Adrianus van. "The Origin of the Name Tyropoeon in Jerusalem." *Zeitschrift für die Alttestamentliche Wissenschaft* 91 (1979): 170–76.

Sheppard, Gerald T. "Canonization: Hearing the Voice of the Same God through Historically Dissimilar Traditions." *Interpretation* 36 (1982): 21–33.

Sprengling, Martin. "Joel 1:17a." *Journal of Biblical Literature* 38 (1919): 129–41.

Stephenson, F. R. "The Date of the Book of Joel." *Vetus Testamentum* 19 (1969): 224–29.

Stohlmann, Stephen. "The Judaean Exile after 701 B.C.E." In *Scripture in Context II: More Essays on the Comparative Method*, pp. 147–75. Edited by William W. Hallo, James C. Moyer, and Leo G. Perdue. Winona Lake, Ind.: Eisenbrauns, 1983.

Stuart, Douglas. *Hosea–Jonah*. Word Biblical Commentary 31. Waco, Tex.: Word, 1987.

Taylor, Archer. "A Riddle for a Locust." In *Semitic and Oriental Studies: A Volume Presented to William Popper*, pp. 429–32. Edited by Walter J. Fischel. Berkeley: University of California Press, 1951.

Thiering, Barbara E. *Redating the Teacher of Righteousness*. Australian and New Zealand Studies in Theology and Religion 1. Sydney: Theological Explorations, 1979.

Thompson, John A. "The Date of Joel." In *A Light unto My Path: Old Testament Studies in Honor of Jacob M. Myers*, pp. 453–64. Edited by H. N. Bream, R. D. Heim, and C. A. Moore.

Gettysburg Theological Studies 4. Philadelphia: Temple University Press, 1974.

――――. "Joel's Locusts in the Light of Near Eastern Parallels." *Journal of Near Eastern Studies* 14 (1955): 52–55.

――――. "The Use of Repetition in the Prophecy of Joel." In *On Language, Culture, and Religion: In Honor of Eugene A. Nida*, pp. 101–10. Edited by Matthew Black and William A. Smalley. The Hague/Paris: Mouton, 1974.

Tournay, Raymond J. "Relectures bibliques concernant la vie future et l'angélologie." *Revue Biblique* 69 (1962): 481–505.

Treves, Marco. "The Date of Joel." *Vetus Testamentum* 7 (1957): 149–56.

Van der Meiden, L. H. "De Vertaling van het woord מוֹרֶה in Joel 2:23." *Gereformeerd Theologisch Tijdschrift* 51 (1951): 136–39.

VanGemeren, Willem A. "The Spirit of Restoration." *Westminster Theological Journal* 50 (1988): 81–102.

Waloft, Z., and S. M. Green. "Regularities in Duration of Regional Locust Plagues." *Nature* 256 (1975): 484–85.

Waltke, Bruce K., and Michael O'Connor. *An Introduction to Biblical Hebrew Syntax.* Winona Lake, Ind.: Eisenbrauns, 1990.

Watts, John D. W. *The Books of Joel, Obadiah, Jonah, Nahum, Habakkuk, and Zephaniah.* Cambridge Bible Commentary on the New English Bible. Cambridge: Cambridge University Press, 1975.

Weingreen, Jacob. "The Title Môrēh Ṣeḏeḳ." *Journal of Semitic Studies* 6 (1961): 162–74.

Weiser, Artur. *Das Buch der zwölf kleinen Propheten*, vol. 1: *Die Propheten Hosea, Joel, Amos, Obadja, Jona, Micha übersetzt und erklärt.* 7th ed. Das Alte Testament Deutsch 24. Göttingen: Vandenhoeck & Ruprecht, 1979.

Weiss, M. "In the Footsteps of a Biblical Metaphor." *Tarbiz* 34 (1964/65): 107–28, 211–23, 303–18 [Hebrew].

Whiting, John D. "Jerusalem's Locust Plague." *National Geographic Magazine* 28/6 (Dec. 1915): 511–50.

Whitley, Charles F. "ʿbt in Joel 2:7." *Biblica* 65 (1984): 101–2.

Wolff, Hans W. *Dodekapropheton.* Vol. 2: *Joel und Amos.* Biblischer Kommentar Altes Testament 14/2. Neukirchen-Vluyn: Neukirchener Verlag, 1969.

――――. *Joel and Amos: A Commentary on the Books of the Prophets Joel and Amos.* Translated by Waldemar Janzen, S. Dean McBride, Jr., and Charles A. Muenchow. Edited by S. Dean McBride, Jr. Hermeneia. Philadelphia: Fortress, 1977.

Zimmerli, Walther. *Erkenntnis Gottes nach dem Buche Ezechiel: Eine theologische Studie.* Abhandlungen zur Theologie des Alten und Neuen Testaments 27. Zurich: Zwingli, 1954.

Superscription (1:1)

1 The word of the LORD that came to Joel son of Pethuel.

1 The word of the LORD that came to Joel son of Pethuel:

I. The Locust Plague: The Immediate Disaster (1:2–20)
A. Effect and Extent of the Disaster (1:2–12)
1. Elders and Citizens (1:2–4)

2 Hear this, O elders!
>Pay attention, all you who live in the land!

Has this ever happened in your lifetime,
>or in the lifetime of your fathers?

3 Tell your children about it,
>and let your children tell their children,
>and their children tell another generation.

4 What the flying locust left, the adult locust has eaten;
>what the adult locust left, the hopper has eaten;
>what the hopper left, the leaping locust has eaten!

2 Hear this, O elders,
>give ear, all inhabitants of the land!
>Has such a thing happened in your days,
>or in the days of your ancestors?

3 Tell your children of it,
>and let your children tell their children,
>and their children another generation.

4 What the cutting locust left,
>the swarming locust has eaten.

What the swarming locust left,
>the hopping locust has eaten,

and what the hopping locust left,
>the destroying locust has eaten.

1:1. The introductory formula אֲשֶׁר הָיָה אֶל דְּבַר־יְהוָה (the word of the LORD that came to) is also found in Hosea 1:1, Micah 1:1, and Zephaniah 1:1; similar wording occurs in Jeremiah 1:2, Ezekiel 1:3, Jonah 1:1, and Zechariah 1:1. The formula דְּבַר־יְהוָה (the word of the LORD) occurs over two hundred times in the Old Testament, largely in the Prophets, introducing individual oracles. יוֹאֵל (Joel) has the sense of *Yahweh is God.* פְּתוּאֵל (Pethuel) connotes enticed or persuaded by God; the Septuagint, the Old Latin, and the Syriac versions read בתואל, the same name as Abraham's nephew, the father of Rebekah (Gen. 22:22–23; 24:15–50). The etymological significance of the names, however, is not developed or otherwise

alluded to in the book, and consequently has no direct bearing on the exegesis.

2. The verbs שָׁמַע (hear) and הַאֲזִין (pay attention) are often found in parallel cola at the onset of a discourse or oracle as a "summons to receive instruction" (Gen. 4:23; Deut. 32:1; Judg. 5:3; Job 33:1; 34:2, 16; Ps. 49:2 [1]; Isa. 1:2, 10; 28:23; 32:9; Jer. 13:15; Hos. 5:1; see Wolff, *Joel and Amos,* p. 20). Chapter 1 is characterized by the interlocking recurrence of numerous terms: the "elders" (זְקֵנִים) and "all inhabitants of the land" (כֹּל יֹשְׁבֵי הָאָרֶץ) are mentioned again in 1:14, forming an inclusio that sets off 1:2–14.

3. סַפֵּרוּ (tell): In many contexts the root סְפַר connotes more than a casual or conversational retelling; it appears to suggest a more formal recitation

---

1:1. The brief note in the superscription that Joel was the son of Pethuel is the only explicit biographical information we have about this prophet; other inferences can be drawn about him from the internal evidence of the book (see the introductory discussions of date and authorship). The fact that there are no additional details about the date or circumstances of his prophecy suggests that he was well known to his contemporaries so that no further specification of shared information would be expected (Keller, *Joël,* p. 118; Allen, *Joel,* p. 45; see Prinsloo, *Theology of the Book of Joel,* p. 11, for the contrary opinion). The book contains no call narrative, nor is there any claim to authority other than that "the word of Yahweh" came to Joel; this was sufficient.

2–3. Judged from the vantage point of form criticism, this section can be evaluated variously. Wolff (*Joel and Amos,* p. 20) describes these verses as a "call to receive instruction" (compare the use of multiple imperatives requiring the audience to listen at the beginning of discourses in Gen. 4:23; Deut. 32:1; Judg. 5:3; Job 33:1; 34:2, 16; Ps. 49:2 [1]; Hos. 5:1). While this is an apt designation for the particular features of these verses, in the larger context 1:2–3 is part of a "summons to communal lamentation." Joel 1:2–12 contains four calls to lament directed at different social groups within the prophet's purview. Verses 2–4 address the most general audience, the elders and inhabitants of the land; other sections address tipplers (vv. 5–7), priests (vv. 8–10), and farmers (vv. 11–12)—specific groups for whom the locust plague would have dire consequences. This first group addressed (elders and inhabitants) is the most general, and the accompanying description of the damage done by the locusts is also in general terms (v. 4), the

more specific population subgroups are accompanied by more specific descriptions of the damage. Note the differences in the imperatives: in verses 2–3 the audience is urged to listen, whereas in the other passages the call is to active participation through lamenting, wailing, mourning, and abasement.

Rhetorical questions often follow such invitations to listen (Allen, *Joel,* pp. 48–49; Wolff, *Joel and Amos,* p. 23; see Isa. 5:4; 28:23–25; 66:8–9; Jer. 2:10–11; Amos 3:3–6); they are also especially common as part of the interrogation in prophetic lawsuits (Mic. 1:1–5; 6:1–11; Mal. 1). The rhetorical questions of verse 3 stress the uniqueness and incomparability of the current disaster (compare the similar note regarding the locust plague in Egypt—Exod. 10:6, 14; see also Deut. 4:32–35; Lam. 1:12).

The Old Testament assigns an important role to the recitation of the deeds, wisdom, and law of Yahweh (Exod. 10:2; 12:26–27; Deut. 6:6–7; 11:19; Josh. 4:6–7; Pss. 22:31–32 [30–31]; 78:1–8; Prov. 4:1–2). Four generations are mentioned in verse 3 (cf. Exod. 20:5), though doubtless the prophet intends an enduring recitation.

Summoning the elders (v. 2) may serve either or both of two functions in this context: (1) they were the leaders of the nation and served to represent the people ("all who live in the land") as a whole; and (2) they were among the oldest of the people and, hence, were the logical group to which to address a question about collective memory ("Has this ever happened in your lifetime or the lifetime of your fathers?"). Yahweh has done to Israel what he had once done to Egypt on Israel's behalf (see Exod. 10:2, 14).

or rehearsal, possibly in a liturgical setting (Pss. 40:6 [5]; 44:2 [1]; 73:28; 78:3–4 [2–3]; 79:13; Jer. 23:28, 32).

4. הַגָּזָם (the flying locust), הָאַרְבֶּה (the adult locust), הַיֶּלֶק (the hopper), הֶחָסִיל (the leaping locust): The Old Testament uses ten different terms to designate locusts and grasshoppers. The four terms for locust here and in 2:25 refer not to differing species of insects (e.g., KJV has palmerworm, locust, cankerworm, caterpillar) but rather to successive stages in the growth and lifecycle of the locust. The locust goes through five molts (instars) before becoming a sexually mature adult. גָּזָם (flying locust; see also Amos 4:9) is derived from a root meaning "cut" and may have developed from a description of the voracious eating of the insect. If these terms identify successive stages in the development of the insect, this term would probably refer to the penultimate stage before the sexually mature adult. In this stage the wings are more fully developed. אַרְבֶּה (adult locust) appears to be the *Leitwort* in the semantic field of terms for locust. It is the most frequent and least specific term in the group. Though אַרְבֶּה (adult locust) is the generic term for locust in this context by virtue of its contrast to the surround-ing terms it is probably a reference to the sexually mature adult, the *imago*. Etymologically it may be related to the term רַב (multitude, many) and may have developed in reference to the swarming of a locust plague. יֶלֶק (hopper; see also Ps. 105:34; Jer. 51:14, 27; Nah. 3:15–16) probably designates the locust in its first instar; this larval stage is often called a "hopper"; the wings are not yet developed, and the insect hops about (for the etymology of this term, see Allen, *Joel*, p. 49). חָסִיל (leaping locust; see also 1 Kings 8:37 par. 2 Chron. 6:28; Ps. 78:46; Isa. 33:4) is etymologically related to a word meaning "consume, finish off"; the cognate verb is used to describe the feeding of locusts (Deut. 28:38). It probably refers to one of the intermediate instars, a pupal or nymph stage during which the insect grows in size and its wings develop within a membranous case. Locusts are voracious in all their instars. One must also allow for the possibility that these terms do not designate successive instars in the development of the locust, but that they may represent differing regional terms, different species or coloration, or simply synonyms piled together for rhetorical effect (Wolff, *Joel and Amos*, p. 27; Allen, *Joel*, pp. 49–50; Keller, *Joël*, p. 109).

One cannot fail to note the absence of reference to the king or his officers at any point in the Book of Joel. When the civil leaders of the nation are addressed, they are the elders (1:2, 14; 2:16); though it is an argument from silence, the most natural assumption is that the Book of Joel was written during a period of Judah's history when the nation was without a monarchy, that is, the postexilic period. However, other prophetic oracles during the period of Judah's monarchy addressed the elders and not the king or royal personnel (Isa. 1:4; Jer. 2:8). See the larger discussion of the date of Joel in the introductory materials.

4. For more detailed discussions of locusts and locust plagues, see Baron, *Desert Locust*; Bennett, "Development of a Locust Plague"; Fishelson, *Fauna Palestina: Insecta*, vol. 3: *Orthoptera, Acridoidea*; Keimer, "Pendeloques en forme d'insectes faisant partie de colliers égyptiens"; Sellers, "Stages of Locust in Joel"; Thompson, "Joel's Locusts in the Light of Near Eastern Parallels"; Waloft and Green, "Regularities in Duration of Regional Locust Plagues"; Whiting, "Jerusalem's Locust Plague."

The Book of Joel provides an example of the practical outworking of the procedure suggested in the dedicatory prayer of Solomon at the com-pletion of the temple. Then Solomon had prayed that the Lord would hear prayers at the temple during locust outbreaks (1 Kings 8:37 par. 2 Chron. 6:28), and God had responded with his pledge to hear such petitions (2 Chron. 7:13). In summoning the citizens of Judah to a lament at the temple, Joel's audience would also witness God's answer to their prayers (2:18–27).

In our generation areas having the potential for a locust outbreak are monitored by international agencies using satellite reconnaissance and other technology; incipient swarms are met by aircraft and trucks carrying powerful pesticides. However, if the locusts are not destroyed or contained shortly after the hatch, once the swarm has formed, control efforts are minimally effective even today. For example, in 1988 the civil war in Chad prevented international cooperation in attacking the hatch, and a destructive swarm spread throughout North Africa devastating some of the poorest nations and threatening Europe as well. It is difficult for modern Western people to appreciate the dire threat represented by a locust plague in earlier periods. Such outbreaks had serious consequences for the health and mortality of an affected population and for a region's economy. Scarcity of food resulting from the swarm's attack would bring the population to subsistence intake or less, would make the spread of disease among a weakened populace easier, would eliminate any trade from surplus food products, and would stimulate high inflation in the costs of food products. Disease outbreaks are further aggravated when swarms die; the putrefaction of the millions of locust bodies breeds typhus and other diseases that spread to humans and animals (see the description in Augustine's *City of God* 3.31). Baron (*Desert Locust*, pp. 3–7) catalogues many locust outbreaks known to have been accompanied by outbreaks of pestilence.

It was only in 1921 that the mystery of the locust was solved. Prior to this date researchers wondered what became of the locust during the years in which there were no outbreaks. In 1921 B. P. Uvarov demonstrated that the swarming locust was none other than an ordinary species of grasshopper. However, when moisture and temperature conditions favored a large hatch, the crowding, unceasing contact, and jostling of the nymphs begin to stimulate changes in coloration, physiology, metabolism, and behavior, so that the grasshopper nymphs make the transition from solitary behavior to the swarming gregarious and migratory phases of the dreaded plague. Plagues continue as long as climatic conditions favor the large hatches. Once entering their gregarious phase, swarms of locusts can migrate great distances and have even been observed twelve hundred miles at sea. The swarms can reach great sizes: a swarm across the Red Sea in 1889 was estimated to cover two thousand square miles. A swarm is estimated to contain up to 120 million insects per square mile (Baron, *Desert Locust*, p.

32). In 1881 an effort in Cyprus to prevent a possible outbreak of locusts by digging up and destroying their egg cases netted thirteen hundred tons of their egg masses. Locusts were the eighth plague on Egypt described in Exodus (Exod. 10:4–19); images of locusts were already carved in sixth-dynasty tombs at Saqqara over three-quarters of a millennium earlier (Baron, *Desert Locust*, p. 2; for Egyptological evidence, see Keimer, "Pendeloques en forme d'insects").

The lifespan of individual locusts is also influenced by temperature and other climatic conditions. In one swarm incubation was 14 days; the hopper period, 38 days; the immature stage, 45 days; and the breeding stage, 30 days—for a total of 127 days (Baron, *Desert Locust*, p. 34). During breeding the female lays approximately 250 to 300 eggs in individual pods dug in suitable soil, each pod containing 70 to 80 eggs. The hatch of an egg-field portends the swarm to follow. In the words of one entomologist (cited in Baron, *Desert Locust*, p. 41), "So far as the eye could see they were boiling out. Every inch of open ground appeared to be bubbling young locusts as pod after pod, many of them only a couple of inches apart, gave up its contents. . . . Within three days the whole of a vast egg-field had been hatched out and the hoppers were ready to march."

The sequence of four terms designating stages in the locust lifecycle in 1:4 differs from that in 2:25. Thompson ("Joel's Locusts") regards the order in 1:4 as reflecting the historical sequence of successive stages in which the swarm attacked Judah in Joel's day, whereas the order in 2:25 reflects the logical order of the lifecycle, beginning with the adult locust (see Allen, *Joel*, pp. 49–50).

I. The Locust Plague: The Immediate Disaster (1:2–20)
A. Effect and Extent of the Disaster (1:2–12)
2. Drunkards (1:5–7)

5 Wake up, you drunkards, and weep.
  Wail, all you who drink wine,
    because the must is kept
      from your mouths.
6 For a nation has come against my land,
    mighty and without number;
  its teeth are the teeth of a lion,
    it has the incisors of a lioness.
7 It reduces my vine to desolation,
    my fig tree to collapse;
  it strips it bare and discards it,
    its branches left white.

5 Wake up, you drunkards, and weep;
    and wail, all you wine-drinkers,
  over the sweet wine,
    for it is cut off from your mouth.
6 For a nation has invaded my land,
    powerful and innumerable;
  its teeth are lions' teeth,
    and it has the fangs of a lioness.
7 It has laid waste my vines,
    and splintered my fig trees;
  it has stripped off their bark and thrown
      it down;
    their branches have turned white.

5. הָקִיצוּ (wake up) is ordinarily used in reference to waking from sleep, but is used also in reference to waking from a drunken stupor (Prov. 23:35). בְּכוּ (weep) and הֵילִלוּ (wail) routinely accompany lamentations and need not reflect mourning rites of a Tammuz/Baal fertility cult (Kapelrud, *Joel Studies*, pp. 19–23). עָסִיס (must) is ordinarily translated as "fresh wine" or "sweet wine." This is favored by the meaning of the verbal root עָסַס (trample, crush) in Malachi 3:21 [4:3], as well as by contexts which suggest freshly squeezed fruit (Joel 4:18 [3:18]; Amos 9:13). The freshly squeezed juice or "must" would be called "sweet" since fermentation had not consumed the natural sugars in the juice (compare the Greek term γλεῦκος, though not the LXX equivalent in this passage). However, Isaiah 49:26 makes it clear that one could become drunk from drinking עָסִיס. The Septuagint construes עָסִיס with יַיִן in Joel 1:5 (οἱ πίνοντες οἶνον εἰς μέθην, those who drink wine to drunkenness) and appears to show a similar understanding. Depending on the relationship of the parallel phrases in Song of Solomon 8:2, it is possible that עָסִיס represents a fruit juice fortified with even more concentrated sugars in order to achieve a higher alcohol content in the final beverage; in this case it would be among the strongest alcoholic beverages available in the ancient world prior to distillation. The sense of the verse is affected by the choice: if unfermented must is intended, the drunkards wail for lack of even the must to make their potables; if a stronger beverage is intended, it refers to the lack of the choice potable. Since the context in Joel 4:18 [3:18] appears to favor unprocessed must, this would appear appropriate also here in 1:5: the disaster of 1:5 is reversed in 4:18 [3:18].

6. עָלָה עַל (has come against) is a common idiom for the approach of a hostile force (1 Kings 20:22; 2 Kings 17:3; 18:9; Jer. 50:3; Ezek. 38:16). עָצוּם (mighty) has a military connotation in 2:2, 5, where it occurs in association with עַם (army/people). לָבִיא (lioness) could be masculine or feminine. The phenomenon should probably be compared with English semantics in cases like the word *dog* which can refer to either sex in the absence of specific modifiers. However, in the phrase *dog or bitch*, *dog* becomes marked for gender as masculine. The two terms for lion are probably marked for gender by virtue of their cooccurrence.

7. שָׂם . . . לְשַׁמָּה (it reduces . . . to devastation) describes the devastation left behind by an invading army in Jeremiah 4:7, which also uses the image of a lion (see Keller, *Joël*, p. 111).

---

5. A locust plague would be a "sobering" thought indeed for heavy drinkers. The supplies of alcoholic beverages would rapidly disappear as a result of the defoliation, and even after the locust outbreak had ended, production would be down for a period while vegetation recovered. It is commonly recognized that disasters promote the tendency to tipple, but no alcoholic beverages would be available except at prohibitive prices as imports from regions beyond the impact of the plague. In selecting drunkards as one of the social groups summoned to a national lament, the prophet singles out those who ordinarily cared little for religion or for much else happening around them (Allen, *Joel*, p. 50). Just as abundant wine could symbolize divine blessing (Ps. 104:15; Song of Sol. 5:1; Joel 4:18 [3:18]; Amos 9:13), here the lack of wine is the product of divine judgment. The often boisterous and rowdy merriment accompanying drink and a good harvest would not be heard in Israel (1:11–12).

6–7. Designating Israel/Judah as "my land" is more common in exilic and postexilic literature than in earlier literature (2 Chron. 6:27; 20:11; Jer. 2:7; Ezek. 36:5, 38:16; cf. Lev. 25:23–24). Israel was not just "my land," but "my vine" and "my fig tree"; the prophet in using the imagery of God's devotion to the land brings us into the realm of paradise imagery. God had planted a garden in Eden, and he had also planted his vine in the land of Israel (Isa. 5:1–7; Ezek. 15; 17); it was God who saw to the fertility of both. The locust plague represents the undoing of the paradisaical abundance of God's garden; the prophecy ends with its restoration both in the near future (2:18–27) and in an eschatological future (4:18–21 [3:18–21]).

The locusts in the exodus plague were also described as innumerable (Exod. 10:4–6, 12–15; Ps. 105:34), a description also of other armies and population groups (1 Chron. 22:16; 2 Chron. 12:3; Ps. 104:25; Song of Sol. 6:8; Nah. 3:3), and in Joel's second description of the Lord's army (2:11). Locusts are described as an invading army (Prov. 30:27); and an invading force is likened to locusts, an army "that cannot be counted" (Jer. 46:23).

The literatures of many nations liken the locust to a variety of animals. In evaluating Joel's comparison of locusts to lions, Baron (*Desert Locust*, p. 3) comments that "the mouth parts of . . . the Desert Locust do bear a strong resemblance to a lion's muzzle surmounted by nose and eyes, so much so that Egyptian faience workers embodied this aspect especially in their representation of the Desert Locust." The golden, tawny color of the insect in its gregarious phase may also have contributed to the comparison with lions. Thompson ("Joel's Locusts," p. 53) cites a couplet from a twelfth-century A.D. Egyptian poet describing the locust as having the "breast of a lion." The lion is often used in the Old Testament as an image of invincible power (Keller, *Joël*, p. 111; see Gen. 49:9; Num. 23:24; 24:9; 2 Sam. 17:10; Job 4:10–11; Ps. 22:14, 22 [13, 21]; Prov. 30:30; Jer. 4:7; 5:6; Amos 3:4). John may be dependent on Joel in his similar characterization of the locust as having the teeth of a lion (Rev. 9:8). Note also the comparison with a horse in Joel 2:4.

Though vine and fig tree are used here as metaphors for Israel/Judah, the prophet describes quite vividly the result of a locust swarm. Vegetation is not only defoliated, but also desiccated, that is, stripped of its bark. This is the work of the teeth mentioned in 1:6 (Wolff, *Joel and Amos*, p. 29) and leaves the white cambium exposed. Following a locust outbreak, the energies of many plants are diverted to repairing damages and return to fruitful production is further delayed. Figs were one of the mainstays of the economy of Israel. The fig is depicted in Jotham's parable as among the trees asked to rule over others (Judg. 9:10–11); the destruction of the vine and fig tree could serve as an illustration of economic calamity (Jer. 5:17; Borowski, *Agriculture in Iron Age Israel*, p. 114). Possession of vine and fig tree is symbolic of an ideal prosperity (2 Kings 18:31 par. Isa. 36:16; Jer. 5:17; Mic. 4:4; Zech. 3:10). Fig and vine recur as a pair in 1:12 and 2:22.

I. The Locust Plague: The Immediate Disaster (1:2–20)
A. Effect and Extent of the Disaster (1:2–12)
3. Priests and Farmers (1:8–12)

8 Mourn the way a virgin wrapped in sack-
    cloth
    mourns for the husband of her youth.
9 Grain offerings and libations have been
    cut off
    from the temple of the Lord.
    The priests grieve,
    those who minister to the Lord.
10 Fields are destroyed;
    the land grieves,
for the grain is destroyed,
    the new wine is dried up,
    the fresh oil fails.
11 Abase yourselves, farmers;
    wail, you who tend the vines,
about the wheat and the barley,
    because the harvest in the field is de-
    stroyed.
12 The vine has dried up,
    the fig tree has failed;
the pomegranate, the palm, the apri-
    cot—
    all the trees of the orchard are dried
    up.
Even joy has dried up among the chil-
    dren of men.

8 Lament like a virgin dressed in sackcloth
    for the husband of her youth.
9 The grain offering and the drink offering
    are cut off
    from the house of the Lord.
    The priests mourn,
    the ministers of the Lord.
10 The fields are devastated,
    the ground mourns;
for the grain is destroyed,
    the wine dries up,
    the oil fails.
11 Be dismayed, you farmers,
    wail, you vinedressers,
over the wheat and the barley;
    for the crops of the field are ruined.
12 The vine withers,
    the fig tree droops.
Pomegranate, palm, and apple—
    all the trees of the field are dried up;
surely, joy withers away
    among the people.

8. אֵלִי (mourn) was apparently read by the Septuagint translators as "to me" (אֵלַי = πρός με). This and the fact that this imperative lacks a defined vocative, along with some other minor difficulties, have prompted many to suggest a rather extensive textual revision for 1:8–9 (see the discussion in Wolff, *Joel and Amos*, p. 18). Since this imperative is feminine singular, it presumably refers to the city of Jerusalem or the land of Judah. The use of the term בְּתוּלָה (virgin) may have influenced its gender (compare the vocative *virgin daughter/s* with geographical names [2 Kings 19:21; Isa. 23:12; 47:1; Jer. 14:17; 18:13; 31:4, 21; 46:11; Lam. 1:15; 2:13]; see Allen, *Joel*, p. 52). Note also the other feminine singular nouns in the context (land, vine, fig tree). שַׂק (sackcloth) was ordinarily woven from goat hair and was therefore usually black in color; it was commonly worn during occasions of personal and communal mourning (Gen. 37:34; 2 Sam. 3:31; 21:10; Isa. 3:24; 15:3; Jer. 48:37; Lam. 2:10; see Wolff, *Joel and Amos*, pp. 29–30). בַּעַל is commonly used as a term for "husband" (Gen. 20:3; Exod. 21:3; Hos. 2:18 [16]). בַּעַל נְעוּרֶיהָ (husband of her youth) occurs only here. Some have regarded this collocation as

a contradiction in terms; a virgin is not likely to have a husband. However, the difficulty dissolves when we understand marriage customs in Israel properly. נְעוּרֶיהָ (youth) connotes the time before marriage and includes the time of betrothal (Jer. 2:2). In Israel betrothal was the stage after the prospective groom had paid the bride price (מֹהַר) but before the consummation of marriage. During this stage the groom-to-be could be called "husband" and the prospective bride "wife" (Gen. 29:21; Deut. 22:23–24; cf. Deut. 28:30), though the marriage was not yet consummated (see the accompanying comments and the helpful excursus in Wolff, *Joel and Amos*, p. 30).

9. הָכְרַת (have been cut off): The entire passage is woven around recurring terms. Just as the wine was "cut off" (כָּרַת) from the mouths of drunkards (1:5), so also grain offerings and libations are cut off (כָּרַת) from the temple ritual. מִנְחָה וָנֶסֶךְ (grain offerings and libations) probably refers to the offering of meal (moistened with a liquid) that accompanied the daily morning and evening sacrifice of a lamb (Exod. 29:38–40; Num. 28:3–8), though other sacrifices were accompanied by a cereal offering and libation as well (Lev. 23:18; Num.

---

8. The time of harvest was preeminently a time of thankfulness, celebration, and joy—much like a wedding. But instead of joy, there would be sackcloth, lamentation, pathos, tragedy. The pathos is at its height in the illustration the prophet chooses: Israel is to mourn like a young woman whose betrothed dies before the consummation of marriage; a time of anticipation and eagerness ends in frustration, disappointment, and sadness. One wonders if Joel is not drawing here from the imagery of Jeremiah 16:9, "I am going to banish from this place, in your days and before your eyes, the voice of mirth and the voice of gladness, the voice of the bridegroom and the voice of the bride" (NRSV). Compare too the mourning of Jephthah's daughter (Judg. 11:34–40). Weddings were the time for multicolored festal garments (Ps. 45:14–16 [13–15]; Song of Sol. 4:11), but these are replaced with a widow's black sackcloth.

Kapelrud (*Joel Studies*, pp. 19–21, 31–33) sees in this lament of a bride for her baal (husband) the lament of a divine consort for the deceased deity in an ancient Near Eastern fertility cult, a relationship like that between Ishtar and Tammuz or between Baal and Anat. This background for the passage is quite improbable. For Israel's prophets the fertility cult of Canaan was an unthinkable contradiction of Yahwism; it is also improbable

that the fertility cult played any significant role in the postexilic period. The Old Testament describes the relationship between Israel and her God using the image of husband and wife (e.g., Ezek. 16:8–43; Hos. 1–3) and indicts the nation for looking to the baals for agricultural prosperity. In the analogy this verse introduces, the prophet may intend his readers to think of Israel as Yahweh's bride: just as in verses 5–7, land, vine, and fig tree are metaphors for Israel, so also it is Virgin Israel that will lament. But here the analogy breaks down: a bride may lament for her deceased groom, but Yahweh does not die. It is also possible that the prophet is simply drawing an analogy between the anticipation of joy at a wedding and the joy of harvest, such that the relationship between Yahweh and Israel was not in the prophet's purview. The focus is not on a sacred marriage in a fertility cult, but on the failure of joy and rejoicing with the failure of crops (1:12). There is also some potential ambiguity in the text as to whether the virgin laments the death of her groom or their estrangement and her desertion (Isa. 54:4–8). Death seems to be the more natural explanation in light of the emphasis on the end of vegetable life.

9–12. The locust plague would not only bring privation to the populace, but the routines of wor-

6:15–17; 15:24; 29; see Allen, *Joel*, p. 53). Liquids used in libations included wine, beer, oil, and water. It is commonly argued that the combination of the cereal offering and libation is found only in postexilic texts and that its occurrence in Joel argues for its postexilic date (e.g., Wolff, *Joel and Amos*, p. 31; Chary, *Les prophètes et le culte*, pp. 198–200), though this line of argument is contradicted by others (Rudolph, *Joel*, p. 45; Ahlström, *Joel and the Temple Cult*, pp. 14–17; Allen, *Joel*, p. 53; Kapelrud, *Joel Studies*, p. 37). Cereal offerings and libations occur together in sacrificial rituals in texts that are considered preexilic (1 Kings 18:29–36; Hos. 9:4; Mic. 6:7). אָבְלוּ (grieve): This verb also recurs in 1:10. מְשָׁרְתֵי (those who minister) occurs also in 1:13 and 2:17. In postexilic literature it is a common designation of the priests (2 Chron. 13:10; 23:6; 29:11; Ezek. 45:4–5; 46:24), though it is also found in the singular in preexilic texts (1 Sam. 2:18; 3:1; see the discussion in Ahlström, *Joel and the Temple Cult*, pp. 17–18).

10. אָבְלָה (grieves): Though it is a subjective judgment, the use of recurrent terms and alliteration gives the passage a mournful or solemn cadence. Terms containing the phoneme שׁ are particularly frequent. Verses 11–12 exhibit a carefully worked interplay between the alliterative verbs בּוֹשׁ (be ashamed) and יָבֵשׁ (be dry). Note the way in which the syllables שֹׂד and שֹׂד function alliteratively in this verse. Both words in the second clause (אָבְלָה אֲדָמָה) begin with an ʾaleph and end with an *a* vowel marked by the letter *he*. The effect of these devices and others in the pericope make for a text pleasing to the ear when read orally. דָּגָן (the grain) is the general term for cereals or grains, primarily wheat and barley. תִּירוֹשׁ (new wine) is regarded by most as "new wine" or "must." It is the juice that overflows the vats after pressing (Prov. 3:10; Joel 2:24); it is the juice still in the cluster (Isa. 65:8), the liquid used to make wine (Mic. 6:15). Others regard it as synonymous with יַיִן; Hosea 4:11 suggests it could have contained alcohol (see Borowski, *Agriculture in Iron Age Israel*, p. 113).

11. הֵבִישׁוּ (abase yourselves) and הֵילִילוּ (wail) may be either perfects or imperatives. The Septu-

agint treats the first as a perfect and the second as an imperative; the Vulgate reads both as perfects. The use of imperatives in 1:5, 8, 13 would favor that reading in these two instances. אִכָּרִים (farmers) and כֹּרְמִים (you who tend the vine, i.e., vine-dressers) were ordinarily the landless agricultural workers who were tenant farmers, often on royal estates, and were among the poorest members of society; their labors are described in 2 Kings 24:14; 25:12; 2 Chronicles 26:10; Isaiah 61:5; Jeremiah 40:9–10; 52:16 (see Graham, "Vinedressers and Plowmen"; Rainey, "Wine from the Royal Vineyards"; on vv. 10–12, see Mallon, "Stylistic Analysis of Joel 1:10–12").

12. רִמּוֹן (pomegranate) was considered a symbol of fertility, possibly because of the large number of seeds in each fruit (Borowski, *Agriculture in Iron Age Israel*, p. 117). Its fruit could be eaten; the juice could be drunk fresh, fermented, or used to make a syrup. It was used as a frequent motif on the priestly vestments and in sanctuary architecture. תָּמָר (the palm) also had many uses. The fruit and juice of the date palm could be eaten, drunk, fermented, or used to make a syrup (דְּבַשׁ); the leaves were woven for mats, baskets, and other domestic goods (Borowski, *Agriculture in Iron Age Israel*, p. 127). According to a citation in Bewer (*Obadiah and Joel*, p. 79) palms are particular favorites for the locust diet. תַּפּוּחַ (the apricot) is not known with certainty; though traditionally identified as the apple, others suggest instead quince, apricot, or citron (see the discussion of Borowski, *Agriculture in Iron Age Israel*, pp. 129–30). The term occurs in a number of place-names in the Bible (Josh. 12:17; 15:34; 16:8; 17:8) and, therefore, must refer to a fruit cultivated in Israel in preexilic times (see Ahlström, *Joel and the Temple Cult*, p. 3). מִן־בְּנֵי (among the children): The uncontracted form (as opposed to the customary מִבְּנֵי) is commonly identified as a characteristic of late Hebrew; the uncontracted form is quite common in Chronicles (1 Chron. 4:42; 5:18; 9:3, 30, 32; 12:17, 26–27; 24:3; 26:10; 27:3, 10, 14; 2 Chron. 20:14, 19; 34:12; see Ahlström, *Joel and the Temple Cult*, p. 21).

---

ship in the temple would be interrupted. The morning and evening offerings required flour, wine, and oil, but now these were destroyed. Grain, wine, and oil are frequently listed together in the Old Testament (e.g., Num. 18:12; Deut. 7:13; 11:14; 12:17; 14:23; 18:4; 28:51; 2 Chron. 31:5; 32:28; Neh. 5:11). These three crops represented the three major types of vegetation in

Israel: grasses, shrubs, and trees; they are used here as representative of all agricultural products. For the landless tenant farm workers, the disaster was compounded: not only no food to eat or seed to plant, but the rent due to overlords would not be forthcoming. The joy attending the harvest (Isa. 9:3 [2]) had dried up with the crops (see Deut. 28:33, 42, 51).

I. The Locust Plague: The Immediate Disaster (1:2–20)
B. Summons to Fasting and Prayer at the Temple (1:13–14)

13 Put on sackcloth and lament, O priests!
  Wail, you who minister at an altar!
Come spend the night in sackcloth,
  you who minister to my God,
for grain offerings and libations
  are withheld from the temple of your
  God.
14 Proclaim a fast! Call an assembly!
  Gather the elders, all who dwell in the
  land,
    to the temple of the LORD your God,
  and cry out to the LORD.

13 Put on sackcloth and lament, you
  priests;
  wail, you ministers of the altar.
Come, pass the night in sackcloth,
  you ministers of my God!
Grain offering and drink offering
  are withheld from the house of your
  God.
14 Sanctify a fast,
  call a solemn assembly.
Gather the elders
  and all the inhabitants of the land
to the house of the LORD your God,
  and cry out to the LORD.

13. חִגְרוּ (put on sackcloth) is ordinarily accompanied by שַׂק (sackcloth) as in 1:8; it is used absolutely also in Isaiah 32:11. The omission of שַׂק in 1:13 may be due to its occurrence in the next line. H. Dressler ("Ugaritic *uzr* and Joel 1:13") appeals to this absolute use in attempting to provide a translation for a disputed passage in a Ugaritic text. סִפְדוּ (lament) connotes also the gestures of lamentation, such as striking the chest (Wolff, *Joel and Amos*, p. 32). בֹּאוּ (come) in this context may suggest a sacral procession (Allen, *Joel*, p. 57). אֱלֹהָי (my God): the Septuagint (with θεῷ) appears to have read אֱלֹהִים (God), whereas the Vulgate (*dei mei*) agrees with the Masoretic Text. There is nothing intrinsically improbable about the Masoretic Text in this instance, and one can readily appreciate why the Septuagint translator or an earlier scribe may have added the final *mem* (contra Wolff, *Joel and Amos*, p. 19; Bewer, *Obadiah and Joel*, p. 86; Rudolph, *Joel*, p. 39). אֱלֹהָי (my God) forms an aesthetically pleasing parallel to אֱלֹהֵיכֶם (your God) in the next line. כִּי (for): Frankfort ("Le כִּי de Joël 1:12") argues that this particle

should be translated as "because" instead of as an asseverative "surely, indeed, yea!"

14. קַדְּשׁוּ (proclaim): Another translational equivalent of this word is "sanctify" (lit. set apart as holy). The use of this root gives this fast a specifically sacral character (cf. 2:15–16; 4:9 [3:9]). צוֹם (a fast): See also 2:12, 15. קִרְאוּ (call) refers to the promulgation of the proclamation, while קַדֵּשׁ refers to specific ritual detail. עֲצָרָה (an assembly): Proclamation of an assembly included a gathering of the people as well as a prohibition against work (Lev. 23:36; Num. 29:35; Deut. 16:8); it ordinarily followed an official proclamation (Ahlström, *Joel and the Temple Cult*, p. 55; Segal, *Hebrew Passover*, p. 209; see also Kutsch, "Die Wurzel עצר im Hebräischen"). אִסְפוּ (gather): See 2:10, 16; 4:15 [3:15]. זְקֵנִים (the elders): The use of this word along with כֹּל יֹשְׁבֵי הָאָרֶץ (all who dwell in the land) forms an inclusio with 1:2 (Prinsloo, *Theology of the Book of Joel*, p. 27). Both verses 13 and 14 are characterized by extensive reuse of vocabulary from the earlier pericopes; in verse 13 note the following: חָגַר (1:8), הֵילִל (1:5, 11), מְשָׁרֵת (1:9), שַׂק (1:8), מִנְחָה וָנֶסֶךְ (1:9; cf. 2:14).

13–14. There has been considerable debate whether 1:13–14 belongs properly with the preceding group of summonses to lament or itself constitutes a different *Gattung* ("summons to fasting and prayer"; Rudolph, *Joel*, p. 46). The use of vocatives, imperatives, recurrent vocabulary, and an inclusio between 1:2 and 1:14 clearly ties these verses to what precedes as one more summons to lament. On the other hand, these verses represent a shift toward what follows by providing specific instructions regarding the place, purpose, and ritual detail for the lament.

Temple personnel maintained a watch through the night apparently on a regular basis (1 Chron. 23:30; Pss. 92:2–4 [1–3]; 134:1), but in these difficult days their numbers would increase (see

2 Sam. 12:16) and a lament liturgy would be observed. The rough, black sackcloth would contrast sharply with the customary splendor of priestly garb. The suspension of the regular cycle of worship due to the lack of the necessary sacrifices would not result in an idle priesthood; rather, a new rite takes the place of the daily worship.

One cannot help but notice the absence of any reference to a king or royal officials in this summons of the national leadership—only the cultic and secular leaders are summoned. The setting of the book as a whole appears to be a time when the temple is in existence, but when Israel has no monarchy, that is, during the postexilic period.

I. The Locust Plague: The Immediate Disaster (1:2–20)
C. The Complaint and Prayer (1:15–20)

15 Alas, the day!
  The day of the Lord is near,
    it comes like devastation from the Devastator!
16 Is not food cut off before our very eyes?
    Joy and gladness are cut off from the temple of our God.
17 The seeds are parched beneath their clods;
    storehouses are in ruins,
    granaries in disrepair,
      because the grain has withered away.
18 Even the cattle moan,
    and the herds are perplexed,
      because they have no pasture.
    The flocks too are suffering.
19 I call out to you, O Lord!
    A fire has consumed the grazing lands in the wilderness,
    a flame burns through the trees of the field.
20 The wild animals too look to you,
    for the water sources have dried up,
    and a fire has consumed the grazing lands in the wilderness.

15 Alas for the day!
  For the day of the Lord is near,
    and as destruction from the Almighty it comes.
16 Is not the food cut off
    before our eyes,
  joy and gladness
    from the house of our God?
17 The seed shrivels under the clods,
    the storehouses are desolate;
  the granaries are ruined
    because the grain has failed.
18 How the animals groan!
    The herds of cattle wander about
  because there is no pasture for them;
    even the flocks of sheep are dazed.
19 To you, O Lord, I cry.
  For fire has devoured
    the pastures of the wilderness,
  and flames have burned
    all the trees of the field.
20 Even the wild animals cry to you
    because the watercourses are dried up,
  and fire has devoured
    the pastures of the wilderness.

15. אֲהָהּ (alas): The Syriac version repeats this word twice and the Septuagint three times. Compare the similar formulas in Isaiah 13:6, Ezekiel 30:2–3, Obadiah 15, and Zephaniah 1:7. שֹׁד מִשַּׁדַּי (devastation from the Devastator): Note the striking assonance in these words, a technique also used in the preceding verses. The translation seeks to capture this feature (compare Allen, *Joel*, p. 59: "mighty ruin from the Almighty"; and Bewer, *Obadiah and Joel*, p. 86: "overpowering from the Overpowerer"). The prophet's linking of the verbal root שָׁדַד (destroy) and the divine title שַׁדַּי may be an example of a popular etymology;

the etymological meaning of the title has never been established with confidence. The traditional translation "Almighty" derives from παν-τοκράτωρ in the Septuagint. The other most common etymology relates the title to the Akkadian word *šadû* (mountain; e.g., "God of the mountain, mountain dweller"); other solutions have also been proposed. The term occurs as a divine title forty-eight times in the Old Testament (thirty-one times in Job).

16. עֵינֵינוּ (our eyes): In some Septuagint manuscripts the pronominal suffixes on this word and אֱלֹהֵינוּ (our God) are second-person plural: τῶν

---

15. In this section we move from the various summonses to lamentation to the lament itself. In 1:14 the nation is instructed to call out to Yahweh in a lament at the temple; 1:15–20 provides a summary of the content of their cry. The complaint proper recites the plight of the nation (vv. 15–18) and ends in a prayer for relief (vv. 19–20) from the disaster as it affects both humans and animals. Though there is wide agreement that these verses constitute part of a lament liturgy, not all concur (see the summary of the debate in Prinsloo, *Theology of the Book of Joel*, pp. 33–34). This section is not only joined to the preceding due to its logical place in a lament liturgy, but also by the continued use of recurring vocabulary and assonance as in 1:2–14 (see the Exegesis).

In verse 15 the locust plague as the manifestation of divine wrath is viewed as a harbinger of the yet greater and more dreadful day of Yahweh. The prophet draws on earlier canonical traditions regarding the day of the Lord and presumes his audience's familiarity with them. In the prophetic traditions of the Old Testament, the day of the Lord was the day of Yahweh's holy war against evil, particularly against the Gentile nations that had opposed or oppressed Israel. However, the prophets were quick to show that the day of the Lord came against all evil, not just evil among the Gentiles, but evil within the covenant people, so that Israel too would experience periodic judgment that anticipated that terrible day. As this theme is developed in Joel's prophecy, the day of the Lord threatens the continued existence of the covenant people (1:2–2:11); but it is a day whose consequences can be averted through repentance (2:12–17), so that it becomes instead a day of blessing for God's people (2:18–3:5 [2:18–32]) and judgment on their enemies (4:1–2 [3:1–2]). During her history prior to the time of Joel, Israel had

experienced periodic outbreaks or foretastes of the day of the Lord in the invasions of foreign nations; the locusts are likened to such a foreign invader in 1:6 and 2:6. The Babylonian invasion leading up to the destruction of Jerusalem in 586 B.C. had been the day of the Lord in the eyes of exilic and postexilic Judah, but the postexilic community was not now beyond the threat of divine punishment due to its own wickedness (Ezra 9:13–15; see Allen, *Joel*, p. 60).

The origin of the concept of the day of the Lord in Israel's religious traditions has been one of the most thoroughly analyzed and debated subjects in Old Testament studies (see the summary of this history in Prinsloo, *Theology of the Book of Joel*, pp. 35–36).

At an earlier stage a number of scholars regarded 1:15 as an interpolation on the part of a later glossator seeking to assimilate the originally independent chapters (1–2) to the later apocalyptic chapters (3–4). This view was originally expounded by B. Duhm and was also the position of Bewer (*Obadiah and Joel*, p. 86). More recent scholarship, as it has generally come to appreciate the unity of the book, tends to view this position as an example of "incautious, arbitrary analysis and amputation on inadequate grounds" (Jones, *Isaiah 56–66 and Joel*, p. 148; see the comments in the Introduction).

16. This verse speaks of the helplessness of human beings in the face of a locust outbreak. In the face of a constant hubris on the part of the human race, there are many ways in which the Creator has chosen to remind proud humans of their impotence, even in the face of the least of God's creatures. Human beings could no more hold back the locusts than they could arrest the tides or stop the changing phases of the moon— they could only sit back and watch.

ὀφθαλυῶν ὑμῶν and θεοῦ ὑμῶν. This removes the verse from the lament proper and makes it an appeal to the priests. The first-person forms are common in communal laments (compare the first-person singular in 1:19). Note again the characteristic reuse of vocabulary: כָּרַת also occurs in 1:5, 9.

17. עָבְשׁוּ פְּרֻדוֹת תַּחַת מֶגְרְפֹתֵיהֶם (the seeds are parched beneath their clods): This clause represents the most difficult philological problem in the Book of Joel. Three of the first four words are *hapax legomena*. Numerous efforts have been made to provide a solution (beyond the commentary literature, see Rudolph, "Ein Beitrag zum hebräischen Lexikon"; Nestle, "Joel 1:17"; Sprengling, "Joel 1:17a," p. 129). עָבֵשׁ (parched) is commonly related to an Arabic verb meaning "shrivel," or to the Mishnaic Hebrew verb עָפֵשׁ (rot). פְּרֻדוֹת (the seeds) is ordinarily related to an Aramaic and Syriac cognate meaning "berry, pebble," and hence "seed, grain"; Sprengling relates it instead to "rifts, watercourses" on the basis of the use of the cognate verb in Genesis 2:10; and Rudolph relates it to the verbal root "set aside, divide" and suggests "reserves, stores, provisions." מֶגְרְפֹתֵיהֶם (their clods) has cognates in Arabic and Aramaic meaning "shovel"; Borowski (*Agriculture in Iron Age Israel*, p. 53) suggests that the implement in view was dragged behind animals to level the ground. In Jewish exegetical tradition the term was ordinarily taken in the sense of clods (רְגָבֵיהֶם). With these in mind, a translation "the grain lies shriveled/is rotting beneath their shovels/clods" appears reasonable. However, it is difficult to relate this to the larger context concerning a locust plague, or even to specific agricultural practices otherwise attested, unless we are to understand it as enunciating the effects of a drought, so that seed which has been sown is not germinating. Kapelrud (*Joel Studies*, pp. 65–66) repoints the preposition תַּחַת (under) to תֵּחַת, a niphal imperfect of the verb חָתַת (be dismayed), and suggests the following translation: "Shrunk are the grains, disheartened are their irrigation spades, empty are the store-houses, collapsed lie the barns, for the corn has dried up." The ancient versions show widely differing translations and cannot be used with confidence to reconstruct the text here; they show either that the text was already corrupt in antiquity or that the translators at the least were not familiar with the vocabulary used here. The net impression is that the versions are trying to cope with what was already a difficult passage. The Septuagint (ἐσκίρτμσαν δαμάλεις ἐπὶ ταῖς φάτναις αὐτῶν, heifers danced at their mangers) is probably to be explained as follows: either פְּרְדָּה (she-mule) or פָּרוֹת (heifers) was read for פְּרֻדוֹת (the seeds); עָכַס (shake, rattle—Isa. 3:16) for עָבֵשׁ (parched); and רֶפֶת (stable, stall) or a cognate for מֶגְרְפֹתֵיהֶם (their clods). Others suggest that ἐσκίρτησαν is an error in the Septuagint for ἐσκλήσαν (from σκέλλω, dry up, parch, wither;

The relationship between the two lines can be conceived in at least two ways: (1) the food that is cut off in verse 16a is the grain offerings and libations that are no longer available to the temple, and hence joy and gladness are cut off from the temple (note the use of *kārat* [cut] in 1:9 in reference to the grain offerings and libations), or (2) the general plight of a hungry population in verse 16a is reflected in its specific consequences for the temple. These two senses come together in the commands authorizing worshipers to partake in particular offerings brought to the temple (Lev. 7:15–18). The fellowship offerings allowed the worshiper to enjoy fellowship with God in a meal at his sanctuary; as that fellowship is interrupted by the sinfulness of the people that prompted the plague, so also the food itself is no longer available. The grain offerings in particular were to be eaten by the priests (Lev. 6:14–18); the loss of these offerings would have dire consequences for cultic personnel.

17. The vocabulary of the Old Testament is rich with terms describing various facilities for storing grain; archeological excavations likewise reveal the use of subterranean facilities (grain pits, silos, cellars) and above-ground facilities (granaries, storehouses, public and private storerooms). These differed in construction, storage method (bulk or container), and ownership (public or private); see Borowski (*Agriculture in Iron Age Israel*, pp. 71–83) for a description of these structures. The precise significance of the two terms used here, *ʾōṣārôt* (storehouses) and *mammĕgūrôt* (granaries), is not known with confidence.

The uncertainty surrounding the first four words in the verse makes it somewhat difficult to establish the relationship of the verse as a whole to what precedes. Verses 17–20 appear to be describing the effects of drought instead of a locust plague. Perhaps we are to infer that a drought followed the outbreak of the locusts and compounded the disaster; copious rains came as a solution to this part of the disaster (2:23). Defoliation also has the effect of lowering the water table, increasing the dryness of the soil, and withering any vegetation for grazing that may have

compare the Syriac version; see Sprengling, "Joel 1:17a," p. 129). The Vulgate (*conputruerunt iumenta in stercore suo*, beasts rot in their dung) may reflect an understanding of מֶגְרְפֹתֵיהֶם (their clods) in a derived sense of the root גָּרַף (sweep away) as "sweepings," and hence "dung." Symmachus's reading (ηὐρωτίασαν σιτοδοχεῖα ἀπὸ τοῦ χρισμάτων αὐτῶν, the granaries have rotted from their plaster) appears to have developed from reading מֶגְרְפֹתֵיהֶם (their clods) as "plaster," for which a graphically similar Hebrew term is unclear. Theodotion is known in this instance only from a Syriac translation, and the retroversion to Greek is difficult and debated (see Rudolph, "Ein Beitrag zum hebräischen Lexikon," p. 245; Sprengling, "Joel 1:17a," pp. 129–41). The Targum's "jarcovers" may have derived from reading מְגוּפָתְהוֹן. This brief survey is sufficient to indicate that the problem with Joel 1:17 is not a new one. Other modern efforts also show considerable variation. The New English Bible has, "The soil is parched, the dykes are dry." Rudolph ("Ein Beitrag zum hebräischen Lexikon," p. 246) translates, "The stored up provisions have rotted under their coverings." Barring further discoveries in epigraphy and philology, the first four words of the verse remain something of an enigma; it is not possible to establish their meaning with confidence.

18. מַה־נֶּאֶנְחָה בְהֵמָה (even the cattle moan): The translators of the Septuagint appear to have read נֶאֶנְחָה (moan) as נֵנִיחָה, a hiphil first-person plural

form from the verb נוּחַ (deposit). For the Masoretic Text's נָבֹכוּ (are perplexed; from the root בּוּךְ, be perplexed, confused), the Septuagint has ἔκλαυσαν, reflecting the more common root בָּכָה (weep), which occurs also in 1:5 and 2:17. Note the recurrence of בְהֵמָה in 1:20. Some (e.g., Stuart, *Hosea–Jonah*, p. 239) read נֶאֶשְׁמוּ (are suffering) as a biform of שָׁמֵם (be desolate). If it is derived from its apparent root אָשֵׁם (bear punishment, suffer) this would be the only occurrence of the verb in the niphal.

19–20. אֵלֶיךָ (to you): The pronominal referents shift from first-person plural (1:17–18) to direct address to Yahweh (1:19–20); the complaint itself gives way to prayer. Prinsloo (*Theology of the Book of Joel*, p. 31) calls attention to the structural symmetry of verses 19–20:

19a:	אֵלֶיךָ	20a:	אֵלֶיךָ
19b:	כִּי	20b:	כִּי
19c:	וְ	20c:	וְ

The repetition of the phrase אֵשׁ אָכְלָה (a fire has consumed) in verses 19a and 20c forms an inclusio; man (v. 19) and beast (v. 20) alike suffer the consequences. This solidarity of man and animal is also described in Exodus 9–11; Deuteronomy 20:14; 28:50–51; Psalm 135:8 (Keller, *Joël*, p. 118). For the formula "to you, O Yahweh, I cry," compare Psalm 28:1; 30:9 [8]; 86:3 (cf. Pss. 3:5 [4]; 18:7 [6]; 55:17–18 [16–17]).

---

survived the locusts. The prophet describes the disrepair of the storage facilities, perhaps since normal maintenance was not done in the absence of crops to store. Just as foreign invaders confiscated crops (Judg. 6:3–6), so also the locusts take the food (Stuart, *Hosea–Jonah*, p. 244).

18. All living creatures look to God for their food (Pss. 104:10–18, 21; 145:15; 147:8–9). The lowing and bleating of the cattle in their distress become their prayer to their Creator; it is joined to the prayer of the prophet himself (1:19). The locust plague had subjected that land, once flowing with milk and honey, to want, privation, and futility, so that the whole creation groans in its suffering, looking for redemption (Rom. 8:20–22; see Allen, *Joel*, p. 62). If the "dumb" animals could recognize their Creator's judgment and might and turn to him in prayer, could not Israel? Calvin's comment (*Joel*, p. 39) is helpful; he notes the "implied comparison between the feeling of brute animals and the insensibility of the people; as though he [the prophet] said, 'There is certainly

more intelligence and reason in oxen and other brute animals than in you; for the herds groan, the flocks groan, but ye remain stupid and confounded!'" (see Jones, *Isaiah 56–66 and Joel*, p. 150).

19–20. Compare Psalm 65:14 [13]; Jeremiah 9:9–10 [10–11]; 23:10. The description of the disaster, the complaint itself, gives way to prayer. The "I" that speaks is presumably the prophet, but could also be a priest leading the lament liturgy.

Once again there is some ambiguity regarding the relationship of these verses to the locust plague (see the Exposition of 1:17). The fire could conceivably be a literal flame compounding the other disasters, but it is more probably a metaphor: either the drought has had the same effect as a grass or forest fire, or it is a description of the locusts themselves, whose noisy advance through the fields, orchards, and forests sounded like an onrushing firestorm; this latter appears to be the image in 2:3, 5. Fire is an important motif in biblical portrayals of judgment and theophany; however the fire is understood in this instance, it emanated from God and reflected his judgment.

The disaster drove not only domesticated animals, which depend on human beings to some extent, to their own lament (1:18), but even the wild animals as well are driven to look to God. Their water and food are gone as well.

The water supply was perhaps the most crucial concern for a city under attack (Gen. 26:18; 2 Kings 3:19, 25; 2 Chron. 32:4; see Stuart, *Hosea–Jonah*, p. 245). A city cannot resist the onslaught of an enemy when the water is gone.

II. The Day of the Lord: The Impending Disaster (2:1–17)
A. Cry of Alarm, Warning of Attack (2:1-2)

2 Blow a trumpet in Zion!
    Sound the alarm on my holy moun-
        tain!
    Let all who live in the land tremble!
For the day of the LORD is coming—
    indeed it is near!
  ² A day of darkness and gloom,
    a day of clouds and obscurity;
  Like dawn spreading over the moun-
    tains,
    a great and powerful army comes,
    the likes of which there never was of
      old,
      nor will ever be again through the
      years of all generations.

2 Blow the trumpet in Zion;
    sound the alarm on my holy moun-
        tain!
  Let all the inhabitants of the land trem-
    ble,
    for the day of the LORD is coming, it is
      near—
  ² a day of darkness and gloom,
    a day of clouds and thick darkness!
  Like blackness spread upon the moun-
    tains
    a great and powerful army comes;
  their like has never been from of old,
    nor will be again after them in ages to
      come.

2:1. כִּי־בָא (for . . . is coming): Prinsloo (*Theology of the Book of Joel*, p. 41) notes a progression between the formula in 1:15, כִּי . . . יְהוָה יוֹם קָרוֹב (the day of the LORD is near, it comes . . .) and that in 2:1b, כָּרוֹב כִּי יוֹם־יְהוָה כִּי־בָא (for the day of the LORD is coming . . . it is near!)—certainly one can say that there is a variation in the formula, but that it denotes progression or a greater urgency is not so easily determined. יוֹם־יְהוָה (the day of the LORD): Joel's description of the day of the Lord and of the appearance of the Lord's own army (2:1–11) includes language and motifs similar to many other passages, but appears uniquely dependent on Isaiah 13:1–13 (see the excursus in Wolff, *Joel and Amos*, p. 47). The Lord's army appears on "the mountains" (הֶהָרִים) in Joel 2:2, 5 and Isaiah 13:4; they are a "great army" (עַם רַב) in Joel 2:2 and Isaiah 13:4 (cf. Joel 2:5, 11).

2. חֹשֶׁךְ (darkness), אֲפֵלָה (gloom), עָנָן (clouds), עֲרָפֶל (obscurity): In his use of the four terms describing the darkness of the day of Yahweh, Joel appears to be quoting Zephaniah 1:15, the only other passage in which the same sequence and number of terms occur; other passages compound synonyms for darkness in connection with theophany (Exod. 20:18, 21; Deut. 4:11; 5:22–23; 1 Kings 8:12 par. 2 Chron. 6:1; Ps. 97:2) or in images of judgment and misery (Exod. 10:22; Isa. 60:2; Jer. 13:16; 23:12; Ezek. 34:12; Amos 5:18–20). Naturally the two foci—the day of Yahweh's appearing and a day of judgment—come together on the day of the Lord. כְּשַׁחַר (like dawn): Some commentators have found the simile of darkness spreading like dawn (שַׁחַר) an improbable oxymoron and suggest repointing to "black, blackness" (שְׁחֹר; see the remarks of Wolff, *Joel and Amos*, p. 44). The emendation is unwarranted (see the Exposition).

2:1. The blasting trumpet was the alarm sounded to warn of an impending attack (Jer. 4:5; 6:1; Ezek. 33:2–4; Hos. 5:8). The image of a watchman occurs often in the Old Testament to depict the prophets (Isa. 21:11–12; 52:8; 56:10; Jer. 6:17; Ezek. 3:17; Hos. 9:8; Mic. 7:4). Ezekiel had likened himself to a watchman on the wall responsible for warning of an attack (Ezek. 33:1–7); failure to sound the alarm would have made him responsible for the deaths that followed. Here Joel too sounds the alarm. Israel's prophets had a prominent role in holy war; they provided battle oracles and even instructions for the conduct of warfare (1 Kings 20; 22; 2 Kings 1; 3:14–19; 6:8–7:2; 13:14–20; 2 Chron. 11:1–4; 20:14–17). Joel is in effect giving another battle oracle—but it is the Lord's army coming against Israel on the day of the Lord. As with Ezekiel, if the people will hear the alarm and heed the summons of another trumpet to national fasting and repentance (2:15), the disaster can be averted.

Joel's version of the day of the Lord reverses Israel's hopes. Instead of myriads of thousands of the winged hosts of the heavenly army coming to the protection, aid, and vindication of the nation, Joel describes a cloud of winged creatures coming rather in devastating judgment (Kline, *Images of the Spirit*, pp. 119–20).

2. The locusts had darkened the skies with their teeming swarms, but the darkness that spreads here is the darkness attending God's presence with his army (2:31; see the Exegesis). Rather than the dawn bringing the light of another day, this dawn would bring darkness (Amos 5:18, 20).

Much of the language here reminds us of the language of Hebrews 12:18–29 and its reflection on events at Sinai and in the heavenly Jerusalem. There were darkness and gloom, a trumpet blast, a consuming fire (Joel 2:3–5), and no escape (2:3). John too uses locustlike creatures in his later announcement of an apocalyptic threat (Rev. 9:1–10).

In describing this plague as unparalleled (2:2; cf. 1:2–3), Joel is drawing attention to Exodus 10:14: what the Lord had once done to another nation in order to redeem Israel, he now does to Israel; where once he had fought in her behalf, he now comes to war against her.

Although Israel had driven out the "great and powerful army" of other nations when she came into the land (Deut. 4:38; 7:1, 17–19; 9:1), there would be no destroying this army coming from the Lord (Jones, *Isaiah 56–66 and Joel*, p. 155).

Stephenson ("Date of the Book of Joel") regards 2:2 and 3:4 [2:31] as speaking of solar and lunar eclipses that occurred in 402, 357, and 336 B.C.; he then uses these eclipses as a means of dating the Book of Joel. The argument is curious, as it is full of citations from medieval literatures from Belgium, Italy, Germany, and England in which scribes describe lunar eclipses as if the moon were sprinkled with blood. Since these and other comparisons are similar to the language of the biblical text, Stephenson concludes that the biblical texts must also be speaking of eclipses. It is far more reasonable to infer instead that these medieval sources were influenced by their knowledge of the

Bible in choosing to describe eclipses this way. Apocalyptic literature and descriptions of theophany in general tend to include cosmic reflexes attending the appearance of God (see the Exposition of 2:10–11). Stephenson's arguments should probably be ignored; they take stereotypical language for theophany or the phenomena attending a locust outbreak as eclipses and attempt to date the book on the basis of this erroneous identification.

II. The Day of the Lord: The Impending Disaster (2:1–17)
B. The Divine Army as Locusts (2:3–11)

3 Before it a fire burns,
   and behind it a flame blazes.
 Before it the land was like the garden of
   Eden,
   and behind it, a devastated wilderness.
 There is no escape from it.
4 Its appearance is like that of horses,
   they run like cavalry.
5 They sound like chariots;
   they skip over the mountaintops.
 They sound like lapping flames,
   devouring chaff.
 They are like a mighty army drawn up
   for battle.
6 Nations are terrified before them;
   every face contorts in dread.
7 They run like warriors
   and scale walls like men of war.
 Each marches straight ahead;
   they do not deviate from their course.
8 One does not crowd the other;
   each marches on his way.
 They hurtle against the defenses,
   they will not break off.
9 They range through the city,
   they run on the wall;
 They climb into houses,
   and go through windows like thieves.
10 Before them the land trembles,
    the heavens shake;
 the sun and moon grow dark,
   and the stars recall their light.
11 The LORD gives his orders to his army,
    for his soldiers are most numerous,
    powerful to do his will;
    for great is the day of the LORD,
    so dreadful, who can endure it!

3 Fire devours in front of them,
   and behind them a flame burns.
 Before them the land is like the garden of
   Eden,
   but after them a desolate wilderness,
   and nothing escapes them.
4 They have the appearance of horses,
   and like war-horses they charge.
5 As with the rumbling of chariots,
   they leap on the tops of the mountains,
 like the crackling of a flame of fire
   devouring the stubble,
 like a powerful army
   drawn up for battle.
6 Before them peoples are in anguish,
   all faces grow pale.
7 Like warriors they charge,
   like soldiers they scale the wall.
 Each keeps to its own course,
   they do not swerve from their paths.
8 They do not jostle one another,
   each keeps to its own track;
 they burst through the weapons
   and are not halted.
9 They leap upon the city,
   they run upon the walls;
 they climb up into the houses,
   they enter through the windows like
   a thief.
10 The earth quakes before them,
    the heavens tremble.
 The sun and the moon are darkened,
   and the stars withdraw their shining.
11 The LORD utters his voice
    at the head of his army;
 how vast is his host!
   Numberless are those who obey his
   command.
 Truly the day of the LORD is great;
   terrible indeed—who can endure it?

3. לְפָנָיו (before it): There is some ambiguity regarding the antecedent of the pronominal suffixes in this verse. Though in the abstract the reference of the pronominal suffix on לְפָנָיו (before it) and אַחֲרָיו (behind it) could be either "God" or the "army" (Keller, *Joël*, p. 125), the antecedent to אַחֲרָיו (behind it) in verse 3 is probably the same as for the same form in verse 2, which is the "great army" of verse 2. In the final analysis it makes little difference: the army is Yahweh's, and he is its commander. The double use of both לְפָנָיו (before it) and אַחֲרָיו (behind it) makes for an effective contrast between conditions before and after the appearance of the locust army. אֵשׁ (a fire): The image of fire recurs; in 1:19–20 it appears to refer to a drought, but here it refers to the flames accompanying the divine army and/or as an extension of the locust metaphor to describe the sound of the locust attack as a raging firestorm. כְּגַן־עֵדֶן (like the garden of Eden): Ezekiel also draws on the reversal of Eden as a motif (Ezek. 28:13; 31:9–18; 36:35; see also Isa. 51:3); if Joel is dependent on Ezekiel for this image, it would require a postexilic date for Joel. Of course, biblical imagery treating Israel as God's garden, field, orchard, or vineyard is much broader and more frequent and belongs to the same conceptual realm. Agricultural prosperity or its loss is a prominent motif in the Old Testament, a portrayal of paradise lost or regained (Joel 4:18 [3:18]; Amos 9:13–15). לוֹ (from it): The antecedent of this form is also ambiguous. It could refer to "anyone" or to "the land" (see Allen, *Joel*, p. 65).

4. יְרוּצוּן (they run): This verb, like all the imperfects in verses 4–9, makes use of the archaic וּן (ûn) ending. Various commentators have suggested that the effect of the repeated use of this longer ending adds weight or power to the description of the attack (Bewer, *Obadiah and Joel*, p. 98; Rudolph, *Joel*, p. 56; Wolff, *Joel and Amos*, p. 46; Allen, *Joel*, p. 71; Prinsloo, *Theology of the Book of Joel*, p. 42). While these older forms may have imparted a sonority to the reading of the passage, it is again difficult to describe with confidence how the original hearers would have perceived this essentially aesthetic understanding of the device.

5. כְּקוֹל (sound like; lit. like the sound of) occurs twice in this verse. This parallels Isaiah 13:4, which also has a double use of קוֹל. Note the use of

---

3–5. The prophet likens the invading "locusts" to fire and horses. The noise made by a locust swarm has often been likened to the sound of a forest fire, and the effect of their passing is similar: nothing but charred, devoured vegetation remains in their wake. Imagine the sound familiar to almost every child, that of a grasshopper flitting about in the grass; multiply this by thousands of millions in leaping and flying frenzy. The droning of their distant fluttering becomes the roar of a firestorm as the swarm reaches the hearer. Just as an enemy army leaves behind scorched earth, so the locusts strip the land. The fact that such noise is made by the locusts facilitates Joel's description of the appearance of the divine army; theophanies in the Bible commonly have an auditory component (see the Exegesis of 2:5). Fire is, of course, one of the main modes of theophany in the Bible. For the fire that burns before and after, see Psalm 50:3; 97:3. Zechariah also described Judah as surrounded by the theophanic pillar of fire, but it was in blessing instead of judgment (Zech. 2:8–9 [4–5]).

Other literatures have also likened locusts to horses and cavalry. A German word for locust, *Heupferd*, etymologically means "hay horse"; in Italian, *cavalletta* is a term for the locust, and means "little horse." An Egyptian poet from the twelfth century A.D. likened the head and mouth of the locust to those of a horse (Thompson, "Joel's Locusts," p. 53); a similar comparison is found in an Algerian tale, an anonymous text from Aleppo, the story of Tawaddud in the *Arabian Nights*, and other texts (Taylor, "Riddle for a Locust"). Here, however, the point of the comparison is probably not the shape of the head and mouth, but rather the horse as a symbol of power and might (Isa. 31:1–3; Hos. 14:4 [3]; Mic. 5:9 [10]; Hag. 2:22; Zech. 9:10; 12:4). John would make the same comparison (Rev. 9:7). Chariots are also a particular mode of theophany (see the Exegesis of 2:5).

In the preexilic period a tradition of the inviolability of Jerusalem arose in Israel and was reinforced in the defeat of her enemies, particularly the army of Assyria under Sennacherib. Zion learned of her vulnerability to divine judgment, however, when the army of Babylon destroyed the city and exiled much of the population. Here the prophet reminds the nation of that vulnerability to an army sent from Yahweh.

The paradise motif is of great importance in the Bible. Though humankind was driven from the garden paradise that God had prepared for his image-bearer in Eden, God would eventually bring

רָקַד (they skip), which also appears in Isaiah 13:21 (see Wolff, *Joel and Amos*, p. 47; Ahlström, *Joel and the Temple Cult*, pp. 4–6). מַרְכְּבוֹת (chariots) are common images in descriptions of theophany (2 Kings 2:11–12; 6:17; Ezek. 1; cf. 1 Chron. 28:18) as are other noises (קוֹל) associated with military imagery (Exod. 19:16, 19; Num. 10:9; 2 Sam. 5:24 par. 1 Chron. 14:15; Isa. 13:4). Fire (אֵשׁ) and flame are perhaps the most frequent image of theophany (Gen. 15:17; Exod. 3:1–6; 19:18; 40:38; Lev. 10:2; Num. 9:15–16; Deut. 5:22–26; 18:16; Judg. 6:21; 1 Kings 18:24, 38; 2 Kings 1:10–12; 2:11–12; etc.). קַשׁ (chaff) is ordinarily used as an image of judgment in reference to its being dispersed in winnowing or by fierce wind (for chaff as burned, see Matt. 3:12; Luke 3:17). עֲרוּךְ (drawn up) is commonly used in military contexts in the sense of deploy for battle, draw up in battle order/array (Gen. 14:8; Judg. 20:22; 1 Sam. 17:8; etc.).

6. יָחִילוּ (are terrified): Compare once again the use of חוּל (יְחִילוּן) in a similar context in Isaiah 13:8. כָּל־פָּנִים קִבְּצוּ פָארוּר (every face contorts in dread): This phrase, which occurs also in Nahum 2:11, is difficult. The Septuagint, which translates it πᾶν πρόσωπον ὡς πρόσκαυμα χύτρας (every face is like a scorched pot), appears to have read פָּרוּר (pot; compare Vulgate, *ollam*) for פָּארוּר, and possibly כְּקִיץ (like the heat) or כְּבִץ (like the silt; Stuart, *Hosea–Jonah*, p. 248) for קִבְּצוּ. Others translate using the presumed etymology פּוּר (boil, heat) and suggest "every face gathers heat, becomes flushed." This approach may furnish another point of contact with Isaiah 13:8, where the result of the appearance of the divine army is that faces are aflame. Others suggest an etymology from the

root פָּאר (brightness) so that "gather brightness, recall brightness" (cf. 2:10; 4:15 [3:15]) is understood as "become pale." Clearly the context favors the effect of the divine army on the countenances of those who see its approach (see the discussions by Görg, "Eine formelhafte Metaphor"; and Schüngel, "Noch einmal zu קבצו פָארור").

7. חוֹמָה (walls): The reference to the wall here and in 2:9 has played an important role in efforts to date the book (see the Exegesis of 2:9). אִישׁ (each): When this word is used in the position of an apparent subject of a plural verb in Hebrew it is regularly translated "each" (see v. 8). וְלֹא יְעַבְּטוּן (they do not deviate): This phrase offers another philological crux. The root עבט occurs in the qal or hiphil in the somewhat technical legal sense of take or give a pledge (Deut. 15:6, 8; 24:10), a sense foreign to the context and improbable for a cooccurrence with אָרְחוֹתָם (their course). This would be the only occurrence in the piel. It is possible to suggest an extended meaning for this stem of the verb in the sense of exchange or change, that is, "they will not change their course." The Septuagint (ἐκκλίνωσι) and Vulgate (*declinabunt*) both give the sense of decline, fall away, and have in part prompted several emendations. Bewer (*Obadiah and Joel*, p. 102) and others opt for reading the verb עָוַת (bend, make crooked); while this yields acceptable sense, the phonetic or aural confusion seems improbable, and it does involve change in two of the three root consonants. The same is also true for the emendation to יְמוּן from the root נטה (turn aside). Leibel ("יְעַבְּטוּן") suggests עָרַב (exchange, take pledge; see also Loewenstamm, "יְעֻרְתוּן = יְעַבְּטוּן?"; Ahlström, *Joel and the*

---

his chosen people into a land flowing with milk and honey. Israel was God's garden, his vineyard, his planting. The floral motifs that decorated the tabernacle and temple reminded Israel of the garden dwelling of God. Here the locusts turn God's garden into desolate chaos. Joel will return to this theme; paradise lost becomes paradise restored (2:21–27), in anticipation of a greater paradise to come (4:18 [3:18]; for other uses of the paradise motif in the Old Testament, see the Exegesis of 2:3).

The statement that "there is no escape" (v. 3) also introduces another prominent biblical theme, the remnant motif. Throughout the Old Testament various natural disasters or military actions threaten the survival of God's people. The remnant is that person or group that undergoes divine judgment for sin, but yet survives or escapes to

become the nucleus of a renewed people of God in whom the nation's hopes are focused. The locusts threatened the survival of God's people; how much more so the pending appearance of the divine army! Yet there will be those who survive, those who call on the name of the Lord (3:5 [2:32]).

6. Perhaps the most common response to theophany is fear; fear is the predictable consequence of the appearance of the Lord and his army (e.g., Gen. 3:10; Exod. 3:6; Deut. 5:21–23 [24–26]; Pss. 96:9; 97:4; Isa. 13:8; Jer. 4:9; 5:22; Amos 3:8; Mic. 7:17; Matt. 14:26–27; 17:6; Luke 1:12; 2:9).

7–8. Armies are commonly likened to locusts (Judg. 6:5; 7:12; Isa. 33:4; Jer. 46:23; 51:14, 27); here that order is reversed, and the locusts take on the character of an invading army. The seemingly orderly, quasi-military advance of the locusts was also noted in wisdom literature (Prov. 30:27).

Temple Cult, pp. 11–13; Whitley, "ʿbṭ in Joel 2:7"). Whitley argues for an interchange of the gutturals ח and ע, and sees עבט as a variant form of חבט (beat down), thus accounting for the sense of *decline* in the ancient translations. This too seems like philological special pleading. Ahlström (*Joel and the Temple Cult*, p. 12) notes the chiastic relationship in the series of verbs in verses 7b–8a:

On the basis of this relationship he suggests that עבט and דחק give almost the same verbal idea.

8. גֶּבֶר בִּמְסִלָּתוֹ יֵלֵכוּן (one does not crowd the other): The Septuagint (καταβαρυνόμενοι ἐν τοῖς ὅπλοις αὐτῶν πορεύσονται, they go weighed down with their weapons) is wide of the Masoretic Text, and it is difficult to provide a reasonable retroversion to account for the Septuagint translation (see Wolff, *Joel and Amos*, p. 38). The *Vorlage* of the Septuagint appears to have contained or misread כָּבֵד for גֶּבֶר, but this is only the first suggestion in a series of difficulties. הַשֶּׁלַח (the defenses): The Masoretic Text points this word as a noun (weapon, spear, lance), though such would not be a good weapon against locusts (Allen, *Joel*, p. 72). Several other possibilities have been suggested: The word could be cognate to Akkadian *šalḫu* (frontwall), and would form a fitting parallel with verse 9a (see Loewenstamm, "וּבְעַד הַשֶּׁלַח יִפֹּלוּ"). Others relate this occurrence to the phrase *waters of Shiloah* in Isaiah 8:6, so that the disaster comes through the Shiloah water system (see Ahlström, *Joel and the Temple Cult*, pp. 12–13; Leibel, "עבר בשלח"). The Targum reads ולאתר דאינון שליחין (to the place where they are sent). לֹא יִבְצָעוּ (they will not break off): בָּצַע has the basic meaning "cut off, break off." The verb has been interpreted in a number of ways: (1) "they are not cut," that is, not wounded (KJV), or (2) "they do not break off" from their course, or from their ranks (NIV), or "are not halted" (NRSV). (3) Ahlström (*Joel and the Temple*

Cult, p. 12), appealing to an Arabic cognate and Isaiah 38:12, suggests "cut down, cut in pieces" and reads לֹא as a *lamed emphaticum*. The sense of *break off from their course* fits well as a parallel with the first two lines of the verse; uncertainty about the third line complicates our determination of the sense with confidence.

9. חוֹמָה (wall): Many scholars (e.g., Gray, Cornill, Marti, Weiser, *Joel*, p. 114; Treves, "Date of Joel," p. 151; see the comments of Myers, "Date of Joel," p. 191) argue that the mention of the wall in 2:7, 9 indicates that the date of the composition of Joel must be after the reconstruction of the wall of Jerusalem in the time of Nehemiah. This position has now largely been abandoned. Though extensive damage was done to the walls of Jerusalem (2 Kings 25:10; 2 Chron. 36:19; Jer. 52:14) the statements that at the time of Nehemiah the breaches in the wall (פְּרֻצִים—Neh. 2:13; 4:1) were repaired (cf. Neh. 3:8) indicate that the entire wall was not leveled during the destruction of the city in 586 B.C.; further, had the walls been leveled in their entirety Nehemiah and his workers could scarcely have completed the repairs in fifty-two days (Neh. 6:15). Ahlström (*Joel and the Temple Cult*, pp. 114–15) compares the references to the wall in 2:7, 9 to the reference to the temple in Jeremiah 41:5: though the temple had been destroyed, individuals could still bring offerings "to the temple of Yahweh"; sufficient structure remained after the destruction that the temple could still be identified, and mentioning it in this context does not imply that it had already been rebuilt. בָּתִּים (into houses): Note again a parallel with Isaiah 13: the divine army plunders the houses (Isa. 13:16; see also Exod. 10:6). Repetition of vocabulary in verses 7–9 (יֵלֵכוּן, יַעֲלוּ, יְרוּצוּן, חוֹמָה, גִּבּוֹרִים גֶּבֶר) adds a certain drama and intensity to the description of the attack (Prinsloo, *Theology of the Book of Joel*, p. 43).

10. רָעֲשׁוּ (shake): B. Childs ("Enemy from the North," pp. 188–90) has shown that רָעַשׁ developed into a technical term, particularly in the postexilic period, for designating a return of chaos at the end of the era. Many of the uses of this verb

---

9. This verse in particular appears to be elaborating on Exodus 10:5–6. Thievery is an apt metaphor for both locusts in their violent taking for their own use the products of the labors of others and as an image of the day of the Lord (Matt. 24:43–44). Stuart (*Hosea–Jonah*, pp. 228, 251) calls attention to Joel's dependence on Mosaic covenant sanctions in his descriptions of the difficulties befalling Judah (Deut. 28:25, 49, 52).

10. The darkening of the skies and obscuring of the sun during the day (2:2) are commonly noted features of a locust plague. However, locusts ordinarily are inactive and do not fly during the night. Here the language moves beyond the metaphor and speaks as well of the darkening of the moon and stars, that is, the prophet has left the locust metaphor and now describes the phenomena of the day of the Lord.

designate ordinary shaking or trembling; other occurrences are associated with theophany (Judg. 5:4; Pss. 18:8 [7]; 68:9 [8]) and others with a return to primeval chaos (Pss. 46:4 [3]; 77:18 [19]). In the Prophets divine judgment is often described as a return to chaos with the accompanying shaking of the heavens and earth (Isa. 13:13; 24:18–20; Jer. 4:23–26; Ezek. 38:18–20; Hag. 2:6, 7, 21; cf. Joel 4:16 [3:16]; see also Kessler, "Shaking of the Nations"). Earlier critical scholarship commonly disputed the unity of the Book of Joel and distinguished between the prophet who gave oracles about a locust plague and a later editor/prophet who added the apocalyptic material pertaining to the day of the Lord. On this basis 2:10–11 was commonly viewed as an insertion by a later interpolator (see, e.g., Bewer, *Obadiah and Joel*, pp. 103–4). Most recent scholarship recognizes the unity of the book. Compare once again parallels with Isaiah 13: the response in the heavens at the appearance of the Lord's army (Isa. 13:10), and the shaking of the heavens and earth (Isa. 13:13).

11. קוֹלוֹ (his orders; lit. his voice): Biblical descriptions of a theophany commonly have an auditory component (see the Exegesis of 2:5). Yahweh's voice is ordinarily associated with thunder and lightning (Exod. 19:18–19; Pss. 18:14 [13]; 29:3–4; 46:7 [6]; Amos 1:2; Hab. 3:10). כִּי (for): See below. רַב מְאֹד מַחֲנֵהוּ (his soldiers are most numerous): For the theme of the innumerable divine host, see also 1 Chronicles 12:22; innumerability is, of course, part of the comparison with the locust plague (1:6; Exod. 10:12–14; Judg. 7:12; Ps. 105:34; Jer. 46:23; Nah. 3:15–17). כִּי (untranslated): See below. עָצוּם עֹשֵׂה דְבָרוֹ (powerful to do his will): The Septuagint has ὅτι ἰσχυρὰ ἔργα λόγων αὐτοῦ (for the deeds of his words are mighty), apparently taking ם of עָצוּם with the following word and understanding עֹשֵׂה as a plural (see Wolff, *Joel and Amos*, pp. 38–39). כִּי (for): The three כִּי clauses are most naturally taken as asseverative or affirmative; the sense is *indeed* or *surely* (Prinsloo, *Theology of the Book of Joel*, p. 44; see Waltke and O'Connor, *Introduction to Biblical Hebrew Syntax*, § 39.3.4e). Some consider the three כִּי clauses as denoting the reasons why Yahweh gives orders to his army ("because his soldiers are numerous, because they are powerful to do his will, because the day of Yahweh is great and dreadful"). While כִּי clauses may introduce subordinate ideas that are often understood causally, to the present writer the idea of cause seems less apparent in this context. The point is not so much *why* Yahweh gives orders as it is the prophet's awe before the unfolding theophany. The translation offered resorts to the common practice of rendering כִּי as

---

11. These cosmic phenomena that attend the day of the Lord are also attested for other theophanies; the forces of nature attend the appearance of the Divine Warrior (4:15–16 [3:15–16]; Judg. 5:4–5; Pss. 18:8 [7]; 68:8–9 [7–8]; 77:19 [18]; Isa. 13:10–13; 24:18–20; Jer. 4:23–26; Ezek. 38:19–20; Amos 8:8–9; Nah. 1:5–6; Hag. 2:7, 21). The Lord appears as the commander of the heavenly host, shouting his orders to his warriors; created order is extinguished and plummets to the starless night of primeval chaos. The work of creation is annulled (Keller, *Joël*, p. 126) as the cosmos convulses in congruence with the divine judgment.

The rhetorical question "who can endure?" implies the obvious answer: no one (cf. Mal. 3:2). The Lord, who had so often fought for Israel, now comes against his own people.

The relationship between the descriptions of the locust plague in chapter 1 and 2:1–11 is one of the major debates in the history of the exegesis of Joel. There are a number of representative positions with intermediate variations, each having advocates both ancient and modern. I will sketch the representative approaches under three categories.

Some interpreters regard chapter 2 as containing simply another description either of the same locust plague or of the outbreak of another historical locust plague in the season following that described in chapter 1. This approach in effect denies the metaphorical character of chapter 2 and argues instead that actual locusts are described as God's army (2:25). A recent representative of this tack is Jack Lewis ("Joel"). No one seriously disputes that locusts are described in 2:1–11, and that the phenomena described there (darkness, noise, invincibility, being driven by the wind into the sea, stench, etc.) reflect the realities of a locust plague. Further, the statement (2:25) that the Lord will repay Judah for the *years* devoured by the locusts may imply more than one outbreak.

Others regard the description in chapter 2 either as a metaphor for an anticipated invasion by a foreign army, one of Israel's traditional foes, or as an allegory for all of Israel's traditional enemies. On this approach a recent locust outbreak (chap. 1) becomes the harbinger of an even greater invasion by a historical foe. The Targum and a marginal gloss in one Septuagint manuscript are representative of this approach (see the Exegesis of 2:25). A

"for"—this term in English is more neutral, that is, not as strongly marked for causality, though it admits of this understanding. נוֹרָא (dreadful): The Septuagint has ἐπιφανὴς (manifest, apparent, revealed), apparently reading the niphal נִרְאָה. This pericope (2:1–11) is set off by the introductory formula "blow a trumpet in Zion," by the concern with the day of the Lord that both begins and ends the section, and by the unified content, a description of a locust army. Keller (Joël, pp. 120–23) suggests that 2:1–11 is arranged in a chiasm; slightly modified from Keller's suggestion, it would look as follows:

> A. The day of the Lord nears (2:1–2a)
> B. Arrival of the army (2:2b)
> C. Ravages of the army: chaos (2:3)
> D. Conduct of the soldiers (2:4–6)
> D´. Conduct of the soldiers (2:7–9)
> C´. Ravages: chaos (2:10)
> B´. Yahweh's army (2:11a)
> A´. The day of the Lord (2:11b)

recent commentator who identifies the foe in 2:1–11 with the Assyrians or Babylonians is Stuart (Hosea–Jonah, pp. 206, 232–34, 250); Stuart also considers the description of the locust plague in chapter 1 to be metaphorical for a historical enemy. The invaders are described as an army on the march; the consequence of their invasion is that the Gentiles rule over Jerusalem (2:17—though see the Exegesis). It is Gentile armies that are judged in chapter 4 [3] (vv. 4–14, 19), and Judah is promised that she will no longer be humiliated before the Gentiles (2:19, 26–27). All recognize some contact between Joel and Exodus 10; the locust plague in Exodus occurred in connection with a victory over the most powerful nation of that period, and victory over some other powerful nation should be expected in connection with Joel. Israel's traditional foes were primarily armies from the north (2:20). Other elements from the exodus events are used by other prophets in reference to Assyria and Babylon (Stuart, Hosea–Jonah, p. 234). Traditional foes of Israel are also described as insects (Isa. 7:18). But other aspects of the text do not fit an actual army very well, for example, the darkening of the sky (2:2) or leaping over the mountains (2:5). It would also be curious to find the locusts likened to an army if an army is what is actually intended, that is, the metaphor is in some sense neutralized by the simile.

The approach adopted in this commentary, and perhaps favored by the majority of modern commentaries, regards the second description of the locust invasion as an extended metaphor based on the locust outbreak described in chapter 1; the prophet uses the recent plague as a harbinger of the impending day of the Lord, the day of judgment when the Lord himself will come at the head of his own heavenly army in holy war against evil. The threat in this case will not come from some particular historical foe, but from the Lord's own army (2:11). This approach is favored by the extensive use of language in 2:1–11 that is most often reserved to describe theophanies. It also preserves the metaphorical character of the language: God's army is often *likened* to human armies. Allen (Joel, p. 64) describes the earlier motifs of the locust plague as "taken up and transposed into a higher key, a more strident setting and a faster pace" in 2:1–11, such that they cannot be reduced to another description of an encounter between Judah and a mass of insects. Further, in the concluding section of the book, the Lord not only promises Judah relief from the effects of the recent locust outbreak, but also freedom from the eschatological day of judgment. All in Israel who call on the name of the Lord will be saved (2:32 [3:5]), and the Lord will be a refuge for his people (4:16 [3:16]), whereas the nations will then face the divine army (4:1–3, 9–15 [3:1–3, 9–15]). The fact that the prophet devotes so much space to his description of the removal of an apocalyptic threat suggests that his second description of a locust army was where this threat was originally introduced.

Each of these approaches and their variations yield reasonably coherent and plausible scenarios for understanding the relation of the two accounts, but it is the opinion of this writer that the last described understanding best accounts for the data and reflects the flow of the argument in the book as a whole. Yet it must also be asked whether the ambiguity regarding the relationship of chapters 1 and 2 felt by modern readers of Joel is the fortuitous product of our not knowing the circumstances of its original composition, or whether such ambiguity is the deliberate product of the author. If Joel is indeed a liturgical text, the very ambiguity within the book would facilitate its use and application in other contexts than that which originally prompted the book, and in this sense could be a deliberate ambiguity.

II. The Day of the Lord: The Impending Disaster (2:1–17)
C. Offer of Repentance (2:12–14)

12 Even now, says the LORD,
　　turn to me with all your heart,
　　with fasting, weeping, and
　　mourning.
13 Rend your hearts, and not your gar-
　　ments,
　　and turn to the LORD your God,
　for he is gracious and compassionate,
　　slow to anger, unfailingly faithful,
　　and he relents from doing harm.
14 Who knows but that he may turn and
　　relent,
　　and leave a blessing behind him,
　　grain offerings and libations for the
　　LORD, your God.

12 Yet even now, says the LORD,
　　return to me with all your heart,
　　with fasting, with weeping, and with
　　mourning;
13 rend your hearts and not your clothing.
　Return to the LORD, your God,
　　for he is gracious and merciful,
　　slow to anger, and abounding in stead-
　　fast love,
　　and relents from punishing.
14 Who knows whether he will not turn
　　and relent,
　　and leave a blessing behind him,
　a grain offering and a drink offering
　　for the LORD, your God?

12. יְהוָה־נְאֻם (says the Lord) is most often found at the introduction of a prophetic oracle. Here it is found on the border of the transition from a description of the divine army (2:1–11) to a prophetic summons to a national lament (2:12–14; see Prinsloo, *Theology of the Book of Joel*, pp. 52–55). It serves to separate 2:1–11 from what follows. The Septuagint adds ὁ θεὸς ὑμῶν (= אֱלֹהֵיכֶם).

13. לְבַבְכֶם קִרְעוּ (rend your hearts): Tearing the garments commonly preceded donning sackcloth in acts of grief and lament. This is the only occasion in the Old Testament where the writer instructs the people to rend their hearts instead of their clothes, that is, no outward act of penance and lament would suffice where an inward change was required. The thrust of the image is similar to the command to circumcise the heart (Deut. 10:16; 30:6; Jer 9:25). כִּי (for) introduces the reason why they should turn to Yahweh. It is because of his character displayed in the sequence of words beginning with חַנּוּן (he is gracious). While this precise sequence of words describing the grace of Yahweh occurs only in one other passage (Jon. 4:2), similar lists of his gracious attributes are common in the Old Testament (Exod. 34:6–7; Num. 14:18; Neh. 9:17; Pss. 86:15; 103:8; 145:8; Nah. 1:3). Joel appears to consciously cite Jonah

4:2 since that passage alone agrees with Joel's list completely and since the context of Jonah 3:9a, 10b is also quoted in Joel 2:14. נִחָם (he relents): Wolff (*Joel and Amos*, p. 49) notes that the presupposition of repentance on God's part is always the repentance of the people in response to the prophetic word, as taught by both Jonah and Joel. What was held up before Israel in the account of Nineveh and Jonah is here proclaimed directly to Jerusalem by Joel. The fact that God is gracious, compassionate, long-suffering, and unfailingly faithful culminates in his "repenting of evil." Many scholars have seen in this list of divine attributes a fragment of a liturgical confession or creed (see Ahlström, *Joel and the Temple Cult*, pp. 23–24). Readers of the Bible are often discomfited by the idea of God's repenting of evil. How does a holy and unchangeable God repent of evil? Clearly this is anthropomorphic language to describe from a human vantage what appears to be God's response to our repentance. Some of the theological difficulty is eased if we translate the phrase הָרָעָה עַל־וְנִחָם by other acceptable equivalents, for example, "relent from the harm, injury [he purposed]" (see Jon. 3:10b).

14. יוֹדֵעַ מִי (who knows): For other occurrences of this question in reference to God, see Jonah

---

12. This verse begins a transition. The prophet's description of the recent disaster (chap. 1) and the threat of an even greater disaster (2:1–11) end, and in their place is an offer of grace and repentance. The same Lord, master of the apocalyptic hosts, takes the initiative in offering and inviting the nation to repentance (Craigie, *Twelve Prophets*, p. 101). The language of verse 12 is in many ways reminiscent of 2 Chronicles 7:14. When Solomon prayed that God would hear the prayer of his people in times of locust outbreaks or other disasters (2 Chron. 6:28), God had responded by promising that "if my people who are called by my name humble themselves, and pray and seek my face, and turn from their wicked ways, then I will hear from heaven, and will forgive their sin and heal their land. Now my eyes will be open and my ears attentive to the prayer that is made in this place" (2 Chron. 7:14–15, RSV). God is keeping his promise to Solomon—the repentant prayer offered in his temple will bring healing for the land.

13. The urgency of repentance is a common theme in the Bible—*now* is the time for a decision (2:12) if one is to escape the decision of God in judgment (4:12, 14 [3:12, 14]). John the Baptist's preaching was similar (Matt. 3:1–12; Luke 3:7–18). In Yahweh's call to "turn to me" (v. 12) we are

reminded that sin always involves a breach of relationship. Repentance must be more than a matter of external ritual compliance; it must be a matter of the heart (Prov. 4:23; 1 John 3:18). The holy God who judges sin is also a God of compassion and mercy (see the Exegesis for other passages that take up this theme—particularly the relationship of these verses to Jon. 4:2).

14. Yet even in the face of repentance, God remains sovereign. Repentance no more controls him than do the magic incantations of pagan priests. Neither the rite nor sincere contrition automatically guarantees the result (Keller, *Joël*, p. 129).

One of the great mysteries of the Book of Joel is the silence of the prophet on the nature of the national sins that prompted the locust plague and the further threats of divine judgment. Though the people are urged to repent, the text is silent regarding the nature of their transgressions; no specific covenant violations are reported as the inciting reasons for the sanctions against the nation. The only sin mentioned in the book is drunkenness, and it appears instead in an illustration of the consequences of the locust outbreak (1:5). This silence may also be explained by the earlier suggestion that the book was originally a

3:9a and 2 Samuel 12:22. Joel appears to be citing the Jonah context (see the Exegesis of v. 13). בְּרָכָה (a blessing) is defined in the second line of the verse: מִנְחָה (grain offerings) and נֶסֶךְ (libations). See also 1:9, 13.

---

liturgical text for a service of national lament; the fact that no specific transgressions are named broadens the number of situations to which this liturgy could be applied.

II. The Day of the Lord: The Impending Disaster (2:1–17)
D. Summons to Fasting and Prayer at the Temple (2:15–17)

15 Blow a trumpet on Zion!
 Proclaim a fast! Call an assembly!
16 Gather the people.
 Proclaim a convocation.
  Summon the elders.
 Gather the children,
  even those who nurse at the breast.
 Let the bridegroom leave his chamber,
  and the bride, her canopy.
17 Let the priests weep between the porch
  and the altar;
   let those who minister to the Lord
   say,
 "Do not make your inheritance a reproach,
  a taunt among the nations.
 Why should they say among the peoples,
  'Where is their God?'"

15 Blow the trumpet in Zion;
  sanctify a fast;
 call a solemn assembly;
16 gather the people.
 Sanctify the congregation;
  assemble the aged;
 gather the children,
  even infants at the breast.
 Let the bridegroom leave his room,
  and the bride her canopy.
17 Between the vestibule and the altar
  let the priests, the ministers of the
  Lord, weep.
 Let them say, "Spare your people, O
  Lord,
  and do not make your heritage a
  mockery,
 a byword among the nations.
 Why should it be said among the peoples,
  'Where is their God?'"

15. תִּקְעוּ (blow) is second-person plural and is probably addressed to the cultic functionaries. שׁוֹפָר (trumpet) is a ram's horn used on a wide variety of occasions in the Old Testament. Trumpets were blown at royal inaugurations (1 Kings 1:34; 2 Kings 11:14 par. 2 Chron. 23:13) as part of raising an army or launching an attack (Num. 10:6–9; Josh. 6:4–13; Judg. 7:18–20; 1 Sam. 13:3; Jer. 51:27; Ezek. 7:14), as part of a cultic procession or to inaugurate religious observances (Num. 10:10; 1 Chron. 15:24, 28; 16:6; 2 Chron. 20:28), and as a warning of an approaching army (Ezek. 33:3, 6; Joel 2:1). Contrast the warning blast in Joel 2:1 with the identical phrase reporting the trumpet blast as a summons to religious observance in 2:15. תִּקְעוּ (blow) is the first of seven imperatives followed by their objects in verses 15–16a. This sequence lends an almost staccato urgency to the prophet's summons, an urgency appropriate to the threat. קַדְּשׁוּ־צוֹם (proclaim a fast!) introduces a statement similar to that of 1:14a. Just as the locust plague of chapter 1 prompted a fast and assembly, so too the threatened day of Yahweh would prompt yet another fast and assembly (see the Exegesis of 1:14).

16. קָהָל (convocation) can be applied to a wide variety of gatherings, but it is predominantly an assembly for religious purposes (Num. 10:7; 20:10; Deut. 9:10; 10:4; 18:16; 2 Chron. 20:5; 30:25; Neh. 5:13). עוֹלָלִים (the children): Biblical Hebrew has a large semantic field for terms designating children at various stages of growth. The precise significance of some of the terms is not clear; some overlap in the ages designated by various terms is certain. The etymology of עוֹלָלִים (children) is dubious. When it occurs opposite בַּחוּרִים (young men; Jer. 6:11; 9:20) or בָּנִים (sons; Ps. 17:14), by contrast it designates small children (perhaps "toddlers" or "boys and girls") as opposed to older children. Its association in this context with יוֹנֵק (nurse, suck) as the second object of a double-duty verb appears to distinguish small children from infants or nursing children (cf. 1 Sam. 15:3; 22:19; Jer. 44:7). חֻפָּה (canopy) evolved in postbiblical Judaism to designate the tentlike temporary structure under which wedding ceremonies were conducted; in the Old Testament itself, however, it appears to refer rather to the room (tent) in which the marriage was consummated (2 Sam. 16:22; Ps. 19:6 [5]; see Allen, *Joel*, p. 76).

17. הַכֹּהֲנִים (the priests): For the priests as "ministers of Yahweh," see the Exegesis of 1:9. חֶרְפָּה (reproach): The Lord's disfavor and judgment are often described in terms of his making Israel or other nations an object of scorn, ridicule, scoffing, horror, mocking, or reproach (Deut. 28:37; 2 Chron. 7:20; 29:8; Pss. 44:14 [13]; 79:4; Jer. 18:16; 19:8; 24:9; 25:9, 18; 29:18; 42:18; 44:8; 48:27; 51:37; Ezek. 5:14–15; 23:32; 36:15; Dan. 9:16; Mic. 6:16). Famine in particular is cause for

---

15. The call to repentance gives way to liturgical instruction (1:14–15). The trumpet that had sounded the alarm for an impending attack (2:1) now summons the people to fasting, prayer, and repentance. This trumpet does not call for mounting the ramparts to defend against an invincible foe, but rather for staffing the temple in a service of national repentance (Allen, *Joel*, p. 67).

16. The law provided that newlywed and betrothed men be exempted from military duty (Deut. 20:7; 24:5), but neither bride nor groom would be exempted from this duty. The consummation of the marriage could wait (Judg. 15:1–2; 2 Sam. 13:10). The Bible also suggests that women with suckling children were exempted from cultic observances (1 Sam. 1:21–24, and possibly 2 Kings 11:2–3), but both mother and child would participate in this service. In singling out both these groups, the prophet is stating the urgency of repentance in the face of the threatened day of the Lord: nothing short of the participation of all the people would suffice. Disaster was uniquely severe for pregnant women and nursing mothers (Matt. 24:19 par. Mark 13:17 par. Luke 21:23; Luke 23:29). A similar summons is found in a Ugaritic text (see Ahlström, *Joel and the Temple Cult*, pp. 56–57).

17. The position of the priests between the porch and the altar (2:17) was essentially a mediatorial position, between the altar where sacrifice was made and the dwelling of God. It was in this place that Zechariah had been killed (2 Chron. 24:21; Matt. 23:35); this was the place where Ezekiel saw the leaders of Israel with their backs turned to the Lord and worshiping the sun (Ezek. 8:16).

The prayer of the priests has two requests: one for mercy for the people and the other that Yahweh act in self-interest to uphold his own glory and might before the nations. Divine self-honor is also appealed to in other contexts (2 Kings 19:34; Pss. 6:6 [5]; 74:18–23; 79:4, 10, 12; 88:12 [11]). For the connection of famine and scorn, see Ezekiel 34:29.

the scorn of the nations (Ezek. 34:29; cf. Joel 2:19). לִמְשָׁל־בָּם גּוֹיִם (a taunt among the nations): The Masoretic Text is translated in the Septuagint as "that the Gentiles should rule over them." If this is correct, it is not synonymous with the preceding line, but rather elaborates upon it; the priests pray that God not make his inheritance a reproach and that, further, he not allow Gentiles to rule over the people. However, the context does not raise the issue of Gentile rule, unless the locust metaphor in 2:1–11 refers to a historical Gentile enemy. In light of the fact that the noun מָשָׁל (proverb, taunt, byword) is occasionally parallel to

חֶרְפָּה (scorn, reproach; cf. Ps. 44:14–15 [13–14]; Jer. 24:9), it may be that the phrase should be repointed so that the priests pray that God not make his inheritance a reproach, and not allow his people to be a byword among the nations. Taking the phrase in this sense also perfects the parallel with the last line of the verse in which the prophet quotes the taunt of the nations ("Where is their God?"). It does, however, also require understanding גּוֹיִם in a syntactically infrequent use as the synonymous antecedent to the pronominal suffix of בָּם (see Wolff, *Joel and Amos*, p. 39; Bewer, *Obadiah and Joel*, p. 118).

III. The Lord's Answer (2:18–4:21) [3:21]
A. To the Immediate Disaster: Locusts (2:18–27)
1. Removal of the Threat (2:18–20)

18 The LORD was jealous for his land;
 he looked with compassion on his
  people.
19 The LORD answered and said to his people,
 Behold, I am sending to you
  the grain, new wine, and fresh oil, and
   you will have enough of them;
 and I will not make you a reproach
  among the nations again.
20 I will remove the northern army far
  from you;
 I will drive it away into a dry and desolate land.
Its advance force will go into the eastern
  sea;
 its rear guard, into the western sea.
Their stench will ascend;
 their smell, arise,
  for they have done great things.

18 Then the LORD became jealous for his
  land,
 and had pity on his people.
19 In response to his people the LORD said:
 I am sending you
  grain, wine, and oil,
  and you will be satisfied;
 and I will no more make you
  a mockery among the nations.
20 I will remove the northern army far
  from you,
 and drive it into a parched and desolate land,
 its front into the eastern sea,
  and its rear into the western sea;
 its stench and foul smell will rise up.
  Surely he has done great things!

18. וַיְקַנֵּא (was jealous): Jealousy is an attribute of God (Exod. 20:5; 34:14; Deut. 4:24; 5:9; 6:15; 32:16, 21; Josh. 24:19; Ps. 79:5; Ezek. 16:38, 42; 23:25; 36:6; Nah. 1:2; Zeph. 1:18; Zech. 1:14; 8:2; 1 Cor. 10:22). There is a significant difficulty with the sequence of tenses in 2:15–18. At some point, at least by verse 19, there is a transition from instructions about the ritual lament to narration. Theodotion has ζηλώσει . . . φείσεται, taking the two verbs as jussives with a single conjunction, thereby joining verse 18 to the prayer of verse 17 (see Wolff, *Joel and Amos*, p. 57). The pointing in the Masoretic Text marks this transition to narration here at the beginning of verse 18 (note the transition to *waw*-consecutives with the imperfect). Bewer (*Obadiah and Joel*, pp. 107–9) argues that the imperatives in verses 15–17 should be repointed as perfects, and thus the narration should begin in verse 15; this would ease what he considers an abrupt transition if the narrative were begun in either verse 17 or verse 18. Others have also repointed the *waw*-consecutives in verse 18 to read as jussives with a conjunction, so that the material in verse 18 continues the content of the prayer of the priests in verse 17, that is, "may the Lord be jealous . . . , and may he have mercy." The Masoretic Text is acceptable as it stands, however. Scholars who feel the need to ease the abrupt transition from liturgical instruction and prayer to the narrative introducing the salvation oracle (v. 18) need also to account for the same abrupt transition from complaint to salvation oracle in other psalms of communal lament (e.g., Pss. 12:6 [5]; 60:8 [6]; 85:9 [8]). The structure as it is in the Masoretic Text pointing reflects precisely that same abrupt shift from complaint to salvation oracle as in the psalms of communal lament. Note also the indication of a transition in the change from address to Yahweh (second-person, v. 17) to speaking of him (third-person, v. 18; see Prinsloo, *Theology of the Book of Joel*, p. 65).

19. הַדָּגָן וְהַתִּירוֹשׁ וְהַיִּצְהָר (the grain, new wine, and fresh oil): These three commodities represent the agricultural produce of three distinct types of vegetation: grasses, bushes, and trees. Grain, wine, and oil occur together here, in 1:10 and 2:24, and in numerous other passages (Lev. 23:13; Num. 18:12; Deut. 7:13; 11:14; 12:17; 14:23; 18:4; 28:51; 2 Chron. 31:5; 32:28; Neh. 5:11; 10:37, 39; 13:5, 12; Jer. 31:12; Hos. 2:10 [8], 24 [22]; Hag. 1:11; see the Exegesis of 1:10). חֶרְפָּה (reproach): See the Exegesis of 2:17.

20. הַצְּפוֹנִי (the northern army, lit. the northerner): In Canaanite mythology the north was the home of the gods; the Bible contains similar allusions to the divine abode (Job 37:22; Ps. 48:3 [2]; Ezek. 1:4). The king of Babylon boasted that he would sit in the northern assembly (Isa. 14:12–13). It is striking that the temple in Jerusalem was also on the north side of the city. Alongside this imag-

---

18. This verse marks the transition to the second half of the book. To this point the prophet has described the devastation of a recent locust outbreak (chap. 1), an even greater apocalyptic threat (2:1–11), and the service of repentance in the temple (2:12–17). Now we hear the response of Yahweh to the people's lament. Just as there had been two threats, one present and the other future, so there are two elements in the divine response: the present crisis will be removed (2:18–27), and the future will bring blessing for Judah (3:1–5 [2:28–32]; 4:17–21 [3:17–21]) and judgment for her enemies (4:1–16 [3:1–16]). As with other laments, the prayer of the people is answered in an oracle of salvation (2 Chron. 20:15–17; Pss. 12:6 [5]; 60:8 [6]; 85:9 [8]).

19. The national prayer as expressed by the priests had two elements (2:17), and the response addresses both (2:19): mercy for the people in the reversal of calamity, and Yahweh's acting to uphold his own honor before the nations. In the midst of their suffering, God remembers his covenant and brings relief (Gen. 8:1; 2 Chron. 36:20–23). It is striking—with the concern expressed in the book about the lack of grain offerings and libations for the temple (1:9, 13; 2:14)—that when the Lord restores the crops his expressed object is that his people will have their fill (2:19); the temple is not mentioned.

The recovery from the locusts and the restoration of prosperity are harbingers of an even greater day to come; where the locusts had been harbingers of an even greater disaster, recovery is a foretaste of an even greater blessing (4:18 [3:18]).

20. The "northerner" is another example of almost studied ambiguity in Joel: it could apply equally well to the locusts, to Israel's historical enemies, or to an apocalyptic foe (see the Exegesis).

The direction of locust migrations is primarily determined by the wind, an influence noted also in Exodus 10:19. Verse 20 embraces all points of the compass: the northerner, the eastern and western seas, and the south ("a dry and desolate land") (see Dahood, "Four Cardinal Points"). A similar image of judgment is used in Zechariah

ery of the north as the site of the divine abode, the Bible also uses the "land of the north" as a way of designating Israel's great historical enemies who came primarily from that direction (Assyria, Babylon, Persia—Isa. 41:25; Jer. 1:13–15; 4:6; 6:22; 10:22; 13:20; 15:12; 25:9, 26; 46:10, 20, 24; 50:3, 9, 41; Ezek. 26:7; 38:6, 15; 39:2; Dan. 11; Zech. 2:6; 6:6–8); other descriptions of Israel's traditional enemies should be included in this list, even though the term *north* is not specifically connected with them (Isa. 5:26–29; 13:1–13; Nah. 2:2–10; 3:1–3; Hab. 1:5–11). While the references to the enemy from the north in the preexilic period are primarily to historical enemies, in the later literature the enemy from the north increasingly takes on a "trans-historical, apocalyptic coloring" (Childs, "Enemy from the North," p. 195), so that the enemy is ascribed superhuman characteristics and is associated with the chaos motif. Verse 20 describes part of the return to order from chaos, the return to Eden from desolation. Perhaps we are to think here that the two motifs have been fused: the apocalyptic army, the army of Yahweh, comes from the site of the divine abode (see Ahlström, *Joel and the Temple Cult*, pp. 32–34). וּשְׁמָמָה (desolate): The Septuagint has καὶ ἀφανιῶ (and I

will render invisible), which appears to translate וּשְׁמָמָה as a verb form; this seems a more probable explanation than Wolff's suggestion (*Joel and Amos*, p. 54) that the Septuagint does not translate the word. צַחֲנָתוֹ (stench) is a *hapax legomenon*, but does occur in Aramaic and postbiblical Hebrew. כִּי הִגְדִּיל לַעֲשׂוֹת (for they have done great things): This clause appears to refer to the northern army, saying that it had done great things. It is tempting to see the entire clause as an erroneous doublet or gloss from 2:21b where it refers less problematically to Yahweh, but there is no support from textual tradition for this change (see Wolff, *Joel and Amos*, p. 55). The extensive use of repetition in Joel (see Thompson, "Repetition in the Prophecy of Joel") also makes excision on conjectural grounds improbable; the repetition serves to reinforce both the parallels and the contrast between Yahweh and the locusts. For other examples of verbs repeated with a different subject for contrast, see 2:13–14 (return), 21–23 (rejoice and be glad); 3:5 [2:32] (call); 4:6–8 [3:6–8] (sell). The Targum adds בִּישׁ ([he has done] evil things), clearly assigning the clause to the northern army and not Yahweh (Stuart, *Hosea–Jonah*, p. 256).

2:6. Large locust swarms have been encountered as much as twelve hundred miles at sea (Hubbell, "Locust," p. 282).

Many observers have also noted the stench from the putrefaction of the millions of locust bodies when a swarm dies. Contaminants from this decay easily entered water supplies, so that pestilence and disease epidemics came also to be associated with locust outbreaks in antiquity. In *The City of God* (3.31), Augustine remarks that

when Africa was a Roman province it was attacked by an immense number of locusts. Having eaten everything, leaves and fruits, a huge and formidable swarm of them were drowned in the sea. Thrown up dead upon the coast, the putrefaction of these insects so infected the air as to cause a pestilence so horrible that in the Kingdom of Masinis-

sa alone 800,000 and more are said to have perished. Of 30,000 soldiers in Utique, only 10,000 remained.

The bodies of drowned locusts have on a number of occasions been observed piled three to four feet high on the coasts around the Red Sea (Baron, *Desert Locust*, p. 4). A similar stench has been noted on many battlefields.

Since the northerner in this context appears to refer not only to the removal of the locusts, but also to the removal of that apocalyptic army, the sea in this context evokes imagery of primeval chaos. The sea, which mythologically stood opposed to Yahweh and created order, becomes the receptacle for the corpses of his foes. Yahweh, who led the attack, has become the Defender and Redeemer of his people.

III. The Lord's Answer (2:18–4:21) [3:21]
A. To the Immediate Disaster: Locusts (2:18–27)
2. Healing of the Land (2:21–24)

21 Do not fear, O land!
　　Rejoice and be glad,
　　for the LORD has done great things.
22 Do not fear, O wild animals,
　　for the pastures will become green,
　　trees will bear their fruit,
　　　the fig and the vine will yield their
　　　wealth.
23 The children of Zion will rejoice;
　　they will be glad in the LORD their
　　God.
　　He will give them the early rains for vin-
　　dication;
　　　he will cause the rain to fall upon
　　　them,
　　　　the former rain and the latter
　　　　rain as before.
24 The threshing floors will be full of
　　grain;
　　　the vats will overflow with wine and
　　　oil.

21 Do not fear, O soil;
　　be glad and rejoice,
　　for the LORD has done great things!
22 Do not fear, you animals of the field,
　　for the pastures of the wilderness are
　　　green;
　　the tree bears its fruit,
　　　the fig tree and vine give their full
　　　yield.
23 O children of Zion, be glad
　　and rejoice in the LORD your God;
　　for he has given the early rain for your
　　vindication,
　　　he has poured down for you abundant
　　　rain,
　　　the early and the later rain, as before.
24 The threshing floors shall be full of
　　grain,
　　　the vats shall overflow with wine and
　　　oil.

21. גִּילִי . . . אַל־תִּירְאִי (do not fear . . . rejoice): Note the compositional technique: the admonitions not to fear and to rejoice move from the land (v. 21), to the animals (v. 22), to humankind (v. 23). The order is from periphery to center (Ahlström, *Joel and the Temple Cult*, pp. 6–7), inanimate to animate to human.

22. אַל־תִּירְאוּ בַּהֲמוֹת שָׂדַי (do not fear, O wild animals): The second-person masculine imperative is occasionally used with a feminine subject (בְּהֵמָה, animal) before the subject is mentioned; that is, the masculine plural is a common or zero form (cf. Ruth 1:8b and Amos 4:1; see Joüon §150a, and Wolff, *Joel and Amos*, p. 55). חֵילָם (their wealth): חַיִל ordinarily connotes strength, power, but is used here metaphorically for "produce." The Targum has פֵּירֵיהוֹן (their fruit).

23. הַמּוֹרֶה לִצְדָקָה (the early rains for vindication): There is a potential ambiguity in this phrase and יֹרֶה צֶדֶק (Hos. 10:12). Both מוֹרֶה and יֹרֶה can derive from verbs or nouns meaning either "teacher, teach," or "rain." This ambiguity is the reason why these two passages may be the origin or legitimation of the important figure at Qumran, the מוֹרֵה הַצֶּדֶק (teacher of righteousness). At Qumran the teacher of righteousness was either the founder of the community or that individual whose interpretation of Torah became normative among them, the definitive interpreter of Scripture for the Qumran sectarians. An extensive scholarly literature is devoted to identifying this individual and his functions (see Ahlström, "*Hammōreh liṣdāqāh* in Joel 2:23"; Jeremias, *Der Lehrer der Gerechtigkeit*; Michel, *Le Maître de justice*; Rabinowitz, "Guides of Righteousness"; Roth, "Teacher of Righteousness and the Prophecy of Joel"; Sellers, "Possible Old Testament Reference to the Teacher of Righteousness"; Thiering, *Redating the Teacher of Righteousness*; Van der Meiden, "De Vertaling van het woord מוֹרֶה in Joel 2:23"; Weingreen, "Title Môrēh Ṣedeḳ"). A personal interpretation of the phrase is found in the Targum (מַלְפֵיכוֹן בְּדֵכוּ), Vulgate (*doctorem iustitiae*), and Symmachus (τὸν ὑποδεικνύοντα). Rabbinic teaching did associate teaching and rain

(see Wolff, *Joel and Amos*, p. 55; Ahlström, *Joel and the Temple Cult*, pp. 98–110). In spite of the considerable debate surrounding the teacher of righteousness at Qumran and the relationship of that individual/institution to Joel 2:23, the concern in the immediate context with the return of precipitation and the reversal of drought would appear to favor heavily the conclusion that in this verse the prophet is referring to rain. מוֹרֶה is parallel in this verse to three other terms for rain in the next line. Nevertheless, a number of scholars have continued to maintain an individual/messianic interpretation of the phrase into the present time (see the summary in Allen, *Joel*, pp. 92–93). It is not impossible that the prophet is deliberately invoking an ambiguity. In line with frequent allusions to other prophetic literature, the prophet contemplates not only an end to the immediate famine, but also an end to the famine of hearing the word of God (Amos 8:11; cf. Joel 3:1–5 [2:28–32]). The individual/messianic interpretation of the verse is of great antiquity. For מוֹרֶה (the early rains), the Septuagint (τὰ βρώματα), Old Latin (*escas*), and Syriac (*mᵉkwltᵉ*) appear to depend on the reading בְּרִיָה (food). לִצְדָקָה (for vindication) also admits of several translations: "prosperity" (Prov. 8:18), "vindication" (in the sense of salvation or deliverance), or "righteousness" (in the sense of a reward for ethical rightness). The context does not provide clear indications in this instance. גֶּשֶׁם (rain) is the general term for rainfall. בָּרִאשׁוֹן (as before; lit. in the first) is ordinarily used in the sense of in the first month (Gen. 8:13; Exod. 12:18; Num. 9:5; Ezek. 29:17; 30:20; 45:18, 21); however, in all these instances the phrase is part of a date notation that includes day numbers. The Targum (בְּיֶרַח נִיסָן) explicitly interprets and translates it as "in the month Nisan," which creates a significant difficulty: מוֹרֶה (former rain) begins to fall in October/November, whereas the first month, Nisan, is March/April (Jones, *Isaiah 56–66 and Joel*, p. 169). The Septuagint (καθὼς ἔμπροσθεν) appears to reflect either כְּרִאשׁוֹן or כְּבָרִאשׁוֹן, which provides the best sense for the passage (compare the Vulgate and Syriac versions). The verse com-

---

21–23. Three areas had been affected by the locust outbreak and accompanying drought: the land, animals, and humankind (1:16–20). Now all three are mentioned again in the reversal of the recent plague. Where joy and gladness had once perished (1:16), they are restored. God's withholding of rain and dew was understood as a covenant sanction (Lev. 26:18–20; Deut. 28:23–24), whereas

his sending it afresh was a sign of blessing and a right relationship between Israel and her God (Lev. 26:3–4; Deut. 11:13–14).

24. Israel would yet be God's garden again, and in an even richer sense in the future (4:18 [3:18]). The threshing floors and vats (2:24) would overflow yet once again—when God judged the nations (4:13 [3:13]).

pounds the terms for rain. מוֹרֶה (former rain) and וְשֶׁ מַלְק (latter rain) form a merism for the rainy season (Allen, *Joel*, p. 93). The former rains come in October/November and soften the ground to facilitate plowing and germination, whereas the latter rains occur in March/April and swell the crop before harvest; the timing or failure of either of these rains could spell disaster for the Israelite farmer (Deut. 11:13–17).

24. בָּר (grain) is the clean grain after winnowing (Jer. 23:28; see Borowski, *Agriculture in Iron Age Israel*, pp. 67–68, 89). הַיְקָבִים (the vats): Archeological finds show at least three different types of presses; Borowski (*Agriculture in Iron Age Israel*, p. 111) associates three biblical terms with these three types of structure: (1) the press hewn into rock (יֶקֶב—here), (2) a press built of stone and mortar within a city (גַּת—see 4:13 [3:13]), and (3) a portable stone press (פּוּרָה). Verses 21–24 have been variously identified as a cultic hymn (Allen, *Joel*,

p. 90), an assurance oracle answering a plea (Wolff, *Joel and Amos*, p. 58), or an exhortation to praise (Jones, *Isaiah 56–66 and Joel*, p. 167; cf. Prinsloo, *Theology of the Book of Joel*, pp. 71–72). Such diversity is evidence that form-critical genre identifications are not always hard and fast, but admit of some fluidity. Clearly the prophet is exhorting people and creation to praise God, and is providing assurance of divine blessing. Bewer (*Obadiah and Joel*, pp. 113–14), in a stance far more characteristic of an older stage of critical scholarship, argues that verses 21–27 are in an incorrect position since they interrupt the speech of Yahweh. He reconstructs the order of the passage as 2:20, 25–26a, 21–24; he also identifies verses 26b–27 as a later gloss. These are entirely conjectural suggestions. See the Exegesis of 2:15–17, and compare the abrupt transition from divine oracle to praise in Psalm 12:8–9 [7–8]; 85:11–14 [10–13].

III. The Lord's Answer (2:18–4:21) [3:21]
A. To the Immediate Disaster: Locusts (2:18–27)
3. Restoration of Prosperity (2:25–27)

25 I will repay you for the years that the locust devoured—
the hopper, the leaping locust, and
the flying locust,
my great army that I sent against you.
26 You will have food and have your fill;
you will praise the name of the LORD
your God,
who has done wondrous
things for you,
and my people will not be put to shame
again.
27 You will know that I am in the midst of
Israel;
I am the LORD your God, and there is
no other,
and my people will not be put to shame
again.

25 I will repay you for the years
that the swarming locust has eaten,
the hopper, the destroyer, and the cutter,
my great army, which I sent against
you.
26 You shall eat in plenty and be satisfied,
and praise the name of the LORD your
God,
who has dealt wondrously with you.
And my people shall never again be put
to shame.
27 You shall know that I am in the midst
of Israel,
and that I, the LORD, am your God and
there is no other.
And my people shall never again
be put to shame.

25. הַשָּׁנִים (the years). Many have suggested repointing this word as הַשְּׁנַיִם (two, double), that is, "I will repay you double for what the locusts have eaten" (Isa. 61:7; Jer. 16:18; 17:18; Zech. 9:12). However, these other passages use מִשְׁנֶה. Where the term שָׁנִים is used in this idiom, it is without the article and the direct object marker (Exod. 22:3, 6, 8 [22:4, 7, 9]), suggesting that the Masoretic Text's pointing is correct. A locust outbreak in one year carries with it diminished harvests in the following year as well. הָאַרְבֶּה (the locust): For the significance of this and the other terms for locusts, see the Exegesis of 1:4. The order of terms in this passage is different from the earlier occurrence of these terms. While the order in 1:4 may reflect the historical sequence in which the successive stages appeared in Jerusalem, the order in 2:25 reflects the life-cycle order. Wolff (*Joel and Amos*, p. 55) suggests that the change in order of the terms shows that originally only the familiar term for locust was used here, and that the other terms reflect secondary expansions; however, this argument cuts both ways—one could argue that a secondary expansion would far more probably pedantically reflect the original order. The Targum provides an interpretation of the terms for locust in this instance; the locusts are, respectively, "peoples, tongues, governments, and kingdoms." This line of interpretation is even more specific in manuscript Q of the Septuagint, which has a gloss that reads "Egyptians, Babylonians, Assyrians, Greeks, Romans." Here the interpretive question regarding the locust metaphor is settled: the locusts represent a series of historical powers. These translations, of course, have no value for textual criticism, but are of interest for the history of interpretation. חֵילִי (army) occurs with this sense also in 2:11.

26. לֹא־יֵבֹשׁוּ (not be put to shame): This phrase appears again at the end of the next verse. It is an obvious possibility to suggest that this initial occurrence is an intrusive, erroneous repetition or gloss (see Wolff, *Joel and Amos*, p. 56). Thompson ("Repetition in the Prophecy of Joel") concludes that the extensive repetition in Joel is part of a conscious literary art, and in particular that the double occurrence of this phrase in these verses represents epiphora, a rhetorical signal closing a section of the text; compare the repetition of the phrase *fire has consumed the grazing lands in the wilderness* in 1:19–20. The personal shame felt by farmers (1:11–12) became national shame before the day of the Lord (2:17)—both sorts of shame are relieved.

27. וִידַעְתֶּם כִּי בְקֶרֶב יִשְׂרָאֵל אָנִי (you will know that I am in the midst of Israel): This is a variation of "you will know that I am the Lord," the more common "recognition formula." Here fulfilment of prophetic word accredits not only the prophet, but also the Lord he represents. The recognition formula is preceded almost without exception in the Old Testament by a reference to some act of Yahweh (Zimmerli, *Erkenntnis Gottes nach dem Buche Ezechiel*, p. 40; Prinsloo, *Theology of the Book of Joel*, pp. 74–75).

25–26. For the locust vocabulary, see the Exegesis of 1:4 and 2:25. Once again the prophet reports no concern on the part of God about the meal offerings and libations in the temple; God is concerned, rather, that his people have plenty (see the Exposition of 2:18–20).

27. Among the things the nation was to learn from these events was that Yahweh was in their midst, and that there was *none other*. Idolatry is not mentioned as a problem in Israel in the Book of Joel, though the nation did have a long track record of looking to the baals for fecundity and rain. The central demand of the covenant for exclusive loyalty to Yahweh alone is reiterated once again; loyalty and worship are due him because of his mighty deeds in saving Israel yet again and because of his compassion and mercy.

God acts to accredit himself—just as the fulfilment of prophecy accredited his messengers the prophets (Deut. 18:21–22), so his bringing to pass that which he had promised was a way in which the people would know he was God in their midst (2:27). The idols could not do this (Isa. 41:23–28; 43:8–13). As surely as the locust plague would end, so too his people would no longer be put to shame (2:17, 27; 4:17 [3:17]).

It is an oft-demonstrated biblical principle that those whom God loves, he chastens. Here the chastening of Judah has borne its harvest of righteousness and peace (Heb. 12:11) in renewed prosperity, renewed worship, and a renewed knowledge of God.

III. The Lord's Answer (2:18–4:21) [3:21]
B. To the Impending Disaster: The Day of the Lord (3:1–4:21) [2:28–3:21]
1. Salvation for Israel (3:1–5) [2:28–32]
a. All to Be Prophets (3:1–2) [2:28–29]

3 And it will come to pass after these things
that I will pour out my spirit on all flesh;
your sons and daughters will prophesy.
Your old men will dream dreams,
and your young men will see visions.
2 Also on slaves and slave girls
in those days will I pour out my spirit.

28 Then afterward
I will pour out my spirit on all flesh;
your sons and your daughters shall prophesy,
your old men shall dream dreams,
and your young men shall see visions.
29 Even on the male and female slaves,
in those days, I will pour out my spirit.

3:1 [2:28]. אַחֲרֵי־כֵן (after these things; lit. after this) seems unambiguously to signify temporal sequence (e.g., 2 Chron. 20:35; Jer. 16:16; 34:11). Joel has presented two threats: the immediate threat (chap. 1) and the apocalyptic threat (2:1-11). The prophet has given the Lord's answer to the immediate threat (2:18-27), and now turns to the apocalyptic threat and events in the future (3:1-4:21 [2:28-3:21]). W. VanGemeren ("Spirit of Restoration") argues instead that the phrase is not to be understood sequentially, but simply as a transition to an explication of 2:27, so that the era of blessing recorded in 2:18-27 and 3:1-5 [2:28-32] overlap, and the blessings spoken of in 2:18-27 are not fulfilled until Pentecost. While the hyperbolic language of 2:18-27 clearly points beyond itself in

an ultimate sense, as the prophet himself understood (4:17-18 [3:17-18]), it is hard to escape the fact that the prophet intends his readers to understand 3:1-5 [2:28-32] as sequential to 2:18-27. Note that Acts 2:17 has ἐν ταῖς ἐσχάταις ἡμέραις (in the end of time) instead of the Septuagintal reading of μετὰ ταῦτα (after this). אֶשְׁפּוֹךְ אֶת־רוּחִי (I will pour out my spirit): The Spirit of God is commonly associated with water in the Bible, and the means of investiture is often associated with pouring (Isa. 44:3; Ezek. 39:29; Zech. 12:10; cf. Acts 2:17-18). This imagery is critical to apprehending the New Testament understanding of baptism (see Manns, *Le Symbole eau-esprit dans le Judaïsme ancien*, pp. 53-56). וְנִבְּאוּ (will prophesy): In the Old Testament, the Spirit of God is

---

3:1-2 [2:28-29]. The prophet has described the immediate threat (chap. 1) and an apocalyptic threat (2:1-11). He has given the Lord's answer of recovery and deliverance to the immediate disaster caused by the locusts (2:18-27). He now turns to the issue of the apocalyptic threat. In dealing with the threatened day of the Lord and the future, the prophet distinguishes between the fate of Judah (3:1-5 [2:28-32]) and the Gentiles (4:1-17 [3:1-17]). For Zion, the day of Yahweh will become a day of salvation and vindication, whereas the nations will face the full fury of Yahweh in holy war.

This most famous oracle from Joel is also tied to its context in several other ways. The theme of "pouring out" in effect elaborates on the concern of the preceding context with a drought; the drought will be overcome in undreamed of ways. Judah will not only have water, but living water in the Spirit of God (see the comments on Amos 8:11 below). Joel's use of the "recognition formula" in 2:27 invokes the fulfilment of prophecy as an authentication of Joel's message and of God's acts; from this introduction of prophetic fulfilment, Joel goes on to describe a day when all Israel will have the prophetic gift.

While it is important to see the place and function of 3:1-5 [2:28-32] in the Book of Joel itself, it is also important to view it in its largest canonical context. Particularly in 3:1-2 [2:28-29] the prophet appears to be drawing on two events narrated in Numbers 11:1-12:8. Moses' desire for relief from his burden prompts God to send his Spirit on seventy elders. This outpouring is confirmed by their subsequent possession behavior and ecstatic speech. Eldad and Medad, though physically isolated from the larger group by their

being in the camp, also show the same evidence of enduement by God's Spirit. Joshua's objection prompts the response of Moses: "Would that all the LORD's people were prophets, and that the LORD would put his spirit on them!" (Num. 11:29, RSV). In the incident that follows, perhaps prompted by their jealousy at this shared authority, Aaron and Miriam become critical of Moses (Num. 12:1-8). While Deuteronomy 18 emphasizes the continuity between Moses and the prophets, Numbers 12 emphasizes the discontinuity: God spoke with Moses face-to-face and clearly, but with the prophets he speaks in dreams and visions.

Joel appears to be reflecting on this earlier narrative. God is going to answer Moses' prayer. He will pour out his Spirit on all Israel, and all Yahweh's people will become prophets. Key vocabulary from Numbers 11-12 is repeated: God's people will prophesy (Num. 11:25-29; Joel 3:1 [2:28]); the revelatory means that characterize prophets (dream and vision—Num. 12:6) will characterize all (Joel 3:1 [2:28]). The Spirit will possess "young men" (*baḥûrîm*—Joel 3:1 [2:28]; Num. 11:28). Possession by God's Spirit will not be the privilege of the few, but the experience of all (Num. 11:25; 12:6; Joel 3:1 [2:28]). The issue of the extent of shared prophetic authority unites Numbers 11-12, and it is the issue addressed by Joel. Other motifs unite the passages as well. In both, the lack of food is cause for complaint or lament (Num. 11:4-6, 18-23, 31-34; Joel 1-2). The removal of the famine of food is accompanied by the Spirit's effusion; one cannot but wonder if Joel is not also drawing an image from Amos 8:11, so that the end of a famine is also an end of the famine of hearing the word of God. Both contexts also reflect a judi-

preeminently the spirit of prophecy. Possession by the Spirit in the Old Testament is the means of prophetic enduement. (For the association of spirit and prophecy, see Num. 11:25–29; 1 Sam. 10:6–10; 18:10; 19:20–23; 1 Kings 22:22–23 par. 2 Chron. 18:21–22; 2 Kings 2:15; Neh. 9:30; Ezek. 13:3; Zech. 7:12; 13:2.) The Targum adds a term making the reference to the Spirit more explicit: רוּחַ קֻדְשִׁי (my holy Spirit). The Septuagint appears to show the influence of Numbers 11:17, 25 (Wolff, *Joel and Amos*, p. 56): ἀπὸ τοῦ πνεύματός μου (portions of my spirit); contrast τὸ πνεῦμά μου in Aquila and Symmachus, which agrees with the Masoretic Text. זְקֵנֵיכֶם (your old men): While the elders are referred to elsewhere in Joel 1:2, 14; 2:16) apparently in their more official capacity as

city leaders, here, by virtue of the contrast with young men, the focus is rather on age. חֲלֹמוֹת יַחֲלֹמוּן (will dream dreams): The prophet appears to be drawing from Numbers 11:24–12:8 (cf. the Exposition). Two of the means of prophetic revelation specified in Numbers 12:6 are vision (מַרְאָה) and dream (חֲלוֹם); so too in 3:1, dream and vision are the means of prophetic revelation. (For dreams as a mode of prophetic revelation, see Deut. 13:2–6 [1–5]; 1 Sam. 28:6, 15; Jer. 23:25, 28, 32; 27:9; 29:8; for visions, see 2 Chron. 9:29; 32:32; Isa. 28:7; 30:10; Jer. 14:14; 23:16; Lam. 2:9, 14; Ezek. 7:26; 12:27; 13:9, 16; 22:28; Dan. 9:24; Hos. 12:10; Mic. 3:6; Zech. 13:4.) בַּחוּרֵיכֶם (your young men): This term also evokes an association with Numbers 11:28.

---

cial function in the possession of the Spirit. Moses' surrogates would serve as judges (Num. 11:17; cf. Exod. 18:13–27); the eschatological outpouring of God's Spirit is conjoined with the Lord's coming in judgment on the nations (Joel 3:4 [2:31]; 4:12, 14 [3:12, 14]).

It is important that the modern reader not miss the radical character of what Joel announces. In the world of ancient Israel, the free, older Jewish male stood at the top of the social structure; most of Israel's prophets had belonged to this group. Joel envisages a sociological overhaul: the distinctions between old and young ("your old men . . . your young men"), slave and free ("slaves and slave girls"), and male and female ("your sons and daughters," "slaves [masc.] and slave girls") are swept aside. This statement from Joel must be contrasted with the ancient daybreak prayer of the Jewish male: "I thank you God that I was not born a Gentile, a slave, or a woman."

The New Testament, of course, understands the phenomena of Pentecost as the fulfilment of Joel's prophecy (Acts 2:14–21). There the outpouring of the Lord's Spirit induced possession behavior that characterized the experience of Israel's prophets (Num. 11:25). This "ecstatic" behavior resembled drunkenness (Acts 2:13), a theme already touched on in Joel (1:5), and a sentiment also expressed by Jeremiah (Jer. 23:9; cf. 1 Sam. 1:13–14; Eph. 5:18). Protestant theology is accustomed to speaking of the "priesthood of all believers"; perhaps in light of Acts 2 and Joel 3:1–5 [2:28–32]), we must also speak of the "prophethood of all believers." The coming of the Spirit at Pentecost inaugurated a new age, the age when Moses' prayer is realized and all God's people are endued with the Spirit of prophecy. The possession of the Spirit would

never again be the restricted preserve of a few; all who call on the name of the Lord (3:5 [2:32]) now have the equippage and the obligation incumbent upon prophets to bear witness to their generation. This enduement with the Spirit of prophecy belongs to the general office of the church—rich and poor, young and old, male and female; the privilege of proclaiming God's truth to a waiting world is not the province of the special office alone.

There can be little doubt in this context that Joel intends *all flesh* to refer to Israel alone—the phrase *all flesh* is explicated as *your* sons and daughters, slaves, young and old; the fortunes of Judah are contrasted to those of the Gentiles (4:1–17 [3:1–17]). Yet Paul understands that Joel spoke better than he knew. In Christ that greatest barrier of all was destroyed—the barrier between Jew and Gentile (Rom. 10:12). Paul applies Joel's oracle to the true Israel, the elect Israel and not simply Israel according to the flesh (Rom. 9:6–15). Those who call on the Lord are those whom the Lord has called (3:5 [2:32]), both Jew and Gentile.

It may well be that Paul also has Joel's prophecy in mind in Galatians 3:27–28. In using an argument from baptism, Paul brings us immediately into the motific realm of the outpouring of God's Spirit. One significance of baptism is that all who are baptized into Christ have "put on" Christ. This use of *endyō* ("clothe, dress") recalls the usage of *lābēš* ("clothe") to describe prophetic investment by the Spirit in the Old Testament (Judg. 6:34; 1 Chron. 12:19 [18]; 2 Chron. 24:20). Paul sees the significance of baptism into Christ as meaning that in Christ all are one—no distinction should be made between Jew and Gentile, slave and free, male and female.

2 [2:29]. הַשְּׁפָחוֹת (slave girls): Of the two terms for a female slave in Hebrew (אָמָה, שִׁפְחָה), שִׁפְחָה appears to designate a female worker less closely assimilated to the employing family than the אָמָה (contrast Ruth 2:13; 3:9). This further enhances the breadth and inclusiveness of Joel's vision of the outpoured Spirit. Acts 2:18 appears to follow Septuagint texts which insert μου twice: "my servants, my servant girls." אֶשְׁפּוֹךְ אֶת־רוּחִי (will I pour out my Spirit): This phrase forms an inclusio around verses 1–2.

In the New Testament one commonly thinks of the portrayal of God's Spirit in the Johannine material as the Comforter and as the agent in regeneration; in the Pauline corpus, the Spirit is preeminently the Spirit of the coming age already inaugurated in the work of Christ. It is primarily in Luke-Acts that we encounter the preeminent portrayal of the Spirit of God as the Spirit of prophecy. Luke presents God's Spirit: (1) as enabling the preaching and teaching of John the Baptist, Jesus, and the early church (Luke 1:15, 17, 67; 2:25–27; 3:16, 22; 4:1, 14, 18; 12:10–12; Acts 1:2, 8; 2:4–38; 6:5, 10; 7:51–55; 15:32; 19:6); (2) as providing instruction and revelation about the future (Luke 1:39–45, 67; Acts 10:19; 13:4; 21:10–11); and (3) as empowering miracles (Luke 10:21; 11:13; Acts 10:38). With such pervasive interest in the Spirit and prophecy, it is not surprising to find Joel 3:1–5 [2:28–32] developed within Luke's writings.

III. The Lord's Answer (2:18–4:21) [3:21]
B. To the Impending Disaster: The Day of the Lord (3:1–4:21) [2:28–3:21]
1. Salvation for Israel (3:1–5) [2:28–32]
b. Deliverance for the Remnant (3:3–5) [2:30–32]

³ I will place signs in the heavens,
    and on the earth, there will be blood
    and fire and columns of smoke.
⁴ The sun will be turned to darkness,
    and the moon to blood
before the coming of the day of the Lord,
    that great and dreadful day.
⁵ And it will be that all who call on the
    name of the Lord will be saved,
for on Mount Zion and in Jerusalem
    there will be an escape,
    as the Lord has said,
among the survivors whom the Lord
    calls.

³⁰ I will show portents in the heavens
    and on the earth, blood and fire and
    columns of smoke.
³¹ The sun shall be turned to darkness,
    and the moon to blood,
before the great and terrible day of the
    Lord comes.
³² Then everyone who calls on the name
    of the Lord shall be saved;
    for in Mount Zion and in Jerusalem
    there shall be those who escape, as
    the Lord has said,
    and among the survivors shall be
    those whom the Lord calls.

3 [2:30]. וָאֵשׁ דָּם (blood and fire): These two are commonly joined in images of judgment (Isa. 9:5; Ezek. 21:32; Rev. 8:7). תִּימְרוֹת (columns) appears to derive from תָּמָר (date palm); the shape of the tree lends itself to translation in the more common English metaphor of "mushroom clouds," which image unfortunately may give rise to fanciful apocalyptic speculations (see Dahood, *Ugaritic-Hebrew Lexicography*, p. 51; and "Hebrew *tam-rûrîm* and *tîmārôt*"). The citation of this verse in

Acts 2:19 appears to follow an expansionistic and late Septuagint text.

4 [2:31]. גָּדוֹל (great) and נוֹרָא (dreadful) are also used in describing the day of Yahweh in 2:11.

5 [2:32]. בַּשְּׂרִידִים (among the survivors): The Septuagint has καὶ εὐαγγελις όμενοι (and those who proclaim good news), apparently reading וּמְבַשְּׂרִים for the Masoretic Text's וּבַשְּׂרִידִים (among the survivors). Aquila and Theodotion (καὶ ἐν τοῖς καταλελειμμένοις) support the Masoretic Text.

3–4 [2:30–31]. Cosmic convulsions accompany the day of Yahweh (2:10–11); the created order reacts to the presence of the Divine Warrior at the head of his army. But in this oracle, the phenomena of the day of Yahweh are part of a day of deliverance and blessing for Israel. The remnant motif is prominent: the remnant undergoes divine wrath and judgment, but survives to become the nucleus of a renewed people of God in the future. Here Zion undergoes the ordeal of divine wrath, but there is escape, there are survivors (3:5 [2:32]).

From the vantage point of the New Testament, John the Baptist had warned that Jesus would baptize with the Spirit and fire. When Peter appeals to this passage from Joel, the fire that comes with the Spirit is not the flame of judgment flashing from the presence of a holy God, but tongues of fire. Other images come to the fore. It is fire that purges lips (cf. Isa. 6:6–7) and empowers for witness (Acts 1:8). The pillar of fire and cloud that once dwelled inaccessible above the Most Holy Place now dwells within people. Where once no one could approach that fire, now those in Zion can undergo the ordeal of the fiery presence of God in safety. The answer to the question "who can endure [that day]?" (Joel 2:11) is given: the repentant who call on the Lord will survive that day. No longer does Yahweh dwell in a small room in a building made of wood and stone—now he will dwell within humans, each of his people becoming a living temple.

5 [2:32]. This verse is one of those sublime statements of Scripture which integrate in a single breath what has always been for theologians a paradox, that tension between moral responsibility and the sovereignty of God (cf. Esther 4:14; Matt.

26:24; Acts 2:21). Those who call on the name of Yahweh are those whom he calls (cf. Acts 2:23). True Israel is not Israel as reckoned by genealogical descent, but Israel as reckoned by divine election. Peter said that the promise of God's Spirit was "to you and to your children and to all who are far off, every one whom the Lord our God calls to him" (Acts 2:39, RSV).

Joel confirms his dependence on and use of earlier canonical material by using a quotation formula, "As Yahweh has said." His source appears to be Obadiah 17a, which is confirmed by his allusion to the second half of Obadiah 17a in 4:17 [3:17].

Verse 5 is also important in the New Testament. Christians become known as those who called on the Lord; Peter leaves no doubt that "calling on the name of the Lord" meant calling on the name of Jesus, the only name by which we must be saved (Acts 4:12; cf. Acts 4:9–12; 9:14, 21; 22:16; 1 Cor. 1:2; 2 Tim. 2:22). Paul argues that there is no difference between Jew and Gentile, and that all who call on the name of the Lord will be saved (Rom. 10:12).

Joel 3:1–5 [2:28–32] is, of course, the most well known passage in the book and has been the object of considerable scholarly interest. In addition to the commentary literature, see Bourke, "Le Jour de Yahvé dans Joël"; Buis, "Étude biblique (de la Semaine de la Pentecôte) (Joel 3:1–5, Acts 2:14–40): Le don de l'Esprit Saint et la prophétie de Joël"; Buis, "Joel announce l'effusion de l'Esprit"; Evans, "Prophetic Setting of the Pentecost Sermon"; Gelin, "L'Annonce de la Pentecôte (Joël 3:1–5)."

III. The Lord's Answer (2:18–4:21) [3:21]
B. To the Impending Disaster: The Day of the Lord (3:1–4:21) [2:28–3:21]
2. Judgment on the Nations (4:1–17) [3:1–17]
a. Slavery for Slavers (4:1–8) [3:1–8]

4 For behold, in those days and at that time
  when I restore the fortunes of Judah and Jerusalem,
² I will gather all nations,
  I will bring them down to the Valley of Jehoshaphat,
and I will enter litigation with them there
  concerning my people, my inheritance Israel,
    whom they have scattered among the nations,
  and concerning my land,
    which they have divided.
³ They cast lots for my people;
  they gave a boy as the price for a prostitute,
    and they sold a girl for wine, and drank.
⁴ Furthermore, what are you to me,
  O Tyre and Sidon, all you regions of Philistia?
Are you trying to repay me for something?
  Or are you trying to get even with me?
Quickly, speedily I will return
  your payment on your own head,
⁵ because you took my silver and my gold,
  and you carried my goodly treasures to your own temples.
⁶ You sold the sons of Judah and Jerusalem to the sons of the Greeks,
  so that you could remove them far from their own borders.
⁷ Behold, I will arouse them to leave that place to which you sold them,
  and I will bring your deeds on your own head.
⁸ I will sell your sons and daughters by means of the sons of Judah,
  and they will sell them to the Sabeans, to a distant nation,
  for the Lord has spoken.

3 For then, in those days and at that time,
  when I restore the fortunes of Judah and Jerusalem,
² I will gather all the nations
  and bring them down to the valley of Jehoshaphat,
and I will enter into judgment with them there,
  on account of my people and my heritage Israel,
    because they have scattered them among the nations.
  They have divided my land,
³ and cast lots for my people,
  and traded boys for prostitutes,
    and sold girls for wine, and drunk it down.
⁴ What are you to me,
  O Tyre and Sidon, and all the regions of Philistia?
Are you paying me back for something?
  If you are paying me back,
I will turn your deeds back upon
  your own heads swiftly and speedily.
⁵ For you have taken my silver and my gold,
  and have carried my rich treasures into your temples.
⁶ You have sold the people of Judah and Jerusalem to the Greeks,
  removing them far from their own border.
⁷ But now I will rouse them to leave the places to which you have sold them,
  and I will turn your deeds back upon your own heads.
⁸ I will sell your sons and your daughters into the hand of the people of Judah,
  and they will sell them to the Sabeans, to a nation far away;
  for the Lord has spoken.

4:1 [3:1]. בַּיָּמִים הָהֵמָּה (in those days): This introductory formula (cf. Jer. 33:15; 50:4, 20) refers back to 3:1 [2:28]; a somewhat similar chronological note sets off the last oracle (4:18 [3:18]). אָשִׁיב אֶת־שְׁבוּת (I restore the fortunes): The phrase שׁוּב שְׁבוּת (Deut. 30:3; Job 42:10; Pss. 14:7; 53:7 [6]; 85:2 [1]; 126:4; Jer. 30:18; 32:44; 33:11, 26; 48:47; 49:6, 39; Ezek. 16:53; 29:14; Hos. 6:11; Zeph. 2:7; 3:20) constitutes a much debated crux in Old Testament study. An extensive literature discusses the meaning of the phrase (for summaries of the current state of the question, see Holladay, *Root Šûbh in the Old Testament*, pp. 110–14; and Bracke, "*Šûb šᵉbût*"). Depending on the decision made regarding the etymology of the noun שְׁבוּת, the phrase can be translated "return the captivity" (from the verb שָׁבָה, take captive) or "restore the fortunes, bring about the restoration of" (from the verb שׁוּב, return). Individual contexts favor viewing the phrase as a reference to return from captivity (Jer. 29:14; Ezek. 29:14; Zeph. 3:20), while others appear to have no reference to captivity and favor a turn of fortune (Job 42:10; Ezek. 16:53). The phrase seems ambiguous in Joel 4:1 [3:1]. While certainly not speaking of the Babylonian exile (Jerusalem is well populated and, more important, the temple is in operation), the prophet does speak of a dispersion, a scattering of Judah among the nations (4:2b [3:2b]) and of a period of captivity in slavery for Judeans (4:3–8 [3:3–8]). On the other hand, the introductory words "in those days and at that time when I" appear to relate this passage to the larger reversal of fortunes for Judah spoken of in the preceding context. Note the assonance in verses 1–12 using the consonants שׁב (שְׁבוּת and אָשִׁיב in v. 1; אָשִׁיב in v. 4; הֲשִׁבֹתִי in v. 7; אָשִׁיב in v. 12—see Allen, *Joel*, p. 107); the use of assonance also characterizes earlier portions (see the Exegesis of 1:10).

2. וְקִבַּצְתִּי אֶת־כָּל־הַגּוֹיִם (I will gather all nations): The nations are spoken of as gathered on a number of occasions, whether to war against Jerusalem, to receive divine judgment, or to go to war with Yahweh (see Isa. 43:9; 66:18; Ezek. 38:8; Hos. 10:10; Mic. 4:11; Zeph. 3:8; Zech. 12:3; 14:2; Matt. 25:32; Rev. 20:8). The gathering of the nations is picked up again as a theme in verse 11. עֵמֶק יְהוֹשָׁפָט (the Valley of Jehoshaphat): This valley is otherwise unknown. There are several theories as to its identity. Some have associated it with the Valley of Beracah (2 Chron. 20:26) where Jehoshaphat had enjoyed a great victory. It is the only valley otherwise associated with that king. However, since that valley is some distance from Jerusalem and near Tekoa, and since it already clearly has another name, this suggestion does not have much to commend it. Others associate it with the Tyropoeon Valley, the swale that runs from north to south through the city of Jerusalem, just to the west of the temple platform and the Ophel ridge (see van Selms, "Origin of the Name Tyropoeon in Jerusalem"). This identification is primarily based on etymology. The term *Tyropoeon* (first known from Josephus, *Jewish War* 5.140) derives from a Greek term meaning "cheese makers, cheese mongers." The Valley of Jehoshaphat is also known in verse 14 as עֵמֶק הֶחָרוּץ (Valley of the Verdict). However, חָרוּץ (verdict) is also a term for "cheese" (1 Sam. 17:18). Van Selms argues that the designation of the valley west of the temple as the "Valley of the Cheese Mongers" arose from Josephus's own metanalysis of the Hebrew word. Van Selms finds corroborating evidence in the *Kethiv* for שַׁעַר הָשְׁפוֹת (Dung Gate) in Nehemiah 3:13; the *Kethiv* הָשְׁפוֹת is another term for cheese or curds (2 Sam. 17:29) and may underlie the Aramaic term תֹּפֶת (Tophet) as a name for the area. Tradition has ordinarily associated the valley with

---

4:1–2 [3:1–2]. The nation had been threatened by both an immediate disaster (locusts) and an ultimate disaster (the day of the Lord). The Lord answered the national contrition with a promise of relief from the immediate disaster (2:18–27) and with the removal of the eschatological threat (3:1–5 [2:28–32]). The threat of invasion by the Lord's army is now lodged against the Gentiles instead (4:1–16 [3:1–16]). The change in the fortunes of Judah is directly related to the change in heart reported in 2:12–13 (Allen, *Joel*, p. 108). The Gentiles who had earlier rejoiced in Judah's humiliation (2:17, 26–27) now face an even greater trial. Joel may be elaborating on Zephaniah 3:8.

The initial section of the chapter (4:1–8 [3:1–8]) is presented as a lawsuit. The accused are summoned (vv. 1–2a), the accusations read (vv. 2b–3), the accused cross-examined and interrogated (v. 4a–b), and the verdict announced (vv. 4c–8) (see the Exegesis of 4:2 [3:2]). Lawsuits in the ancient Near East and in the Bible usually ended either with instructions on how to heal the breach in relations or with the threat of military incursion and judgment. Here only the latter option is offered.

This passage in Joel should be compared with similar passages depicting eschatological judgment in a valley (Ezek. 39:11; Zech. 14:4–5; cf. Isa.

the Kidron Valley on the eastern side of the temple and the Ophel ridge, between Jerusalem and the Mount of Olives. This explanation is favored by the fact that the Kidron is perhaps the most prominent topographical feature around Jerusalem and by the fact that other theophanies or visions are set east of the city (e.g., Ezek. 10:19; 47:1–12). Presumably the fountain that flows from the temple of Yahweh (Joel 4:18 [3:18]) also flowed into this valley east of the city (see Ezek. 47:1–12; Zech. 14:3–8). If in verse 18 Joel is dependent on Ezekiel 47, the argument for identifying the Valley of Jehoshaphat with the Kidron would be reasonably strong. Designating the valley by the name of that earlier king would then be a paronomasia on the name of Jehoshaphat (Yahweh judges) as the name for the place of judgment; the Chronicler indulged in a similar paronomasia on the king's name (2 Chron. 19:4–11; see Dillard, *2 Chronicles*, pp. 129–30). This traditional identification is the preeminent reason for the great Jewish necropolis in the valley to this day; burial in the place of Yahweh's self-vindication before the nations was highly prized. Others see no need to correlate the Valley of Jehoshaphat with some particular feature of the topography of Jerusalem but prefer to recognize the paronomasia in the name and to regard it as a feature of an apocalyptic geography in Joel's vision. (See also the discussions by Freund, "Multitudes, Multitudes in the Valley of Decision"; Haupt, "Valley of the Gorge"; dell'Oca, "El Valle de Josafat.") וְנִשְׁפַּטְתִּי (I will enter litigation): The purpose of this assembly of the nations is that Yahweh may announce his lawsuit against them; the niphal of שָׁפַט is commonly used in the sense of entering into a judicial proceeding or controversy. Verses 2–3 show elements of a prophetic lawsuit, including the announcement of

the suit (v. 2a) and the listing of charges (vv. 2b–3). Verses 4–8 should probably be included within this lawsuit, as they contain rhetorical questions typical of lawsuit interrogations (v. 4), further specifications of charges (vv. 5–6), and an announcement of sentence (vv. 7–8). יִשְׂרָאֵל (Israel) in this verse should not be thought of as referring to the northern kingdom; rather it reflects the practice, reasonably common in postexilic literature, of designating Judah by this name. The restoration community apparently considered itself in some sense the legal and spiritual successor of the larger nation. אַרְצִי (my land) is also more common in late and postexilic sources (2 Chron. 7:20; Isa. 14:25; Jer. 2:7; 16:18; Ezek. 36:5; 38:16; see also Joel 1:6).

3. גּוֹרָל (lots): The scene is that of dividing plunder after a battle (Obad. 11; Nah. 3:10). הַיֶּלֶד (a boy): Human life is so cheap that a boy is given as the fee for using a prostitute, and a girl (הַיַּלְדָּה) as the price of drink. בַּזּוֹנָה (for a prostitute): The use of the preposition בְּ in this construction is often called the *beth* of price (e.g., Ps. 44:13 [12]; Amos 2:6). The Septuagint mistakenly has καὶ ἔδωκαν τὰ παιδάρια πόρναις, and the Vulgate has *et posuerunt puerum in prostibulo*, both meaning "they gave the boys into prostitution." The Targum and the Syriac version translate the idiom correctly (see Wolff, *Joel and Amos*, p. 71). The prepositional phrase with בְּ introduces what the sellers receive in both clauses, not what those sold become.

4. הַגְּמוּל (repays; lit. recompense, benefit [BDB, p. 168]): The precise nuancing of the phrases using גְּמֻל is difficult. The noun may be a reward or payment; used with the piel of שָׁלֵם (be complete [BDB, p. 1022]) it suggests the idea of repayment. וְאִם (untranslated): There is a question of how to

---

22:1; Jer. 7:32; 19:6; Zech. 12:11—Jones, *Isaiah 56–66 and Joel*, p. 180).

3. The gravity of the sins of the nations against Judah can only be measured against the backdrop of the redemption God had provided for his people. God had brought Israel out of slavery; he had brought them into a land given to them in perpetuity as the inheritance secured in their redemption. The nations in effect had set themselves to undo the redemptive work of God. In the postbattle revelry of dividing the spoils they took Judeans back into slavery and drove them from their land. Dividing the land was Yahweh's prerogative (Josh. 13–22; Mic. 2:1–5), and he would not brook its being taken by others.

There is a sense in which any society can be measured by the treatment accorded its children. In ancient Israel children, largely because they were defenseless, were the particular object of the care of God and the protection of the law. The treatment accorded Judean children by Gentile nations showed the depths of their crimes (Keller, *Joël*, p. 147). The treatment of Judah's children by the nations is in sharp contrast to what God intends for them (3:1–2 [2:28–29]).

4. The enemies mentioned in this pericope (vv. 4–8; Tyre, Sidon, Philistia) are some of the traditional foes of Israel, though minor in comparison with Assyria or Babylon. Since these lesser enemies are mentioned, the date for the book

understand וְאִם. In Hebrew the first in a series of "yes/no" questions is ordinarily introduced with the interrogative ה, and the remaining questions in the series with אִם. Taken as a series of questions, the translation becomes "Are you repaying me? Are you trying to get even with me? Quickly, speedily, I will. . . ." This approach was taken by the Septuagint and the New English Bible. However, according to Masoretic Text pointing, ה on הַגְּמוּל is the definite article instead of the interrogative marker. וְאִם also introduces conditional sentences; in this case the translation would be, "Are you repaying me? If you are trying to get even with me, then quickly, speedily. . . ." This approach was followed by the Vulgate, the King James Version, and the New International Version. גֹּמְלִים (get even): The verb גָּמַל itself often has negative connotations (Deut. 32:6; Pss. 7:5 [4]; 137:8); hence, the translation "get even." קַל מְהֵרָה (quickly, speedily): Both of these words are ordinarily read as adverbs. If מְהֵרָה is read as an imperative, the sense becomes "do it quickly. I am going to return. . . ."

5. מַחֲמַדַּי (my . . . treasures) may be used in reference to temple treasures (2 Chron. 36:18–19), but that does not appear to be the use here. There is no record of any Tyrian or Philistine plundering of the temple in Jerusalem; presumably the passage

speaks of other plunder taken along with the slaves after warfare or raids. הֵיכְלֵיכֶם (your own temples) is also ambiguous: it can refer either to temples or palaces.

6. מְכַרְתֶּם (you sold): Prinsloo (*Theology of the Book of Joel*, p. 96) notes the verbal relationship between verses 6 and 8: וּבְנֵי יְהוּדָה . . . מְכַרְתֶּם (you sold the sons of Judah) in verse 6a becomes יְהוּדָה וּמָכַרְתִּי . . . בְּיַד בְּנֵי (I will sell . . . by means of the sons of Judah) in verse 8a. לְמַעַן הַרְחִיקָם (so that you could remove them far) in verse 6b becomes רָחוֹק אֶל־גּוֹי (to a distant nation) in verse 8b. The situation of the Judeans and their captors is completely reversed. בְּיַד (by means of): Instead of the customary sense of means or instrumentality for בְּיַד, the Septuagint has εἰς χεῖρας (sold to), which would more properly translate מָכַרְל (in vv. 6a, 8b). הַיְּוָנִים (the Greeks): The mention of the Greeks comports most naturally with a postexilic date for the Book of Joel, but it must also be stressed that it does not establish it. The Greeks are mentioned in trading contact with the eastern Mediterranean in Assyrian inscriptions from the eighth century B.C.; material remains from excavations suggest trading contact with Palestine by the seventh century (see Rudolph, *Joel*, pp. 81–82; Kapelrud, *Joel Studies*, pp. 154–55; Myers, "Date of Joel," pp. 178–85).

itself would most naturally fit a period before the rise of Assyrian power in the Levant or after the decline of Babylonian power, that is, in the ninth century B.C. or in the postexilic period. A postexilic date has been argued throughout this volume (see the Introduction); Tyre, Sidon, and Philistia are also the objects of oracles against foreign nations in Zechariah early in the postexilic period (Zech. 9:1–8). Phoenician involvement in slave trading is denounced in the Bible as early as the eighth century (Amos 1:6–9); as two of the great trading hubs of the Near East, Tyre and Sidon were naturally involved in slave trade as well as almost all other commodities (Ezek. 27:13). Tyre and Sidon had been a thorn in Judah's side (Ezek. 28:24). Ezekiel denounced Judah's neighbors (Ammon, Moab, Edom, Philistia—Ezek. 25) because they sought a share of Judah's territory after its downfall. Tyre in particular was an opportunist and saw an enhancement of her own fortunes through taking over Judean trade: "Aha, broken is the gateway of the peoples; it has swung open to me; I shall be replenished, now that it is wasted" (Ezek. 26:2, NRSV; see Katzenstein, *History of Tyre*, p. 322). The enmity with the Philis-

tines ran from the time of the judges into the postexilic period; Ezekiel also describes the malice and hostility they had directed toward Judah (Ezek. 25:15–17).

The *lex talionis* (Exod. 21:24; Lev. 24:18, 20; Deut. 19:21) of the Old Testament appears there in many guises. Those who exported Judeans far to the west will in turn be exported to the east; those who enslaved Judeans will be slaves; those who were enriched by the slave trade will serve to enrich others. God had redeemed his people from a land of slavery, and he will not suffer their enslavement again.

5–6. The crimes committed by these nations against Judah have also been committed against God. It was his silver and gold (v. 5), his land and his people (v. 2), so the crimes are "against me" (v. 4). Allen (*Joel*, p. 109) finds in this lawsuit echoes of another trial announced by Jesus, when the nations would be gathered and judged for their treatment of his brothers and himself (Matt. 25:31–46). Yahweh, who is the champion and defender of the widow, the orphan, and the poor, is also the champion of his oppressed people; he is their advocate in the court (Prov. 22:22–23; 23:11).

8. לִשְׁבָאִים (to the Sabeans): The Sabeans dominated the trade routes to the Arabian world until the mid-sixth century B.C. when hegemony over these routes passed to the Mineans. Myers concludes ("Date of Joel," pp. 185–90) that this information also provides a terminus for the Book of Joel: Joel could not be dated after the fifth century B.C. Once again, the data most naturally comport with this reading: the Sabeans are likely to have been mentioned at a time when they were either dominant in these trade routes or at least continued to be somewhat active. However, all that can be deduced from the verse itself is that South Ara-

bia and Sheba were the destination of the captives. Sheba may have been chosen simply as the opposite geographical extreme from the Greeks; the passage does not provide strict warrant for concluding that the Sabeans themselves necessarily conducted the trade. The wording admits of two understandings: (1) the Judeans would sell their former oppressors to the Sabeans, traders who would in turn sell them to a far land; or (2) the Judeans would sell their captives to the Sabeans, to a far land (understanding לִשְׁבָאִים and אֶל־גּוֹי רָחוֹק as synonyms). The brokers in this transaction are the "sons of Judah" instead of the Sabeans; Sheba

---

7–8. It is striking that in their polemic against the nations and their idols, the prophets never appeal to the loftier ethics of their religion, or the greater sublimity of their theology, or the beauty of the temple architecture; their boast is always that it is Yahweh who controls history, and that it is his ability to fulfil his word that demonstrates that he is God (Deut. 18:21–22; Isa. 41:21–24; 43:8–13; 44:6–8, 24–26; 46:11; 48:3–6). Tyre was in antiquity a much more populous city than the modern city. Arrian (*Anabasis* 2.24.4–5), who describes that city on the eve of its conquest by Alexander the Great, reports that thirty thousand people, including women and children, were sold into slavery after the siege and battle in 332 B.C. (Katzenstein, *History of Tyre*, pp. 10–11). A similar fate at the hands of Alexander awaited the descendants of the Philistines who inhabited Gaza after holding out for two months. It is highly probable that Jewish brokers participated in the sale of the slaves. Even what happens in distant places is under the control of Yahweh: "The LORD has spoken" (v. 8).

Although the scholarly pendulum has swung away from bifurcating Joel into an earlier locust prophet (chaps. 1–2) and a later eschatologist (chaps. 3–4) toward a greater appreciation of the unity of the book, the discussion has not abated with reference to 4:4–8 [3:4–8]. Scholars continue to debate two major issues pertaining to these verses: Are they original with the composition of Joel or a subsequent insertion? Are the verses written in poetry or prose?

Numerous features in 4:4–8 [3:4–8] suggest that this is a secondary or independent composition inserted into the text. In addition to the fact that many consider it a prose section within the otherwise poetic material of Joel, it does interrupt the flow of the context in several respects. While the larger context (vv. 1–3, 9–21) deals with universal

judgment of the nations, these verses focus on particular enemies otherwise unmentioned in the book. The punishment of these nations does not occur in the Valley of Jehoshaphat in war with Yahweh, but rather by a principle of *lex talionis*; their sons and daughters will also be sold into slavery. The larger context is devoted to eschatological, transhistorical, and climactic judgment, whereas verses 4–8 appear to speak of historically realized reversals that result in slavery. Verses 4–8 also introduce a number of lexical items which do not figure in the remainder of the book, for example, *gāmal* and *gĕmûl*; in verse 3 the children are referred to using the root *yld*, whereas in verses 4–8 the chosen phrases all use *ben*. The independent status of verses 4–8 is also indicated by its concluding formula, "Yahweh has spoken" (see Wolff, *Joel and Amos*, pp. 74–75).

While there is certainly much that would suggest regarding 4:4–8 [3:4–8] as secondary in its present position, other features favor its integrity. The materials in verses 4–8 fit within the larger rubric of a lawsuit (see Exegesis and Exposition of 4:2 [3:2]) and are a natural part of it. Though they are not necessarily present, oracles against foreign nations are routinely part of prophetic books, so much so that one expects to find them. Verses 4–8 appear to be an exposition of verses 2–3: the subjects of dividing the land, scattering the population, and selling the children lead to charges of slaving and plundering against particular nations. Alternatively, however, it could also be argued that *mākar* (sell) served as a catchword that triggered the inclusion of verses 4–8, otherwise independent at this point. Ahlström (*Joel and the Temple Cult*, pp. 134–35) sees no reason that the prophet himself could not have been prompted to include this oracle in the same way. Specific enemy nations are also mentioned in verse 19,

appears rather to be the destination. For לִשְׁבָאיִם the Septuagint has εἰς αἰχμαλωσίαν (to captivity), possibly a corruption of לְשְׁבִי or לִשְׁבוּת. The Masoretic Text is favored by the use of geographi-

cal terms at opposite ends of the ancient Near Eastern world. "To captivity in a distant land" may have eased for the Septuagint translators the awkwardness of an appositive.

---

though not as many commentators suggest excising this passage from its context.

The debate over whether the section is poetry or prose is, of course, related to the preceding question. A prose section falling within an otherwise poetic book could be suspect as a secondary insertion. The question of whether a passage is poetry or prose is not as simple as a neat binary "yes" or "no." The distinctions between prose and poetry in Hebrew fall rather on a continuum instead of into two hermetically sealed bins. The boundary between elevated prose and rudimentary poetry is hard to call. The verses could be viewed as prose because they show a narrative progression from charges to sentencing, and they

do not contain the elevated figures of speech associated with poetry. However, on the other hand, it is possible to scan the lines in a poetic parallelism, so that they show that element most fundamental to Hebrew poetry. The ambiguity attaching to this question is well illustrated in the two major reference editions of the Hebrew Bible: BHK prints the lines as prose, whereas BHS arranges the text as poetry (Allen, *Joel*, p. 29; Prinsloo, *Theology of the Book of Joel*, p. 96). Yet even were one able to conclude confidently that the section was prose, it may not entirely warrant the conclusion that verses 4–8 are secondary; changes between poetry and prose sections are not uncommon in other prophetic books, for example, Zechariah 11, 13.

III. The Lord's Answer (2:18–4:21) [3:21]
    B. To the Impending Disaster: The Day of the Lord (3:1–4:21) [2:28–3:21]
        2. Judgment on the Nations (4:1–17) [3:1–17]
           b. Holy War against Evil (4:9–17) [3:9–17]
               (1) Summons to Battle (4:9–11) [3:9–11]

⁹ Cry this aloud among the nations,
    Sanctify a war!
Stir up the warriors!
    Let all men of war come near and go up!
¹⁰ Beat your plows into swords,
    and your pruning hooks into spears!
Let the one who is weak say, "I am a warrior!"
¹¹ Hurry, come, all you nations round about;
    let them gather there!
Bring down your warriors, O LORD!

⁹ Proclaim this among the nations:
    Prepare war,
        stir up the warriors.
    Let all the soldiers draw near,
        let them come up.
¹⁰ Beat your plowshares into swords,
    and your pruning hooks into spears;
    let the weakling say, "I am a warrior."
¹¹ Come quickly,
    all you nations all around,
    gather yourselves there.
Bring down your warriors, O LORD.

9. מִלְחָמָה קַדְּשׁוּ (sanctify a war!): Where the nation was earlier instructed to sanctify a fast (1:14; 2:15–16), now the nations are instructed to "sanctify war"; we are clearly brought into the realm of holy war ideology (Jer. 6:4; 22:7; 51:27–28). הָעִירוּ (stir up): Note also the use of this verb in verse 7. God who roused his people from their slavery will now rouse the nations to bring them to judgment.

10. אִתֵּיכֶם (your plows): The verse is an ironic parody on Isaiah 2:4 and Micah 4:3. The familiarity of these two passages has probably immortalized forever in English the translation of אֵת as "plowshare," though this is probably incorrect; the term was more likely used of a hand tool, perhaps either a kind of hoe or adze or some other cutting tool resembling a pruning knife. The pruning knife had a curved blade and resembled a sickle, though smaller (see Borowski, *Agriculture in Iron Age Israel*, pp. 108–9). Turning agricultural implements into military equipment was a genuine possibility in times of war in earlier periods of Israel's national existence (1 Sam. 13:20–21); with the advent of a standing army, stockpiled arms, and more readily available iron during the period of the monarchy, such exigencies became less likely and would represent a necessary step only in all-out war (see Mariottini, "Joel 3:10"). הַחַלָּשׁ (the one who is weak): This is the only occurrence of the noun חַלָּשׁ (weak). The verbal root suggests more than simply weak; it connotes prostrate or disabled (Job 14:10).

11. עוּשׁוּ (hurry) is a *hapax legomenon*. The Septuagint, Targum, and Syriac version give the sense of assemble, perhaps influenced by נִקְבְּצוּ (let them gather) in the next clause; there is no clear etymological basis for this significance. Some also emend to עוּרוּ (stir, rouse) on the basis of the occurrence of that verb in the context (vv. 7, 9). Others (perhaps RSV?) emend to חוּשׁוּ (hasten). Rudolph (*Joel*, p. 77) appeals to several Arabic cognates that have the sense of *run fast* or *hurry*. All fit the context reasonably well. נִקְבְּצוּ (let them gather) is a niphal perfect third-person plural; one anticipates in the context another imperative. Allen (*Joel*, p. 107) considers it an irregular form of the imperative, whereas others emend to the expected הִקָּבְצוּ (e.g., Wolff, *Joel and Amos*, p. 72). Rudolph (*Joel*, p. 77) transposes the last five words of verse 11 to the end of verse 12, as the result of a hypothetical copying error that was erroneously corrected. The Septuagint reads all of the first three verbs as imperatives, whereas the Targum presupposes a jussive; both of these versions may already be coping with the same difficult text we now have before us. שָׁמָּה (there): The accents in the Masoretic Text join this word with the last clause, "There bring down your warriors, O LORD," whereas the Septuagint joins it with verse 11a (note line scanning in BHS). הַנְחַת יְהוָה גִּבּוֹרֶיךָ (bring down your warriors, O LORD): This clause has long been considered problematic. The Septuagint has ὁ πραῢς ἔστω μαχητής (the meek will be a hero), which may derive from a Hebrew text resembling הַנַּחַת יְהִי גִבּוֹר (Allen, *Joel*, p. 107) or גִּבּוֹר

---

9. The pericope opens with a summons to battle (Isa. 13:3; Jer. 6:4; 46:3; 51:27–28). Zion had often been attacked in the past, but this would be the last time. There is a great irony in this summons: the nations believe they are being called to do battle, but really it is to hear God's sentence of judgment against them. There is no real doubt about the outcome.

There is an urgency in the text that lends it an almost staccato pace; Jones (*Isaiah 56–66 and Joel*, p. 184) notes that there are fifteen imperatives in verses 9–14, a fact giving vivid expression to the frantic tenor of the passage.

10. Earlier prophets had spoken of a time when the nations would turn their instruments of war into productive implements of pastoral life (Isa. 2:4; Mic. 4:3); Joel reverses that image. Craigie's comment (*Twelve Prophets*, p. 116) is apropos: "But, when the nations were assembled in the valley, fully equipped for battle, they would receive a

shock; they would find there the Judge of all the nations, and in their hands they would be holding the incriminating evidence of their own history of violence." The prophetic books of the Old Testament abound with oracles against individual nations of antiquity; this sort of specific pronouncement regarding particular nations is found in the immediately preceding passage (vv. 4–8). Here, however, we have an oracle against all nations; the total mobilization of the enemy matches the total summons to prayer and lament in chapter 2.

11. Alongside this summons to the nations, the prophet gives voice to his own prayer, a prayer which contains another summons (v. 11b), this time to the armies of heaven who will execute the Lord's judgment. This sole mention of the presence of Yahweh's warriors establishes the outcome: the nations will be vanquished (Keller, *Joël*, p. 151).

הָעֵז יְהֹוָה; this clause would then be synonymous with verse 10b, and some argue it should be transposed there. The Targum and the Vulgate agree with the Masoretic Text, but derive הַנְחַת from the verb חָתַת (be shattered, dismayed; BDB, p. 369), yielding, "There Yahweh will cause to fall/break the power of your warriors" (see Wolff, *Joel and Amos*, p. 73). Either of these readings could arguably fit the context better than the Masoretic Text. In the Masoretic Text the prophet injects a brief, one-line prayer to Yahweh; the remainder of 4:9–12 [3:9–12] appears to address the nations, and this short prayer would interrupt this uniformity. Nevertheless, it must also be said that the Masoretic Text as it stands is not a difficult text and also fits the context. הַנְחַת (bring down) is a hiphil imperative from נָחַת (bring down). The nations are summoned, and it is not unreasonable to expect a call for the appearance of the Lord's own army (see 2 Chron. 20:22; Isa. 13:3; Zech. 14:5). For a similar brief prayer injected into a vision by the prophet, compare Zechariah 3:5 (though here too text-critical issues may cloud the question). Verses 9–11 constitute a summons to war (see Bach, *Die Aufforderungen zur Flucht und zum Kampf*, pp. 51–104; cf. Isa. 13:2–3; Jer. 6:4–5; 46:3–4; 49:14; Obad. 1; Mic. 4:14 [5:1]; Nah. 2:1, 5). Messengers or heralds are mustering an army for battle in the Valley of Jehoshaphat. Though the messengers are not identified specifically, other passages suggest they are emissaries from the heavenly council (Miller, "Divine Council and the Prophetic Call to War"; see 1 Kings 22:19–21; 2 Chron. 20:15–17; Amos 3:7–9). The messengers who summon the armies of the nations may well themselves be part of the heavenly hosts (4:11b [3:11b]).

III. The Lord's Answer (2:18–4:21) [3:21]
B. To the Impending Disaster: The Day of the Lord
(3:1–4:21) [2:28–3:21]
2. Judgment on the Nations (4:1–17) [3:1–17]
b. Holy War against Evil (4:9–17) [3:9–17]
(2) Events in the Valley of Jehoshaphat (4:12–17) [3:12–17]

12 Let the nations stir;
let them come up to the Valley of Jehoshaphat,
for there I will sit to render judgment on
all the nations round about.
13 Swing the sickle,
for the harvest is ripe.
Come and tread,
for the winepress is full!
The vats are overflowing,
for their wickedness is great!
14 Hordes! Hordes in the Valley of the Verdict!
For the day of the Lord is near in the
Valley of the Verdict.
15 The sun and the moon grow dark,
and the stars recall their light!
16 The Lord roars from Zion,
he raises his voice from Jerusalem,
and the heavens and earth shake.
The Lord is a refuge for his people,
a stronghold for the children of Israel.
17 And you will know that I am the Lord
your God,
he who dwells on Zion, my holy
mountain.
Jerusalem will be holy,
and foreigners will never violate her
again.

12 Let the nations rouse themselves,
and come up to the valley of Jehoshaphat;
for there I will sit to judge
all the neighboring nations.
13 Put in the sickle,
for the harvest is ripe.
Go in, tread,
for the wine press is full.
The vats overflow,
for their wickedness is great.
14 Multitudes, multitudes,
in the valley of decision!
For the day of the Lord is near
in the valley of decision.
15 The sun and the moon are darkened,
and the stars withdraw their shining.
16 The Lord roars from Zion,
and utters his voice from Jerusalem,
and the heavens and the earth shake.
But the Lord is a refuge for his people,
a stronghold for the people of Israel.
17 So you shall know that I, the Lord your
God,
dwell in Zion, my holy mountain.
And Jerusalem shall be holy,
and strangers shall never again pass
through it.

12. אֵשֵׁב (I will sit): Sitting is the posture of a judge (see Exod. 18:14; Ruth 4:2; Pss. 9:8–9 [7–8]; 122:5; Prov. 20:8; Isa. 16:5; 28:6; Jer. 26:10; Matt. 19:28; 27:19; Luke 22:30; Acts 23:3; 1 Cor. 9:3; James 4:11).

13. מַגָּל (sickle) was the principal tool used in harvesting. The material from which the blade was made reflected the technological progress of ancient Israel; earliest examples were of flint, followed by bronze, and eventually iron, though some blades of the earlier materials continued to be used after the later materials had been introduced. Numerous examples have been found in excavations (Borowski, *Agriculture in Iron Age Israel*, pp. 59, 61–62). The blade was attached to a wooden handle; the reaper grasped stalks with one hand and cut using the sickle in the other. In this context the image is of the grape harvest (v. 13b–c). בָּשַׁל (ripe) ordinarily connotes *cook* or *boil*; this is its only occurrence in the qal in the sense of be ripe or ripen (the hiphil occurs in Gen. 40:10, also in reference to grapes; see Lewy, "Miscellanea Nuziana," pp. 9–11, n. 2). Ripeness as an image is associated with judgment (see Isa. 17:5; 28:4; Jer. 24:2; 48:32; Hos. 2:9; Amos 8:1–2; Nah. 3:12; Matt. 13:39; Rev. 14:15, 18). Who is speaking in this verse, and to whom is it spoken? It seems clear that the speaker is Yahweh, and he addressees either his army (as summoned in v. 11b) or Israel, or the two acting in concert to exact judgment on the nations (see Prinsloo, *Theology of the Book of Joel*, p. 102).

14. הֲמוֹנִים (hordes!) is ambiguous; it can refer either to crowds or hordes (Vulgate *populi*; Aquila συναγωγαί; Theodotion πλῆθη), or to noise or tumult (LXX ἦχοι). In this context the former sense would emphasize the numbers gathered in the valley; the latter sense, the confusion, chaos, or noise of battle (see 2 Chron. 20:2; Isa. 13:4; 17:12). הֶחָרוּץ (the verdict) appears to derive from a verbal root having the sense of cut or decide, and hence, decision. Others have associated it with a type of cheese (חָרִיץ; see the Exegesis of 4:2 [3:2]), or a type of agricultural implement, "valley of the threshing tool" (Bewer, *Obadiah and Joel*, p. 140). It is presumably the same valley as the Valley of Jehoshaphat.

15. See the Exegesis of 2:10b.

16. יִשְׁאָג (roars): For Yahweh's roaring in thunder, see Jeremiah 25:30 and Amos 1:2 (see also Job 37:4; Ps. 29; Joel 2:11). For the shaking of heaven and earth, see the Exegesis of 2:10b. Yahweh is described as a refuge and stronghold also in Psalm 46:2 [1] (see Ps. 48).

12–13. The Lord's warriors (v. 11b) have a task: they will tread the winepress in the valley. The metaphor is made the more poignant since a valley may resemble a great winepress hewn into the stone; the armies of the nations assembled for battle in the Valley of the Verdict had really gathered themselves into the winepress of God.

14. The prophet has used images from viniculture with great skill. The locust plague had earlier deprived the drunkards of Judah of their drink (1:5), but with the reversal of the plague, the vats would once again overflow (2:24). Now the hordes (4:14 [3:14]) of the nations gather in Jerusalem, in many ways resembling the swarms of locusts that had earlier ravaged the city; but their fate is to be cut down in an eschatological harvest and crushed in the winepress of God. The Valley of the Verdict will flow with their blood, while the mountains and valleys of Judah would flow with wine (v. 18). John would later draw on Joel in his description of the eschatological harvest (Rev. 14:14–20). Agricultural images occur throughout the Bible. God's image-bearers were placed in a garden and ultimately driven from it; the tabernacle and temple ornamentation visibly present the garden of God in the midst of his people and offer the possibility of renewed fellowship with the Creator. Israel is God's vineyard (Isa. 5) and will yet become a paradise (Joel 4:18 [3:18]).

Many preachers have appealed to verse 14 for an evangelistic thrust; their audiences are addressed as "multitudes in the Valley of Decision" who must decide their fate. There is a problem with that use of this passage: in Joel the hordes do not gather to make a decision, but to hear one; they will not be deciding their fate, for God has already decreed it. The time for decisions is now past.

15. This verse repeats some of the imagery used in 2:10. The measure of time is arrested; the unfolding of history submits to the influence of a violent restraint (Keller, *Joël*, p. 152).

16. The God whose thundering voice causes the universe to reverberate is also a refuge to his people. Nahum makes a similar point when he says that Yahweh takes vengeance on his enemies and rebukes the sea (Nah. 1:2, 4), yet he is a stronghold for "those who take refuge in him" (Nah. 1:7 nrsv). Our perception of God depends on our relationship to him (see Ps. 18:25–28 [24–27]).

17. וִידַעְתֶּם (and you will know): See the Exegesis of 2:27 on the recognition formula. וְזָרִים (and foreigners): The prophetic hope of Jerusalem's freedom from foreign intrusion is one aspect of the theme of the inviolability of Zion; Joel has already addressed this theme in the promise of God that Jerusalem never again be the object of ridicule and humiliation (2:19, 26–27). The same theme is also found in Isaiah 52:1; Zechariah 9:8; 14:21. For Jerusalem's designation as "holy," see also Jeremiah 31:40 and Zechariah 8:3.

---

17. The prophet has used the recognition formula ("you will know that I am the Lord") twice, once in connection with the salvation of God's people (2:27) and once in connection with his judgment on the Gentiles (4:17 [3:17]); both are reasons to acknowledge the sovereignty of God.

Other prophets also give expression to their hopes for a future Jerusalem that is a holy city (Isa. 52:1; Zech. 14:20–21; Rev. 21:2). Joel looks to a day when the entire city is suffused with the presence of God, the city become sanctuary. Zechariah too looks to a day when Yahweh will dwell (*šākan*) in the city, and the entire city will be taken within the walls of the pillar of fire (Zech. 2:5–17 [1–13]).

III. The Lord's Answer (2:18–4:21) [3:21]
B. To the Impending Disaster: The Day of the Lord
(3:1–4:21) [2:28–3:21]
3. Blessing for the People of God (4:18–21) [3:18–21]

18 And it shall come to pass in that day
that the mountains will drip must,
the hills will flow with milk,
and all the streambeds of Judah
will run with water.
A fountain will issue from the temple of
the Lord,
and it will water the Valley of the
Acacias.
19 Egypt will become a desolate waste,
and Edom will become a desolate wilderness,
because of the violence done to the sons
of Judah,
because they shed innocent blood in
their land.
20 Judah will endure forever,
and Jerusalem, for lasting generations.
21 Shall I let their bloodguilt go unpunished?
I will not let it go unpunished,
for the Lord dwells in Zion.

18 In that day
the mountains shall drip sweet wine,
the hills shall flow with milk,
and all the stream beds of Judah
shall flow with water;
a fountain shall come forth from the
house of the Lord
and water the Wadi Shittim.
19 Egypt shall become a desolation
and Edom a desolate wilderness,
because of the violence done to the people of Judah,
in whose land they have shed innocent blood.
20 But Judah shall be inhabited forever,
and Jerusalem to all generations.
21 I will avenge their blood, and I will not
clear the guilty,
for the Lord dwells in Zion.

18. בַּיּוֹם הַהוּא (in that day): This chronological introductory formula links with 3:1 [2:28] and 4:1 [3:1] (see the Exegesis of 4:1 [3:1]). עָסִיס (must) and חָלָב (milk) form a pair representative of all plant and animal products; the absence of עָסִיס had been reason for the drunkards' lament in 1:5. נַחַל הַשִּׁטִּים (the Valley of the Acacias) is otherwise unknown. נַחַל (valley) is a wadi, a dry watercourse which carries water ordinarily only after rains. שִׁטִּים (acacia trees) is also the name of a location northeast of the Dead Sea in the plains of Moab (Num. 25:1; 33:49), though this context would not suggest that locale. Clearly this verse invites comparison with other texts announcing an eschatological fountain opening in the temple of Yahweh (Ezek. 47:1–12; Zech. 13:1; 14:3–9). Ezekiel describes the stream from the temple as flowing down the Kidron Valley east of Jerusalem and into the Dead Sea; he relates this flow of water to the fecundity of fruit trees there (47:12). Since Joel's fountain also flows out of the temple, and since Joel appears also to be dependent on Ezekiel and Zechariah, the most natural identification for the Valley of the Acacias would be the Kidron or another wadi tributary feeding into its system in the area. If the Kidron Valley is already identified in Joel 4 [3] both as the Valley of Jehoshaphat and as the Valley of Decision, it is also possible that yet another designa-

tion is used here. Some acacias still grow in the Kidron Valley. The wood was also used for the construction of furnishings for the tabernacle (Exod. 25–27; 30; 35–38), and therefore has an association with Israel's sanctuaries. The acacia is today common in the dry regions of the Negeb and Sinai. The imagery then could be that of the abundance of water: there would be plenteous water even where acacias grow. Bewer (*Obadiah and Joel*, p. 142) identifies the valley with a wadi west of Jerusalem, so that the water from the temple flows to the west instead of the east as in Ezekiel's vision. Compare the flow of water both east and west in Zechariah 14:8; Jerusalem sits astride the watershed of the Judean hill country, and rainfall in the city to this day flows in part toward the Mediterranean and in part toward the Dead Sea (see also Luria, "And a Fountain Shall Come Forth"; and Milik, "Notes d'épigraphie et topographie palestiniennes"). Milik identifies the Valley of Acacias with the Wadi Qaddum, a ravine located between the Mount of Olives and the village of Bethany.

19. חֲמַס בְּנֵי יְהוּדָה (violence done to the sons of Judah): Joel alludes to Obadiah 10: Edom had earlier been indicted for its violence directed toward "your brother Jacob." The pouring out of the

18. The book comes to an end with a paean for the blessings of God. Drought and famine had earlier plagued the land, but both are swept away. To the issue of famine, the prophet describes the mountains flowing not with mere subsistence levels of foodstuffs, but with the luxury of wine. Where once there was drought, the prophet describes the watercourses of Judah as full of water and a fountain opened in the temple of Yahweh. The sanctuary which itself had once been deprived of grain and libations now becomes the source of fertility. The image of a fountain in the Lord's temple is also taken up by Ezekiel (Ezek. 47) and Zechariah (Zech. 13:1; 14:3–8). Ezekiel associates the imagery with abundant harvests (Ezek. 47:12), while Zechariah relates it to the geological convulsions that accompany eschatological holy war against the nations (Zech. 14:3–8). John takes up both images; after the eschatological battle, he describes the New Jerusalem coming down from heaven with its river of life (Rev. 20:1–22:6). Agricultural motifs are often used in the Hebrew Bible as symbols of the blessedness of the future (Zech. 3:10); Joel's language recalls the imagery of Amos 9:13–15. The issues

that precipitated the crisis (drought and famine) are taken up in the conclusion; just as the nations would never again humiliate Jerusalem, so it would never be bereft of crops. The land becomes the garden of God; just as a river issued from Eden (Gen. 2:10), so a river flows from paradise restored (cf. Pss. 36:9 [8]; 46:5 [4]; 65:11 [10]; 87:7; Isa. 8:6; 33:21).

19. The prophet turns once again to traditional foes of Israel. Not only the Phoenicians and Philistines (vv. 4–8), but also Edom and Egypt will experience judgment for their conduct toward God's chosen people. The text does not provide direct clues regarding which atrocities or violence by Edom and Egypt are intended. In the case of Egypt the events of 609 B.C. associated with the death of Josiah, the deportation of Jehoahaz, and the installation of Jehoiakim (2 Kings 23:29–36) could be in view. The death of Josiah may well be at least part of the "innocent blood" with which the prophet is concerned. In the case of Edom, incursions into Judah either at the behest of Babylon or to take advantage of the Babylonian threat around 587 B.C. could be intended (Ps. 137:7; Lam. 4:21–22). Isaiah also uses imagery of the winepress to describe

Spirit (3:1–2 [2:28–29]) contrasts with this indictment for pouring out innocent blood.

20. לְדוֹר וָדוֹר (forever): See 2:2 (and 1:3).

21. וְנִקֵּיתִי דָּמָם (shall I let their bloodguilt go unpunished?): At first glance the verse appears to contain self-contradictory clauses: דָּמָם לֹא־נִקֵּיתִי וְנִקֵּיתִי (I will declare them innocent of their bloodshed, I will not not declare [them] innocent). This tension has given rise to a number of solutions. The issues revolve around the translation of נִקֵּיתִי and the questions of who shed the blood and whose blood was shed (דָּמָם). Allen (*Joel*, p. 117) reads the first clause as a question: "Shall I leave their bloodshed unpunished? I will not. . . ." In this case דָּמָם refers to the Judean blood shed by Egypt and Edom (4:19 [3:19]). One is reluctant to suggest a rhetorical question when no interrogative words or particles mark it; however, such unmarked questions are also found elsewhere in the Old Testament. Some suggest that the Septuagint (ἐκδικήσω) and the Syriac version read נָקַמְתִּי for the first occurrence of נִקֵּיתִי: "And I will avenge their blood, I will not leave it unpunished" (cf. Hos. 1:4, LXX). However, the Septuagint uses ἐκδικεῖν elsewhere as a translation of the verb נָקָה (Zech. 5:3), so that the warrant for suggesting an alternative text with נָקַם is thereby reduced (see Allen, *Joel*, p. 117; Rudolph, *Joel*, p. 78). The verb נָקָה embraces the roughly opposite senses of to purge, cleanse, or remove and to declare innocent or let go unpunished. Even if a textual emendation is not needed, it is improbable that the same

verb was used in opposite senses in such a proximate context. Prinsloo (*Theology of the Book of Joel*, pp. 113–14), Keller (*Joël*, p. 153), and Ahlström (*Joel and the Temple Cult*, pp. 95–96) read the negative לֹא as an emphatic or affirmative particle, so that the sense becomes "I will declare their bloodshed innocent, yea, I will declare innocent." This does not require a modification of the consonantal text, but only a change in vocalization. Ahlström takes the further step of reading נָקָה as cognate of an Akkadian verb *nequ* (pour out) so that the text then is understood to say, "I will pour out their blood, yea, I will pour it out"; this equation with the Akkadian verb is philologically improbable. A further option understands דָּמָם as the blood of Gentiles shed by Judeans; in contrast to the blood shed by the Gentile nations which will be avenged, the bloodshed committed by the Judeans ("which I had not pardoned") will be pardoned. This reads the entirety of verses 20–21 as a contrast with verse 19. The violence that is being overlooked could be viewed as sin forgiven in Judah or as the violence done in their participation in Yahweh's vengeance on the nations. This translation understands the verse without textual or vocalization change, reads נִקֵּיתִי the same in both instances, and does not require suggesting a rhetorical question for the first clause (cf. also 4:6 [3:6]): it was wrong for Gentile nations to sell Judean slaves, but no condemnation is offered when Judeans do the reverse.

God's judgment on Edom (Isa. 63:1–6). If we understand *their land* (v. 19) as a reference to Egypt and Edom, this indictment may be instead for crimes committed against Judean slaves who had also been sold to distant places. Both Egypt and Edom had a long history of enmity with Israel, extending back to the exodus. The fate of Egypt and Edom is to become a desolate waste, precisely what the locusts and drought had done to Judah. God intends to pour out (*šāpak*) his Spirit on Judah (3:1 [2:28]), but these nations had poured out their innocent blood. Yahweh himself becomes the blood avenger for his people (Gen. 4:10; Deut. 19:1–13; Heb. 12:24; Rev. 6:10).

20–21. Yahweh will not allow violence toward Jerusalem and his people to go unpunished, because he dwells in Zion (v. 21). Yahweh will be a refuge for his people (v. 16), but there will be no refuge when he seeks to avenge their blood. God will not terminate his relationship with his people. Today, the church stands as a decisive testimony to the fact that God has not abandoned his promise of offspring (see 2 Sam. 7:12). The Lord still dwells in Zion (Heb. 12:22–23; 1 Pet. 2:6; Rev. 14:1) in keeping with his promise.

Amos

Introduction

Author

The prophet Amos came from Tekoa (1:1), a village some ten miles south of Jerusalem and six miles south of Bethlehem in Judah. We know nothing about his family. We do not know how old he was when he prophesied, nor how long he lived. In fact we know nothing about him beyond the little he has said about himself. It is significant that Amos chose to remain largely faceless, because this attitude reflects what should be the true spirit of a prophet, epitomized by the last of the prophets of the old covenant, who said, "He must increase, but I must decrease" (John 3:30).

Amos probably grew up in Tekoa, and learned there the related skills of a shepherd (1:1) and a livestock breeder (7:14). His work must have required him to travel, however, because he was also a dresser of sycamore-fig trees (7:14), which are not found more than one thousand feet above sea level and grow nowhere near Tekoa (which lies over two thousand feet above sea level), but in the lower lands of the Jordan Valley and on the shores of the Dead Sea and the Mediterranean. Moreover, Tekoa is only a day's journey from Samaria, and it is possible that Amos pursued his various callings in the north as well as the south. It seems reasonable to suppose, therefore, that his professions carried him to different parts of his own country and probably to neighboring countries as well (see Craigie, "Amos the *nōqēd* in the Light of Ugaritic").

If this is so, Amos may have gained some knowledge of the surrounding nations, including their history (1:3–2:3). He certainly knew the history of the divided kingdom. He was familiar with the atrocities committed against Israel during the Syro-

To my father and mother— who repented when the Lord warned them and who are now with Him.

Contributor:
Jeffrey J. Niehaus,
B.A., M.A.,
M.Div., Ph.D.
Professor of
Old Testament,
Gordon-Conwell
Theological Seminary.

315

Israelite wars (1:3). He knew of the deportations of Israelites by the Philistines and their sale as slaves (1:6) and of the similar behavior of the Phoenicians who broke international treaties (1:9). He knew how the Ammonites had ripped open the pregnant women of Gilead (1:13), and he was aware also of Edom's remorseless pursuit of his brother (Judah) with the sword during the uprising of Jehoram's reign (1:11; see also 2 Chron. 21:16–17). But he also knew something of the history of foreign nations, for he tells us that Moab had burned to lime the bones of the king of Edom (2:1).

Amos was also familiar with the history of God's covenant people and with the covenant itself, as his numerous allusions to the law make clear (e.g., 2:4, 8, 11; 3:1; 4:7, 9–11; 5:11). Such knowledge was appropriate to prophets, for they were primarily covenant-lawsuit messengers. Prophets were appointed by God to bring suit against the Lord's people when they rebelled against the law that the Lord gave through his servant Moses. Some knowledge of that law was, therefore, appropriate, if not essential, to the prophetic calling, just as some knowledge of the Old Testament is apparent in Jesus' apostles—and, especially, in Paul—who function with prophetic authority in the New Testament. Amos had not studied to be a prophet (7:14), however, but the Lord sovereignly called him to be one. Amos ministered primarily to the northern kingdom (7:15), although his prophecies also addressed the sins of Judah (2:4–5; cf. 9:11).

The sovereign nature of his calling is of great spiritual importance. Amos did not seek to be a prophet by joining a prophetic school or guild (7:14). God made him a prophet and gave him his message. The fact that God's message was unpopular (2:12) and that it provoked a strong reaction in official quarters (7:12–13) did not deter Amos from taking his stand (7:14–15) and prophesying (7:16–17). Amos's faith, which was based on his intimacy with God (3:7; cf. John 15:15), may be difficult for us to comprehend, but God desires a similar intimacy of faith from all his people (Jer. 31:33–34; John 14:21).

Date and Situation

The ministry of Amos spanned the reigns of King Uzziah of Judah (791–740 B.C.) and King Jeroboam II of Israel (793–753 B.C.). The precise dates of his prophetic activity cannot be known for certain, but it is likely that he prophesied late in Jeroboam's reign, perhaps in the early 760s.

One factor that supports a date later in Jeroboam's reign is the level of prosperity in Israel that the prophecy of Amos describes. Jeroboam was a successful king by worldly standards. In accordance with a prophecy of Jonah son of Amittai (2 Kings 14:25),

Jeroboam restored the borders of Israel to the boundaries that existed at the time of the Israelite defection from the united kingdom. There was peace between Israel and Judah during Jeroboam's reign. On the international scene, Egypt and Babylon were weak. Syria (Aram), which had so troubled Israel late in the ninth century (2 Kings 10:32–33; 13:7), had been subjugated by the Assyrian king Adad-nerari III (810–783). The subjugation of Syria gave Israel the opportunity to expand and reclaim its borders. After the death of Adad-nerari III, however, Assyria had its own troubles. Assyria also entered a period of quiescence, for, with the rise of the kingdom of Urartu under Argisti I and Sarduri II (810–743), the Assyrians found themselves challenged from the north. They were in no position to threaten Israel.

Israel prospered during the long and secure reign of Jeroboam II. However, the affluence, which Amos's prophecy describes, could not have come about quickly, but only some years after Israel's fortunes had been restored under Jeroboam. That would have been a considerable time after the recapture of alienated territory earlier in his reign. Amos, then, must have prophesied toward the end of Jeroboam's reign, and a date around 760 is generally accepted. Concrete support for this date includes the reference to an earthquake, which has been dated to this period (see the Exposition of 1:1). Later, under Tiglath-pileser III (744–727 B.C.), Assyria regained its military might and expanded to the north and west. Judah became an Assyrian vassal, and Damascus, which in the past had been a buffer state between Israel and Assyria, became part of the Assyrian Empire (2 Kings 16:7–9). Tiglath-pileser III was followed by his son, Shalmaneser V (726–722 B.C.), who pursued his father's policy of westward expansion and forced King Hoshea of Israel to become his vassal (2 Kings 17:3). Hoshea misguidedly rebelled, however, relying for help on Egypt (2 Kings 17:4), but that help never came. In a punitive invasion, typical of Assyria, Shalmaneser laid siege to Samaria, the capital of Israel, and after three years the city fell (722 B.C.), bringing to an end the kingdom of Israel (2 Kings 17:5–6).

Amos may have delivered the oracles this book records at different places in the northern kingdom, including Samaria and Bethel. We cannot know for sure; it is certain only that he fulfilled some of his prophetic ministry at Bethel (7:10–17).

Style and Structure

Unlike the oracles of earlier prophets (except those of Joel, if he may be dated in the ninth century B.C.), Amos's words, like those of his contemporaries Isaiah, Hosea, and Jonah, were preserved in writing. It was essential that the people preserve these great covenant-lawsuit messages because they were reminders of Israel's history, and they set forth promises of restoration and redemption, which related to the nation.

Amos's book falls naturally into three sections: chapters 1–2, 3–6, and 7–9. The first two chapters are essentially prefatory, with a brief superscription and introduction, followed by a lengthy poem against the chief nations bordering on Israel, and against Israel itself. The next four chapters consist of three covenant lawsuits and ancillary oracles of exile and judgment. The last three chapters comprise a series of five visions, followed by longer or shorter explanations, and interrupted by an autobiographical account of Amos's confrontation with Amaziah, the (high) priest at Bethel.

The book clearly has a purposeful structure. Since Amos is a covenant-lawsuit messenger, it is appropriate that his words take the form of covenant-lawsuit addresses. Herbert B. Huffmon ("Covenant Lawsuit in the Prophets," p. 285) diagrams the covenant lawsuit as follows:

I. A description of the scene of judgment
II. The speech by the judge
    A. Address to the defendant
        1. Reproach (based on the accusation)
        2. Statement (usually in the third person) that the accused has no defense
    B. Pronouncement of guilt
    C. Sentence (in second or third person)

This form is not unique to the Old Testament, for it occurs in the annals of the Hittite king Mursilis II (ca. 1325 B.C.; see Götze, *Die Annalen des Muršiliš*) and in the Middle Assyrian *Tukulti-Ninurta Epic* (Thompson and Hutchinson, "Excavations on the Temple of Nabû"; Thompson and Mallowen, "British Museum Excavations at Nineveh, 1931–32"; Lambert, "Three Unpublished Fragments of the Tukulti-Ninurta Epic"). The following passage from the Hittite annals, in which Mursilis brings covenant lawsuit against a rebellious vassal, illustrates the form (translated from Götze, *Die Annalen des Muršiliš*, pp. 46–47):

9) But I [Mursilis] sent an emissary to Uḫḫa-LU-iš,
10) and wrote to him: "My servants, who came to you—
11) when I demanded them back from you, you did not
12) send them back to me. And you have treated me like a mere child,
13) and abused me. Now then! We will do battle against each other!
14) And may the Storm God, my Lord, decide our trial by combat!"

This pericope may be analyzed as follows:

> introduction: lines 9–10a
> historical review: lines 10b–11a
> indictment: lines 11b–13a
> judgment: lines 13b–14

This covenant-lawsuit pattern is essentially the same as the form identified by Huffmon, with the introduction presenting the scene and the plaintiff (in the Old Testament, the plaintiff was also the judge, Yahweh), the historical review presenting the basis of the accusation, the indictment presenting the accusation itself, and the judgment presenting the pronouncement of guilt and the sentence. The covenant-lawsuit form was apparently common in the ancient Near East (see, for example, the *Tukulti-Ninurta Epic* in Thompson and Hutchinson, "Excavations on the Temple of Nabû," pp. 130, 133).

Because these lawsuit documents deal with covenant breaking, their literary form derives from the second-millennium covenant form itself, as the following parallel shows:

Covenant	*Covenant Lawsuit*
introduction of suzerain	introduction of plaintiff/judge
historical prologue	historical review
stipulations	indictments
summons to witnesses	summons to witnesses
oath (= response to a call to obedience)	call to repentance
blessings/curses	judgment (enactment of curses)

It seems apparent that the bulk of Amos's oracles, which are also covenant-lawsuit documents, are built on this form. The covenant-lawsuit form is found in all three sections of the book. For instance, the oracle against Aram, which begins the international judgment poem in the first section, is structured as follows:

> introduction of plaintiff and judge (1:3a)
> introduction of defendant (1:3a)
> indictment (1:3b)
> judgment (1:4–5)

Likewise, the much longer covenant lawsuit that begins the second section:

> introduction of plaintiff and judge (3:1a)
> introduction of defendant (3:1b)
> indictment (3:2)
> confirmation of covenant-lawsuit messenger (3:3–8)
> summons to witnesses (3:9a)

> indictment (3:9b–10)
> judgment (3:11–15)

Covenant lawsuit elements also appear in the ancillary oracles that conclude the third section, as the first of them illustrates:

> introduction of defendant (5:18a)
> introduction of judge (5:18a)
> judgment warning (5:18b–20)
> indictment (5:21–23)
> call to repentance (5:24)
> indictment (5:25–26)
> judgment (5:27)

The covenant-lawsuit genre that governs to a large degree the structure of Amos's book also governs its style. In particular, it clarifies the matter of the two third-person sections—the superscription (1:1) and the encounter between Amos and Amaziah (7:10–17)—which have usually been considered the product of another author.

Relevant to this discussion are Hittite second-millennium suzerain-vassal treaties, which have been useful in dating and elucidating the covenantal structure of portions of the Pentateuch, particularly Deuteronomy. One aspect of this relationship that has not received sufficient attention, however, is the shift that regularly occurs between the third-person and first-person singular in these treaties and in biblical books.

The Hittite treaties without exception display such a shift. Thus, the treaty between the Hittite king Mursilis and Duppi-Tessub of Amurru begins:

> These are the words of the Sun Mursilis, the great king, the king of the Hatti land, the valiant, the favorite of the Storm-god, the son of Suppiluliumas, the great king, the king of the Hatti land, the valiant.
>
> Aziras was the grandfather of you, Duppi-Tessub. He rebelled against *my* father, but submitted again to *my* father. (*ANET*, p. 203, italics added)

Note that, after the superscription or preamble in the third person, identifying the great king, there is a shift to the first person as the treaty or covenant gets underway with the historical prologue. In other words, the great king is introduced in the third person, then begins to speak in the first person.

A similar shift is apparent in the structure of Deuteronomy. For example, 1:1–9 says:

> These are the words that Moses spoke to all Israel beyond the Jordan— in the wilderness, on the plain opposite Suph, between Paran and Tophel, Laban, Hazeroth, and Di-zahab. . . . Beyond the Jordan in the land of Moab, Moses undertook to expound this law as follows:

> The LORD *our* God spoke to *us* at Horeb. . . .
> At that time *I* said to you. . . .

Like the Hittite treaties, Deuteronomy begins in the third person. This time, however, it is not the Great King, but his covenant mediator who represents him and is introduced in the third person. And the narrative continues with a lengthy historical prologue in the first person (1:6–4:43), just as in the second-millennium Hittite treaties.

The Old Testament prophets also exhibit a similar stylistic device. The prophetic books regularly begin with a superscription or preamble in the third person, identifying the name of the covenant-lawsuit messenger of the Great King. There follows a shift to the first person as the covenant lawsuit continues.

This parallel between Hittite treaties, Deuteronomy, and the prophetic books is not accidental, but is intrinsic to the covenant and covenant-lawsuit forms (the covenant-lawsuit form is an outgrowth of the covenant form itself). Likewise, the shift from a third-person introduction to a first-person historical review/lawsuit procedure is common to both forms.

There is more to be said, however, for the Hittite treaties also manifest occasional shifts from first to third person, and back again, within the treaty or covenant itself. In a treaty between Suppiluliuma and King Mattiwaza of Mitanni, for example, we find the standard shift from third to first person after the introduction of the treaty or covenant. But then it shifts back to the third person ("In the days of the father of the king of Hatti land, the land Isuwa rebelled"), and then again to the first person ("Now the people, who had escaped *my* grasp, went to Isuwa land"; Weidner, *Politische Dokumente aus Kleinasien*, pp. 1–7, lines 1–15).

There are numerous examples of this type of shift. They indicate that shifts between third and first person are not uncommon in covenantal literature. These may be expected (as we regularly find them in the prophets) between the preamble or superscription and the main body of the covenant lawsuit. They may also be found within the body of the covenant lawsuit itself.

This fact has considerable implications for the question of authorship in the Old Testament prophetic books. It is not unreasonable, for example, to suppose that the third-person portions of Jeremiah, traditionally ascribed to Baruch, may be original to Jeremiah himself. The Book of Jeremiah may reflect this ancient Near Eastern stylistic practice. If that is so, the words near the end of that book are quite literally true: "The words of Jeremiah end here" (Jer. 51:65, NIV).

The implications for Amos are also clear. It is possible that we should ascribe to Amos not only the superscription, but also the third-person account of the confrontation between Amos and Amaziah (7:10–17).

As a covenant-lawsuit messenger, Amos regularly employs what has been called messenger formulas: "Thus says the LORD," (1:3), "Says the LORD" (1:5), "Oracle of the LORD" (2:11). He also employs the charge to listen which stems from covenantal usage: "Hear this word" (3:1). In these cases he is reminiscent of the mediator-prophet Moses, who often summoned the people to hear Yahweh's words or commands (e.g., Deut. 4:1; 5:1). Amos also reports oaths that Yahweh has sworn (4:2; 6:8; 8:7), a form that conveys with special force the Lord's intent, which, as a prophet, Amos was privileged to receive.

The phraseology of the Prophecy of Amos illustrates the covenant background against which it was written, as the following list of select words and phrases shows (pentateuchal references are not exhaustive).

Amos	Phrase/Concept	Pentateuchal Reference
1:1	the words of Amos	Deut. 1:1
1:9	remember covenant	Gen. 9:15; Exod. 2:24; 6:5; Lev. 26:42–45
2:4	keep statutes	Exod. 15:26; Deut. 4:40
	walk after	Deut. 4:3; 11:28; 13:5 [4]
2:7	pervert justice	Exod. 23:6
2:10; 9:7	brought you up from Egypt	Gen. 50:24; Exod. 3:8
2:10	inherit the land	Gen. 15:7; Num. 33:53; Deut. 2:31
3:1	hear this word	Deut. 4:1; 5:1; 6:4
3:7	his servants the prophets	Deut. 34:5, 10
4:4	tithes every three days/years	Deut. 14:28; 26:12
4:5	burn sacrifices	Lev. 1:9
	leavened bread as a thank-offering	Lev. 2:11; 7:12–15
	freewill offerings	Lev. 22:17–25
	love	Deut. 6:5
4:6	return to Yahweh	Deut. 4:30; 30:2
4:9	blight and mildew	Deut. 28:22
	vineyards, olive trees	Deut. 28:30, 39–40
4:10	I sent plague among you	Lev. 26:25; Deut. 28:20–21, 48
4:12	prepare to meet your God	Exod. 19:15–17
4:13	on the heights of the earth	Deut. 32:13
5:4	seek Yahweh	Deut. 4:29
5:6	Yahweh like a consuming fire	Deut. 4:24
5:11	futility curse on houses	Deut. 28:30a
	futility curse on vineyards	Deut. 28:30b, 39
5:20	gloom as covenant curse	Deut. 28:29
	accept offerings	Lev. 1:4; 7:18; 19:7; 22:27
5:26	images that you fashioned for yourselves	Exod. 20:4; 32:1, 23; Deut. 5:8
5:27	exile far from home	Deut. 28:36, 64–68; 29:27 [28]
6:1	first of the nations	Num. 24:20
6:11; 9:9	Yahweh is commanding	Exod. 34:11; Deut. 26:16
7:2	locusts eating the vegetation of the land	Exod. 10:12, 15
7:9	desolation and waste of high places and sanctuaries	Lev. 26:30–31
7:11, 17	exile away from the land	Deut. 29:27 [28]
7:16	preach (drip)	Deut. 32:2
8:4	needy and oppressed	Deut. 15:11; 24:14–15
8:5	open the granaries	Gen. 41:56
	false weights	Lev. 19:36; Deut. 25:14
	false measures	Lev. 19:35
8:9	noon is dark	Deut. 28:29
8:11	famine	Deut. 28:48
	scarcity of Yahweh's words	Deut. 4:28–29; 32:20
9:8	destroy from the face of the land	Deut. 6:15
9:12	over whom my name is pronounced	Deut. 28:10
9:15	land that I have given to them	Num. 20:12, 24; 27:12
	Yahweh your God	Gen. 27:20; Exod. 8:24 [28]; Lev. 11:44; Num. 10:9; Deut. 1:10

It is clear from these parallels that Amos draws frequently on the covenantal ideology and phraseology of the books of Moses. Most of these literary echoes come from those books that contain the historical prologue, laws (covenant stipulations), and blessings/curses of the Lord's covenant with his people, that is, Exodus–Deuteronomy.

As a poet, Amos shows architectonic skill and power, using structure and repetition to bring his oracles to a climax. The long poem against the nations that forms the first section of the book is an example of this. The poem takes, in part, the form of a geographical chiasmus: Syria to the northeast (1:3–5), Philistia to the southwest (1:6–8), Tyre to the northwest (1:9–10), and Edom, Ammon, and Moab to the southeast (1:11–2:3). The focus then shifts to Judah in the south (2:4–5), before coming home to Israel (2:6–16) (see Stuart, *Hosea–Jonah*, pp. 290–91). Moreover, the poem builds to a climax by going the round of foreign nations before turning to Judah and—surprisingly and appallingly—to Israel herself. The power of this oracle is further established by the repetition of important phrases, for example, "for three rebellious acts of A and for four, I will not reverse it," a classic example of x/x+1 parallelism (e.g., 1:3); "and I will send fire against A, and it will eat up the royal citadels of B" (e.g., 1:4); and the threats, "I will cut off" and "they will go into exile" (both 1:5).

Repeated phrases or structures are significant elsewhere in Amos. For instance, the device of repetition draws 3:3–8 to a climax. In this passage a series of parallel rhetorical questions with implicit but obvious answers leads inevitably to the conclusion that Yahweh does indeed reveal his plans to the prophets, and that a prophet has no choice but to prophesy.

Reiterated structure also characterizes the vision section (7:1–9:10), which includes a dialogue between Amos and Yahweh (7:1–9). These visions have a climactic aspect. The first two prompt intercession on the part of Amos and the Lord relents (7:1–3, 4–6). But the last three (7:7–9; 8:1–3; 9:1–4) entail Yahweh's explanation of why judgment must come.

Amos draws on another genre that involves repetition: the divine or royal titulary, that is, the naming of the god (or king), followed by a series of epithets that describe him. This literary form, common in the ancient Near East, appears in 4:13, 5:8, and 9:5–6. Typically, the epithets are in the form of participles, although these are often intermixed with verbs in the perfect. A famous illustration comes from the law code of King Hammurabi of Babylon:

> Hammurabi, the shepherd, called by Enlil, am I;
> the one who makes affluence and plenty abound;

who provides in abundance all sorts of things for Nippur-
   Duranki;
the devout patron of Ekur;
the efficient king, who restored Eridu to its place;
who purified the cult of Eabzu;
the one who strides through the four quarters of the world;
who makes the name of Babylon great;
who rejoices the heart of Marduk, his lord. (*ANET*, p. 164)

This form occurs elsewhere in the Bible in Isaiah 44:24–28 (for examples from ancient Near Eastern annals, see King, *Annals of the Kings of Assyria*, pp. 28–29, 32–33).

Most interesting for our discussion of Amos is the frequency with which such titularies occur in the Assyrian annals. We find them not only at the beginning of the annals, but interspersed throughout, at the beginning of each new annual report. For instance, the report of Tiglath-pileser's second-year campaigns begins with a titulary (King, *Annals of the Kings of Assyria*, pp. 46–47):

Tiglath-pileser, valiant hero,
who opens ways through the mountains,
who subdues the insubmissive,
who overthrows all fierce foes.

It is further significant that many of the Assyrian campaigns were against rebellious vassals—that is, covenant vassals who had broken covenant, just as the vassal Israel had broken covenant with her Lord.

The appearance of these titularies in Amos (as in Isaiah) stresses the power and indeed the sovereignty of Yahweh, just as the Babylonian and Assyrian titularies stressed the sovereignty and power of their gods and kings. The purpose of titularies in the Babylonian and Assyrian materials is to underscore the authority of the god and the kings who (as in the case of Hammurabi) gave the laws and (as in the case of Tiglath-pileser I) who punished the rebels who broke covenant.

The Amos titularies are simply brief examples of their genre. They were most likely composed by Amos to fit his purposes, as were the Babylonian and Assyrian examples. Amos's titularies may well contain traditional epithets of Yahweh, as their Mesopotamian counterparts contain epithets of the gods to which they refer. This does not mean that Amos's titularies are fragments of a hypothetical ancient hymn, as some have thought (Watts, "Old Hymn"; Stuart, *Hosea–Jonah*, pp. 347–48).

Another literary device that Amos employs is the summary quotation. He uses it in 4:1 to characterize the wealthy "cows" of Bashan who idly demand drinks from their husbands. It appears also in 6:13 to portray those who vainly boast of military strength ("a pair of horns") that they themselves have acquired. In 8:5–6 we see it again where it dramatizes the greed of merchants who cannot wait for the holy days to pass so they can cheat the poor. In 9:10 this device represents those who deny that judgment is coming.

Amos's summary quotations make use of irony, another device that plays an important part in his book. Irony represents a reversal of what is normal or expected. It gives poignancy and bite to the word of rebuke and judgment. Thus, it was a powerful tool for the prophet. We find irony in Amos's use of the divine/royal titulary, for he applies it not only to God, but also to the Lord's sinful people:

> Hear this word, you cows of Bashan
>   on Mount Samaria,
> who oppress the poor,
> who crush the needy,
>   who say to their husbands,
>   "Bring, that we may drink!"   (4:1)

This use of irony is especially stinging because it is addressed to women of wealth and stature, who may have secretly felt that they deserved to be addressed in a style accorded to gods and royalty.

Amos's use of irony coincides with paranomasia as he pronounces judgment: "Woe . . . to the distinguished men of the '*first* of the nations'" (6:1), who "anoint themselves with *first-class* oils (6:6), for they "will go into exile as the *first* [lit. at the head] of the exiles" (6:7). The judgment that he announces is expressed in part by futility curses, which by their nature are ironic. For example,

> Houses of dressed stone you have built,
>   but you will not live in them;
> pleasant vineyards you have planted,
>   but you will not drink their wine.   (5:11)

One of the ironies that God brings on Israel is that of historical reversal. Amos's allusions to the nation's experience in Egypt are of this kind. The Lord reminds them, "I myself brought you up from the land of Egypt" (2:10). He goes on to remind them of his covenant faithfulness to them in the promised land (2:11). But, as the bulk of Amos's prophecy shows, Israel rebelled against her Maker. In ironic reversal, the Lord afflicted them as he had afflicted Egypt. He sent locusts to devour their gardens and groves, just as he had sent locusts against Egypt (4:9; see Exod.

10:1–20; Ps. 105:33–34). He sent plagues among them "after the manner of Egypt" (4:10). But they did not repent at these covenant warnings. So he declared, "I will pass through your midst" (5:17), bringing judgment and destruction, just as he had passed through the land of Egypt in judgment in Moses' day (Exod. 12:12).

If Amos reflects ironically on the exodus, he also reflects ironically on the conquest. The Lord reminds Israel, "I myself destroyed the Amorite from before them" (2:9). But Israel, in her rebellion and idolatry, has become as bad as or worse than the ones she had displaced. So the Lord declares of the sinful kingdom, "I will destroy it from the face of the land" (9:8).

Theology

The depiction of God in the prophecy of Amos is similar to the depiction of him we find in the first pages of the Pentateuch. In three divine titularies, Amos portrays God's sovereign power over the world (visible and invisible) he has created. He formed the mountains and made the wind (4:13). He draws water from the seas to bring rain upon the earth (5:8; 9:6). He makes the night day, and the day night (4:13; 5:8). He formed the Pleiades and Orion (5:8). And, in the invisible realm, he has built his temple in the heavens (9:6). He also made humans in his image, and he alone is God. For that reason, God will not tolerate idolatry (5:26), which in reality is the worship of demons (Deut. 32:16–17; 1 Cor. 10:20), for God does not want people whom he has made in his image to abase themselves before demons.

Sovereign over the world, Amos's God is also the Lord of the nations. As Lord he is also Judge. He can, and does, raise up one nation against another in judgment (1:3–2:3)—a process that will continue until the Lord's return (for he is now, as always, "the Judge of all the earth" [Gen. 18:25]). The Lord is also the Judge of Israel, his covenant people. He brought them up out of Egypt and led them forty years in the wilderness to possess the land of the Amorite (2:9–10). He gave them Torah and commandments, which, however, they did not obey (2:4). He gave them Nazirites as emblems of holiness and prophets to keep them in his way (2:11), but the people frequently responded in rebellion. When God must find his people guilty of covenant breaking, he raises up another nation against them (6:14). As sovereign Lord of all, he is able to do this; as Judge of all the earth, he must.

Yet the Lord is a loving God who desires the life, not the death, of his sinful people. Above all, he desires a relationship with his people. According to Amos, that relationship finds its most intimate expression in the prophet's calling. The Lord and his prophet are like two who walk together (3:3). He reveals his secrets to his servants, the prophets (3:7), just as he did long ago (Gen. 20:7) to the prophet Abraham (Gen. 18:17). But God desires a relationship with all his people. He has known them in the past (3:2) and wants to restore that relationship with them (4:8, 14–15). So his plea to a wayward land is, "Seek me and live" (5:4; cf. 1 Tim. 2:3–4).

Anthropology

If much of biblical theology is the story of salvation, much of biblical anthropology is the story of sin. Since the leaven of sin is at work in all humanity, it is at work in God's chosen people as well. So, when Amos attacks the sins of the nations, along with those of Judah and Israel, he is speaking the mind of God about a fallen humanity and a rebellious people.

The nations in Amos's day hold a mirror to our own age. They did not care for solemn international treaties, but voided them at the first hope of success (1:9). In war, their treatment of the foe was so inhumane that it was likened to threshing (1:3). Taking people into exile and selling them into slavery were common (1:6, 9). Ancestral relations were ignored as brother pursued brother with the sword (1:11). Soldiers cut open pregnant women with swords (1:13). People even sought vengeance on the dead by burning their bones (2:1). As modern events have shown, no nation is so cultured that it cannot stoop to such atrocities. Both ancient and modern history show our desperate need of God's covenant lordship and the redeeming power of the Holy Spirit, to bear his fruit and to form Christ in us, the hope of glory.

Amos attacks two major areas of sin frequently indicted by other prophets: idolatry and social injustice. Israel's root problem was, of course, spiritual. The nation was religious, but only superficially. Idolatry was commonplace (2 Kings 17:14–17; Amos 5:26). So were violence and injustice (2:6–8; 4:1). In fact, such things normally appear together for, as people turn to worship that which is less than God (i.e., demons, who want to destroy humanity), they lose more of God's image and become like the objects of their worship (Ps. 135:15–18; Rom. 1:18–32), desiring, like Satan himself, to destroy other humans.

The Lord had warned Israel in the form of hunger, thirst, blight, locusts, plagues, and military defeat. But they had refused to see his hand in these (4:6–11). Judgment was certain (4:12). The nature of the impending judgment is portrayed in a series of verbal and visionary prophecies that portend wholesale destruction and exile. The Lord only chastises those whom he loves, however. His judgment is really a sign of his commitment to his covenant people. He promises the restoration and redemption of "David's collapsing tent" (9:11–12) and the ultimate future of his people is portrayed in a concluding section (9:13–15), almost evocative of Eden in its lushness and blessedness.

Analysis

Select Bibliography

Ackroyd, Peter R. "The Meaning of Hebrew דּוֹר Considered." *Journal of Semitic Studies* 13 (1968): 3–10.

Baltzer, Klaus. *Das Bundesformular.* Wissenschaftliche Monographien zum Alten und Neuen Testament 4. Neukirchen: Neukirchener Verlag, 1960.

Barré, Michael L. "The Meaning of Þ ʾšybnw in Amos 1:3–2:6." *Journal of Biblical Literature* 105 (1986): 611–31.

Bartina, Sebastian. "'Vivit Potentia Beer-Šeba!' (Amos 8:14)." *Verbum Domini* 34 (1956): 202–10.

Borger, Riekele. *Einleitung in die assyrischen Königsinschriften,* vol. 1: *Das zweite Jahrtausend v. Chr.* Handbuch der Orientalistik 1:5:1. Leiden: Brill, 1961.

———. *Die Inschriften Asarhaddons, Königs von Assyrien.* Archiv für Orientforschung Beiheft 9. Graz: Weidner, 1956.

Bright, John. *A History of Israel.* 3d ed. Philadelphia: Westminster, 1981.

Cassuto, Umberto. *Biblical and Oriental Studies,* vol. 2: *Bible and Ancient Oriental Texts.* Translated by Israel Abrahams. Jerusalem: Magnes, 1975.

———. *The Documentary Hypothesis and the Composition of the Pentateuch.* Translated by Israel Abrahams. Jerusalem: Magnes, 1961.

Cogan, Morton. *Imperialism and Religion: Assyria, Judah and Israel in the Eighth and Seventh Centuries* B.C.E. Society of Biblical Literature Monograph Series 19. Missoula, Mont.: Scholars, 1974.

Couroyer, B. "L'Arc d'Airain." *Revue Biblique* 72 (1965): 508–14.

Craigie, Peter C. "Amos the *nōqēd* in the Light of Ugaritic." *Studies in Religion* 11 (1982): 29–33.

———. *The Book of Deuteronomy.* New International Commentary on the Old Testament. Grand Rapids: Eerdmans, 1976.

Cross, Frank M. *Canaanite Myth and Hebrew Epic: Essays in the History of the Religion of Israel.* Cambridge: Harvard University Press, 1973.

Crowfoot, John W., and Grace M. Crowfoot. *Early Ivories from Samaria.* Samaria-Sebaste 2. London: Palestine Exploration Fund, 1938.

Dahood, Mitchell. "Hebrew-Ugaritic Lexicography II." *Biblica* 45 (1964): 393–412.

———. "Hebrew-Ugaritic Lexicography IX." *Biblica* 52 (1971): 337–56.

———. "*Nādâ* 'to Hurl' in Ex 15:16." *Biblica* 43 (1962): 248–49.

Davidson, Andrew B. *Hebrew Syntax.* 3d ed. Edinburgh: T. & T. Clark, 1901.

Donner, Herbert, and Wolfgang Röllig. *Kanaanäische und aramäische Inschriften.* 3 vols. Wiesbaden: Harrassowitz, 1962–64.

Dossin, Georges. "Les Archives Épistolaires du Palais de Mari." *Syria* 19 (1938): 105–26.

Driver, Samuel R. *The Books of Joel and Amos.* 2d ed. Cambridge Bible for Schools and Colleges. Cambridge: Cambridge University Press, 1915.

Ebeling, Erich, Bruno Meissner, and Ernst F. Weidner. *Die Inschriften der altassyrischen Könige.* Altorientalische Bibliothek 1. Leipzig: Quelle & Meyer, 1926.

Gerstenberger, Eberhard. "The Woe-Oracles of the Prophets." *Journal of Biblical Literature* 81 (1962): 249–63.

Gevirtz, Stanley. *Patterns in the Early Poetry of Israel.* Studies in Ancient Oriental Civilization 32. Chicago: University of Chicago Press, 1963.

Gibson, John C. L. *Canaanite Myths and Legends.* 2d ed. Edinburgh: T. & T. Clark, 1977.

Gordon, Cyrus H. *Ugaritic Textbook.* Analecta Orientalia 38. Rome: Pontifical Biblical Institute, 1965.

Götze, Albrecht. *Die Annalen des Muršiliš.* Leipzig: Hinrichs, 1933. Reprinted Darmstadt: Wissenschaftliche Buchgesellschaft, 1967.

Grayson, Albert K. *Assyrian Royal Inscriptions.* 2 vols. Records of the Ancient Near East 1–2. Wiesbaden: Harrassowitz, 1972–76.

Held, Moshe. "Studies in Comparative Semitic Lexicography." In *Studies in Honor of Benno Landsberger on His Seventy-fifth Birthday, April 21, 1965,* pp. 395–406. Edited by Hans G. Güterbock and Thorkild Jacobsen. Assyriological Studies 16. Chicago: Oriental Institute, University of Chicago, 1965.

———. "The *yqtl-qtl (qtl-yqtl)* Sequence of Identical Verbs in Biblical Hebrew and in Ugaritic." In *Studies and Essays in Honor of Abraham A. Neuman,* pp. 281–90. Edited by Meir Ben-Horin, Bernard D. Weinryb, and Solomon Zeitlin. Leiden: Brill for the Dropsie College, 1962.

Hillers, Delbert R. "Amos 7:4 and Ancient Parallels." *Catholic Biblical Quarterly* 26 (1964): 221–25.

Hirsch, Hans. "Die Inschriften der Könige von Agade." *Archiv für Orientforschung* 20 (1963): 1–82.

Holladay William L. "Once More, ʾanāk = 'Tin,' Amos 7:7–8." *Vetus Testamentum* 20 (1970): 492–94.

———. *The Root Šûbh in the Old Testament, with Particular Reference to Its Usages in Covenantal Contexts.* Leiden: Brill, 1958.

Holma, Harri. *Die Namen der Körperteile im Assyrisch-Babylonischen: Eine lexikalisch-etymologische Studie.* Helsinki: Suomalaisen Tiedeakatemian Kunstantama, 1911.

Horst, Friedrich. "Die Visionsschilderung der alttestamentlichen Propheten." *Evangelische Theologie* 20 (1960): 193–205.

Huffmon, Herbert B. "The Covenant Lawsuit in the Prophets." *Journal of Biblical Literature* 78 (1959): 285–95.

———. "The Treaty Background of Hebrew *Yādaʿ*." Bulletin of the *American Schools of Oriental Research* 181 (1966): 31–37.

Iwry, Samuel. "New Evidence for Belomancy in Ancient Palestine and Phoenicia." *Journal of American Oriental Studies* 81 (1961): 27–34.

Jeremias, Jörg. *Theophanie: Die Geschichte einer alttestamentlichen Gattung.* Wissenschaftliche Monographien zum Alten und Neuen Testament 10. Neukirchen-Vluyn: Neukirchener Verlag, 1965.

Keil, Carl F. *The Twelve Minor Prophets.* 2 vols. Translated by James Martin. Biblical Commentary on the Old Testament 10. Reprinted Grand Rapids: Eerdmans, 1977.

King, Leonard W. *Annals of the Kings of Assyria.* London: British Museum, 1902.

Knudtzon, Jürgen A. *Die El-Amarna-Tafeln mit Einleitung und Erläuterungen.* 2 vols. Leipzig: Hinrichs, 1915. Reprinted Aalen: Zeller, 1964.

Kugel, James L. *The Idea of Biblical Poetry: Parallelism and Its History.* New Haven: Yale University Press, 1981.

Lambert, Wilfred G. "Three Unpublished Fragments of the Tukulti-Ninurta Epic." *Archiv für Orientforschung* 18 (1957–58): 38–51.

Landsberger, Benno. "Tin and Lead: The Adventures of Two Vocables." *Journal of Near Eastern Studies* 24 (1965): 285–96.

Langdon, Stephen H. *Die neubabylonischen Königsinschriften.* Translated by Rudolf Zehnpfund. Vorderasiatische Bibliothek 4. Leipzig: Hinrichs, 1912.

Luckenbill, Daniel D. *Ancient Records of Assyria and Babylonia.* 2 vols. Chicago: University of Chicago Press, 1926–27.

———. *The Annals of Sennacherib.* Oriental Institute Publications 2. Chicago : University of Chicago Press, 1924.

McComiskey, Thomas E. "Amos." In *The Expositor's Bible Commentary,* vol. 7, pp. 267–331. Edited by Frank E. Gaebelein. Grand Rapids: Zondervan, 1985.

———. "The Hymnic Elements of the Prophecy of Amos: A Study of Form-Critical Methodology." *Journal of the Evangelical Theological Society* 30 (1987): 139–58.

Mays, James L. *Amos: A Commentary.* Old Testament Library. Philadelphia: Westminster, 1969.

Mendenhall, George E. "The Census Lists of Numbers 1 and 26." *Journal of Biblical Literature* 77 (1958): 52–66.

Millard, Alan R. "Saul's Shield Not Anointed with Oil." *Bulletin of the American Schools of Oriental Research* 230 (1978): 70.

Moran, William L. "The Ancient Near Eastern Background of the Love of God in Deuteronomy." *Catholic Biblical Quarterly* 25 (1963): 77–87.

———. "A Note on the Treaty Terminology of the Sefîre Stelas." *Journal of New Eastern Studies* 22 (1963): 173–76.

———. "Review of Das Bundesformular, by Klaus Baltzer." *Biblica* 43 (1962): 100–106.

Moscati, Sabatino (ed.). *An Introduction to the Comparative Grammar of the Semitic Languages: Phonology and Morphology*. Porta Linguarum Orientalium n.s. 6. Wiesbaden: Harrassowitz, 1964.

Neuberg, Frank J. "An Unrecognized Meaning of Hebrew *dôr*." *Journal of Near Eastern Studies* 9 (1950): 215–17.

Oppenheim, A. Leo. *Ancient Mesopotamia: Portrait of a Dead Civilization*. Revised by Erica Reiner. Chicago: University of Chicago Press, 1977.

Ouellette, Jean. "Le Mur d'Étain dans Amos 7:7–9." *Revue Biblique* 80 (1973): 321–31.

Paul, Shalom M. *Amos: A Commentary on the Book of Amos*. Edited by Frank M. Cross. Hermeneia. Minneapolis: Fortress, 1991.

Piepkorn, Arthur C. *Historical Prism Inscriptions of Ashurbanipal*, vol. 1: *Editions E, B_{1-5}, D, and K*. Assyriological Studies 5. Chicago: University of Chicago Press, 1933.

Rad, Gerhard von. "The Origin of the Concept of the Day of Yahweh." *Journal of Semitic Studies* 4 (1959): 97–108.

Robinson, Theodore H., and Friedrich Horst. *Die zwölf kleinen Propheten*. Handbuch zum Alten Testament 14. Tübingen: Mohr, 1938 [Amos by Robinson].

Rost, Paul. *Die Keilschrifttexte Tiglat-Pilesers III*. 2 vols. Leipzig: Pfeiffer, 1893.

Roth, Wolfgang M. W. "The Numerical Sequence x/x + 1 in the Old Testament." *Vetus Testamentum* 12 (1962): 300–311.

Schramm, Wolfgang. "Die Annalen des assyrischen Königs Tukulti-Ninurta II (890–884 v. Chr.)." *Bibliotheca Orientalis* 27 (1970): 147–60.

Scott, R. B. Y. "Weights and Measures of the Bible." *Biblical Archaeologist* 22 (1959): 22–40.

Sellers, Ovid. R. "Weights and Measures." In *The Interpreter's Dictionary of the Bible*, vol. 4, pp. 828–39. Edited by George A. Buttrick. Nashville: Abingdon, 1962.

Smith, George A. *The Book of the Twelve Prophets, Commonly Called the Minor*. Rev. ed. 2 vols. New York: Harper, 1928.

Soden, Wolfram von. *Akkadisches Handwörterbuch*. 3 vols. Wiesbaden: Harrassowitz, 1965–81.

Sollberger, Edmond. "Samsu-ilūna's Bilingual Inscriptions C and D." *Revue d'Assyriologie* 63 (1969): 29–43.

Sollberger, Edmond, and Jean-Robert Kupper. *Inscriptions Royales Sumériennes et Akkadiennes*. Littératures Anciennes du Proche-Orient 3. Paris: Cerf, 1971.

Sperber, J. "Der Personenwechsel in der Bibel." *Zeitschrift für Assyriologie* 21 (1918–19): 23–33.

Streck, Maximilian. *Assurbanipal und die letzten assyrischen Könige bis zum Untergange Ninevehs*. 3 vols. Vorderasiatische Bibliothek 7. Leipzig: Hinrichs, 1916.

Stuart, Douglas. *Hosea–Jonah*. Word Biblical Commentary 31. Waco, Tex.: Word, 1987.

———. "The Sovereign's Day of Conquest." *Bulletin of the American Schools of Oriental Research* 221 (1976): 159–64.

Thompson, John A. "Ammon, Ammonites." In *The Illustrated Bible Dictionary*, vol. 1, pp. 40–43. Edited by James D. Douglas et al. Leicester: Inter-Varsity, 1980.

Thompson, R. Campbell. *The Prisms of Esarhaddon and Ashurbanipal Found at Nineveh, 1927–8*. London: British Museum, 1931.

Thompson, R. Campbell, and Richard W. Hutchinson. "The Excavations on the Temple of Nabû at Nineveh." *Archaeologia* 79 (1929): 103–48.

Thompson, R. Campbell, and Max E. L. Mallowan. "The British Museum Excavations at Nineveh, 1931–32." *University of Liverpool Annals of Archaeology and Anthropology* 20 (1933): 71–127.

Thureau-Dangin, François. *Une Relation de la Huitième Campagne de Sargon (714 av. J.-C.)*. Paris: Geuthner, 1912.

———. *Die sumerischen und akkadischen Königsinschriften*. Vorderasiatische Bibliothek 1:1. Leipzig: Hinrichs, 1907.

Vaux, Roland de. *Ancient Israel*, vol. 1: *Social Institutions*; vol. 2: *Religious Institutions*. Translated by John McHugh. London: Darton, Longman & Todd/New York: McGraw-Hill, 1961.

Watts, John D. W. "An Old Hymn Preserved in the Book of Amos." *Journal of Near Eastern Studies* 15 (1956): 33–39.

Weidner, Ernst F. "Die Feldzüge und Bauten Tiglatpilesers I." *Archiv für Orientforschung* 18 (1957–58): 359–60.

———. *Die Inschriften Tukulti-Ninurtas I. und seiner Nachfolger*. Archiv für Orientforschung Beiheft 12. Graz, 1959.

———. "Die Kämpfe Adadnarâris I. gegen Ḫanigalbat." *Archiv für Orientforschung* 5 (1928–29): 89–100.

———. *Politische Dokumente aus Kleinasien: Die Staatsverträge in akkadischer Sprache aus dem Archiv von Boghazköi*. Boghazköi-Studien 8–9. Leipzig: Hinrichs, 1923.

Wellhausen, Julius. *Skizzen und Vorarbeiten*, vol. 5: *Die kleinen Propheten übersetzt, mit Noten*. Berlin: Reimer, 1893.

Winckler, Hugo. *Die Keilschrifttexte Sargons*. 2 vols. Leipzig: Pfeiffer, 1889.

Wolff, Hans W. *Joel and Amos: A Commentary on the Books of the Prophets Joel and Amos*. Translated by Waldemar Janzen, S. Dean McBride, Jr., and Charles A. Muenchow. Edited by S. Dean McBride, Jr. Hermeneia. Philadelphia: Fortress, 1977.

Yadin, Yigael, Yohanan Aharoni, Ruth Amiran, Trude Dothan, Immanuel Dunayevsky, and Jean Perrot. *Hazor II: An Account of the Second Season of Excavations, 1956*. Jerusalem: Magnes, 1960.

Superscription (1:1)

1 The words of Amos, who was one of the shepherds of Tekoa, which he saw concerning Israel in the days of Uzziah, the king of Judah, and in the days of Jeroboam, the son of Joash, the king of Israel, two years before the earthquake.

1 The words of Amos, who was among the shepherds of Tekoa, which he saw concerning Israel in the days of King Uzziah of Judah and in the days of King Jeroboam son of Joash of Israel, two years before the earthquake.

1:1. דִּבְרֵי עָמוֹס (the words of Amos): This phrase refers to the oracles of the prophet, as in Jeremiah 1:1. It is similar to covenant formulas frequently found in ancient Hittite vassal treaties, for example, "Thus (speaks) the Sun, Šuppiluliuma, the great king, the king of Hatti, the hero" (Weidner, *Politische Dokumente aus Kleinasien*, pp. 58–59 [*umma* ^d^*Šamši* ^m^*Šu-ub-bi-lu-li-u-ma šarru rabû šar mât Ḫa-at-ti qarradu*]; see also pp. 76–77, 88–89). Deuteronomy, which is the Old Testament covenant document par excellence, begins with the formula אֵלֶּה הַדְּבָרִים (these are the words [that Moses spoke]). The opening words of the Prophecy of Amos are thus appropriate to Amos's role as a covenant-lawsuit messenger. אֲשֶׁר־הָיָה (who was) is a relative clause with עָמוֹס (Amos) as antecedent. נֹקְדִים (shepherds): The root *nqd* in Ugaritic appears to describe functionaries who may have been suppliers of sheep to the royal palace of the temple. King Mesha of Moab was a *noqēd* who was obligated to supply the king of Israel with lambs and wool (2 Kings 3:4). In Arabic, however, the root connotes a small breed of sheep with excellent wool, a shepherd of such sheep being a *naqqad*. Perhaps Arabic reflects the nuance that sets the *nōqĕdîm* apart from ordinary shepherds, thus designating a shepherd of such sheep. It is difficult to be certain. At any rate, Amos was not an ordinary shepherd (*rōʿeh*) but a supplier of certain types of small animals. תְּקוֹעַ (Tekoa) is a village on high ground, twelve miles south of Jerusalem and six miles south of Bethlehem. Its good pasture land attracted many shepherds. אֲשֶׁר חָזָה (which he saw): This phrase has דִּבְרֵי עָמוֹס (the words of Amos) as its antecedent. It is unusual for a prophet to "see a word" (Isa. 1:1; Mic. 1:1). חָזָה broadly connotes receiving a revelation, a "word of Yahweh," as in Isaiah 2:1 and Micah 1:1. For Uzziah and Jeroboam, see the Introduction. הָרַעַשׁ (the earthquake): See the Exposition of 1:1.

1:1. The opening words make it clear that what follows is a covenant lawsuit commanded by Israel's suzerain, the Lord himself. The words are those of Amos, but those that he "saw" or received by divine revelation. Thus, the words of this lawsuit are really the words of the Lord himself. He is able to send not only the words, but also the messenger, and whom he sends, he empowers. So even Amos, who was only a shepherd of choice sheep, is sent by the Great Shepherd to his choice sheep, for they must hear his voice. The Lord himself has empowered Amos and given him authority to deliver his message against a rebellious people, as the often employed messenger formula *thus says Yahweh* affirms again and again throughout the book. Amos as a shepherd is a type of Christ, the "good shepherd," the "prophet" who was to come (Deut. 18:15–20; John 7:40). And Amos, a mere shepherd, might have asked about the words he must speak, "Who is equal to such a task?" (2 Cor. 2:16, NIV). But as subsequent experience would show, he could also affirm that, "Unlike so many, we do not peddle the word of God for profit. On the contrary, in Christ we preach before God with sincerity, like men sent from God" (2 Cor. 2:17, NIV). We who bear the words of God today must do no less as we address his sheep.

Amos refers to an earthquake. This earthquake was a memorable event in an earthquake-prone region. It was remembered as an act of divine judgment in Zechariah 14:5 ("you shall flee as you fled from the earthquake in the days of King Uzziah of Judah"). A date around 760 B.C. has been proposed on the basis of archeological findings (Yadin et al., *Hazor II*, pp. 24–26, 36–37). The suggestion that some of Amos's sayings "appear to predict an earthquake as a vehicle for carrying out the covenant destruction/death curses" (Stuart, *Hosea–Jonah*, p. 299) is unlikely. The examples Stuart cites (3:14–15; 6:11; 9:1, 9) are all in the context of punishment that enemies were to inflict on the nation (e.g., 9:1, "strike the capital," "cut them off at the head"; 9:9–10, "I will shake up the house of Israel among all the nations, as one shakes with a sieve, but not a pebble shall fall to the ground. By the sword they shall die—all the sinners of my people"). These passages express the shattering results of war—not predictions of an earthquake.

Introduction (1:2)

2 He said,
"Yahweh roars aggressively from Zion
and thunders from Jerusalem,
and the pastures of the shepherds mourn
and the top of Carmel withers."

2 And he said:
The LORD roars from Zion,
and utters his voice from Jerusalem;
the pastures of the shepherds wither,
and the top of Carmel dries up.

2. וַיֹּאמַר (he said): If 1:1 introduces "the words of Amos," 1:2 gives the first of them. The speaker is Amos, to judge from the antecedent verse. The subject of Amos's words is a theophanic depiction of impending judgment. יְהוָה (Yahweh): Yahweh is the covenant name and character by which God dealt with his people (see Cassuto, *Documentary Hypothesis*, p. 31). The name may be a qal imperfect form, indicating eternal being (and thus translated by the LXX as ὁ ὤν in Exod. 3:14); it is further explicated in Exodus 3:14 as self-determining and hence self-creating: אֶהְיֶה אֲשֶׁר אֶהְיֶה (I am who I am). The same claim is made for the Egyptian sun god around 2000 B.C.: "I am Atum. . . . I am the great god who came into being by himself" (*ANET*, pp. 3–4, "Another Version of the Creation by Atum"; for other similar declarations, see *ANET*, pp. 367–68; and Luckenbill, *Annals of Sennacherib*, p. 149). The claim of Yahweh, however, is unique, as the fulfilment of his prophecies would prove. מִצִּיּוֹן (from Zion): Zion was the place where Yahweh chose to put his name so that it would be available for his people (as in 1 Kings 9:1–9). The name *Zion* frequently refers to the temple mount that was the Lord's residence (e.g., Pss. 9:12 [11]; 76:3 [2]), but it designates the city of Jerusalem as well (Ps. 48:2–3 [1–2]). The fact that Jerusalem occurs in parallel with Zion here shows that the city is intended. The city of Jerusalem, as well as its temple mount, is the place where God is resident (Isa. 24:23; 31:9; Joel 4:16 [3:16]). It is appropriate, then, that his punishment of covenant transgressors should proceed from this dwelling place. יִשְׁאָג (roars aggressively): The imperfect tenses (יִשְׁאָג, roars; יִתֵּן, lit. gives [the voice]) presage the judgment about to fall on the nations in the subsequent oracles. The roaring of the Lord may precede judgment (Jer. 25:30; Joel 4:16 [3:16]) or blessing (Hos. 11:10). In this passage the verb שָׁאַג warns of imminent danger. It signifies the kind of roaring that a lion does when it is about to attack (as opposed to נָהַם; see BDB, p. 625). יִתֵּן קוֹלוֹ (thunders; lit. gives his voice): The idiom נָתַן קוֹל often signifies thunder in the Old Testament, as well as in the Ugaritic Baal theophanies and in the Akkadian Adad (=Baal) theophanies (for thunder as Yahweh's voice, and Canaanite and Assyrian parallels, see Cross, *Canaanite Myth and Hebrew Epic*, pp. 148–56; and Jeremias, *Theophanie*, p. 89). So in the Sinai theophany קֹלוֹת signifies thunder, as Yahweh appears terrifyingly, but redemptively, to his people (e.g., Exod. 19:16; 20:18). The bicolon is a neat synonymous parallelism ("from Zion" parallels "from Jerusalem"; "roars aggressively" parallels "thunders"), with יְהוָה doing double duty as the subject of both verbs. These words closely parallel Joel 4:16 [3:16], which the NIV translates as "the LORD will roar from Zion and thunder from Jerusalem." יְרוּשָׁלָ‍ם (Jerusalem): See the Exegesis of 2:5. וְאָבְלוּ (mourn) poetically describes the results of drought or destruction (see Isa. 24:7; 33:9; Joel 1:10). For אָבַל (mourn) and יָבֵשׁ (dry up) in parallel, see Jeremiah 12:4 and 23:10. נְאוֹת (pastures): Amos may have had in mind the pastures of Tekoa. As a prophet, his own experiences could form a backdrop to his prophecies. רֹאשׁ הַכַּרְמֶל (the top of Carmel): Carmel (i.e., "the garden land") is a notable promontory, about eighteen miles long and 1,200 to 1,800 feet high, south of the bay of Haifa. It is a forest land rich in orchards and vineyards. The parallelism with נְאוֹת (pastures) indicates the completeness of the coming destruction: it will affect both meadow and high forest. The curse or threat of drought for covenant disobedience appears in the Hittite treaties and in the Mosaic covenant in Leviticus 26:19 and Deuteronomy 28:22–24. There is irony in the verse, for the Lord had long been regarded as a shepherd to those he loved (Gen. 48:15; Ps. 23:1; Hos. 4:16; cf. also Ps. 80:2 [1]). A good shepherd protects his sheep from lions (e.g., David, 1 Sam. 17:34–37), but now Israel's shepherd was to become a lion roaring against his people.

---

2. This verse constitutes an introduction to the main theme of the book: prophecy against Israel. It is a terrible introduction: for Yahweh will roar aggressively like a lion about to pounce on his foe, and he will thunder with such devastation that forest and meadow alike will languish and dry up. The similarity to Joel is ironic. There it was the nations in the "valley of decision" against whom Yahweh would roar in theophanic judgment. But now it is against his own people—who have become like the nations—that he will act. Indeed, Israel's sin is worse than theirs. For they sinned against the God they knew not. But the Lord had revealed himself wonderfully to Israel (2:9–11; 3:1), and he would punish them the more severely for their apostasy. The punishment is the inevitable and just fulfilment of the curse promised in the Mosaic covenant. The fact that Yahweh chose to roar from Zion and thunder from Jerusalem indicates that he found fault with the northern kingdom; but the southern kingdom could take little comfort in that, for it would hardly escape notice (2:4–5)!

I. A Poem of Judgment Against Various Nations
A. Aram (1:3–5)

³ Thus says Yahweh:
"For three rebellious acts of Damascus,
and for four, I will not relent,
because they threshed Gilead
with sharp threshing-boards of basalt.
⁴ I will send fire against the house of
Hazael,
and it will eat up the royal citadels of
Ben-hadad,
⁵ and I will break the bar of Damascus,
and I will cut off the enthroned from
the Valley of Aven,
and the scepter-holder from Beth-eden,
and the people of Aram will go into
exile to Kir,"
says Yahweh.

³ Thus says the Lord:
For three transgressions of Damascus,
and for four, I will not revoke the
punishment;
because they have threshed Gilead
with threshing sledges of iron.
⁴ So I will send a fire on the house of Haza-
el,
and it shall devour the strongholds of
Ben-hadad.
⁵ I will break the gate bars of Damascus,
and cut off the inhabitants from the
Valley of Aven,
and the one who holds the scepter from
Beth-eden;
and the people of Aram shall go into
exile to Kir,
says the Lord.

3. כֹּה אָמַר יְהוָה (thus says Yahweh): This messenger formula introduces a long and powerful poem and recurs at the head of each stanza (1:3, 6, 9, 11, 13; 2:1, 4, 6; see also the Exegesis of אָמַר יְהוָה at 1:5 and אָמַר אֲדֹנָי יְהוָה at 1:8). The poem announces Yahweh's indictment and judgment of eight Syro-Palestinian nations. These include six pagan nations: Syria (1:3–5), Philistia (1:6–8), Phoenicia (1:9–10), Edom (1:11–12), Ammon (1:13–15), and Moab (2:1–3). Ironically, Judah (2:4–5) and Israel (2:6–16) are included, and the long indictment of Israel indicates that she is the main object of Amos's covenant lawsuit. דַּמֶּשֶׂק (Damascus) is the royal city of the Syrian kingdom. David had defeated the Arameans (Syrians), made them vassals, and garrisoned Aram of Damascus (2 Sam. 8:6). During the reign of Solomon, however, Damascus established its independence under Rezon (1 Kings 11:23–25). פִּשְׁעֵי דַמֶּשֶׂק וְעַל־אַרְבָּעָה עַל־שְׁלֹשָׁה (for three rebellious acts of Damascus, and for four): This is a typical example of ascending enumeration, that is, x/x + 1 parallelism (see Roth, "Numerical Sequence"). It does not literally mean three or four sins. Rather, finite numbers are used to aid the imagination: Damascus has sinned not only three times, but four—that is, sin upon sin, many sins. Compare Psalm 62:12 [11]: "Once God has spoken; / twice have I heard this," and Micah 5:4 [5]: "We will raise against them seven shepherds / and eight installed as rulers." The same pattern occurs in Ugaritic poetry, for example, "Two [kinds of] sacrifices does Baal hate, / three, the Rider of the Clouds" (Gordon, *Ugaritic Textbook*, p. 170, no. 51, col. 3, lines 17–18); "Seven years may Baal fail [i.e., not rain], / eight, the Rider of the Clouds" (Gordon, *Ugaritic*

Textbook, p. 245, no. 1 Aqht, lines 42–44). For further discussion, see Gevirtz, *Early Poetry of Israel*, pp. 15–30. פְּשָׁעִים (rebellious acts): The common translation "transgressions" does not express the full semantic range of this word, which frequently conveys a sense of overt rebellion, as, for example, in 1 Kings 12:19: "So Israel has been in rebellion against the house of David to this day"; and in 2 Kings 1:1: "After the death of Ahab, Moab rebelled against Israel." The sense of rebellion is not inappropriate to this context because the wrongs of these nations are implicitly against the Lord. Not least of all are they a violation of the Noahic re-creation covenant: "Whoever sheds the blood of a human, / by a human shall that person's blood be shed; / for in his own image God made humankind" (Gen. 9:6). The Syrians apparently grossly violated God's image in their course of conquest and torture. More broadly, sins against Yahweh's implicitly covenantal relationship with each nation is in view (cf. Jer. 18:1–12, esp. vv. 7–10). לֹא אֲשִׁיבֶנּוּ (I will not relent; lit. I will not reverse it): As elsewhere in this poem (1:6, 9, 11, 13; 2:1, 4), this comment is epexegetical to the punishment that follows, and the third-person masculine singular pronoun ending (in lieu of a neuter, which Hebrew lacks) refers to it. It is the intended punishment that Yahweh will not reverse. The verb שׁוּב (relent) occurs in other contexts expressing the Lord's irreversible decisions. Balak, speaking of God's blessing on Israel, says: "He has blessed, and I cannot revoke it" (Num. 23:20). In Isaiah 43:13 the Lord says of his own irreversible deeds: "I work and who can hinder [שׁוּב] it?" In light of this evidence, the translation "I will not restore it" (see Barré, "Meaning of

3. The word of Yahweh applies not only to his chosen people but to all peoples, because Yahweh is God not only over Israel and Judah, but over all nations. His universal deity is implicit in this powerful volley of oracles against the nations, and indeed in all prophetic oracles against the nations (e.g., Isa. 13:1–23:18; Jer. 46:1–51:64; Ezek. 25:1–32:32). This sovereignty is explicit in Deuteronomy 32:8 ("the Most High gave the nations their inheritance," NIV), where Yahweh is portrayed as the Great King and benefactor over all nations, in a poem that is itself the first model of the covenant-lawsuit genre in the Old Testament, in the book that embodied the form and much of the substance of the Lord's covenant with his people. The Lord indeed had a covenant with his creation at the beginning, and a re-creation covenant with

Noah and, inevitably, with all Noah's descendants, who, like the offspring of Abraham, were "in his loins" when God made a covenant with him. Syria violated that covenant, which included respectful treatment for humans as created in God's image. For that reason, it must be punished. And because its rebellion against God's standards has been multiple and severe—even involving grotesque punishment of its foe by threshing them with threshing boards—Syria's punishment cannot be reversed.

This passage apparently reflects the repeated invasions and conquests by Hazael and his son Ben-hadad during the reigns of Jehu (2 Kings 10:32–33) and Jehoahaz (2 Kings 13:1–7), approximately 842–802 B.C. During the reign of Jehu, the Syrians defeated the Israelites "from the Jordan

ʾšybnw in Amos 1:3–2:6") is possible, but less suitable. עַל־דּוּשָׁם בַּחֲרֻצוֹת הַבַּרְזֶל (because they threshed . . . with sharp threshing boards of basalt): חֲרֻצוֹת (lit. sharp) is a poetical term for a type of threshing board with knives or sharp stones underneath (see the Exposition). This board was approximately seven feet by three feet and is used for threshing even today in Syria. As the driver stands on it, a young ox pulls it around the threshing floor, thus separating the grain from the chaff. בַּרְזֶל (iron or basalt): Basalt, which is plentiful in the volcanic region east of the Jordan, may be intended here (as also perhaps in Deut. 3:11, where the "iron bed" of Og of Bashan is better understood as a basalt sarcophagus; see BDB, p. 793). הַגִּלְעָד (Gilead): The name derives from two Aramaic/Hebrew words, גַּל (hill or heap) and עֵד (witness), used to name the heap of stones that testified to the covenant between Laban and Jacob (see Gen. 31:44–54). It came to be used as the name for the mountainous boundary between Israel and the Arameans. Lying on Israel's border with Syria, Gilead naturally bore the brunt of the Syrian attacks.

4. וְשִׁלַּחְתִּי אֵשׁ (I will send fire): Except for the last oracle (2:6–16) this phrase functions as a refrain in each oracle of the poem (in 1:14 the word יָצַת, kindle, appears in place of שָׁלַח). In the oracle against Israel, a detailed account of disasters replaces the refrain. This phrase is also used by Hosea (8:14) and Jeremiah (17:27; 21:14; 43:12; 49:27; 50:32—all with וְיָצַת). See the Exposition for a discussion of fire in the Old Testament and the ancient Near East. בֵּית חֲזָאֵל (the house of Hazael): These words refer not only to Hazael, but to his royal dwelling as well, as illustrated by the parallel with אַרְמְנוֹת (royal citadels) (compare the phrase אַרְמוֹן בֵּית־הַמֶּלֶךְ, the citadel of the king's house, in 1 Kings 16:18). The double-entendre sharpens the divine affirmation. Elisha predicted Hazael's ascent to the Syrian throne (2 Kings 8:7–15). Hazael was a contemporary of Joram (2 Kings 8:28–29), Jehu (2 Kings 10:32), and Jehoahaz (2 Kings 13:22). בֶּן־הֲדַד (Ben-hadad) means "son of Hadad" (or Adad, also known as Baal, i.e., the storm god; compare the Babylonian name *Bin-addu-natan*) and was a throne-name (as was the name *Pharaoh*) employed by Syrian kings. Ben-hadad I was contemporary with King Asa of Judah and King Baasha of Israel (1 Kings 15:16–18) and possibly is identical with King Rezon of Damascus (1 Kings 11:23–25). Ben-hadad II, or Hadadezer, was a con-

eastward, all the land of Gilead, . . . from Aroer, which is by the Wadi Arnon, that is, Gilead and Bashan" (2 Kings 10:33). They left Jehoahaz no more than "fifty horsemen, ten chariots and ten thousand footmen; for the king of Aram [Syria] had destroyed them and made them like the dust at threshing" (2 Kings 13:7). The language here suggests that the Syrians literally rode over the defeated Israelites with threshing boards—an atrocity comparable to the practice of impaling and skinning alive of which the Assyrians were guilty (Grayson, *Assyrian Royal Inscriptions*, vol. 2, p. 124, §547, annals of Assurnasirpal II). The same language is used with prophetic approval of victorious Jerusalem in Micah 4:13 (see also Prov. 20:26).

The crime cited here is a social crime, as are all the acts to which Amos refers. In this case it was a crime against Israelites, but, as we shall see, not all the oracles relate to Israel. Amos holds the nations responsible for crimes against fellow human beings.

4. Divine judgment will come upon Syria for its atrocities. Yahweh himself will send fire by war—a purging fire that will burn the citadels of Syrian royalty (and the house of Hazael the usurper) and will destroy the household and dynasty that

Hazael had begun to establish. It is the Lord who had allowed Hazael to judge Israel. The judgment came because of Jehoahaz, who "followed the sins of Jeroboam son of Nebat, which he caused Israel to sin" (2 Kings 13:2). So, in afflicting Israel, Syria had carried out the Lord's judgment. But she went too far in doing so, performing uncalled for atrocities. The same pattern appears in the case of Assyria, which God used to judge his people, but which then behaved presumptuously and had to be devoured by punitive fire (Isa. 10:5–19, esp. vv. 16–17). God is sovereign over nations and raises up one to punish another. The warning for all generations is clear. Let no nation think itself exempt from obedience and reverence to God—even if God has used that nation to defeat militarily ("judge") other evil nations: "Shall the ax vaunt itself over the one who wields it, / or the saw magnify itself against the one who handles it?" (Isa. 10:15). Let no nation forget God and boast, as did Assyria, saying, "By the strength of my hand I have done it, / and by my wisdom, for I have understanding" (Isa. 10:13).

Fire was a major instrument of divine judgment in the ancient Near East. It was often used in warfare and was especially considered a means whereby the god purged away rebellious people.

temporary of King Ahab of Israel (1 Kings 20:1–34), and was probably the son of Ben-hadad I. Hazael killed Hadadezer and usurped the throne (2 Kings 8:15); his son was Ben-hadad III (2 Kings 13:3, 24), a contemporary of King Amaziah of Judah and King Jehoahaz of Israel (2 Kings 13:25–14:1). It was Ben-hadad III who made Israel's army "like the dust at threshing" (2 Kings 13:7). Jehoash, in accordance with Elisha's prophecy (2 Kings 13:18–19), defeated Ben-hadad I on three occasions and recovered several Israelite cities (2 Kings 13:25). For the whole verse, compare Jeremiah 49:27.

5. בְּרִיחַ דַּמֶּשֶׂק (the bar of Damascus): Huge bars of wood, bronze, or iron frequently secured the gates of ancient cities (Deut. 3:5; 1 Kings 4:13). וְהִכְרַתִּי (and I will cut off): See also 1:8 and 2:3. The hiphil of כָּרַת regularly indicates annihilation by

war; see Joshua 23:4 (nations in Canaan), Judges 4:24 (Jabin of Hazor), Isaiah 10:7 (nations), and Jeremiah 44:11 (Judah). יוֹשֵׁב (the enthroned) also occurs in 1:8 and possibly connotes "inhabitant" (the LXX has κατοικοῦντας), as it does in Genesis 50:11, Isaiah 5:9, and 6:11. But the masculine participle may also connote one "who sits enthroned"; see Psalm 2:4 ("he who sits [enthroned] in the heaven"), Psalm 22:4 [3] ("enthroned on the praises of Israel"), and Isaiah 10:13 ("those who sat on thrones"; the NIV translates "their kings"). The parallel with תּוֹמֵךְ שֵׁבֶט (the scepter-holder) further suggests this interpretation (for the latter, compare the semantically equivalent Aramaic expression אחז חטר in Donner and Röllig, *Kanaanäische und aramäische Inschriften*, vol. 1, pp. 38–39, no. 214, lines 15, 20, 25). בִּקְעַת־אָוֶן (the Valley of Aven; lit. of idolatry): The identification

---

Tukulti-Ninurta I (1243–1207 B.C.) of Assyria burned alive the people of a hostile city whom he considered rebels against Assur his god (Weidner, *Die Inschriften Tukulti-Ninurtas I.*, p. 3; Grayson, *Assyrian Royal Inscriptions*, vol. 1, p. 104, §693). Israel stoned and burned Achan, his family, and all their possessions, because Achan had broken the injunction of his covenant God (Josh. 7). In the Old Testament, fire sometimes represents divine judgment, for example, Genesis 19:24 (Sodom and Gomorrah), Leviticus 10:1–2 (Yahweh's fire devours Nadab and Abihu for offering presumptuously), and Numbers 11:1–3 (Yahweh burns among the camp because of the people's grumbling). But fire was also an aspect of Yahweh's judgment of his foes, when used in war, for example, in Numbers 31:7–10 (destruction of Midianite cities and encampments at Yahweh's command), Joshua 6:24 (divinely mandated destruction and burning of Jericho), Joshua 8:8 (burning of Ai), and Joshua 11:9 (burning of chariots of the northern coalition)—all of the cases in Joshua, of course, are instances of divinely mandated or "holy war." In both cases, fire was considered a means of purgation. This concept is the source of the stock phrase in Deuteronomy, "You shall burn out the evil from your midst [from Israel]" (Deut. 13:6 [5], Author's Translation; 17:7; cf. 1 Cor. 3:15: "The builder will be saved, but only as through fire"). In this context fire connotes devastating war against Damascus. The first-person masculine singular verb makes it clear that this fire will be the Lord's judgment against Syria.

5. Yahweh gives sovereignty to kings, and he can take it away. The fact that Yahweh is the sub-

ject of the verbs in this oracle stresses this point. He will break the heavy bar on Damascus's gate that protected the city from the foe. He will cut off (exterminate) the allied or vassal kings from "the valley of idolatry" and Beth-eden. So he will put an end to the rule of both Damascus and its covenant allies. The thoroughness of that end is indicated by the fact that the very people of Aram will return to their place of origin and to their original, powerless condition.

Just as Syria was to return to its original home, so Israel was threatened with a return to Egypt for covenant breaking (Deut. 28:68; Hos. 8:13), a warning symbolically fulfilled in Assyria and Babylon and literally fulfilled for many in Egypt (Jer. 43:5–7). Just as Israel was punished by a return to oppression with no state of their own—and return to the very place whence the Lord had led them out and constituted them a nation—so Aram would lose its independence and its kingdom, and return to its original place of subordination. The prophecy came to pass within a generation. Pekah of Israel and Rezin of Damascus (2 Kings 16:5–9; Isa. 7:1–9) attacked King Ahaz of Judah, who sought help from Tiglath-pileser III of Assyria (2 Kings 16:7–8). The Assyrians conquered Damascus, killing Rezin and taking the people into exile to Kir (2 Kings 16:9). The annals of Tiglath-pileser III give a graphic picture of the progressive subjugation and conquest of the kingdom of Damascus (Rost, *Die Keilschrifttexte Tiglat-Pilesers III.*, pp. xxxvi, 14–15, 26–27 [Rezon's tribute], 34–37 [conquest of Rezon's home town and sixteen districts of Damascus], 38–39 [destruction of Rezon]).

is uncertain. It is possibly ancient Syrian Heliopolis, now known as Baalbek in the plain of Coele-Syria. Massive ruins from Roman times and foundations from an earlier period indicate that it was an ancient cult center where the sun and perhaps other deities were worshiped. Macrobius and Lucian report that the cult of the sun was imported there from the Egyptian Heliopolis, an ancient center of solar worship. The name אָוֶן here may be a play on the Egyptian name of the cult center, *Anûnû*, which is אוֹן in Hebrew (Gen. 41:45, 50; 46:20). The pointing of אוֹן as אָוֶן in Ezekiel 30:17 reflects sarcasm. The Septuagint renders אָוֶן in Amos 1:5 as Ὤν—pointing to the possibility that the context refers to a worship center for the sun (that the LXX renders אוֹן in Genesis and אָוֶן in Ezekiel as Ἡλίου πόλεως hardly counts against this identification, as this version does not always translate proper names consistently). If this identification is correct, the intended cult center was about sixty miles north-northeast of Dan. בֵּית עֶדֶן (Beth-eden) is not to be confused with עֵדֶן (Eden) in Genesis 2:8. It is probably the ancient *Bît-adini* of the Assyrian annals, which was a district on the Euphrates about two hundred miles north-northeast of Damascus. It appears in inscriptions of Assurnasirpal II (883–859 B.C.) and Shalmaneser II

(1030–1019 B.C.). It was probably ruled by an allied (vassal) king (1 Kings 20:1, 16 cite some thirty-two kings as allies of Ben-hadad I). The point of the parallelism and of the place-names is that not only Damascus, but its allied territories as well, will be undone. וְגָלוּ (and . . . will go into exile): The Assyrians regularly deported their captives to other lands. This practice prevented their former enemies from rebelling (5:5; 6:7; 7:11, 17). עַם־אֲרָם (the people of Aram), widely spread northeast of Palestine, were known by groups, for example, "Aram of Damascus" (2 Sam. 8:5–6), "Aram of Beth-rehob" (2 Sam. 10:6), and "Aram of Zobah" (2 Sam. 10:6, 8). Genesis 10:23 and 22:20–24 indicate that there were many tribes of these people. Generally they spoke dialects of Aramaic, the language that eventually supplanted Akkadian in Mesopotamia. It became the diplomatic language over much of the ancient Near East (2 Kings 18:26). קִירָה (to Kir): According to Amos 9:7, Kir was the original home of Aram; now it will become their place of exile. אָמַר יְהוָה (says Yahweh): The closing formula emphasizes the fact that this word of doom is from the Lord himself and is thus irreversible. The formula recurs in 1:15; 2:3; 5:16, 17, 27; 7:3; 9:15.

I. A Poem of Judgment Against Various Nations
B. Philistia (1:6–8)

⁶ Thus says Yahweh:
"For three rebellious acts of Gaza,
  and for four, I will not relent,
Because they carried into exile a whole
    population
  to deliver them up to Edom.
⁷ I will send fire against the wall of Gaza,
  and it will eat up her royal citadels,
⁸ and I will cut off the enthroned from
    Ashdod,
  and the scepter-holder from Ashkel-
    on,
and I will turn my hand against Ekron,
  and the remainder of the Philistines
    will perish,"
says the Lord Yahweh.

⁶ Thus says the Lord:
For three transgressions of Gaza,
  and for four, I will not revoke the
    punishment;
because they carried into exile entire
    communities,
  to hand them over to Edom.
⁷ So I will send a fire on the wall of Gaza,
  fire that shall devour its strongholds.
⁸ I will cut off the inhabitants from Ash-
    dod,
  and the one who holds the scepter
    from Ashkelon;
I will turn my hand against Ekron,
  and the remnant of the Philistines
    shall perish,
         says the Lord God.

6. יְהוָה אָמַר כֹּה (thus says Yahweh): On this phrase and on the x/x + 1 parallelism, see the Exegesis of verse 3. עַזָּה (Gaza): Gaza was the southernmost city of the Philistine pentapolis of royal cities (Gaza, Ashkelon, Ashdod, Ekron, and Gath; see Josh. 13:3 and 1 Sam. 6:17). A fertile area at the edge of a desert, it was a natural center for trade. The oracle implies that slave trading was carried on here. Gaza appears to function as a synecdoche (a figure of speech whereby a part stands for the whole), meaning for all of Philistia, for the punishment falls on the other Philistine cities as well (vv. 7–8). גָּלוּת שְׁלֵמָה is the direct object of the infinitive הַגְלוֹתָם (their carrying into exile). We may translate the phrase literally: "Because they carried into exile a complete exile(d group)." It is correctly paraphrased as "entire populations" or the like. Jerome explains it as an exile "so perfect and complete [שָׁלֵם], that not a single captive remained

who was not delivered to the Edomites" (cited in Keil, *Twelve Minor Prophets*, p. 245). לְאֱדוֹם לְהַסְגִּיר (to deliver them up to Edom; lit. to shut up or imprison to Edom) is a hiphil infinitive (Deut. 32:30; Lam. 2:7; Obad. 14).

7. For this refrain, see the Exegesis of verse 4. עַזָּה חוֹמַת (the wall of Gaza) is the defensive wall that surrounded the city (see the Exposition).

8. יוֹשֵׁב (enthroned): See the Exegesis of verse 8. אַשְׁדּוֹד (Ashdod) was one of the five Philistine royal cities (see the Exposition for all these cities). אַשְׁקְלוֹן (Ashkelon) is the third royal city of the pentapolis. יָדִי וַהֲשִׁיבוֹתִי (and I will turn my hand against): יַד (hand) was often a symbol of power in Egyptian, Canaanite, and Mesopotamian idiom. When the Lord "turns his hand" against a nation it bodes disaster for it, as in Isaiah 1:25 (against Jerusalem) and Zechariah 13:7 (against the little ones of a sinful land). עֶקְרוֹן (Ekron) is the fourth

---

6. Gaza stands as representative of all Philistia, who are to be punished for their "rebellious acts." They have sold God's people to Edom. By taking their relatives into slavery, the Edomites have violated their covenant heritage with Israel. Both Israel and Edom stemmed from Abraham's household, since Israel came from Jacob and Edom from Esau (Gen. 25:23–26). Both would have been circumcised according to Isaac's covenantal obedience, following in the covenant made by God with Abraham (Gen. 17:9–14). As Edom violated this fraternal covenant, so Philistia has had a part in that violence by delivering up Israel to captivity in Edom. In the ancient Near East all who aided and abetted covenant breaking came under the wrath of the god who oversaw the covenant. In Mesopotamia that god was Shamash, the mythical sun god. But for Abraham's descendants the covenant god was the living God. So Yahweh would punish Philistia for scorning his covenant with Abraham and selling his people to their treacherous brothers.

Slavery was essential to many ancient civilizations, and prisoners of war regularly became slaves. Assyrian bas-reliefs contain representations of slaves, and there is legislation pertaining to slaves in the Code of Hammurabi (e.g., §§117–19, 175–76, 226–27). The reference here is to events in the reign of Jehoram when Philistines and Arabs penetrated Judah, entering Jerusalem and plundering the palace. They carried off the royal household (2 Chron. 21:16–17), plundered the temple (Joel 4:5 [3:5]), and sold the people into slavery (Joel 4:3, 6 [3:3, 6]; Amos 1:9). Amos 1:11–

12 implies Edomite complicity in these events, which is apparently the background for Obadiah's warning to Edom (vv. 10–14). The Mosaic law forbade kidnapping of individuals (whether for resale or not—Exod. 21:16), and implies this principle on the international level. The chief sin of Philistia, however, is her complicity in violating Edom's ancestral covenantal heritage with God's people.

7. Because of her complicity in Edom's violation of her fraternal covenant, Philistia would be punished with the fire of divine judgment. The judgment would take the form of warfare, in which her wall would be burned and her royal citadels consumed by fire. As in many other cases, Assyria would be Yahweh's divine judgment instrument.

The use of fire to burn and weaken a city wall was a standard practice in ancient Near Eastern warfare. Tiglath-pileser III of Assyria took Gaza (734 B.C.) in the course of his campaign against Israel. We read in his annals, "As to Hanno of Gaza who had fled before my army and run away to Egypt, I conquered the town of Gaza, . . . his personal property, his images . . . and I placed(?) the images of my . . . gods and my royal image in his own palace . . . and declared them to be thenceforward the gods of their country. I imposed upon them tribute" (Rost, *Die Keilschrifttexte Tiglat-Pilesers III.*, pp. 79–83; *ANET*, p. 283).

8. This verse names three of the Philistine royal cities. Yahweh will cut off sovereignty from two of them and turn his hand against the third. That is, he will deprive two of independence and, implicitly, do the same to the third. For him to

royal city. שְׁאֵרִית פְּלִשְׁתִּים (the remainder of the Philistines): Gath, which had already been conquered by Hazael (2 Kings 12:18 [17]) and Sargon II (Luckenbill, *Ancient Records*, vol. 2, p. 31, no. 62; *ANET*, p. 286) is included in this phrase, which announces the eventual obliteration of all the Philistines. Assyria was the primary instrument of judgment against all these cities, and all four are mentioned as vassals of Esarhaddon and Assurbanipal. אֲדֹנָי יְהוִה (the Lord [lit. my Lord] Yahweh) is

a frequent title for God in Amos, occurring twenty times (1:8; 3:7, 8, 11, 13; 4:2, 5; 5:3; 6:8; 7:1, 2, 4 [2 times], 5, 6; 8:1, 3, 9, 11; 9:8). It also occurs in Isaiah (25:8; 40:10; etc.), Jeremiah (1:6; 4:10; etc.), and often in Ezekiel. It is an ancient title, appearing in Genesis 15:2, 8; Deuteronomy 3:24; 9:26; Joshua 7:7; Judges 6:22; and elsewhere. The formula אָמַר אֲדֹנָי יְהוִה (says the Lord Yahweh) occurs four times in Amos (1:8; 3:11; 5:3; 7:6), in Obadiah 1, and 131 times in Ezekiel.

---

turn his hand against a city or land means either their loss of liberty or their destruction. Likewise Gaza, mentioned in verse 7, will be deprived of autonomous existence, for the fires of war will reduce her. All of these curses led to the same thing—the cities were conquered by Assyria and became vassals to that empire. Eventually the ultimate end of the oracle came to pass, and the Philistines ceased to exist not only as an independent league of city-states, but also as an identifiable people group.

Ashdod was located some twenty-one miles north-northeast of Gaza and three miles from the coast. It was a strong and prosperous city, a stopping point on the caravan route between Gaza and Joppa. According to Joshua 11:22 the Anakim, a race of giants, lived there, as well as at Gaza and Gath. Joshua assigned it and Gaza to Judah (Josh. 15:46–47). Judah failed to take it, however, "because they had chariots of iron" (Judg. 1:19). Ashdod was the first city to receive the ark of God after the Philistine defeat of Israelite troops at Ebenezer. Its inhabitants were divinely punished with tumors (1 Sam. 5:1–8). Uzziah captured Ashdod along with Gath, for "God helped him against the Philistines" (2 Chron. 26:6–7). Sargon II (721–705 B.C.) took it toward the end of his reign (Isa. 20:1; *ANET*, p. 284).

Ashkelon lay on the coast, halfway between Gaza and Ashdod. Judah captured it shortly after Joshua's death (Judg. 1:18), and it was later taken by the Philistines. Zechariah prophesied its demise (9:5). It is mentioned, along with Jehoahaz of Judah, as a vassal of Tiglath-pileser III (Rost, *Die Keilschrifttexte Tiglat-Pilesers III.*, pp. 35–41; *ANET*, pp. 282–83).

Ekron was situated twelve miles northeast of Ashdod. It was the northernmost of the pentapolis and the nearest to Judah, lying at the border of Judah and Dan (Josh. 15:11; 19:43). It was the city of the god Baal-zebub (2 Kings 1:2). Joshua assigned it to Judah (Josh. 15:45). After the return of the ark of God from there (1 Sam. 5:10–6:12), the Israelites regained Ekron (1 Sam. 7:14). Subsequently it returned to Philistine hands, but after David's defeat of Goliath the Israelites drove the Philistines back to Ekron (1 Sam. 17:52). The prophecy against it was partly fulfilled when Sennacherib (704–681 B.C.) captured it, killing its officials because of their disloyalty (Luckenbill, *Annals of Sennacherib*, pp. 31–32; *ANET*, pp. 287–88). Esarhaddon (680–669 B.C.) claimed it as vassal (Thompson, *Prisms of Esarhaddon and Ashurbanipal*, p. 25, line 58; *ANET*, p. 291), as did Assurbanipal (668–627 B.C.; Streck, *Assurbanipal*, pp. 139ff.; *ANET*, p. 294).

I. A Poem of Judgment Against Various Nations
C. Phoenicia (1:9–10)

9 Thus says Yahweh:
 "For three rebellious acts of Tyre,
  and for four, I will not relent,
 because they delivered up a whole population to Edom,
  and did not remember the covenant
  of brotherhood.
10 I will send fire against the wall of Tyre,
  and it will eat up her royal citadels."

9 Thus says the LORD:
 For three transgressions of Tyre,
  and for four, I will not revoke the
  punishment;
 because they delivered entire communi-
  ties over to Edom,
  and did not remember the covenant
  of kinship.
10 So I will send a fire on the wall of Tyre,
  fire that shall devour its strongholds.

9. כֹּה אָמַר יְהוָה (thus says Yahweh): On this phrase and on the x/x + 1 parallelism, see the Exegesis of verse 3. צֹר (Tyre, i.e., rock) was one of two major Phoenician cities (the other was Sidon; see the Exposition). עַל-הַסְגִּירָם גָּלוּת שְׁלֵמָה לֶאֱדוֹם (because they delivered up a whole population to Edom): This phrase combines elements from verse 6; however, הַסְגִּירָם (they delivered up, from הִסְגִּיר, to deliver up) replaces הַגְלוֹתָם (they carried into exile) in the phrase עַל-הַגְלוֹתָם גָּלוּת שְׁלֵמָה (because they carried into exile a whole population). לֶאֱדוֹם (to Edom): In verse 6 this construction functions

as an adverbial prepositional phrase modifying לְהַסְגִּיר (to deliver up), but here it modifies הַסְגִּירָם-עַל (because they delivered up). This change does not signal different authorship. Rather, it indicates a different historical reality. Tyre (the Phoenicians) did not take captives, but received them from others and acted as agents for those who took them. Ezekiel (27:13) and Joel (3:6) mention Tyre's role as a slave trader. וְלֹא זָכְרוּ בְּרִית אַחִים (and [they] did not remember the covenant of brotherhood): זָכַר בְּרִית (to remember covenant), an ancient technical term for covenant keeping (see

---

9. Tyre was a colony of Sidon—it is called the daughter of Sidon in Isaiah 23:12. Tyre is mentioned in the Amarna letters (14th century B.C.; Knudtzon, *Die El-Amarna Tafeln*, vol. 1, pp. 384–85, no. 77, line 15; pp. 422–25, no. 89, lines 11, 18, 23, 44, 48). Tyre and Sidon appear in parallel in the Ugaritic "Keret Epic" (14th–12th centuries B.C.; Gibson, *Canaanite Myths and Legends*, p. 87: "Athirat of the two Tyres [i.e., island and mainland] / and Elat of the Sidonians"; *ANET*, p. 145). According to the Egyptian narrative known as "The Journey of Wen-Amon to Phoenicia" (*ANET*, pp. 25–29), Sidon had become a center of commerce by the 11th century B.C.: "As to this Sidon, . . . aren't there fifty more ships there which are in commercial relations with Werket-El?" (*ANET*, p. 27). Tyre was also a commercial city: The Prince of Tyre exclaims, "Aren't there twenty ships here in my harbor which are in commercial relations with Ne-su-Ba-neb-Ded?" (*ANET*, p. 27). Ezekiel 27 paints a vivid picture of Tyre's extensive maritime trade. Tyre was blessed by God with a far-flung mercantile empire. It was further blessed with a covenant of "love" and "brotherhood" between David and Hiram, and between Solomon and Hiram—a relationship that may well have continued, with whatever fluctuations (see Bright, *History of Israel*, pp. 240–41, 258, 285, 329), for generations. But it did not keep covenant faith—Tyre did not remember its covenant with God's people. Rather, it sold them to Israel's real brother Edom, who, devoid of family affection (cf. Rom. 1:31; 2 Tim. 3:3), was an ancient foe of God's covenant lineage (see Gen. 27:41, Esau's plan to murder Jacob). For the sin of covenant breaking, Tyre would be punished.

Kings who entered into covenant together styled themselves brothers. For example, the treaty between Hattusilis III of Hatti and Ramses II of Egypt, begins: "The treaty of Ramses . . . the great king, the king of Egypt, . . . with Hattušiliš,

the great king, the king of Hatti, his brother [aḫ-šú]" (Weidner, *Politische Dokumente aus Kleinasien*, pp. 112–13). Another example is the letter from Burnaburias of Babylon to Amenophis IV of Egypt, in which Amenophis is "my brother," and Burnaburias is "your brother" (Knudtzon, *Die El-Amarna-Tafeln*, vol. 1, pp. 94–95, no. 11, lines 1–2). The Amarna terminology includes aḫḫatum (brotherhood) and aḫḫatum ù ṭabutum (brotherhood and good relations) (see Knudtzon, *Die El-Amarna-Tafeln*, vol. 1, pp. 98–99, no. 11, line 22; pp. 72–73, no. 4, lines 15, 17). In 1 Kings 20:32 Ahab calls Ben-hadad of Syria "my brother." The covenantal relationship in view in Amos 1:9 is apparently the one between Solomon and Hiram of Tyre (1 Kings 5:26 [12]; see 1 Kings 9:13, where Hiram calls Solomon "my brother"). W. Moran shows that the term *ʾoheb* (friend; lit. lover), which describes Hiram's relationship to David, is a technical term indicating a covenant or treaty relationship ("Love of God," p. 80). This was a covenant between Tyre and the Israelites, since Tyre is rebuked for not keeping it, not Edom. Although the Edomites were "brothers," they were not so by covenant (i.e., international treaty), but by family descent. The suggestion of Driver that the treaty to which this verse alludes was between Tyre and other Phoenician cities has no evidence to support it. Driver's complaint that the treaty between Hiram and Solomon was "entered into nearly 300 years previously" (*Joel and Amos*, p. 141) neglects the fact that friendly relations continued between Israel and Phoenicia long after David and Solomon (e.g., in 1 Kings 16:31 Ahab takes Jezebel daughter of King Ethbaal of Sidon for a wife) and that treaty relationships were commonly reratified from one generation to the next in the ancient Near East. There are examples of the renewal of covenantal "brotherhood" from one generation to the next in Ugaritic, Egyptian, Babylonian, Assyrian, and Mitannian treaties

Gen. 9:15; Exod. 2:24; 6:5; Lev. 26:42, 45), is equivalent to שָׁמַר בְּרִית (to keep covenant; see Exod. 19:5; 1 Kings 11:11). בְּרִית אַחִים (the covenant of brotherhood; lit. the covenant of brothers; *brothers* is an abstract plural) is another technical term (see the Exposition).

10. For this refrain, see the Exegesis of verse 4. Once again the punishment is military defeat. Isaiah 23, Jeremiah 25:22, Ezekiel 26–28, and Zechariah 9:3–4 prophesy Tyre's demise as well (see the Exposition).

(Moran, "Treaty Terminology," pp. 174–75; see also the history of the treaty relationship between Assyria and Kassite Babylon in Thompson and Mallowan, "British Museum Excavations at Nineveh," pp. 117–25).

10. Judgment fire is Tyre's reward for breaking covenant. Such was the standard punishment in the ancient Near East. But that common grace understanding was rooted in an eternal reality, for God will punish all covenant breakers with eternal fire. Tyre came under the suzerainty of Assyria and paid tribute to Assurnasirpal II (883–859 B.C.; Grayson, *Assyrian Royal Inscriptions*, vol. 2, p. 149, §597; *ANET*, p. 276), to Shalmaneser III (twice, in 840 and 837 B.C.; *ANET*, p. 280), and to Tiglath-pileser III (in 734 B.C.; Rost, *Die Keilschrifttexte Tiglat-Pilesers III.*, pp. 72–73; *ANET*, p. 283). Sennacherib apparently subdued it and took captives (Luckenbill, *Annals of Sennacherib*, pp. 73, 104). Esarhaddon conquered it (Borger, *Die Inschriften Asarhaddons*, p. 86; see also p. 49) and made a suzerainty treaty with it (Borger, *Die Inschriften Asarhaddons*, pp. 107–9, "Der Vertrag mit Baal von Tyrus"). Assurbanipal besieged it, and received tribute (Piepkorn, *Historical Prism Inscriptions of Ashurbanipal*, pp. 40–45; *ANET*, p. 295). Nebuchadnezzar (604–562 B.C.) besieged it for thirteen years, but in vain (Bright, *History of Israel*, p. 352; Ezek. 29:18). Alexander the Great took it after a seven-month siege in 332 B.C., and thirty thousand of its inhabitants were sold as slaves (Bright, *History of Israel*, p. 413). There may be a note of irony in this latter event, for those who dealt in slaves had now become slaves. Tyre was finally taken by the Saracens in A.D. 1291 and is now only a ruin.

I. A Poem of Judgment Against Various Nations
D. Edom (1:11–12)

¹¹ Thus says Yahweh:
"For three rebellious acts of Edom,
and for four, I will not relent,
because he pursued his brother with the
sword,
and corrupted his bonds of kinship,
and his wrath tore continually,
and he harbored his fury constantly.
¹² I will send fire against Teman,
and it will eat up the royal citadels of
Bozrah."

¹¹ Thus says the LORD:
For three transgressions of Edom,
and for four, I will not revoke the
punishment;
because he pursued his brother with the
sword
and cast off all pity;
he maintained his anger perpetually,
and kept his wrath forever.
¹² So I will send a fire on Teman,
and it shall devour the strongholds of
Bozrah.

11. For the introductory messenger formula יְהוָה כֹּה אָמַר (thus says Yahweh) and the x/x + 1 parallelism, see the Exegesis of verse 3. אֱדוֹם (Edom): The Edomites were descendants of Esau (Gen. 36:9, 43) and nourished a perpetual hatred of the descendants of Jacob (see the Exposition). אָחִיו עַל-רָדְפוֹ בַחֶרֶב (because he pursued his brother with the sword): עַל (because) does double duty in this colon and the next (i.e., and [because] he corrupted his bonds of kinship). This verse refers to events in Jehoram's reign, when Edom revolted and, more immediately, formed an alliance with the Philistines and Arabs to attack Judah; they entered Jerusalem, plundered the palace, and carried off the royal household (2 Chron. 21:16–17). Edom is condemned in previous oracles because of complicity with Tyre (v. 9) and the Philistines (v. 6). In this oracle he is condemned for "pursuing his brother with the sword." רַחֲמָיו (his bonds of kinship) is a form of רַחֲמִים (an abstract plural meaning "bonds of kinship" or "brotherly affection"), a denominative from רֶחֶם (womb) (see BDB, p. 933). The more usual translation, "compassion," lacks adequate significance here, for the fact is that Edom and Israel sprang from the same womb, and it is Edom's lack of brotherly affection and love that has caused him to pursue his brother with the sword. וַיִּטְרֹף לָעַד אַפּוֹ (and his wrath tore continually): טָרַף (tore) occurs in Job 16:9 (with Yahweh as subject: "He has torn me in his wrath") and Psalm 7:3 [2] ("like a lion they will

tear me apart"; רָדַף, pursue, is another term common to both Amos 1:11 and Ps. 7). עֶבְרָתוֹ (his fury): The masculine singular pronominal suffix continues the masculine identification of the nation. The word *fury* properly denotes an overflowing of passion and may be paraphrased as Edom's *irrepressible* fury against his brother. Their hostility continued from the patriarchal era throughout the whole of Edom's existence as a nation. As Genesis 25:23 foretold, however, Edom was usually either subject to his brother Israel or in revolt against him (Gen. 27:39–40). שְׁמָרָה (he harbored): The Masoretic Text points this verb as third-person masculine singular since the third-person feminine singular form is שָׁמְרָה. עֶבְרָתוֹ, which is feminine, cannot be the subject of שְׁמָרָה. The ה is a feminine singular suffix (its referent is Edom) with *mappiq* softened because of the retraction of the stress before a tone-bearing syllable (GKC §58g). The construction says, literally, "His fury—he harbored it constantly"; the suspended topic (his fury) is resumed by the suffix ה. The sense is that Edom jealously tended his fury, as a shepherd might his sheep—he nursed it and loved it constantly. For another instance of שָׁמַר and נֶצַח in conjunction, see Jeremiah 3:5: "Will he be angry forever, / will he be indignant to the end?"

12. For this refrain, see the Exegesis of verse 4. תֵּימָן (Teman): Teman was a grandson of Esau (see the Exposition). בָּצְרָה (Bozrah): Bozrah was the northernmost Edomite city, some thirty-five

---

11. Edom's hatred of Israel is anticipated in Genesis 25:22–23 (see also 27:41; 32:8–12 [7–11]). David conquered Edom and became its suzerain, installing garrisons there (2 Sam. 8:13–14: "And all the Edomites became David's servants" [i.e., vassals in ancient Near Eastern covenant terminology, not individual slaves in the way the Israelites were sold to Edom in Amos 1:6, 9]). Edom revolted during Jehoram's reign (852–841 B.C.; 2 Kings 8:20–22; 2 Chron. 21:8–10) and did not again come completely under Israelite rule. Edom suffered not only at Israelite hands, but also at the hands of Assyrians. It paid tribute to Adad-nerari III (810–783 B.C.; Luckenbill, *Ancient Records of Assyria and Babylonia*, vol. 1, pp. 262–63, §§739–40; *ANET*, p. 281), Tiglath-pileser III (Rost, *Die Keilschrifttexte Tiglat-Pilesers III.*, pp. 72–73; *ANET*, p. 282), Sennacherib (Luckenbill, *Annals of Sennacherib*, p. 30; *ANET*, p. 287), Esarhaddon (Borger, *Die Inschriften Asarhaddons*, p. 60; *ANET*, p. 291), and Assurbanipal (Streck, *Assurbanipal*, p. 139; *ANET*, p. 294). Edom was subse-

quently conquered by Nebuchadnezzar (Jer. 27:1–7; see the Introduction to Obadiah in this series). Edom's sin is intensified by the fact that it violates the love between those who sprang from the same womb. Esau was hostile to Jacob even in the womb, and this hostility continued between the descendant nations. Edom's wrath tore at Jacob repeatedly throughout their history. Here Edom is condemned not only for receiving the Israelites as slaves from Philistia and Tyre, but also for pursuing them with the sword. Edom has not abandoned its anger, but rather harbored and kept its wrath, and loved it. The full outworking of that wrath would come with Edom's exultation at the defeat of Jerusalem by Babylon (Ps. 137:7), of which events in Jehoram's day were a foreshadowing.

12. Teman's descent from Esau is cited in Genesis 36:11, 15. His clan apparently gave its name to a region in Edom. According to Jerome (cited in Driver, *Joel and Amos*, p. 142), the southern part of this district produced many leaders. Teman was

miles north of Petra (Sela). It is mentioned in Genesis 36:33, Jeremiah 49:13, and in parallel with Edom in Isaiah 34:6, 63:1 (the Savior coming with bloodstained garments from Bozrah), and Jeremiah 49:22.

---

also the name of a village fifteen miles from Petra, at which a Roman garrison was stationed. From its Old Testament usage, however, it is clear that the term indicates a region, not a village. The name is used in parallel with Edom (Jer. 49:20) and as a synechdoche for it (Jer. 49:7; Obad. 9; Hab. 3:3). Teman was also famed for wisdom (Job's counselor, Eliphaz, was from Teman; Job 2:11).

The Lord's punishment of Edom is given both specificity and thoroughness by mention of southern and northern sites: Not only will wisdom depart from Teman (Jer. 49:7), it will be destroyed by fire; likewise Bozrah will be consumed. By citing both a major southern region (Teman) and a northern city (Bozrah), Amos condemned all of Edom.

I. A Poem of Judgment Against Various Nations
E. Ammon (1:13–15)

¹³ Thus says Yahweh:
"For three rebellious acts of the children
of Ammon,
and for four, I will not relent,
because they split open the pregnant
women of Gilead
In order to expand their territory.
¹⁴ I will kindle a fire at the wall of Rabbah,
and it will eat up her royal citadels
amid war shout on a day of battle,
amid tempest on a day of stormwind,
¹⁵ and their king shall go into exile,
he and his officials together,"
says Yahweh.

¹³ Thus says the Lord:
For three transgressions of the Ammonites,
and for four, I will not revoke the
punishment;
because they have ripped open pregnant
women in Gilead
in order to enlarge their territory.
¹⁴ So I will kindle a fire against the wall of
Rabbath,
fire that shall devour its strongholds,
with shouting on the day of battle,
with a storm on the day of the whirlwind;
¹⁵ then their king shall go into exile,
he and his officials together,
says the Lord.

13. כֹּה אָמַר יְהוָה (thus says Yahweh): On this phrase and on the x/x + 1 parallelism, see the Exegesis of verse 3. בְּנֵי־עַמּוֹן (the children [lit. sons] of Ammon): The Ammonites were descended from Ben-ammi, half-brother to Moab (see the Exposition). עַל־בִּקְעָם הָרוֹת (because they split open the pregnant women): This particular barbarism was not restricted to Ammonites. It was practiced by Hazael of Syria (see Elisha's prophecy, 2 Kings 8:12), Menahem (2 Kings 15:16), and Assyria (presumably; see Hos. 14:1 [13:16]; cf. 10:14). The idea apparently was to eliminate any descendants who might seek to reclaim the land. Inasmuch as it is pointedly mentioned as a horrible thing in both Old Testament history and prophecy, it might

have been considered an especially heinous offense and especially worthy of punishment. לְמַעַן הַרְחִיב אֶת־גְּבוּלָם (in order to expand their territory; lit. border): לְמַעַן (in order to) expresses purpose here. The heinous act to which this passage alludes was apparently committed in a border raid on Gilead.

14. For this refrain, see the Exegesis of verse 4. The formula is slightly altered here by use of the verb וְהִצַּתִּי (and I will kindle) instead of וְשִׁלַּחְתִּי (and I will send). רַבָּה (Rabbah; lit. the great [city]) is a short form of the fuller reference, "Rabbah of the Ammonites" (Deut. 3:11; 2 Sam. 12:26; 17:27; Jer. 49:2; Ezek. 21:25 [20]). בִּתְרוּעָה (amid war shout): תְּרוּעָה has the basic sense of *shout*. Context deter-

---

13. Ben-ammi, from whom the Ammonites descended, was the child of Lot's younger daughter, and Moab was the child of Lot's older daughter—both by Lot (Gen. 19:30–38). They are called here "sons of Ammon" (and so always in the Old Testament, except 1 Sam. 11:11 [where, however the LXX has "sons of Ammon"] and Ps. 83:8 [7]), probably because they were not as firmly settled as the nations around them. They dwelt south of Aram and north of Moab, bordering on Gilead in the west and southwest. On the eve of the conquest of Canaan, the Lord told Israel not to harass them, "for I will not give the land of the Ammonites to you as a possession, because I have given it to the descendants of Lot" (Deut. 2:19; see also v. 37). Yet they had a history of hostility toward Israel, sometimes successful (Judg. 3:12–14, in collusion with Moab and the Amalekites; 2 Kings 24:1–3, in collusion with the Babylonians, Moabites, and Syrians against Jehoiakim), but usually subdued, for example, by Jephthah (Judg. 10:6–11:33), Saul (1 Sam. 11:1–11; 14:47), David (2 Sam. 8:12; 10:1–14; 12:31), or Yahweh fighting for Jehoshaphat at the wilderness of Tekoa (2 Chron. 20:1–30). The Ammonites also opposed Nehemiah (Neh. 4:1–3 [7–9]). For other oracles against them, see Jeremiah 49:1–2; Ezekiel 21:33–37 [28–32]; 25:1–7 (note their malicious delight in the exile of Judah and the profanation of God's house); Zephaniah 2:8–11.

Since the Ammonites were blood relatives of Israel, the Lord did not allow Israel to have any of their territory, for he himself had given it to them as a possession. The Ammonites were quite unmindful of the Lord's gift, however. They repaid his kindness to them by recurrent attacks on his people. They sought only to expand their own territory, and even cut open pregnant women

to do so. At the least, their barbaric behavior was a rejection of the Noahic covenant (Gen. 9:6), and for it the Ammonites must suffer doom, even as God told Noah.

It was a boast of kings in the ancient Near East that they enlarged their borders. The phrase was standard, for instance, in Assyrian royal typology, as evinced by Adad-nerari I (1305–1274 B.C.; "the one who extends territory and border"; Ebeling, Meissner, and Weidner, *Die Inschriften der altassyrischen Könige*, pp. 60–61), Tukulti-Ninurta I ("the one who extended the borders"; Weidner, *Die Inschriften Tukulti-Ninurtas I.*, p. 8), Tiglath-pileser I ("the god Ashur and the great gods . . . commanded me to extend the border of their land"; Grayson, *Assyrian Royal Inscriptions*, vol. 2, p. 6, §11), and Sennacherib ("thus I extended my land"; Luckenbill, *Annals of Sennacherib*, p. 29, col. 2, line 32). In Isaiah 26:15 the same is truly claimed for the Lord:

> But you have increased the nation, O LORD,
> you have increased the nation; you are glorified;
> you have enlarged all the borders of the land.

14. Rabbah was the capital of Ammon. It was renamed Philadelphia after Ptolemy II Philadelphus (285–246 B.C.). It has been known since the Middle Ages as Amman and is the present-day capital of Jordan. It was located near a source of the Jabbok River, now known as Wadi Amman. The citadel is well situated on a hill 300 to 400 feet high, with the city itself on the Amman (Jabbok) to the south.

The fire that will destroy Rabbah will come by battle. But the prime mover of that battle will be

mines its precise meaning. It connotes a trumpet blast (Num. 10:5) as well as a shout (Josh. 6:5, 20). The context here, with its reference to atrocities and expansion of territory, requires the sense of a war cry. בְּסַעַר (amid tempest): סַעַר (tempest) is used figuratively for hostilities. It describes the anger of the psalmist's foes (Ps. 55:9 [8]); Yahweh's tempest (par. סוּפָה, whirlwind) against Edom, Ammon, Philistia, Tyre, Assyria, and others who are in covenant against Israel (Ps. 83:16 [15]); Yahweh's tempest against the wicked (Jer. 23:19; 30:23); and Yahweh's tempest against the nations (Jer. 25:32). סוּפָה (whirlwind) is associated not only with mortal foes whom the Lord uses as instru-

ments of judgment (e.g., Isa. 5:28; 21:1; Jer. 4:13), but also, and even more often, with the Lord himself in theophanic judgment (Isa. 17:13; 29:6 [with סְעָרָה, tempest]; 66:15; Nah. 1:3; see the Exposition).

15. מַלְכָּם (their king) is the correct reading; the Septuagint and Targum support this reading, not the opposed Μελχόμ (= מִלְכֹּם, i.e., Milcom, the Ammonite national god; see 1 Kings 11:5, 33; 2 Kings 23:13), which is attested by Aquila, Symmachus, the Vulgate (Melchom), and the Syriac. Jeremiah (49:3) borrowed and expanded this verse to read, "For their king [NRSV Milcom] shall go into exile, with his priests and his attendants." The

---

the Lord himself, as the theophanic storm language indicates. Ammon's enemies would storm Rabbah with fire and like a whirlwind; but Yahweh the Lord, not Adad, would help their assailants. God would not do this because of any righteousness on the part of those he used as judgment instruments (Hab. 1–2). Yet the act of judgment is described in theophanic terms. It is so described because the Lord really would be present in the storm of battle, fighting against Ammon. In the Old Testament, as in the ancient Near East, theophanic imagery was used to indicate the active presence of a god in battles against those who refused his rule. So Ammon, who had violated covenant standards, would be judged, and a stormy judgment fire would consume its capital.

In Assyria we also find theophanic judgment imagery associated with the human king who is the god's agent. Assyrian kings regularly thundered and stormed against the foe, as did Adad, the storm god, who helped them: for example, Shalmaneser I (1273–1244 B.C.; Ebeling, Meissner, and Weidner, *Die Inschriften der altassyrischen Könige*, pp. 112–13), Tiglath-pileser I (Grayson, *Assyrian Royal Inscriptions*, vol. 2, p. 12, §28), Sargon II (Thureau-Dangin, *La Huitième Campagne de Sargon*, pp. 36–37; see also pp. 24–25, 52–53), and Sennacherib (Luckenbill, *Annals of Sennacherib*, p. 44, col. 5, line 75). In the Amarna correspondence, Abimilki of Tyre so describes Pharaoh Akhenaton, "who thunders in the heavens like Adad so that the whole land shakes before his voice" (Knudtzon, *Die El-Amarna-Tafeln*, vol. 1, pp. 608–9, no. 147, lines 13–15; the word *thunders* is a smooth rendition of *iddin rigmašu*, gives his voice; compare the Hebrew phrase *natan qôl* in v. 2, on which see the Exegesis). The dual usage of the same terminology—both the god and his

agent, the king, "thunder"—indicates their affinity of purpose (see Cogan, *Imperialism and Religion*, p. 51, n. 51). So here, the theophanic storm language (which parallels ancient Near Eastern storm-theophany concepts) indicates two things: Yahweh will act in judgment against Ammon, but he will use human agents to do so. This we see from the application of theophanic-judgment imagery (by Adad) to human kings and armies in the ancient Near East. It is also made clear by the parallelism in this verse: "Amid war shout" parallels "amid tempest," and "on a day of battle" parallels "on a day of whirlwind."

15. The exile of kings, their officials, their households, and their gods was a common practice in the ancient Near East. Assyrians used it regularly as a punishment for covenant-breaking vassals (see the Exegesis). The Ammonites would experience it because they had so ruthlessly violated not only the bonds of kinship, but also the standards of humanity laid down by God. They would indeed suffer more, for after their defeat by Judas Maccabeus they disappeared from the pages of history. This final result was entirely in accord with God's word (Ezek. 21:33–37 [28–32]; 25:1–7; Zeph. 2:8–11). Ammon was defeated by Shalmaneser III (858–824 B.C.; Luckenbill, *Ancient Records of Assyria and Babylonia*, vol. 1, p. 223, §611; *ANET*, p. 279) and paid heavy tribute to Sennacherib (Luckenbill, *Annals of Sennacherib*, p. 30). Under Nebuchadnezzar, the Babylonians, Arameans, Moabites, and Ammonites harried Judah (2 Kings 24:2; Jer. 35:11) until Nebuchadnezzar himself came to quell Jehoiakim's rebellion (2 Kings 24:10). In league with Tyre, Ammon apparently later revolted against Nebuchadnezzar (Jer. 40:13–41:18; Ezek. 21:23–37 [18–32]). Archeological evidence indicates disruption of sedentary

assumption by Driver (*Joel and Amos*, p. 146; see also BDB, p. 576) that the mention of priests in Jeremiah requires reading Milcom (with the LXX at Jer. 49:3) is specious, because, although gods were regularly taken into exile (Cogan, *Imperialism and Religion*, pp. 22–41, 119–21) and did have priests, they are not mentioned as having princes or officials. Kings had officials, and so "their king" is the best reading here and in Jeremiah 49:3. שָׂרָיו (his officials): "Princes" (RSV) is a possible translation, although the word does not necessarily connote royal offspring. The royal officials and households of covenant breakers were often carried into exile, as the Assyrians boasted, for example, Adadnerari I (Weidner, "Die Kämpfe Adadnarâris I.," p. 90), Tiglath-pileser I (who took both gods and household; Grayson, *Assyrian Royal Inscriptions*,

vol. 2, pp. 8, 13), Tukulti-Ninurta II (Schramm, "Die Annalen des assyrischen Königs Tukulti-Ninurta II.," pp. 148, 156), Tiglath-pileser II (gods and household; Rost, *Die Keilschrifttexte Tiglat-Pilesers III.*, pp. 8–9), Sargon II (household and people; Thureau-Dangin, *La Huitième Campagne de Sargon*, pp. 52–53), Sennacherib (gods and household; Luckenbill, *Annals of Sennacherib*, p. 30), Esarhaddon (household and royal court; Borger, *Die Inschriften Asarhaddons*, p. 48), and Assurbanipal (household and officials; Piepkorn, *Historical Prism Inscriptions of Ashurbanipal*, pp. 70–71). On the basis of Old Testament usage, "officials" is the more appropriate translation (see BDB, p. 978). אָמַר יְהוָה (says Yahweh): See the Exegesis of 1:5.

---

occupation by the Babylonian retributive campaigns of the sixth century B.C. (prophesied in Jer. 49:1–5; see Thompson, "Ammon, Ammonites," p. 43). Ammon later became a Persian province (Neh. 2:10, 19). They regained some measure of prosperity, in accord with God's word (Jer. 49:6). But the last we hear of them is their defeat by

Judas Maccabeus (1 Macc. 5:6–7). This event, along with the other fulfilled catastrophes of these oracles, show Amos to be a true prophet, who spoke the words that he had from the Lord—for whom all things are present, and who predicts what shall be, as if it was.

I. A Poem of Judgment Against Various Nations
F. Moab (2:1–3)

2 Thus says Yahweh:
  "For three rebellious acts of Moab,
    and for four, I will not relent,
  because he burned the bones
    of the king of Edom to lime.
  2 "I will send fire against Moab,
    and it will eat up the citadels of
      Keriyyoth,
  and Moab will die in uproar,
    with exultant shouts, with trumpet
      sounds,
  3 and I will cut off the ruler from her
      midst,
    and all her officials I will kill with
      him,"
  says Yahweh.

2 Thus says the Lord:
  For three transgressions of Moab,
    and for four, I will not revoke the
      punishment;
  because he burned to lime
    the bones of the king of Edom.
  2 So I will send a fire on Moab,
    and it shall devour the strongholds of
      Kerioth,
  and Moab shall die amid uproar,
    amid shouting and the sound of the
      trumpet;
  3 I will cut off the ruler from its midst,
    and will kill all its officials with him,
  says the Lord.

2:1. כֹּה אָמַר יְהוָה (thus says Yahweh): On this phrase and on the x/x + 1 parallelism, see the Exegesis of 1:3. מוֹאָב (Moab): Moab's borders were the Arnon in the north, Edom in the south, the desert in the east, and the Dead Sea in the west (see the Exposition). עַל־שָׂרְפוֹ עַצְמוֹת (because he burned the bones): עַל (because) frequently requires a causal sense because it may designate the basis on which something is done (BDB, p. 753). In this case, the desecration of the king's bones is the ground for the punishment.

2. For the opening refrain, see the Exegesis of 1:4. הַקְּרִיּוֹת (Kerioth) is not a common noun meaning "city," as the Septuagint interprets it (τῶν πό-λεων αὐτῆς, of its cities), but the name of a major city. It is cited as one of the cities of Moab in Jeremiah 48:24, 41 ("the cities," NIV margin). In the Mesha Inscription (Moabite Stone) it appears as a

---

2:1. Ancestral Moab was the grandson of Lot by incest with his older daughter (Gen. 19:30–38). Moabite women seduced Israelites to follow Baal of Peor, and the Lord punished Israel's covenant breaking with a plague that destroyed twenty-four thousand people (Num. 25:1–9). During the period of the judges, Israel "served King Eglon of Moab eighteen years" (Judg. 3:12–14). When Israel repented and prayed, God raised up Ehud, who killed Eglon by trickery and subdued Moab (Judg. 3:15–30). King Mesha of Moab paid tribute to Ahab of Israel (2 Kings 3:4). He rebelled after Ahab's death, but Jehoram of Israel, allied with Jehoshaphat of Judah and the king of Edom, defeated him—quite contrary to Mesha's boast, in the sole surviving Moabite inscription, the Moabite Stone (ca. 830 B.C.), that "Israel has perished forever!" (Donner and Röllig, *Kanaanäische und aramäische Inschriften*, vol. 1, p. 33, no. 181, lines 4–7; vol. 2, p. 168; *ANET*, p. 320). Isaiah prophesied against Moab because of its pride (Isa. 15–16). Zephaniah predicted its destruction for the same reason (Zeph. 2:8–11). Jeremiah portrayed its punishments at some length (Jer. 48). Ezekiel prophesied against it for likening the house of Judah to other nations (Ezek. 25:8–11).

Moab was vassal to several Assyrian kings, including Tiglath-pileser III (Rost, *Die Keilschrifttexte Tiglat-Pilesers III.*, pp. 72–73 [tribute paid by King Salamanu of Moab]; *ANET*, p. 282), Sennacherib (Luckenbill, *Annals of Sennacherib*, p. 30 [King Kammusunadbi]; *ANET*, p. 287), Esarhaddon (Borger, *Die Inschriften Asarhaddons*, p. 60 [King Musuri]; *ANET*, p. 291), and Assurbanipal (Streck, *Assurbanipal*, pp. 138–39 [King Musuri]; *ANET*, p. 294).

Moab had committed a frightful offense, diabolical in its intensity. It had carried its unbrotherly hostility against Edom to the furthest possible extreme. By burning the bones of its king, it indicated a desire for complete destruction of the peace and even the soul of Edom's king for eternity—with obvious implications for its attitude toward Edom as a whole. That this crime is against a non-Israelite underscores the social nature of the crimes these oracles condemn. Amos represents God as holding the nations responsible, not only for sins against his people, but against other nations as well. Crimes against humanity bring God's punishment. This observation is a powerful motivation for God's people to oppose the mistreatment and neglect of their fellow human beings. The place of burial and the remains of the dead were considered sacred in the ancient Near East. Frightful curses were inscribed at the mouths of tombs and on sarcophagi to discourage grave robbers and meddlers (*ANET*, pp. 661–62). It was believed that proper burial guaranteed peace in the afterlife, and possibly immortality itself (see Stuart, *Hosea–Jonah*, pp. 314–15; Piepkorn, *Historical Prism Inscriptions of Ashurbanipal*, pp. 74–77, records that the Assyrian king Assurbanipal boasts how he dealt with the bones of one who had incited war against Assyria: "These bones before the gate in the middle of Nineveh I had his sons crush"). Moab's deed therefore indicates a special contempt and hatred. Josiah took the bones of idolaters at Bethel and burned them on the altar (2 Kings 23:15–16), in accord with the prophecy concerning that place (1 Kings 13:1–2). In the battle with the three kings, Mesha made a concerted effort to break through the lines to the king of Edom, but failed (2 Kings 3:26). Hebrew tradition records that it was this Edomite king whose bones were burned to lime.

2. The doom in store for Moab is the typical one applied to covenant-breaking nations in the ancient Near East. The precise nature of Moabite faithlessness is not clear, although it apparently involved Edom. But the nature of the punishment is clear: the punitive elements of fire will be applied, as in the cases heretofore. Personification of Moab as an individual who will die adds power to the portrayal. It also indicates the corporate solidarity of the nation, an important idea in the ancient Near East. Because of national sin, the nation will die, so completely that it will be like the death of an individual. If Kerioth was the

cult center and was apparently the capital of Moab: "Now the men of Gad had always dwelt in the land of Ataroth, and the king of Israel had built Ataroth for them; but I fought against the town and took it and slew all the people of the town . . . for Chemosh and Moab. And I brought back from there Arel (or Oriel), its chieftain, dragging him before Chemosh in Kerioth, and I settled there men of Sharon and men of Maharith" (ANET, p. 320; Donner and Röllig, Kanaanäische und aramäische Inschriften, vol. 1, p. 33, no. 181, lines 10–14; vol. 2, pp. 168–79). וּמֵת (and [Moab] will die): Through personification the fate of all human beings is applied to the country of Moab. שָׁאוֹן (uproar) has the basic sense of roar. It describes the roar of water (Isa. 17:12) and the din of battle (Hos. 10:14). Here, the context requires the connotation of the tumult of battle because this word occurs in parallel with תְּרוּעָה (exultant shouts; lit. an exultant shout—see 1:14) and שׁוֹפָר קוֹל (trumpet sounds; lit. a sound of a trumpet).

The שׁוֹפָר is a war trumpet or "bugle" of ancient warfare, not a metal trumpet, but a curved ram's horn (Josh. 6:4; Judg. 3:27).

3. וְהִכְרַתִּי (and I will cut off): See the Exegesis of 1:5. שֹׁפֵט (ruler; lit. judge) probably refers to the king in his capacity as lawgiver and administrator of justice. The term is used of King Jotham of Judah (2 Kings 15:5) and God (Gen. 18:25) as King of the earth. The equivalent Akkadian term dajānu (cf. Hebrew דַּיָּן, judge) occurs in Old Babylonian with reference to a king: "The just judge who does not harm anybody but provides justice for those who have been harmed, male as well as female" (CAD, vol. 3 [D], p. 30). אֶהֱרוֹג עִמּוֹ (I will kill with him): The third-person masculine singular ending finds its referent in שֹׁפֵט (ruler): the Lord will slay all of Moab's officials along with the king. Of course, it is not the Lord himself, but his appointed agents, in this case the Assyrians, who will slay them. אָמַר יְהוָה (says Yahweh): See the Exegesis of 1:5.

Moabite capital, then it was an alternate name for Ar-Moab (see Num. 21:15; Isa. 15:1). This is possible, since Ar and Kerioth are not mentioned together in the Old Testament. Ar was located in the Arnon Valley in the north of Moab (Deut. 2:9, 18). As Damascus, the capital of Syria, stands for Syria in 1:5, so here Kerioth stands for Moab.

3. The portrayal of covenant punishment continues, with doom pronounced upon both the ruler of Moab and his officials. If the punishment seems extreme, it is perfectly in keeping with the punishments considered just for rebels in the ancient Near East. In fact, the corporate solidarity of punishment is appropriate, on the reasonable assumption that the officials were fully implicated in the rebellion. This punishment may seem extreme, but it is consistent with ancient Near Eastern punishment of rebellious vassals. For example, the annals of Assurbanipal state: "Dunanu [vassal king of Gambulu] and Samgunu [his brother] . . . whose forefathers had made trouble for my royal ancestors, and who themselves had made difficult the exercise of my sovereignty, to Ashur and Arbela (respectively) I brought them. . . . The tongues of Mannukiahhê, the lieutenant of Dunanu, and Nabûṣalli, a man who was over a city of Gambulu, who had spoken most disrespectfully of my gods, I tore out in Arbela and flayed them. In Nineveh they threw Dunanu on a skinning-table and slaughtered him like a lamb. The other brothers of Dunanu and Šumayya [grandson of Merodachbaladan of Babylon] I killed, their flesh I sent to be gazed at throughout the land" (Piepkorn, Historical Prism Inscription of Ashurbanipal, pp. 74–75). Similar examples may be found in the Old Testament: Achan was punished along with his household (Josh. 7). Because of our limited knowledge, we are not in a position to question the justice of God as he administers judgment. Our place is to trust that God is just. It may be observed that the extremes of punishment for covenant breaking that are evidenced by the Assyrian documents represent a distortion of God's justice: they mete out punishment, but with undue viciousness (for similar Assyrian excess beyond what God had in mind, see Isa. 10:5–19). God's punishment for Achan's household was death by stoning, followed by the burning of remains. But the Assyrians skinned alive, impaled, dismembered, and even buried their captives alive. Moab's punishment was ordained by God and the form of it may become extreme in the hands of her punishers, but punished she must be, for sin will not go unjudged. The certainty of her doom is assured by the final words of the oracle: it is the Lord's proclamation, and it will surely come to pass.

I. A Poem of Judgment Against Various Nations
G. Judah (2:4–5)

4 Thus says Yahweh:
"For three rebellious acts of Judah,
   and for four, I will not relent,
because they have rejected the instruction of Yahweh
   and have not kept his statutes;
because their false gods have led them
   astray,
   the gods their fathers followed.
5 I will send fire upon Judah
   and it will eat up the royal citadels of
   Jerusalem."

4 Thus says the LORD:
For three transgressions of Judah,
   and for four, I will not revoke the
   punishment;
because they have rejected the law of the
   LORD,
   and have not kept his statutes,
but they have been led astray by the
   same lies
   after which their ancestors walked.
5 So I will send a fire on Judah,
   and it shall devour the strongholds of
   Jerusalem.

4. כֹּה אָמַר יְהוָה (thus says Yahweh): On this phrase and on the x/x + 1 parallelism, see the Exegesis of 1:3. יְהוּדָה (Judah) was the fourth son of Jacob (Gen. 29:31–35). The tribe descended from Judah was prominent in the conquest. It was the first tribe to occupy its allotted territory in the southern part of Canaan. Despite God's many blessings, however, Judah broke covenant. This oracle attests to that fact in the words עַל־מָאֳסָם (because they have rejected; lit. because of their rejection of, using an infinitive construct with third-person masculine singular pronominal suffix). The preposition עַל is repeated for the third time in the oracle, but here its sense is different. In the previous bicolon it is translated "for" (e.g., "*for* three rebellious acts of Judah / and *for* four"). Now a twist in usage heightens our attention, for it introduces the acts of disobedience themselves. מָאַס (reject) connotes both the Lord's rejection of people (e.g., 2 Kings 17:20 [the descendants of Israel]; Jer. 6:30 [the wicked]) and their rejection of the Lord (Num. 11:20; Isa. 8:6). Here, as in Jeremiah 6:19, it connotes rejection of divine Torah. תּוֹרַת יְהוָה (the instruction of the LORD): תּוֹרָה (instruction) is often translated "law"; however, this word more properly connotes Yahweh's instruction for his covenant people. The verbal form of the root is יָרָה, which has the sense of *throw* or *shoot* (BDB, p. 434), thus the noun תּוֹרָה connotes the idea of direction and instruction. Since תּוֹרָה regulates human life, it naturally assumes the role and character of law. לֹא שָׁמְרוּ וְחֻקָּיו (and they have not kept his statutes): חֻקָּיו (his statutes) and the accompanying verb (שָׁמַר) repre-

sent covenant terminology. Often occurring in covenant contexts, we find them in Deuteronomy, the Old Testament covenant document par excellence, as well as in other contexts relating to covenantal obligation (Exod. 15:26; Deut. 4:40; 26:17; see also 11:32; 16:12; 1 Kings 3:14; 9:4). Here the Lord speaks to Judah against the background of a gracious covenant relationship that they have heedlessly rejected. כִּזְבֵיהֶם (their false gods; lit. falsehoods or lies): The parallel colon shows that the falsehoods are false gods (the collocation הָלַךְ אַחַר, walk after, has the sense of following false deities in several contexts, e.g., Deut. 8:19; Jer. 11:10; Ezek. 20:16). The application of the word כָּזָב (lie) to false deities implies more than the fact that they do not exist. It means that the people pursued a false principle, that is, that other gods exist besides the Lord. A lie has led them astray from God, just as in Genesis 3:1–6. אֲשֶׁר־הָלְכוּ אֲבוֹתָם אַחֲרֵיהֶם (the gods their fathers followed; lit. after which their fathers walked): In the ancient Near East the concept of walking after someone indicated a subordinate or, in some cases, a suzerain-vassal relationship. The vassal king "walked after" the greater king, for example, in a letter to a king of Mari (18th century B.C.): "There is no king who is strong for himself. Ten to fifteen kings walk after Hammurabi, king [lit. man] of Babylon; likewise after Rim-Sin, king of Larsa; likewise after Ibalpil, king of Eshununna" (translated from Dossin, "Les Archives Épistolaires du Palais de Mari," p. 117, lines 24–29). The Akkadian cognate idiom is *alaku warki* (CAD, vol. 1/2 [A], p. 320). So the Lord's people should

---

4. This verse is full of allusions to the gracious background of the covenant relationship that God's people have enjoyed with him. The people, however, have perversely rejected his divine instruction, and have not kept the way of life he enjoined in his statutes. The chiastic structure emphasizes this point:

a	b
because they have rejected	the instruction of the LORD
b´	**a´**
and his statutes	they have not kept

The structure is elegant, but terrible in its condemnation. The people have believed a lie: they have followed gods who are themselves lies.

When Satan first tempted Eve, he lied to her about the nature of God's commands ("did God say?"), about God's veracity ("you will not die"), and about his own superior interest in her welfare ("you will be like God"). His temptations have been the same ever since. He has led Judah away from God's commands, apparently convincing them that the curses God threatened (Deut. 28:15–68) would not come to pass and that their best interests lay with him. The false gods they have followed are in fact demons, and not gods. Paul makes this clear in 1 Corinthians 10:20 (cf. Deut. 32:13–18). So, allied with the host of Satan, the judgment of Judah is inevitable.

The people mistakenly ascribed to Baal the fertility and prosperity that actually came from the Lord. Hence they mistook Baal as their covenant lord and husband (Hos. 2:4–15 [2–13]). They had stubbornly followed the ways of their fathers and

walk after him (Deut. 13:4). Consequently, Yahweh warns of a curse "if you do not obey the commandments of the LORD your God, but turn from the way which I am commanding you today, to follow [walk after] other gods that you have not known" (Deut. 11:28). To walk after other gods, then, meant to accept and follow them as covenant lords instead of Yahweh. So, in Deuteronomy 4:3, Moses reminds the people of "what the LORD did with regard to the Baal of Peor—how the LORD your God destroyed from among you everyone who followed [walked after] the Baal of Peor" (referring to Num. 25:1–9).

5. For the opening refrain, see the Exegesis of 1:4. יְרוּשָׁלָ͏ִם (Jerusalem): The name *Jerusalem* means "city of peace" (see Heb. 7:2; King Melchizedek of Salem is thereby "king of peace"). It is so attested in Akkadian texts as *uru* (city) *salīmu* (of peace); see, for example, *alu*ú-ru-sa-lim in the Amarna tablets (Knudtson, *Die El-Amarna-Tafeln*, vol. 1, pp. 864–65, no. 287, line 25) and ʿUr-sa-li-im-mu in the annals of Sennacherib (Luckenbill, *Annals of Sennacherib*, p. 32, col. 3, line 15).

---

were deceived by Satan, the prince of this world. We must be alert to the warning in Hebrews 3:13: "Exhort one another every day, . . . so that none of you may be hardened by the deceitfulness of sin."

5. Over 150 years after Amos's prophecy, Nebuchadnezzar II conquered Jerusalem, and fulfilled the prophecy: "In the fifth month, on the seventh day of the month—which was the nineteenth year of King Nebuchadnezzar, king of Babylon—Nebuzaradan, the captain of the bodyguard, a servant of the king of Babylon, came to Jerusalem. He burned the house of the LORD, the king's house, and all the houses of Jerusalem; every great house he burned down. All the army of the Chaldeans who were with the captain of the guard broke down the walls around Jerusalem" (2 Kings 25:8–10; see also Jer. 39:8: "The Chaldeans burned the king's house and the houses of the people, and broke down the walls of Jerusalem"). Jerusalem was the "city of peace." She was the city of the Great King and possessed the temple or "house" of the Lord. The Lord, who had caused his name to dwell there, had truly been the peace of Jerusalem, of Judah, of his people Israel. But he would not dwell with iniquity, nor would he counte-

nance it forever. After many warnings by his servants the prophets, the Lord abandoned his temple (Ezek. 7:20–22; 8:6; 11:22–23). He who was their peace abandoned them because they consistently rejected him in their way of life. God was faithful and fulfilled the word of his prophet (see Isa. 44:26, where we are told that the Lord "carries out the words of his servants / and fulfills the predictions of his messengers," NIV). His abandonment of them to the judgment of fire was well understood in the ancient Near East. But God had in store a better city, the heavenly Jerusalem (Rev. 21:10), the "city that has foundations, whose architect and builder is God" (Heb. 11:10). We look forward to that city, as did Abraham our father in the faith. But as we do so, being strangers and sojourners on this earth, let us not forget that God judges the nations and is actively involved in history to judge and bring down any nation that continues in unrighteousness, just as he did with Judah and Jerusalem (e.g., Jer. 18:1–11, esp. vv. 5–10, which show God's judgment to be generally and continuously active among nations). Let anyone who has an ear listen!

I. A Poem of Judgment Against Various Nations
H. Israel (2:6–16)

6 Thus says Yahweh:
"For three rebellious acts of Israel,
   and for four, I will not relent,
because they sell a righteous man for silver,
   and a needy man on account of a pair
     of sandals.
7 Those who crush against the dust of the
     earth, the head of the poor,
   and the justice of the oppressed they
     pervert;
and a man and his father go in to the
   same girl,
   to profane my holy name.
8 And upon cloaks taken in pledge they
     lay themselves down
   beside every altar,
and the wine of those who have been
     fined they drink
   at the house of their God.
9 Yet I myself destroyed the Amorite from
     before them
   whose height was like height of the
     cedars—
   and strong he was, like oaks—
but I destroyed his fruit from above
   and his roots from below.
10 And I myself brought you up from the
     land of Egypt,
   and led you in the wilderness forty
     years
   to possess the land of the Amorites,
11 And I raised up some of your sons as
     prophets
   and some of your young men as Na-
     zirites—
   is it indeed not so, O children of Isra-
     el?"—
   oracle of Yahweh.
12 "And you made the Nazirites drink
     wine,
   and as for the prophets, you com-
     manded,
'You shall not prophesy at all!'

   oracle of Yahweh!
6 Thus says the Lord:
For three transgressions of Israel,
   and for four, I will not revoke the
     punishment;
because they sell the righteous for silver,
   and the needy for a pair of sandals—
7 they who trample the head of the poor
     into the dust of the earth,
   and push the afflicted out of the way;
father and son go in to the same girl,
   so that my holy name is profaned;
8 they lay themselves down beside every
     altar
   on garments taken in pledge;
and in the house of their God they drink
   wine bought with fines they im-
     posed.
9 Yet I destroyed the Amorite before
     them,
   whose height was like the height of
     cedars,
   and who was as strong as oaks;
I destroyed his fruit above,
   and his roots beneath.
10 Also I brought you up out of the land of
     Egypt,
   and led you forty years in the wilder-
     ness,
   to possess the land of the Amorite.
11 And I raised up some of your children to
     be prophets
   and some of your youths to be nazir-
     ites.
   Is it not indeed so, O people of Israel?
          says the Lord.
12 But you made the nazirites drink wine,
   and commanded the prophets,
   saying, "You shall not prophesy."
13 So, I will press you down in your place,

¹³ See, it is I who press you down,
    as a cart presses down
    which is itself full of sheaves.
¹⁴ And escape shall perish from the swift,
    and the strong shall not reinforce his
      power,
    and the hero shall not deliver himself.
¹⁵ And the bowman shall not stand,
    and the fleet-footed shall not deliver
      himself,
    and the cavalryman shall not deliver
      himself,
¹⁶ and the stout-hearted among the he-
      roes—
    naked shall he flee on that day!"—
    oracle of Yahweh!

¹⁴ Flight shall perish from the swift,
    and the strong shall not retain their
      strength,
    nor shall the mighty save their lives;
¹⁵ those who handle the bow shall not
      stand,
    and those who are swift of foot shall
      not save themselves,
    nor shall those who ride horses save
      their lives;
¹⁶ and those who are stout of heart among
      the mighty
    shall flee away naked in that day,
               says the LORD.

6. יְהוָה אָמַר כֹּה (thus says Yahweh): On this phrase and on the x/x + 1 parallelism, see the Exegesis of 1:3. יִשְׂרָאֵל (Israel): The oracle against Judah is the seventh in the series. The Israelites might have concluded that that one was the last oracle. But now Israel is indicted—and at much greater length than the others. עַל־מִכְרָם (because they sell; lit. because of their selling): מִכְרָם may refer to bribery in civil or criminal judicial proceedings. Such practices were explicitly condemned by the law (Exod. 23:6–8; Deut. 16:18–20) and the prophets (Isa. 1:23; 5:23; Ezek. 22:12, 29; Mic. 3:9–12 [esp. v. 11]). It is also possible that this word refers to the selling of innocent people into slavery for debt (as in 2 Kings 4:1). בַּכֶּסֶף (for silver; lit. for the silver, i.e., for the money to be gained) may mean in order to obtain the bribe or to obtain the price of a slave. צַדִּיק (a righteous man): The root צדק does not necessarily connote righteousness in a moral sense (although that is not excluded); it has a forensic sense as well. Basic to the root is the sense of rightness. In contexts of litigation or dispute the word describes one who is "in the right." Deuteronomy 1:16 states: "Hear the disputes between your brothers and judge fairly [righteously; צֶדֶק], whether the case is between brother Israelites or between one of them and an alien" (NIV). The law was to be applied impartially to all, whether morally righteous or not. אֶבְיוֹן (a needy man) refers to someone who was both poor and powerless. Their rights were to be protected among the Lord's covenant people (Exod. 23:6: "You shall not pervert the justice due to the poor"; Jer. 5:28). It is possible to understand the pairing of צַדִּיק and אֶבְיוֹן as a hendiadys (the righteous needy), but that is not necessary. James L. Kugel (*Idea of Biblical Poetry*, pp. 1–58) argues that Hebrew synonymous parallelism tends to follow the pattern "A is so, and *what's more*, B is so." In other words, so-called synonymous parallelism is not based on absolute synonymity of its parallel elements. The two words in this structure may refer to two groups of people who were oppressed by the ruling classes of Amos's day. Since the common collocation is אֶבְיוֹן (poor) and עָנִי (needy), the departure from that formula may indicate a lack of precise synonymity here. בַּעֲבוּר (on account of) is hyperbole for the extremely low prices for which these people were sold into slavery or debt servitude. נַעֲלָיִם (a pair of sandals): The use of the dual indicates a pair of sandals. There is nothing here to indicate a business transaction involving the symbolic use of a *single* sandal (as Ruth 4:8; cf. Deut. 25:9–10). The issue in

---

6. The Lord's indictment now turns, no doubt unexpectedly, against Israel. The Israelites might have thought the mighty poem complete, with the seventh oracle against Judah delivering the ultimate blast against a rival nation. But it was not so. If the Lord's judgment seemed complete with that oracle, it is made perfect with this one. A series of indictments comes forth, and the first is not light. God's covenant people had a unique privilege: a divinely given Law, divine Torah—instruction—on how to live godly lives in a fallen world. The Law included very particular guidance with regard to the administration of justice and the care of the poor. Justice was to be righteous and the party who was in the right, acquitted. Care of the poor was to be redemptive, as the Lord had redeemed Israel out of Egypt, as seen in Leviticus 25:39–40, 42: "If one of your countrymen becomes poor among you and sells himself to you, do not make him work as a slave. He is to be treated as a hired worker or a temporary resident among you. . . . Because the Israelites are my servants, whom I brought out of Egypt, they must not be sold as slaves" (NIV). Israel had not held to this high standard, however, and so the promise of Deuteronomy 4:5–6 was not fulfilled, where Moses declared, "See, I have taught you decrees and laws as the LORD my God commanded me, so that you may follow them in the land you are entering to take possession of it. Observe them carefully, for this will show your wisdom and understanding to the nations, who will hear about all these decrees and say, 'Surely this great nation is a wise and understanding people'" (NIV). They did not keep God's covenant, so they are faced with God's covenant lawsuit, of which this verse gives the first indictment. Like the preceding oracles, this one follows the essential covenant-lawsuit pattern. It begins with an indictment that includes, initially, social injustice (vv. 6–7a), sexual immorality (v. 7b), and religious abuses (v. 8). The lawsuit then gives a brief historical review of the Great King's generous acts toward his vassal: his destruction of the Amorites (v. 9), the exodus (v. 10), and the raising up of prophets and Nazirites (v. 11). The historical review concludes with a note about Israel's abuse of God's Nazirites and prophets (v. 12). It is followed by a statement of righteous judgment (vv. 13–16). The eighth oracle thus continues the lawsuit pattern (indictment,

365

this verse is apparently unjust sale into slavery. Slavery itself was a legitimate option among the Israelites, but it was intended as a benign institution that was hardly slavery at all. It was based on general human compassion (Exod. 21:2–11, 20–21, 26–27; Lev. 25:39–55; Deut. 15:12–18; 23:16–17 [15–16]).

7. הַשֹּׁאֲפִים (those who crush): There is no need to emend to the root שׁוּף (to bruise) by deleting א (as suggested by BHS and Stuart, *Hosea–Jonah*, p. 307). The homonym שָׁאַף (to crush, trample upon), a byform of שׁוּף (GKC §72p), is well attested in biblical Hebrew (e.g., Pss. 56:2–3 [1–2]; 57:4 [3]; Ezek. 36:3). The use of בְ to achieve the accusative, בְרֹאשׁ, is to be retained, as it occurs with other verbs, for example, בָּחַר and גֵּרַע. The verb also achieves the accusative without בְ (again, like גֵּרַע) at 8:4. עַל־עֲפַר־אָרֶץ (against the dust of the earth): The alliteration of עַל־עֲפַר (against the dust) enhances the poetic impact of this portrayal of a physical evil inflicted on the poor. Amos uses vivid and brutal imagery to convey the socioeconomic evils of exploitation (cf. Isa. 3:15: "What do you mean by crushing my people / by grinding the face of the poor?"). וְדֶרֶךְ עֲנָוִים יַטּוּ (and the justice [lit. way] of the oppressed they pervert): The idea is not that they keep the oppressed from getting anywhere; the sense of דֶרֶךְ with the verb נָטָה is

more particular than that. The use of the verb in judicial contexts is illuminated by Exodus 23:6: "You shall not pervert the justice due to your poor" (cf. Deut. 16:19; 24:17), as well as by Amos 5:12: "And push aside the needy in the gate," that is, "you deprive the poor of justice in the courts" (NIV). The idea is perhaps best expressed in Proverbs 17:23: "The wicked accept a concealed bribe / to pervert the ways [אָרְחֹות] of justice" (see also Job 24:4, 13). We find the same parallelism (עֲנָיִים, poor par. דַּלִּים, oppressed) in Isaiah 11:4 where it says of Messiah, the Shoot of Jesse: "But with righteousness he shall judge the poor, / and decide with equity [justice] for the meek [oppressed] of the earth." וְאִישׁ וְאָבִיו (and a man and his father): Sexual promiscuity is clearly against the divine plan for humanity. From the beginning it was the divine intention that a man and a woman become one flesh in marriage (Gen. 2:24; Matt. 19:4–6). The Lord's covenantal legislation specifically forbids the practice mentioned here (see Lev. 18:7–8). It is significant that sexual perversion was one of the reasons why the land became polluted. Leviticus 18:24 states: "Do not defile yourselves in any of these ways, because this is how the nations that I am going to drive out before you became defiled" (NIV). לְמַעַן חַלֵּל (to profane [my holy name]): לְמַעַן expresses purpose (BDB, p. 775 n. 1).

---

historical review, and announcement of judgment) that has structured each oracle in the poem.

7. The indictment of Israel continues, as Amos attacks injustice against the poor and afflicted, Israel's weakest and most defenseless members. His poetry makes vivid the brutal treatment of people who should receive the special care of those in authority, rather than the brunt of their injustice. The chiastic structure of the bicolon gives elegant articulation to this horrible fact:

a	b
they who crush against the dust of the earth	the head of the poor
b′	**a′**
and the justice of the oppressed	they pervert

Both social injustice and sexual evil come under the spotlight of God's judgment. These evils are contrary to the Torah (God's covenant with his people and the foundation law for their society and nation's existence). When the Lord reminded

them, in Leviticus 18, that because of such sexual evils he was driving out the nations before them, he was not giving an idle reminder. He was making an important point: if they polluted themselves with such sin, as the Canaanites had done, he would drive them out of the land, just as he had driven out the Canaanites. God will not abide iniquity in the earth for long, nor among his people whom he has created to be children of light (Deut. 4:5–6; Rom. 13:12–14; Eph. 5:8–20). We cannot fully understand the nature of the sexual act the writer describes here. It is possible that it was incestuous, for according to the laws of Leviticus 18 and 20 having sexual intercourse with a parent was tantamount to the same act with the other parent (Lev. 18:7–8). In the case Amos describes it may be that the use of the same girl by a father and son violated the laws against incest by amounting to an implied incestuous relationship between father and son. At any rate, the sharing of a female for sexual gratification shows that the father in this example had no concern for fidelity in marriage, and even participated with his son in an act that would certainly encourage him to follow his father's infidelity. The example

The statement is a biting irony. It is not the Israelites' conscious intention to profane Yahweh's name, but their perverse action has that result: the sexual pollution of God's people is profanation of his name. This does not imply that the Lord's name (his essential character) is actually polluted. Rather, his holy character is polluted in the sight of the nations because of the perverse lifestyle of his people. שֵׁם קָדְשִׁי (my holy name; lit. the name of my holiness): God's holiness connotes his total separation from anything evil. The basic meaning of קֹדֶשׁ is that of separateness.

8. בְּגָדִים חֲבֻלִים (cloaks taken in pledge): בְּגָדִים were large square cloaks used as garments by day and coverings by night. If a garment was taken in pledge, it was to be returned by nightfall, according to Exodus 22:25–26 [26–27] (although this passage uses a different Hebrew word for cloak; see also Deut. 24:12–13): "If you take your neighbor's cloak (שַׂלְמָה) in pawn, you shall restore it before the sun goes down; for it may be your neighbor's only clothing to use as cover; in what else shall that person sleep?" A widow's cloak was not to be taken at all (Deut. 24:17). יַטּוּ (they lay themselves down): The direct object is understood. It may be that they are reclining for a feast, as the reference to wine may indicate. Keil understands it this way: "And this they did by every altar, at sacrificial meals, without standing in awe of God" (*Twelve Minor Prophets*, p. 254). The pagans certainly held eating and drinking festivals in their temples (cf. Judg. 9:27). Or, it may be, as Stuart suggests, that they were "bedding down for the night" (*Hosea–Jonah*, p. 317). This statement, however, is connected to the preceding statement by וְ (and). Since this statement occurs in a series of clauses connected by conjunctions, it serves to make Driver's interpretation more likely, that "they lay themselves down there, with their partners in sin" (*Joel and Amos*, p. 153). The occurrence of the verb נָטָה here echoes its use in the previous verse, where it has the sense of turning aside or perverting the justice of the oppressed. Here it relates to another kind of perversion. כָּל-מִזְבֵּחַ (every altar) conveys the sense of multiple altars to Yahweh. These were at various locations: Bethel (3:14), Dan (8:14), Gilgal (Hos. 12:12 [11]), and other local sanctuaries (Hos. 8:11; 10:1–2, 8). Such a plurality was itself a contravention of the original covenantal ideal of a single sanctuary (Deut. 12:5–11). עֲנוּשִׁים (those who have been fined; lit. fined ones): People who were fined may have paid their fines in money or in kind. Perhaps the influential officials levied fines that they used to purchase wine (or they used wine that was made in actual payment of a fine) for their orgies. In either case, the wine was used in an illegitimate way, as the parallelism suggests, for the second bicolon of the verse is parallel with the first: "And upon cloaks taken in pledge they lay themselves down" parallels "and the wine of those who have been fined they drink." Hence, the act of laying themselves down is paralleled by their drinking; if the former is morally wrong, the latter is implicitly wrong also. If we understand this verse as a continuation of the thought of verse 7, the wine drinking had the effect of fueling sexual indulgence. בֵּית אֱלֹהֵיהֶם (the house of their God): This construction is an adverbial accusative (i.e., at the house of their God). In parallel with "beside every altar" in the first bicolon, it indicates any place at which God was served. אֱלֹהִים (God), while plural in construction, is to be understood as an essential singular, indicating the true God, not pagan deities. If the latter were the case we would expect בֵּית (house) to be plural. The strange synchretistic worship of the time was not non-Yahwistic. The people thought they were worshiping the God of their heritage, but they were doing so in the guise of pagan fertility religion.

---

the prophet cites demonstrates the extent to which the people had strayed from the purity of the law that was intended to be their wisdom.

8. The perversion of the justice of the poor and the oppressed by those in authority is gross enough, but their sin extends even further, for they abuse the very cloaks that they have received from the people they oppress. They recline in sexual sin upon the cloaks of the poor, who thus have nothing in which to wrap themselves at night. They drink the wine acquired by fines, but not legitimately as part of a sacred feast (see Exod. 24:11, where Moses, Aaron, Nadab, Abihu, and the seventy elders of Israel ate and drank before God on the mountain; see also Deut. 12:17–18; for similar pagan practices, see Num. 25:1–2; Judg. 9:27)—rather, they drink it as an accompaniment to their sinful indulgence. The poetic parallelism makes it clear enough that both usages are sinful and a desecration of the altars and house of God. Spiritually considered, any oppression and abuse of the poor are also perversions that affect anyone involved, for the believer, too, is a temple of the Holy Spirit (1 Cor. 6:19) whose entire person should be an offering on God's altar (Rom. 12:1).

9. וְאָנֹכִי (yet I myself): The separate use of the pronoun here is deictic (GKC §135a). It establishes a contrast with the adversative *waw* (i.e., "My people have disobeyed me at every turn. Yet it was *I* who destroyed the Amorite," etc.). This form of the first-person pronoun is common in Deuteronomy (e.g., 5:6), which sets forth the Lord's covenant dealing with his people in the exodus and the early stages of the conquest. Amos 2:9–10 alludes to some of these events. In Deuteronomy, as here, the depiction of these events draws attention to Yahweh as the covenant God who has redeemed his people from Egypt and brought them into their inheritance. מִפְּנֵיהֶם הִשְׁמַדְתִּי אֶת־הָאֱמֹרִי (destroyed the Amorite from before them): שָׁמַד (destroy) occurs in similar phrases in Deuteronomy. Deuteronomy 2:21–22, for example, says that Yahweh "destroyed them [the Rephaim] from before the Ammonites" and "destroyed the Horim before them [the sons of Esau]" (see also Josh. 24:8). This stock phrasing does not indicate one writer or school of writers, but is always suitable to a given context or subject matter. In this way it is similar to stock phrasing in other ancient Near Eastern literary traditions (e.g., Assyrian). הָאֱמֹרִי (Amorite) refers to the inhabitants of the territory immediately west of the Jordan, as well as to the inhabitants of Canaan generally. In this context it may recall both the conquest and Moses' signal victories over Sihon and Og, kings of the Amorites (Deut. 2:24–37 [Sihon; see also Num. 21:21–31]; 3:1–11 [Og; see also Num. 21:33–35]). The context does not admit a more precise sense for this word. The theological point central to this reference to the Amorites,

as well as those in Deuteronomy, is that the Lord drove away the foe from before Israel; the people could not have done it by themselves. Moreover, it was because of the iniquity of the Amorites that God destroyed them by the hand of Israel. This was in accordance with the promise to Abraham in Genesis 15:16: "And they [your descendants] shall come back here [i.e., to inherit the land] in the fourth generation; for the iniquity of the Amorites is not yet complete [reached its full measure]." אֲשֶׁר כְּגֹבַהּ אֲרָזִים גָּבְהוֹ (whose height was like the height of cedars): This reference to the Amorites' height recalls the discouraging report of the twelve spies (Num. 13:26–33; Deut. 1:26–28). It also reminds us that God is opposed to all that is lofty and proud. Isaiah 2:12–17 tells us that "the LORD of hosts has a day against all that is proud and lofty, . . . against all the cedars of Lebanon. . . . The haughtiness [גַּבְהוּת] of people shall be humbled." Cedars and oaks are types of loftiness and strength (for cedars, see Ps. 92:13 [12]; Ezek. 31:3; Zech. 11:1; for oaks, see Isa. 2:13; Zech. 11:2). וָאַשְׁמִיד פִּרְיוֹ מִמַּעַל וְשָׁרָשָׁיו מִתָּחַת (but I destroyed his fruit from above and his roots from below): The verb שָׁמַד (destroyed) appears again in this verse retaining the sense of contrast established by וְאָנֹכִי הִשְׁמַדְתִּי in the first line. It may be paraphrased: "Although the Amorite was so mighty, yet I destroyed him." פִּרְיוֹ (fruit) refers to the visible evidence of their national well-being. שָׁרָשָׁיו (his roots) connotes the source of any future well-being. This too will be cut off. The word pair fruit/roots occurs also in Hosea 9:16 ("their root is dried up, / they shall bear no fruit"; see also Job 18:16; Isa. 37:31; and Ezek. 17:9). This word pair

---

9. Yahweh states emphatically that it was he who uprooted the Amorites before Israel in the conquest, which followed and in part fulfilled his covenant with Israel. In the ancient Near East it was commonly understood that military victory was a sign of divine favor and that hostile lands were conquered because the national gods both desired it and were able to accomplish it. How much more, then, should Israel have been aware that it was by the might of the true God alone that they had come into the inheritance promised to their father Abraham! But so far were they from remembering this, that they had turned from him to become like those whom they had supplanted. This course had dire implications, for they were now in danger of becoming like those whom God had punished through them, when he used his people to bring judgment on the Amorites. The

cedarlike loftiness and oaklike strength of the Amorites could not save them from the consequences of their sin. For the Lord of hosts has a day against all that is lofty and proud, and his holy war against the Amorites was but a type of that final day of the Lord, in which he will come with his saints to bring judgment on the earth when the sin of its inhabitants "has reached full measure" (see Gen. 15:16, NIV). Then he will establish that eternal kingdom, of which the Old Testament kingdom was but a type. The judgment on the Amorites is expressed here poetically in terms of root and fruit, as elsewhere this stock pair is used of Israel and of the typical wicked person. The same principle and imagery carry forth in the New Testament, where John the Baptist warns that "the ax is lying at the root of the trees; every tree therefore that does not bear good fruit is cut

also occurs in the Ešmunʿzar Inscription (early 5th century B.C.), in an imprecation against tomb violators, "May they have no root below, and no fruit above" (*ANET*, p. 662; Donner and Röllig, *Kanaanäische und aramäische Inschriften*, vol. 1, p. 3, no. 14, lines 11–12; vol. 2, pp. 19–23).

10. וְאָנֹכִי (and I): The orthographic representation of the pronoun indicates emphasis because it occurs with an already inflected verb. הֶעֱלֵיתִי אֶתְכֶם (I brought you up): הֶעֱלֵיתִי (brought you up) recalls Yahweh's self-identification in the Decalogue (which is itself an example of second-millennium B.C. covenant structure): "I am the Lᴏʀᴅ your God, who brought you out of Egypt, out of the land of slavery" (Exod. 20:2 par. Deut. 5:6, ɴɪᴠ). This echo of the original covenant documents should have had some impact on the Lord's covenant lawsuit here in Amos. עָלָה (go up) is used because the trip from Egypt to the promised land involves a literal ascent from the low, flat ground of Egypt to the higher, mountainous Palestine. אֶתְכֶם (you): The shift from the third-person pronoun in verse 9 ("before them") to the second person here aims the comment more directly at the covenant community whom Yahweh redeemed out of Egypt and whom he now addresses. בַּמִּדְבָּר (in the wilderness): From Yahweh's first command that they worship him in the wilderness (Exod. 5:1), the wilderness had a special place in the history of Israel. There Yahweh led them (Deut. 1:19; 8:15), fought for them (Deut. 1:30–31), and fed them (Deut. 8:16). There, too, he punished Dathan and Abiram, opening the earth to swallow them and their allies (Deut. 11:5), and making his rebellious people wander through it (Deut. 1:40). אַרְבָּעִים שָׁנָה (forty years): The forty years' time of purification was necessary to prepare the people so they would have the faith to undertake the conquest that their parents had refused (Num. 13–14; Deut. 1:19–2:7). לָרֶשֶׁת אֶת־אֶרֶץ הָאֱמֹרִי (to possess the land of the Amorites): This clause is to be taken with both of the preceding clauses: that is, the purpose of both the exodus and the purifying time in the wilderness was that Israel might inherit the land of the Amorites. As noted, this involved (1) judgment on the rule of Egypt, (2) preparation of a faithful people, and (3) use of those people as a judgment instrument against the sinful Amorites. The phrase originates in Genesis 15:7 (the promise to Abraham; see also Num. 33:53; Deut. 2:31; 3:18; 4:5).

11. וָאָקִים (and I raised up): The hiphil of קוּם is used in a variety of ways. It describes the raising up of the tabernacle (Exod. 26:30) and the setting up of stones for the writing of the law (Deut. 27:2) and for a memorial in the Jordan (Josh. 4:9, 20). In connection with the covenant, however, it has the special sense of establishing a covenant. The Lord established (raised up) covenants with individuals (Noah [Gen. 6:18], Abraham [Gen. 17:7], Isaac [Gen. 17:21], and the patriarchs [Exod. 6:4]) as well as with Israel (Lev. 26:9; Deut. 8:18). He also raised up covenant-lawsuit messengers in the persons of prophets (see also Deut. 18:15, 18, where the prophet par excellence, Christ, is anticipated), as well as judges (Judg. 2:18), priests (1 Sam. 2:35), and kings (2 Sam. 7:12). He will raise up the shepherd (king), great David's greater son, to the last (Ezek. 34:23). נְבִיאִים (prophets) is related to Akkadian *nabû* (to call). The Hebrew form is passive, indicating that a prophet is one who is called by Yahweh. נְזִרִים (Nazirites) has the literal sense of

down and thrown into the fire" (Matt. 3:10). The warning is always thus to God's covenant people: take advantage of God's grace, keep in step with the Spirit, and bear good fruit (John 15:5–8; Gal. 5:22–25).

10. The Lord continues the historical review of his gracious acts toward his rebellious vassal. He brought them out of Egypt and made them wander in the wilderness forty years because of their rebellion there—all this to prepare them for the conquest of the promised land. The historical review itself, using phraseology rooted in the covenant and in the exodus experience, could not but recall to any Israelite the mighty and faithful actions of her covenant Lord. But the typology of the historical review has a special value for the church, for the exodus was a demonstration of the Lord's power over Pharaoh, and Pharaoh, who claimed to be a god, was a type of Satan, the god of this world. The Lord's redemption of his people was thus a type of Jesus' redemption of his people out of Satan's kingdom. But more, the preparation of a faithful generation in the wilderness is a type of the sanctifying life experience of the church in the world. And finally, the Lord's victorious leading of his people in the conquest (Josh. 10:42) is a type of Jesus' victorious conquest of the world with his army in the eschatological battle (Rev. 19:11–21). So the life experience of the church sanctifies and prepares her to wage that war for the establishment of the Lord's eternal kingdom.

separated or consecrated ones (see the Exposition). בְּנֵי יִשְׂרָאֵל (children [lit. sons] of Israel) occurs again in 3:1, 12; 4:5; 9:7. נְאֻם־יְהוָה (oracle of Yahweh): The passive participle occurs often as a designation of a divine utterance; only once does the denominative verb occur (Jer. 23:31). The phrase appears frequently in Amos (2:11, 16; 3:10, 13, 15; 4:3, 5, 6, 8, 9, 10, 11; 6:8, 14; 8:3, 9, 11; 9:7, 8, 12, 13), in addition to אָמַר יְהוָה (Yahweh says; 1:5, 15; 2:3; 5:16, 17, 27; 7:3; 9:15) and אָמַר אֲדֹנָי יְהוָה (the Lord Yahweh says; 1:8; 3:11; 5:3; 7:6). After the rhetorical question that challenges Amos's hearers (Is it indeed not so, O children of Israel?), the assertion that this is an "oracle of the LORD" should preclude contradictory response.

12. וַתַּשְׁקוּ אֶת־הַנְּזִרִים יָיִן (and you made the Nazirites drink wine): There is no historical evidence of such a transgression. Perhaps it was a violent attempt to defile them, or it may allude to seduction of the Nazirites from obedience to their vows. לֹא תִּנָּבְאוּ (you shall not prophesy at all!): The use of לֹא (not [at all]) with the imperfect expresses the most emphatic expectation of obedience, as opposed to the weaker jussive with אַל (not; see GKC §107o). The same form is found in the Decalogue, with its firm commands that God's people shall *never* do certain things (e.g., "have no other gods before me," "make for yourself an idol," "lie," "steal," etc.). Here, the people who are disobedient to his covenant commands ironically

---

11. The Lord has shown himself faithful. Not only has he established his covenant with Abraham and his descendants, as promised; he has also raised up prophets (covenant-lawsuit messengers) to recall Israel from covenant disobedience throughout her history.

Abraham is the first prophet mentioned in the Old Testament (Gen. 20:7). As such, and as the mediator of a covenant between God and his family, Abraham was a type of Christ. Moses likewise was a prophet, without equal (Deut. 34:10); as the mediator of the Old Covenant, he was also a type of Christ. There were many prophets in the Old Testament, both unnamed (e.g., 1 Sam. 10:5; 1 Kings 13:11; 18:4) and named, for example, among the nonwriting prophets, Nathan (2 Sam. 7:2), Ahijah (1 Kings 11:29), Jehu (1 Kings 16:7), Elijah (1 Kings 18:36), and Elisha (1 Kings 19:16). The office was a special gift of the Lord, intended to recall the people from covenant disobedience and remind them of the favor of their God. These prophets had brought the Lord's charge to a stubborn people.

The Lord had also raised up Nazirites—people who, as outstanding examples of life consecrated to the Lord, provided visible testimony of the humility of heart and purity of life that are appropriate before the Great King. The Nazirites were a class set aside by holy motivation to live a more austere life dedicated to Yahweh. The law of the Nazirite (Num. 6:1–21) stipulated that one so separated must not drink wine, wine vinegar, or grape juice; must not eat grapes or raisins; must allow his or her hair to grow long and never cut it, so long as the vow of separation obtained; and must remain ceremonially clean. The Old Testament mentions two Nazirites by name, Samson

(Judg. 13:1–5) and Samuel (never called a Nazirite, but see 1 Sam. 1:22).

In the present covenant lawsuit God reminds his people of these facts. In fact, he challenges them: "Is it indeed not so, O children of Israel?" And, as though to show that the answer is obvious and that there is no room for contradiction, Amos seals the point with the abrupt affirmation, "Oracle of the LORD." Such a prophetic challenge, coming against such an intractable people, is also a type (or anticipation) of the challenge made by the supreme prophet—of whom all others are but types—Jesus Christ, who was careful to remind Israel that God had sent his prophets to it (Matt. 21:33–46). The reaction of Jesus' stubborn contemporaries was not entirely favorable: "They wanted to arrest him, but they feared the crowds, because they regarded him as a prophet." Nazirites likewise, not by prophetic words but by extraordinary examples of dedicated living, were raised up to provide visible encouragement toward godliness for Yahweh's people. By God's grace the precepts and examples were there. It was the call of his people to be not only hearers of the word, but doers also. And that call remains the same for the people of God.

The Nazirites, the Rechabites, and the "Sons of the Prophets" (e.g., 2 Kings 2:3) were prophetic subgroups who, for the most part, had a benign effect on Israel. Largely they were groups that reacted against the decline of religious zeal among the Israelites following the conquest. The prophets were the most important spiritual influence in Israelite society. Israelite prophetism (exclusive of the Sons of the Prophets) was composed of individuals who were called of God to proclaim his will to their societies. Amos viewed the prophets and the Nazirites as institutions that God had

order his covenant-lawsuit messengers not to prophesy. Amos heard this command himself from Amaziah the priest of Bethel, who commanded, "At Bethel you shall never prophesy again" (7:10–17, esp. vv. 13, 16; see also Isa. 30:10–11; Jer. 11:21; Mic. 2:6).

13. הִנֵּה (see): The participle gives a sense of immediacy—in this case, an immediate demand for attention—as well as an indication that judgment is imminent. אָנֹכִי (it is I): For the deictic use of the first-person pronoun, see the Exegesis of verse 9. מֵעִיק (who press . . . down): The root עוק is attested only twice in the Old Testament, in Psalm 55:4 [3], where the noun form עָקָה may convey the sense of pressure, and in Psalm 66:11, where it connotes burdens. The picture here is that of a heavily loaded cart that cannot move. תַּחְתֵּיכֶם (down) has the same sense as Greek κατά, here, indicative of pressing down upon someone. It does double duty in the next colon, where it is not Yahweh but the cart, as a simile, that presses down upon the earth. הַמְלֵאָה לָהּ (which is itself full): This phrase is used reflexively, that is, the cart has been filled, or is full.

14. וְאָבַד (and . . . shall perish): וְ logically connects this thought to the preceding. The failure of the swift of foot to find a way of escape is one element in Amos's complex description of the impending catastrophe. אָבַד (perish) establishes the absoluteness of the divine judgment. It is ironic that every place of escape shall perish from the swift. מָנוֹס (escape or place of escape) expresses the idea that no opportunity for escape will exist. וְחָזָק לֹא־יְאַמֵּץ כֹּחוֹ (and the strong shall not reinforce [i.e., strengthen] his power): The use of these two words—the noun חָזָק (strong) and the verb אָמֵץ (piel; reinforce or strengthen)—may express irony, for these words occur in contexts that describe happier occasions in Israel's history: The Lord told Moses to "encourage and strengthen" Joshua, who would lead the people into the promised land (Deut. 3:28; 31:6–7); he told Joshua to "be strong and courageous" on the eve of the conquest (Josh. 1:9). Here, however, these words occur together in a way that might have recalled those earlier and

---

raised up. No doubt this reflects his view of his own prophetic calling (7:14–15).

12. The covenant breakers of Israel not only sin on their own account, they urge or compel others to do so—specifically, the Nazirites, whom they lead, by whatever means, to break their holiness vows by drinking. Ironically, and with the same emphatic negative used in the Decalogue (the quintessence of covenant law), they command God's covenant-lawsuit messengers, the prophets, not to prophesy. This is an abuse of the very ones whom Yahweh had raised up as examples and messengers of holiness. Such abuse is constantly the lot of the Lord's representatives and emissaries, as Jesus early warned his followers: "Blessed are you when people revile you and persecute you and utter all kinds of evil against you falsely on my account. Rejoice and be glad, for your reward is great in heaven, for in the same way they persecuted the prophets who were before you" (Matt. 5:11–12).

13. The Lord announces by a simile the punishment for his people. He will press down upon them, as a load of sheaves presses down upon a cart. The overall sense is that of a pressure from above that defeats the normal function of something—in this case, the cart and, by analogy, God's people. So the sense is broader than being "bogged down." Although it includes that nuance, and indeed three of the subsequent illustrations

involve inability to save by flight ("escape shall perish from the swift," v. 14; "the fleet-footed shall not deliver himself," v. 15; "the cavalryman shall not deliver himself," v. 15). But the other illustrations show the broader intent of the simile, namely, that the normal function will not obtain: "The strong shall not reinforce his power, / and the hero shall not deliver himself" (v. 14); "the bowman shall not stand" (v. 15); "and the stout-hearted among the heroes— / naked shall he flee on that day" (v. 16). This sense will carry through the subsequent verses. It is characteristic of divine judgment that the Lord takes away the normal ability of the one punished to effect his or her own protection. So Achan failed to be able to keep his disobedience hidden (Josh. 7); so Israel cannot save itself by horses and chariots (as in Ps. 33:16–19).

14. The principle announced in verse 13 is explained now by several examples: all place or opportunity of flight will perish from the swift, so that the soldier's swiftness will not serve its normal function; the strong will not be able to reinforce their strength for battle, as they might normally do; even the heroes, the most battle-able of all, will not be able to deliver their lives, let alone fight effectively for the defense of others. The terminology used communicates more than this basic message, however, for just as opportunity for flight will perish from the swift, the swift as well

better days, but now they appear in a context of disaster. יְאַמֵּץ כֹּחוֹ (reinforce his power) is also found in the doom oracle to Nineveh in Nahum 2:2 [1] ("gird your loins; / collect all your strength"). וְגִבּוֹר (and the hero): וְ is the second of four occurrences of this particle. They function as logical connectors in this passage, giving unity to the thought that begins with הִנֵּה in verse 13. גִּבּוֹר properly refers to a soldier who by prowess and stature was unusually well suited to be a mighty warrior. The term applies to the Nephilim who existed before the flood: "These were the heroes that were of old, warriors of renown" (Gen. 6:4). It refers also to Nimrod, who was a "mighty hunter before the LORD" (Gen. 10:8–10), and to Goliath (1 Sam. 17:51). In Isaiah 9:5 [6] it describes the Messiah: "Wonderful Counselor, God the Hero, Everlasting Father, Prince of Peace." יְמַלֵּט נַפְשׁוֹ (shall . . . deliver himself) frequently occurs as a word pair. This expression sometimes refers to people delivering themselves (1 Kings 1:12; Jer. 48:6; 51:6, 45 [in all three Jeremian references, the wording is, literally, "Run, save yourselves"; but this is taken as a hendiadys by the NIV: "Run for your lives!"]; Ps. 89:49 [48]]), but sometimes it is the Lord who delivers them (Pss. 41:2 [1]; 107:20; 116:4). נֶפֶשׁ (soul or self) is cognate with Akkadian *napištu*, which essentially means "throat." In both Akkadian and Hebrew a broader meaning developed, "life" or "self," but the primary meaning is still sometimes apparent; for example, David's cry, "Save me, O God, for the waters have come up to my neck" (Ps. 69:2 [1]). Since breath must come through the throat, the association of the word with life itself is natural: "the Lord Yahweh . . . breathed into his nostrils the breath of life, and the man became a living being" (Gen. 2:7). We should not understand this word to refer here to the immaterial aspect of the human being

(that is, the soul). The word most frequently refers to the whole person. The sense is that the hero will not save his life (himself).

15. וְ (and) continues the litany of events that will characterize Israel's captivity. וְתֹפֵשׂ הַקֶּשֶׁת (and the bowman; lit. the wielder of the bow): Archers were important in ancient warfare, and it was crucial that they stand their ground. This will not be the case, however, when the Lord's judgment falls on the nation. וְקַל בְּרַגְלָיו (and the fleet-footed; lit. light on his feet): Since this expression is flanked by military motifs in the first and third cola it is likely that it refers to soldiers, not civilians. This is supported by the only other occurrence of this phrase in a description of the warrior Asahel as he pursued Abner in the war between the houses of David and Saul (2 Sam. 2:18). לֹא יְמַלֵּט (shall not deliver himself): It is not necessary to emend this verbal form (piel) to a niphal to achieve the reflexive sense ("deliver himself"), for it anticipates the following use of the same verbal form in the concluding phrase, which occurs with נַפְשׁוֹ (himself). Thus, נַפְשׁוֹ does double duty in this sentence (see Keil, *Twelve Minor Prophets*, p. 257, for a similar observation). This device holds the reader in suspense until the end of the verse. The closing phrase is thus a mournful conclusion to Amos's words here. The sentence says, literally: "The swift of foot shall not save—nor the rider of the horse—he shall not save himself." וְרֹכֵב הַסּוּס (and the cavalryman; lit. rider of the horse): This phrase has the basic sense of *rider*. The context establishes the nature of this verbal action with appropriate modifying nouns (chariot, horse, etc.). Here the occurrence of סוּס (horse) indicates riders, not charioteers.

16. וְאַמִּיץ לִבּוֹ (and the stout-hearted; lit. strong in his heart): וְ is the last usage of this particle that ties the oracle together. אַמִּיץ (lit. strong) is cognate

---

(along with the others) will perish. In the past, when Israel was young and about to conquer, and when its holiness was being used by the Lord as an instrument of judgment against the inhabitants of Canaan, Joshua the leader was strengthened and encouraged. But now, when Israel, through disobedience, has become worthy to be cast out of the promised land, its strong men will not be able to "encourage" or reinforce their power. And whereas in the past Israel's heroes had accomplished the conquest, now its heroes will not even be able to deliver themselves in the day of battle. In the midst of all this, however, there is ultimate hope. For it is the Lord who chastises them. And the Lord is, after all, "God the Hero."

"The Lord disciplines those whom he loves, / and chastises every child whom he accepts" (Heb. 12:6, quoting Prov. 3:12). And he must win the battle.

15. The theme continues as the prophet makes it clear that no classes of warrior will be able to perform their expected function on the day of judgment. The archers will not be able to stand ground—their skill and weapons will be of no use. The fleet-footed, able in times of success to pursue and smite the retreating foe, will on that day not even be able to save themselves as, in a turnabout, they flee. The riders, formidable opponents in war because of the massiveness and momen-

with the verb אָמֵץ in verse 14 and no doubt resonates with it in context. גִּבּוֹרִים (heroes): See the Exegesis of verse 14. עָרוֹם (naked) does not connote merely a lack of armor, for, when the word applies to people, it always has the sense of nakedness in the strict sense of the word (see Gen. 2:25; Job 1:21). יָנוּס (shall he flee) does not necessarily imply escape, for flight in battle is generally disastrous (Josh. 10:10–11; 1 Sam. 4:17). בַּיּוֹם־הַהוּא (on

that day) is a phrase common to the prophets. It designates a time frame, which from the perspective of the writer, lies in the future. It frequently refers to the eschaton (Isa. 24:21), but is not limited to it. Here it refers to the time of the events this context describes, that is, the impending captivity. נְאֻם־יְהוָה (oracle of Yahweh): See the Exegesis of verse 11.

---

tum of their steeds in combat, will not be able to save themselves in that day.

16. Just as the strong in verse 14 will not be able to summon or reinforce their strength for the battle, so here the stout-hearted has no recourse but to flee. But again, just as the heroes shall not be able to deliver themselves in verse 14, so here the stout-hearted among the heroes shall flee naked, but, implicitly, not be able to deliver themselves either. For flight in battle is generally disastrous,

as the Old Testament and human experience amply show. This verse completes the short section introduced in verse 13. It illustrates, along with verses 14–15, the principle there stated, that none of the able, skilled, or mighty will be able to do what is expected of them when the judgment of Yahweh comes. Indeed, they will not even be able to deliver themselves, not to mention making an effective stand against the foe.

II. Pronouncements of Judgment (3:1–6:14)
A. Covenant Lawsuit (3:1–15)
1. Historical Background (3:1–2)

3 Hear this word that Yahweh has spoken against you, O children of Israel, against the whole family that I brought up from the land of Egypt.

2 "Only you have I known
from all the families of the earth;
therefore I will visit upon you
all your iniquities."

3 Hear this word that the Lord has spoken against you, O people of Israel, against the whole family that I brought up out of the land of Egypt:

2 You only have I known
of all the families of the earth;
therefore I will punish you
for all your iniquities.

3:1. שִׁמְעוּ אֶת־הַדָּבָר הַזֶּה (hear this word): This solemn command occurs again in 4:1 and 5:1, serving as a unifying element in this section (chaps. 3–6). שִׁמְעוּ (hear) frequently occurs in contexts where the translational equivalent "obey" is most appropriate. The forces at work in these contexts (e.g., Josh 1:18; Jer. 12:17) invest the word with the sense of listen with attention or give heed to. The injunction to hear God's word or commands echoes the language of the covenant itself (e.g., Deut. 4:1; 5:1; 6:4) and occurs regularly in covenant-lawsuit material (e.g., Isa. 1:2, 10; Jer. 2:4; Hos. 4:1) Amos's audience would have understood it against this covenantal background. כָּל־הַמִּשְׁפָּחָה (the whole family): מִשְׁפָּחָה (family) denotes a community of individuals who share a common relationship. Besides the concept of family in the strict sense, it includes the concepts of clan, guild, and nation. The term *family* connotes a whole people in Jeremiah 8:3 ("all the survivors of this evil nation [lit. family, i.e., Judah]," NIV) and 33:24 ("the LORD has rejected the two kingdoms [lit. families] he chose," NIV; Mic. 2:3 and Zech. 14:18 use מִשְׁפָּחָה in a similar way). Although Amos is focusing on Israel here, the phrase affirms that both Israel and Judah constitute a covenant community under Yahweh, a "family," indeed the household of God. The point is affirmed again in verse 2. For the formula אֲשֶׁר הֶעֱלֵיתִי מֵאֶרֶץ מִצְרָיִם (that I brought up from the land of Egypt), see the

Exegesis of 2:10. It is a reminder of the exodus experience, when God showed his saving power and kindness.

2. יָדַעְתִּי (have I known): יָדַע (know) has a wide range of meaning in biblical Hebrew. It includes sexual relations (e.g., Gen. 4:1, "Adam knew his wife," RSV), cognitive knowledge (Gen. 4:9, "I do not know"), recognition (Exod. 1:8, a Pharaoh who did not know Joseph, i.e., did not recognize any claim on the part of Joseph's descendants), and covenantal recognition (e.g., Exod. 33:12, Yahweh knows Moses by name; Ps. 1:6: "the LORD knows the way of the righteous," RSV; Hos. 13:5: "I . . . knew you in the wilderness," RSV). The term not only has a treaty background (see Huffmon, "Treaty Background of Hebrew *Yādaʿ*"), but a general theological background in the ancient Near East (see the Exposition). מִשְׁפְּחוֹת הָאֲדָמָה (the families of the earth): For מִשְׁפְּחוֹת (families), see the Exegesis of verse 1. This phrase occurs first in Genesis 12:3 (cf. 28:14), where Yahweh tells Abram, "In you all the families of the earth shall be blessed." Its use in Amos may reflect this ancient covenantal promise from Genesis. עַל־כֵּן (therefore) introduces a statement of fact, that is, on the basis of the foregoing, such and such is the case (BDB, p. 487). Implicit in the foregoing affirmation of Israel's covenant privilege is the fact that she failed to live up to that privilege. It is because of this (עַל־כֵּן) that Israel will suffer pun-

---

3:1. This verse (in prose) and the following (in verse) together constitute a brief oracle that introduces a series of judgment pronouncements (chaps. 3–6), which is really a further development of the initial pronouncement in 2:6–16. The verse begins with the solemn covenantal command to hear the word that Yahweh has spoken against his children. A similar injunction to hear what God has to say formerly introduced his commands in the Sinai covenant. Now, it introduces his covenant lawsuit against his rebellious people, who are in fact his family. There may be some comfort in the fact that they are his family. The phraseology, which reminds the Israelites of the exodus experience, would also recall his saving power and kindness to them then, when "the LORD your God carried you, just as one carries a child, all the way that you traveled" (Deut. 1:31). But it would also recall their rebelliousness in those days, a tendency that has subsequently born fruit of disobedience, and that must now be punished again, more rigorously than before. If there is any comfort, it will be in this: that their chastisement

proves that they are still God's children, and still in the family.

2. Israel has had the greatest possible privilege. It has been known by the living God, which in the ancient world meant covenantal recognition and oversight on the part of the national god. Some ancient kings claimed that the gods "knew" (or recognized) the kings themselves or their prayers; for example, Hammurabi claimed in his famous prologue that he was "the illustrious prince, whose prayers Adad recognizes" (*ANET*, p. 165). The privileges claimed by kings in the ancient Near East (such as recognition by the gods, election, being loved by the gods, having a priestly function before the gods) parallel the privileges of God's people under the old covenant, but preeminently under the new covenant. All these prerogatives of a redemptive covenantal relationship are implied here by the term *I have known*. In Israel's case, with that knowledge came all the other supposed prerogatives of ancient Near Eastern royalty: election (Deut. 7:6), covenant love (Deut. 4:37; 23:6 [5]), royalty and priesthood (Exod. 19:6:

ishment. There are several other places in Amos where punishment is hinted at but not described (note, e.g., the lack of a specific antecedent for the suffix נּוּ [it] on אֲשִׁיבֶנּוּ [lit. I will not revoke it] in chaps. 1–2; also note the lack of a stated punishment in 4:12). The construction עַל־כֵּן often occurs in covenant lawsuits to pronounce a verdict based upon Yahweh's indictment, which is the case here (and in Isa. 5:25; Jer. 5:6). אֶפְקֹד (I will visit) frequently occurs in contexts depicting the Lord's punishment of the wicked, whether his own covenant people as here (also in Jer. 5:9, 29; Hos. 4:14) or other nations (e.g., Isa. 10:12 [Assyria]; 23:17 [Tyre]; Jer. 27:8 [any nation that will not serve Babylon]). כָּל־עֲוֹנֹתֵיכֶם (all your iniquities): The Lord will cause their iniquities to reappear hauntingly in their national experience. Since the Old Testament concept of sin demands requital (see, e.g., Num. 32:23), this statement is an affirmation of divine punishment.

"You shall be for me a priestly kingdom"). The same prerogatives are ours preeminently now because of the work of Christ. We too are elect (Eph. 1:4), the objects of covenant love (Rom. 5:6–8; Heb. 9:15), and are a royal priesthood (1 Pet. 2:9). Israel had ignored its great blessing of a relationship with God, and so he must punish it. His reminder, that he has known it alone from "all the families [i.e., nations] of the earth," is ironic. This phrase first appeared in the Lord's blessing on their father Abram, and from that blessing and that relationship had come the nation Israel. On the basis of that relationship, Yahweh had delivered his people and made them a nation (Deut. 4:37). Now he must punish them because of that special covenantal relationship. This case illustrates a broader principle, that is, that the Lord has a holy right to punish all sin because he has created all things and is thereby in covenantal relationship with all things (see the Exposition at 1:3). That universal covenant is one of common grace, to be sure, but it still entails judgment. So it is that the Alpha, whose creation of the world was reported in covenantal form in Genesis 1:1–2:3, must be the Omega who will come to judge the world and usher in a new heaven and new earth (Rev. 19–21). In all justice, as he did with his covenant people Israel, he will visit upon the world the effects of their iniquities. And, as then, those who are truly in covenantal relationship with him— those whom he knows—he will redeem. For "this is eternal life, that they may know you, the only true God, and Jesus Christ whom you have sent" (John 17:3).

II. Pronouncements of Judgment (3:1–6:14)
A. Covenant Lawsuit (3:1–15)
2. Affirmation of Prophecy (3:3–8)

<table>
<tr><td>

³ Would a pair go in unison,
    unless they had made an appoint-
    ment?
⁴ Would a lion roar in the forest
    yet have no prey?
Would a young lion thunder from its den
    unless it had taken something?
⁵ Would a bird fall into a ground snare
    if there had been no bait for it?
Would a snare spring up from the dirt
    with nothing to catch?
⁶ Would a trumpet be blown in a city
    and the people not be afraid?
Would there be disaster in a city
    and Yahweh has not caused it?
⁷ For the Lord Yahweh would not do a
    thing
    without revealing his secret plan
    to his servants the prophets.
⁸ A lion has roared;
    who would not fear?
The Lord Yahweh has spoken;
    who would not prophesy?

</td><td>

³ Do two walk together
    unless they have made an appoint-
    ment?
⁴ Does a lion roar in the forest,
    when it has no prey?
Does a young lion cry out from its den,
    if it has caught nothing?
⁵ Does a bird fall into a snare on the earth,
    when there is no trap for it?
Does a snare spring up from the ground,
    when it has taken nothing?
⁶ Is a trumpet blown in a city,
    and the people are not afraid?
Does disaster befall a city,
    unless the LORD has done it?
⁷ Surely the Lord GOD does nothing,
    without revealing his secret
    to his servants the prophets.
⁸ The lion has roared;
    who will not fear?
The Lord GOD has spoken;
    who can but prophesy?

</td></tr>
</table>

3. הֲיֵלְכוּ שְׁנַיִם יַחְדָּו (would a pair go in unison?): The dual ending on שְׁנַיִם connotes a couple. Perhaps it refers to Yahweh and his prophet, or perhaps it is a general term: do any two walk together unless they have agreed to do so? יַחְדָּו (in unison; lit. in its unitedness) normally means "together," but with a background sense of strong unity or oneness (see BDB, pp. 402–3). If the relation between Yahweh and his prophet is implied here, that strong sense is applicable. בִּלְתִּי אִם (unless) also occurs in verse 4. נוֹעָדוּ (they had made an appointment): The Septuagint's γνωρίσωσιν ἑαυ–τούς (know one another), reflects either a metathesis of יָעַד (niphal, make an appointment) to יָדַע, or the presence of יָדַע in its Hebrew *Vorlage*. The word יָעַד (make an appointment) has the sense of meeting at an appointed place or time (Exod. 25:22; 30:6; Josh. 11:5; Job 2:11; Neh. 6:2; see BDB, pp. 416–17).

4. This verse is structured around two bicola that are synonymously parallel: "Would a lion roar . . . ?" parallels "Would a young lion thunder . . . ?" שָׁאַג (roar) and נָתַן קוֹל (lit. to give voice) also appear in parallel in 1:2, where שָׁאַג connotes the roaring of a lion about to attack. Both questions in 3:4 are rhetorical, expecting a "no" answer (GKC §150d). Other parallels are lion / young lion, in the forest / from his den, and yet have no prey / unless he had taken something. אַרְיֵה (lion) and כְּפִיר (young lion) are a stock pair in poetry (e.g., Isa. 31:4). There is no apparent difference between them. מְעֹנָתוֹ (its den; lit. habitation) regularly refers to the dens or lairs of wild animals. It also describes God as a refuge for his people in Deuteronomy 33:27. בִּלְתִּי אִם (unless) recurs here (see verse 3), contributing a rhetorical force of repetition to the context. The verb לָכָד (it had taken something) stands alone and the object is assumed, as also in verse 5.

5. Verse 5 continues the series of rhetorical questions that leads to the devastating conclusion of verses 7–8. עַל־פַּח הָאָרֶץ (into a ground snare; lit.

---

3. This section includes a series of rhetorical questions based on a cause-and-effect structure (vv. 3–6). The series culminates in verse 7, in which the concluding principle is stated. Then verse 8 introduces two more rhetorical questions, based on verses 4 and 7, and these last two questions introduce a series of oracles.

The first in this series of rhetorical questions introduces a relationship between two who have agreed to walk together. This statement may envision any two people found walking in the desert. It would be strange for them to be walking side by side in such a vast expanse if they had not agreed to do so. It is also possible that the relationship between the Lord and his prophet is indicated here, anticipating the point made in verse 7, that the Lord does nothing "without revealing his secret plan / to his servants the prophets." Just as the Lord met with his people in the tent of meeting as they walked through the wilderness, so he meets with his faithful servant, the prophet, as they walk together in the prophet's life calling.

The effect that this question establishes is two people walking together. The cause is their agreeing to do so. This relationship of cause and effect prepares the reader for the climactic cause-and-effect relationship that we find in verse 8.

4. Amos continues the series of rhetorical questions with an example from nature. Would a lion roar—as it does when attacking its prey—if there were no prey? Would a young lion thunder with satisfaction from its den if it had taken nothing?

The obvious answer to both questions is "no." These questions pave the way for the identification of the Lord with the lion in verse 8, where we learn that he is the one who will roar when he is about to pounce on his people, and thunder as he accomplishes his judgment upon them.

In this question, the effect is a lion roaring. The cause is the lion's prey. In each line of this binary structure the point is made that the lion roars when it has successfully stalked and killed an animal. This illustration from nature may have been familiar to Amos in his occupation as a sheepherder.

5. The next rhetorical question gives the coming judgment a sense of inevitability. It continues the idea of cause and effect. Would a bird fall into a snare if it had not been attracted by bait? Would a snare spring to enclose its victim if the victim itself had not sprung it? In the context this question may signal the inevitability of Israel's judgment. Against the Old Testament background, however, the trap or bait may stand for sin: the sin into which the nation had fallen and which had ensnared it. In Ecclesiastes 9:12, the writer uses similar imagery to describe entrapment of a different kind:

> As fish are caught in a cruel net,
>   or birds are taken in a snare,
> so men are trapped by evil times
>   that fall unexpectedly upon them. (NIV)

upon or onto a snare of the earth or ground): פַּח (ground snare) is a stationary snare for birds set up on the ground (bird traps are known from Egyptian records), perhaps a net on a framework (Driver, *Joel and Amos*, p. 161). In Isaiah 24:17–18 this word occurs in a description of the Lord's judgment on sinful people. מוֹקֵשׁ (bait): Probably the primary connotation of this term is bait; later it may have developed the sense of trap (BDB, p. 430). The sense of bait is more appropriate to this context because of the cause-and-effect relationship it establishes. No bird would fall upon a snare unless it had been attracted by bait. לֹא יִלְכּוֹד וְלָכוֹד (with nothing to catch; lit. and indeed does not take anything): The direct object is assumed, as in verse 4. The idea (again a statement of cause and effect) is that the snare would not go into action without something to spring it.

6. Once again, this verse is structured around two bicola, each of which poses a cause-and-effect rhetorical question, to which the obvious answer is "no." שׁוֹפָר (trumpet) was blown on several occasions: to attack in time of war (e.g., Judg. 7:18–19), to halt a military action (2 Sam. 2:28), to warn the citizens of a city or region of the approach or attack of the enemy (Jer. 6:1; Hos. 5:8), to signal the Lord's judgment on nations (e.g., of Babylon, Jer. 51:27), and to announce his redemption of his people (Isa. 27:13). Here, the trumpet is a warning to the citizens of a hypothetical city. רָעָה (disaster; lit. evil): The context requires that evil be understood in the sense of catastrophe, not ethical wrong. It is evil that the Lord brings upon (הָיָה) a city, and its parallel concept in the verse is the warning of military attack. וַיהוָה לֹא עָשָׂה (and Yahweh has not caused it; lit. done it): The direct object is understood. The Old Testament states Yahweh's sovereignty starkly at times, as here and in Isaiah 45:7. But is also clear from the Old Testament that he allows evil for the sake of sanctification (e.g., Job), and most expressly so as a form of judgment for covenant breaking.

But now the Lord warns his people through his servant Amos so that the impending righteous judgment will not be unexpected. He is a God who loves his people and desires them to be saved and ultimately rescued from the snare into which they had fallen. David spoke of rescue from a snare in Psalm 124:6–8:

Praise be to the LORD,
    who has not let us be torn by their teeth.
We have escaped like a bird
    out of the fowler's snare;
the snare has been broken,
    and we have escaped.
Our help is in the name of the LORD,
    the Maker of heaven and earth.   (NIV)

In Amos's question the effect is something ensnared in a trap. In the A line we see a bird struggling in a trap set on the ground. The B line is more general, not specifying a bird; but perhaps the parallel structure requires us again to picture a bird in a trap. The cause in the analogy is a snare set on the ground.

6. The series of questions continues, pressing closer to home. The cause-and-effect situation envisions a military attack against or some disaster coming upon a city and its people. It is this kind of event that is the stuff of which divine judgment is made. The answer to the first question is obvious: Yes, the people would be afraid if a warning were sounded, for the usual fate of a besieged city in the ancient world was defeat. Amos, as a faithful prophet of the Lord, must himself sound a warning of judgment that is not unlike that trumpet blast. In a similar fashion, the prophetic warnings in the Bible as a whole anticipate the trumpet blasts that will sound when the Lord returns with his hosts to work judgment on the earth and redemption for his people.

The evils of judgment are caused (ʿāśâ) by the Lord according to this verse. Thus, the Lord is the one who creates evil. We must remember, however, that the context informs the word rāʿâ with the sense of disaster, not ethical evil (see the Exegesis). The prophet Isaiah echoes the same idea:

I am the LORD, and there is no other.
I form light and create darkness,
I make weal and create woe;
I the LORD do all these things.   (45:6c–7)

Divine judgment is an expression of the Lord's sovereignty (Eph. 1:11). His sovereignty as it relates to Israel requires him as their king to execute judgment upon them for breaking their covenant with him. His sovereignty as it relates to the earth means that as earth's king he must execute judgment upon the earth for all of its covenant breaking (see the Exposition at 1:3). Believers, however, can rejoice in the Lord's sovereignty, because he is their king. The writer of Hebrews (1:8, quoting Ps. 45:7 [6]) said:

7. כִּי (for): The connection of this statement with verses 3–6 is not obvious. It is possible that כִּי denotes proximate causation; that is, the statement introduced by כִּי is the effective cause of the foregoing statements, which now find their rationale in this כִּי clause. The cause-and-effect relationships of this passage have their conclusion in the counsel or plan of Yahweh, which is punishment for his people (vv. 4–6). אֲדֹנָי יְהוִה (the Lord Yahweh): See the Exegesis of 1:8. דָּבָר (a thing) has a broad semantic range. The connotation with which this context energizes the word is that of a thing. The expression עָשָׂה דָּבָר (do a thing) occurs frequently in the Old Testament (e.g., Gen. 22:16). The context here requires the sense of *do anything*. סוֹדוֹ (his secret plan): The various contexts in which this word appears determine several connotations for it. It has the sense of friendly or confidential sharing (e.g., Job 19:19; Ps. 25:14), and it can also connote a council in which plans—whether human (Ps. 64:3 [2]) or of the Lord—are formed. In Jeremiah 23:18, 22, the term occurs in a context rebuking false prophets who did not have access to Yahweh's counsel. Here the word describes Yahweh's secret plan, or confidential counsel, which he shares with his prophets. עֲבָדָיו הַנְּבִיאִים (his servants the prophets) probably has its origin in the designation of Moses as a prophet of God (Deut. 34:10). He was also known as the עֶבֶד־יְהוָה (servant of Yahweh, Deut. 34:5; Josh. 1:1; see also Exod. 14:31; Num. 12:7).

8. אַרְיֵה שָׁאָג (a lion has roared) is a direct echo of הֲיִשְׁאַג אַרְיֵה (would a lion roar . . . ?) in verse 4, which would perhaps recall the rest of the earlier rhetorical question, "Yet have no prey?" Of course it would have prey, and the implication in the early question is now clearer. It is the people who are the prey, and Amos asks of fellow compatriots, מִי לֹא יִירָא (who would not fear?), which parallels מִי לֹא יִנָּבֵא (who would not prophesy?). Both imperfects are to be taken modally, like the other imperfects in verses 3–6. אֲדֹנָי יְהוִה (the Lord Yahweh): See the Exegesis of 1:8.

Your throne, O God, will last for ever and ever,
> and righteousness will be the scepter of your kingdom. (NIV)

But if they had stood in my council,
> they would have proclaimed my words to my people
> and would have turned them from their evil ways
> and from their evil deeds. (NIV)

7. The series of questions suddenly comes to an end and the conclusion confronts us. As this verse intimates, the Lord draws his prophets into a personal relationship with himself. They are privy to his counsel, receiving a clear statement of his confidential plans. It is not that Yahweh does nothing at all without telling the prophets; rather, he does nothing by way of covenant-lawsuit judgment without telling them. He tells them as well of impending judgments in the area of common grace, as was the case with Abraham (who was a prophet, Gen. 20:7), whom God informed about the impending judgment on Sodom and Gomorrah (Gen. 18:17). He may reveal to them his plans for humankind in general, or for particular groups, as he did with Abraham. Most often, the Lord reveals his plans for his own people. That is the case here in verse 7. Those plans may be indicated pictorially, as in verses 4–6, and will appear in greater detail later. The Lord brought the true prophets into this relationship with himself because he desired that through them his people might learn to know his good will and his ongoing care for them. This is clear from Jeremiah's rebuke of the false prophets in 23:22:

The designation of the prophets as servants of the Lord complements the previous description of the privilege they have in sharing the Lord's secret intentions. Not only do they learn about the divine plan, but as servants they carry out a specific task. They are spokesmen for God who announce his will to the people. The phrase *his servants the prophets* also occurs later in the historical books (2 Kings 17:13, 23; 21:10; 24:2) and in the prophets (Jer. 7:25; 25:4; 26:5; 29:19; 35:15; Ezek. 38:17; Dan. 9:10; Zech. 1:6). Of course, all the Lord's people are his servants (Lev. 25:55), and it was Moses' wish that all of them would be prophets (Num. 11:29). The prospective fulfilment of that wish was to appear later, through another prophet (Joel 3:1–2 [2:28–29]).

The cause-and-effect relationship in this verse is not as clear as it was in the preceding. Certainly the prophetic pronouncements of doom did not *cause* God's judgment. We must look to the next verse to learn the lesson of cause and effect.

8. The last verse in this section consists of two bicola that are, like those in verses 3–6, rhetorical questions involving cause-and-effect relationships. These questions make clear what was lurking in the other questions in the series. The Lord has roared a message of impending judgment. This is the cause. Upon hearing it, who would not prophesy? The appearance of a prophet is the effect. Thus Amos's lesson on cause and effect is a substantiation of his role as a prophet. The cause of his appearance in the northern kingdom as a prophet is not monetary gain (7:14), but the impulsion of the divine will that Amos could not resist.

The two bicola in this verse are externally synonymous:

a	b
a lion has roared	who would not fear?
a´	b´
the Lord Yahweh has spoken	who would not prophesy?

The parallelism makes it clear that Yahweh is like a lion, and his speaking is like a lion's roar. This concept occurs elsewhere (e.g., 1:2; Jer. 25:30; Joel 4:16 [3:16]). The resultant fear, which is inevitable, is paralleled by the inevitability of prophecy. The parallel may indicate that such covenant-lawsuit prophecy, although it proceeds from a confidential relationship (v. 7), is still terrible to the prophet, as well as to his hearers.

II. Pronouncements of Judgment (3:1–6:14)
A. Covenant Lawsuit (3:1–15)
3. Oracle: Witnesses, Indictment, Judgment (3:9–11)

9 Proclaim upon the royal citadels in Ashdod
and upon the royal citadels in the
land of Egypt,
and say, "Assemble yourselves upon the
mountains of Samaria,
and see the great disorders within her,
and the oppression in her midst."
10 "And they do not know how to do
right"—
oracle of Yahweh—
"those who store violence and destruction in their royal citadels."
11 Therefore, thus says the Lord Yahweh:
"An adversary—and around the land!
And he will bring down your strongholds from you,
and your royal citadels will be plundered."

9 Proclaim to the strongholds in Ashdod,
and to the strongholds in the land of
Egypt,
and say, "Assemble yourselves on
Mount Samaria,
and see what great tumults are within it,
and what oppressions are in its
midst."
10 They do not know how to do right, says
the Lord,
those who store up violence and robbery in their strongholds.
11 Therefore thus says the Lord God:
An adversary shall surround the land,
and strip you of your defense;
and your strongholds shall be plundered.

9. הַשְׁמִיעוּ עַל־אַרְמְנוֹת (proclaim upon the royal citadels): הַשְׁמִיעוּ (proclaim) does double duty, governing this colon as well as the next. It is a plural imperative, perhaps indicating other prophets or functioning as a literary device similar to the commands in Isaiah 40:3, 6. In this case the address is to hypothetical persons and is used for literary effect. Similar plural commands appear elsewhere in the prophets (Isa. 57:14; 62:11; Jer. 5:1, 10, 20; Hos. 5:8; 8:1). The imperative of this word occurs elsewhere in the prophetic literature, especially in Jeremiah. The identical phrase occurs in Jeremiah 4:16: הַשְׁמִיעוּ עַל־יְרוּשָׁלַ͏ם (proclaim against Jerusalem). Here, however, עַל does not mean "against" the royal citadels, because the purpose of this command is to summon Ashdod and Egypt, not to condemn them. עַל is perhaps best rendered "upon," indicating that the hypothetical figures who summon Philistia and Egypt are standing on the pinnacles of the cities of these nations. אַרְמְנוֹת (royal citadels) is used frequently in chapters 1–2; see the Exegesis of 1:4. אַשְׁדּוֹד (Ashdod) echoes 1:8. The Septuagint has Ἀσσυρίος (Assyria), perhaps correctly. Assyria was a frequent parallel for Egypt (as in Isa. 7:18; 19:23–25; Jer. 2:18, 36; Hos. 7:11; Mic. 7:12), and perhaps the Septuagint translators thought they were correcting an error. If Ashdod is the orig-

inal reading, it is then echoed by שֹׁד (destruction) in verse 10 (a suggestion made in the first edition of Smith's *Twelve Prophets*, vol. 1, p. 145, but not retained in his second edition). It appears that the purpose of this oracle is to summon nations, known for their cruelty to Israel, to witness the cruelty within its capital. Since Assyria was not at this time a perennial enemy of Israel, Ashdod, which represents the Philistines, is thus an appropriate nation to address in this regard. וְאִמְרוּ (and say) is another plural imperative, as in Isaiah 62:11. הֵאָסְפוּ (assemble yourselves) is a plural imperative that is now directed to Ashdod and Egypt. שֹׁמְרוֹן עַל־הָרֵי (upon the mountains of Samaria). עַל means "upon" here, as in the first two cola. The Septuagint has the singular ὄρος (mountain), but this is probably an effort to "correct" the plural, making it consistent with the singular occurrences that follow (e.g., Mount Samaria in 4:1 and 6:1). In those places, however, Samaria, situated alone on her mountain, is addressed; here, the people of two nations (or their leaders) are summoned to come to the mountains that surround Samaria. They are to witness a kind of oppression of which even they would not be guilty—Israel oppressing her own people. The verb וּרְאוּ (see), a plural imperative addressed to imaginary spectators, does double

---

9. This oracle begins with an elegant structure that befits its stately, if ironic, summons:

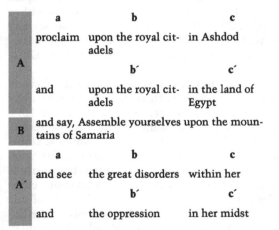

	a	b	c
A	proclaim	upon the royal citadels	in Ashdod
	and	upon the royal citadels (b´)	in the land of Egypt (c´)
B	and say, Assemble yourselves upon the mountains of Samaria		
	a	b	c
A´	and see	the great disorders	within her
	and	the oppression (b´)	in her midst (c´)

This structure consists of a bicolon with synonymous parallelism and a double-duty verb, a hinge colon (the call to assemble), and a second bicolon with synonymous parallelism and a double-duty verb. Formally, the second half reflects the first: the messengers' command to "see" reflects the Lord's command to "proclaim."

The structure indicates that the whole process has a certain rightness and inevitability. It is the task of these messengers—Amos and perhaps other prophets—to proclaim upon the rooftops the summons that the Lord has given them—a summons to observe the oppression within the northern kingdom. It is ironic that the summons should sound from the royal citadels of Ashdod and Egypt, since these places were known for their oppression and wrongdoing. These pagans are summoned to station themselves on the mountains that surround Samaria, to witness the disorders and oppression within her. The implication is that Israel's wrongs outdo their own. Those disorders are not what the Lord desires for his people or, indeed, his world. They arise from sinful hearts that nurture bloodshed and idolatry. It takes little imagination to realize that the first sin of bloodshed was also a sin of idolatry, for Cain sacrificed his brother on the altar of his own ego. Indeed all sins lead to the opposite of peace, just as did the sin of the people of the northern kingdom. Thus it is that Jesus says, "Blessed are peacemakers, for they shall be called children of God!" God's children are called to be makers of *šalôm*,

duty, controlling both מְהוּמֹת רַבּוֹת (great disorders) and עֲשׁוּקִים (oppression). The former phrase is the antithesis of שָׁלוֹם (peace or wholeness) in 2 Chronicles 15:5: "In those times it was not safe [שָׁלוֹם] for anyone to go or come, for great disturbances afflicted all the inhabitants of the lands." Ezekiel condemned Jerusalem for being רַבַּת הַמְּהוּמָה (full of tumult; lit. great disorders, Ezek. 22:1–5). עֲשׁוּקִים (oppression) is an abstract plural noun, occurring also in Job 35:9: "Men cry out under a load of oppression" (NIV); and Ecclesiastes 4:1: "Again I looked and saw all the oppression that was taking place under the sun" (NIV).

10. נְכֹחָה (right) is a feminine form of the masculine adjective and substantive נָכֹחַ, which has a similar sense. Basically this root denotes something in front. The feminine form has the sense of straightness. Since this context reflects moral concerns we may translate the word "just" or "right." נְאֻם־יְהוָה (oracle of Yahweh): See the Exegesis of 2:11. הָאוֹצְרִים (those who store): The verbal form of this word connotes storing up treasures (e.g., 2 Kings 20:17 par. Isa. 39:6; Isa. 23:18). Ironically, however, the oppressors have stored up שֹׁד חָמָס (violence and destruction). אַרְמְנוֹתֵיהֶם (royal citadels) just occurred in verse 9 (see the Exegesis

of 1:4). Because the oppressors store in their royal citadels the plunder gained from their own people, those very citadels will be plundered (v. 11).

11. לָכֵן (therefore) introduces the consequence of the previously listed sins (vv. 9–10); it is repeated in 4:12; 5:11, 13, 16; 6:7; and 7:17 (3:2 uses the similar עַל־כֵּן, therefore). אֲדֹנָי יְהוִה (the Lord Yahweh) is repeated from verses 7–8 (see the Exegesis of 1:8). צָר וּסְבִיב הָאָרֶץ (an adversary—and around the land!): There is no need to emend וּסְבִיב (and around) to יְסוֹבֵב (will surround), with צָר (adversary) as the subject, as the Syriac, Targum, and Vulgate seem to imply. וְ here is explanatory (moreover, [it] surrounds the land; see GKC §154a, n. 1). וְהוֹרִד מִמֵּךְ עֻזֵּךְ (and he will bring down your strongholds from you) recalls the covenantal curse in Deuteronomy 28:52: "They [a distant nation] will lay siege to all the cities throughout your land until the high fortified walls in which you trust fall down" (NIV). מִמֵּךְ (from you) underscores the exposure of the people to danger as their strongholds are pulled down away from them. They are left with no protection. וְנָבֹזּוּ (and . . . be plundered) complements the preceding clause by vividly describing the reality of what that clause anticipates.

---

which is the Hebrew word for peace or wholeness. God's children in Samaria did the opposite: they created great disorders and oppression. Qoheleth saw that this was the way of the world, for he said in Ecclesiastes 4:1:

> I saw the tears of the oppressed—
> and they have no comforter;
> power was on the side of their oppressors—
> and they have no comforter. (NIV)

This is the way of the world, and will be to the end, but it is not to be the way of God's children.

10. Samaria's degeneration is so complete that it does not know how to do what is clearly right and just. Its people deviate from the path of covenant righteousness. Its leaders store up unjust gain in their royal citadels. They are storing up and treasuring the violence against their people and the destruction of their nation for which they are responsible. For that reason, the terrible irony of judgment awaits them.

When Amos says "violence and destruction" (ḥamas wašōd) he employs metonomy of cause: he states the cause, "violence and destruction," but intends the effect, that is, the wealth that was acquired and stored up as a result of the nation's violence and destruction. These words form a stock pair in the prophetic literature (e.g., Isa.

60:18 [in parallelism]; Jer. 6:7; 20:8; Ezek. 45:9; Hab. 1:3 [in reverse order]; 2:17 [in parallelism]). *Ḥamas* (violence) connotes violence done to people, including even the violence of false witness (Exod. 23:1; Deut. 19:16), as well as attempted physical harm (2 Sam. 22:3, 49) and bloodshed (Judg. 9:24: "The violence done to the seventy sons of Jerubbaal"). *Šōd* (destruction) tends to connote ruination by seizure of property (e.g., Obad. 5; Mic. 2:4).

11. The disaster in view is an outworking of covenantal curses, such as those in Deuteronomy 28:49–52. An adversary will surround the land, pull down the high walls in which Israel trusted, and plunder the royal citadels in which it stored up unjust gain. The irony is apparent, for Israel once balked at entering the promised land because of the "sky-high" walls of the Canaanite cities (Deut. 1:26–28). The Lord proved the folly of this fear by demolishing the strong walls of Jericho (Josh. 6). But now it is his people who, having high walls in the promised land, have themselves become like Canaanites in their immorality and social injustice. So they, in their turn, will have their walls, their strongholds in which they trusted, brought down. The Lord will allow the adversary to bring them down, and the Lord will allow the citadels to be plundered.

II. Pronouncements of Judgment (3:1–6:14)
A. Covenant Lawsuit (3:1–15)
4. Oracle (3:12)

¹² Thus says Yahweh:
"As the shepherd rescues from the lion's
mouth
a couple of leg bones, or a scrap of an
ear,
so shall the children of Israel be rescued,
who recline in Samaria on the side of
a divan,
and in Damascus, on a couch."

¹² Thus says the Lord: As the shepherd rescues from the mouth of the lion two legs, or a piece of an ear, so shall the people of Israel who live in Samaria be rescued, with the corner of a couch and part of a bed.

12. יְהוָה אָמַר כֹּה (thus says Yahweh): See the Exegesis of 1:3. כַּאֲשֶׁר (as) introduces the protasis of the comparison clause here. כֵּן (so) takes up the apodosis in the fourth line. יַצִּיל (rescues) has the sense of snatch; the context pictures a shepherd who is able to recover only a few parts of a sheep that a lion has torn to pieces. הָרֹעֶה (the shepherd): The article (הָ) functions to denote a person who cannot be defined (GKC §126q), thus a shepherd, any shepherd. כֵּן fills out the comparison. Just as the hypothetical shepherd snatches only a few remaining parts of the sheep, so all that will remain of Israel will be broken fragments of her proud and opulent past. הַיֹּשְׁבִים (who recline; lit. sit): Some translate this participle as "dwell" (e.g., rsv), but the niv is probably nearer the mark with

the translation "sit." The image is that of royalty (especially the king and the wealthy of Assyria) reclining on a divan beside the table. The Romans also were known for this mode of luxurious dining and relaxation. מִטָּה בִּפְאַת (on the side of a divan) is the side or edge of a couch close to the table. עֶרֶשׂ וּבִדְמֶשֶׁק should be repointed וּבְדַמֶּשֶׁק with the Septuagint (ἐν Δαμασκῷ), yielding "and in Damascus on a couch," taking "couch" as an adverbial accusative. S. Fränkel suggests that דְּמֶשֶׁק represents the metathesized form of an Arabic noun, *midaqs* (edge; cited in Driver, *Joel and Amos*, p. 165). The resulting parallelism could support such a reading: "on the side of a divan" and "on the edge of a couch."

---

12. This oracle, which begins with "thus says Yahweh" states an awful certainty. It pictures a shepherd who has found a wild animal devouring one of his lambs. The shepherd is too late. He can only snatch the remaining pieces of the lamb from the animal's bloody mouth—"a couple of leg bones, or a scrap of an ear." In the same way Israel will be devoured in the coming catastrophe. The nation will die and only a few dismal remnants of its once proud past will remain. The nation will perish, devoured by the Assyrian hordes.

If we are correct in pointing *ûbidmešeq* to read "and in Damascus . . . ," the resultant scenario is historically conceivable. Jeroboam II recaptured Damascus (2 Kings 14:28), and wealthy Israelites might have lived and traded in the vassal state. Amos speaks of it as Aramean (1:3, 5; 5:27), but this was with a prophetic perspective on the punishment yet to befall the city (1:5). The alternative reading, "damask," is tempting, but there is no evidence that Damascus produced that fabric in Amos's day.

II. Pronouncements of Judgment (3:1–6:14)
A. Covenant Lawsuit (3:1–15)
5. Oracle: Witnesses, Judgment (3:13–15)

¹³ "Hear and testify against the house of
    Jacob"—
  oracle of the Lord Yahweh, the God of
    hosts—
¹⁴ For on the day that I punish Israel for its
    sins,
  I will punish the altars of Bethel,
and the horns of the altar will be cut off
  and they will fall to the ground.
¹⁵ And I will strike the winter house
  along with the summer house,
and the houses of ivory will perish
  and the mansions will come to an
    end"—
  oracle of Yahweh.

¹³ Hear, and testify against the house of Ja-
    cob,
  says the Lord GOD, the God of hosts:
¹⁴ On the day I punish Israel for its trans-
    gressions,
  I will punish the altars of Bethel,
and the horns of the altar shall be cut off
  and fall to the ground.
¹⁵ I will tear down the winter house as
    well as the summer house;
  and the houses of ivory shall perish,
and the great houses shall come to an
    end,
says the LORD.

13. שִׁמְעוּ (hear): See the Exegesis of verse 1. The imperative here, as with the subsequent verb, is plural (see the Exegesis of verse 9). הָעִידוּ (testify; hiphil) is typical of juridical proceedings, in particular of covenant and covenant-lawsuit material in which the Lord himself testifies (Deut. 8:19; Pss. 50:7; 81:9 [8]; Mal. 2:14) or calls heaven and earth to do so (Deut. 4:26; 30:19; 31:28). בְּבֵית יַעֲקֹב (against the house of Jacob): בְּ (against) occurs frequently with הָעִיר in the sense of *witness against* (Deut. 4:26; 30:19; 31:28). בֵּית יַעֲקֹב (house of Jacob) appears first in Genesis 46:27, then Exodus 19:3, and often thereafter in the prophets (e.g., Isa. 2:5; Jer. 2:4; Ezek. 20:5; Mic. 2:7). It is a frequent surrogate for Israel, recalling its familial connections with the great patriarch. נְאֻם־אֲדֹנָי יְהוָה (oracle of the Lord Yahweh): See the Exegesis of 2:11. אֲדֹנָי יְהוָה (the Lord Yahweh): See the Exegesis of 1:8. הַצְּבָאוֹת אֱלֹהֵי (the God of hosts, or the God of armies): צְבָאוֹת occurs in 4:13; 5:14, 15, 16, 27; 6:8, 14; 9:5, and many times in the Book of Psalms (80:8 [7], 15 [14]) and Jeremiah 38:17; 44:7; 46:10. אֱלֹהֵי צְבָאוֹת is a less common title for the Lord than יְהוָה צְבָאוֹת (Yahweh of hosts/ armies). Both titles indicate the Lord's command over powerful armies, either of angels (Josh. 5:14; cf. 2 Kings 6:17) or, less commonly, of men (Isa. 13:4). These titles, "the Lord Yahweh" and "the God of hosts," occur together only here in Amos. Since this is an expanded title, it emphasizes the majesty of the God who brings lawsuit against his people.

14. בְּיוֹם פָּקְדִי פִשְׁעֵי־יִשְׂרָאֵל עָלָיו (on the day that I punish Israel for its sins; lit. on the day of my visitation of Israel's sins upon it) is a covenant-lawsuit formula. פָּקְדִי (punish): See the Exegesis of verse 2. עַל־מִזְבְּחוֹת בֵּית־אֵל וּפָקַדְתִּי (I will punish the altars of Bethel): When פָּקַד (visit) occurs without a direct object, as it does here, it brings the attention of the initiator of the action into the experience of the indirect object (in this case, מִזְבְּחוֹת altars). Thus, the Lord will give active attention to these altars in that he will destroy them. For examples of פָּקַד עַל without a direct object, see Isaiah 10:12 and Jeremiah 44:13 (see the Exegesis of Hos. 1:4). The basic formula, עַל . . . פָּקַדְתִּי בְּיוֹם פָּקְדִי (on the day of my punishment . . . I will punish upon), is found first in Exodus 32:34: וּבְיוֹם פָּקְדִי וּפָקַדְתִּי עֲלֵיהֶם חַטָּאתָם (when the time comes for me to punish, I will punish them for their sin, NIV), with the infinitive construct and converted perfect as here. In Jeremiah 27:22 it occurs in a positive sense: "And there they shall stay, until the day when I give attention to them, says the LORD. Then I will bring them up and restore them to this place" (see also Isa. 27:1). מִזְבְּחוֹת בֵּית־אֵל (the

13. The command to hear and testify against the house of Jacob announces the testimony concerning the guilt of the accused, which is an essential part of covenant-lawsuit proceedings. Normally this testimony is given by the Lord or by the heavens and the earth. Perhaps the latter are implied here. In any case, it is the sovereign Lord, Yahweh, the God of armies heavenly and earthly, who so commands. And if he commands the trial, who shall tell him to stop?

The plural address introduced by *šimʿû* (hear) may be simply a literary device similar to the one noted earlier (see the Exegesis of v. 9). The address is to no one in particular, but echoes the juridical nature of the adversarial relationship that the Lord establishes here with the people of the northern kingdom. The prophet calls them "the house of Jacob," a term that he may have intended to recall the nation's ancient covenantal heritage (Gen. 35:9–12).

14. The prophecy draws upon phraseology found in the original covenant documents. The Lord's "visitation" would not be to restore, as in the promise of Jeremiah, but to execute the covenantal punishment that must precede restoration. The Lord deals with sin not only by forgiving it, but also by removing it. Forgiveness comes in the form of justification, but removal comes in the form of sanctification. The Lord is going to sanctify his people by putting an end to their sins of idolatry at Bethel. By establishing idolatry there, Jeroboam set his nation on a course of evil that was to end in destruction. The horns of the altar at such a temple could never provide true sanctuary, nor could they legitimately bear the blood of an atoning sacrifice. So the Lord, the God of true atonement who is a sanctuary for his people, will put an end to the satanic counterfeit at Bethel, in accord with the prophecy uttered at its institution. We who follow in the footsteps of Christ may also be tempted to the terrible

altars of Bethel): The plurality of altars indicates polytheistic worship that Yahweh will punish. קַרְנוֹת הַמִּזְבֵּחַ (the horns of the altar) probably refers to the altar of burnt offering, which was the main altar. Both the altar of burnt offering (Exod. 27:2) and the altar of incense (Exod. 30:2) had horns. In the case of sin on the part of a priest (Lev. 4:7) or unintentional sin by the community (Lev. 4:18), the blood of a bull was to be put on the horns of the altar of incense. When a leader (Lev. 4:25) or a member of the community sinned unintentionally (Lev. 4:30, 34) blood was applied to the horns of the altar of burnt offering.

15. וְהִכֵּיתִי (and I will strike): נָכָה in the hiphil regularly occurs in accounts of war. It may have humans (e.g., Deut. 2:33; 4:46; Josh. 8:21; 10:10) or the Lord (e.g., Exod. 3:20; 12:12, 29) as its subject. בֵּית־הַחֹרֶף (the winter house) parallels בֵּית הַקַּיִץ (the summer house). עַל (along with) cannot have the sense of *on* here because two different types of houses are in view. It is best to understand it in the sense of accompa-

niment (BDB, p. 755). וְאָבְדוּ (and . . . will perish): Perishing was a result of divine judgment (e.g., Num. 16:33; Deut. 4:26; Judg. 5:31; Job 4:9; Ps. 73:27; Jer. 10:15). Pagans thought the same. For example, Mesha, king of Moab, reported that "Omri, king of Israel, . . . humbled Moab many years, for Chemosh [the Moabite god] was angry at his land [i.e., Moab]. And his son followed him and he also said, 'I will humble Moab.' In my time he spoke (thus), but I have triumphed over him and over his house, while Israel has perished forever" (*ANET*, p. 320; see also 2:1). Like his contemporaries, Mesha considered that such victories, including the perishing of his enemies, were a divine conquest and judgment upon the foe. בָּתֵּי הַשֵּׁן (the houses of ivory) were houses whose walls were paneled or inlaid with ivory. Ahab had such a house (1 Kings 22:39; see also Ps. 45:9 [8]) and the "beds of ivory" at Amos 6:4). וְסָפוּ (will come to an end): This verb is used only three other times in the qal (Esther 9:28; Ps. 73:19; Isa. 66:17), and once (disput-

---

error of an idolatry—be it illicit sex, money, power, or false doctrine. If we fall to any of these, we may need severe chastisement to advance our sanctification. How much better to flee from them (1 Cor. 6:18; 1 Tim. 6:11; 2 Tim. 2:22) and to put on the full armor of God (Eph. 6:10–18).

The plurality of altars of which this verse speaks ("altars of Bethel") was deeply rooted in Israel's past. Jeroboam I made a calf of gold for Israel to worship at Bethel (1 Kings 12:25–33). He erected one altar (1 Kings 13:1), but others were subsequently added. Hosea prophesied against Bethel (Hos. 10:5, 15), and the altar and sanctuary were subsequently destroyed by Josiah (2 Kings 23:15–16), as had been prophesied by "a man of God . . . [from] Judah" during Jeroboam's reign (1 Kings 13:1–3).

15. The possession of both a winter house and summer house was a remarkable luxury in Amos's day, as witnessed by the fact that even some foreign kings might not boast of it. A roughly contemporary inscription of King Barrakab of Samʾal (ca. 730 B.C.) reads: "My fathers, the kings of Samʾal, had no good house. They had the house of Kilamu, which was their winter house and also their summer house" ("Barrakab of Yʾdy-Samʾal," *ANET*, p. 655;

Donner and Rӧllig, *Kanaanäische und aramäische Inschriften*, vol. 1, p. 40, no. 216, lines 15–19; vol. 2, p. 233). The luxury of Israel, which allowed for summer and winter homes and homes inlaid with ivory, was great. The day of great wealth and great houses was coming to an end, however. The righteous judgment of the Lord would come upon them.

The destruction of these symbols of affluence focused on the root causes of Israel's spiritual sickness in Amos's day. The nation basked in its wealth, but the people did not understand that the homes to which they went to escape the summer's heat, and the ivory inlays that they lovingly fingered, were symbols of impending destruction. God had raised up a prophet to tell them these things. God had placed a prophetic burden on him. The lion had roared and he could not forebear to prophesy. If the oppression within Samaria's walls had ceased and if the people had bowed to the covenant demands of their suzerain in covenant loyalty, God's hand would have been stayed. They did not, nor did Amos believe they would. That is why he sees no hope for the nation, but instead places his hope in a restored remnant (9:12).

edly) in the hiphil (Jer. 8:13; see BDB, pp. 692–93). In Isaiah it is applied to those who practice abominations. In Psalm 73 it is applied to the evildoers: "How suddenly are they destroyed, / completely swept away by terrors!" (NIV). רַבִּים בָּתִּים (mansions; lit. great houses): The transla-

tion "great" is preferable to "many" because of the parallelism with בָּתֵּי הַשֵּׁן (houses of ivory). The houses, or mansions, of the wealthy and privileged are meant. נְאֻם־יהוה (oracle of Yahweh): See the Exegesis of 2:11.

II. Pronouncements of Judgment (3:1–6:14)

    B. Covenant Lawsuit (4:1–13)

        1. Indictment of Social Sin, Judgment (4:1–3)

4 Hear this word, you cows of Bashan
    on Mount Samaria,
who oppress the poor,
who crush the needy,
    who say to their husbands,
      "Bring, that we may drink!"
² The Lord Yahweh has sworn by his holi-
    ness:
    "Even now, days are coming upon
      you,
when they will take you with hooks,
    and the remnant of you with fish-
      hooks.
³ And through breaches you shall go forth,
    each woman straight ahead,
    and you will let go dominion"—
    oracle of Yahweh.

4 Hear this word, you cows of Bashan
    who are on Mount Samaria,
who oppress the poor, who crush the
    needy,
    who say to their husbands, "Bring
      something to drink!"
² The Lord GOD has sworn by his holiness:
    The time is surely coming upon you,
when they shall take you away with
    hooks,
    even the last of you with fishhooks.
³ Through breaches in the wall you shall
    leave,
    each one straight ahead;
    and you shall be flung out into Har-
    mon,
says the LORD.

4:1. שִׁמְעוּ הַדָּבָר הַזֶּה (hear this word): See the Exegesis of 3:1. שִׁמְעוּ (hear) is construed as masculine, even though it is addressed to women. It probably represents a blurring of distinctions between genders in the spoken language (GKC §135o). There is a similar use of the masculine in Isaiah 32:11: "Tremble [חִרְדוּ, masculine plural imperative], you complacent women" (NIV). פָּרוֹת הַבָּשָׁן (you cows of Bashan): הַבָּשָׁן (lit. the Bashan) generally appears with the definite article. Bashan was a fertile area east of the Jordan. The Old Testament mentions its "choice rams" (Deut. 32:14, NIV) and "fertile pasturelands" (Mic. 7:14, NIV). The conclusion of the verse makes it clear that the cows of Bashan are the corrupt and voluptuous women of Samaria. בְּהַר שֹׁמְרוֹן (on Mount Samaria): See the Exegesis of 3:9. These words describe the influential women of Samaria as sleek, well-fed cattle grazing on the hillsides overlooking Samaria, the center of uncaring indolence. הָעֹשְׁקוֹת (who oppress) and הָרֹצְצוֹת (who crush) comprise a word pair, also found together in Deuteronomy 28:33: עָשׁוּק וְרָצוּץ, literally, oppressed and crushed, but rightly taken as a hendiadys meaning "cruel oppression" by the NIV, and 1 Samuel 12:3: אֶת־מִי עָשַׁקְתִּי אֶת־מִי רַצּוֹתִי, "Whom have I defrauded? Whom have I oppressed?" The abstract noun עֲשׁוּקִים (oppression) occurred earlier in 3:9. דַּלִּים (the poor) and אֶבְיוֹנִים (the needy) are a stock pair in poetry and poetic parallelism, as in 1 Samuel 2:8; Psalm 72:13; 82:4

(see the Exegesis of 2:7). These words are not absolute synonyms because certain contexts invest דָּל with a sense of weakness and poverty, while אֶבְיוֹן generally connotes the sense of need. The linguistic force that the parallel structure creates, however, establishes these words as functional synonyms emphasizing the concept of poverty. This emphasis is appropriate to this context, which sets forth the misuse of wealth and the negative effects of greed. אֲדֹנֵיהֶם (their husbands): The masculine plural suffix is an acceptable stylistic license (see the comment on שִׁמְעוּ, hear, at the beginning of this paragraph). The loftier noun, אָדוֹן, instead of the more common בַּעַל (both of which mean "lord," and are used for "husband"), may indicate husbands of high rank or social standing. For the former as "husband," see Genesis 18:12, for the latter, see Hosea 2:18 [16].

2. נִשְׁבַּע אֲדֹנָי יְהוִה בְּקָדְשׁוֹ (the Lord GOD has sworn by his holiness): God swears: by his life (6:8), by the pride of Jacob (8:7), by his right hand (Isa. 62:8), by his great name (Jer. 44:26), and, as here, by his holiness (Ps. 89:36 [35]). The Lord's holiness enforces the oath and guarantees its validity. יְהוָה אֲדֹנָי (the Lord Yahweh): See the Exegesis of 1:8. כִּי (untranslated) introduces an object clause indicating the content of the oath, literally: "The Lord Yahweh has sworn that. . . ." הִנֵּה יָמִים בָּאִים (even now, days are coming): The deictic particle הִנֵּה frequently occurs with participles (as here) to desig-

---

4:1. The prophecy turns now to the privileged women of Samaria. They, as well as the male population, have oppressed the poor and crushed the needy by their greed. They are likened to cows of Bashan because this area was known for its well-fed cattle. The three feminine plural participles that introduce the three consecutive cola in this verse ("who oppress," "who crush," "who say") follow one another in the pattern of an ancient Near Eastern divine or royal titulary (a sequence of titles or epithets employing relative clauses or participles parallelistically). See, for example, the introduction to Hammurabi's law code (ANET, pp. 164–65, starting at col. 1, line 50), as well as in Isaiah 44:24–28 ("I am the LORD, who made all things, / who alone stretched out the heavens, / who by myself spread out the earth," etc.). Whether the women "press their husbands to supply them with the means for enjoying a joint carouse" (Driver, Joel and Amos, p. 168) or "demand the household service that, according to normal practice, they themselves should be providing" (Stuart, Hosea–Jonah, p. 332), the proph-

ecy denounces them primarily for their appetites. For other prophetic words against such women, see Deuteronomy 28:56–57 and Isaiah 32:9–13.

2. The Lord has sworn by his holiness that severe punishment will come upon the "cows of Bashan." God's holiness is an appropriate guarantor of the oath in this context because it is his holiness that the oppressing classes of Amos's day violated. The holiness they sullied by their disobedience had become the guarantor of their punishment. These women were far from holy. They had broken the covenant in many ways. But the Lord remains holy and swears by his holiness as a sign that he will surely enforce his covenant.

God swears by his holiness in Psalm 89:36–37 [35–36], where he says, "Once and for all I have sworn by my holiness; / I will not lie to David. / His line shall continue forever, / and his throne endure before me like the sun" (NRSV). In this passage the Lord's holiness is the guarantor of the oath because God cannot violate his holiness. He cannot lie or forsake his promise. And when the Lord swore to Abraham, he swore by himself,

nate future time (GKC §116p). Here it indicates a sudden change of fortunes, through divine judgment, as in 8:11 and 9:13 (see also 1 Sam. 2:31; 2 Kings 20:17 par. Isa. 39:6; and fifteen times in Jeremiah—e.g., 7:32; 9:24 [25]; 14:19). וְנִשָּׂא אֶתְכֶם (when they will take you; lit. he or one will take): וְנִשָּׂא (piel), an impersonal third-person masculine singular verb, with the enemy as the understood subject, does double duty for both cola. וְ (when) with the perfect tense presents the logical consequence of the participle בָּאִים (coming) and may be translated temporally (GKC §112x). אֶתְכֶם (you): For the masculine plural pronominal suffix, see the Exegesis of verse 1. בְּצִנּוֹת (with hooks) is the plural of צִנָּה, the feminine equivalent of צֵן (thorn, hook). There is another possibility, for צִנּוֹת (hooks) is attested in Hebrew in the feminine plural with the sense of shields, which may indicate that these women were carried off on shields (see McComiskey, "Amos," p. 303). In this view, the companion word סִירוֹת would designate a receptacle of some kind, perhaps for boiling fish. וְאַחֲרִיתְכֶן (and the remnant of you) has the feminine plural pronominal suffix, as we expect. This word indicates the last, that is, the remaining people.

בְּסִירוֹת דּוּגָה (with fishing hooks): סִירוֹת is the feminine plural of סִיר (thorn, hook). The relationship of this word to דּוּגָה (fish) may indicate that "fish hooks" are meant here. This construct phrase serves as ballast variant in the second colon. In the view taken here, the parallelism of hooks and fish hooks indicates that the women who were once sleek "cows" will be caught like fish and dragged away.

3. וּפְרָצִים (and through breaches) is an adverbial accusative indicating where they will go forth. The walls of their city will be "breached," and the women will be led forth into captivity. אִשָּׁה נֶגְדָּהּ (each woman straight ahead): Ironically, these words recall the somewhat similar words in Joshua 6:5, 20, אִישׁ נֶגְדּוֹ (lit. each man straight ahead), where the Israelites were to charge through the broken walls of Jericho. וְהִשְׁלַכְתֶּנָה (and you will let go; lit. cast away) is pointed as a hiphil, but the Septuagint renders it as a hophal (ἀπορριφήσεσθε), reflecting a difference of only one vowel. The passive sense that results from reading this verb as a hophal (be cast out) is appropriate to the *hapax legomenon* that follows, for הַהַרְמוֹן may be the name of a place. In this con-

---

because there was no greater guarantor of his promise (Heb. 6:13).

The Lord will always be faithful to his covenant, both to purge and to restore. Purging is in view here. The women who were first addressed as cows are now viewed in another way. As fish are dragged out of the water, these women will be dragged out of their comfortable places. In the ancient Near East, captives were often led by ropes through the nose or lip. Their captors even cut off hands, ears, and tongues, blinding, impaling, and skinning their captives alive. Assyrian reliefs show captives being led away by ropes fastened to a hook that pierced the nose or lower lip. The annals of the tenth year of Tiglath-pileser I report that the Assyrian king captured thirty Nairi kings and "put [ropes] in their noses" (King, *Annals of the Assyrian Kings*, pp. 116–20, 125–26, line 9; Weidner, "Die Feldzüge und Bauten Tiglat-pilesers I."). For the suggestion that *sinnot* is "ropes, reigns," see Holma (*Die Namen der Körperteile*) and Paul (*Amos*, p. 131). For other biblical references to hooks, see 2 Chronicles 33:11; Ezekiel 19:4, 9; Habakkuk 1:15; and ironically Isaiah 37:29 par. 2 Kings 19:28.

Even these prospects pale, however, beside the eternal punishment that awaits those who reject the love of God. As Jesus said in Matthew 10:28:

"Do not be afraid of those who kill the body but cannot kill the soul. Rather, be afraid of the One who can destroy both soul and body in hell" (NIV). Our call, like ancient Israel's, is a serious one, for the one who swore by his holiness has also said in Matthew 5:48: "Be perfect, therefore, as your heavenly Father is perfect" (NIV).

3. The destruction of Samaria is graphically apparent in this description. There will be breaches in the walls, and the once arrogant women of the city will go forth through those breaches. As the previous verse indicated, their captors will drag them forth with fish hooks. The phraseology here may echo the phraseology at the conquest of Jericho long ago, when the Israelites went *straight ahead* across the rubble of shattered walls to conquer the Lord's foes (see the Exegesis). Now, the rebellious women of his people will go *straight ahead* into the exile. No longer will they enjoy the lofty authority that they once abused.

This prospect for the affluent women of the northern kingdom is a vivid illustration of the uncertainty of earthly possessions. If these people had sought for the spiritual wealth of the knowledge of God, they would have found eternal riches. Instead their greed drove them ultimately to lives that were empty. Their wealth could not satisfy the soul.

text we should retain the pointing of the hiphil on the principle of *lectio difficilior*. The Vulgate reads *proiciemini* and the Syriac version is paraphrastic. הַהַרְמוֹנָה (dominion): The ancient translations generally understand this form as a place-name, Harmon. The Syriac version and Symmachus both have Armenia. Jerome has "Et proiiecimini in locis Armeniae, quae vocantur Armona." The Septuagint has εἰς τὸ ὄρος τὸ Ρεμμαν (to Mount Rimmon; see Judg. 20:45, 47). In these cases the ה that terminates the form is locative. Others have taken it in the sense of אַרְמוֹן (palace)—so the AV and Gesenius (see Keil, *Twelve*

Minor Prophets, p. 269), but a vague reference to an unknown palace is of little help. If it is a place-name, it remains unknown. It is possible to identify the word as a byform of Talmudic *harmânaʾ* (royal power or dominion), as Rashi has done (Keil, *Twelve Minor Prophets*, p. 269). The surfacing of such a form only once in an ancient Near Eastern text is not an anomaly, and the meaning is not inappropriate to the context. However, it must be admitted that no solution is certain at present. נְאֻם־יְהוָה (oracle of Yahweh): See the Exegesis of 2:11.

II. Pronouncements of Judgment (3:1–6:14)
B. Covenant Lawsuit (4:1–13)
2. Indictment of Religious Sin (4:4–5)

4 "Come to Bethel and rebel,
    to Gilgal and magnify rebellion;
do bring in your sacrifices every morn-
    ing,
    and your tithes every three days!
5 And burn some leavened bread as a
    thank-offering,
and proclaim freewill offerings pub-
    licly,
for this is what you love to do, O chil-
    dren of Israel"—
oracle of the Lord Yahweh.

4 Come to Bethel—and transgress;
    to Gilgal—and multiply transgres-
    sion;
bring your sacrifices every morning,
    your tithes every three days;
5 bring a thank-offering of leavened bread,
    and proclaim freewill offerings, pub-
    lish them;
    for so you love to do, O people of Isra-
    el!
says the Lord GOD.

4. בֹּאוּ בֵית־אֵל (come to Bethel): בֹּאוּ does double duty: "Come to Bethel . . . [Come] to Gilgal." בֵית־אֵל (Bethel) means "house of God." It became the chief sanctuary of the northern kingdom when Jeroboam I made it an idolatrous alternative to Jerusalem (see also 3:14; 7:13). וּפִשְׁעוּ (and rebel): See the Exegesis of 1:3 for a similar usage of this word. הַגִּלְגָּל (Gilgal; lit. the Gilgal): The name *Gilgal* has the sense of circle or wheel (it occurs with the sense of wheel in Isa. 28:28). The origin of the name is uncertain. The article may indicate that it was a common noun, perhaps designating a circle of stones (Josh. 4:8). Joshua 5:9 records a popular etymology tracing the origin of the name to God's rolling away the reproach of Egypt from the people. Hosea uses Gilgal in a word play in 12:12 [11]: "Do they sacrifice bulls in Gilgal? / Their altars will be like piles of stones [כְּגַלִּים] / on a plowed field" (NIV). וְהָבִיאוּ (do bring in; lit. and bring in) governs this clause as well as its companion clause. לַבֹּקֶר (every morning; or, in the morning): See below. זִבְחֵיכֶם (your sacrifices) connotes blood sacrifices, involving slaughtered animals eaten at feasts (see BDB, pp. 257–58), as opposed to grain or cereal offerings. לִשְׁלֹשֶׁת יָמִים (every three days; or, in three days, i.e., on the third day) more likely has the sense of every three days since the idea of

on *the third day* is generally rendered בַּיּוֹם הַשְּׁלִישִׁי. Since שְׁלֹשֶׁת (three) is in construct with יָמִים (days) it designates a period of three days (cf. שְׁלֹשֶׁת יָמִים in Judg. 19:4). לְ may thus function distributively, yielding a sense of every three days. If this is so, we may view לְ on בֹּקֶר (morning) in the previous clause in the same way (every morning). מַעְשְׂרֹתֵיכֶם (your tithes): Tithes were to be given every three years (Deut. 14:28; 26:12). As in the case of the previous clause, Amos's command involves exaggeration of formal piety and thus reflects irony. If, however, the phrase has the sense of in three days or on the third day, punctuality in sacrifice is commanded.

5. וְקַטֵּר (and burn) is the piel infinitive absolute, which functions as an imperative (GKC §113bb). This verb regularly occurs in sacrificial contexts (e.g., Lev. 1:9, hiphil; Jer. 7:9, piel). מֵחָמֵץ (some leavened bread) is the direct object of the verb; with the partitive use of the preposition (מִן) it is an adverbial accusative indicating how the leavened bread was to be used (GKC §118m). According to Leviticus 7:12–15, the thank-offering was to consist of unleavened cakes of bread that were burned on the altar. Leavened cakes were also to be offered, but not burned: "You must not turn any leaven or honey into smoke as an offering by

---

4. Both Bethel and Gilgal enjoyed an illustrious history in the Lord's dealings with his people. The patriarch Jacob saw the Lord at Bethel, and gave the place its name, "house of God." It was a sanctuary for many years and was one of the places where Samuel judged (1 Sam. 7:16). Jeroboam had placed the golden calf there, and thus began a disastrous course for the nation. Gilgal was Israel's base camp early in the conquest. Samuel confirmed Saul as king at Gilgal. In Amos's time the worship of the Lord had deteriorated so that it was actually rebellion against God.

The parallel words *rebel* (*pišʿû*) and *magnify rebellion* (*harbû lipšoaʿ*) are from the same root. The B line intensifies the thought of the A line by multiplying the concept (see Kugel, *Idea of Biblical Poetry*, pp. 1–57). In their zeal to offer sacrifices more frequently than required by the law they actually increased their rebellion. The tithe was to be brought every three years according to the law (Deut. 14:28); they brought them every three days. They offered their individual sacrifices more frequently than the law required (every morning). This increase in the law's requirements increased their rebellion because the people failed to obey the heart of the law, which was to love their fellow citizens. The more they observed the

ritual of the law, the more they ignored its true purpose, and thus they increased their rebellion.

It is, therefore, ironic that the prophet commands the people to be punctual and even excessive in their tithes and sacrifices. What good will punctuality do where sin is rampant? What help is excessive sacrifice where rebellion characterizes the people? So it is with us, who are called, like ancient Israel, not to sacrifice but to mercy (Matt. 9:13).

5. The prophet commands the people here to do what they are already doing ("for this is what you love"). He orders them to sacrifice in the wrong way by burning leavened bread. Presumably, they did this as an added gesture of appeasement, as though God were interested in the sacrifice itself rather than in the spiritual condition of his people. He also commands them to call publicly for freewill offerings, which is a contradiction in terms, for freewill offerings were individual offerings that would hardly result from a universal summons.

In the first case that this verse describes, the people went further than the law requires by burning leavened bread on the altar, whereas the law required the burning only of unleavened bread in the thank-offering and sacrifice of well-being

fire to the LORD" (Lev. 2:11; cf. 6:17). They were rather to be eaten by the priest. Here, the people are enjoined to burn leavened bread, which is contrary to the law. וְקָרְאוּ . . . הַשְׁמִיעוּ (and proclaim . . . publicly; lit. and proclaim . . . make it heard): The two verbs form a hendiadys emphasizing the public nature of the proclamation. The נְדָבוֹת (freewill offerings) were to be spontaneous gestures on the

part of an individual (see Lev. 22:18–25; Deut. 12:6). Here, however, the people are to proclaim them publicly, that is, everyone will be urged to bring them. כִּי כֵן אֲהַבְתֶּם (for this is what you love to do; lit. for so you love): כִּי (for) introduces the basis for the preceding injunctions. נְאֻם אֲדֹנָי יְהוָה (oracle of the Lord Yahweh): See the Exegesis of 1:8 and 2:11.

(Lev. 7:12–13). In the second case, the universal proclamation, bordering on compulsion, would impose the obligation of offering sacrifice when it should have proceeded from an individual's grateful spirit. As it is, the people had become like the nations around them. They did not love the Lord, and so were not able to love their neighbors. They loved the sacrificial system more than they loved their poor and oppressed neighbors. They were loyal to a religious ritual, which they thought

could appease God, irrespective of their moral and spiritual condition. Jesus embodied the prophetic spirit when he called us to love the Lord our God with all our heart, mind, soul, and strength, and our neighbor as ourselves. He told us also, "If you love me, you will keep my commands." Not the least of these commands is "to present your bodies as a living sacrifice, holy and acceptable to God" (Rom. 12:1).

II. Pronouncements of Judgment (3:1–6:14)
B. Covenant Lawsuit (4:1–13)
3. Historical Review of Past Judgments (4:6–11)

6 "I even gave you
  cleanness of teeth in all your cities,
    and want of food in all your localities,
  yet you did not return to me"—
    oracle of Yahweh.
7 "I withheld from you the winter down-
    pours,
    with yet three months to the harvest,
  and I made it rain over one city,
    and over another city I did not make
      it rain;
  one field would be rained on, but a field
    over which you did not make rain
      dried up.
8 And two or three cities would stagger
    to one city to drink water,
    but they could not get enough;
  yet you did not return to me"—
    oracle of Yahweh.
9 "I struck you with blight and mildew;
    the multitude of your gardens and
      vineyards
    and fig trees and olive trees the locust
      would devour;
  yet you did not return to me,"
    oracle of Yahweh.
10 "I sent plague among you after the man-
    ner of Egypt;
  I killed your young men with the
    sword,
    along with your captured horses,
    and I made the stench of your camps
      go up into your nostrils;
  yet you did not return to me"—
    oracle of Yahweh.
11 "I overthrew some of you
    as when God overthrew Sodom and
      Gomorrah,
    and you were like a stick snatched
      out of the burning;
  yet you did not return to me"—
    oracle of Yahweh.

6 I gave you cleanness of teeth in all your
    cities,
    and lack of bread in all your places;
  yet you did not return to me,
    says the Lord.
7 And I also withheld the rain from you
    when there were still three months to
      the harvest;
  I would send rain on one city,
    and send no rain on another city;
  one field would be rained upon,
    and the field on which it did not rain
      withered;
8 so two or three towns wandered to one
    town
    to drink water, and were not satisfied;
  yet you did not return to me,
    says the Lord.
9 I struck you with blight and mildew;
    I laid waste your gardens and your
      vineyards;
    the locust devoured your fig trees and
      your olive trees;
  yet you did not return to me,
    says the Lord.
10 I sent among you a pestilence after the
    manner of Egypt;
    I killed your young men with the
      sword;
  I carried away your horses;
    and I made the stench of your camp
      go up into your nostrils;
  yet you did not return to me,
    says the Lord.
11 I overthrew some of you,
    as when God overthrew Sodom and
      Gomorrah,
    and you were like a brand snatched
      from the fire;
  yet you did not return to me,
    says the Lord.

6. וְגַם־אֲנִי (I): גַּם (untranslated) emphasizes the pronoun; perhaps "yea" is an appropriate translational equivalent. נִקְיוֹן שִׁנַּיִם (cleanness of teeth): נִקְיוֹן (cleanness) is a noun related to the verb נָקָה, which connotes a verbal idea akin to English equivalents such as be free, be empty, be clean. Cleanness of teeth connotes the absence of food, that is, famine. בְּכָל־עָרֵיכֶם (in all your cities) indicates the widespread distribution of famine, appropriate to the corporate nature of their sin. וְחֹסֶר לֶחֶם (and want of food) informs the context with the same basic sense as its companion clause (נִקְיוֹן שִׁנַּיִם). Both clauses describe lack of food. The sense of the first phrase is clarified by its companion. The Lord has sent hunger and want upon them, as he had warned he would in cases of covenantal disobedience (Deut. 28:47–48). מְקוֹמֹתֵיכֶם בְּכֹל (in all your localities): The word עָרֵיכֶם (your cities) in the parallel clause energizes the word מָקוֹם (lit. place) with the sense of an inhabited place, thus, a locality. וְלֹא־שַׁבְתֶּם עָדַי (yet you did

not return to me): This phrase stems from Israel's covenant, as in Deuteronomy 4:30, 30:2 (cf. Hos. 14:2–3 [1–2]; see also Holladay, *Root Šûbh in the Old Testament*, pp. 116–21). It is a call to return to the Lord after covenantal punishment for their sins. נְאֻם־יְהוָה (oracle of Yahweh): See the Exegesis of 2:11.

7. וְגַם אָנֹכִי (I): The first-person common singular pronoun is deictic, as in 2:9. Here the expression has אָנֹכִי not אֲנִי as in 4:6. Perhaps this is for further emphasis or elegant variety. הַגֶּשֶׁם (the winter downpours) denotes the rains of winter, from late October through late February, which were essential for the crops to develop sound initial growth. Then would come the "latter rains" of March and April, followed by harvest in May. וְהִמְטַרְתִּי (and I made it rain): The words נְאֻם־יְהוָה (oracle of Yahweh), which end this section (vv. 7–8), as well as the other logical sections in verses 1–11, indicate that the Lord is the subject of this verb. The Septuagint construes this verb and its companion in

---

6. The sinfulness and idolatry of his people have extended so far that they have made an idol of the Lord's sacrificial system. Their loyalty is to it, rather than to him. In order to bring the people back to himself, the Lord sent them famine. The prophet describes this graphically as "cleanness of teeth." Against the background of their covenant with the Lord, the people should have recognized a divine message in their want of food, for just this thing was foretold should they break covenant and turn away from him. The very structure of the oracle underscores the Lord's action on their behalf, as well as the irony of their response. They were so blinded by their sin—including their mistaken substitution of the ritual service of the Lord for the Lord himself—that they failed to understand the signs of the times. Christians who may be prone to substitute devotion to ritual, or to worship, or even to sacrificial works, for devotion to the Lord, may well heed this warning.

The words *yet you did not return to me* are in contrast to the first colon. The structure of the oracle illustrates this fact:

	a	**b**
A	I even gave	you
B	cleanness of teeth and want of food	in all your cities in all your localities
	b′	**a′**
A′	yet you did not return to	me

The contrast between the first and last cola of the oracle is clear, and the chiasmus heightens its effect. The two cola flank the central bicolon, which tells both what the Lord sent and what the response to it should have been (i.e., return to him, which is what did *not* happen). Again, the phrase *oracle of the LORD* rounds off a brief but pointed oracle.

7. The prophet continues the litany of catastrophes that the nation had suffered. Not only had they experienced widespread famine (v. 6), but now we learn that they had suffered a drought just before the harvest. The particle *gam* (even) has the sense of *on top of famine, I sent drought.*

This section depicts the prophet's philosophy of history. To him, God was not merely transcendent above, but active in, history. Historical event could reflect the divine will because the Lord had chosen to bring punishment on his people in the realm of nature should they violate his covenant with them (Deut. 28:22–24). The Lord had warned the people that covenant disobedience would bring dire consequences. Now he has fulfilled his promise. As Creator of heaven and earth, he has all authority in heaven and earth to send or withhold rain, to make the earth fertile or hard as iron from drought. The curse of drought, here portrayed, was threatened in the original covenantal documents (e.g., Lev. 26:19; Deut. 28:23–24). Such curses were well known in the ancient Near East, for example, in the second-millennium Hittite treaties. The elements were even called to witness

the line (אַמְטִיר) as future tense, but the conclusion of verse 8 (yet you did not return to me) rules this out. The parallelism of perfect-imperfect forms of the same verb is a classic example of the *qatal-yaqtul* pattern (Held, "*Yqtl-qtl* [*qtl-yqtl*] Sequence of Identical Verbs") and warrants taking both verbs as perfects. (Alternately, however, the sequence of a perfect and imperfect might be taken as denoting action that continued for a longer or shorter period; see GKC §107b.) חֶלְקָה (field; lit. portion of ground) is a divided portion of ground, such as might be purchased by or allotted to an individual or a household (e.g., Gen. 33:19; Deut. 33:21). Yahweh would make rain over one portion, but not over another. לֹא אַמְטִיר (you did not make rain): The Septuagint understands this verb as a first-person singular (βρέξω), apparently in an effort to smooth out the irregularity caused by the sudden shift to the second person. But shifts of person and number are common in ancient Near Eastern documents (see the Introduction).

8. וְנָעוּ (and . . . would stagger) also occurs in 8:12. This verb denotes an action akin to waving or trembling (Judg. 9:9; 1 Sam. 1:13). In contexts dealing with intoxication the verb connotes staggering. In Lamentations 4:14 it depicts confused wandering. Here it connotes the desperately thirsty condition of the people as they stagger in search of water. שְׁתַּיִם שָׁלֹשׁ . . . לִשְׁתּוֹת (two or three . . . to drink): These words are alliterative in what is an otherwise prosaic verse. Perhaps this alliteration reinforces the sense of desperation for water. וְלֹא יִשְׂבָּעוּ (but they could not get enough; lit. not be satisfied): The sibilant (שׂ) in this verb may be an appropriate extension and attenuation of the alliteration in this verse, underscoring the fact that their desperate need for water could not be satisfied. This may reflect the covenantal curse in Leviticus 26:26, which states that, as a result of covenant disobedience, the people will eat but not be satisfied, exactly as here (cf. Hos. 4:10; Mic. 6:14). וְלֹא־שַׁבְתֶּם עָדַי (yet you did not return to me): See the Exegesis of verse 6. נְאֻם־יְהוָה (oracle of Yahweh): See the Exegesis of 2:11. This phrase rounds off the oracle, giving it a sense of authority.

9. בַּשִּׁדָּפוֹן וּבַיֵּרָקוֹן (with blight and mildew): This word pair occurs in the covenantal curse in Deuteronomy 28:22, in Solomon's prayer (1 Kings 8:37), and in Haggai 2:17 (which echoes the

---

the treaties in case of covenant disobedience, because those same elements would be used by the gods to punish covenant disobedience. For example, in a treaty between Mursilis of Hatti and Duppi-Tessub of Amurru (ca. 1325 B.C.), we read, in the lengthy concluding invocation of the gods, at the end of the list of gods, "the mountains, the rivers, the springs, the great Sea, heaven and earth, the winds and the clouds—let these be witnesses to this treaty and to the oath" ("Treaty Between Mursilis and Duppi-Tesub of Amurru," *ANET*, p. 205). So, in Deuteronomy 4:26 Yahweh calls heaven and earth to witness against his people should they turn away from him; and in Deuteronomy 28:23 he warns, "The sky over your head shall be bronze, and the earth under you iron," as a result of the punitive drought he will send. The verb placement in this verse creates a chiasmus:

a	**b**
and I made it rain	over one city
b´	**a´**
and over another city	I did not make it rain

This chiastic parallelism contributes an elegant, almost curselike dimension to a verse that is otherwise prosaic.

8. Because of the sporadic nature of the rainfall, the people of two or three cities will go to another city in hope of getting water to drink. They will be so weak that they will stagger in their journey, but they will not get enough water to satisfy their thirst. As in the covenantal curse involving bread or food, so also there will not be enough water to go around. Even if one gets a little, it will not be enough. Alliteration emphasizes the point as the oracle comes to a close. The concluding refrain, repeated from verse 6, indicates the reason for the drought. It is because the Lord wanted to get the attention of the people by punishing them. This punishment was in accord with their covenant with him, for the Lord wanted them to return to him and be healed. Their hard hearts, however, would not allow them to understand what the Lord was doing (as in Isa. 6:9–10). The same was true of a later generation (Acts 28:25–27), through whose hardness of heart we Gentiles have been blessed with the revelation of God's salvation (Acts 28:28). May we strive in humility not to make the mistake of ancient Israel (Heb. 3:12–19).

9. Again, the Lord makes it clear through his covenant-lawsuit messenger that he has done to his rebellious people the very things he warned them about in the original covenant documents. The blight of plants blasted by the hot wind, as well as the mildew that strikes them and prevents fruition, were anticipated by the curse section of

present oracle). הָרְבּוֹת (the multitude) is a hiphil infinitive construct used as a substantive (GKC §114c) in construct with the following four nouns (gardens, vineyards, fig trees, and olive trees) and as the direct object of the verb יֹאכַל (would devour). It is possible, but less likely, that this is a temporal clause (when your gardens and your vineyards and your fig trees and your olive trees increased, KJV). Stuart construes this as a protasis-apodosis structure: "When your gardens and vineyards increased, / Locusts would devour your fig trees and olive trees" (Stuart, Hosea–Jonah, p. 335). In any case, there is no need to emend to הֶחֱרַבְתִּי (I laid waste, RSV), with Wellhausen (Skizzen und Vorarbeiten, p. 79), Driver (Joel and Amos, p. 173), and Wolff (Joel and Amos, p. 210). Vineyards (כַּרְמֵיכֶם) and olive trees (זֵיתֵיכֶם) appear in the covenantal curse section of Deuteronomy 28:30, 39–40. וּתְאֵנֵיכֶם (and your fig trees) sometimes forms a word pair with גֶּפֶן (vine), indicating prosperity (1 Kings 5:5 [4:25]; Mic. 4:4). הַגָּזָם (the locust; lit. the shearer or cutter): Joel 1:4 and 2:25 vividly describe the devastation the locust could cause (see BDB, p. 160). Ironically, the punishment described here is similar to that which the Lord inflicted on Egypt before the exodus, a pun-

ishment that Psalm 105:33–34 describes in somewhat similar terms (he struck, vines, fig trees, locusts [אַרְבֶּה], young locusts [יֶלֶק]). The terminology here is Deuteronomic (Deut. 28:38–42). עָדַי וְלֹא־שַׁבְתֶּם (yet you did not return to me): See the Exegesis of verse 6. נְאֻם־יְהוָה (oracle of Yahweh): See the Exegesis of 2:11. As in the previous verses, the last phrase underscores the authority of the oracle by identifying its source, the Lord himself.

10. שִׁלַּחְתִּי בָכֶם דֶּבֶר (I sent plague among you): This phrase also has a covenantal background (see Lev. 26:25: וְשִׁלַּחְתִּי דֶבֶר בְּתוֹכְכֶם, I will send pestilence among you). These words echo the curse section of Deuteronomy: שָׁלַח occurs in 28:20, 48 and דֶּבֶר in 28:21. In Deuteronomy 28:27, 60 the Lord threatens his people with all the diseases of Egypt. The Septuagint has θάνατος (death) for דֶּבֶר (plague), but this does not necessarily indicate a different Hebrew Vorlage because the Septuagint frequently translates דֶּבֶר by θάνατος. In all probability it is an expansive translation for sake of clarity or explanation. בְּדֶרֶךְ מִצְרַיִם (after the manner of Egypt): This phrase occurs also in Isaiah 10:24, 26 (cf. Ezek. 20:30) and means "in the way that Egypt" or "after the manner of Egypt." The Lord has sent plague among his people in the way

Deuteronomy. The locust plague that devoured their gardens, vineyards, fig trees, and olive trees was also a divine act of judgment. Perhaps the greatest irony of all was that the Lord was bringing upon his own rebellious people the same afflictions he had brought on Egypt, when Pharaoh resisted God.

The reference to the "multitude [harbôt] of your gardens and vineyards" reflects the affluence of the time in which Amos lived. There was abundance of food, but God destroyed it with decay. This passage illustrates the temporality of riches and possessions, of which Jesus spoke as well: "Do not store up for yourselves treasures on earth, where moth and rust consume" (Matt. 6:19).

This section demonstrates that God's judgments often came from a loving hand. It was painful for the people to watch the produce of the field wither and their food supply dwindle. It was frightening for them to observe the desolate aftermath of a locust plague. All this, however, was meant to restore their broken relationship with God and to show them that he was the author of life. This desire of the Lord to restore his erring people to himself echoes plaintively in the refrain: "Yet you did not return to me" (vv. 6, 8, 9, 10, 11).

Chastisement is often God's loving display of concern for his children (Heb. 12:6).

The references to the curses of Deuteronomy should have quickened the minds of the people to recollect their rich heritage, but their hearts were hard. As a result of their hardness of heart they experienced the ultimate irony, for God considered them virtually the same as enemies who had never turned to him in the first place. The warning is grave; we find it in the New Testament as well: "For if, after they have escaped the defilements of the world through the knowledge of our Lord and Savior Jesus Christ, they are again entangled in them and overpowered, the last state has become worse for them than the first" (2 Pet. 2:20).

10. It is ironic that the Lord does to his people the same thing he had done to the Egyptians. Surely this was to warn the people that they had become like the Egyptians in their pagan practices and lack of social conscience. The poignant words *I killed your young men with the sword* have, along with so much in this section, a covenantal background. In Exodus 22:22–23 [23–24], for example, the Lord threatens the very thing he has done here. He says that, if the people take advantage of widows and orphans, "I will certainly hear

that (just as) he sent plague among the Egyptians at the time of the exodus. הָרַגְתִּי בַחֶרֶב בַּחוּרֵיכֶם (I killed your young men with the sword): See the Exposition. עִם שְׁבִי סוּסֵיכֶם (along with your captured horses): The NRSV has an interpretive translation: "I carried away your horses." שְׁבִי may refer either to the state of captivity or to the captives themselves. The preferable sense of the word here is captive, because it is in construct with סוּסֵיכֶם (your horses), yielding, literally, the captivity of your horses, that is, those horses that had been taken captive (see BDB, p. 985). בְּאֹשׁ מַחֲנֵיכֶם וּבְאַפְּכֶם וָאַעֲלֶה (and I made the stench of your camps go up into your nostrils): ו on וּבְאַפְּכֶם may be emphatic, "Right up into your nostrils" (lit. and into your nose). In some instances similar to this ו has the function of "and that" (GKC §114p). The sense here would thus be that God made the stench of the camps go up, and that into their nostrils. בְּאֹשׁ (stench), besides here, occurs only twice in the Old Testament (Isa. 34:3; Joel 2:20). In Isaiah 34:3 it connotes the stench of the dead among the nations as the Lord judges them. In Joel 2:20 it is the stench of the northern army after the Lord destroys it. In both cases, it occurs with the qal of עָלָה (go up), but here with the hiphil. וְלֹא־שַׁבְתֶּם עָדַי (yet you did not return to me): See the Exegesis of verse 6. נְאֻם־יְהוָה (oracle of Yahweh): See the Exegesis of 2:11.

11. הָפַכְתִּי (I overthrew) is used of the Lord at the overthrow of Sodom and Gomorrah: "And he

overthrew those cities" (Gen. 19:25; compare the allusion to the same event, with the same verb, in Jer. 20:16). בָּכֶם (some of you): בְּ (some) is understood here as partitive (GKC §119m). וְאֶת־עֲמֹרָה כְּמַהְפֵּכַת אֱלֹהִים אֶת־סְדֹם (as when God overthrew Sodom and Gomorrah; lit. like God's overthrowing Sodom and Gomorrah): כְּ frequently determines a temporal sense for clauses (Davidson, *Hebrew Syntax*, §145a). The identical phrase occurs in Isaiah 13:19, as it does in Jeremiah 50:40. This idea is rooted in the covenantal warning in Deuteronomy 29:22 [23]: אֲשֶׁר הָפַךְ יְהוָה . . . כְּמַהְפֵּכַת סְדֹם וַעֲמֹרָה (like the destruction of Sodom and Gomorrah, . . . which the LORD destroyed [in his fierce anger]). There, as here, the verb הָפַךְ (overthrew) and its cognate verbal noun (overthrow or overthrowing—used only in these phrases in the Old Testament) appear together. The same phrase occurs in Jeremiah 49:18 against Edom. כְּאוּד (like a stick): The root אוד contains the idea of curved or bent; thus it connotes a stick, rather than a larger log. The fuller phrase, כְּאוּד מֻצָּל מִשְׂרֵפָה (like a stick snatched out of the burning), gives a vivid idea of the manner of Israel's rescue (for this idea, see Isa. 1:9). A slightly different form of the phrase appears in Zechariah 3:2: אוּד מֻצָּל מֵאֵשׁ (a brand plucked from the fire). וְלֹא־שַׁבְתֶּם עָדַי (yet you did not return to me): See the Exegesis of verse 6. נְאֻם־יְהוָה (oracle of Yahweh): See the Exegesis of 2:11.

---

their cry. My anger will be aroused, and I will kill you with the sword; your wives will become widows and your children fatherless" (NIV). There is a similar thought in Jeremiah 11:22 ("the young men shall die by the sword"). Plague and the sword often appear in conjunction with famine as covenant-lawsuit curses (Jer. 14:12; 21:7, 9; Ezek. 5:12, 17; 6:11). Here, as in 2:3, it is not the Lord himself, but his appointed judgment instruments (the Assyrians) who will do the actual killing.

11. This verse ends the section 4:6–11. In this subsection, the Lord reminds his people of all the judgments he has sent. Now he recalls the fact that he overthrew some of them like Sodom and Gomorrah. The event to which this refers is not certain. It seems to reflect successful military attacks against cities or territories of the northern kingdom. It may reflect all the devastating attacks suffered by Israel and would certainly recall the invasions by Syria (2 Kings 13:4–7). The language is Deuteronomic (see Deut. 29:21–23 [22–23]).

Like Sodom and Gomorrah, the whole land would become a burning waste of salt and sulfur. Such destruction would come from the Lord in the form of famine (Deut. 28:47–48), drought (Deut. 28:23–24), blight and mildew (Deut. 28:22), locusts (Deut. 28:38), and disease (Deut. 28:21–22, 27, 60). It would also come by Israel's conquerors (Amos 4:10; Deut. 28:25–26), for it was a regular practice of the Assyrian kings to sow the ground of a conquered area with salt, so that nothing would grow there again. This was especially the case with rebellious vassals. The Assyrians seem to have intended the complete sterilization and eradication of the enemy city so that even its surrounding territory would no longer support life (see Grayson, *Assyrian Royal Inscriptions*, vol. 1, p. 60, n. 119; Ebeling, Meissner, and Weidner, *Die Inschriften der altassyrischen Könige*, king 21 [Shalmaneser I], no. 1, col. 2, lines 6–11; Thompson, *Prisms of Esarhaddon and Ashurbanipal*, p. 34, col. 5, lines 5–8 [Assurbanipal]). Thus, the point of comparison with Sodom and Gomorrah is not the issue of earthquake or divine intervention; rather, it has to do with the *result* of the Lord's judgments: the land would be as devastated as Sodom and Gomorrah were, once the various calamities had done their work.

The northern kingdom was snatched like a stick out of the burning. That is, it was burnt, but not destroyed. This too is evidence of divine love. The Lord did not allow the termination of the nation in its history of conflicts, but kept it from absolute destruction. This is a picture of God's grace, but the people rejected his gracious providence. Once again we hear, "Yet you did not return to me."

To the prophet, history was a book of theology. He could read divine grace on every page. Unfortunately for Israel, the book Amos read did not have a happy ending. There is a finality to the words *you did not return to me*. We shall hear more about the threat veiled in these words in the next verse.

II. Pronouncements of Judgment (3:1–6:14)
B. Covenant Lawsuit (4:1–13)
4. Judgment Announced (4:12)

12 "Therefore thus will I do to you, O Israel—
    because this is what I will do to you,
    prepare to meet your God, O Israel!"

12 Therefore thus I will do to you, O Israel;
    because I will do this to you,
    prepare to meet your God, O Israel!

12. לָכֵן כֹּה אֶעֱשֶׂה־לָּךְ (therefore thus will I do to you): לָכֵן (therefore) introduces the logical consequence of the foregoing statement. אֶעֱשֶׂה (will I do) is future because it indicates the Lord's resolve to act on the basis of Israel's patent disobedience. עֵקֶב כִּי־זֹאת אֶעֱשֶׂה־לָּךְ (because this is what I will do to you): זֹאת (this) has no apparent referent (see the Exposition). הִכּוֹן לִקְרַאת־אֱלֹהֶיךָ (prepare to meet your God): הִכּוֹן (prepare) is the hiphil of כּוּן (to be firm, sure). It occurs in several contexts with the sense of preparing one's heart for God, as the context here requires (1 Sam. 7:3; Job 11:13). The word occurs as a niphal participle in Exodus 19:15 to describe the preparation of the people to meet God (in vv. 17, 19).

---

12. The Lord affirms that he will do something, because of what has gone before. And what has gone before? The continued sin of his people and the calamities based on the covenant sanctions of Deuteronomy. The Lord exercised restraint in these calamities in order to save his people from the total destruction that a full unleashing of covenantal judgment would bring. Because of this, they are "like a stick snatched out of the burning" of total judgment (v. 11). But all this has been to no avail. The many warnings—in the form of famine, drought, blight and mildew, locusts, plague, and disaster in war—have not achieved their purpose of recalling the people to the Lord. Therefore, because he has done these things repeatedly and warned them repeatedly, he will now carry out the covenant curses.

Amos does not state what the divine judgment will be. The words he speaks leave us wondering: "Thus will I do to you, O Israel—because this is what I will do to you." The failure to state the punishment fills the hearer with dread uncertainty. Amos did the same thing in 1:3, 6, 9, 11, 13; 2:1, 4, 6, where the suffix on *ăšîbennû* (I will not relent) has no stated referent. This word states, literally, "I will not revoke it" (see the Exegesis of 1:3). It must refer to the punishment, but we are not told so. Here, the stark omission in Amos's words intensifies his gloomy forecast.

II. Pronouncements of Judgment (3:1–6:14)
B. Covenant Lawsuit (4:1–13)
5. Identification of the Lord and Judge (4:13)

[13] For behold:
    The one who forms mountains,
    the one who creates wind,
    and the one who reveals to human-
      kind its musings;
  the one who makes dawn and darkness,
    and the one who treads on the heights
      of the earth—
  Yahweh God of hosts is his name!

[13] For lo, the one who forms the moun-
    tains, creates the wind,
    reveals his thoughts to mortals,
  makes the morning darkness,
    and treads on the heights of the
      earth—
  the Lord, the God of hosts, is his name!

13. כִּי הִנֵּה (for behold) commands immediate attention. כִּי (for) gives the reason why Israel must prepare to meet God: because he is the mighty God whose description follows. יוֹצֵר הָרִים (the one who forms mountains; lit. former of mountains) is the first of a series of five titles. יוֹצֵר (forms) denotes the potter's work, but often describes the Lord's activity as well. For example, the Lord formed animals and man (Gen. 2:7–8, 19), the earth (Isa. 45:18), and the people of Israel (Isa. 43:1, 21; 44:2, 21, 24). וּבֹרֵא רוּחַ (the one who creates wind; lit. creator of wind). The verb בָּרָא (create) is used only of God's creative activity in the Old Testament (e.g., Gen. 1:1; Isa. 40:28; 43:1, 15; 45:12, 18). וּמַגִּיד (and the one who reveals; lit. one who brings to the fore, declares): The hiphil participle continues the series of divine titles. לְאָדָם (to humankind) connotes humanity in general here, since God has the power to reveal to all of us our innermost thoughts. מַה־שֵּׂחוֹ (its musings; lit. what is his musing or meditation): שֵׂחוֹ (its musings) is a *hapax legomenon*. The singular suffix probably refers to humanity, not to the Lord Yahweh. The word שֵׂחַ (thought) is a byform of שִׂיחַ (complaint, musing), which is used elsewhere only of humankind. In 1 Kings 18:27 it refers to Baal, indicating that he is *not* God. עֹשֵׂה שַׁחַר עֵיפָה (the one who makes dawn and darkness): The Septuagint places καὶ (and) between the nouns, and some Hebrew manuscripts add *waw*. This does not necessarily reflect the original wording, however, for this may be asyndeton. This literary device is common in Hebrew poetry, and is thus appropriately interpreted by the Septuagint. The phrase indicates that Yahweh is the maker, not only of dawn and darkness, but of everything in between. אֶרֶץ וְדֹרֵךְ עַל־בָּמֳתֵי (and the one who treads on the heights of the earth; lit. and the treader on, etc.): This phrase occurs in Micah 1:3, where it refers to the Lord (Job 9:8 uses יָם [sea] instead of אֶרֶץ [earth]). Similar phrases occur with reference to Israel in Deuteronomy 32:13 ("He set him atop the heights of the land") and Isaiah 58:14 ("I will make you ride upon the heights of the earth"). For further discussion of high place, see the Exegesis of 7:9. יְהוָה אֱלֹהֵי־צְבָאוֹת (Yahweh God of hosts): See the Exegesis of 3:13.

---

13. This verse expands upon the theme of the preceding. There, Israel was commanded to prepare to meet its God. Here, the nature of that God is revealed in a series of participial phrases that function as epithets or titles. However, the verse is not simply a doxology as some have called it. Because of the series of participles, it is a typical example of an ancient Near Eastern divine titulary, of which the inscriptions give many instances (see also 4:1 and 9:5).

After a declaration that the Lord would continue his covenantal discipline of his people, comes a reminder of who the Lord is. A contemporary would have instantly recognized the literary form of this verse. It is a list of divine titles frequently occurring in inscriptional literature. The Lord is described as majestic in power. He is the one who, like a potter, formed the mountains and created the wind. He reveals the innermost thoughts and makes the day and night. He treads upon the heights of the earth. Israel might well take warning from such a God. God still reveals our thoughts. By the Holy Spirit, operative through his word, he reveals our innermost thoughts to us (Heb. 4:12). The one who makes day and night is also the true light. Overcoming darkness (John 1:5), he has come into the world and illumines all people (John 1:9). And he exalts us with Jesus Christ even above the heights of the earth, namely, in the heavens (Eph. 2:6).

Redaction and form critics frequently attribute this hymn and those found in 5:8–9 and 9:5–6 to a later hand. For an opposing view, see McComiskey, "Hymnic Elements of the Prophecy of Amos." There is no reason why this "hymn" cannot be an exalted statement by Amos of the awesome power of God to judge.

II. Pronouncements of Judgment (3:1–6:14)
C. Covenant Lawsuit—Lament Form (5:1–17)
1. Introduction (5:1)

5 Hear this word
  that I am taking up against you,
  a lament, O house of Israel.

5 Hear this word that I take up over you in
lamentation, O house of Israel:

5:1. שִׁמְעוּ אֶת־הַדָּבָר הַזֶּה (hear this word): See the Exegesis of 3:1. אֲשֶׁר אָנֹכִי נֹשֵׂא (that I am taking up): The antecedent of אֲשֶׁר (that) is הַדָּבָר (word). אָנֹכִי (I) may indicate Yahweh or his spokesman, the prophet, who after all is speaking the Lord's word. נֹשֵׂא (taking up) is often used with regard to laments (Jer. 7:29; Ezek. 19:1; 26:17). עֲלֵיכֶם (against you): עַל can connote either over or, in contexts of prophetic condemnation, against. The context calls for the latter meaning here. קִינָה (a lament) is in apposition to דָּבָר (word) and further defines that word. בֵּית יִשְׂרָאֵל (O house of Israel) is synonymous with בֵּית יַעֲקֹב (house of Jacob) in 3:13 and is sadly ironic, for Jacob was renamed Israel by virtue of his wrestling with God and prevailing (Gen. 32:23–29 [22–28]). Now, however, the Lord must deal with a people who have forgotten how to lay hold on their Lord and seek his blessings.

5:1. This verse begins the next section, which is itself the first of two large sections (5:1–17; 5:18–6:14) that deal with the fall of the northern kingdom. The prophet commands attention by announcing a lament for the people. This lament is not *over* the Lord's people, but *against* them, in the manner of prophetic condemnations of the Lord's enemies. The fact that the message is a lament has special impact, because one does not lament what has not yet happened. Indeed, the disaster described in the following verse has not yet come. The prophetic lament, however, indicates that it is as good as accomplished, for what the Lord's prophet foretells will occur, and the approaching disaster that he laments will surely come to pass.

The lament consists of four clearly identifiable parts: (1) a description of the tragedy (vv. 2–3); (2) a call to react (vv. 4–6 and 14–15); (3) a direct address to the fallen (vv. 7–13); and (4) a summons to mourning (vv. 16–17). Stuart's excellent discussion compares its structure with David's lament over Saul and Jonathan (*Hosea–Jonah*, p. 344): "We have here more than a mere elegy," says Stuart. "It is a judgment elegy, artfully crafted—a prophetic dirge for Israel in which Yahweh speaks to and against Israel as well." The same may be said of Ezekiel's elegies over Tyre (Ezek. 27) and Egypt (Ezek. 32).

II. Pronouncements of Judgment (3:1–6:14)
C. Covenant Lawsuit—Lament Form (5:1–17)
2. Description of Tragedy (5:2–3)

2 "Fallen—she will not rise again—
  is the virgin, Israel:
abandoned on her land;
  there is no one to raise her."
3 For thus says the Lord, Yahweh:
  "The city that goes forth a thousand,
  will have a hundred left.
That which goes forth a hundred,
  will have ten left
  for the house of Israel."

2 Fallen, no more to rise,
  is maiden Israel;
forsaken on her land,
  with no one to raise her up.
3 For thus says the Lord GOD:
The city that marched out a thousand
  shall have a hundred left,
and that which marched out a hundred
  shall have ten left.

2. נָפְלָה (fallen) is a perfect tense indicating completed action: Israel is seen prophetically as already having fallen (prophetic perfect)—her fall accomplished by all the covenantal curses, not least of which is the sword of the foe. לֹא־תוֹסִיף קוּם (she will not rise again): תּוֹסִיף (again) is from יָסַף, which has the basic sense of *add*. The statement is, literally, "nor will she add to rise." The English requires the sense *again*. בְּתוּלַת יִשְׂרָאֵל (the virgin, Israel): The construct relationship does not indicate possession, that is, "a virgin *of* Israel" (Deut. 22:19), but apposition, since Israel is the subject of the lament. The same phrase occurs in Jeremiah 18:13; 31:4, 21 (similar phrases are "virgin daughter Zion" [2 Kings 19:21; Isa. 37:22; Lam. 2:13], "virgin daughter Babylon" [Isa. 47:1], and "virgin daughter Egypt" [Jer. 46:11]). בְּתוּלַת (virgin): In Ugaritic mythology, the word *btlt* (virgin) may reflect the sense of *consort*. The term is applied to Anat, the consort of El, chief god of the Ugaritic pantheon. נִטְּשָׁה (abandoned): That is, left to perish where she has fallen; the verb also occurs in Ezekiel 29:5 and 32:4. מְקִימָהּ (to raise her) is the hiphil

of קוּם (stand). In covenant contexts the word has the sense of *establish*: The Lord establishes covenant (Gen. 6:18; 9:11; 17:7; Exod. 6:4; Deut. 8:18), oath (Gen. 26:3; Jer. 11:5), and the people of his covenant (Deut. 28:9). An identical phrase is applied to the earth in Isaiah 24:20: "It falls, and will not rise again."

3. כִּי (for) introduces the reason for the fall predicted in the preceding verse: military disaster will bring about the ultimate demise of the kingdom. כֹּה אָמַר (thus says): See the Exegesis of 1:3. אֲדֹנָי יְהוִה (the Lord Yahweh): See the Exegesis of 1:8. אֶלֶף (a company, usually translated "a thousand"), מֵאָה (a platoon, usually translated "a hundred"), and עֲשָׂרָה (a squad, usually translated "ten"): These words probably do not represent precise numerical equivalents, but military units of graduated size, whose numbers were likely smaller than their names would appear to indicate (see Mendenhall, "Census Lists of Numbers 1 and 26"; and de Vaux, *Ancient Israel*, vol. 1, p. 216; for Israel's military units, see 1 Sam. 10:19; 17:18; 18:13; 22:7; 2 Sam. 18:1). תַּשְׁאִיר (will have . . . left):

---

2. This verse begins the lament promised in verse 1. It is an elegiac couplet, with each bicolon taking the form of a longer (three-beat) colon, followed by a shorter (two-beat) colon. For the form, see 2 Samuel 1:17–27; 3:33–34; Ezekiel 19:1–14; 26:17–18; 32:2–16; as well as most of the Book of Lamentations. The pattern of long and short cola finds a counterpart in the Latin elegiac couplet, a six-foot line followed by a five-foot line. In this way, ancient poetry apparently reflected the long-short pattern in the wailing of mourners over the fallen. This verse, along with the next, comprises the first section of the lament, the description of the tragedy.

The prophet addresses Israel as a virgin (*bĕtûlâ*), which may reflect Israel's status as bride of Yahweh. The prophetic perfect views Israel as already fallen. Thus, his lament is appropriate. She has fallen because of the Lord's curses, not least of which was defeat by the pagan foe. She has been abandoned to die in her own land. The structure of the verse indicates the hopelessness of her case. She has fallen, and there is none to raise her up. Only the Lord could raise her up, but he is the one who has punished her. What a contrast between this portrait and the saving grace of Jesus! He passed through the crowd of mourners who believed Jairus's daughter dead, took her by the hand, and said, "Child, get up!" Surely all have sinned, and all are worthy of abandonment and

death. But the God who wounds us also heals us and extends his hand to raise us into life.

The reference to Israel fallen in her own land reflects an awful irony. Israel fell in the midst of the inheritance that God had promised her. Her fall does not imply God's unwillingness to keep his promise, but it witnesses to the failure of his people to keep their covenantal obligations. Israel's fall was permanent. It would never rise again. However, the Lord had affirmed his intention to restore his people (Lev. 26:44–45), which restoration finds its ultimate realization in the church.

3. Military disaster, as the previous verse hints, will be the proximate cause of Israel's collapse (see also 3:11–12). The ultimate cause is their covenant breaking, including their social sins (2:6–7; 3:15), rejection of God's prophets (2:12), abuse of the Nazirites (2:12), and idolatry (3:14; 5:26). Their catastrophe, which will be worse than decimation, was foretold in the original covenant documents (see Deut. 32:15–18, 28–30). The fulfilment of this passage occurred at the captivity of the northern kingdom. We should not press the numerals here. Their purpose is to create the impression of severe populational diminution.

The lament meter ends at this verse as we hear the reason for the lament over Israel's fall. It is the Lord's word. He has determined the impending demise of the nation. These words recall the

411

The verbal action of שָׁאַר describes the process of remaining. In all its stems it is associated with something that survives (Exod. 10:19; 1 Sam. 9:24; Ruth 1:3). The disaster that will befall the people

is reminiscent of the prophetic judgment in Deuteronomy 32:30 (cf. Isa. 30:17). בֵּית יִשְׂרָאֵל (house of Israel): See the Exegesis of verse 1.

---

haunting words of 3:6a: "Would there be disaster in a city / and the LORD has not caused it?"

The warning is to us as well. We are warned that love of money is idolatry (Col. 3:5), and we live in a nation whose acculturated Christianity is too comfortable with pride, envy, deceit, and other evils. God calls his people to holiness, and

his holy wind blows through his church, exposing and toppling idolatrous ministries in a judgment that must begin with the "house of Israel," the household of God. Those who are "wise and understand this" (Deut. 32:29, NIV) will repent of their sins and turn again to serve the living God.

II. Pronouncements of Judgment (3:1–6:14)
C. Covenant Lawsuit—Lament Form (5:1–17)
3. Call to Lament (5:4–6)

⁴ For thus says Yahweh to the house of Is-
rael:
"Seek me so that you may live!
⁵   But do not seek at Bethel,
and you shall not go to Gilgal,
    and you shall not cross the border to
    Beer-sheba;
for Gilgal will surely go into exile,
    and Bethel will become trouble."
⁶ Seek Yahweh so that you may live,
    lest he break out like fire in the house
    of Joseph,
    and it consume, and there be none to
    quench it for Bethel.

⁴ For thus says the Lᴏʀᴅ to the house of Is-
rael:
Seek me and live;
⁵ but do not seek Bethel,
and do not enter into Gilgal
    or cross over to Beer-sheba;
for Gilgal shall surely go into exile,
    and Bethel shall come to nothing.
⁶ Seek the Lᴏʀᴅ and live,
    or he will break out against the house
    of Joseph like fire,
    and it will devour Bethel, with no one
    to quench it.

4. כִּי (for) answers to the כִּי in verse 3. These particles introduce the broadest of causalities: Israel is fallen (v. 2), because (כִּי) the Lord affirms her destruction (v. 3); because (כִּי) of the foregoing the Lord pleads for their return to him. His desire is that they should turn to him and live (see Deut. 32:46–47). כֹּה אָמַר יְהוָה (thus says Yahweh): See the Exegesis of 1:3. לְבֵית יִשְׂרָאֵל (to the house of Israel) echoes the same phrase in the preceding verse and ties the present call for repentance to the previous prophecy of disaster. דִּרְשׁוּנִי (seek me): One might seek the Lord by a prophet or an oracle (e.g., Gen. 25:22; Exod. 18:15; 1 Sam. 9:9; Jer. 37:7) or by desiring him, that is, by wanting his oversight and will in one's life. The Lord promised, through his prophet Moses, to be available to those who would seek him, even in exile (Deut. 4:29: "If you search after him with all your heart and soul"; cf. Lam. 3:25). דָּרַשׁ and its synonym בָּקֵשׁ are used in Deuteronomy 4:29 (cf. David's charge to Solomon in 1 Chron. 28:9). Sadly, the Lord's people usually did not seek him (Isa. 9:12 [13]; 31:1; Jer. 10:21). וִחְיוּ (so that you may live; lit. and live): The

sequence of two imperatives warrants our understanding the second in the sense of an assured result or consequence (as in Gen. 42:18: "Do this and [i.e., so that] you will live"; GKC §110a; and see Deut. 30:6; Ezek. 37:14).

5. וְאַל־תִּדְרְשׁוּ בֵּית־אֵל (but do not seek at Bethel): The context requires an adversative sense for וְ in English. These words are in contrast to the phrase *seek me, so that you might live* (v. 4). The Lord, having told the people to seek him, now warns them that they are not to seek him at Bethel. אַל (do not) introduces a negative command. תִּדְרְשׁוּ (seek): The repetition of this verb creates a sense of emphasis. בֵּית־אֵל (Bethel) is probably not the direct object of the verb (as in the NRSV), but an adverbial accusative, telling *where* they are not to seek, that is, at Bethel. In this case the direct object is understood, namely, "me" (i.e., the Lord), doing double duty from the previous verse. It is, however, possible that דָּרַשׁ (seek) answers to תָּבֹאוּ (go) in the next line, thus having the sense of seeking out Bethel—that is, making it the object of their going (לֹא תָבֹאוּ, do not go). On the basis of the

---

4. As the coordinate clauses of verses 3–4 indicate, the Lord punished his people to get their attention. He did not desire their utter destruction; he wanted them to turn back to him and seek him that they might live. For life is in God alone, and in his Christ (John 5:26).

The concept of life ("seek the Lord so that you may live") in the Old Testament does not always imply eternal life. In the legal material it often connotes a viable relationship to the inheritance (Lev. 18:5, 28; Deut. 30:16–18). The nation lost its life through disobedience and perished. The prophet states that their national vitality will again flourish if they seek the Lord. While Amos held little hope that the people would repent, he nevertheless held out the offer of grace to them.

One seeks the Lord by desiring his oversight of life. The people had only to relearn the Lord's ways and gracious requirements. If they had humbly returned to him, their nation would have continued to live and they would have retained the land of promise.

God's redemptive faithfulness would eventually restore his people, as he promised in Deuteronomy 30:6: "The LORD your God will circumcise your heart and the heart of your descendants, so that you will love the LORD your God with all your heart and with all your soul, in order that you may live." And only with God was such salvation pos-

sible, as he himself told them, much later, through his prophet Ezekiel (37:12–14).

We, too, have no recourse but to seek the one true God and find life in him. It has been said that God is not open to the casual enquirer. But it has also been said that God "rewards those who seek him" (Heb. 11:6). The task of the believer is to seek him earnestly. Jesus must be the object of our prayers and our whole desire. Our God is found in Jesus Christ, who has told us that "because I live, you also will live" (John 14:19). The concept of life in the New Testament applies to the believer now (John 10:10) as well as eternally (John 17:3).

5. The prophet warned the people to seek the Lord, not Bethel. Both Bethel and Beer-sheba were rich with religious associations. At Bethel, Abraham sacrificed and called upon the Lord (Gen. 13:3–4); when Jacob was fleeing from Laban he received a revelation from "the God of Bethel" (Gen. 31:13)—a direct connection to the dream he had there twenty years earlier when fleeing to Laban (Gen. 28:10–22); Jacob subsequently worshiped at Bethel after reconciliation with his brother Esau (Gen. 35:1–14); it was still a sanctuary in the time of Samuel, who visited it on his annual circuit (1 Sam. 7:16); and a company of prophets lived there during the time of Elijah (2 Kings 2:3). At Beer-sheba, Abraham called upon the Lord (Gen. 21:31–33); the Lord appeared there

former suggestion, the people sought the Lord in a ritual or oracular sense, for they were not accustomed to seek him truly for himself (as v. 4 commands). The command is twofold: not only are they not to seek him at Bethel, but they are not to seek him in the superficial way in which they have, that is, at Bethel. הַגִּלְגָּל לֹא תָבֹאוּ (and you shall not go to Gilgal; lit. and to Gilgal you shall not go) is also an adverbial accusative, specifically an accusative of place expressing the idea of direction toward (GKC §118d–f). הַגִּלְגָּל (Gilgal): See the Exegesis of 4:4. לֹא (not) indicates an emphatic command, which is stronger than אַל with the jussive (GKC §107o) in the previous clause. תָבֹאוּ (go) occurs with דָּרַשׁ (seek) in Deuteronomy 12:5: "But you shall seek the place that the Lord your God will choose out of all your tribes as his habitation to put his name there. You shall go there." תַּעֲבֹרוּ וּבְאֵר שֶׁבַע לֹא (and you shall not cross the border to Beer-sheba; lit. and [to] Beer-sheba you shall not cross over): The negative command here, again, is emphatic. This repeated negative enhances the sense of parallelism in both cola. בְּאֵר שֶׁבַע (Beer-

sheba) was an ancient holy place (see the Exposition). כִּי הַגִּלְגָּל גָּלֹה יִגְלֶה (for Gilgal will surely go into exile): כִּי (for) gives the reason for the foregoing interdictions. They should not go to Gilgal any longer, because that city will cease to exist. גָּלֹה יִגְלֶה (surely go into exile): The combination of the infinitive absolute and the finite form of the verb creates emphasis, that is, "Gilgal will *surely* go (GKC §113l–r). The Lord is leaving no doubt. The colon is rich in consonance and word play (*gilgal, galoh, yigleh*), an emphatic device used to drive the point home. גָּלֹה (exile): See the Exegesis of 1:5. וּבֵית-אֵל יִהְיֶה לְאָוֶן (and Bethel will become trouble): יִהְיֶה (will become) with the preposition ל indicates becoming, that is, coming into a different state or condition (BDB, p. 226). אָוֶן (trouble) is ironically substituted for אֵל (God) in the name *Bethel* (see Hos. 4:15; 5:8; 10:5).

6. דִּרְשׁוּ . . . וִחְיוּ (seek . . . so that you may live): See the Exegesis of verse 4. פֶּן-יִצְלַח כָּאֵשׁ (lest he break out like fire): The basic sense of יִצְלַח (break out) appears to be akin to the English word *rush* (BDB, p. 852). Contexts inform the word with its

to Isaac (Gen. 26:23–25) and to Jacob (Gen. 46:1–5); Samuel's sons served there as judges (1 Sam. 8:1–2). Josiah desecrated the high places "from Geba to Beer-sheba" in his reform (2 Kings 23:8), sparked by Hilkiah's discovery of the "book of the law" in the temple during its renovation (2 Kings 22). People from the northern kingdom probably went there on pilgrimage (see 8:14). Beer-sheba lay in the far south of Judah, about fifty miles south-southwest of Jerusalem. So, when people went there on pilgrimage, they would have to "cross over" the border. The Lord now forbids such pilgrimages. The three cola form a neat pattern of chiasmus followed by parallel structure:

a	b
but do not seek	at Bethel
b´	**a´**
and to Gilgal	you shall not go
b´´	**a´´**
and to Beer-sheba	you shall not cross the border

The structure drives home the point of the Lord's message, and is followed by a warning reason as to why such seeking of Yahweh will not only be fruitless, but no longer allowed. This structure, along with two emphatic imperatives and a striking example of consonance near the

end, all contribute to a sense of strong interdiction in this verse. The people of the northern kingdom have been counseled, indeed commanded, to seek the Lord in the previous verse. Now, however, they are told that the very ways in which they have thought to seek him—at Bethel, at Gilgal, and even by long pilgrimages to Beer-sheba—are not the ways they must now pursue; for Gilgal will go into exile and Bethel is headed for trouble. Truly, God now wants his people to seek him and not his shrines—nor even his word at his shrines. So today, he desires a people who will love him and seek him for himself.

The prophet warned the people not to seek the Lord in the religious sanctuaries, because they would soon be no more. In this way he drew a contrast between the pagan concept that the deity may be localized at pagan shrines and the concept of God as a spirit. Jesus observed the same truth (John 4:23–24).

6. Amos has been quoting the Lord; now he speaks on his own behalf. He repeats God's command of verse 4, "Seek me so that you may live," but now with "the Lord" as the direct object, since Amos, not Yahweh, is the speaker. But even if Amos speaks here, his words are still a prophetic warning from the Lord to his people.

As a true representative of the Lord, Amos seeks the reconciliation of God and his people (cf. 2 Cor. 5:18). He warns them that, as the Lord has

distinctive nuances. For example, it describes the Holy Spirit coming forcefully on Samson (Judg. 14:6, 19; 15:14), Saul (1 Sam. 10:6; 11:6), and David (1 Sam. 16:13), and also of an evil spirit from God coming forcefully on Saul (1 Sam. 18:10). Here it describes the forceful activity of the Lord against the nation. כָּאֵשׁ (like fire): For the comparison of Yahweh with fire, see Deuteronomy 4:24: "For the LORD your God is a devouring fire [אֵשׁ אֹכְלָה], a jealous God" (cf. Jer. 4:4). בֵּית יוֹסֵף (in the house of Joseph): This structure is an adverbial accusative, indicating where the fire will break out (GKC §118d). This term denotes

the tribes of Ephraim and Manasseh, and so covers the areas that contain Bethel (Ephraim) and Gilgal (Manasseh). These are the only sanctuaries of concern in the north; Beer-sheba (v. 5), being in the south, is not an object of this oracle of doom. וְאָכְלָה וְאֵין־מְכַבֶּה (and it consume, and there be none to quench it; lit. no quencher): The unexpressed subject (it) is the consuming fire of Yahweh, which is indeed the Lord himself. וְאֵין־מְכַבֶּה (and there be no quencher): With regard to the inextinguishable nature of the Lord's judgment fire, see Isaiah 1:31; Jeremiah 4:4; 21:12 (cf. also Matt. 3:12; Mark 9:48).

---

already revealed, he is a "consuming fire" (Deut. 4:24, NIV). The judgment he brings will come in the form of his very self, a holy fire in whose presence sinful people cannot stand (e.g., Exod. 19:16–25; Deut. 5:20–23 [23–26]). Jeremiah later gave a similar command to the people of the southern kingdom (4:4).

Today, believers have a similar role, as ministers of reconciliation, to warn the world about the wrath of a holy God. For a season he has made salvation available through his Son, but that season will not last forever.

The sense of life as the viable relationship of the nation to their inheritance (v. 4) finds support in the structure of this verse. The command is followed by the result of their disobedience to it. If they seek the Lord they will live. If they do not, they will experience the judging fire of God. This fire will consume Bethel, for there will be none to quench it. In this structure life is defined by its antithesis, which is the death of the nation represented by the destruction of its most important sanctuary—Bethel.

II. Pronouncements of Judgment (3:1–6:14)
C. Covenant Lawsuit—Lament Form (5:1–17)
4. Direct Address to the Fallen (5:7–13)

7 You who turn justice to wormwood,
    and throw righteousness into the
      dirt!
8 The one who made the Pleiades and Ori-
    on,
    and the one who turns black darkness
      to morning,
    and darkens day into night,
  the one who summons the waters of the
    sea,
    and pours them out upon the surface
      of the earth—
  Yahweh is his name—
9 the one who flashes forth destruction
    upon the strong,
    as destruction comes upon the forti-
      fied city.
10 They hate the one who reproves in the
    gate,
    and they abhor the one who speaks
      the truth.
11 Therefore: because you trample upon
    the poor,
    and you take an exaction of grain
      from him—
  houses of dressed stone you have built,
    but you will not live in them;
  pleasant vineyards you have planted,
    but you will not drink their wine.
12 For I know that your transgressions are
    many,
    and that your sins are numerous,
  afflicters of the righteous, takers of a ran-
    som—
    and they deprive the needy of justice
      in the gate!
13 Therefore the prudent shall cease at
    that time,
    for it will be an evil time.

7 And, you that turn justice to worm-
    wood,
    and bring righteousness to the
      ground!
8 The one who made the Pleiades and Ori-
    on,
    and turns deep darkness into the
      morning,
    and darkens the day into night,
  who calls for the waters of the sea,
    and pours them out on the surface of
      the earth,
  the Lord is his name,
9 who makes destruction flash out against
    the strong,
    so that destruction comes upon the
      fortress.
10 They hate the one who reproves in the
    gate,
    and they abhor the one who speaks
      the truth.
11 Therefore because you trample on the
    poor
    and take from them levies of grain,
  you have built houses of hewn stone,
    but you shall not live in them;
  you have planted pleasant vineyards,
    but you shall not drink their wine.
12 For I know how many are your trans-
    gressions,
    and how great are your sins—
  you who afflict the righteous, who take a
    bribe,
    and push aside the needy in the gate.
13 Therefore the prudent will keep silent
    in such a time;
    for it is an evil time.

7. הַהֹפְכִים לְלַעֲנָה (you who turn justice to wormwood): The definite article (הַ) is vocative (GKC §126e). Amos continues to speak to those he addressed in verse 6 with the plural imperatives *seek* and *live.* לַעֲנָה (wormwood) is a bitter plant, mentioned elsewhere in prophecy (Jer. 9:14 [15]; 23:15; Lam. 3:15, 19; see also Prov. 5:4; Amos 6:12). For לְלַעֲנָה the Septuagint has εἰς ὕψος (upward), perhaps reflecting a Hebrew *Vorlage* of לְמַעְלָה (upside down). The Masoretic Text has this expression in Judges 7:13: וַיַּהַפְכֵהוּ לְמַעְלָה (it [a Midianite tent] turned upside down). The structure of this verse seems to support the emendation from "wormwood" to "upside down," for the words *upward* and *earthward* answer to one another chiastically:

a	**b**	**c**
you who turn	upward	justice
c′	**b′**	**a′**
and righteousness	earthward	you throw

This emendation, like many in Old Testament poetry, however, is doubtful in the light of 6:12, where the word לַעֲנָה (wormwood) is parallel to רֹאשׁ (poisonweed) in a statement similar to the one here. מִשְׁפָּט (justice) frequently occurs in contexts that require the sense of justice. In the prophetic corpus, contexts sometimes require a sense close to true religion, that is, the practice of the ethical intent of the Mosaic law. וּצְדָקָה (and . . . righteousness) underscores the ethical sense of its companion word מִשְׁפָּט (justice) in this verse. For this pair used in parallelism, see 6:12; Isaiah 5:7; 11:4. לָאָרֶץ הִנִּיחוּ (you throw . . . into the dirt; lit. earthward) has roughly the significance of "trampling underfoot."

8. עֹשֵׂה (the one who made; lit. the maker) along with וְהֹפֵךְ (and the one who turns; lit. and the turner) and הַקּוֹרֵא (the one who summons; lit. the summoner) represents another divine titulary, with another series of participial phrases. The form occurred earlier in 4:1, 13. כִּימָה (the Pleiades; perhaps the Group or Flock; see BDB, p. 465) possibly designates a "group" or "flock" of stars. The Pleiades is an open galactic star cluster in the constellation Taurus; it has seven prominent stars and is visible to the naked eye. וּכְסִיל (and Orion; perhaps the Fool; see BDB, p. 493): Driver (*Joel and Amos*, p. 182) suggests that Orion, a "brilliant and conspicuous constellation, was originally some fool-hardy, heaven-daring rebel, who was chained to the sky for his impiety." This constellation is known classically as "the Hunter." For the Pleiades and Orion together, see Job 9:9 and 38:31, where they appear in a context depicting God's incomparable wisdom and power. וְהֹפֵךְ (and the one who turns) is the same participle applied to those "who turn justice to wormwood" in verse 7. Undoubtedly this is another use of prophetic

---

7. In this new subsection, the prophet addresses those who have distorted justice, making it bitter poison. These people have scornfully cast righteousness to the ground, where it may be trampled by anyone who passes. By turning justice to wormwood, the prophet means that the oppressing classes of his day perverted justice. They did not render the requirements of the Mosaic law impartially. They ignored its social concerns and used it for their own advantage. For the poor, the unjust administration of the law created bitterness and suffering (for a further discussion of *mišpat*, see the Exegesis).

The section beginning at verse 1 presages doom for the northern kingdom because they have despised righteousness by throwing it to the ground. There is a lesson here for today, for the Lord calls his church to righteousness (Matt. 3:15). In Matthew 5:20 he called for righteousness that exceeds that of the Pharisees. The religion of Amos's day was a precursor of the later Pharisaical religion in that the purpose of the law was distorted and its heart destroyed.

8. Another series of divine epithets serves to remind Amos's audience of the nature of the God with whom they must deal. The literary structure facilitates his thought. The first bicolon is chiastically structured, with a participle and a perfect:

a	**b**	**c**
and who turns	to morning	black darkness
c′	**b′**	**a′**
and day	to night	he darkens

The pattern is similar to that in the divine titulary in Isaiah 44:27. This series of majestic descriptions illustrates the futility of resisting the Lord. It is ironic that the same verb used to describe the perversion of justice in the previous verse (*hapak,* turn) is here applied to the Lord, "who *turns* black darkness to morning." By God's grace, the contrast between human sinfulness and divine holiness is not unbridgeable. Jesus said, "Very truly, I tell you, you will weep and mourn, but the world will rejoice; you will have pain, but your pain will turn into joy. . . . So you have pain

irony. צַלְמָוֶת (black darkness) is not a composite of צֵל (shadow) and מָוֶת (death); it is cognate with Akkadian *ṣalmatu* (black, dark). It has this meaning elsewhere in the Old Testament, for example, Psalm 23:4; Job 24:17. הַקּוֹרֵא לְמֵי־הַיָּם (the one who summons the waters of the sea): For similar expressions of Yahweh's power over the sea and the rain, see Job 12:15b; 36:27–30. יְהוָה שְׁמוֹ (Yahweh is his name) also occurs in 9:6 and Jeremiah 33:2.

9. הַמַּבְלִיג (the one who flashes forth) might mean "to cause to flash forth" or possibly "to stream over" (with Dahood, "Hebrew-Ugaritic Lexicography IX," p. 340, n. 2). The root has the meaning "to gleam or smile" in Psalm 39:14 [13]; Job 9:27; 10:20. שֹׁד . . . . וְשֹׁד (destruction . . . destruction): The repetition of these words may seem "inelegant" (Driver, *Joel and Amos*, p. 184), but that alone is no cause for emendation. מִבְצָר (the fortified city) denotes a city with strong walls for defense. The use of the terms *strong* and *fortified city* recalls claims made in the Assyrian annals that rebellious vassals had "trusted in their own strength" (e.g., Tiglath-pileser I, King, *Annals of the Kings of Assyria*, pp. 35–36, col. 1, lines 68–69) or "trusted in their mighty walls" (e.g., Assurnasirpal II, King, *Annals of the Kings of Assyria*, p. 293, col. 1, line 114; see also pp. 79–80, col. 6, lines 11–14, 17–18). So here, the strength of the true covenant God would prove stronger than that of his rebellious vassal people. וְשֹׁד . . . . יָבוֹא (as destruction . . . comes) is a circumstantial clause joined by ו (*waw*) to a participial clause, as in Genesis 38:25 (GKC §142e). The Septuagint has ἐπάγων (who brings), perhaps reflecting a Hebrew *Vorlage* with יָבִיא (hiphil) or an emendation to the same. The hiphil participle that heads this line seems to support the change, but we retain the qal with the Masoretic Text because the destruction in the second colon may be viewed as coming as a result of the Lord's flashing it forth. The verse is designed not only to make clear the divine power of the Lord, but also to underscore the divine authority that is his, as the tightly structured, chiastic statement leaves no doubt that he can produce such destruction.

10. בַּשַּׁעַר (in the gate) was a complex of rooms along a corridor built into a city wall. It could

---

now; but I will see you again, and your hearts will rejoice, and no one will take your joy from you" (John 16:20, 22).

This doxology is also considered by redaction critics to be the addition of a later hand (see the Exposition of v. 13), mainly because of its apparent intrusiveness. It seems logically unconnected to the preceding discussion. We can, however, find a similar apparently disconnected pericope in Amos (6:9–10). It is possible that the seemingly intrusive nature of this "hymn" is a mark of Amos's style.

9. The divine titulary continues, with the power and authority of the Lord clearly displayed. The structure of this section is similar to verse 8 and is chiastic, with a participle in the first colon corresponding, in this case, to an imperfect in the second:

a	b	c
the one who flashes forth	destruction	upon the strong

b´	c´	a´
as destruction	upon the fortified city	comes

The repetition of the word *destruction* emphasizes the doom that will come upon the rebellious people. The previous verse shows that the Lord was almighty in the natural realm; this verse shows him almighty in the human realm. The strong may trust in their strength and the rebellious in their fortified cities, but the Lord will bring destruction on them. There is irony in the echo of ancient Near Eastern allegations against rebellious vassals, for the people of Amos's day had not understood a spiritual principle that God had made clear: the power of the covenant Lord was stronger than any human power.

Amos painted an accurate picture of the Lord in these words. The people of his day did not believe that God would judge them. They apparently castigated Amos for predicting judgment (9:10). Here, Amos affirmed that God judges wickedness. His statement should have engendered fear of God in the hearts of his hearers, but it appears that his message was largely unheeded.

10. The chiastic structure of this verse imparts both elegance and power to its message:

a	b
they hate	the one who reproves in the gate

b´	a´
and the one who speaks truth	they abhor

house guards, but also afforded a place for the discussion and settlement of disputes (see Deut. 21:19; 22:15; 25:7; Ruth 4:1–2, 11; Job 5:4 ["in court," NIV]; 31:21; Ps. 127:5). מוֹכִיחַ (the one who reproves) is one who, either as judge or advocate, seeks to impeach or reprove the wrongdoer (Job 13:9–10; 22:4–5). The same phrase occurs in Isaiah 29:21 ("the defender in court," NIV). וְדֹבֵר תָּמִים (and . . . the one who speaks truth) occurs only here; it may also have the sense of a person who speaks up for the blameless. The ambiguity is probably intentional. יְתָעֵבוּ (they abhor) is a much stronger term than שָׂנֵא (hate), so that the second colon represents the structure of parallelism identified by Kugel (*Idea of Biblical Poetry*, pp. 1–58) as "A is so, and *what's more*, B is so."

11. לָכֵן (therefore) introduces the consequence that follows. יַעַן (because) introduces the reason for the consequence. יַעַן בּוֹשַׁסְכֶם (because you trample; lit. because of your trampling): The shift from third-person plural in the previous verse to second-person plural here is typical of ancient Near Eastern covenant documents (discussed in the Introduction). בּוֹשַׁסְכֶם is a *hapax legomenon* and probably a byform of בּוּס (to trample), with interchange of שׁ and ס, a frequent switch in the Old Testament. וּמַשְׂאַת־בַּר (and . . . an exaction of

grain): מַשְׂאַת (exaction) is from נָשָׂא (lift) and has several English translational equivalents related to the verbal idea (burden, uplifting, tax, exaction). The context here describes oppression of the poorer classes and thus requires the sense of grain exacted from the poor by the wealthy oppressing classes. בָּתֵּי גָזִית (houses of dressed stone) would be unusually costly and solid houses, as opposed to, for example, mud-brick houses (e.g., Isa. 9:9 [10], where the inhabitants of Ephraim and Samaria say with pride that they will rebuild the fallen bricks with dressed stone). בְּנִיתֶם (you have built) continues the address to the oppressing classes. The word order of the entire bicolon reflects the original covenantal curse in Deuteronomy 28:30b: "You shall build a house, but not live in it" (cf. Zeph. 1:13; contrast Isa. 65:21–22). וְלֹא תֵשְׁבוּ אֶת־יֵינָם כַּרְמֵי־חֶמֶד נְטַעְתֶּם (pleasant vineyards you have planted, / but you will not drink their wine): This curse also reflects the original covenantal wording in Deuteronomy 28:39: "You shall plant vineyards and dress them, but you shall neither drink the wine nor gather the grapes" (cf. Deut. 28:30c ["You shall plant a vineyard, but not enjoy its fruit"] and Zeph. 1:13). For other examples of the "futility curse," see Deuteronomy 28:30a, 31 and Micah 6:15.

For the close appearance (in chiasm, as here) of the terms *hate* and *abhor*, see Psalm 5:6b–7 [5b–6]. The chiastic structure adds both elegance and emphasis to the message. It is a portrayal of hatred: hatred on the part of the oppressors and hatred for those who would expose them.

This verse vividly affirms the words (v. 7) preceding the divine titulary. It shows how the people described there turned justice to wormwood and contributes to the litany of sins in verses 11–12. When the influential people in any society despise truth, there is little basis for a stable society.

Those who hated the children of light in Amos's day, and those who hate them today, will one day stand in a "court" where they are powerless to resist the light that will expose all. How much better, then, to be a child of light and live by the truth. For "those who do what is true come to the light, so that it may be clearly seen that their deeds have been done in God" (John 3:21).

11. Amos excoriates the privileged classes of Israel because they abuse the poor. The word *therefore* (*lākēn*) establishes the logical result of their rejection of truth and justice. Because they violated the social dimension of the law by bilk-

ing the poor to enrich their own coffers, these oppressing classes will find that the houses they built with ill-gotten gain will be left empty and they will not enjoy the fruits of their luxury. The exile will take them from their luxurious homes and pleasant gardens. Once again the prophet shows the futility of earthly gain. It is better to grasp the eternal (Matt. 6:19; Mark 10:21 par. Luke 18:22). The privileged classes in Amos's day did not take account of the poor as fellow children in God's kingdom. They did not take care of the underprivileged; rather they lorded it over them. The same attitude was encountered by Jesus when he spoke to his disciples in Matthew 20:25–28: "You know that the rulers of the Gentiles lord it over them, and their high officials exercise authority over them. Not so with you. Instead, whoever wants to become great among you must be your servant, and whoever wants to be first must be your slave—just as the Son of Man did not come to be served, but to serve, and to give his life as a ransom for many" (NIV). The Lord's word to our land today may not be much different from his warning by Amos; his word to his people today is surely no different than his word to his first disciples.

12. יָדַעְתִּי כִּי (for I know): כִּי (for) introduces the reason for the threat in the previous verse: it is the sin of the oppressing classes—sin that the Lord knows full well. Perhaps these people believed the Lord was not aware of their sin (Job 22:13–14; Ps. 73:11). רַבִּים פִּשְׁעֵיכֶם (that your transgressions are many) also occurs in Jeremiah 5:6. עֲצֻמִים (numerous) has as one of its nuances the idea of strength, hence, "virulent." The words in this bicolon are often found either together or in parallel, for example, רַב parallels עָצוּם in Psalm 35:18; 135:10; Micah 4:3; פְּשָׁעִים parallels חַטָּאִים in Psalm 51:5 [3] and Isaiah 44:22; the latter two are used together in Psalm 25:7; 32:1; 59:4 [3]; and Isaiah 43:25. צַדִּיק (the righteous): See the Exegesis of 2:6. לֹקְחֵי כֹפֶר (takers of a ransom): Numbers 35:31 forbade the taking of כֹּפֶר (atonement) money for the life of a murderer. Murder was to be punished by death, and the law prohibited the ransom of a murderer. אֶבְיוֹנִים (the needy): See the Exegesis of 2:6. שַׁעַר (the gate): See the Exegesis of verse 10. הִטּוּ (and they deprive; lit. they turn aside): By turning the needy aside in the gate, they turn them out of court.

That is, they deprive them of justice (as in 2:7). For the spirit of the verse, see 2:6.

13. לָכֵן (therefore): This word, which frequently introduces judgment sayings in Amos (4:12; 5:11, 16; 6:7), introduces the general consequence of the foregoing societal wrongs. יִדֹּם (shall cease): There are three roots דמם: (1) to stop or stand still, (2) to wail, or (3) to perish. Either the first or third root may be intended here: that is, stopping what they are doing (as in Ps. 35:15: "Tore at me without ceasing") or ceasing to exist (as in Jer. 49:26; 50:30: "All her soldiers shall be destroyed"). The phraseology of the two verses from Jeremiah is almost identical to that here. Here, it means "cease, perish." כִּי עֵת רָעָה הִיא (for it will be an evil time): The עֵת רָעָה (evil time) is a time of judgment (see Ps. 37:19; Jer. 15:11; Mic. 2:3). This phrase states the reason why the prudent will perish; it is because the times will be so bad that goodness will not be tolerated. It is also possible, however, that this sentence states that those who are prudent will not speak out in this time of great evil because it will be to no avail (McComiskey, *Amos*, p. 313).

---

12. The threat in the previous verse is based on the Lord's knowledge of the people's sins. He accuses them of afflicting the righteous (i.e., those who are in the right in a case) and of depriving the needy of justice. The verse contrasts the treatment given the rich and the poor. Those in authority are accused of taking bribes. This type of bribe (see the Exegesis) was given for the life of a murderer. The inference is that the rich were able to buy their way free even from the most heinous of crimes, while the needy did not receive the justice the law required. The verse is reminiscent of the treatment of the poor Amos described in 2:6.

The sins that Amos addressed were issues of eternal importance. Similar issues face us today, as social sins are an expression of the sinful nature. When God judges a nation he does not judge an abstraction, but a people. The cry of Jesus at the outset of his ministry must also be the cry of his church in the last days: "Repent, for the kingdom of heaven has come near" (Matt. 4:17).

13. The times that lie ahead will be worse than the present. Things will get so bad that even the prudent, who up until now have been abused, will diminish. As a nation deepens in sin, wisdom becomes increasingly rare. Moses said that the people would not have enough understanding to see where their sins were leading them (see also Jer. 49:7–8; Obad. 8):

> They are a nation void of sense;
>   there is no understanding in them.
> If they were wise, they would understand
>   this;
>   they would discern what the end would
>   be. (Deut. 32:28–29, NIV)

If Amos's implication is that those who are wise will not speak out because of the futility of opposing their influential leaders, it underscores the wickedness of his society. The prophets were concerned with the health of their society. Their social concern should also find reflection in the church.

The pattern applies to believers also, for the beginning of wisdom is the fear of the Lord (Prov. 9:10), and Jesus affirmed that there would be little reverence for God in the end times (Matt. 24:9–14).

II. Pronouncements of Judgment (3:1–6:14)
C. Covenant Lawsuit—Lament Form (5:1–17)
5. Brief Exhortation (5:14–15)

14 Seek good, and not evil,
    so that you may live, and it may be
      so,
  That Yahweh, God of hosts is with you,
    as you have claimed.
15 Hate evil, but love good,
    and establish justice in the gate;
  maybe Yahweh God of hosts
    will be gracious to the remnant of Jo-
      seph.

14 Seek good and not evil,
    that you may live;
  and so the Lord, the God of hosts, will be
    with you,
    just as you have said.
15 Hate evil and love good,
    and establish justice in the gate;
  it may be that the Lord, the God of
    hosts,
    will be gracious to the remnant of Jo-
      seph.

14. דִּרְשׁוּ־טוֹב וְאַל־רָע (seek good, and not evil): Compare Isaiah 1:16–17: "Cease to do evil, / learn to do good." דָּרַשׁ (seek): See the Exegesis of verse 4. Here the people are commanded to seek good in an ethical sense, for the counterpart of טוֹב (good) is רָע (evil). לְמַעַן תִּחְיוּ (so that you may live) is the functional equivalent of the imperative וִחְיוּ (and live) in verse 4. וִיהִי־כֵן (and it may be so) and its companion verb תִּחְיוּ are understood here as dependent on the conjunction לְמַעַן (so that). That תִּחְיוּ is imperfect indicates that it is not certain that they will live, but it is a possibility contingent on their seeking God (GKC §107x). Amos proceeds to tell his audience what it is that will follow, namely, the Lord's presence with them. יְהוָה אֱלֹהֵי־צְבָאוֹת (Yahweh God of hosts): See the Exegesis of 3:13. אִתְּכֶם (with you) expresses the deepest need of God's people, anticipated also in Isaiah 7:14 (Immanuel; cf. Matt. 1:23). כַּאֲשֶׁר אֲמַרְתֶּם (as you have claimed; lit. said): Apparently, the people have claimed that the Lord was with them, even though he was not. The ground of their false

confidence was in part their devotion to the sacrificial system (4:4–5).

15. שִׂנְאוּ־רָע וְאֶהֱבוּ טוֹב (hate evil, but love good): The contrast in this context permits a mild adversative sense for *waw* in the English translation. The command here is more forceful than the one in the previous verse: The people are not merely to "seek good, and not evil," but, rather, they are to "hate evil, and love good." This may mean to love the Lord, who alone is good. מִשְׁפָּט (justice) is the noun form of שָׁפַט (to administer justice). In ethical contexts, particularly in the Prophets, it has the sense of the administration of the spirit of the Mosaic law in everyday life—thus, justice, fairness, and respect for one's fellow citizen. בַּשַּׁעַר (in the gate): See the Exegesis of verse 10. יְהוָה אֱלֹהֵי־צְבָאוֹת (Yahweh God of hosts): See the Exegesis of 3:13. שְׁאֵרִית יוֹסֵף (the remnant of Joseph): In Amos's time, the northern kingdom could hardly be described as a "remnant," for Joash (2 Kings 13:22–25) and Jeroboam II (2 Kings 14:26–28) had restored the kingdom to greatness (2 Kings 10:32–33; 13:3, 7; see the Exposition).

---

14. In language reminiscent of verse 4, where Amos commanded the people to seek the Lord and live, he now commands them to seek good and not evil so that they may live. The two commands are similar, for although seeking good rather than evil may not seem tantamount to seeking God himself, in the deepest sense it is the same because good is the result of knowing God.

Here, life is the result of seeking good. In verse 4 it is the result of seeking the Lord directly. This statement underscores the fact that an ethical response to God was essential for the people's retention of the land. The law made it clear that so long as they obeyed God they would continue to enjoy a viable relationship to the land God had promised (see the Exposition of v. 4). Moses affirmed this in Deuteronomy 30:15–18. The ethical good the people sought would promote their national welfare.

The Lord did not reveal his goodness to his people simply for their own sakes, but also that they might be a testimony to the nations (Deut. 4:6–8), for he is a God "who desires everyone to be saved and to come to the knowledge of the truth" (1 Tim. 2:4). So he has revealed to us his goodness in Jesus Christ, not simply for our own sakes: he wants us to take the news of his goodness to the ends of the earth. In that very context came our

Lord's promise, "And remember, I am with you always, to the end of the age" (Matt. 28:20).

15. The prophet commands the people to love good and hate evil. The Lord's judgment must come, for he knows their evil hearts and he knows that his own faithfulness to the covenant requires judgment. Yet, if they will turn and seek the good, a remnant can be spared. It is a question of seeing one's true good in God and holding fast to him.

Amos refers to the nation as a remnant. This word (šĕʾērît) basically describes something left over. In its theological usages in the Prophets it speaks of the people through whom God continues to effect his promises. Perhaps Amos refers to the future state of the nation after the Assyrian decimations, or possibly he holds out the hope that God will preserve a remnant and through them fulfill his gracious promises.

When he calls to his people to establish justice (mišpaṭ) in the gate, he refers to the just administration of the Mosaic law in the seat of government. It was in the gates that the leaders of Israel's cities convened to administer their affairs. Here, however, these leaders wove their nets of intrigue in which they ensnared the poor and used the law to their own advantage. If justice existed in the gates the poor would have had sustenance and the nation would have enjoyed the blessing of their God.

II. Pronouncements of Judgment (3:1–6:14)
C. Covenant Lawsuit—Lament Form (5:1–17)
6. Conclusion (5:16–17)

¹⁶ Therefore, thus says Yahweh, God of
hosts, the Lord:
"In all the squares there will be wailing,
and in all the streets they will say,
'Woe, woe!'
And they will call the farm laborer to
mourning,
and [they will call], 'Wailing!' to the
professional mourners.
¹⁷ And in all the vineyards there will be
wailing,
for I will pass through your midst,"
says Yahweh.

¹⁶ Therefore thus says the Lord, the God
of hosts, the Lord:
In all the squares there shall be wailing;
and in all the streets they shall say,
"Alas! alas!"
They shall call the farmers to mourning,
and those skilled in lamentation, to
wailing;
¹⁷ in all the vineyards there shall be wail-
ing,
for I will pass through the midst of
you,
says the Lord.

16. לָכֵן (therefore): See the Exegesis of 4:12. יְהוָה כֹּה־אָמַר (thus says Yahweh): See the Exegesis of 1:3 and 1:5. These two phrases are combined here, as in 7:17 and elsewhere (e.g., Isa. 29:22; 37:33; Jer. 5:14; Mic. 2:3). אֱלֹהֵי צְבָאוֹת (God of hosts): See the Exegesis of 3:13. אֲדֹנָי (the Lord): See the Exegesis of 1:8. רְחֹבוֹת (squares), large open spaces frequently near the city gate (Neh. 8:1), and חוּצוֹת (streets) occur in similar parallel in Isaiah 15:3: "In the streets they wear sackcloth, / on the roofs and in the public squares" (NIV). מִסְפֵּד (wailing) connotes a loud howl of mourning, as in Micah 1:8: "I will howl like a jackal / and moan like an owl" (NIV). הוֹ is a *hapax legomenon*; it usually appears in the fuller form, הוֹי (as in 5:18; 6:1; 1 Kings 13:30; Isa. 1:4; 5:22; Jer. 22:18). וְקָרְאוּ (and they will call) is a converted perfect. The verb does double duty in this bicolon, with אִכָּר (farm laborer) in the first colon and מִסְפֵּד (wailing) in the second as its direct objects. The subject of this verb is probably the same as that for יֹאמְרוּ (they will say), that is, the citizens who throng the streets crying out in lamentation. These people will cry to the farmers who are outside the city limits, as well as to the professional mourners, to join them in their outpouring of woe. אִכָּר (farm laborer) is probably a farm hand rather than a farm owner. The word occurs only six other times (2 Chron. 26:10; Isa. 61:5; Jer. 14:4; 31:24; 51:23; Joel 1:11). אֵבֶל (mourning) is generally mourning for the dead or the dying; see Micah 1:8, where the word is in parallel with מִסְפֵּד (wailing) as here. יֹדְעֵי נֶהִי (the professional mourners; lit. the knowers of or those skilled in mourning song[s]): The participle denotes those who were highly skilled in a particular art, whether or not as professionals. For this use of the participle, see Genesis 25:27 ("Esau was a skillful hunter"); 1 Samuel 16:16 ("someone who is skillful in playing the lyre"); and 1 Kings 9:27 ("sailors who were familiar with the sea"). נֶהִי (mourning song) occurs only six other times (Jer. 9:9 [10], 17 [18], 18 [19], 19 [20]; 31:15; Mic. 2:4). For a similar scene of mourning, see Mark 5:38–39.

17. וּבְכָל־כְּרָמִים מִסְפֵּד (and in all the vineyards will be wailing): This colon parallels the first colon of this long octastich: "In all squares will be wailing." כִּי (for) tells why there will be such great lamentation: אֶעֱבֹר בְּקִרְבְּךָ (I will pass through your midst). The idiom here is not עָבַר לְ, as Stuart maintains (*Hosea–Jonah*, p. 350), but עָבַר בְּ. However, the meaning is not to be sought in Leviticus 26:6, where a sword passes through the land. Rather, the meaning is found in Exodus 12:12,

---

16. As the lament draws to a close, the Lord presents a vivid picture of the way the people will lament. There will be wailing in the public square and cries of "woe, woe" in the streets. Even farm laborers will be summoned to leave their work (or perhaps, by reason of the devastation, they will no longer have any proper work) to join in the mourning. The victims are commanded to call out to the professional mourners, "Wailing"—that is, "Wail for us now!" The wailing, cries of "woe," and mourning songs are for the judged and dying nation. Micah had this lament over Judah:

For this I will lament and wail;
  I will go barefoot and naked;
I will make lamentation like the jackals,
  and mourning like the ostriches.
For her wound is incurable.
  It has come to Judah. (Mic. 1:8–9)

A righteous God must judge a sinful people—and a sinful world. But his love is more powerful than death, and we see that love as Jesus passes through the crowd of professional mourners and mockers and imparts life to the dead by the power of God. That same life is ours, through him who died for us.

It is the Lord of hosts who announces the fact that the people will lament, a name that connotes the numerous hosts of heaven. It is a vast array that God governs. The name expresses the power and authority of the God who acts in history, controlling the events that cause the people to mourn. The Lord himself says that he will pass through their midst (v. 17), which illustrates the immanence of God in history. The title *Lord of hosts* depicts his transcendence; the fact that he is in the midst of Israel expresses his presence in human events. In view of this prophetic lesson, let us be holy as he is holy, so that we may have him in our midst and represent him well to a perishing world as ministers of reconciliation (2 Cor. 5:18).

17. This verse is a continuation of the previous and concludes the lament begun at verse 2. The lamentation concludes with a dreadful statement of cause. The people have every reason to lament, because the Lord will soon pass through them, just as he passed through the land of Egypt on the night of the passover. That was a triumphant moment for God's people, for the children of darkness were stricken, but the children of God were spared.

Once again the prophet refers to a symbol of the people's affluence, for he singles out the vineyards

where the Lord says of his impending judgment on Egypt: וְעָבַרְתִּי בְאֶרֶץ־מִצְרַיִם (for I will pass through the land of Egypt). This collocation, coming straight from the passover narrative in Exodus, would have had a chilling effect on those who knew that context, for Yahweh now uses the same phrase to declare that he will now pass through *their* midst. The idea of having the Lord

"in your midst" also stems from the exodus experience, for at that time, as a people set apart (though even then rebellious), they could experience Yahweh "in their midst" (see Exod. 17:7; 34:9; Num. 11:20; 14:14; Deut. 6:15; 7:21; 23:15 [14]; and, negatively, Exod. 33:3; Deut. 31:17). יְהוָה אָמַר (says Yahweh): See the Exegesis of 1:5.

(see the Exposition of v. 11). In the midst of the very thing that represents their rebellion against God, there appears divine judgment. The context

of their misplaced devotion became a stark image of their national doom.

II. Pronouncements of Judgment (3:1–6:14)
D. Announcements of Judgment (5:18–6:14)
1. Warning about the Day of Yahweh (5:18–20)

¹⁸ Woe to you who desire the day of Yah-
weh.
   What good will the day of Yahweh be
   to you?
It will be darkness, and not light.
¹⁹ It will be as if a man fled from a lion
   but a bear met him;
yet he got home,
   and leaned with his hand against the
   wall,
   but a serpent bit him.
²⁰ Will it not be darkness, the day of Yah-
   weh, and not light—
and gloom without brightness to it?

¹⁸ Alas for you who desire the day of the
   Lord!
   Why do you want the day of the
   Lord?
It is darkness, not light;
¹⁹   as if someone fled from a lion,
   and was met by a bear;
or went into the house and rested a hand
   against the wall,
   and was bitten by a snake.
²⁰ Is not the day of the Lord darkness, not
   light,
   and gloom with no brightness in it?

18. הוֹי (woe): See the Exegesis of verse 16. הַמִּתְאַוִּים (you who desire) is taken as a direct address, introducing a woe oracle (see Gerstenberger, "Woe-Oracles of the Prophets"). As such, it addresses those who are to receive judgment. יוֹם יְהוָה (the day of Yahweh) is the great and terrible day of the Lord's coming as a conqueror to establish justice in the earth (see von Rad, "The Day of Yahweh"; and Stuart, "Sovereign's Day of Conquest"). Joel prophesied that day as one of terrible judgment and destruction (Joel 1:15–18; 2:11), although it would entail also a redemptive outpouring of the Lord's Spirit (Joel 3:1–5 [2:28–32]). See also Isaiah 2:12; 13:6–13; Obadiah 15; Zephaniah 1:7, 14. לָמָּה־זֶּה לָכֶם יוֹם יְהוָה (what good will the day of Yahweh be to you? lit. what is this, to you, the day of the Lord?): This translation seems more accurate than "Why would you have . . . ?" (RSV) or "Why do you want . . . ?" (NRSV), for the question does not ask *why* they want that day, but instructs them as to the nature of the day about which they are obviously misled. Essentially the same construction appears in Genesis 27:46, where Rebekah asks, לָמָּה לִּי חַיִּים (what good will my life be to me? lit. for what, to me, life?). For this interpretation see BDB, p. 554. וְלֹא־אוֹר הוּא־חֹשֶׁךְ (it will be darkness, and not light) may recall the affirmation in verse 8 that the Lord

"turns black darkness to morning" as an attribute of his almighty power. Darkness and light appear in contrast, signifying good or disaster, here and in, for example, Isaiah 5:30; 9:1 [2]; 59:9; Jeremiah 13:16; Lamentations 3:2.

19. הָאֲרִי (the lion) once frequented Palestine. הַדֹּב (the bear) appears along with הָאֲרִי in David's boast that he could rescue his father's sheep from a lion or a bear (1 Sam. 17:34–37). Both animals appear in Lamentations 3:10, and Hosea 13:7–8 applies similar terminology to the Lord. וּבָא הַבַּיִת (yet he got home; lit. yet or and he came [in]to the house): The subject of the verb is the same individual who encountered the lion and the bear and has now managed to make it home. וְסָמַךְ יָדוֹ (and leaned with his hand): יָד (hand) is an adverbial accusative, telling *how* the individual leaned. הַנָּחָשׁ וּנְשָׁכוֹ (but a [lit. the] serpent bit him): The pattern of this verse is intensely ironic and expresses the unavoidability of disaster. Isaiah uses the same technique (Isa. 24:17–18).

20. הֲלֹא (will it not) introduces a question expecting an affirmative answer (BDB, p. 520). This verse in effect repeats, in an emphatic interrogative, the statement of verse 18. In that verse we read, "The day of Yahweh . . . will be darkness, and not light." Now we read, "Will it not be darkness, the day of Yahweh, and not light?" For the

---

18. This is the first verse of a warning (vv. 18–20) about the day of the Lord. The verse also begins a new woe oracle (vv. 18–27) subsequent to the lament of verses 1–17. This woe oracle begins in an unexpected way, addressing those who have desired the day of the Lord. With a false confidence, they assumed that the Lord was on their side and would establish them at his coming. This is an insight into the popular view of the day of the Lord. Evidently the people of Amos's time viewed the day of the Lord only as a time when he vindicates his people and punishes evildoers. Since many of the people of Amos's day believed themselves exempt from God's wrath (9:10), they apparently saw this time of divine intervention as a time of hope and deliverance. Amos corrects their erroneous theology in the vivid simile that follows in verse 19.

What good will the day of the Lord do them, the prophet asks. It will not be a redemptive day, as they might have hoped, but a day of reckoning. The sovereign Lord, who daily darkens day into night, will turn their day into darkness. Only later would the same Lord come with a greater salvation than they could ever dream:

The people who walked in darkness
  have seen a great light;
those who lived in a land of deep darkness—
  on them light has shined. (Isa. 9:2)

19. By depicting the utter unavoidability of disaster, this verse describes the darkness that the day of the Lord (v. 18) will entail. The simile Amos uses is highly emotional. We ourselves feel the relief that Amos's hypothetical person felt at escaping from the lion and the bear. Leaning breathlessly against the wall at home, the relieved individual feels secure; no harm can come here. But a serpent that has crawled into a crevice in the wall lurks near one arm, and then strikes. The people may feel secure in Zion, believing in their "temple theology," but God will reach them even in the city where he chose to put his name. Let the church today be prophetic, as the day of the Lord draws near. Let our gospel be whole: the good news of salvation from coming judgment. Then we shall be faithful sentinels (Ezek. 3:16–21; 33:1–9). Then we shall be true ministers of reconciliation.

20. After a simile that explains how terrible the day of the Lord will be, Amos reiterates the sub-

pair darkness / light, see the Exegesis of verse 18. וְאֹפֶל (and gloom) is a *hapax legomenon*. A feminine cognate (אֲפֵלָה) with the sense of gloom appears in the original covenant literature as a curse to be expected for disobedience (Deut. 28:29: "You shall grope about at noon as blind people grope in darkness"). For gloom as an aspect of judgment and the day of the Lord, see Isaiah 8:22

and Joel 2:2 ("a day of darkness and gloom"). לֹו וְלֹא־נֹגַהּ (without brightness to it) balances וְלֹא־אֹור (and not light) as וְאֹפֶל (and gloom) balances חֹשֶׁךְ (darkness). This symmetrical balance of line, so typical of Semitic poetry, sets forth the gloomy prospect of the day of the Lord in phraseology that is at once insistent and starkly beautiful.

---

stance of verse 18 in the form of a question. "Will it not be darkness, the day of the LORD, and not light?" The question expects the answer "yes." It will indeed be a day of darkness and gloom, with no brightness in it. As there has been no brightness of righteousness in the people, so the Lord's redemptive brightness will not dawn on them. As they have loved the ways of darkness, a day of darkness and gloom will descend upon them. Isaiah prophesied a glorious future for Zion:

Arise, shine; for your light has come,
  and the glory of the LORD has risen upon
  you.

For darkness shall cover the earth,
  and thick darkness the peoples;
but the LORD will arise upon you,
  and his glory will appear over you.
Nations shall come to your light,
  and kings to the brightness of your
  dawn. (Isa. 60:1–3)

But it was to be otherwise for the deceived sinners of the north. We, too, who live in a generation that loves darkness, should heed the warning of Amos and walk as children of light.

II. Pronouncements of Judgment (3:1–6:14)
D. Announcements of Judgment (5:18–6:14)
2. Indictment and Judgment of False Religiosity and Idolatry (5:21–27)

21 "I reject with utter hatred your feasts,
  and I do not take pleasure in your solemn assemblies.
22 For though you offer up burnt offerings,
  I will neither accept your grain offerings,
  nor regard your peace offerings of fattened cattle.
23 Take away from me the din of your songs,
  that I may not hear the music of your lyres.
24 But let justice roll on like the waters,
  and righteousness like an ever-flowing wadi.
25 Did you bring sacrifices and grain offerings to me
  in the wilderness for forty years, O house of Israel?
26 But you have carried around Sakkuth your king
  and Kaiwan—your images—
  the star of your gods,
  which you fashioned for yourselves.
27 I will exile you beyond Damascus,"
  says Yahweh—God of hosts is his name.

21 I hate, I despise your festivals,
  and I take no delight in your solemn assemblies.
22 Even though you offer me your burnt offerings and grain offerings,
  I will not accept them;
  and the offerings of well-being of your fatted animals
  I will not look upon.
23 Take away from me the noise of your songs;
  I will not listen to the melody of your harps.
24 But let justice roll down like waters,
  and righteousness like an everflowing stream.
25 Did you bring to me sacrifices and offerings the forty years in the wilderness, O house of Israel? 26You shall take up Sakkuth your king, and Kaiwan your star-god, your images, which you made for yourselves; 27therefore I will take you into exile beyond Damascus, says the Lord, whose name is the God of hosts.

21. שָׂנֵאתִי מָאַסְתִּי (I reject with utter hatred; lit. I hate, I reject): These verbs form a hendiadys, compounding the Lord's indignant rejection of their religious festivals. For מָאַס (reject), see the Exegesis of 2:4. חַגֵּיכֶם (your feasts) does not connote feasts in general, but the three major feasts designated by this term: the feast of unleavened bread, the feast of weeks, and the feast of booths (Exod. 23:14–17; 34:22–25; Deut. 16:9–17). The term also indicates the pilgrimages to such feasts. Note the Arabic cognate, *haj*, which is the term used today for the pilgrimage to Mecca. וְלֹא אָרִיחַ בְּ (and I do not take pleasure in): אָרִיחַ (take pleasure) has as its basic sense *to smell*. The term comes from the realm of burnt offering, and alludes to רֵיחַ נִיחֹוחַ (smell of sweet savor or pleasing aroma) that ascended from the burning sacrifice. עַצְּרֹתֵיכֶם (your solemn assemblies) appears here in parallel with חַגִּים (feasts). It designates the three major annual gatherings (Lev. 23:36; Num. 29:35; Deut. 16:8), and can even designate an assembly in honor of Baal (2 Kings 10:20). For a sentiment similar to the present context, see Isaiah 1:13.

22. כִּי אִם (for though) introduces a tricolon in which the protasis implicitly applies to the apodosis (the two subsequent cola) as well (i.e., *though* they make grain or peace offerings, he will not accept them either). תַּעֲלוּ־לִי עֹלֹות (you offer up burnt offerings): עֹלֹות (burnt offerings) is a cognate accusative with the verb עָלָה (תַּעֲלוּ). It is commonly used of the whole burnt offering (e.g., Gen. 8:20; Exod. 32:6; Lev. 14:20; Deut. 12:13–14). For the law of the burnt offering, see Leviticus 1. מִנְחֹתֵיכֶם (your grain offerings) has *gift* as its basic connotation. It refers, for example, to Jacob's gift of domesticated animals to his brother Esau (Gen. 32:14–16 [13–15]), as well as to Israel's gift to his son Joseph (Gen. 43:11). When it refers to sacrifices it views them as gifts offered to God (e.g., Gen. 4:3–5; Num. 16:15; 1 Sam. 2:17, 29). Specifically, it connotes grain or cereal offerings (e.g., Exod. 29:41; Lev. 2:1; Num. 4:16). For the law of the grain offering, see Leviticus 2. לֹא אֶרְצֶה (I will not accept): Basic to the sense of רָצָה is the idea of pleasing. The context here informs the word with an idea akin to favorable response. God will not look favorably on their sacrifices or regard them as pleasing gifts. וְשֶׁלֶם (your peace offerings): שֶׁלֶם occurs only here in the singular. It denotes what is called the peace offering (RSV), the fellowship offer-

---

21. Here, as in 4:4–5, the Lord affirms that, because their hearts have turned from him and they use religion only as a mechanical means of pleasing (or appeasing) their God, he has no interest in the people's attachment to the cultic system that he himself instituted. The Lord is interested in their hearts, not in their sacrifices. Isaiah conveyed a similar sentiment to Judah and Jerusalem when he declared:

Bringing offerings is futile;
  incense is an abomination to me.
New moon and sabbath and calling of convocation—
  I cannot endure solemn assemblies with iniquity.
Your new moons and your appointed festivals
  my soul hates. (Isa. 1:13–14)

How much does the church today need to learn this lesson? How many attend "solemn assemblies," falsely believing that their ritual attendance pleases God? But now, as then, God desires not our attendance, not even our pilgrimages, but ourselves.

22. The Lord has stated that he "rejects with utter hatred" (v. 21) Israel's religious observances. Now he expresses this thought in a concise protasis-apodosis structure. He tells them that, if they offer whole burnt offerings, grain offerings, or offerings of well-being, he will not take pleasure in them or even regard them. These offerings were important aspects of Israel's levitical heritage. Why would the prophet represent the Lord as rejecting his own institutions? The reason is that these offerings had become ends in themselves. The offerers had rejected the heart of the law, which was love for one's neighbor (Matt. 22:37). By observing religious rituals they were lulled into thinking that they were fulfilling the whole law and giving God his rightful due.

The presence of the poor and oppressed, however, witnessed to their failure to please God. The neglected widow and the poor child in dirty rags were theological statements condemning the attitudes of the oppressors. Amos viewed the sacrifices as objects of God's hatred because they furthered the spiritual ignorance of the people by giving them a false sense of security.

The burnt offering was the most frequently offered sacrifice. It involved the sprinkling of blood, after which the pieces of the animal were burned. The grain offering accompanied the animal sacrifices. One handful was burned and the priest kept the rest. The offering of well-being (or

ing (NIV), or the sacrifice of well-being (NRSV). This type of sacrifice involved a communion meal in which a sacrificial animal was eaten (e.g., Exod. 20:24; 24:5). For the law of the peace offering, see Leviticus 3. Burnt offerings and peace offerings occur often together, as in Leviticus 9:22; Judges 20:26; 21:4; 1 Samuel 13:9; 1 Kings 9:25; and elsewhere. מְרִיאֵיכֶם (lit. your fattened calves) together with שֶׁלֶם denotes the peace offerings of your well-fed calves.

23. הָסֵר מֵעָלַי (take away from me; lit. from upon me): The singular imperative הָסֵר represents a shift from the plural forms that have characterized the Lord's general address to Israel to this point. Such shifts, however, are consistent with shifts in person and number in the ancient Near East, in both prose and poetry. For the issue as it relates to second-millennium Hittite treaties and Deuteronomy, see Baltzer, *Das Bundesformular* (and the review by Moran) and Sperber, "Der Personenwechsel in der Bibel." מֵעָלַי (from me): The Lord commands the people to take away the din of their songs. Their souless worship is thus represented as a burden to the Lord (as in Isa. 1:14, "Your new moons and your appointed festivals . . . have become a burden to me"). הֲמוֹן שִׁרֶיךָ (the din of your songs) also appears in Ezekiel 26:13 in a prophecy against Tyre. הֲמוֹן (din) has a broad semantic range. It describes the sound of falling rain (1 Kings 18:41) as well as the roar of a crowd (1 Sam. 14:19). The context here describes the people's songs, not in terms of their melody, but

the noise they create. זִמְרַת נְבָלֶיךָ (the music of your lyres): These words appear together in Psalm 81:3 [2]: "Begin the music, strike the tambourine, / play the melodious harp and lyre" (NIV). Music was an important part of Israelite worship, but it became something that God detested. לֹא אֶשְׁמָע (that I may not hear) should be understood modally with a sense of purpose, following the initial imperative, "take away" (GKC §107q). For the phraseology of the verse, see Ezekiel 26:13, where the verb occurs in the niphal. The Lord's promise that he will not "regard" (v. 22) or "hear" (v. 23) their sacrifices and worship may have Deuteronomy 31:17–18 and 32:20 as its background.

24. וְיִגַּל (but let . . . roll on) is from גלל (roll, roll along), not גלה (uncover), as interpreted by the Targum and Jerome (*et revelabitur* = וְיִגָּל). For the parallelism of מִשְׁפָּט (justice) and צְדָקָה (righteousness), see the Exegesis of verse 7. כְּנַחַל (like a wadi): The English word *stream* (NRSV) hardly captures the idea. A wadi in the Middle East is a narrow valley, often a deep channel, through which rapid torrents of water gush during the rainy season, but which may have only a trickle of water or be completely dry in the summer. אֵיתָן (ever-flowing) is an elative form (see Moscati, *Comparative Grammar of the Semitic Languages*, p. 80, §12.14) from the root יתן, which in Arabic has the sense of *be perpetual* or *never failing* (BDB, p. 450), and which in Ugaritic is the equivalent of Hebrew נתן (to give; Gordon, *Ugaritic Textbook*, p. 416, no. 1169); hence, the nuance *ever-giving* or *renewing*.

---

peace offering) was a communal offering. It required animal sacrifice and was followed by a communal meal.

23. Israel has worshiped the Lord with ritual punctiliousness, even to excess (4:4–5), but he has rejected their feast days and solemn assemblies (v. 21). He rejected their burnt offerings, grain offerings, and offerings of well-being (v. 22), and now he rejects their songs and the music of their lyres. The former he describes, devastatingly, as a "din," the sort of noise made by torrential waters or the thundering wheels of an army's chariots. The rejection here is like the one that the Lord later pronounced upon pagan Tyre in Ezekiel 26:13: "I will put an end to your noisy songs, and the music of your harps will be heard no more" (NIV).

Like a pagan nation, Israel had grown prosperous and felt herself secure. But she paid no attention to the one who provided her prosperity and security. Unlike a pagan nation, she should have known the one that was the source of all her good.

She worshiped him formally, but her heart was far from him. And now he is exposing her empty worship for what it is, before he comes in judgment.

24. The Lord states his desire here again (see vv. 14–15) so that there may be no doubt. He does not desire religious assemblies or rituals, he does not desire sacrifices or skilled musicianship. He wants worship in spirit and in truth. True worshipers of the Lord, who do worship in spirit and in truth, will bear the true fruit of the Spirit in their private lives and in their public conduct. In their society, justice will flow like healing waters (Ezek. 47:1–12), and righteousness like a perennial wadi.

Once again the prophet speaks of justice (see the Exegesis and Exposition of v. 15). He pictures it as rolling on like an abundant, never-ending stream. While desert wadis could dry up in the heat of summer, Amos pictures one that does not. The wadi of his analogy does not cease to supply water to the parched wilderness. In his day the wadi of justice was barely a trickle or had dried up

The identical phrase occurs in Deuteronomy 21:4. For its use as a substantive, see Exodus 14:27: "Moses stretched out his hand over the sea, and at dawn the sea returned to its normal depth [אֵיתָנוֹ]" (cf. Ps. 74:15: "ever-flowing streams").

25. הֲ (did . . .): The interrogative particle clearly introduces a rhetorical question, the expected answer being "no" (GKC §150d). זְבָחִים (sacrifices): See the Exegesis of 4:4. מִנְחָה (grain offerings): See the Exegesis of verse 22. הִגַּשְׁתֶּם־לִי (you bring . . . to me): This verb occurs together with ל in Malachi 2:12, where it describes the act of bringing a grain offering (cf. Mal. 3:3). The emphasis of the colon is not on לִי (to me) but on the words זְבָחִים וּמִנְחָה (sacrifices and grain offerings). Such had in fact been brought to the Lord during the wilderness wanderings; see Exodus 18:12 (sacrifices brought by Jethro) and Leviticus 9:8–24 (sin offerings, burnt offering, sacrifices of well-being, and grain offering administered by Aaron). The point of the rhetorical question, however, is not to establish, that such had *never* been brought. Rather, it is to emphasize that sacrifices and grain offerings alone are not of primary importance to the Lord. For essentially the same thought, see Jeremiah 7:22–23. In fact the sacrificial system was preplanned for a settled condition, that is, after the conquest, when agriculture and animal husbandry would provide the elements of the sacrifices (Exod. 34:23–24; Num. 15:2–5; Deut. 18:1–5; see also Craigie, *Deuteronomy*, p. 218). For מִדְבָּר (the wilderness) and אַרְבָּעִים שָׁנָה (forty years), see the Exegesis of 2:10. בֵּית יִשְׂרָאֵל (house of Israel): See the Exegesis of verse 1.

26. וּנְשָׂאתֶם (but you have carried around): Context requires an adversative sense for וְ. The tense is perfect, but not converted (NRSV). This is something the Israelites *have done*. It may be, as Stuart suggests, that they carried the gods (idols) around atop standards (*Hosea–Jonah*, p. 355; see also *ANEP*, figs. 305, 535; see the Exposition). סִכּוּת (Sakkuth; instead of the MT's *sikkuth*) is misunderstood by the Septuagint as σκηνὴν (tent or tabernacle) and by the Vulgate as *tabernaculum*. Sakkuth was a name of Adar, Assyrian god of war and the chase. מַלְכְּכֶם (your king) is misunderstood by the Septuagint as Μολὸχ (Molech). Sakkuth is called a king because the name *Sakkuth* means "king of decision," that is, "chief arbiter" in war. כִּיּוּן (Kaiwan): The Septuagint's Ῥαιφάν is apparently a corruption of the Hebrew; it is further corrupted in the quotation in Acts 7:43 (Ῥεμφάν). The

---

altogether. He calls for the people to turn to God in revival. If they had, they would have found the blessings the law promised coming to them in national health and spiritual refreshment.

25. The spirit of this rhetorical question is much like that later posed by Jeremiah in 7:21–23: "This is what the LORD Almighty, the God of Israel, says: Go ahead, add your burnt offerings to your other sacrifices and eat the meat yourselves! For when I brought your forefathers out of Egypt and spoke to them, I did not just give them commands about burnt offerings and sacrifices, but I gave them this command: Obey me, and I will be your God and you will be my people. Walk in all the ways I command you, that it may go well with you" (NIV). The point in both passages is the same. The Lord is not saying that he did not give them commands regarding burnt offerings, sacrifices, and grain offerings; rather, his chief concern is the proper observance of these rites. His desire is that his people should love him with all of their heart, soul, and strength (Deut. 6:5) and live in obedience to him because they love him. Instead, they have loved his religious system (Amos 4:5).

The people had placed ritual over heart obedience. When God called them out of Egypt, his chief concern was that they follow him in humble obedience. The words to which Jeremiah refers reflect the giving of the law at Sinai (Exod. 19:5). The Lord said, "Obey me." The people in Amos's day had elevated the ritual of the law above its primary concern, which was obedience to God in all areas of life, not just religious ritual observances.

Today, there are those who are more in love with the church than with Christ, people who are more preoccupied with choir robes and candle holders than with an encounter with the living God. Can we imagine that the God who is the same yesterday, today, and forever will wink at this misdirected love? Let God's people learn from their history, and let us return to our first love.

26. The Lord knows what his people have done and he is not pleased. They have not only missed the point of the previous verse, namely, that he wants worship from the inner person and not mere external ritual. They have even gone in the other direction. They have not only preferred external ritual; they have made physical, tangible idols so that they might worship a visible thing. Such worship is not only absurd, it actually has terrible spiritual consequences. The people of Israel could not know then what we know now:

Assyrian equivalent is *ka-ai-va-nu*, the name of Saturn; Syriac, *Keʾwān*; Arabic, *Kaiwan*. צַלְמֵיכֶם (your images): The term applies to idols both in the Old Testament (e.g., Num. 33:52; 2 Kings 11:18; Ezek. 7:20) and in Mesopotamian inscriptions (e.g., *CAD*, vol. 16 [Ṣ], pp. 78–85). The word is plural, hence it cannot be taken with Kaiwan alone. The antecedents here are both Sakkuth and Kaiwan. כּוֹכַב אֱלֹהֵיכֶם (the star of your gods): The phrasing is awkward, but the antecedent is Kaiwan, that is, Saturn. אֲשֶׁר עֲשִׂיתֶם לָכֶם (which you fashioned for yourselves): Old Testament polemic against idolatry often emphasizes the human-made nature of idols, and hence the absurdity of worshiping these merely human productions (Isa. 41:21–24; 44:12–20; Jer. 10:1–16). But such worship is not only silly, for both Testaments make it clear that to worship such idols is to worship demons (Deut. 32:16–17; 1 Cor. 10:20). Worse still, to worship demons means to take on their characteristics (see the Exposition).

27. וְהִגְלֵיתִי אֶתְכֶם (I will exile you) is a converted perfect announcing the punishment that will follow as a result of the sins already mentioned in the oracle. For the identical phrasing (but with unconverted perfect), see Jeremiah 29:7, 14. לְדַמֶּשֶׂק מֵהָלְאָה (beyond Damascus): הָלְאָה (beyond) appears elsewhere in both a temporal sense (e.g., Lev. 22:27; Num. 15:23; 1 Sam. 18:9; Isa. 18:2, 7; Ezek. 39:22; 43:27) and a spatial sense (Gen. 19:9; 35:21; Num. 17:2 [16:37]; 32:19; 1 Sam. 10:3; 20:22, 37; Jer. 22:19). It has the latter sense here. דַמֶּשֶׂק (Damascus): See the Exegesis of 1:3. For anyone in Amos's day, exile beyond Damascus would have implied exile to Assyria in the northeast. This occurred just ten years later, in 722, when Shalmaneser III captured Samaria and deported the Israelites to Assyria (2 Kings 17:3–6). Exile far from home was one of the original covenantal curses (Deut. 28:36, 64–68; 29:27 [28]). אָמַר יְהוָה (says Yahweh): See the Exegesis of 1:5. אֱלֹהֵי־צְבָאוֹת (God of hosts): See the Exegesis of 3:13.

---

just as we, who open up to God's love in Jesus Christ, receive thereby his Spirit dwelling in us and remaking us into his likeness, so those who worship idols open themselves up to receive the spirits of what they worship and so are transformed into their likeness: "Those who make them . . . shall become like them" (Ps. 135:18). This truth, made polemically and ironically in Psalm 135, is manifestly true today in the subtler forms of idolatry—be the "idol" one of lust, deception, selfishness, political ideology, or whatever. Anyone who sins habitually by elevating any sinful desire or attitude above the Lord, and hence idolizing it, invites Satan's influence.

It was a regular practice in the ancient Near East to carry "gods" (idols) around. A text from Uruk describes gods being carried from their chambers in the temple to a central court, where meat was set before them on a gold platter, and then removed, possibly to be eaten later by the king (Oppenheim, *Ancient Mesopotamia*, p. 193; cf. pp. 188–89). The Assyrian king Esarhaddon had his gods carried out to the hunt. Indeed, the gods were carried about in processions in both the temple and the city, and in many respects paralleled the king in his processions, activities, and even, in extant reliefs, in his dress (Oppenheim, *Ancient Mesopotamia*, pp. 184–87). Consequently, the idea is not that the Israelites will carry their gods with them into exile (which would connect this verse with the next), for a conquering enemy would do that. Indeed, it was a regular practice for the conqueror to carry off the gods or idols of the vanquished as evidence that their own gods had conquered and captured the gods of the foe. The practice is well attested in Assyria by the stock phrase *I took their gods* (*CAD*, vol. 7 [I/J], p. 102; Cogan, *Imperialism and Religion*, pp. 22–41, 119–21). Rather, the Israelites themselves have carried the idols around on various occasions, as was common ancient practice.

27. The Lord does not threaten idly, and all that he decrees shall come to pass. So he now promises exile "beyond Damascus," which to an Israelite would have clearly implied captivity by Assyria. Ten years later, this tragedy came to pass. So today, we live in a world that has broken its creation covenant with God. Idolatry of every kind is rife. And the same Lord has promised to return in judgment (Matt. 25:31–45). Let God's people consider how to lead "lives of holiness and godliness, waiting for and hastening the coming of the day of God" (2 Pet. 3:11–12).

II. Pronouncements of Judgment (3:1–6:14)
D. Announcements of Judgment (5:18–6:14)
3. Woe Oracle Against Israel's Complacency (6:1–7)

6 "Woe to those who are at ease in Zion,
 and to those who are confident on
  Mount Samaria—
to the distinguished men of the "first of
 the nations,"
to whom the house of Israel comes.
² Cross over to Calneh, and see,
 and go from there to Great Hamath,
 and go down to Gath of the Philistines.
Are you better than these kingdoms,
 or is their territory larger than your
  territory?
³ You who thrust away the evil day,
 and bring near a reign of violence.
⁴ Who lie upon divans inlaid with ivory,
 and are sprawled out on their couches;
 and eat the pick of the flock,
  and calves from the fattening stall.
⁵ Who sing frivolous songs to the sound of
 the lyre—
 like David they invent for themselves
  musical instruments.
⁶ Who drink from basins of wine
 and with first-class oils they anoint
  themselves,
 but they do not grieve over the ruin of
  Joseph.
⁷ Therefore, now,
 they will go into exile as the first of
  the exiles,
 and the loud partying of those who
  are sprawled out will pass away."

6 Alas for those who are at ease in Zion,
 and for those who feel secure on
  Mount Samaria,
the notables of the first of the nations,
 to whom the house of Israel resorts!
² Cross over to Calneh, and see;
 from there go to Hamath the great;
 then go down to Gath of the Philistines.
Are you better than these kingdoms?
 Or is your territory greater than their
  territory,
³ O you that put far away the evil day,
 and bring near a reign of violence?
⁴ Alas for those who lie on beds of ivory,
 and lounge on their couches,
and eat lambs from the flock,
 and calves from the stall;
⁵ who sing idle songs to the sound of the
 harp,
 and like David improvise on instruments of music;
⁶ who drink wine from bowls,
 and anoint themselves with the fin-
  est oils,
 but are not grieved over the ruin of Joseph!
⁷ Therefore they shall now be the first to
 go into exile,
 and the revelry of the loungers shall
  pass away.
 from the entrance of Hamath to the
  Wadi of the Arabah."

6:1. הוֹי (woe): See the Exegesis of 5:16. הַשַּׁאֲנַנִּים (those who are at ease): This is the first of a series of participles that introduce each category under condemnation in this oracle. This verb generally has a bad connotation (as in Isa. 32:9), but not always (Isa. 32:18; 33:20). בְּצִיּוֹן (in Zion): See the Exegesis of 1:2. וְהַבֹּטְחִים (those who are confident) has the connotation of false confidence, as it does in Isaiah 32:9, 11, where it and הַשַּׁאֲנַנִּים appear in parallel. הַר שֹׁמְרוֹן (Mount Samaria): See the Exegesis of 3:9. Like his contemporaries (i.e., Isa. 9:7–20 [8–21]; Hos. 6:11; Mic. 1:3–16), Amos received a prophecy that addressed both kingdoms (see 2:4–5). Perhaps Amos mentions Zion first in order to dispense with it and move on to the major address to Israel, as in 2:6–16. נְקֻבֵי (the distinguished men): נקב means to pierce. It also connotes the related verbal sense of designate, as in Genesis 30:28 where it refers to designating one's wages (BDB, p. 666). The word occurs in the niphal in Numbers 1:17 to refer to men who were נִקְּבוּ בְּשֵׁמוֹת (designated by name). It also describes leaders in worship (1 Chron. 16:41), as well as those designated to distribute freewill offerings to rural and small-town priests (2 Chron. 31:19) or to assist the Levites in the temple (Ezra 8:20). Here it indicates people of privilege and rank, who might judge

cases brought to them. The subsequent phrase indicates that the people came to these notables for various reasons, thus they must have held positions of influence. רֵאשִׁית הַגּוֹיִם (the first of the nations) occurs also in Numbers 24:20 (of Amalek). Israel, thanks to the efforts of Jeroboam II, had subdued Syria and recovered territory, including Hamath (2 Kings 14:23–29; see Amos 6:2). She had become powerful and prosperous and might well fancy herself "the first of the nations." לָהֶם וּבָאוּ (to whom . . . comes; lit. and they come to them): That is, people (the house of Israel) come to the distinguished rulers for help or judicial decisions. בֵּית יִשְׂרָאֵל (house of Israel): See the Exegesis of 5:1.

2. כַּלְנֵה (to Calneh): The identification of this city is uncertain. Calneh appears in Genesis 10:10, as one of four important Babylonian cities that were centers of the kingdom of Nimrod (Babel, Erech, and Accad are the others—note, however, that the NRSV translates כַּלְנֵה as "all of them," not as a proper name). Perhaps it is identical to Calno, which is mentioned in Isaiah 10:9 as recently conquered by Assyria. Sargon II mentions a Kulunu as one of his conquests in 710 B.C. (the name appears as Zirlaba or Zarilab, but can also be read as Kulunu; see Driver, *Joel and Amos*, p.

6:1. A second woe oracle begins here, this time addressed to both Zion and Samaria. Like other prophets of his time, Amos was inspired by God to speak words of warning and judgment against both kingdoms. Both kingdoms were going astray from the way of the Lord and engaging in idolatry and social injustice. The ease that the inhabitants of Samaria enjoy is fleeting and their confidence is false. Isaiah warned the inhabitants of Zion in a similar way in 32:9–15.

This binary structure balances "those who are at ease" with "those who are confident." The B line informs the "ease" of the A line with a sense of relaxed security. These people were secure in their homes—confident that no great harm would come to the nation.

Amos blasts their false confidence by pronouncing another woe oracle. He tries to impress on them the fact that those who trust in themselves or in their position of worldly security trust in vain. There is only one sure ground of confidence, as the psalmist declared, "O LORD of hosts, / happy is everyone who trusts in you" (Ps. 84:13 [12]). The distinguished of Israel had a false confidence about being the elite of the "first of the nations." If, however, they had only considered, they would

have remembered Balaam's oracle against Amalek: "First among the nations was Amalek, / but its end is to perish forever" (Num. 24:20).

Amos says that the people came to those distinguished leaders. How ironic! They came for counsel and direction to those who counseled peace. The parallel structure relates "distinguished men" with "those who are at ease" and "those who are confident." The people probably shared the confidence of their leaders that God would not let his people suffer great harm. Amos, however, had the right counsel: "Woe!"

2. This verse surveys other cities, ranging all the way from Mesopotamia in the east, through Syria, to Philistia in the west. It then poses the question, to both Zion and Samaria: "Are you better than these kingdoms?" The question has two answers, for in a material sense they were better. In another and far more important sense, however, the answer to the question was "no." The irony of the question would have been apparent to all who heard it, for the outward comparison with other kingdoms invited a positive response. The prophet, however, uses the interrogative, and the context, which reinforces it, demands a negative answer. Although Zion and Samaria should have

196). Tiglath-pileser III mentions a Kullani that he conquered, probably in northern Syria, in 738 B.C. (Rost, *Die Keilschrifttexte Tiglat-Pilesers III.*, pp. 20–21, line 125; see *ANET*, p. 282). This latter might be the present-day Kullanhou, near Tel Arpad (note that Arpad and Calno are mentioned together in Isa. 10:9). חֲמַת רַבָּה (Great Hamath) is so designated to distinguish it from "Little Hamath"—a common practice in the ancient Near East, for example, Great Sidon and Little Sidon (see *ANET*, p. 287). Hamath was located on the Orontes River in upper Syria, about 150 miles north of Dan. It was to be the northern boundary of Israel according to Numbers 34:8, Joshua 13:5, and 2 Kings 14:25 (cf. Amos 6:14). The Lord left Hivites there to test Israel (Judg. 3:3). Hamath had its own king in David's day (King Toi or Tou, 2 Sam. 8:9–10). But it was restored to Israel by Jeroboam II (2 Kings 14:23–28). It later came under Assyrian control (implied in 2 Kings 18:34), being defeated on successive occasions by Shalmaneser III in 854 B.C. (*ANET*, pp. 277–80), Tiglath-pileser III in 740 B.C. (Rost, *Die Keilschrifttexte Tiglat-Pilesers III.*, pp. 22–23, line 131; see *ANET*, p. 283), and Sargon II in 720 B.C. (Winckler, *Die Keilschrifttexte Sargons*, vol. 1, pp. 103–5; see *ANET*, p. 285). Babylon subsequently ruled it (Jer. 39:5). Much later, Antiochus Epiphanes (ca. 175–164 B.C.) ruled it and renamed it Epiphaneia after himself. It still exists today, as Hama, with a largely Muslim population. וּרְדוּ (and go down): A traveler from the highlands of central Palestine would have to descend to the coast, where the Philistine cities, including Gath, were situated (compare the phrases *go up from Egypt* and *bring up out of Egypt;* see the Exegesis of 2:10). גַּת־פְּלִשְׁתִּים (Gath of the Philistines) was one of the pentapolis of Philistine royal cities (see the Exegesis of 1:6). It is omitted in the list of Philistine cities in 1:6–8 (see also Zeph. 2:4–5; Zech. 9:5–6), probably because it was under Judah's control in Amos's day. Its location is uncertain, but it lay on the border between Judah and Philistia, between Socoh and Ekron (1 Sam. 17:1, 52). It may perhaps be found in Tell eş-Şâfi, on a hill at the foot of Judah's mountains, about ten miles east of Ashdod and eleven miles southeast of Ekron. הַטוֹבִים מִן (are you better than): הַ is interrogative, implying a negative answer (BDB, pp. 209–10). מִן (than), here and in the following colon, is comparative: larger than. The referents are obviously Israel and Judah (or, more precisely, Zion and Samaria, v. 1), but whether the phrase should be interpreted as second or third person (i.e., "are you better?" or "are they [Zion and Samaria] better?") is uncertain. The interpretation that refers טוֹבִים to the other kingdoms disrupts the poetic structure and makes for a difficult interpretation, with which, for example, Smith (*Twelve Prophets*, p. 179, n. 4) wrestles in vain, concluding that the verse is a contradictory insertion. Since the preceding verse is a direct command, it seems more natural to see a continuing

---

been better than the other kingdoms because of God's favor, they had in fact become like the nations around them and were thus liable to the same judgments that would befall them. Indeed, the same instrument of judgment that brought many of these nations down would be the instrument that would put an end to Israel.

The structure of the bicolon is implicitly chiastic, with considerable rhetorical impact as a result:

a	b	c
are you	better than	these kingdoms
c′	b′	a′
or is their territory	larger than	your territory?

Dating of the oracle cannot be precise, but it is unnecessary to suppose that it is a late eighth-century insertion into the text (Wellhausen, *Skizzen und Vorarbeiten*, p. 84). The point is not that

"these kingdoms have fallen to Assyria, so how can you, Zion and Samaria, hope to fare better?"— for they had not yet fallen to Assyria in Amos's day. Rather, the comparison is ironic. To understand this, we must understand the final bicolon, taking the last colon first. The last colon asks, "Is their territory greater than your territory?" The answer is "no," for none of these cities commanded territories greater than those commanded by Zion and Samaria. Now we can understand the question posed by the first colon: "Are you better than these kingdoms?" The obvious answer, at least in a material sense, is "yes." The whole verse, in other words, is set up to remind Zion and Samaria of their advantages: they are bigger and (materially at least) better than these others. And yet there is a deep irony. For the interrogative implies a negative answer—and the answer, sadly, must be negative, when it comes to what really matters. For Zion and Samaria *should* be better in a moral sense, since they alone, of all the king-

second-person address here. הַמַּמְלָכוֹת הָאֵלֶּה (these kingdoms), that is, those just mentioned by cities: Calneh, Great Hamath, and Gath of the Philistines. אִם (or) introduces the second clause of this double question (GKC §150h). It is not clear that אִם imparts greater emphasis to the second clause, or that the restatement of the idea in different words in the second clause is emphatic. Both clauses set forth the idea from different perspectives. גְּבוּלָם (their territory) has the basic sense of border or boundary, hence, the territory contained within the border or boundary (BDB, pp. 147–48). The same is true of Akkadian *miṣru* (*CAD*, vol. 10 /2 [M], pp. 114–15).

3. הַמְנַדִּים (you who thrust away) continues the second-person masculine plural address begun in verse 2. The verb נדה I (piel) is rare in the Old Testament, occurring otherwise only in Isaiah 66:5, מְנַדֵּיכֶם (your own people who . . . reject you). It reflects Akkadian *nadû* (throw, overthrow) and seems to imply an overthrow or rejection of any divine day of judgment (Dahood, "*Nadâ* 'to Hurl' in Ex 15:16," p. 249, n. 2, understands the verb as "escape from"; Iwry, "New Evidence for Belomancy," p. 34, interprets it as "cast"). יוֹם רָע (the evil day; lit. a day of evil) is a *hapax legomenon* in the singular; the plural, "days of evil," occurs in Psalm 49:6 [5] ("evil days . . . / when wicked deceivers surround me," NIV) and 94:13 ("you [i.e., Yahweh] grant him [i.e., the man Yahweh disciplines] relief from days of trouble / till a pit is dug for the wicked," NIV). The kindred phrase יוֹם רָעָה can likewise indicate a day of evil fortune (Pss. 27:5; 41:2 [1]; Eccles. 7:14) or a day of divine judg-

ment (Jer. 17:17–18; 51:2; Prov. 16:4). Amos uses related phrases elsewhere: "day of battle" and "day of the whirlwind" (1:14), "that day" (2:16; 8:3, 9, 13; positively, 9:11), "the day I punish Israel" (3:14), "the day of the LORD" (5:18, 20), "a bitter day" (8:10). When יוֹם (day) occurs in construct with some quality it functions as a characteristic genitive in which the word יוֹם denotes an indefinite period of time qualified by the accompanying substantive. Here it designates an evil time that is to come on the nation. וַתַּגִּישׁוּן (and [you] bring near): The hiphil verb does not readily have the sense of produce via divination (Stuart, *Hosea–Jonah*, p. 358). The only example of usage that comes close to this meaning is in Isaiah 41:21–22: "Bring your strong ones" (i.e., deities—this is the correct translation of עַצֻּמוֹתֵיכֶם, not "your arguments" [NIV] or "your proofs" [NRSV]; see the discussion in BDB, p. 783); "Let them bring them [their idols], and tell us what is to happen." There is considerable difference in meaning between bringing idols to see if they can foretell the future, and the approach of שֶׁבֶת חָמָס, the "reign of violence" that is the object of נָגַשׁ. There is insufficient evidence that the hiphil of this verb was a technical term used to imply that deities would forecast such a time of violence (see BDB, p. 329, on חָמָס). What the people have overthrown is the idea of the coming day of evil—the day of the Lord—and in its stead they have enthroned violence (see Driver, *Joel and Amos*, p. 197).

4. הַשֹּׁכְבִים (who lie): This is not a reference to sleeping, but to eating in a reclined position, as the last two clauses of the verse make clear. Since

---

doms mentioned, have Yahweh's special revelation. They should be better, but they are not.

3. The participle *hamĕnaddîm* (thrust away) continues the address to the dissolute leaders that began in verse 1. Evidently they were rejecting Amos's prediction of a day of judgment. By doing so they were also discouraging the people from repenting of their disobedience to the covenant standards, and thus they were bringing near the reign of violence. If the people did not heed Amos's call to exercise justice (5:24), they would experience the judgment of which the prophet warned. The longer they put off repentance, the closer they brought the "evil day." It is typical of fallen humans that we don't want to believe in a righteous and holy God. It is also typical that we don't want to believe that such a God will come in righteous indignation to judge the earth. So the Israelites were not unusual in wanting to thrust

far off any idea of an evil day, a terrible day of judgment, that their Lord would bring upon them. But even more so, as the Lord's covenant people, they were reluctant to think that they were offensive in his sight. Yet again, precisely because they were his covenant people they had a revealed standard, his covenant, by which they could have known that they were far from him and ripe for judgment—had they wanted to know him truly and to know their own status before him. But such was not the desire of their hearts. And so today, since the final historical revelation of God in Jesus Christ, people have not been willing to recognize that they are accountable and that a day of evil, the day of the Lord, is coming.

4. The condemnation here is similar to that in 3:12. Some Israelites were living in shameless luxury, while others were oppressed (2:6–7; 3:9–10; 4:1). They lay around on divans inlaid with ivory,

a series of participles with the definite article introduces each category under condemnation in this oracle (see the Exegesis of v. 1), those who "eat" the pick of the flock are simultaneously those who "lie" upon divans. The rebuke here recalls the words of 3:12. מִטּוֹת שֵׁן (divans inlaid with ivory; lit. ivory divans): For a description of these divans of wood inlaid with ivory, see Crowfoot and Crowfoot, *Early Ivories from Samaria*; *ANEP*, figures 125–32. The phrase is a *hapax legomenon*, but compare the "ivory throne" of Solomon (1 Kings 10:18 par. 2 Chron. 9:17). Amos mentions "houses of ivory" in 3:15. Sennacherib boasted that he received "ivory couches" and "great ivory seats" from Hezekiah (Luckenbill, *Annals of Sennacherib*, p. 34, col. 3, lines 43–44). וּסְרֻחִים (and are sprawled out): The root idea of this verb is overrunning or exceeding. Here, it contemptuously describes those who "sprawl" at banquets. וְאֹכְלִים (and eat) does double duty for this colon and the next. The active participle lacks the definite article, which is a clear indication that it does not begin a new category of rebuke, but simply continues the category already being addressed, that is, those who lie on ivory divans and sprawl on their couches. They do these things in a context of dining, as in 3:12. כָּרִים מִצֹּאן (the pick of the flock): כַּר (he-lamb or battering-ram; Akkadian *kirru*) occurs only once in the singular, in a phrase that indicates that it could refer to a lamb of fine quality: "Send the lamb [as tribute] to the ruler of the land" (Isa. 16:1 JB); see also Deuteronomy 32:14: "Fattened lambs and goats, / with choice rams of Bashan" (NIV). This evidence,

along with the present context, indicates a choice lamb on which the wealthy were dining. וַעֲגָלִים מִתּוֹךְ מַרְבֵּק (and calves from the fattening stall; lit. tying place): The fattening stall or tying place was where the calves were kept for fattening. Virtually the same phrase, עֶגְלֵי מַרְבֵּק (calves of the fattening stall), is used in a simile of prosperity in Malachi 3:20 [4:2], and it describes well-fed Egyptian mercenaries in Jeremiah 46:21 (cf. a stall-fed, fattened calf in 1 Sam. 28:24).

5. הַפֹּרְטִים (who sing frivolous songs) is a *hapax legomenon*. In Leviticus 19:10 פֶּרֶט connotes something broken or fallen off. While we cannot be certain of its sense, the context here apparently requires the idea of some frivolous verbal accompaniment to music. עַל־פִּי (to the sound of) literally means "at the mouth of (i.e., at the command of)" something, thus, "according to what a thing dictates" or "according to the measure" of a thing. So here, the words of the songs come forth as the music of the harp dictates—that is, according "to the sound of the lyre." נֵבֶל (lyre): See the Exegesis of 5:23. כְּדָוִיד חָשְׁבוּ (like David they invent): חָשְׁבוּ nowhere else applies to David, and there is no evidence that he invented musical instruments. He did, of course, create many songs (2 Sam. 23:1), and it is tempting to emend כְּלֵי־שִׁיר (musical instruments, as in 2 Chron. 34:12) to כָּל־שִׁיר (all sorts of songs). However, the Hebrew term (כֵּלִים) for musical instruments is well attested elsewhere in relation to musicianship under David's rule (e.g., 1 Chron. 23:5; 2 Chron. 29:26–27; both references perhaps signifying instruments invented by

---

sprawled out in utter abandon on their couches while they dined on the choice animals of the flock. Some of these sleek Israelites have already been addressed ironically as "cows of Bashan" (4:1). Moses prophesied concerning them with similar irony:

> He [the LORD] nursed him [Israel] with hon-
> ey from the crags,
> with oil from flinty rock;
> with curds from the herd, and milk from the
> flock,
> with fat of lambs and rams;
> Bashan bulls and goats. . . .
> Jeshurun grew fat, and kicked.
> You grew fat, bloated, and gorged!
> He abandoned God who made him,
> and scoffed at the Rock of his
> salvation. (Deut. 32:13–15)

In ironic prophecy, the Israelites became like what they ate—sleek and heavy, heavy of understanding, forgetting the Rock and Savior who gave them birth (Deut. 32:18).

5. The privileged classes of Israel were living like kings, and Amos likens them to a king—David, to be exact. They sang at their banquets and composed songs at their feasts. Their songs, however, were of a kind different from David's, for they were frivolous songs. There is irony here, for David made songs for the glory of God, but they made songs to the glory of their feasts. It might be said of them that "their god is their belly" (Phil. 3:19). They were not serving the Lord, but their own appetites. So today a warning from the apostle stands for the church, against people who "do not serve our Lord Christ, but their own appetites" (Rom. 16:18). As in the days of Israel, so

David), and there is no evidence in the versions for emending the Masoretic Text.

6. הַשֹּׁתִים (who drink) is another in the sequence of participles with the definite article (see v. 1). יַיִן בְּמִזְרְקֵי (from basins of wine): We must translate the preposition בְּ with the sense of *from*, as elsewhere in the Old Testament and Ugaritic. מִזְרָק (basin) occurs with both masculine and feminine plural inflections. It is similar to words used to describe the throwing of blood against the altar (Exod. 27:3; 38:3; Num. 4:14; 7:13, 19). The root זרק (Lev. 1:5, 11; 3:2, 8, 13) means to "throw" or "cast," not "to sprinkle." The basins were apparently large, and were probably fashioned of valuable metal (as were the offerings for the dedication of the altar of the Mosaic tabernacle [Num. 7:13]). Out of such large and costly basins the wealthy of Israel drink wine. וְרֵאשִׁית שְׁמָנִים (and with first-class oils) is an adverbial accusative, denoting material. The phrase is a *hapax legomenon* in the Old Testament, but its meaning is clear. The cognate phrase *šamnu rēštû* occurs in Assyrian inscriptions, describing oil used for anointing idols and inscriptions (von Soden, *Akkadisches Handwörterbuch*, vol. 3, p. 1157). Oil was important for anointing the body, especially after washing, for it refreshed and protected the skin in a hot climate. Usually plain olive oil was used (Deut. 28:40; Mic.

6:15), but the wealthy might have added spices and perfumes to it (Mark 14:3–5). רֵאשִׁית (first-class) recalls the same word in verse 1 ("the first of the nations"). יִמְשָׁחוּ (they anoint themselves) often occurs in contexts of consecration. It may refer to the consecration of a prophet (Elisha by Elijah, 1 Kings 19:16), a king (Judg. 9:8; 1 Sam. 16:13), or a priest (Exod. 28:41). It also connotes the consecration of articles, such as Saul's shield (2 Sam. 1:21; cf. Isa. 21:5; the leather shield was "anointed" with oil to keep it from becoming dry and brittle; see Millard, "Saul's Shield") and the Mosaic tabernacle and its vessels (Exod. 29:36; 30:26; Lev. 8:10–11). וְלֹא נֶחְלוּ (but they do not grieve over): The context requires an adversative sense for וְ. נֶחְלוּ (grieve over) has the basic sense of being sick (see Dan. 8:27, niphal, as here; here it connotes to be sick with grief. שֵׁבֶר יוֹסֵף (the ruin of Joseph): This phrase occurs only here, but the noun שֵׁבֶר (ruin) occurs elsewhere in the context of national ruin (i.e., "the injuries of his people" [Isa. 30:26], "the wound of my people [Jer. 6:14; cf. 8:21; 10:19; 14:17; 30:12, 15; Lam. 2:13], "your [the king of Assyria's] wound" [Nah. 3:19]). יוֹסֵף (Joseph): See the Exegesis of 5:6; the phrase *remnant of Joseph* occurs in 5:15.

7. לָכֵן (therefore): See the Exegesis of 3:11. עַתָּה (now) gives a sense of immediacy to the state-

---

today, the Lord will not tarry in disciplining his people.

6. Those who banquet are addressed now in another light, as those who drink wine from basins. The basins they use are very large and probably of costly metal and design, so that both luxury and drunkenness are attacked at the same time. The wealthy also spare no expense in care for their bodies, but anoint themselves with first-class oil, finely scented and perfumed. But in their luxury and self-indulgence, they pay no heed to the condition of their land, which is going to ruin. They are like the prophets excoriated by Jeremiah:

> They have treated the wound of my people
> carelessly,
> saying, "Peace, peace,"
> when there is no peace. (Jer. 6:14)

Because of this, those who now enjoy wine in basins and anoint themselves with first-class oil—who consider themselves the "first of the nations" (v. 1)—will suffer a terrible irony, as Moses prophesied long ago: "You shall plant vineyards and dress them, but you shall [not] drink the

wine. . . . You shall have olive trees throughout all your territory, but you shall not anoint yourself with oil" (Deut. 28:39–40).

Likewise, Jesus had a warning for those who enjoyed the best that this life could offer, but with no thought about the oppressed, whose oppression made such superfluous wealth possible (Luke 16:19–26).

The first two cola of this verse produce a chiasmus:

a	**b**
who drink	from basins of wine
b´	**a´**
and with first-class oils	they anoint themselves

The chiasmus accentuates the luxury of their lifestyle and contrasts vividly with their indifference to the ruin of Joseph.

7. "Therefore" introduces the conclusion. The audience should know what to expect. The leaders of Jerusalem and Samaria, who had fancied themselves at the "head" of the nations (v. 1), would now find themselves at the "head" of the

ment: the doom will come soon. יִגְלוּ (go into exile): See the Exegesis of 1:5. בְּרֹאשׁ גֹּלִים (as the first of the exiles; lit. at the head of the exiles) indicates that they will lead the way into exile *from* Israel, as they led the way in revelry and injustice *in* Israel. The phrase ironically echoes רֵאשִׁית הַגּוֹיִם (the first [i.e., occupying the "head" place] of the nations), at the beginning of the oracle in verse 1. וְסָר (and . . . will pass away): For the verb in this sense, see Isaiah 11:13 ("the jealousy

of Ephraim shall depart"); for the hiphil imperative, see Amos 5:23. מִרְזַח סְרוּחִים (the loud partying of those who are sprawled out): The sense of loud partying is indicated by the basic denotation מִרְזַח, which seems to be "a cry" (BDB, p. 931). It appears in the sense of a mourning cry in Jeremiah 16:5 (translated, however, "a funeral meal" in the NIV. סְרוּחִים (those who are sprawled out): See the Exegesis of verse 4.

---

exiles. The word plays on "chief or head" (v. 1) and "head" (v. 7) and on "nations" (v. 1) and "exiles" (v. 7) are not apparent in English, but are clear in Hebrew, so that the irony between the introduction of the oracle and its conclusion would be clear.

Once again Amos makes the manifestations of the nation's covenant violations the focal point of

divine judgment. He mentioned their houses and vineyards in 5:11, and said that the people would not enjoy them. Now, he says, their loud partying will pass away. Their revelry dulled their sensitivity to God, and it too will be no more.

II. Pronouncements of Judgment (3:1–6:14)
D. Announcements of Judgment (5:18–6:14)
4. Judgment Announced Against Pride and Unrighteousness (6:8–14)

8 The Lord Yahweh has sworn by himself—
oracle of Yahweh, God of hosts—
"I abhor the pride of Jacob,
and his royal citadels I hate,
and I will deliver up each city and everything in it.
9 And if even ten men are left in a single house, they will die." 10 And when a man's kinsman and burner lifts him up to take the body out of the house, and says to whomever is in the recesses of the house, "Is there anyone still with you?" and the other shall say, "No one." Then he shall say, "Hush! For the Yahweh's name must not be invoked.
11 For even now Yahweh is commanding,
and he will pound the large house to pieces,
and the small house to bits.
12 Would horses run on a crag,
or would one plow a crag with oxen?
But you have turned justice to poison-weed,
and the fruit of righteousness to wormwood.
13 You who rejoice in Lo-debar,
you who say, "Is it not by our own strength
that we took Karnaim for ourselves?"
14 "For even now I am raising up against you, O house of Israel"—
oracle of Yahweh, the God of hosts—
"A nation, and they will oppress you

8 The Lord GOD has sworn by himself
(says the LORD, the God of hosts):
I abhor the pride of Jacob
and hate his strongholds;
and I will deliver up the city and all that is in it.
9 If ten people remain in one house, they shall die. 10And if a relative, one who burns the dead, shall take up the body to bring it out of the house, and shall say to someone in the innermost parts of the house, "Is anyone else with you?" the answer will come, "No." Then the relative shall say, "Hush! We must not mention the name of the LORD."
11 See, the LORD commands,
and the great house shall be shattered to bits,
and the little house to pieces.
12 Do horses run on rocks?
Does one plow the sea with oxen?
But you have turned justice into poison
and the fruit of righteousness into wormwood—
13 you who rejoice in Lo-debar,
who say, "Have we not by our own strength
taken Karnaim for ourselves?"
14 Indeed, I am raising up against you a nation,
O house of Israel, says the LORD, the God of hosts,
and they shall oppress you from Lebo-hamath
to the Wadi Arabah.

8. יְהוָה אֲדֹנָי (the Lord Yahweh): See the Exegesis of 1:8. נִשְׁבַּע . . . בְּנַפְשׁוֹ (has sworn by himself; lit. by his life or soul): For נִשְׁבַּע (has sworn), see the Exegesis of 4:2. The phrase occurs otherwise only in Jeremiah 51:14. It is essentially the same in meaning as the more common נִשְׁבַּע בִּי (to swear by myself) applied to the Lord (see Gen. 22:16; Exod. 32:13; Isa. 45:23; Jer. 22:5; 49:13). נְאֻם־יְהוָה (oracle of Yahweh): See the Exegesis of 2:11. אֱלֹהֵי צְבָאוֹת (God of hosts): See the Exegesis of 3:13. מְתָאֵב אָנֹכִי (I abhor): The verb תאב (piel) is a *hapax legomenon*. It is probably a byform of the more common תעב (to abhor or abominate) in which the gutteral was softened from ע to א. תָּעַב occurs in parallel with שָׂנֵא (hate) here, in 5:10, and in Psalm 5:6–7 [5–6]. For the deictic use of the first common singular pronoun, see the Exegesis of 2:9. אֶת־גְּאוֹן יַעֲקֹב (the pride of Jacob) also occurs in 8:7 and Psalm 47:5 [4]. גָּאוֹן (pride) may indicate either the attitude itself (Isa. 16:6; Hos. 5:5) or, by metonymy of the effect, the things that generate pride (Ps. 47:5 [4]; Nah. 2:3 [2]; Zech. 9:6). In Psalm 47:5 [4], however, it clearly stands for the promised land itself ("He chose our inheritance for us, / the pride of Jacob," NIV). So here, Yahweh abhors the land/inheritance/pride of Jacob, just as he hates Jacob's royal citadels. יַעֲקֹב (Jacob): See the Exegesis of 3:13. אַרְמְנֹתָיו (his royal citadels): See the Exegesis of 1:4. וְהִסְגַּרְתִּי (and I will deliver up): See the Exegesis of 1:6. עִיר וּמְלֹאָהּ (each city and everything in it; lit. a city and its fullness)

is not *the* city (i.e., Samaria), since the definite article is lacking. Rather, the indefinite noun is used collectively, "each or every city." For the phrase *X and everything in it*, compare "the earth and everything in it" (Deut. 33:16; Pss. 24:1; 50:12; 89:12 [11]; Isa. 34:1), "the sea and everything in it" (1 Chron. 16:32; Pss. 96:11; 98:7; Isa. 42:10). Assyrian kings regularly boasted both of the numerous cities that they had taken (Isa. 10:8–11) and of their total pillaging (Isa. 10:13–14).

9. וְהָיָה (and . . . ; lit. and it will be) is a converted perfect, introducing a future situation. אִם־יִוָּתְרוּ (if even [ten men] are left): For the niphal verb used in contexts of judgment or disaster, leaving few or no survivors, see 2 Samuel 13:30; 17:12; Psalm 106:11; Zechariah 13:8. עֲשָׂרָה אֲנָשִׁים (ten men): On עֲשָׂרָה (ten), see the Exegesis of 5:3. The use of ten in this fashion may indicate the smallest fighting unit remaining, or just a small number left after disaster has struck. In all probability it is the latter because the context does not inform the concept with military connotations. בְּבַיִת אֶחָד (in a single house): The identical phrase occurs also in Exodus 12:46 (the passover regulations) and 1 Kings 3:17. The usage leaves open the question whether Amos means only that there are ten people left in any given house, or whether he means that there is only one house left standing after the devastation. However we view it, we must not lose sight of the fact that this is a

---

8. This oracle begins on a solemn note. The Lord has sworn by himself. In this context, the prospect is frightful, for if the Lord swears by himself, he can swear by none truer and none greater (Heb. 6:13–14). What he swears is certain. The Lord abhors the pride of Jacob, that is, he hates the pride of the people of the northern kingdom, as well as the factors that bolster such pride, such as its ill-gotten wealth (2:6–7; 3:9–10; 5:11–12), military ability (2:14–16; 5:3), and sumptuous religious decorum (4:4–5). The structure of the bicolon, which declares his abhorrence and hatred, lends impact to the content. The parallelism is structured chiastically:

a	**b**
I abhor	the pride of Jacob
b´	**a´**
and his royal citadels	I hate

The chiasm enhances the rhetorical impact of the statement, as in verse 6.

There can be no doubt about the Lord's attitude, for they have forgotten that he is the source of all their well-being (2:9–11). As a result, their punishment will be similar to that inflicted later on Judah, whose prophet lamented, "He has delivered into the hand of the enemy / the walls of her palaces" (Lam. 2:7). The Lord would "deliver up" each city and everything in it.

9. The picture is bleak. If a group of people are left alive in a house after the ravages of divine judgment, they, too, shall die. This hypothetical picture is intended to affirm the thoroughness of the judgment. If some people have hidden themselves in a house hoping to escape the invading armies, they will not be successful. They cannot escape the ravages of the invasion.

hypothetical situation introduced by אִם (if). We are to envision people huddled in fear of the devastation Amos describes.

10. וּנְשָׂאוֹ (and when [he] lifts him up) is an infinitive construct, introducing a temporal clause. The verb is used here of carrying a corpse to burial, as in the case of Jacob (Gen. 47:30; 50:13), Asahel (2 Sam. 2:32), and Saul (1 Chron. 10:12). דּוֹדוֹ וּמְסָרְפוֹ (a man's kinsman and burner; lit. his kinsman and his burner). Because the suffix on וּנְשָׂאוֹ (lifts up) is masculine singular, מְסָרְפוֹ (burner) is an appositive to דּוֹדוֹ (kinsman), that is, they are one and the same person. דּוֹד, translated "kinsman," basically means "loved one," and might be an uncle, another relation, or even a close friend (see Isa. 5:1 and BDB, p. 187). מְסָרֵף (burner) is understood as a byform of מְשָׂרֵף. It possibly indicates an honorary funeral fire; see 2 Chronicles 16:14: "They laid him [Asa] on a bier covered with spices and various blended perfumes, and they made a huge fire in his honor [lit. burned for him a very great burning]" (NIV) (see also Jer. 34:5). Here, there are so few people left that only one person, a relative or close friend, must perform the whole funeral, including any such honorary burning as might be arranged. It is also possible that so many have died that their bodies must be burned to prevent disease. Burning of bodies was not an acceptable funeral practice in Israel, although it occurred in the case of certain sexual sins (Lev. 20:14; 21:9), Achan's disobedience (Josh. 7:15, 25), and Saul and Jonathan (1 Sam. 31:12). Less likely is the interpretation of Mays (*Amos*, p. 119), who cites Robinson (*Zwölf kleinen Propheten*, p. 94) to the effect that מְסָרֵף means "kinsman on the mother's side" and is a synonym of דּוֹד. עֲצָמִים (corpse; lit. bones): The masculine plural is used

only here to represent not merely the bones, but the entire corpse. Elsewhere the feminine plural is so used (e.g., Gen. 50:25; Exod. 13:19; 1 Chron. 10:12). בְּיַרְכְּתֵי (in the recesses of [the house]) connotes the remote parts of some area, such as the depths of a cave (1 Sam. 24:4 [3]), Sheol (Isa. 14:15), a ship (Jon. 1:5), or the innermost parts of a house (Ps. 128:3). The survivor is pictured as cowering or hiding in the innermost recesses of the house. אֶפֶס (no one; lit. end, limit, or cessation [i.e., of anyone else's being here]): The word occurs in parallel or in tandem with אַיִן (nothing or nonexistence) in Isaiah 40:17 and 41:12. Here we have the sequence אֶפֶס הַעוֹד עִמָּךְ וְאָמַר ("is there anyone still with you?" and the other [lit. and he] shall say, "No one"). Similar phrasing occurs in Zephaniah 2:15: עוֹד אֲנִי וְאַפְסִי (I am, and there is no one else); see also Isaiah 45:6 and 46:9. הָס (hush!) also occurs in 8:3. The interjection occurs elsewhere to enjoin silence—before the Lord's coming judgment (Zeph. 1:7), his arising to redeem his people (Zech. 2:17 [13]), or in his presence (Hab. 2:20). In a secular setting, it occurs when Eglon king of Moab fatally commands his attendants to leave him (Judg. 3:19). It is inflected as a verb in Nehemiah 8:11, where the Levites seek to quiet the people on the sacred day when the Torah was read (a hiphil occurs in Num. 13:30). כִּי (for): The conjunction gives the reason for the silence enjoined. לֹא לְהַזְכִּיר בְּשֵׁם יְהוָה (Yahweh's name must not be mentioned): Perhaps הַזְכִּיר (mention) has the sense of *invoke* here, as it does in Isaiah 48:1: "You who take oaths in the name of the LORD / and invoke the God of Israel" (NIV). If this is the case, the prohibition is not against speaking the Lord's name because it might draw his attention toward the survivor, nor is it a matter of some unevidenced funerary

---

10. The desolate picture continues. Survivors are few in the land. A relative (perhaps an uncle or some other relation—at least a close friend) comes to bury the corpse of a loved one. Calling out and asking if there are any others, the answer comes from far within the house: "No one." There is someone there who is afraid to venture forth. The relative says, "The Lord's name is not to be invoked." Desolate as the situation is, one must not turn to the Lord for help. Ironically, the very disaster that has engulfed them has come directly from the Lord!

It is but a fulfilment of the curses delineated long ago in the original covenant:

> In the street the sword shall bereave,
> and in the chambers terror,
> for young man and woman alike,
> nursing child and old gray head. (Deut. 32:25)

11. This verse makes clear just how, or on what authority, the devastation of households (vv. 9–10) will proceed—the Lord himself calls for it. Since his people did not obey the laws and

"prayer or invocation to Jehovah" (Driver, *Joel and Amos*, p. 201). Rather, it would be a covenantal invocation to Yahweh for aid, and such a call is utterly inappropriate, because he is now accomplishing his role as covenant judge, punitively visiting his people.

11. כִּי (for) introduces the reason for the devastation depicted in verse 8. הִנֵּה (even now) is a deictic particle that possesses a sense of immediacy. It often occurs with a participle in prophetic pronouncements regarding the future (4:2; Isa. 3:1; Jer. 8:17; 11:22). יְהוָה (Yahweh): See the Exegesis of 1:2. מְצַוֶּה (is commanding): This participial form often appears in covenantal passages where the Lord commands covenant obedience (Exod. 34:11; Deut. 26:16), as well as where he commands punitive judgment against his rebellious people (Jer. 34:22). וְהִכָּה (and he will pound; i.e., smite, strike): The verb also occurs in 3:15, where, as here, houses are destroyed. There, too, the Lord speaks of himself as doing the striking or pounding. In both cases, it is understood that the agent whom he commands (cf. 6:14) will actually carry out the destruction. The verb does double duty, applying to both cola. הַבַּיִת הַגָּדוֹל (the large house) and הַבַּיִת הַקָּטֹן (the small house): The parallelism forms a merismus and indicates that all houses, large or small, will be demolished. The alliteration (five of the seven words in the colon start with *h*) emphasizes the point. רְסִיסִים (pieces) is a *hapax legomenon*, but the meaning is clear both etymologically and from context (BDB, p.

944). בְּקָעִים (to bits) occurs elsewhere only in Isaiah 22:9 (the "breaches" of the city of David). As is clear from its usage there and its etymology (root בקע, to cleave, break open, or break through), it portrays a facade or surface that has been cleft, and hence reduced to fragments.

12. הַיְרֻצוּן . . . סוּסִים (would horses run . . . ?): The incomplete action of the imperfect verb calls for the sense: Do (would) horses run . . . ? The following questions are obviously contrary to nature. בַּסֶּלַע (on a crag; lit. the crag) is a steep and possibly inaccessible cliff. It would have been a dangerous place to ride and an unthinkable place to plow. The word סֶלַע (crag) serves both clauses. This observation obviates repointing בִּבְקָרִים (with oxen) to בְּבָקָר יָם (the sea with an ox; i.e., or does one plow the sea with an ox?), made by, for example, Driver (*Joel and Amos*, p. 202), Mays (*Amos*, p. 120), and Wolff (*Joel and Amos*, p. 284). אִם־יַחֲרוֹשׁ (or would one plow . . . ?): The subject is indefinite. For the function of אִם in double questions, see the Exegesis of verse 2. כִּי (but; see BDB, p. 474) introduces the rationale for the previous questions: just as those things are unnatural, so what you (Israel) are doing is unnatural. הֲפַכְתֶּם (you have turned) does double duty, applying to poisonweed as well as to wormwood in the second colon. לְרֹאשׁ (poisonweed) probably is not simply a reference to poison (see Deut. 29:17 [18] and Hos. 10:4 for metaphorical uses of poison), because the poison involved is a plant derivative (Stuart, *Hosea–Jonah*, pp. 361–62) and רֹאשׁ here is parallel to לַעֲנָה (wormwood), which is also a plant. צְדָקָה

---

decrees that he commanded them in the days of Moses, they will now suffer the invasion he is commanding. The invader, acting as the Lord's agent, will destroy all houses, large and small, and will both eradicate (v. 9) and carry away into exile (v. 7). The houses will be thoroughly destroyed, pounded into bits and pieces, as the Lord virtually makes war on his own rebellious people.

When the text expresses the command of God in the form of a participle, it expresses the immanency of God in the circumstances so described. The Lord is commanding—he is at work within time controlling events so that his judgment may fall on his rebellious people. This passage reveals an aspect of God that we must not forget. He judges sin in his own people. We must fear God, as well as love him.

12. Amos propounds two absurd questions: "Would horses run on a crag?" "Would one plow a crag with oxen?" The obvious answer to both questions is "no." Horses can scarcely run on a crag without falling to their death. Nor would one plow on a crag. Not only would it be dangerous, but there would be no arable soil. However unnatural these propositions might seem, Israel has done something even more unnatural. They have turned justice to poison and the fruit of righteousness to wormwood. This is natural in the fallen world, but Israel was to be different. The Lord had chosen it alone out of all the families of the earth (3:2). It knew God's standards and when it departed from them, he sent his servants the prophets. One of those prophets depicted the unnaturalness of the disobedience of his people in another metaphor:

וּפְרִי (and the fruit of righteousness) answers to מִשְׁפָּט (justice) in the first colon. The structure of these words in parallel serves to round out the concept of the ethical response to God that the author had in mind. פְּרִי (fruit) as a metaphor appears both positively and negatively in the Old Testament, positively in Proverbs 11:30 ("the fruit of the righteous is a tree of life") and Isaiah 3:10; negatively in Hosea 10:13 ("fruit of lies"), Proverbs 1:31, and Micah 7:13 ("fruit of their doings"). The phrase *the fruit(s) of righteousness* occurs in the New Testament in Philippians 1:11 and James 3:18 (cf. Matt. 7:15–20; 12:33). For מִשְׁפָּט (justice) in parallel with צְדָקָה (righteousness), see the Exegesis of 5:7. לַעֲנָה (wormwood): See the Exegesis of 5:7.

13. הַשְּׂמֵחִים (you who rejoice) continues the second-person masculine plural address begun in verse 12 (see also verse 3). לֹא דָבָר (Lo-debar) was a town near the border in Gilead, some three miles east of the Jordan and twelve miles south of the Sea of Galilee. The name means, literally, "no thing or word" (the LXX has ἐπ᾽ οὐδενὶ λόγῳ, over no word; Symmachus, ἀλόγως, wordless; the Vulgate, *in nihili*, in nothing), an interpretation adopted by some moderns, for example, Keil (*Twelve Minor Prophets*, p. 303) and Driver (*Joel and Amos*, p. 203), but rejected by others, for example, Wellhausen (*Skizzen und Vorarbeiten*, p. 86), Wolff (*Joel and Amos*, p. 286), and Stuart (*Hosea–Jonah*, p. 362, n. 13a). If the name has significance here, it expresses irony: Israel rejoices in "nothing." This rebuke would be in the category of other prophetic rebukes employing לֹא (not) in compounds, for example, "no people" (Deut. 32:21), "not God" (Deut. 32:17), "not of mortals" (Isa. 31:8), and לֹא־אֶהְיֶה (not I AM) in Hosea 1:9, where the Lord says, "Name him Lo-ammi [not my people], for you are not my people and I am not [לֹא־אֶהְיֶה, not I AM] your God"—thus declaring that, for his rejected people, he will no longer be the great I AM of Exodus 3:14. Both interpretations, however, are true and probably both are intended (see Smith, *Twelve Prophets*, pp. 182–83). Israel now rejoices in the conquest of Lo-debar by Jeroboam II; yet, because they attribute this feat to their own strength, they in fact rejoice in "nothing." They enjoy only an ephemeral advantage. הֲלוֹא בְחָזְקֵנוּ (is it not by our own strength . . . ?): This phrase appears only here. The usual phraseology for such overweening pride includes the noun יָד (hand), that is, יָדִי or יָדֵינוּ (our/my power; lit.

What more was there to do for my vineyard
    that I have not done in it?
When I expected it to yield grapes,
    why did it yield wild grapes? (Isa. 5:4)

Amos is a master of the use of metaphorical language based on aspects of nature. The people did not see how absurd they were in poisoning themselves with their violation of the covenantal regulations. The law was intended to be their wisdom (Deut. 4:6–8), but they had turned their backs on it. Like the foolish actions in Amos's metaphor, the nation was foolish as well.

Of course, the fruit of righteousness was not possible for Old Testament saints in the way it is for us, since they did not have Spirit as we do (John 7:37–39). We today can be filled with "the harvest of righteousness that comes through Jesus Christ for the glory and praise of God" (Phil. 1:11). We can also grow into peacemakers, ministers of the gospel of reconciliation between God and human, after the likeness of our Master. And we are encouraged to do so by the assurance that "a harvest of righteousness is sown in peace for those who make peace" (James 3:18).

13. Israel apparently rejoices over Lo-debar and Karnaim, cities recently conquered by Jeroboam II. The cities themselves are not of cardinal significance, but their names have a special significance in this context. Israel is rejoicing in what it has done through its own strength. This is a fatal attitude. It imagines substantial victory where there is, in fact, nothing. It fancies that it has horns of power, when in fact it has merely taken them to itself and, like Zedekiah's handmade horns, they will gore nothing.

The people boasted that they had conquered in their own strength (*běḥazqěnû*). Isaiah met this attitude as well. In 10:13 he applies a somewhat similar concept to Assyria. His phraseology, attributing such arrogance to Assyria, is especially ironic because Assyrian kings regularly denigrated their foes by asserting that the enemy "trusted in his own strength," while the pious Assyrian "trusted in Aššur, my lord!" For example, Tiglath-pileser I comments that the Muski and their five kings "trusted in their own strength," whereas he defeated them "with

our/my hand), as in Deuteronomy 32:27 ("our hand is triumphant") and Isaiah 10:10 ("my hand," said of Assyrian power; cf. Isa. 10:13). לְקַחְנוּ (we took): לָקַח (take) is used often of military conquest (e.g., Num. 21:25; Deut. 3:4; Josh. 11:16, 23; 1 Sam. 7:14). Driver (*Joel and Amos*, p. 203), however, asserts that "*lakaḥ* . . . is not the word properly used of taking a town (*lakhad*)." לָנוּ (for ourselves): Since the preceding verb (לָקַח) is sufficient to express the fact of Israel's conquest, the prepositional phrase is additional and emphasizes Israel as the ones who have conquered. This reflects their attitude of pride. קַרְנָיִם (Karnaim) is a dual noun meaning "a pair of horns." The full name of the city is Ashteroth-karnaim (Astarte of Horns). Situated on the plain of Bashan on the way to Damascus, it was a strategic site. It is mentioned in the context of Chedorlaomer's defeat of the Rephaim who lived there (Gen. 14:5), and it was among the large fortified towns (1 Macc. 5:26) captured by Judas Maccabeus (1 Macc. 5:43–44). Understood as a town name, the word may also be taken literally, as "horns" (the LXX has κέρατα; the Vulgate, *cornua*). Again, both meanings were probably intended (Smith, *Twelve Prophets*, p. 182).

14. כִּי הִנְנִי (for even now I; lit. for here I am): This concluding verse of the oracle recalls verse 11. It indicates the means by which the smashing of Israel's houses will be accomplished. הִנֵּה with the first-person common singular pronoun occurs in Genesis 6:13; 22:1, 7, 11; Isaiah 65:1. מֵקִים (am raising up) describes the Lord's raising up a foe against his people in judgment. See Habakkuk 1:6, where this phrase occurs in a similar context. For the hiphil of the verb in general, see the Exegesis of 2:11. בֵּית יִשְׂרָאֵל (O house of Israel): See the Exegesis of 5:1. נְאֻם־יְהוָה (oracle of Yahweh): See the Exegesis of 2:11. אֱלֹהֵי הַצְּבָאוֹת (the God of hosts): See the Exegesis of 3:13. גּוֹי (nation) generally connotes a people whom the writer considers a political entity, as opposed to an ethnic group (עַם) (see the Exegesis of verse 1). וְלָחֲצוּ (and they will oppress): לָחַץ (oppress) is often used of oppression by a foreign power, for example, Jabin of Hazor (Judg. 4:3); the Egyptians, Amorites, and five other powers (Judg. 10:12); Aram (2 Kings 13:4, 22); and enemies in general (Ps. 106:42). חֲמָת עַד־נַחַל הָעֲרָבָה מִלְּבוֹא (from the entrance of Hamath to the Wadi of the Arabah): See also 2 Kings 14:25. Here the Lord tells Israel that she will be completely overcome, from the northern to the southern

---

trust in Aššur, my Lord" (King, *Annals of the Kings of Assyria*, p. 36, col. 1, lines 68–70). Much later, Assurbanipal claims that King Tarhaka of Egypt and Ethiopia "forgot the might of Ashur and Ishtar and the great gods, my lords, and trusted in his own strength," whereas the Assyrian king defeated him "with the help of Ashur, Bêl, Nabû, the great gods, my lords, who walk beside me" (Piepkorn, *Historical Prism Inscriptions of Ashurbanipal*, pp. 30–33, lines 55–56, 75–76; cf. Amos 5:9). But the piety claimed by Assyrian kings was really appropriate to the Lord's people, who should have trusted in their God, and not in their own strength.

14. The oracle concludes with a statement of coming judgment. But more, it concludes by telling how the judgment would be accomplished. The Lord will raise up a nation against his people. That nation will quickly strip Israel of all that it had regained under Jeroboam II. Circumstances had favored Jeroboam's successes, for during his reign the surrounding powers—Egypt, Syria, Assyria—were relatively weak, so that his conquests were comparatively

easy (Bright, *History of Israel*, pp. 257–59). Still, those conquests had been in accord with the prophecy of Jonah son of Amittai (2 Kings 14:25), so Jeroboam, and Israel, had enjoyed God's favor. But they had not been faithful to their Lord, and the God who could have protected a faithful Israel would soon bring judgment in the form of a resurgent Assyria. This nation would conquer Israel from "the entrance of Hamath to the Wadi of the Arabah."

The Lord does not operate differently today. He had given Israel much, but they had not desired him. They had not been faithful. They had trusted in the resources they had amassed for themselves. But it was for them, as it was for the man in the parable: "And I will say to my soul, 'Soul, you have ample goods laid up for many years; relax, eat, drink, be merry.' But God said to him, 'You fool! This very night your life is being demanded of you. And the things you have prepared, whose will they be?' So it is with those who store up treasures for themselves but are not rich toward God" (Luke 12:19–21).

border. חֲמָת (Hamath): See the Exegesis of verse 2. נַחַל הָעֲרָבָה (the Wadi of the Arabah): הָעֲרָבָה (Arabah) is a deep valley carved by the Jordan as it flows into the Dead Sea, hence the name *Sea of the Arabah* (Deut. 3:17; Josh. 3:16; 2 Kings 14:25). The Wadi of the Arabah has been tentatively identified as the Wadi el-Ahsa, the southern stream that separated Moab and Edom.

III. Prophetic Visions (7:1-9:15)
   A. Visions of Judgment Turned Aside (7:1-6)
      1. Vision of Locusts (7:1-3)

7 So the Lord Yahweh showed me [a vision], and see! he was forming a locust swarm, when the spring planting was beginning to grow—that is, the spring planting after the king's mowing. **2** And when they had finished eating the vegetation of the land, I said, "O Lord Yahweh, forgive! How can Jacob endure, since he is so small?"

3 The Lord changed his mind about this.
   "It shall not be," said Yahweh.

7 This is what the Lord GOD showed me: he was forming locusts at the time the latter growth began to sprout (it was the latter growth after the king's mowings). **2**When they had finished eating the grass of the land, I said,

   "O Lord GOD, forgive, I beg you!
      How can Jacob stand?
      He is so small!"

3 The LORD relented concerning this;
      "It shall not be," said the LORD.

7:1. כֹּה הִרְאַנִי אֲדֹנָי יְהוִה (So the Lord Yahweh showed me [a vision]; lit. caused me to see): כֹּה (so) generally introduces something that follows (BDB, p. 462). Thus, this oracle appears to be unrelated to the foregoing material. This phrase occurs only in Amos, in 7:1, 4, 7, and 8:1. It is a variant of the expression, "Thus (or so) says (or said) Yahweh," for which see the Exegesis of 1:3. הִרְאַנִי, the hiphil of רָאָה (to see), is used to denote divine causation of either dreams (Gen. 41:28) or visions (Jer. 24:1; Zech. 2:3 [1:20]; 3:1). The qal is also used in connection with divine visions (1 Kings 22:17, 19; Isa. 6:1; Ezek. 1:1, 4; 8:2). אֲדֹנָי יְהוִה (the Lord Yahweh): See the Exegesis of 1:8. וְהִנֵּה (and see!) expresses immediacy (as it does in 2:13). יוֹצֵר (was forming): The participial form is often used of the Lord as the maker or former, for example, of the eye (Ps. 94:9), of Israel (Isa. 43:1), of his servant from the womb (Isa. 49:5), of light (in parallel with "create darkness," Isa. 45:7), of the earth (Isa. 45:18), and of all things (Jer. 10:16). It occurs in Amos elsewhere in 4:13. Here, it is used of the Lord as the former of a locust swarm that he will use to judge Israel. In the present case, the participle indicates an action, now in progress, that will culminate in Israel's disaster. גֹּבַי (locust swarm) occurs elsewhere only in Nahum 3:17 in a simile describing the sudden disappearance of Assyrian rulers when Nineveh falls. A byform of גֵּבֶה (similar to שָׂדֶה/שָׂדַי and שָׂרָה/שָׂרַי), it is related to the root גבה (to collect; hence, a swarm or collection). It apparently denotes locusts swarming from the ground when their eggs hatch in the spring (the Arabic jabaʾa means "to come forth suddenly"). עֲלוֹת הַלָּקֶשׁ בִּתְחִלַּת (when the spring planting was beginning to grow; lit. at the beginning of the growth or going up of the spring planting): For similar phrases, compare "as the dawn began to break" (Judg. 19:25); "a column of smoke began [הֵחֵלָּה] to rise" (Judg. 20:40); "as a shock of grain comes up" (Job

---

7:1. This verse begins a lengthy unit that contains five visions (7:1–3; 7:4–6; 7:7–9; 8:1–3; 9:1–4) and an autobiographical section (7:10–17) relevant to the third vision. The first four visions are similarly structured, as the following schema (adapted from Stuart, *Hosea–Jonah*, p. 368) shows:

7:1–3	Vision of locusts	a. Yahweh imparts the vision
		b. Amos intercedes
		c. Yahweh relents
7:4–6	Vision of fire	a. Yahweh imparts the vision
		b. Amos intercedes
		c. Yahweh relents
7:7–9	Vision of tin	a. Yahweh imparts the vision
		b. Yahweh interrogates Amos
		c. Amos replies
		d. Yahweh explains and judges
8:1–3	Vision of summer fruit	a. Yahweh imparts the vision
		b. Yahweh interrogates Amos
		c. Amos replies
		d. Yahweh explains and judges

This structure is, however, not unique to Amos, but appears as well in other prophetic visions, as the following analysis illustrates:

Jer. 1:11–12	Vision of almond branch	a. Yahweh imparts vision
		b. Yahweh interrogates Jeremiah
		c. Jeremiah replies
		d. Yahweh explains and judges
Jer. 1:13–19	Vision of boiling pot	a. Yahweh imparts vision
		b. Yahweh interrogates Jeremiah
		c. Jeremiah replies
		d. Yahweh explains and judges
Jer. 24:1–10	Vision of fig baskets	a. Yahweh imparts vision
		b. Yahweh interrogates Jeremiah
		c. Jeremiah replies
		d. Yahweh explains and judges

The last example concludes not only with a sentence, but also with a promise of good to the "good figs" (Jer. 24:4–7). It is similar to Amos's visions not only in structure, but also in its use of the formula *the Lord asked me* (Amos 7:8) and its use of *rʾh* (see).

The Lord gives Amos a vision of what may come. It is a judgment that is consistent with the Lord's covenantal warnings. He had warned in Deuteronomy 28:42 that locusts would come and devour all that they had. Here, in Amos, the

5:26). לֶקֶשׁ (spring planting) derives from the root לקשׁ (to be late; BDB, p. 545). Apparently the word designates crops (or grass) that begin to grow after the latter (spring) rains of March and April. לקשׁ occurs in the Gezer Calendar (Donner and Röllig, *Kanaanäische und aramäische Inschriften*, vol. 1, p. 34, no. 182, line 2; vol. 2, p. 181; *ANET*, p. 320). The destruction of such crops would mean the ruin of both farmers and livestock. וְהִנֵּה (that is) draws attention to the following, and so is translated as a demonstrative (GKC §147b). גִּזֵּי הַמֶּלֶךְ (the king's mowings): גֵּז (mowings) may also be translated "shearings," as the same word, גֵּז (shearing or mowing; cf. Akkadian *gizzu*), root גזז (to shear), is also used of sheep shearing (e.g., Deut. 18:4; Job 31:20). This is the only mention of any royal mowing. First Kings 18:5 is often cited in support of such an event, but a straightforward reading of the text reveals nothing like an annual royal mowing.

2. אִם (when), while a conditional particle, frequently yields to a temporal sense in English when it accompanies a perfect verb. The perfect tense, with its emphasis on completed action, views the event as culminated, thus "when" is an appropriate translation in many contexts (e.g., Num. 21:9). כִּלָּה (had finished) has as its subject the locust swarm mentioned in the previous verse. Driver (*Joel and Amos*, p. 206, n. 1) says of this phrase that "the Hebrew . . . is peculiar, and can scarcely be right." In fact, the phrase is not unusual, for it follows the pattern of וְהָיָה אִם + perfect + perfect or imperfect; see, for example, Genesis 38:9 ("whenever he went in to his brother's wife, he spilled his semen"); Numbers 21:9; Judges 6:3. עֵשֶׂב (vegetation) means not just grass, but plants in general, as in Genesis 1:11. The entire phrase is almost identical to one in Exodus 10:12, 15: וְיֹאכַל אֶת־כָּל־עֵשֶׂב הָאָרֶץ ([and [the locusts will] . . . eat every plant in the land); a similar account is found in Psalm 105:35. אֲדֹנָי יְהוִה (Lord Yahweh): See the Exegesis of 1:8. סְלַח־נָא (forgive!) occurs elsewhere only in Numbers 14:19. The imperative occurs elsewhere only in these two

---

locusts were to come just when the plants were beginning to grow—just when the promise of spring seemed fullest and sweetest. We are not to believe that the plague actually occurred, because the Lord changed his mind.

A locust plague, particularly after the king had taken his share of the harvest, would have been devastating. We do not know of the custom in which a king took a share of the harvest (it may have been a form of taxation). Apparently, though, this was the case in Amos's day. It would have required a great deal of food to support the court and the military, which would have reduced the amount of food available for the people. Now what remained was threatened by locusts.

In several prophetic visions, conversation plays an important role, as it does here. The conversation in verses 2–3 is an integral part of the visionary experience (see also vv. 5–6, 8–9; 8:2–3). Similarly, conversation in divinely imparted dreams occurs in other ancient Near Eastern records, for example, the dream-vision of Gudea of Lagash in which his god commands him to build a temple (Thureau-Dangin, *Die sumerischen und akkadischen Königsinschriften*, pp. 92–95, cylinder A, col. 4, line 14 through col. 5, line 18), dreams recorded at Mari (*ANET*, pp. 623–24, texts a and b), Samsuiluna's dream visitation by divine emissaries (Sollberger, "Samsu-iluna's Bilingual Inscriptions," lines 32–88), and the dream-vision of Astarte reported by Assurbanipal (Piepkorn, *His-*

torical Prism Inscriptions of Ashurbanipal, pp. 64–67).

2. Now Amos learns of the outcome of the plague he sees in this vision. The land is stripped of all its vegetation. Such a judgment could result in the starvation of all living things. This judgment harks back to the Lord's judgment on Egypt, where the Lord also judged a proud and sinful nation. Now Israel was eligible for the same judgment (Deut. 28:27, 60–61, 68). Earlier in Israel's history, when they had rebelled at the report of the twelve spies and longed again for Egypt, Moses the great covenant mediator interceded and, on the basis of the *greatness* of the Lord's covenant mercy, asked him to forgive his rebellious people. Now, in a later time, another prophet intercedes with the same prayer: "Forgive!" He bases his prayer of intercession not on the Lord's greatness, however, but on the fact that "Jacob is so *small*." Little Jacob, who, for all his craftiness, needed a mother's help to get a father's blessing and preserve his life, now needs parental help if he is to endure—this time the help of his heavenly Father, who alone can save. Amos appeals to the nation's smallness. It seems incongruous that he should do this in view of the vast holdings and affluence of the northern kingdom in the eighth century B.C. The nation must have seemed small, however, in view of the devastating plague he witnessed. Sometimes adversity places things in their proper perspective.

passages and in Daniel 9:19. The verb is used in general of the Lord's forgiveness (Exod. 34:9; 1 Kings 8:30, 34, 36, 39, 50; Ps. 25:11; Jer. 33:8). מִי (how; lit. as who) is adverbial; the particle asks, "In what condition or capacity?" (so Ruth 3:16; Isa. 51:19; cf. the Akkadian *mî*; see BDB, p. 566). יָקוּם (can [Jacob] endure; lit. stand): The imperfect should be translated modally. For the verb in contexts of standing or enduring under judgment, see Joshua 7:12–13; Psalm 1:5; Lamentations 1:14; Nahum 1:6. For יַעֲקֹב (Jacob), see the Exegesis of 3:13. כִּי קָטֹן הוּא (since he is so small): The final pronoun completes the sentence, but is also probably emphatic—he, Jacob, is so small. The mention of Jacob's smallness harks back to the patriarchal narrative, in which Jacob is described as Rebekah's יַעֲקֹב בְּנָהּ הַקָּטָן (her younger son Jacob; Gen. 27:15, 42). In the earlier context, his mother's wisdom got him the paternal blessing and prevented Esau's plans to murder him. Now, again, Jacob needs his Father's kindness if he is to survive.

3. נִחַם (changed his mind) essentially means "to groan inwardly," usually in remorse or repentance about something. עַל (about) creates the collocation נִחַם עַל (change one's mind or repent about); several contexts apply to the Lord to describe arrested punishment (Exod. 32:12, 14; Jer. 18:8; Joel 2:13; Jon. 3:10). All these contexts use the phrase נִחַם עַל־הָרָעָה to designate the idea of changing one's mind about the evil the Lord intended to bring. זֹאת (this) is feminine abstract, which Hebrew uses in this fashion when it is impossible to determine the gender of the foregoing (GKC §122q). Since זֹאת refers back to the threat and its reversal, there is no gender one can assign to the concept. Thus, the feminine construction of זֶה (this) appears here. לֹא תִהְיֶה (it shall not be): The imperfect implies incomplete action. The negative particle לֹא (not) combines with the imperfect to negate the possibility of this ever happening. אָמַר יְהֹוָה (said Yahweh): See the Exegesis of 1:5.

---

3. The Lord changed his mind about the locusts (vv. 1–2). God relented as a result of prayer on the part of the prophet. Moses, who was also a prophet, prayed for God's people when they had made and worshiped the golden calf. God answered Moses' prayer (Exod. 32:12, 14): "Turn from your fierce anger; relent and do not bring disaster on your people. . . . Then the LORD relented and did not bring on his people the disaster he had threatened" (NIV). Amos's intercessory prayer had a similarly powerful result. The Lord promised that the punishment will *never* happen. Amos's example may be an encouragement to the Lord's people today.

This vision may lead us to think that all will go well for the nation; all the prophet has to do is pray, and the problem will go away. Perhaps he has only to pray and the captivity he foresaw will not occur. We must wait, however, for the third vision.

III. Prophetic Visions (7:1–9:15)
A. Visions of Judgment Turned Aside (7:1–6)
2. Vision of Fire (7:4–6)

⁴ So the Lord Yahweh showed me [a vision], and see! the Lord Yahweh was calling for a judgment ordeal by fire, and it ate up the great deep and ate up the land. ⁵ And I said, "O Lord Yahweh, cease! How can Jacob endure, since he is so small?"
⁶ The Lord changed his mind about this. "This also shall not be," said the Lord Yahweh.

⁴ This is what the Lord GOD showed me: the Lord GOD was calling for a shower of fire, and it devoured the great deep and was eating up the land. ⁵Then I said,
"O Lord GOD, cease, I beg you!
How can Jacob stand?
He is so small!"
⁶ The LORD relented concerning this;
"This also shall not be," said the Lord GOD.

4. כֹּה הִרְאַנִי (so . . . showed me [a vision]): See the Exegesis of verse 1. אֲדֹנָי יְהוָה (the Lord Yahweh): See the Exegesis of 1:8. וְהִנֵּה (and see!): See the Exegesis of verse 1. קֹרֵא (was calling) occurred earlier in 5:8, where it was used in a brief divine titulary. Here, as in other cases, it indicates present progressive activity on the part of the Lord, describing him as summoning instruments of judgment. The author's interpretation of לָרִב בָּאֵשׁ (for a judgment ordeal by fire) follows Hillers ("Amos 7:4 and Ancient Parallels"). A similar expression occurs in Isaiah 66:15–16, where Isaiah uses גַּעֲרָתוֹ (his rebuke) and וּמִשְׁפָּט (will execute judgment) in association with fire. The judgment ordeal is a covenant-lawsuit procedure, instituted by the Lord and eventuating in judgment (see Jer. 25:31; Hos. 4:1; 12:3 [2]; Mic. 6:2). וַתֹּאכַל (and it ate up) is a converted imperfect. וְאָכְלָה (and ate up) is perfect tense and not converted. Rather, it retains its past sense, so that the vision represents a complete destruction, as did the first vision (v. 2). For the idea of fire devouring, see 1:4. תְּהוֹם רַבָּה (the great deep): This phrase describes the ocean (Gen. 7:11), the Red Sea at Israel's crossing (Isa. 51:10), and, figuratively, the Lord's justice (Ps. 36:7 [6]; cf.

Akkadian *tâmtu).* הַחֵלֶק (the land; lit. the portion) is singular and thus does not refer to fields or plots. Nor is it to be understood as the Lord's people (Deut. 32:9), in opposition to the great deep, which Keil (*Twelve Minor Prophets,* p. 308) understands to be the nations. Rather, it is the land, for that is a more natural antithesis to the ocean. The land of Israel itself is their portion (Mic. 2:4; see BDB, p. 324).

5. אֲדֹנָי יְהוָה (the Lord Yahweh): See the Exegesis of 1:8. חֲדַל־נָא (cease!): This expression does not appear elsewhere, but the imperative occurs a number of times, sometimes as a plea to the Lord to cease his activity (Job 7:16; 10:20). Yahweh's punishments are also said to cease, for example, the thunder and hail (Exod. 9:29, 33).

6. נִחַם יְהוָה עַל־זֹאת (Yahweh changed his mind about this): See the Exegesis of verse 3. גַּם (also) denotes addition. The sense is that this second threat *also* shall not become a reality. הִיא (this) has as its antecedent the second vision of punishment. For the feminine construction of this pronoun, see the Exegesis of verse 3. אָמַר אֲדֹנָי יְהוָה (said the Lord Yahweh): See the Exegesis of 1:3 and 1:8.

---

4. The Lord shows Amos a second vision that is even more terrible than the first. In this vision the Lord summons a fire that devours both the great deep and the land of Israel itself. Such a vision seems hyperbolic, but it is consistent with the Lord's power and the thoroughness of his judgment. The fire is powerful enough to consume the great deep, as well as the land of Israel, which the Lord had apportioned to his people. The extent of judgment described by Amos echoes Deuteronomy 32:22: "For a fire is kindled by my anger, / and burns to the depths of Sheol; / it devours the earth and its increase, / and sets on fire the foundations of the mountains." Possibly there is an allusion here to the idea that the mountains were conceived of as rooted in the sea (see Jon. 2:7 [6]), so that Amos's description implies destruction of mountains, earth, and sea. The removal of the sea (see Rev. 21:1) in a Canaanite context implies the removal of all powers of evil and death, as Cassuto argues (*Biblical and Oriental Studies,* pp. 80–102). The explanation offered by Keil—that the ocean represents the pagan nations—seems highly interpretive, and the evidence cited to support it is scanty. Keil feels that "the idea of a fire falling upon the ocean, and consuming it, and then beginning to consume the land of Israel, by which the ocean was bounded, . . . would be too monstrous"

(*Twelve Minor Prophets,* pp. 308–9). But such a vision is consistent not only with hyperbolic descriptions in the Old Testament (e.g., Ps. 97:5: "The mountains melt like wax before the LORD), but also with New Testament revelation of the truth toward which such images point (2 Pet. 3:10).

5. With the exception of *ḥădal* (cease) instead of *sĕlaḥ* (forgive), this verse is identical to the second half of verse 2. Here again, the intercessory prayer of the prophet averts disaster. How devotedly, how passionately—with how much spiritual understanding—are God's people interceding for a world ripe for fiery judgment? If we are to intercede, let us be like Amos and walk with God (3:3). Then we may have some confidence that our intercession will have effect. In a small but important way, we will be like our master and teacher, of whom we read: "Christ Jesus, who died, yes, who was raised, who is at the right hand of God, who indeed intercedes for us" (Rom. 8:34; cf. Isa. 53:12).

6. Again, the Lord changes his mind. He had intended to destroy by fire (vv. 4–5), but he will refrain. As in the previous vision, he changed his mind because of the intercession of a righteous man. Let such examples remind God's people of the power of prayer and of the importance of righteousness.

III. Prophetic Visions (7:1–9:15)
B. Visions of Judgment Not Turned Aside (7:7–9:10)
1. Vision of Tin (7:7–9)

7 So he showed me [a vision], and see! the Lord was standing above a wall of tin, and in his hand was tin. 8 And the Lord said to me, "What do you see, Amos?" And I said, "Tin." And Yahweh said, "See! I am placing tin in the midst of my people Israel. I will no longer pass over them.

9 "And the high places of Isaac shall be desolated,

and the sanctuaries of Israel shall be laid waste,

and I will rise up against the house of Jeroboam with a sword."

7 This is what he showed me: the Lord was standing beside a wall built with a plumb line, with a plumb line in his hand. 8 And the Lord said to me, "Amos, what do you see?" And I said, "A plumb line." Then the Lord said,

"See, I am setting a plumb line

in the midst of my people Israel;

I will never again pass them by;

9 the high places of Isaac shall be made desolate,

and the sanctuaries of Israel shall be laid waste,

and I will rise against the house of Jeroboam with the sword."

7. וְהִנֵּה כֹּה הִרְאַנִי (so he showed me [a vision], and see!): See the Exegesis of verse 1. The phrasing here is identical, except that אֲדֹנָי יְהוָה (the Lord Yahweh) is omitted. The Septuagint's κύριος, followed by the Vulgate's *dominus*, apparently supplements the phrasing to bring it into conformity with verses 1 and 4. אֲדֹנָי (the Lord): See the Exegesis of 1:8. נִצָּב (standing) is a reflexive niphal: the Lord stationed himself. Whereas God relented (נִחַם), in the preceding visions, we now feel that he is unyielding. The Akkadian semantic equivalent, *izuzzum* (to stand/take one's stand), often describes enemy troops taking their stand for battle in Assyrian royal annals (see Ebeling, Meissner, and Weidner, *Inschriften*, pp. 52–55). עַל means above, as it does in 9:1 (see also Gen. 24:13, 43; 28:13; Exod. 17:9); however, the range of this preposition is broad and its sense is largely determined by the structure of the context. חוֹמַת אֲנָךְ (a wall of tin): אֲנָךְ (tin) is a *hapax legomenon*. The meaning of this word, earlier conjectured to be either tin or lead (so BDB, p. 59, and hence plummet or plumbline; KB, p. 69, Senkblei, plummet), from Akkadian *anâku*, which was likewise thought to mean either tin or lead (so von Soden, *Assyrisches Handwörterbuch*, vol. 1, p. 49), is now known to mean tin only, like its Akkadian original (so Landsberger, "Tin and Lead," followed by *CAD*, 1/2 [A], pp. 127–30; see the discussion of the history of interpretation in Holladay, "*ᵃnak* = 'Tin,' Amos 7:7–8"). It is thus possible that חוֹמַת אֲנָךְ connotes a wall of tin. References to walls of

metal in the ancient Near East sometimes have military connotations, for example, Ramses II's boast to his troops that "I am your wall of iron," and the similar comment of Seti I that he was "a great wall of bronze protecting his soldiers" (see Couroyer, "L'Arc d'Airain"). Likewise, Abdimilki of Tyre wrote to Pharaoh, "You are the sun who rises above me, and a wall of bronze erected for me" (Knudtzon, *Die El-Amarna-Tafeln*, vol. 1, pp. 610–11, no. 147, line 53). In all these examples, both biblical and extrabiblical, the significance of the wall is military. In the Old Testament, Jeremiah 15:20 speaks of "a fortified wall of bronze," and in Ezekiel 4:3 we find "an iron wall [קִיר]." The wall may thus symbolize Assyria's military might that Israel was to experience. It is also possible that אֲנָךְ represents a lead weight or plumbline. Thus אֲנָךְ would be "a wall of a plumbline" or "a plumb wall," that is, a vertical wall (see the Exposition). וּבְיָדוֹ אֲנָךְ (and in his hand was tin): Under the former view, אֲנָךְ (tin) anticipates the declaration of the following verse that the Lord is going to put tin (a military force) into the midst of his people. On the basis of the latter view, the Lord stands in the midst of his people, on or beside (עַל) the vertical wall, holding a plumbline in his hand.

8. וַיֹּאמֶר יְהוָה אֵלַי מָה־אַתָּה רֹאֶה עָמוֹס (and Yahweh said to me, "What do you see, Amos?"): This question also occurs in 8:2 (see also Jer. 1:11, 13; 24:3). אֲנָךְ (tin): See the Exegesis of the previous verse. For the theory that אֲנָךְ is a play on similar-

---

7. The third vision pictures a wall of metal, symbolizing great military strength—an image that was probably familiar to Amos and to others in the ancient Near East. The metal is tin, and the word used for it is a *hapax legomenon* in the Old Testament, but known from Akkadian. The use of this Akkadian word is no accident. For Akkadian was the language of Assyria, and in a few years the Lord would use Assyria to punish Israel. In the preceding visions God may have seemed vacillating, in that he responded unconditionally to the prophet's prayer. In the third vision, however, there is an atmosphere of determination: God *stations himself* (niṣṣāb) above this wall of tin. The Akkadian semantic equivalent often appears in Assyrian royal annals to describe enemy troops taking up their position for attack. His position above the wall is a commanding one—perhaps suggesting also his position of authority over the Assyrian Empire which he will use as a judgment instrument. In his hand is some of the tin—sym-

bolic of Assyrian power—which will come from the east to conquer Israel. (Similarly, in 9:1, the Lord appears above the altar, showing his authority over it as, from that position, he destroys the temple.) The traditional interpretation, that the Lord stands with a *plumbline* in his hand by a *vertical* wall (ḥômat ʾănāk—"wall of a plumbline")—all representative of a "standard" by which he will judge his people—rests on an old misunderstanding of the term for "tin." In the third vision, then, the Lord imparts to Amos both a sight and a term which indicate the impending Assyrian invasion.

8. The Lord asks Amos what he sees, as though to lead him pedagogically into a full understanding of the vision. He does this, because this vision, unlike the others, will be fulfilled, and it is important that the prophet grasp it. Amos replies that he sees ʾănāk (see v. 7 for explanation). The Lord now explains the meaning of this otherwise curious vision. He is even now in the process of placing the ʾănāk in Israel's midst. The vision is fore-

sounding words such as אָנַק (moaning) or אָנַח (groaning), see Horst ("Das Visionsschilderung der alttestamentlichen Propheten"), Ouellette ("Le Mur d'Étain dans Amos 7:7–9"), and Stuart (*Hosea–Jonah*, pp. 372–73). The theory compares the use of אֲנָךְ in verse 7 with the use of קָיִץ (summer fruit) in 8:1–2, and the use of אֲנָךְ in verse 9 with the use of קֵץ (end) in 8:2 (see the Exegesis of 8:1–2). Just as קָיִץ (summer fruit) in 8:1–2 prepares the reader or hearer for the word play with קֵץ (end) in 8:3, so here the use of אֲנָךְ (tin) in 7:7 is supposed to prepare the reader or hearer for the use of אֲנָךְ (moaning) in 7:8. The obvious problem, however, is that in 8:1–3 the word play involves two *different*, but similar-sounding words, whereas here the same word is simply repeated. The point of אֲנָךְ in 7:8 does not depend on a word play—for there is no word play. אֲדֹנָי (the Lord): See the Exegesis of 1:8. הִנְנִי שָׂם (see! I am placing): For this construction, see the Exegesis of 6:14. The particle and the participle express immediacy: The Lord is even now in the process of doing what he says. בְּקֶרֶב עַמִּי (in the midst of my people): For the Lord in the midst of the people, see Numbers 14:14. The phrase עַמִּי יִשְׂרָאֵל (my people Israel) also occurs in Jeremiah 7:12; 12:14; Ezekiel 25:14; 36:12. לֹא־אוֹסִיף עוֹד (I will no longer; lit. I will not add again [to pass over them]) also occurs in 8:2 (also compare the phrases *shall enter you no more* in Isa. 52:1 and *I will no longer have pity on the house of Israel* in Hos. 1:6). עֲבוֹר לוֹ (pass over them; lit. pass over him [i.e., Israel, Yahweh's people]) also occurs in 8:2. The complete idiom, however, is עֲבוֹר עַל־פֶּשַׁע לְ (to pass over the transgression of someone), as in Micah 7:18 (see also Prov. 19:11).

9. וְנָשַׁמּוּ (and . . . shall be desolated): The verb in the niphal is used of the desolation of lands (e.g., Jer. 12:11; Ezek. 29:12; Zech. 7:14), highways (Lev.

26:22; Isa. 33:8), cities (Isa. 54:3; Ezek. 36:35; Amos 9:14), and altars (Ezek. 6:4), and generally of the results of divine judgment. בָּמוֹת (the high places) were elevated sites, either natural (e.g., 1 Kings 3:2; 2 Kings 17:10) or constructed (Jer. 7:31; 1 Kings 11:7; 2 Kings 17:9). Used for idolatrous worship, they were patterned after Canaanite high places (Deut. 12:2). The term, apart from its religious significance, denotes a hill or natural eminence (e.g., Deut. 32:13; 2 Sam. 1:19). The Semitic equivalents are Akkadian *bamâtu* (open country) and Ugaritic *bmt* (high place): "The high places [i.e., hills, mountaintops] of the earth shook [when Baal spoke—i.e., thundered]" (Gibson, *Canaanite Myths and Legends*, p. 65, no. 4, col. 7, lines 34–35). יִשְׂחָק (Isaac) is a softened form of יִצְחָק and also occurs in verse 16; Psalm 105:9; and Jeremiah 33:26. It appears only here and in verse 16 as a synonym of Israel. מִקְדְּשֵׁי יִשְׂרָאֵל (the sanctuaries of Israel) appears only here, but compare "the holy places of the LORD's house" (Jer. 51:51). The sanctuaries, as the root קדשׁ (holy, separate) indicates, were set aside for worship—but in this case, for idolatrous worship. יֶחֱרָבוּ (shall be laid waste): The verb (qal) appears frequently with the sense of drying up (e.g., Gen. 8:13; Ps. 106:9; Isa. 44:27), hence, in general, becoming desolate or waste, said of lands (e.g., Isa. 60:12), cities (e.g., Jer. 26:9), and altars (Ezek. 6:6). וְקַמְתִּי עַל־בֵּית יָרָבְעָם (and I will rise up against the house of Jeroboam): The same phrase occurs in Isaiah 31:2 ("he [i.e., Yahweh] will rise against the house of the evil doers"). For קוּם as a warlike idiom, see Isaiah 14:22. בֶּחָרֶב (with a sword): The sword is symbolic of the conqueror (Assyria), whom the Lord will raise up (קוּם, hiphil) against Israel (6:14). For the sword as a symbol of judgment, see Exodus 5:3; Leviticus 26:25; Deuteronomy 32:25; Isaiah 1:20.

---

boding: The Lord has come into Israel's midst. We should not be surprised to read of subsequent judgment, as the Lord will no longer pass over his people. For long years he let them go on in their misguided worship and their unjust administration of the Mosaic law. Now he will no longer allow that. His grace gives place to judgment. It is important that we have a full knowledge of God that includes all his attributes. Otherwise we shall have a god of our own making.

9. The first two cola of this tricolon employ language reminiscent of Leviticus 26:30–31 (high places, waste places, desolate, sanctuaries), one of

the curse sections (Lev. 26:14–46) in the original covenantal documents. The two cola are exactly parallel, with chiasmus:

a	**b**
and shall be desolated	the high places of Isaac
b´	**a´**
and the sanctuaries of Israel	shall be laid waste.

The final colon "wraps it up," asserting that "I will rise against the house of Jeroboam with a sword," thus tying the final colon to the preceding by means of a word play on *yeḥĕrābû* (shall be laid waste) and *beḥāreb* (with a sword). The use of three proper names, Isaac, Israel, and Jeroboam, not only structures the tricolon, but also contributes to a sense of thoroughness: the judgment will be complete—on sanctuaries, people, and royal household. The Lord is faithful, both to bless and to curse. Long before, in the original covenant documents, he had promised blessings if Israel obeyed and curses if she rebelled. One of the curses was the destruction of idolatrous places of worship (Lev. 26:30–31). The high places (*bāmôt*) were the pagan sanctuaries where the people of the northern kingdom carried on their strange synchretistic worship. They figured prominently in the ancient world. King Mesha of Moab boasted, "I made this high place for Chemosh" (Donner and Röllig, *Kanaanäische und aramäische Inschriften*, vol. 1, p. 33, no. 181, line 3; vol. 2, p. 168). Josiah desecrated the high places that "King Solomon of Israel had built for Astarte the abomination of the Sidonians, for Chemosh the abomination of Moab, and for Milcom the abomination of the Ammonites" (2 Kings 23:13). Josiah also demolished the altar and high place at Bethel (2 Kings 23:15). But the judgment that the Lord would bring would be more complete than Josiah's reformation.

III. Prophetic Visions (7:1–9:15)
B. Visions of Judgment Not Turned Aside (7:7–9:10)
2. Autobiographical Interlude (7:10–17)

10 And Amaziah, the priest of Bethel, sent word to Jeroboam, the king of Israel: "Amos has conspired against you in the very heart of the house of Israel! The land cannot endure all his words! 11 For thus says Amos: 'By the sword shall Jeroboam die, and Israel shall surely go into exile away from his land.'" 12 And Amaziah said to Amos, "O seer, flee swiftly to the land of Judah, and earn your living by prophesying there.
13 "At Bethel you shall never prophesy again,
> for it is a royal sanctuary,
> and it is a temple of the kingdom."

14 But Amos answered, and said to Amaziah, "I was not a prophet, and I was not a prophet's disciple, but I was a livestock breeder, and a sycamore-fig dresser. 15 But Yahweh took me from tending the flock, and Yahweh said to me, 'Go, prophesy to my people Israel.'
16 "But now, hear the word of Yahweh,
> you who say,
> 'You shall never prophesy against Israel,
> and you shall never preach against the house of Isaac.'

17 Therefore thus says Yahweh:
> 'Your wife shall be a prostitute in the city,
> and your sons and your daughters shall fall by the sword,
> and your land shall be parceled out by measure,
> and as for you, you shall die in an unclean land,
> and Israel shall surely go into exile away from his land.'"

10 Then Amaziah, the priest of Bethel, sent to King Jeroboam of Israel, saying, "Amos has conspired against you in the very center of the house of Israel; the land is not able to bear all his words. 11For thus Amos has said,
> 'Jeroboam shall die by the sword,
> and Israel must go into exile
> away from his land.'"

12 And Amaziah said to Amos, "O seer, go, flee away to the land of Judah, earn your bread there, and prophesy there; 13but never again prophesy at Bethel, for it is the king's sanctuary, and it is a temple of the kingdom."
14 Then Amos answered Amaziah, "I am no prophet, nor a prophet's son; but I am a herdsman, and a dresser of sycamore trees, 15and the LORD took me from following the flock, and the LORD said to me, 'Go, prophesy to my people Israel.'
16 "Now therefore hear the word of the LORD.
> You say, 'Do not prophesy against Israel,
> and do not preach against the house of Isaac.'

17 Therefore thus says the LORD:
> 'Your wife shall become a prostitute in the city,
> and your sons and your daughters shall fall by the sword,
> and your land shall be parceled out by line;
> you yourself shall die in an unclean land,
> and Israel shall surely go into exile away from its land.'"

10. אֶל . . . וַיִּשְׁלַח (and [Amaziah] sent word . . . to; lit. sent to): The collocation שָׁלַח אֶל connotes the sending of a message (2 Sam. 11:6). For the same idiom with לֵאמֹר (represented here by quotation marks), see Genesis 38:25 and 1 Kings 20:5. The literal meaning of אֲמַצְיָה (Amaziah) is "Yahweh is mighty." As is often—and sadly—the case with Old Testament theophoric names, the name is far from being an indication of the character or godliness of its bearer. כֹּהֵן בֵּית־אֵל (the priest of Bethel): The construct state requires כֹּהֵן (priest) to be definite. This may indicate that Amaziah was the high priest, that is, *the* priest of consequence at Bethel, the central sanctuary of the northern kingdom. בֵּית־אֵל (Bethel): See the Exegesis of 4:4. יָרָבְעָם (Jeroboam) apparently means "the people increase" (an alternative possibility is "the people contend"; see BDB, p. 914). קָשַׁר עָלֶיךָ (has conspired against you) has as its basic sense the idea of binding. Several contexts energize it with the sense of joining together to conspire against someone. The context here requires the sense of con-

spire. בְּקֶרֶב בֵּית יִשְׂרָאֵל (in the very heart [lit. midst] of the house of Israel): Amos appropriately does his prophetic (although not treasonous) work "in the heart or midst of the house of Israel," since it is Samaria, the center of that kingdom, which has "oppression in her midst" (3:9, on which see the Exegesis). בֵּית יִשְׂרָאֵל (the house of Israel): See the Exegesis of 5:1. הָאָרֶץ (the land) is Israel considered as a geopolitical entity. לֹא־תוּכַל . . . לְהָכִיל ([the land] cannot endure; lit. contain): Perhaps Amaziah is portraying Amos's prophesying as so abundant that the land cannot contain it—as though the land were being overrun by a flood. The use of כִּיל (hiphil) in kindred passages supports this interpretation (Jer. 6:11; 10:10; Joel 2:11). The Old Testament usage implies a sense of inability to contain the Lord's wrath or as here, words of divine wrath, as the sense of Amaziah's statement. אֵת־כָּל־דְּבָרָיו (all his words): For similar phrasing in the context of a prophetic message considered burdensome, see Jehoiakim's reaction to "all the words" of Jeremiah (Jer. 36:24–26).

---

10. This verse begins an autobiographical section that includes Amaziah's message to Jeroboam (vv. 10–11), Amaziah's rebuke of Amos (vv. 12–13), and Amos's reply (vv. 14–17). The section is narrated in the third person, but this does not per se make it biographical (see the Introduction). The use of third person in autobiographical narrative is well attested in the Old Testament (e.g., the third-person narratives of Jeremiah, concluding at Jer. 51:64 with "the words of Jeremiah end here," NIV—but not including chap. 52, which was possibly written by Baruch) and commonplace in the ancient Near East. Examples of the latter category include the historical prologues of Hittite treaties (e.g., Suppiluliuma-Mattiwaza in Weidner, *Politische Dokumente aus Kleinasien*, pp. 2–5, no. 1 verso, lines 10–14) and the annals of the Assyrian kings (e.g., Assur-bel-kala in King, *Annals of the Kings of Assyria*, pp. 128–49; and Borger, *Einleitung in die assyrischen Königsinschriften*, vol. 1, pp. 138; Tukulti-Ninurta II in Schramm, "Die Annalen des assyrischen Königs Tukulti-Ninurta II.," pp. 148–54, 156–58; and Assurnasirpal II in King, *Annals of the Kings of Assyria*, pp. 269–72, lines 46–54, and pp. 306–7, lines 34–38)—all of which demonstrate third-person narrative intermixed with first-person narrative, as in Jeremiah, and even longer stretches of third-person narrative than here (especially the Assur-bel-kala text).

This autobiographical section illustrates the

official reaction to Amos's prophesying, as well as the Lord's reaction (v. 17). Amaziah sent word to Jeroboam about Amos, whom he says had conspired against the king by his words. Amos's message must have been quite powerful, for Amaziah said that the land cannot contain it. His reaction is the typical reaction of darkness against light. Later, Jeremiah faced the same problem in the southern kingdom, and still later, in John 3:19–20, the greatest of the prophets articulated the foundational principle that we see at work in these Old Testament examples: "This is the verdict: Light has come into the world, but men loved darkness instead of light because their deeds were evil. Everyone who does evil hates the light, and will not come into the light for fear that his deeds will be exposed" (NIV).

Amaziah's accusation was unfounded. Amos was not conspiring against Jeroboam or even Israel. But his prophesying against both could certainly have given that impression. Later, Jeremiah was considered treasonous (i.e., as one who favored Babylon) because of his prophecies against Judah (Jer. 26:7–11; 37:11–38:4). The verb *qāšar* (conspire) is used of Baasha, who conspired against Nadab (son of Jeroboam I), killing him and succeeding him as king (1 Kings 15:27–28); and of Shallum, who conspired against Zechariah (son of Jeroboam II), assassinating him and succeeding him as king (2 Kings 15:10–12), thus helping to fulfill Amos's prophecy of verse 9.

11. כִּי (for) gives the reason why the land cannot bear Amos's words: it is because Amos has predicted the destruction of the land. כֹּה אָמַר עָמוֹס (thus says Amos): This formula applies most frequently to the Lord in the Old Testament, particularly in the Pentateuch and prophetic literature. Occasionally it applies to others as well (e.g., Pharaoh, Exod. 5:10—perhaps ironically, as a contrast to Yahweh). Here it introduces the direct speech of Amos. חֶרֶב (sword) frequently functions as a metonomy for a violent death or death in war (Jer. 14:15; Isa. 1:20). יָרְבְעָם (Jeroboam): See the Exegesis of verse 10. יִשְׂרָאֵל גָּלֹה יִגְלֶה (Israel shall surely go into exile): This phraseology is identical to that at 5:5 ("for Gilgal will surely go into exile"), with the substitution of Israel for Gilgal (which equally represented all Israel). For the word play in the original phrase, see the Exegesis of 5:5. מֵעַל אַדְמָתוֹ (away from his land): This language, "away from one's land," is rooted in the curse section (Deut. 29:27 [28]) of the original covenant documents and appears subsequently in the histories of Israel (2 Kings 17:23) and Judah (2 Kings 25:21)—both again with גלה (see also Jer. 12:14; 27:10; and esp.

52:27). The third-person masculine pronoun ending characterizes Israel as masculine, as in 3:14 and 4:12.

12. חֹזֶה (O seer) is a noun form of חָזָה, which has the sense of see, but also connotes the idea of seeing visions (Isa. 1:1; Ezek. 12:27). Thus, חֹזֶה denotes a seer. This word appears to have become a common designation for prophets. לֵךְ בְּרַח־לְךָ (flee swiftly; lit. go, flee): These two imperatives probably form a hendiadys, commanding the swiftest possible flight. This phrase occurs only here. The idiom בְּרַח־לְךָ (flee; lit. flee for yourself) enjoins hasty flight in the presence of danger or threatening anger, as in Genesis 27:43 and Numbers 24:11. וֶאֱכָל־שָׁם לֶחֶם (and earn your living . . . there; lit. and eat bread there): For this phrase as an idiom for "earn a living," see Genesis 3:19 and 2 Kings 4:8 (BDB, p. 37, however, interprets the phrase in Amos 7:12 to mean "spend one's life"). Prophets were remunerated for their word (e.g., 1 Sam. 9:7–8; 1 Kings 18:19; Mic. 3:5, 11). הִנָּבֵא (prophesying) seems to have as its basic sense *to speak for another*. This is its sense in passages

---

11. Amaziah quotes Amos with a formula that ironically recalls the traditional prophetic messenger formula, "Thus says the LORD." Amaziah goes on to paint Amos's words in the worst possible light, attributing to him the prediction that Jeroboam himself would die by the sword. This misrepresentation is probably deliberate, making Amos appear as bad as possible in the king's eyes. But the other prophecy that Amaziah quotes is true. It echoes almost identically Amos's prediction of exile (5:5). That prediction was grounded in the original covenant warnings that foretold the day when all the nations would ask, "Why has the LORD done this to this land?" (Deut. 29:23 [24]), and the answer comes in Deuteronomy 29:24–27 [25–28]: "It is because this people abandoned the covenant of the LORD, the God of their fathers, the covenant he made with them when he brought them out of Egypt. . . . Therefore the LORD's anger burned against this land, so that he brought on it all the curses written in this book. In furious anger and in great wrath the LORD uprooted them from their land and thrust them into another land, as it is now" (NIV).

The threat that Jeroboam will die by the sword is probably an echo of Amos's prophecy of verse 9: "And I will rise up against the house of Jeroboam with a sword." Such words might imply the death of Jeroboam himself by the sword (so Keil, *Twelve*

Minor Prophets, p. 311), although there is no conclusive evidence for this (see 2 Kings 14:29). Either Amaziah was quoting a prophecy by Amos that is no longer extant, or he was misquoting Amos's prophecy at verse 9, either accidentally, or, as seems more probable, to put Amos's words in the worst light before the king.

12. Amaziah commands Amos to flee swiftly to the south and earn his living there. There is no evidence that Amaziah was authorized by the king to say this. Nor is there evidence of any response by Jeroboam to the word that Amaziah had sent him (vv. 10–11). From what we know of Jeroboam (e.g., 2 Kings 14:24), he would not have liked what he heard of Amos's ministry, whether he heard of it from Amaziah or anyone else. But there is no record of any hostile reaction on his part, such as Ahab's imprisonment of Micaiah (1 Kings 22) or Jehoiakim's methodical slicing and burning of the scroll of Jeremiah's prophecies (Jer. 36). Amaziah is apparently speaking on his own account, because, as priest of the official cultus in the north, he feels Amos's prophecies keenly (3:14; 4:4–5; 5:4–6, 21–27). He commands Amos to go to the south, where his prophecies against the north would presumably find more acceptance.

Amaziah's desire to be rid of the unwelcome prophet is typical of the reaction of false religion against God's true light. So in Jesus' day, most of

where the word is informed by context (for the noun, see Exod. 7:1–2; Deut. 18:18; Jer. 1:5–6, 17).

13. בֵּית־אֵל (Bethel): See the Exegesis of 3:14. לֹא־תוֹסִיף (you shall [never prophesy] again): The hiphil of יסף (to add) plus an infinitive means "to do [something] again" and is a frequent construction (BDB, p. 415). The negative particle לֹא (not) plus the imperfect expresses an emphatic negative command, that is, "You shall not at all, at any time, prophesy again at Bethel." כִּי (for) gives the reason or justification for the preceding negative command. מִקְדַּשׁ־מֶלֶךְ (a royal sanctuary): מִקְדָּשׁ most frequently designates the tabernacle and the temple in the Old Testament. In keeping with the concept of the verbal root (קדשׁ), the noun denotes

something devoted to the sphere of the holy. Thus, a sanctuary was an area devoted to the sacred, not the profane. מֶלֶךְ (royal) was apparently the royal sanctuary. הוּא (it), in this clause and the next, gives a degree of emphasis to its referents: for *this* is a royal sanctuary. בֵּית (temple): The parallel structure of these clauses probably invests בֵּית with a sense similar to that of מִקְדָּשׁ (sanctuary), hence temple.

14. לֹא־נָבִיא אָנֹכִי (I was not a prophet): This verbless clause is best translated as a past tense (with the LXX: ἤμην, I was) for two reasons: (1) because to translate it as present contradicts the fact that Amos *is* a prophet (see 3:3, 7–8) and (2) because it comports well with the context, which recalls

---

the official priesthood and religious officials reacted against that greatest of the prophets, because he said what they did not want to hear.

Amaziah called Amos a "seer" (ḥozeh). This term is well attested, both for seers in the royal employ, for example, the following seers of David: Gad (2 Sam. 24:11 par. 1 Chron. 21:9), Heman (1 Chron. 25:5), Asaph (2 Chron. 29:30), and Jeduthun (2 Chron. 35:15); these four are also identified as prophets (2 Sam. 24:11; 1 Chron. 25:1). In Isaiah 29:10 the plural terms *prophets* and *seers* occur in parallel lines. The word is thus appropriate to Amos as a prophet. It is also apropos in view of the fact that he "saw" (ḥazâ) his prophetic message in the first place (1:1).

The words *eat there bread and there prophesy* (a literal translation) form a complex statement, probably a hendiadys (and so translated), but also structured chiastically:

a	b	c
eat (verb)	there (adverb)	bread (direct object)
b´	a´	
there (adverb)	prophesy (verb)	

13. Amaziah ranks himself among those cited in 2:12 as commanding the Lord's prophets not to prophesy. The phrases *royal sanctuary* and *temple of the kingdom* are parallel, but in high prose rather than poetry. Amaziah couches his command in stately rhetoric, befitting the chief priest of the northern kingdom's chief sanctuary. Both phrases are *hapax legomena*. But their meaning is clear. From the beginning, when Jeroboam I established idolatrous worship at Bethel and Dan (see 3:14), the northern kings had a major influence on

the cultus, for example, Omri (1 Kings 16:25–26), Ahab (1 Kings 16:30–33) and Jezebel (1 Kings 18:4, 19), Ahaziah (1 Kings 22:52–54 [51–53]), and Jehoash (2 Kings 13:10–11).

However stately Amaziah's rhetoric, it is without authority, as subsequent events (e.g., vv. 16–17) will show. The Lord deals swiftly with those who threaten his prophets (e.g., the men of Anathoth, Jer. 11:18–23) or persecute them (e.g., Pashhur, Jer. 20:1–6). Likewise he punished those who killed Jesus, the greatest of the prophets. They too, like Amaziah, were motivated to preserve their kingdom and temple (John 11:48). But the result was the same with them, because they could not recognize that the Lord had visited them by his prophet (Luke 19:42–44).

14. This verse introduces Amos's reply to Amaziah and states what Amos was, and was *not*, in the southern kingdom, before the Lord called him. It lays the foundation for the brief account of that divine calling. Amaziah has, implicitly if not explicitly, accused Amos of prophesying as a professional, in order to make a living (v. 13). To this Amos replies (vv. 14–15) that, to the contrary, he never was in a prophetic guild, neither was he ever a prophet in that sense nor in any other sense. He followed agricultural trades, being a livestock breeder and a dresser of sycamore-figs. His declaration sets the stage for the bold, simple statement that (although he was neither a prophet nor a prophet's disciple, but rather an agricultural tradesman) the Lord called him and commanded him to prophesy to his people Israel (v. 15).

By translating the verbless clauses *I was not a prophet*, and *I was not a prophet's disciple* there is no need for alternate translations like "No! I am a prophet, but not a son of a prophet," or "I am indeed [reading lû' for lō'] a prophet, but not a son

what Amos *was* before he became a prophet (see the Exposition). כִּי (but) is adversative (BDB, p. 474). בּוֹקֵר (a livestock breeder) is related to בָּקָר (large cattle or oxen). This does not necessarily contradict the suggestion in 1:1 that Amos was a נֹקֵד (shepherd). Rather, he seems to have been a man of several trades. בּוֹלֵס (dresser), a *hapax legomenon*, is related to Ethiopic *balas* (fig or sycamore), hence, it connotes something akin to "handle or dress the sycamore-fig." The שִׁקְמִים (sycamore-fig) is a tree that flourished in the lower

lands, for example, Egypt (Ps. 78:47) and the Shephelah (1 Kings 10:27; 1 Chron. 27:28).

15. וַיִּקָּחֵנִי יְהוָה (but Yahweh took me). Context calls for an adversative function for וְ (but). The verb לָקַח (take) always indicates the sovereign choice and power of God when he is the subject (Gen. 2:21–22; 5:24; 1 Kings 11:37; Job 1:21). Note in particular the close parallel in 2 Samuel 7:8: "I took you . . . from following the sheep [מֵאַחַר הַצֹּאן = מֵאַחֲרֵי הַצֹּאן here] to be prince over my people

of a prophet." The parallelism of the clauses underscores the meaning:

a	b
I (was) not a prophet	and I (was) not a son of a prophet

a´	b´
I (was) a livestock breeder	and (I was) a sycamore-fig dresser

The structure supports a past-tense, parallel translation, and renders less likely a present-tense translation of the first two clauses, and even less likely an adversative translation (as above). Amos is responding here to Amaziah's command in the preceding verse to go south and earn his living by prophesying there. He is making the point that he did not earn his living there by prophesying, because he followed agricultural trades. Nor, implicitly, if he returned home, need he prophesy there to earn a living now. But Amaziah's command also implied that Amos was a "professional prophet," that is, one of the "sons of the prophets" (e.g., 1 Kings 20:35; 2 Kings 2:3, 5, 7, 15; 4:1, 38; 5:22), one trained in a professional prophetic guild to earn his living by prophesying. Amos's response will also answer this point, informing Amaziah that it was by no such means that he became a prophet, but by Yahweh's direct calling (v. 15). Consequently, Amos will presumably one day return to his earlier callings, since he is not a guild prophet. As Wellhausen (*Skizzen und Vorarbeiten*, p. 89) observes, Amos is "an extraordinary messenger . . . his mission is only a temporary interruption of his regular calling."

Amos was a sycamore-fig dresser as well as a breeder of livestock. A dresser of sycamore fruit pierced the fruit to make it edible. "The fruit is infested with an insect (the *Sycophaga crassipes*), and till the 'eye' or top has been punctured, so that the insects may escape, it is not eatable" (W. R. Smith, cited in Driver, *Joel and Amos*, p.

212). Or, the term may refer to the practice of slitting the sycamore-fig before it ripens—a process that ensures that it will turn sweet (Wolff, *Joel and Amos*, p. 314). This task is referred to in the Septuagint as *knizōn* (pricking or nipping). Amos apparently did this along with shepherding and being a herdsman. Since his work may have carried him far from home, the fact that sycamore-figs cannot grow at the altitude of his native Tekoa stands in no way against his claim to the trade of sycamore-fig dresser. For the disclaimer here, compare, in a contrasting sense, Zechariah 13:4–5.

15. Amos replies to Amaziah's challenge with an affirmation of his own divine election. He did not study to be a prophet, nor did he seek to earn his living by that profession (vv. 13–14). Rather, the Lord called him to it from a totally different sphere of employment (v. 14). The phraseology, in which Amos couches the brief narrative of his calling, evokes the Lord's sovereign choice of David, whom he also took from tending flocks to shepherd his people Israel. Amos's use of the very phraseology applied to David may be intended to remind Amaziah that a true prophet, like a true king, became so by divine election (king, Deut. 17:15; prophet, Deut. 18:15; cf. Amos 2:11). Amos cites the Lord's command, "Go, prophesy," perhaps as a counter to the general northern response to the Lord's prophets ("you shall not prophesy at all," 2:12), and certainly as a counter to Amaziah's command, "At Bethel you shall never prophesy again" (v. 13). Amaziah has brought to the contest the full weight of his authority as chief priest of Bethel, but Amos has brought the full weight of the Lord's command.

In an act comparable to the Lord's choice of David, he took Amos from tending the flock and commanded him to prophesy to his people Israel. This is not an incidental parallel, for who could have denied that the mighty King David was indeed a man chosen by the Lord? And if David,

Israel." עַמִּי יִשְׂרָאֵל (my people Israel): See the Exegesis of verse 8.

16. וְעַתָּה (but now): וְ (but) is adversative in this context. וְעַתָּה is a standard introduction for oracles (e.g., Isa. 43:1; 44:1; Jer. 18:11). שְׁמַע דְּבַר־יהוה (hear the word of Yahweh): Compare the command *hear this word* in 3:1. The phrase is a standard oracular introduction and occurs seven times in the singular (here; 1 Kings 22:19; 2 Kings 20:16; Isa. 39:5; Jer. 22:2; 34:4; Ezek. 21:3) and twenty times in the plural (e.g., 2 Kings 7:1; Isa. 1:10; Jer. 2:4; and, with אֵת, Ezek. 34:7). Only here are the two introductory phrases *but now* and *hear the word of the Lord* combined. אַתָּה אֹמֵר (you who say) is a stock phrase expressing challenge in dialogue (e.g., Exod. 2:14; 33:12; 1 Kings 18:11, 14). The phrase introduces what Amaziah has commanded Amos. This preliminary material forms the indictment against the priest. The indictment is followed by a statement of coming judgment, as is standard in prophetic lawsuits. לֹא תִנָּבֵא (you shall never prophesy): See the Exegesis of 2:12 and 7:13. לֹא תַטִּיף (you shall never preach): נָטַף has the basic sense of drip (Judg. 5:4: "And the heavens poured, / the clouds indeed poured water"; the metaphorical use meaning "to preach" is found in Ezek. 21:2 [20:46]; 21:7 [2]; Mic. 2:6, 11). The parallelism and the field of Old Testament usage indicate a sense of fluency as the unction of the

Spirit gives utterance. יִשְׂרָאֵל (Israel): See the Exegesis of 5:1. בֵּית יִשְׂחָק (the house of Isaac): It is clear from the parallel structure that the expression means, in effect, the northern kingdom. For although Israel can be inclusive of both the north and the south, in Amos it designates the northern kingdom. Only secondarily does it imply both kingdoms. On the form יִשְׂחָק, see the Exegesis of verse 9.

17. לָכֵן כֹּה־אָמַר יהוה (therefore thus says Yahweh): See the Exegesis of 5:16. This phrase introduces the verdict, based on the foregoing indictment (v. 16), and comes forth in poetical form, with increased power. תִזְנֶה (shall be a prostitute): The verb and its related noun have the sense of engaging in prostitution (e.g., Gen. 38:24; Josh. 2:1) or promiscuity (Deut. 22:21), yet it almost always occurs with theological overtones connoting idolatry (e.g., Exod. 34:15; 2 Chron. 21:13; Isa. 1:21; Jer. 2:20; Ezek. 6:9; Hos. 1:2). The latter sense is not intended here, however (see the Exposition). וּבָנֶיךָ וּבְנֹתֶיךָ בַּחֶרֶב יִפֹּלוּ (and your sons and your daughters shall fall by the sword): For the full expression, see Ezekiel 24:21. For "your sons and your daughters" in covenant curses, see Deuteronomy 28:32, 53; in covenant lawsuits, see Jeremiah 5:17 and Ezekiel 23:25. The phrase *will fall by the sword* is typical in prophetic oracles (e.g., Isa. 3:25; 13:15; Jer. 39:18; Ezek. 5:12; Hos. 7:16;

---

so then Amos. But Amaziah did not recognize Amos's divine calling and mission. If he had, he would have realized in his own life the promise made later by Jesus: "Whoever welcomes a prophet in the name of a prophet will receive a prophet's reward" (Matt. 10:41).

16. Amos continues his response to Amaziah with an oracle introduced by standard phrases. Amaziah must have expected a strong statement from the prophet, but before the oracle comes, Amos repeated Amaziah's own commands to him. These commands function now as evidence for the prosecution. The judgment will be severe (v. 17).

Amos reflects on what Amaziah has said. Amaziah has commanded him to go south and prophesy (v. 12). Consequently, it is quite impossible that Amos now accuses Amaziah of "forbidding him to prophesy—period" (i.e., that Amaziah is actually forbidding him to prophesy in either kingdom, since "house of Isaac" implies Judah also—see Stuart, *Hosea–Jonah*, p. 377), unless the implication is that if he may not prophesy in the north, then he cannot prophesy at all, since the

north is where Yahweh has called him to prophesy.

17. Amos now directs an oracle from the Lord directly at Amaziah. As is frequent in Old Testament and New Testament punishments, both the sinner and his household are punished (e.g., Josh. 7; Matt. 18:25). Amaziah's wife will be forced from her position of high regard as the wife of the priest of Bethel and will become a prostitute in the city itself, where she may be seen in her disgrace by those who knew her. His sons and daughters will fall by the sword, slain by the conqueror. His land will be parceled out by the Assyrians, and Amaziah himself will die in their unclean land—meaning, of course, that he will be exiled there and never return. And, to add emphasis, the Lord repeats Amaziah's own words against him, declaring that "Israel shall surely go into exile away from his land."

The reference to Amaziah's wife does not imply that she will be raped, for the verb is never used in this sense, although such was the lot of some women when judgment came (e.g., Deut. 28:30; Isa. 13:16; Zech. 14:2). The idea is, rather, that

cf. Deut. 32:25). אַדְמָתְךָ (your land) is used in several senses, in both the Old Testament and in Amos. It can refer to the whole earth (e.g., Gen. 28:14; Amos 3:2), the earth in the sense of dirt or soil (Gen. 2:7; Amos. 3:5), land as a personal possession (Gen. 47:18, 22; Prov. 12:11; 28:19; Amos 7:17), or a particular land (e.g., Egypt, Gen. 47:26; Assyria, Amos 7:17). It frequently denotes the promised land of Israel (e.g., Exod. 20:12; Deut. 4:40; Josh. 23:13; Amos. 5:2; 7:11, 17; see the Exposition). וְאַתָּה . . . תָּמוּת (and as for you, you shall die): For a prophetic judgment of death against other disobedient priests, see 1 Samuel 2:34 (Eli's sons) and Jeremiah 20:1–6 ("and you, Pashhur, and all who live in your house, shall go into captivity, and to Babylon you shall go; there you shall die, . . . you and all your friends, to whom you have prophesied falsely"—v. 6). אֲדָמָה טְמֵאָה (an unclean land) is a *hapax legomenon*; similar concepts of

land defilement occur in Joshua 22:19 ("if your land [אֶרֶץ] is unclean [i.e., has somehow become unclean], cross over into the Lord's land"), Micah 2:10 (the land of Israel is made unclean by false prophesy and oppression), and Zechariah 13:2 ("on that day, says the Lord of hosts, I will cut off the names of the idols from the land [אֶרֶץ], so that they shall be remembered no more; and also I will remove from the land [אֶרֶץ] the prophets and the unclean spirit"). Hosea expresses a similar concept against Israel: "They shall not remain in the land [אֶרֶץ] of the Lord; / but Ephraim shall return to Egypt, / and in Assyria they shall eat unclean food" (9:3). Banishment to such a land would be especially disagreeable to a priest, such as Amaziah, for whom ritual "cleanness" was a daily consideration (see Lev. 11). On Israel's exile, see the Exegesis of verse 11.

Amaziah's wife will engage in prostitution in order to provide for herself (cf. Isa. 4:1). The fact that her prostitution will take place "in the city" may well indicate heightened disgrace for a woman of high position (Wellhausen, *Skizzen und Vorarbeiten*, p. 90).

The word *ʾădāmâ* (land) has three senses in this verse: a plot of land (Amaziah's, as discussed below), a pagan land (implicitly, Assyria, in the next colon), and Israel (in the concluding line = v. 11). The use of this word in more than one sense in one verse finds a ready parallel in Genesis 47:26: "So Joseph made it a statute concerning the land of Egypt, and it stands to this day, that Pharaoh should have the fifth. The land of the priests alone did not become Pharaoh's." For land in the sense of property, see also Genesis 47:18, 19, 20, 22, 23. Amos's pronouncement against Amaziah's land could either mean the land of Israel (Stuart, *Hosea–Jonah*, p. 378) or Amaziah's own holdings (Keil, *Twelve Minor Prophets*, p. 313; Driver, *Joel and Amos*, p. 213; Mays, *Amos*, p. 140; Wolff, *Joel and Amos*, pp. 315–16). The latter is far more likely, not, as Wolff suggests, because the same word is used of "an individual plot of ground" in

3:5, for it is used there simply in the sense of the ground or dirt from which a snare springs into action. Rather, the context is one of personal address to Amaziah: it is *his* wife, *his* sons and daughters, who will be affected. Even the last line of the oracle, which speaks of Israel, is personal, because it is a verbatim quote of what Amaziah said earlier (v. 11), and so *his* words return to him now as a personalized barb. The similarity of this phrase to Micah 2:4 ("among our captors he parcels out our fields") further argues in favor of this interpretation. The use of a measure or measuring line, however, "would suit an interpretation of אדמה [*ʾădāmâ*, land] as referring to either the substantial holdings of an individual landowner or the total territorial possession of Israel (cf. Mic. 2:4–5)" (Wolff, *Joel and Amos*, p. 316), since the word can be used for the measurement of a small space (e.g., the length of a man, 2 Sam. 8:2), a city (Jerusalem, Zech. 2:5 [1]), or a land (Argob, Deut. 3:4, 13). In context it may indicate the parceling out of Amaziah's substantial holdings. For the thought, see Jeremiah 6:12.

III. Prophetic Visions (7:1–9:15)
B. Visions of Judgment Not Turned Aside (7:7–9:10)
3. Vision of Summer Fruit (8:1–3, 4–14)
a. The Vision (8:1–3)

8 So the Lord Yahweh showed me [a vision],
> and there was a basket of summer fruit.

2 And he said, "What do you see, Amos?" And I said, "A basket of summer fruit." And Yahweh said to me,
> "The end has come to my people Israel;
> I will no longer pass over them.

3 And the temple songs will change to howls on that day"—
> oracle of Lord Yahweh. "They will cast out abundant corpses, everywhere—Hush!"

8 This is what the Lord GOD showed me—a basket of summer fruit. 2 He said, "Amos, what do you see?" And I said, "A basket of summer fruit." Then the LORD said to me,
> "The end has come upon my people Israel;
> I will never again pass them by.

3 The songs of the temple shall become wailings in that day,"
says the Lord GOD:
"the dead bodies shall be many,
> cast out in every place. Be silent!"

8:1. כֹּה הִרְאַנִי אֲדֹנָי יְהוִה (so the Lord Yahweh showed me [a vision]): See the Exegesis of 7:1. יְהוִה אֲדֹנָי (the Lord Yahweh): See the Exegesis of 1:8. הִנֵּה (untranslated) is an emphatic particle that draws our attention to the basket (a similar use of הִנֵּה occurs in 2:13). כְּלוּב (a basket) was apparently used to collect fruit from trees. The word seems to denote some sort of wicker or woven container, since its only other occurrence signifies a cage for birds (Jer. 5:27). קָיִץ (summer fruit) denotes ripe fruit, as in 2 Samuel 16:1–2; Isaiah 16:9; 28:4. The root meaning of the word is "summer" or "summer heat" (BDB, p. 884). Its significance lies in its resemblance to קֵץ (end) in the next verse ("the end has come to my people Israel") for it sets the stage for the punning interpretation. Compare the word play on שָׁקֵד (almond tree) and שֹׁקֵד (watching) in Jeremiah 1:11–12, where the Lord gives Jeremiah a vision of the branch of an *almond tree* and explicates it by saying that he, the Lord, is *watching* over his word to see that it is fulfilled.

2. וַיֹּאמֶר (and he said): This question-and-response sequence also occurs in 7:8. הַקֵּץ (the end): For קֵץ (end) as a pun on קָיִץ (summer fruit), see the Exegesis of the previous verse. עַמִּי יִשְׂרָאֵל (my people Israel): See the Exegesis of 7:8.

3. וְהֵילִילוּ (and [the temple songs] will change to howls; lit. will howl): This verb is intransitive, as elsewhere in the Old Testament. שִׁירוֹת הֵיכָל (the temple songs): Although the plural form is unattested elsewhere, it is the expected plural of שִׁירָה (song), which is well attested in unbound (Exod. 15:1) and bound (Isa. 5:1; 23:15) forms. There is no need to emend it to שָׁרוֹת (songstresses or female singers), as do, for example, Wellhausen (*Skizzen und Vorarbeiten*, p. 90) and Wolff (*Joel and Amos*, p. 317). בַּיּוֹם הַהוּא (on that day): See the Exegesis of 2:16. נְאֻם אֲדֹנָי יְהוִה (oracle of the Lord Yahweh): See the Exegesis of 1:8 and 2:11. רַב הַפֶּגֶר (abundant corpses) gives the reason for the howling. It is not introduced by כִּי so it stands out starkly in this sentence (see the Exposition). בְּכָל־מָקוֹם (everywhere; lit. in every place): The phrase occurs only four other times in the Old Testament (Num. 18:31; Deut. 12:13; Prov. 15:3; Mal. 1:11). Without the preposition it occurs once in a positive sense (Josh. 1:3), and once in a negative, prophetic context, as here (Isa. 7:23: "On that day every place where there used to be a thousand vines, worth a thousand shekels of silver, will become briers and thorns"). הִשְׁלִיךְ (they [it. he or one] will cast out): Yahweh is not the subject of this verb (Keil, *Twelve Minor Prophets*, p. 314), but rather occurrs with an indefinite subject, that is, one or they. הָס (hush!): Exactly as in 6:10 (on which see the Exegesis).

8:1. The Lord again causes Amos to see a vision, which has no obvious significance in itself, but whose meaning becomes clear in its interpretation. The Lord's method of revelation here illustrates his sovereignty. He alone can give the vision. He alone can interpret it (e.g., Gen. 41:15–16; Dan. 2:27, 45, 47). Indeed, the same was even true of our Lord's parabolic teaching (Matt. 13:10–18).

2. The Lord interrogates Amos, as he did in an earlier vision in 7:7–9. As was the case there, so here, the vision will be fulfilled. Therefore the Lord speaks with Amos about it, so that he will be sure to understand its import. We see an important truth illustrated by this conversation (as also in 7:8). The Lord takes into his confidence those whom he desires to understand his words and his works (cf. 3:7; Gen. 18:17–19). So, much later, when his disciples asked him, "Why do you speak to the people in parables" (Matt. 13:10), Jesus answered them: "The knowledge of the secrets of the kingdom of heaven has been given to you, but not to them. Whoever has will be given more, and he will have an abundance. Whoever does not have, even what he has will be taken from him" (vv. 11–12, NIV).

3. Amos portrays the end of Israel. On that day, the temple songs, whose "din" the Lord could no longer tolerate (5:23), will be transformed into howling. The reason for this is that there will be so many dead bodies that they will be cast out without a decent burial. This is a fate typical of conquered cities in the ancient Near East, especially those conquered by Assyria (see Nah. 3:19: "For who has ever escaped your endless cruelty?"). Assyrian cruelty included piles of the heads and/or hands of the slain, heaped up at a conquered city's gates as a warning to others who might contemplate rebellion. The picture of desolation here is reminiscent of 6:10, where the command "hush!" indicates the futility of calling for help. Assyria would be one instrument by which the Lord would bring this about. Ironically, a similar fate was soon to befall Assyria, as the prophet Nahum said:

> Piles of dead,
>> heaps of corpses,
> dead bodies without end—
>> they stumble over the bodies! (3:3)

And, sadly, a similar fate would befall Judah, which also fell away from the Lord (Jer. 16:4).

III. Prophetic Visions (7:1–9:15)
B. Visions of Judgment Not Turned Aside (7:7–9:10)
3. Vision of Summer Fruit (8:1–3, 4–14)
b. Indictments and Explanation of Coming Judgments (8:4–14)

4 Hear this, you who crush the needy,
  even exterminating the oppressed
    people of the land,
5 Saying: "When will the New Moon be
    past,
  that we may market grain,
and the sabbath,
  that we may open the granaries,
lightening the ephah and weighting the
    shekel,
  and cheating with false scales?
6 So that we may buy the poor for silver,
  and a needy man for a pair of sandals,
  and sell the refuse of wheat as grain?"
7 Yahweh has sworn by the pride of Jacob,
  "I will never forget all of their deeds.
8 Shall not the land shake on account of
    this,
  and everyone who dwells in it mourn,
and all of it rise like the Nile,
  and be tossed about and recede like
    the Nile of Egypt?"
9 "On that day"—
  oracle of the Lord Yahweh—
  "I will make the sun set at noon,
  and I will darken the land in broad
    daylight.
10 I will turn your feasts to mourning,
  and all your songs to laments;
I will put sackcloth upon all loins,
  and baldness upon every head;
I will make it like the mourning for an
    only son,
  and its end like a bitter day.
11 Even now days are coming"—
  oracle of the Lord Yahweh—
  "when I will send a famine into the
    land,
not a famine of bread,
and not a thirst for water,
  but of hearing the words of Yahweh.

4 Hear this, you that trample on the
    needy,
  and bring to ruin the poor of the land,
5 saying, "When will the new moon be
    over
  so that we may sell grain;
and the sabbath,
  so that we may offer wheat for sale?
We will make the ephah small and the
    shekel great,
  and practice deceit with false balanc-
    es,
6 buying the poor for silver
  and the needy for a pair of sandals,
  and selling the sweepings of the
    wheat."
7 The LORD has sworn by the pride of Ja-
    cob:
  Surely I will never forget any of their
    deeds.
8 Shall not the land tremble on this ac-
    count,
  and everyone mourn who lives in it,
and all of it rise like the Nile,
  and be tossed about and sink again,
    like the Nile of Egypt?
9 On that day, says the Lord GOD,
  I will make the sun go down at noon,
  and darken the earth in broad day-
    light.
10 I will turn your feasts into mourning,
  and all your songs into lamentation;
I will bring sackcloth on all loins,
  and baldness on every head;
I will make it like the mourning for an
    only son,
  and the end of it like a bitter day.
11 The time is surely coming, says the
    Lord GOD,
  when I will send a famine on the land;
not a famine of bread, or a thirst for wa-
    ter,
  but of hearing the words of the LORD.

¹² And they shall stagger from sea to sea,
    and from north to east they shall has-
      ten,
  to seek the word of Yahweh,
  but they shall not find it.
¹³ In that day the beautiful maidens and
    young men
  will grow faint for thirst.
¹⁴ Those who swear by the shame of Sa-
    maria,
  and say, 'As your god lives O Dan,'
  and, 'As the way to Beer-sheba lives'—
    they will fall, and will not rise again."

¹² They shall wander from sea to sea,
    and from north to east;
  they shall run to and fro, seeking the
    word of the Lord,
  but they shall not find it.
¹³ In that day the beautiful young women
    and the young men
  shall faint for thirst.
¹⁴ Those who swear by Ashimah of Sama-
    ria,
  and say, "As your god lives, O Dan,"
  and, "As the way of Beer-sheba lives"—
    they shall fall, and never rise again.

4. שִׁמְעוּ־זֹאת (hear this): See the Exegesis of 3:1. הַשֹּׁאֲפִים (you who crush): See the Exegesis of 2:7. אֶבְיוֹן (the needy): See the Exegesis of 2:6 and 4:1. לְשַׁבִּית (even exterminating): The infinitive plus *waw*, following a verb, expresses an idea of intention, effort, or being in the act of (GKC §114p). The sense here, however, is not that of intention or purpose, for the rich and powerful would not actually seek to eliminate the poor, who are their source of income. Rather, they crush the needy, and in so doing effectively exterminate the oppressed people from the land. עֲנָוֵי (the oppressed) presents a minor *kethiv–qere* problem. Should we read עֲנָוֵי (*qere*) from עָנִי (the poor), or עֲנָוֵי (*kethiv*) from עָנָו (the humble)—both from root ענה III (to oppress)? Either way, the translation is much the same, and in any case the former is probably a biform of the latter (BDB, p. 776). אֶרֶץ עֲנָוֵי (the oppressed people of the land) also occurs in Job 24:4; Psalm 76:10 [9]; Isaiah 11:4; Zephaniah 2:3. For the word pair needy/oppressed, see Deuteronomy 15:11; 24:14–15; Proverbs 30:14; 31:20. For the general thought, see Proverbs 30:14.

5. לֵאמֹר (saying) introduces the quotation. יַעֲבֹר (be past) does double duty, applying to Sabbath as

well as new moon. הַחֹדֶשׁ (the new moon) was a festival of the Mosaic covenant, celebrated once every four weeks. It involved burnt, grain, and wine offerings, along with a goat as a sin offering (Num. 28:11–15). It was ranked among the other appointed feasts (Num. 10:10; Isa. 1:14; Hos. 2:13 [11]) and Sabbaths (2 Kings 4:23; Isa. 1:13; Ezek. 46:3; Hos. 2:13 [11]; cf. Col. 2:16) and was popularly observed (e.g., 1 Sam. 20:5, 18, 24). Consequently, by custom if not explicitly by law, the people did not buy and sell at this time. שֶׁבֶר וְנַשְׁבִּירָה (that we may market grain; lit. cause others to buy grain): The context requires a modal translation. The seventh day was a day of rest, founded on God's acts of creation (Exod. 20:8–11) and redemption (i.e., new creation; Deut. 5:12–15). Work was forbidden on this day, not simply that people might honor God (Exod. 20:10), but that like God, in whose image they were made, they might rest (Exod. 20:11; cf. Mark 2:27). וְנִפְתְּחָה־בָּר (that we may open the granaries; lit. the wheat): See Genesis 41:56: "And since the famine had spread over all the land, Joseph opened all the storehouses, and sold to the Egyptians." אֵיפָה לְהַקְטִין (lightening [lit. to make small] the ephah):

---

4. Amos here begins a new oracle that, like 2:6, is directed against those who oppress the poor, "exterminating the oppressed of the land." He does not mean that the privileged are so ruthless that they set out to exterminate the oppressed classes. After all, the oppressed are their livelihood. Rather, by their ruthless greed, they in effect gradually exterminate the needy, by whose exploitation they have gotten unjust wealth.

The world will have poor people until the Lord returns: "For you always have the poor with you" (Matt. 26:11; see also Deut. 15:11). The poor and needy have always been objects of compassion in the Lord's eyes (Exod. 23:11; Deut. 15:7–11; Pss. 69:34 [33]; 72:4, 12–13; Isa. 25:4). So we are reminded that Jesus came "to bring good news to the poor" (Luke 4:18), and that "God [has] chosen the poor in the world to be rich in faith and to be heirs of the kingdom that he has promised to those who love him" (James 2:5). Let the church today, then, like Jesus and Paul, continue to "remember the poor," for that, as the apostle said, was "the very thing I was eager to do" (Gal. 2:10 NIV).

5. The oppressing classes of Amos's day could not wait for the holidays to be over so that they could again go about the business of getting gain for themselves at the expense of the poor. The people could not engage in business on the new

moon or Sabbath. The oppressors whom Amos addressed observed the law by keeping its stipulations regarding these holidays, but they failed to observe the heart of the law by continuing to disregard the plight of the poor and helpless among them.

God intended these laws for the nation's benefit, as Moses declared in Deuteronomy 4:5–6: "See, I have taught you decrees and laws as the LORD my God commanded me. . . . Observe them carefully, for this will show your wisdom and understanding to the nations, who will hear about all these decrees and say, 'Surely this great nation is a wise and understanding people'" (NIV).

Amos also says that they weighted the shekel, a standard weight equaling F(²⁄₅) ounce (11.5 grams). These merchants used shekels heavier than the standard. The shekels were placed in one bowl and the customer's silver in the other (Sellers, "Weights and Measures," pp. 828, 831–32; Scott, "Weights and Measures of the Bible," pp. 32–39). So, against the merchant's illegally heavy shekels, the customers would pay out more than they should—and for an adulterated product! The deception could go even further: in excavations at Tirzah, shops from the eighth century were found with two sets of weights, one for buying and one for selling (Mays, *Amos*, p. 144). Much earlier, Hammurabi's law code said: "If a merchant lent

The infinitive plus ל indicates motive or attendant circumstances (GKC §114o; see the Exposition). וּלְהַגְדִּיל שֶׁקֶל (and weighting the shekel) and וּלְעַוֵּת (and cheating): For the use of these two infinitives, see the Exegesis of verse 4. מֹאזְנֵי מִרְמָה (with false scales) is an adverbial accusative indicating material or means.

6. לִקְנוֹת (so that we may buy) is an infinitive construct with ל. It indicates purpose, as in verse 5. בַּכֶּסֶף (for silver): The words *buy the poor for silver* echo 2:6 ("they sell a righteous man for silver"). These expressions indicate a brutal attitude toward the poor, righteous or otherwise. The privileged treat them like objects, for buying or sell-

---

grain or money at interest and when he lent it at interest he paid out the money by the small weight and the grain by the small measure, but when he got it back he got the money by the large weight (and) the grain by the large measure, that merchant shall forfeit whatever he lent" (*ANET*, p. 169, §94). A related law is this: "If a woman wine seller, instead of receiving grain for the price of a drink, has received money by the large weight and so has made the value of the drink less than the value of the grain, they shall prove it against [variant: they shall bind] that wine seller and throw her into the water" (*ANET*, p. 170, §108). In the "Hymn to the Sun God," found in fragments in the library of Assurbanipal (668–627 B.C.), is this observation: "He who handles the scales in falsehood, / He who deliberately changes the stone weights and lowers their weight, / will make himself lie for the profit and then lose his bag of weights" (*ANET*, p. 388, col. 2, lines 51–53). Such practices also were against Yahweh's covenant—producing weights that were not "honest weights" is condemned in Leviticus 19:36—and ensured Yahweh's judgment (Mic. 6:11). The interpretation that this refers to "overweighting the . . . 'shekel' . . . so that the buyer thought he was getting more than he really was when he saw his grain weighed in the scales against the shekel" (Stuart, *Hosea–Jonah*, p. 384) rests on a mistaken assumption that the grain, rather than the purchase money, was weighed against the shekels. This is unlikely, since it would take a lot of shekels, at $F(\frac{2}{5})$ ounce, to balance a usable amount of grain. (Who, after all, would buy wheat in units of $F(\frac{2}{5})$ ounce, to make bread?) Also, the interpretation is self-contradictory, for if the shekels were overweight, the customers would receive *more* grain, and not less, than they thought they were getting. Finally, the verse illustrates the general commercial difference between weights and measures: the grain was sold in measures, but paid for in weights (Hammurabi's law code §94, cited above, also illustrates this distinction.) So it would have made no sense to put grain in the scales against shekels.

The law says in Leviticus 19:35–36: "Do not use dishonest standards when measuring length, weight or quantity. Use honest scales and honest weights, an honest ephah and an honest hin. I am the LORD your God, who brought you out of Egypt" (NIV). And in Deuteronomy 25:13–16: "Do not have two differing weights in your bag—one heavy, one light. Do not have two differing measures in your house—one large, one small. You must have accurate and honest weights and measures, so that you may live long in the land the LORD your God is giving you. For the LORD your God detests anyone who does these things, anyone who deals dishonestly" (NIV).

One of the ways the people disobeyed the law according to Amos 8:5 was in their "lightening the ephah." This is not that they express a desire to lighten the ephah or weight the shekel (although in fact they do these things), but, rather, that they express a desire to market grain and open the granaries to sell grain, and then "lightening the ephah," "weighting the shekel" and "cheating with false scales" as they sell. The ephah was a standard measure equaling $F(\frac{3}{5})$ bushel (22 liters). The merchants sell a reduced amount as if it were a full measure, thus cheating their customers. It is no longer "an honest ephah" (Lev. 19:36), but a "scant measure that is accursed" (Mic. 6:10). Such deception was clearly contrary to Yahweh's covenant (Deut. 25:14: "Do not have two differing measures in your house—one large, one small").

6. This verse concludes a short portrayal of the injustice rampant in Israel. The net effect of the people's deceit is that the poor and needy must pay the going rate for adulterated goods, and thereby become so impoverished that they must sell themselves to the very ones who have impoverished them. The Mosaic covenant provided for slavery in Leviticus 25:39–43, but it is obvious from the context that the privileged of Israel had no concern for that law or for any other, except the law of self-aggrandizement, which they had laid down for themselves.

ing. On דַּלִּים (the poor) and אֶבְיוֹן (a needy man), see the Exegesis of 2:7. נַעֲלִים (a pair of sandals) in parallel with כֶּסֶף (silver) indicates that the poor were forced to sell themselves (as slaves; see Lev. 25:39–43) for a small amount of silver (see Job 24:9–12). מַפַּל בָּר (the refuse [lit. fallings] of wheat) is erroneously rendered by the Septuagint as καὶ ἀπὸ παντὸς γενήματος (and from every product), reflecting a Hebrew *Vorlage* of וּמִכָּל בָּר. It indicates the bran or unfilled grain that fell (root נפל) to the floor when wheat was threshed. The landed gentry mixed this with the wheat and sold an adulterated product, thus making the poor pay for worthless chaff. No doubt, this impoverished them further so that they had to sell themselves as slaves.

7. נִשְׁבַּע יְהוָה (Yahweh has sworn): See also 4:2, where Yahweh swears by his holiness, and 6:8, where he swears by his life or soul. גְּאוֹן יַעֲקֹב (the pride of Jacob): As noted at 6:8, the phrase may indicate either Israel's attitude of pride or the things that encourage pride, such as military power, independence, and affluence. It may even refer to the Lord himself after the analogy of 1 Samuel 15:29, where the Lord is "the Glory of Israel," or Micah 5:3 [4], where we read that the promised ruler from Bethlehem will shepherd "in

the majesty [גְּאוֹן] of the name of the LORD his God." Most likely, however, we should understand it as we do in Psalm 47:5 [4], where it refers to Israel's inheritance, that is, the promised land itself. אִם־אֶשְׁכַּח לָנֶצַח (I will never forget) is, literally, "if I ever forget." This phrase introduces a standard Old Testament self-imprecatory oath (see the Exposition). For לָנֶצַח plus שָׁכַח, see Psalm 9:19 [18] and, without ל, 13:2 [1]. כָּל־מַעֲשֵׂיהֶם (all of their deeds) has several senses in the Old Testament. It is used positively of the Lord's works (Pss. 103:22; 145:9–10, 17; Dan. 9:14) and of the deeds of his people, which, in fact, are Yahweh's accomplishments (Isa. 26:12). It is used (apparently, both positively and negatively) of the works of all humans as the Lord observes them (Ps. 33:15). It is also used negatively of one man's work—Qoheleth—as being vanity (Eccles. 2:11) and, here, of Israel's deeds as sinful.

8. הַעַל (shall . . . on account of . . . ?): The interrogative particle introduces a rhetorical question, clearly expecting an affirmative answer. עַל (on account) is to be taken with זֹאת (this). These particles form a collocation with the sense of *at this* (Jer. 31:26) or *on account of this* (BDB, p. 754). זֹאת may refer to the sin of Israel, delineated in the previous verses (vv. 4–6), but more than likely it

---

7. The Lord now swears, not by his holiness (4:2) nor by himself (6:8), as before, but by the "pride of Jacob." Given its use earlier in Amos (6:8) and in Psalm 47:5 [4], there can be little doubt what this phrase means. The Lord is swearing by the very land that he swore to give to Abraham's descendants, to Israel. But he does so ironically, for they have polluted the land by their oppression and idolatry. So, like the Canaanites before them, they rendered themselves unfit by their deeds to inhabit it. But the Lord, all of whose works are righteous (Dan. 9:14), will not forget the unrighteous works of Israel. And to remove all doubt, he swears a self-imprecatory oath to that effect. And he swears by that same land that was such an important part of the original covenant, as much as to say, "I gave you this land by covenant, but now by covenant lawsuit I drive you out of it, and I swear this by the land itself, so that you may have no doubt of my intentions!" The full form of this oath is: "If I do (or fail to do) so-and-so, then may such-and-such happen to me." The form is truncated here, as often (e.g., Gen. 14:23; Num. 14:23), and, since a literal translation of the truncated form is awkward, it is generally translated as a negative: "I will *not* do (fail to do) so-and-so

(allow so-and-so to happen)." For the full form, and the same introduction as here, see Psalm 137:5: "If I forget you, O Jerusalem, / let my right hand wither!"

8. The Lord makes it clear that horrible things will happen in the land, because he has resolved to punish it for its sin. He asks a negative rhetorical question, "Shall the land not shake on account of this?" And the question demands a positive response (even more than a positive statement of coming judgment would have). The land will surely shake, it will rise and be tossed about and recede again, just as the waters of the Nile rise, are tossed about by the wind, and recede. In light of other Old Testament passages, this imagery clearly indicates a coming flood of judgment, in the form of an invading nation. Assyria will flood the land, so that the land itself may be said to "rise" with the influx. The invading flood will toss the land about, just as a flood tosses things about when it flows through a region. Then the flood will recede, so that the land itself sinks down with the outflow. What is left? A devastated and impotent vassal state. Because of this judgment, all the inhabitants of the land will mourn.

refers to the Lord's announced judgment (v. 7), for זֹאת is an abstract feminine particle that occurs in Amos to refer to the thought of a previous section (7:3, 6). In this case it refers to the content of the divine oath in the previous verse. לֹא־תִרְגַּז (shall not [the land] shake): The shaking implies upheaval or devastation. The land will tremble under the burden of the impending tragedy and, as a result, the people will be in turmoil (see 1 Sam. 14:15; Isa. 14:16). הָאָרֶץ (land) does not refer to the earth, because the judgment is on Israel, not on the whole earth. Compare the prophetic perfect in Joel 2:10, where the land shall shake before the onslaught of locusts that the Lord brings. בָּהּ וְאָבַל כָּל־יוֹשֵׁב (and everyone who dwells in it [shall] mourn): On אָבַל (mourn), see the Exegesis of 1:2. כָּל־יוֹשֵׁב בָּהּ (everyone who dwells in it) also occurs in Hosea 4:3. וְעָלְתָה (and rise) is associated with flooding in several passages (Isa. 8:7; Jer. 46:7–8; 47:2). כָאֹר (like the Nile) is a defective form for כִּיאֹר, as its parallel with כִּיאֹר מִצְרַיִם (the Nile of Egypt) in the next colon shows (see also the repeti-

tion of the same word at 9:5). וְנִגְרְשָׁה (and be tossed about) is used here of the Nile, but elsewhere of the sea (Isa. 57:20). It describes the surface as tossed about by wind or storm. Here, it is the storm of the Lord's judgment. וְשָׁקְעָה (and recedes; lit. sinks) is a softened form of וְנָשְׁקָעָה, as is apparent from the latter's appearance in 9:5 (שָׁקְעָה). The verb also describes fire dying down (Num. 11:2; cf. also Ezek. 32:14). It is important to consider this verse in its connection with what follows, where the Lord promises to make the sun go down at noon and to darken the moon (v. 9). Much of the terminology of this verse (רגז, ארץ, אבל, יושב) occurs in similar passages that describe divine judgment in terms of seismic and heaven-changing events (e.g., Isa. 24:1–7; Jer. 4:27–28; Joel 2:1, 10). And all of these judgments, with their attendant signs and mournings, anticipate the return of Christ in judgment (see Matt. 24:29–30; Rev. 1:7).

9. וְהָיָה בַּיּוֹם הַהוּא (on that day; lit. and it will be, on that day) is a standard introductory phrase in the prophets (e.g., Isa. 7:18; Jer. 4:9; Ezek. 38:18;

Similar language is used of the Lord's judgment in other prophecies, where we read that the Lord is going to "lay waste the earth . . . and scatter its inhabitants . . . [so that] the world languishes and withers" (Isa. 24:1–4); that "the earth shall mourn, / and the heavens above grow black" (Jer. 4:28); and that "the earth quakes before them [i.e., the punishing army of the Lord], / the heavens tremble. / The sun and the moon are darkened, / and the stars withdraw their shining" (Joel 2:10).

All of these prophecies anticipate the final judgment, when, as Jesus prophesied, "The sign of the Son of Man will appear in heaven, and then all the tribes of the earth shall mourn" (Matt. 24:30).

9. The prophecy of disaster continues, connecting the coming of darkness with the shaking of the land and the mourning of its people mentioned in the previous verse. The coming disaster predicted in the original covenantal curse (Deut. 28:29: "You shall grope about at noon as blind people grope in darkness") must be fulfilled. Likewise Jeremiah, in language clearly related to the covenant curse, warned Judah:

> Give glory to the LORD your God
>   before he brings darkness,
> and before your feet stumble
>   on the mountains at twilight;
> while you look for light,
>   he turns it into gloom
> and makes it deep darkness. (Jer. 13:16)

That the Lord will make the sun set "at noon," and "darken the land in broad daylight," echoes the covenant curse in Deuteronomy 28:29, as do similar passages in the prophets, for example, Isaiah 59:10 ("we stumble at noon as in the twilight"); Jeremiah 15:8 ("I have brought . . . a destroyer at noonday"); 15:9 ("her sun went down while it was yet day"); 13:16 (cited above). On the sun darkening at a time of judgment, see Joel 2:10; 3:4 [2:31]; 4:15 [3:15]; Micah 3:6 ("the sun shall go down upon the prophets, / and the day shall be black over them"). As the latter indicates, the imagery here not only builds on the covenant curse, but expresses symbolically the sudden, unexpected setting of Israel's sun and the darkening of her day, just when the sun seemed at its zenith of prosperity and power. The verse has nothing directly to do with solar eclipses, although eclipses did occur then as now (e.g., a total eclipse for Israel on 9 February 784 B.C., and a partial eclipse on 15 June 763 B.C.), and their occurrence may have suggested the imagery—the sun seeming to "set" at midday—which we find in Deuteronomy and elsewhere in the prophets.

This and other Old Testament prophecies of the day of the Lord may have drawn their imagery from natural phenomena such as solar (and lunar) eclipses, but they expressed a far more important truth. It has been well said that "every judgment that falls upon an ungodly people or kingdom, as the ages roll away, is a harbinger of the approach

Hos. 1:5; Joel 4:18 [3:18]; Mic. 5:9 [10]), occurring only here in Amos. בַּיּוֹם הַהוּא (on that day): See the Exegesis of 2:16. נְאֻם (oracle): See the Exegesis of 2:11. אֲדֹנָי יְהוִה (the Lord Yahweh): See the Exegesis of 1:8. וְהֵבֵאתִי הַשֶּׁמֶשׁ (I will make the sun set): The verb בּוֹא (to go in, qal) is often used of the sun "going in" or "setting" (e.g., Gen. 15:12, 17; Lev. 22:7). The affirmation that the Lord can make the sun set clearly affirms his supremacy, and illustrates, too, that the sun is, after all, just one of his creations. The same point is made in 5:8, where in similar language Yahweh is called "the one who . . . darkens [חָשַׁךְ, hiphil, as here] day into night." בַּצָּהֳרָיִם (at noon) indicates noon, when the sun is highest in the heavens. וְהַחֲשַׁכְתִּי לָאָרֶץ (I will darken the land): The hiphil of חָשַׁךְ appears in a similar affirmation in 5:8. לָאָרֶץ (the land) does not refer to the earth because Israel is in view, not the whole world (note in the subsequent verse: *your* feasts, *your* songs). בְּיוֹם אוֹר (in broad daylight) occurs only here, but its sense is obvious. The companion phrase בַּצָּהֳרָיִם gives this phrase the sense of *daylight*.

10. וְהָפַכְתִּי (I will turn): See 4:11, where Yahweh "overthrew some of you." הָפַךְ with לְ forms a collocation that frequently requires the English sense *turn into* (Exod. 7:17; 1 Sam. 10:6). חַגֵּיכֶם (your feasts): See the Exegesis of 5:21. לְאֵבֶל (to mourning): See the Exegesis of 5:16. שִׁירֵיכֶם (your songs): See the Exegesis of 5:23. לְקִינָה (to lament): See the Exegesis of 5:1. מָתְנַיִם (loins) is generally understood to refer to the middle of the body, that is, the hips and lower back. M. Held ("Studies in Comparative Semitic Lexicography," p. 405) suggests that this word describes the linkage of muscles connecting the upper and lower parts of the body (note its parallelism in Job 40:16 with בֶּטֶן,

belly). In most contexts it is sufficient to understand this term to refer to the hips or lower back (2 Sam. 20:8; Ezek. 47:4). שָׂק (sackcloth) is a rough material not meant for wearing. Clothing one's self with sackcloth indicated the mournful state of the wearer's soul, for whom the comforts of life no longer mattered. קָרְחָה (baldness): The shaving of heads in conjunction with mourning was proscribed in the Mosaic covenant (Deut. 14:1) because of its pagan associations (e.g.; in Moab, with wearing of sackcloth, Isa. 15:2–3 and Jer. 48:37; in Tyre, with sackcloth and dust poured on their heads, Ezek. 27:30–31). Ironically, shaving the head was prophesied for Israel and Judah (Mic. 1:16; with sackcloth in Isa. 3:24). שַׂמְתִּיהָ (I will make it): The feminine pronominal suffix refers to the preceding, that is, all of their former "sunshine" (v. 9) and gaiety. It is the feminine abstract and thus may refer to an entire concept, not simply a single grammatical entity (see the Exegesis of v. 8). כְּאֵבֶל יָחִיד (like the mourning for an only son): See Jeremiah 6:26 and Zechariah 12:10. This was perhaps the most bitter mourning of all, since progeny in the ancient world meant continuity of family and was the closest one might hope to come to immortality. וְאַחֲרִיתָהּ כְּיוֹם מָר (and its end like a bitter day): Compare "the end will be bitter" in 2 Samuel 2:26, and "in the end she is bitter as wormwood" in Proverbs 5:4. As these and other passages indicate, the word מָר (bitter) has tragic overtones in such contexts, indicating destruction that comes as a result of wrong behavior. אַחֲרִיתָהּ (its end): The feminine suffix on this word functions in the same way as on the first word in the colon.

---

of the final judgment" (Keil, *Twelve Minor Prophets*, p. 317).

10. The oracle continues in an ironic litany of reversals. Israel's religious feasts are unclean in the Lord's sight, because the people who partake of them mix idolatry with worship of the Lord (see the Exposition of v. 14). His judgments here are ironic in themselves, being reversals of the expected course of things; but they are also ironic because it has been Israel that, hitherto, has "turn[ed] justice to wormwood" (5:7) and "justice to poison-weed" (6:12). As a fitting punishment for their perversion, the Lord will now turn all their good to bad.

Israel had aroused the Lord's jealousy by polluting themselves with idolatry and concomitant social sin. They had acted as though they were

"stronger than he," and could have their own way. But God would not be mocked. He would turn their feasts into mourning and their songs into lamentation. He would bring such sorrow upon them that they would wear sackcloth and shave their heads in mourning. The mourning would be intense—like that over the loss of an only child. And the end of all their revelry and excess would be bitterness.

What we see here on the historical plane is a type of what one day will occur when the Lord judges not one nation, but all the earth. But the result of that judgment will be "weeping and gnashing of teeth" (Matt. 8:12), who had the opportunity to obey their Lord, but went their own way instead.

11. יָמִים בָּאִים (days are coming): See the Exegesis of 4:2. נְאֻם אֲדֹנָי יְהוִה (oracle of the Lord Yahweh): See the Exegesis of 1:8 and 2:11. וְהִשְׁלַחְתִּי רָעָב בָּאָרֶץ (when I will send a famine into the land): רָעָב (famine) is clarified and intensified by the following synonymously parallel bicola: לֹא־רָעָב לַלֶּחֶם (not a famine of bread) and לֹא־צָמָא לַמַּיִם (not a thirst for water). רָעָב (famine) and צָמָא (thirst) do double duty here and in the last colon, where they are taken with the infinitive construct לִשְׁמֹעַ (of hearing) (see the Exposition). לִשְׁמֹעַ אֵת דִּבְרֵי יְהוָה (of hearing the words of Yahweh): Scarcity of Yahweh's prophetic words was a curse stemming from the original covenant (Deut. 4:28–29; 32:20; see also Hos. 3:4). A similar situation occurred late in the period of the judges, when "all the people did what was right in their own eyes" (Judg. 21:25) and, consequently, we are told that "the word of the LORD was rare in those days; visions were not widespread" (1 Sam. 3:1). This absence of Yahweh's word is a clear sign of his divorce (albeit temporary—Hos. 2:4 [2], 18–22 [16–20]) from his people (see also Luke 17:22).

12. וְנָעוּ (and they shall stagger): See 4:8, where the verb applies to people of various cities staggering about in search of water. Here it describes the people staggering about in search of the word of the Lord. מִיָּם עַד־יָם (from sea to sea): The phrase occurs also in Psalm 72:8 and Zechariah 9:10, where it denotes the ends of the earth (see the Exposition). וּמִצָּפוֹן וְעַד־מִזְרָח (and from north to east) complements the preceding phrase. The two directions are normally mentioned along with south and west, as in 1 Kings 7:25 par. 2 Chron. 4:4; Psalm 107:3; and Zechariah 14:4. North and east occur together to represent the directions from which the Mesopotamian conqueror comes (with, no doubt, much of the same flavor here), in Isaiah 41:25 (see also Dan. 11:44). יְשׁוֹטְטוּ (they shall hasten): The verb שׁוּט (to wander, polel) can connote the action of searching back and forth in a city's streets (Jer. 5:1), of traveling about to increase knowledge (Dan. 12:4), or of the eyes of God roaming about over the earth (2 Chron. 16:9; Zech. 4:10). It is also used, in the qal, of Satan (Job 1:7; 2:2), of those who wander about seeking the manna (Num. 11:8), and of the search for soldiers (2 Sam. 24:2, 8). The picture is that of fruitless pursuit of God's word. לְבַקֵּשׁ אֶת־דְּבַר־יְהוָה (to seek the word of Yahweh) does not appear elsewhere in

---

11. In consequence of their sins, the Lord's people will receive the worst of punishments: not famine, nor thirst, but a famine and thirst for his words. This punishment is terrible, and indeed worse than any material punishment, because, as they already knew from the wilderness wanderings, and as Moses had told them in Deuteronomy 8:3, "[The LORD] humbled you, causing you to hunger and then feeding you with manna, . . . to teach you that man does not live on bread alone but on every word that comes from the mouth of the LORD" (NIV).

Famine (*rāʿāb*) and thirst (*ṣāmāʾ*), or related statives, appear together in seven other Old Testament passages, sometimes, as here, in conjunction with *leḥem* (bread) and *mayim* (water): Deuteronomy 28:48, which forms some of the background for the present curse ("you shall serve your enemies whom the LORD will send against you, in hunger and thirst, in nakedness and lack of everything"); 2 Samuel 17:29; Nehemiah 9:15 ("for their hunger you gave them bread from heaven, and for their thirst you brought water for them out of the rock"); Proverbs 25:21 ("if your enemies are hungry, give them bread to eat; / and if they are thirsty, give them water to drink"); Isaiah 5:13; 29:8; and 32:6.

12. This verse continues the thought of the last. Because of their hunger and thirst after the "words

of the LORD," the people will wander "from sea to sea." This is a difficult expression, but we are probably right to adopt Wolff's view (*Joel and Amos*, pp. 330–31) that it designates "the uttermost boundaries of the earth." It is apparently the Hebrew equivalent of the more ample Akkadian phrase, "from the upper sea to the lower sea" (*ultu tamti elīti adi tamti šaplīti*, from the upper sea to the lower sea; i.e., from the Mediterranean to the Persian Gulf), a stock phrase (with minor variations) in Mesopotamian literature, especially royal inscriptions and annals, for example, Sargon I (Hirsch, "Die Inschriften der Könige von Agade," p. 42, no. 6, lines 48–59), Sargon II (Thureau-Dangin, *La Huitième Campagne de Sargon*, p. 22, line 126), Tukulti-Ninurta I (Weidner, *Die Inschriften Tukulti-Ninurtas I.*, p. 11, no. 5, lines 1–6), Assurbanipal (Thompson, *Prisms of Esarhaddon and Ashurbanipal*, p. 34, col. 4, lines 19–20), Nebuchadnezzar (Langdon, *Die neubabylonischen Königsinschriften*, p. 112, line 21), and Nabonidus (Langdon, *Die neubabylonischen Königsinschriften*, p. 220, lines 41–42). Like the Mesopotamian phrase that it echoes, it indicates the limits of Akkadian, Assyrian, and (later) Babylonian adventurism and conquest. It does not, therefore, indicate a lesser extent (e.g., from the Dead Sea to the Mediterranean), because it applies to the seeking of the people after the Lord has judged them,

the Old Testament, but its sense is amplified by similar expressions (2 Sam. 21:1; Ps. 27:8; Isa. 51:1; Lam. 1:11; Hos. 5:6; Mal. 2:7). וְלֹא יִמְצָאוּ (but they shall not find it): The direct object is understood. For the phrase, see Hosea 2:9 [7]: "She [i.e., Israel] shall pursue her lovers, / but not overtake them"—with the same two verbs in contrast as here. Again, the direct object of the verb *find* is understood. There, ironically, it describes Israel's fruitless search for the Baals whom she loved, after the Lord has punished her. Here, it refers to her fruitless search for the word of the Lord, as part of the punishment. In Ecclesiastes 8:17 the same pair, seek/find, is used of a fruitless search for an understanding of all that God has done under the sun.

13. בַּיּוֹם הַהוּא (in that day): See the Exegesis of 2:16. תִּתְעַלַּפְנָה (will grow faint): עלף has the sense *to cover* in the hithpael, that is, to "cover or hide oneself (with night)," or "to faint or swoon" (see Keil, *Twelve Minor Prophets*, p. 318). However, since the verb describes Jonah's state of enervation in which he is still able to talk with God, it does not indicate there a state of total unconsciousness (Jon. 4:8), but rather of utter weakness and helplessness (as in v. 14 below). See also Isaiah 51:20: "Your children have fainted [pual], /

they lie at the head of every street." הַבְּתוּלֹת (the beautiful maidens) indicates young women of marriageable age. It occurs with (or in parallel to) הַבַּחוּרִים (young men) in Psalm 148:12; Isaiah 23:4; Lamentations 1:18; 2:21; and Zechariah 9:17. Even the young and robust men and women will be at the end of their strength. בַּצָּמָא (for thirst): See verse 11, where the thirst is a spiritual thirst for the words of the Lord. Here, however, the thirst is obviously physical. It is a punishment they have experienced before (4:7–8), but will now experience even more terribly.

14. הַנִּשְׁבָּעִים (those who swear): For the verb, see the Exegesis of 4:2. The participle (niphal) with the definite article can describe those who swear by the Lord (e.g., Isa. 48:1; Zeph. 1:5) or those who swear by a false god (Molech, Zeph. 1:5), as here (see the Exposition). בְּאַשְׁמַת שֹׁמְרוֹן (by the shame of Samaria): Some have suggested an original pointing of אֲשֵׁמָה on the grounds that a deity known as אֲשִׁימָא (Ashima), worshiped by settlers from Hamath in Syria, is mentioned in 2 Kings 17:30 (for discussion, see Wolff, *Joel and Amos*, p. 323). But there is no evidence for this cult earlier at Samaria. The related verb אָשֵׁם (to be guilty) is used of Baal worship in Hosea 13:1. The shame of Samaria might therefore be the altar and temple of

---

that is, after conquest and exile, when they will reside in the empire of the Assyrians, whose kings used the phrase so often to describe the limits of their enterprise. Thus, this expression indicates the full extent of the Assyrian Empire, that is, from the Mediterranean to the Persian Gulf. The people's search, however, will be fruitless. They will seek the word of the Lord, but they will not find him. Their search will be similar to the view of Qoheleth, who sees humanity as seeking to understand all that goes on (in the Lord's providence) under the sun, but not finding it out. It will resemble the state of humans under common grace, without a personal revelation of the Lord, because the Lord will be absent—he will have withdrawn from them for a season. On the other hand, it will not be like humans under common grace, because Israel had God's revealed word, and they understood (from that word and from prophecy) what was going on "under the sun." But there would be no new, fresh revelation of the Lord, and that temporary absence would be felt very keenly, and would be their worst punishment.

13. The oracle takes a slight turn, proceeding from the idea of spiritual thirst for "the words of the Lord" in the previous two verses, to that of physical thirst, because the people cannot find

water. This recalls the curses of 4:6–8, where the judgments on nature come because the people did not turn to the Lord.

14. The Lord announces the end of idolatry in Israel. The "shame" of Samaria (presumably its Asherah worship), the golden calf at Dan, the pilgrimage route to Beer-sheba—all these will come to an end, for the people who gave them meaning shall fall by the Lord's judgment and never rise again. The pagan practices of the people are vividly described in 2 Kings 17:7–17.

The prophet castigates those who "swear by the shame of Samaria." To swear by a god in the ancient world meant to take that god as your own god. The Israelites were commanded to swear by the Lord (Deut. 6:13; 10:20). The idolatrous swore by what were in reality "not gods" (Jer. 5:7), but were, demons (Deut. 32:17). Swearing had to do with oaths (under the sanction of a god or gods), whether between two individuals on a personal matter (e.g., friendship between David and Jonathan, 1 Sam. 20:42) or between nations in a treaty (e.g., the covenant between the Gibeonites and Israel, Josh. 9:18–20). In the covenant between Rahab and the spies, Rahab requested, "Swear to me by the Lord" (Josh. 2:12).

Baal and the Asherah pole (Asherah was a consort of Baal) set up during the reign of Ahab in Samaria (1 Kings 16:32–33) and still there in the days of Jehoahaz (2 Kings 13:6), or it might refer to the golden calf at Bethel set up by Jeroboam I (Amos 3:14; 7:13). In support of the latter option, compare the similar phraseology in Deuteronomy 9:21: "Then I took the sinful thing you had made, the calf, and burned it with fire" (the phrase *the sinful thing* refers to a golden calf like that at Bethel). Indeed, the other golden calf, at Dan, is alluded to in the next colon of Amos 8:14 ("as your god lives, O Dan"). But that colon is obviously parallel to what follows ("as the way to Beer-sheba lives") and not to this. Since it would have been easy enough for Amos to say "the shame of Bethel" if he had meant Bethel, it is more likely that he refers to the Asherah worship at Samaria. The people swear by this idol, which is in reality their shame. The shame of Samaria here contrasts ironically with the pride of Jacob in verse 7. חֵי אֱלֹהֶיךָ דָּן (as your god lives, O Dan) is the typical introduction to an oath (see "as Pharaoh lives" in Gen. 42:15–16 and "as the LORD lives" in 1 Sam. 14:39). The god referred to here is, of course, the golden calf established by Jeroboam I. חֵי דֶּרֶךְ בְּאֵר־שֶׁבַע (as the way to Beer-sheba lives): On Beer-sheba, see the Exegesis of 5:5. This oath parallels the foregoing. It would seem, therefore, that דֶּרֶךְ (way) should parallel אֱלֹהֶיךָ (your god) in the previous colon. The issue, then, is the meaning of דֶּרֶךְ. Cyrus Gordon (*Ugaritic Textbook*, p. 387, no. 702), Mitchell Dahood ("Hebrew-Ugaritic Lexicography II," p. 404), and *HALAT* (p. 223, no. 7) have understood some uses of דֶּרֶךְ in the Hebrew Bible in light of Ugaritic *drkt* (dominion or might). Bartina ("Vivit Potentia Beer-Šeba!") and Stuart (*Hosea–Jonah*, p. 382, n. 14b) have applied this understanding to the word here and interpret the phrase as "the power of Beer-sheba."

However, the existence of a Hebrew דֶּרֶךְ = Ugaritic *drkt* is not at all assured. Neuberg ("Unrecognized Meaning of Hebrew *dôr*") and Ackroyd ("The Meaning of Hebrew דּוֹר Considered," p. 4) have proposed repointing to דֹּרְךָ, in light of Ugaritic *dr* (circle or assembly). The allusion then would be to an assembly of gods: "your pantheon, Beer-sheba." A bilingual Phoenician-Hittite inscription (ca. 720 B.C.), found at Karatepe, mentions "the eternal sun god and the whole circle/assembly of the sons of the gods [*wkl dr bn ʾlm*]" (Donner and Röllig, *Kanaanäische und aramäische Inschriften*, vol. 1, p. 6, no. 26, col. 3, line 19; vol. 2, p. 37). However, although the people worshiped other gods, there is no evidence that syncretism in Israel ever developed to such a degree that there was a formally proclaimed pantheon, so that this suggestion also remains conjectural. The best alternative, unless more compelling evidence appears, is to translate it as above. It is not odd that such an oath should appear, nor that such an inanimate thing ("the way") should be said to "live." Arabs swear by inanimate things, for example, "by the life of this fire, or of this coffee!" Moslems swear "by the sacred way to Mecca" and "by the pilgrimage, and the height of Mina, where the pious host stone Satan" (all three examples are cited in Driver, *Joel and Amos*, p. 220). וְנָפְלוּ וְלֹא־יָקוּמוּ עוֹד (and they will fall, and will not rise again) is a fairly common idea in the prophets, for example, the earth "falls, and will not rise again" (Isa. 24:20); pagan kings "fall and rise no more, because of the sword that I am sending among [them]" (Jer. 25:27). Positively, Israel says, "When I fall, I shall rise" (Mic. 7:8). Amos 5:2 ("fallen—she will not rise again—is the virgin, Israel") reflects 8:14. She has fallen, and will not rise again. The opposites affirm the sureness of the sentence.

Israel had slipped from monotheism into a kind of syncretism, like that in Judah, where Zephaniah prophesied against

those who bow down on the roofs
   to the host of the heavens;
those who bow down and swear by the
   LORD,

but also swear by Milcom. (Zeph. 1:5)

In vain had the Lord commanded them to worship him alone, and to have no other gods besides himself. They had tried to serve two masters: the Lord, and the god of this world.

III. Prophetic Visions (7:1–9:15)
C. Vision of the Lord above the Altar (9:1–10)
1. The Vision (9:1–4)

9 I saw the Lord standing above the altar,
   and he said,
 "Strike the capital so that the thresholds
   shake,
     and cut them off at the head, all of
       them,
   and those who remain I will kill with the
     sword,
       none of their fugitives shall flee,
       and none of their escapees shall es-
         cape.
² If they dig down to Sheol,
     my hand will snatch them from
       there.
   If they ascend to heaven,
     I will bring them down from there.
³ If they hide themselves at the top of Carmel,
     I will search them out and snatch
       them from there.
   If they conceal themselves from my
     sight on the ocean floor,
     I will command the serpent from
       there, and it will bite them.
⁴ If they go into captivity before their enemies,
     I will command the sword from there
       and it will slay them.
   And I will fix my eye upon them,
     for evil, and not for good."

9 I saw the Lord standing beside the altar,
   and he said:
 Strike the capitals until the thresholds
   shake,
     and shatter them on the heads of all
       the people;
   and those who are left I will kill with the
     sword;
       not one of them shall flee away,
       not one of them shall escape.
² Though they dig into Sheol,
     from there shall my hand take them;
   though they climb up to heaven,
     from there I will bring them down.
³ Though they hide themselves on the top
     of Carmel,
     from there I will search out and take
       them;
   and though they hide from my sight at
     the bottom of the sea,
     there I will command the sea-serpent,
       and it shall bite them.
⁴ And though they go into captivity in
     front of their enemies,
     there I will command the sword, and
       it shall kill them;
   and I will fix my eyes on them
     for harm and not for good.

9:1. אֲדֹנָי (the Lord): See the Exegesis of 1:8. עַל נִצָּב (standing above): See the Exegesis of 7:7; possibly, however, עַל is to be taken here as standing "beside" (as in 1 Kings 13:1). הַמִּזְבֵּחַ (the altar): See the Exegesis of 2:8 and 3:14. From these passages it is clear that, while there were numerous altars at Bethel, Dan, and elsewhere, it is meaningful to talk of *the* altar in the north (i.e., at Bethel; see 3:14: "And the horns of *the* altar will be cut off"). So the argument of Keil (*Twelve Minor Prophets*, pp. 320–21), that "*the* altar" must signify the altar at Jerusalem ("the altar *par excellence*"), is without warrant and also does not fit the present context, in which the Lord is aiming punishment against Israel in particular. הַךְ (strike): The one to whom this and the following command ("cut them off") are directed is not apparent, but probably it was an angel. The verb נכה (hiphil) occurs in connection with the Lord's judgments and the "destroyer" in two passages, once with Yahweh as subject (Exod. 12:13) and once with the angel as subject (2 Kings 19:35). Perhaps here, too, the destroying angel is to be understood as the one who does the striking. הַכַּפְתּוֹר (the capital) describes the rounded ornament on the shaft and branches of the golden lampstand (Exod. 25:31, 33–36), hence, the rounded part at the top of a column. וְיִרְעֲשׁוּ הַסִּפִּים (so that the thresholds shake): The verb expresses purpose after the imperative; it does not connote merely "until the thresholds shake" (NRSV). The purpose is to cause them to shake (GKC §109f). הַסִּפִּים (the thresholds) are the stone bases of the door, with holes cut in them to accommodate the doorposts (Judg. 19:27; Isa. 6:4). וּבְצַעַם בְּרֹאשׁ כֻּלָּם (and cut them off at the head, all of them): There is ambiguity here, for it is unclear whether to take the masculine plural pronominal suffixes ("them . . . them") as referring to the tops of the columns (so Stuart, *Hosea–Jonah*, p. 391: "*All* [כלם] pillars were to be razed"), or to take the

first as referring to the pillar and thresholds and the second as referring to the people, on whom presumably the ruin would fall (so Keil, *Twelve Minor Prophets*, p. 320: "And smash them upon the head of all of them"; p. 323: "And smash them to pieces, i.e., lay them in ruins upon the head of all"). Both endings might even refer to the people who would die in the catastrophe, since the same masculine plural pronominal suffix occurs in the following colon: אַחֲרִיתָם (*those* who remain I will kill with the sword). The command is to cut off or smash the heads of all the people (i.e., all those in the temple). The ambiguity is probably purposeful, since the smiting of the temple will result in the death of many. A comparison with Judges 16:29–30 is appropriate. בַּחֶרֶב אֶהֱרֹג (I will kill with the sword): Whoever escapes death in the temple, the Lord will kill with the sword. Here, as in 2:3 and 4:10, it is not the Lord himself who does the killing, but his chosen judgment instruments (Assyrians). For the covenantal background of the phrase *I will kill with the sword*, see the Exposition of 4:10. לֹא־יָנוּס לָהֶם נָס (none of their fugitives shall flee; lit. there shall not flee of them a fugitive): For נוס (flee), see the Exegesis of 2:16; here, as there, the flight is, implicitly, from a warlike pursuer. לָהֶם (their, of them) is used here and in the following colon to define those of whom the predicates ("shall not flee," "shall not escape") are affirmed, that is, the Israelites (BDB, p. 512, no. 5aa). The use of the imperfect and active participle in the same clause enhances the poetic effect by consonance (*yānûs, nas*), as do the endings, *-let . . . -lît*, in the parallel clause: וְלֹא־יִמָּלֵט לָהֶם פָּלִיט (and none of their escapees shall escape). The meaning of the latter is, of course, that no one who might seem to have escaped will actually get free: The Lord's judgment will catch up with them and put an end to them.

9:1. A fifth and final vision begins here. It is, in a sense, a complement to the vision in 7:7–9. Whereas in the other four visions (7:1–3, 4–6, 7–9; 8:1–3) Amos acted as an intercessor or a respondent to the Lord's questions, he has no active part in this vision. Probably this is meant to emphasize the separateness of the Lord from humans, and the finality of his decision to judge his sinful people.

This vision of Amos's prophecy reveals the Lord standing above the altar, probably the altar of the temple at Bethel. He gives a command to strike the sanctuary, which probably represents the syn-

chretistic religion of the northern kingdom. It is significant that the misguided religion of this kingdom is what will destroy the people according to this vision. The use of this literary device eloquently crystallizes Amos's message concerning the destructive course the nation had taken when it persisted in its distortion of true Yahwism (see the Exposition of Hos. 10:15 in this volume).

The prophet speaks with finality here. There will be no escape. The warning in this section applies to all false religion. It is possible for superficial religion to lull its adherents into a state of false security.

2. אִם (if) introduces the first of a series of five protasis-apodosis statements (vv. 2–4), all of which begin with אִם (if) plus an imperfect verb (stating the contrary-to-fact condition), followed by מִשָּׁם (from there) plus an imperfect verb (stating the Lord's action in pursuit of them). All of these cola express the fact that those who flee will not be able to escape the Lord. יַחְתְּרוּ (they dig down) with the preposition בְּ (in or into) indicates "to break through" (in this case, into Sheol), as in Ezekiel 8:8; 12:5, 7, 12 (breaking through a wall). שְׁאוֹל (Sheol): In many instances שְׁאוֹל connotes the grave, but several times it functions as a great depth opposite of heaven (Job 11:8; Ps. 139:8; see also Deut. 32:22), as it does here. It is clear that שְׁאוֹל has no theological sense here (hell, pit) because of the similar metaphorical language in the next verse that speaks of "the top of Carmel" and "the ocean floor." תִּקָּחֵם (will snatch) pictures Israel as taken for judgment while in flight from the Lord. יַעֲלוּ (they ascend): Ascent to heaven can

be real, as in the case of Elijah (2 Kings 2:11), or pretentious, as in the case of Babylon (Isa. 14:13). Here, in a figure, it indicates the impossibility of flight from Yahweh. מִשָּׁם אוֹרִידֵם (I will bring them down from there): For the identical phraseology, also in a contrary-to-fact clause, see Obadiah 4 (against Edom: "Though your nest is set among the stars, / from there I will bring you down").

3. בְּרֹאשׁ הַכַּרְמֶל (at the top of Carmel): See the Exegesis of 1:2 and the Exposition of 9:3. אֲחַפֵּשׂ (I will search them out) connotes diligent seeking in the piel. It is used of Yahweh's searching Jerusalem with lamps, to punish the complacent (Zeph. 1:12). מִנֶּגֶד עֵינַי (from my sight) is, literally, "from before my eyes." See Jeremiah 16:17 ("for my eyes are on all their ways; they are not hidden from my presence, nor is their iniquity concealed from my sight"); 23:24; Job 13:20; and, in a different sense, Hosea 13:14 ("Compassion is hidden from my eyes"). The impossibility of concealing oneself (סתר, niphal) from Yahweh was made clear in

---

2. In the first of a series of contrary-to-fact clauses, the Lord makes it clear that it is impossible for his guilty people to flee from him. Their sin has brought them to this state, and there is no recourse. If only they had known the God with whom they had to deal, of whom David long ago had sung:

Where can I go from your Spirit?
  Or where can I flee from your presence?
If I ascend to heaven, you are there;
  if I make my bed in Sheol, you are there.
If I take the wings of the morning
  and settle at the farthest limits of the
    sea,
even there your hand shall lead me,
  and your right hand will hold me
    fast. (Ps. 139:7–10)

How good it would have been for Israel, if they had held fast to their Lord. But they turned from him to idols and forsook the protection of his mighty hand. So now their Lord announced that that same hand would be able to snatch them even from the depths of Sheol, if they sought to escape him there. And even if they could ascend to the heavens, he would bring them down again.

The word pair Sheol/heaven occurs several places in parallel to indicate the range of the Lord's dominion (Deut. 32:22; Job 11:8). A similar pair, heaven/earth, occurs in the covenant lawsuit (Deut. 32:1; Isa. 1:2), appropriately so, since God

created heaven and earth (Gen. 1:1). The pair is a merismus for "everything" that humans know of—and the Lord's presence/dominion extend beyond it! A similar pair occurs in Akkadian, *šamu ù erṣetu* (heaven and earth; *CAD*, vol. 4 [E], pp. 309–11). For the thought here, see Psalm 139:8. The use of *yād* (hand) is an anthropomorphism, as is often the case in the Old Testament. This is especially ironic against the covenantal background, since it was "by a mighty hand and an outstretched arm" that the Lord delivered his people from Egypt (e.g., Deut. 4:34). But now he will use that mighty hand to capture and punish his fleeing people.

There is no place the people can go from the Lord's presence. This verse complements the preceding assertion (v. 1) that none of the people will be able to escape the Lord. For a similar idea, see Isaiah 2:19; Hosea 10:6–8; Luke 23:30; Revelation 6:16.

3. This verse contains the third and fourth in the series of protasis-apodosis clauses that express the impossibility of flight from the Lord. Like the first two clauses in the previous verse, these two clauses are externally synonymous; they express the impossibility of concealment in terms of great height or depth. Even if the Israelites flee to the top of Carmel and try to hide among its thick forest cover, the Lord will diligently seek them out and snatch them away for punishment (by using the Assyrians). Even if they found Carmel inadequate as a hiding place and tried to conceal them-

Israel's wisdom literature (e.g., Job 34:21–22). הַיָּם בְּקַרְקַע (on the ocean floor): Numbers 5:17 refers to the earth floor of the tabernacle and 1 Kings 6:15–16, 30 to the floor of the temple (cf. Akkadian *qaqqaru*, ground, earth). If the top of Carmel could not provide adequate refuge, the sea was the only place left. And even if they could flee to the ocean floor and try to conceal themselves there, Yahweh would punish them. נָחָשׁ (serpent): For serpent bites as covenantal punishment, see the Exegesis of 5:19. Yahweh had sent fiery or venomous serpents to punish his wayward people in the wilderness (Num. 21:6–9), and he could again send fiery serpents in covenant-lawsuit punishment (e.g., to Judah, Jer. 8:17). But here another kind of serpent is meant, a sea snake or serpent, perhaps even a sea monster, such as Leviathan (Isa. 27:1).

4. יֵלְכוּ בַשְּׁבִי (they go into captivity): This would be a fulfilment of an original covenant curse (Deut. 28:41); it is subsequently fulfilled (e.g., Lam. 1:5, 18; Ezek. 12:11). לִפְנֵי אֹיְבֵיהֶם (before their enemies) implies that they are driven by their ene-

mies. For the phrase *to go into captivity before the enemy*, see Lamentations 1:5. הַחֶרֶב (the sword) functions as a covenantal judgment instrument in 4:10 (also 7:9, 11, 17) and, more immediately, in 9:1. The phrase *I will command the sword* pictures the Lord as sending (Jer. 9:15 [16]; 24:10), bringing (Ezek. 5:17; 29:8), or calling for (Jer. 25:29; Ezek. 38:21) the sword in acts of covenantal punishment. וַהֲרָגָתַם (and it will slay them): By metonymy of the adjunct, the sword is spoken of as slaying them, whereas it is actually the foe wielding the sword who will do it. וְשַׂמְתִּי עֵינִי עֲלֵיהֶם (and I will fix my eye upon them): This stock phrase is usually in the plural, and so here the Septuagint (still consistent with the consonantal MT) translates it as plural. The phrase is elsewhere used in a favorable sense (e.g., Gen. 44:21; Jer. 24:6; 39:12). לְרָעָה וְלֹא לְטוֹבָה (for evil, and not for good): See Jeremiah 21:10 ("for I have set my face against this city for evil and not for good"); 39:16; 44:27 ("I am going to watch over them for harm and not for good").

---

selves from the Lord's sight on the ocean floor, the Lord would command a serpent to bite them.

The prophet says that they will not be able to hide on Mount Carmel. Carmel, at some 1,800 feet above sea level, may not seem very high, but its contrast with the sea is striking. Projecting into the water, it was the last point of land to which one might flee and still be in Israel. It was thickly forested at the top, and the forest provided cover as a hiding place for robbers even in the first century A.D. The promontory had many limestone caves, which Driver (*Joel and Amos*, pp. 221–22) cites as possible hiding places. But since the top of Carmel is mentioned, it is more likely that its dense forest is the intended hiding place. There is a warning in store here for everyone, believers included:

> The LORD is in his holy temple;
> the LORD's throne is in heaven.

His eyes behold, his gaze examines humankind. (Ps. 11:4)

And again: "Before him no creature is hidden, but all are naked and laid bare to the eyes of the one to whom we must render an account" (Heb. 4:13).

4. After extremes of flight (vv. 2–3), most if not all of which would have been impossible, we encounter a concrete possibility. The prophet speaks of the reality of the captivity. Even if Israel is taken captive by their enemies, the Lord will be against them. The fulfilment of this curse took the form of the resettlement of the northern tribes after the Assyrian conquest, which was a standard Assyrian practice intended to discourage rebellion. The policy was so effective that the exiles came to be referred to as the "lost tribes." For this reason, too, Samaritans came to be looked down upon as impure, and not God's people (see John 4:9).

III. Prophetic Visions (7:1–9:15)
C. Vision of the Lord above the Altar (9:1–10)
2. Identification of the Lord and Judge (9:5–6)

5 The Lord, Yahweh of hosts,
  who touches the earth, and it melts,
    and all who dwell in it mourn,
  and all of it rises like the Nile,
    and it recedes, like the Nile of Egypt;
6 the one who builds his temple in heaven,
    and founds his vault above the earth,
  the one who summons the waters of the
      sea,
      and pours them out upon the surface
      of the earth—
Yahweh is his name!

5 The Lord, GOD of hosts,
  he who touches the earth and it melts,
    and all who live in it mourn,
  and all of it rises like the Nile,
    and sinks again, like the Nile of
      Egypt;
6 who builds his upper chambers in the
      heavens,
    and founds his vault upon the earth;
  who calls for the waters of the sea,
    and pours them out upon the surface
      of the earth—
the LORD is his name.

5. אֲדֹנָי יְהוִה (the Lord Yahweh): See the Exegesis of 1:8. הַצְּבָאוֹת (of hosts): See the Exegesis of 3:13. This word appears in this phrase with the definite article only here, but it occurs often enough without the article (Ps. 69:7 [6]; Isa. 3:15; Jer. 2:19). הַנּוֹגֵעַ בָּאָרֶץ וַתָּמוֹג (who touches the earth, and it melts): For similar expressions of the awesome presence of the Lord, see Psalm 104:32 ("who touches the mountains and they smoke"); 46:7 [6] ("he utters his voice, the earth melts"); and (hithpael) Nahum 1:5 ("the mountains quake before him and the hills melt"). The phraseology of the last three cola in Amos 9:5 is virtually identical with that of 8:8, where the phrases appear in a question (see the Exegesis of 8:8). Here they appear as part of a divine titulary. The difference is significant. For here we are told who will be able to produce the devastating effects prophesied in 8:8. The differences between the two otherwise are minimal, with 9:5 using the plural, כָל־יוֹשְׁבֵי בָהּ אָבְלוּ (all who dwell in it mourn), instead of the singular, אָבַל כָּל־יוֹשֵׁב בָּהּ (everyone who dwells in it mourn), omitting an active equivalent for גרשׁ

(be tossed about), and using the qal instead of the niphal of שׁקע (to recede).

6. הַבּוֹנֶה (the one who builds) continues the divine titulary (similar constructions in 4:1, 13) with the active participle, further illustrating the Lord's abilities. The participle is used elsewhere as an epithet of the Lord as "the builder of Jerusalem" (Ps. 147:2 NJB). מַעֲלוֹתָו (his temple; lit. stairs) is to be taken as plural, contra the Septuagint (ἀνάβασιν αὐτοῦ). The word denotes "ascent(s)" (e.g., the superscription on each of Pss. 120–34). Several interpreters understand it as עֲלִיּוֹת (the upper room[s]; Ps. 104:3) to which one must ascend (Keil, *Twelve Minor Prophets*, p. 326). This rendering, however, may be too modest. The word frequently connotes steps in the Old Testament (Exod. 20:26; 1 Kings 10:19–20; Ezek. 40:6, 22, 26, 31, 34, 37). It seems likely, if we interpret this word against the background of God's total revelation, that the steps to his heavenly temple (Exod. 26:30; cf. Rev. 11:19) are intended as metonomy, that is, the part for the whole, so we may translate the phrase as "his temple" (the NIV has "his lofty

---

5. A short divine titulary follows the announced punishment. It is not, however, a "hymnic fragment" (Watts, "Old Hymn," pp. 33–34). It is a divine titulary, like its counterparts in 4:13 and 5:8. Ancient Near Eastern inscriptions contain similar brief titularies, often rehearsing some attributes of a king. They appear several times throughout the narrative (e.g., the annals of Tiglath-pileser I; see King, *Annals of the Kings of Assyria*, pp. 46–47, col. 2, lines 85–88; p. 52, col. 3, lines 32–34; p. 63, col. 4, lines 40–42; p. 72, col. 5, lines 42–43; pp. 74–75, col. 5, lines 64–66). In the Assyrian annals these brief titularies were meant to affirm the power and authority of the one whose deeds were being recounted. So here, the titularies are meant to affirm the power and authority of the one who has judged and will judge. (The Assyrian king was usually carrying out covenant judgment against rebellious vassals, and so is Yahweh.) These are no more fragments of a hymn than were their Assyrian counterparts, which, like them, are nevertheless written in a hymnic style that was very ancient, appearing in the prologue of Hammurabi's law code (*ANET*, pp. 164–65), with antecedents in Sumerian inscriptions of even earlier date (see Sollberger and Kupper, *Inscriptions Royales Sumériennes et Akkadiennes*).

This titulary states that it is the Lord who has the power to search out and find his fleeing people

(vv. 2–4). The Lord has a powerful title here: "The Lord Yahweh of hosts." This title asserts that the one who is truly Lord is the one who will do it. The verse resumes the language of 8:8, to illustrate further the Lord's awesome power, for the Lord will be the one to accomplish that terrible punishment. Let none doubt his authority or power. When the Lord touches mountains, they melt, and when he lifts his voice or touches the land, it melts. Such language illustrates his power in terms of fire, one of the most devastating weapons known to the ancients. But it also foreshadows that final day of the Lord, which "will come like a thief, and then the heavens will pass away with a loud noise, and the elements will be dissolved with fire, and the earth and everything that is done on it will be disclosed" (2 Pet. 3:10).

6. The divine titulary continues by emphasizing the awesome nature of the one who brings covenant lawsuit (and who will bring covenant punishment) upon his people. He is the one who has built his temple in heaven and founded the arch of heaven itself above the earth. He draws water from the sea and causes it to rain upon the earth. If he can do all this, building the invisible and commanding the visible, how much more will he be able to rain down punishment upon a rebellious people! The first bicolon of this verse is chiastic:

palace"). אֲגֻדָּתוֹ (his vault) is a difficult word to interpret since its attested meanings do not clearly correspond to the present passage. It can mean a *bunch* of hyssop (Exod. 12:22), the *band* of a yoke (Isa. 58:6), or a *band* of soldiers (2 Sam. 2:25). The talmudic אֲגַד and Aramaic אֲגַד both mean "to bind." So it is taken by, for example, Keil (*Twelve Minor Prophets*, p. 326) and Driver (*Joel and Amos*, p. 223), as equivalent to רָקִיעַ (firmament), that is, something "bound or fitted together," hence, an arch or vault. Support for this comes from Arabic *ijad* (arch, i.e., of stones fitted together). A related idea, employing the term חוּג (vault or horizon, i.e., the "circle" of the heavens), occurs in Job 22:14 ("thick clouds enwrap him, so that he does not see, / and he walks on the dome of heaven"), Proverbs 8:27 ("when he established the heavens, I was there, / when he drew a circle on the face of the deep"), and Isaiah 40:22 ("it is he who sits above the circle of the earth, / and its inhabitants are like grasshoppers"). The translation "his storerooms" depends implicitly on the

parallelism with מַעֲלוֹתָו (his upper chamber) (Stuart, *Hosea–Jonah*, p. 389). However, parallelism does not demand strict synonymity (e.g., heaven and earth, though parallel in this bicolon, are not synonymous in meaning, but only in function within the parallelism; the same is probably true of temple and vault). עַל־אֶרֶץ יְסָדָהּ ([and] founds [his vault] above the earth): For the Lord's founding the earth itself, see Psalm 78:69; 102:26 [25]; Proverbs 3:19; and Isaiah 51:13. Similar phraseology occurs in Psalm 24:2: "He [the Lord] has founded it [the earth] on the seas." The remainder of the verse repeats exactly the second half of 5:8 (on which see the Exegesis). But there is no need to assume that this repetition is "secondary," and not part of the original text (as does Wolff, *Joel and Amos*, p. 337, n. w; see also p. 216). It is far from unusual for a poet or prophet to repeat phrases or sentences, either within a poem or oracle (e.g., Ps. 42:6–7 [5–6] par. v. 12 [11] par. Ps. 43:5; Isa. 2:11 par. v. 17) or between oracles (e.g., Jer. 49:26 par. 50:30; Amos 8:8 par. 9:5).

a	b	c
the one who builds	in heaven	his temple
c´	b´	a´
and his vault	above the earth	founds.

The elegant structure lends power to the utterance: there must be no doubt that the Creator is the one who brings suit against his people. For the titulary as a whole, see Jeremiah 31:35.

III. Prophetic Visions (7:1–9:15)
C. Vision of the Lord above the Altar (9:1–10)
3. Judgment Announced (9:7–10)

7 "Are you not like the Cushites to me, O
    Israelites?"—
  oracle of Yahweh—
"did I not bring Israel up from the land of
    Egypt,
    and the Philistines from Caphtor, and
    Aram from Kir?

8 Even now the eyes of the Lord Yahweh are against the sinful kingdom, and I will destroy it from the face of the land—except that I will not completely destroy the house of Jacob"—oracle of Yahweh. 9 "For even now I am commanding, and I will shake up the house of Israel among all the nations, as one shakes with a sieve, and not a pebble shall fall to the ground." 10 "By the sword they shall die—all the sinners of my people, those who say, 'You shall never approach or confront us with evil.'"

7 Are you not like the Ethiopians to me,
    O people of Israel? says the Lord.
Did I not bring Israel up from the land of
    Egypt,
    and the Philistines from Caphtor and
    the Arameans from Kir?
8 The eyes of the Lord God are upon the
    sinful kingdom,
    and I will destroy it from the face of
    the earth
    —except that I will not utterly de-
    stroy the house of Jacob,
                 says the Lord.
9 For lo, I will command,
    and shake the house of Israel among
    all the nations
as one shakes with a sieve,
    but no pebble shall fall to the ground.
10 All the sinners of my people shall die by
    the sword,
    who say, "Evil shall not overtake or
    meet us."

7. הֲלוֹא (are . . . not?) is the first of two negative interrogatives (the second being "did . . . not?") that introduce the two rhetorical questions. כְּשִׁיִּם כִּבְנֵי (like the Cushites; lit. sons of the Cushites): Cush was a son of Ham (Gen. 10:6). The land (modern Ethiopia) that bore his name appears in Egyptian inscriptions as *Kesh* (see Isa. 11:11; 18:1; 20:3–5). נְאֻם־יְהוָה (oracle of Yahweh): See the Exegesis of 2:11. הֶעֱלֵיתִי (did I . . . bring?) does triple duty, having Israel, the Philistines, and Aram as direct objects. God's bringing Israel up from Egypt also occurs in 2:10. פְּלִשְׁתִּיִּם (the Philistines) are condemned in 1:6–9. מִכַּפְתּוֹר (from Caphtor) is probably Crete, although the Septuagint here and in Deuteronomy 2:23 renders it as Καππαδοκίς (Cappadocia).

8. הִנֵּה (even now) gives a sense of urgency, as in 2:13. עֵינֵי אֲדֹנָי יְהוָה (the eyes of the Lord Yahweh):

See the Exegesis of verses 3–4. אֲדֹנָי יְהוָה (the Lord Yahweh): See the Exegesis of 1:8. בַּמַּמְלָכָה הַחַטָּאָה (against [or, upon] the sinful kingdom): The eyes of the Lord may be on (בְּ) an object for good (Deut. 11:12; Ps. 101:6) or ill (Job 7:8 and here; hence, "against"). Here, the Lord's eyes are against (בְּ) the sinful kingdom. מַמְלָכָה (kingdom) indicates here the northern kingdom only, not both north and south. This is clear from the reference to the house of Jacob later in line 3 of this verse. הָאֲדָמָה וְהִשְׁמַדְתִּי אֹתָהּ מֵעַל פְּנֵי (and I will destroy it from the face of the land): The shift from third-person masculine singular ("the eyes of the Lord Yahweh") to first-person common singular in the same verse is a stylistic feature attested in other ancient Near Eastern documents (see the Introduction). הִשְׁמַדְתִּי (destroy): See the Exegesis of 2:9. The same phrase occurs in the original covenantal materials: "The

---

7. This verse is an ironic historical review, which introduces a judgment oracle. Two rhetorical questions structure this prose verse, which introduces the Lord's intent to sift his people (vv. 8–9).

The Lord will now disabuse Israel of any sense of specialness. As his covenant people they were special, but he opens their eyes to the fact that he has brought other people from one land to another, and he has enabled other people to conquer the inhabitants of those new lands and settle in their place. Indeed, he has even fought for those people, just as he fought for Israel in Canaan. The only difference between Israel and the Philistines, Ethiopians, or Arameans is that Israel had entered into covenant relationship with the Lord. Much was expected of them, because the Lord had given them much. But Israel had broken the covenant, and for that reason had become profane in the Lord's eyes and was now considered no better than the accursed descendants of Ham: "Are you not like Cushites to me, O Israelites?"

The Philistines are called "the remnant of the coastland of Caphtor" in Jeremiah 47:4 (the translations of Aquila and Symmachus read "Cappadocia" here). Deuteronomy 2:23 relates their origin and settlement: "As for the Avvim, who had lived in settlements in the vicinity of Gaza, the Caphtorim, who came from Caphtor, destroyed them and settled in their place." This is said in the context of Yahweh's bringing people into new territories and enabling them to conquer (or, rather, Yahweh conquering for them; see Deut. 2:20–22) and settle there. So here he justly says that he

"brought the Philistines from Caphtor." On Aram and Kir, see the Exegesis of 1:5.

8. The eyes of the Lord, from which his rebellious people cannot hide (vv. 2–4), are now set against the sinful kingdom. Their destruction for covenantal disobedience was threatened long before, by Moses in Deuteronomy 4:26: "I call heaven and earth as witnesses against you this day that you will quickly perish from the land that you are crossing the Jordan to possess. You will not live there long but will certainly be destroyed" (NIV). Joshua also gave a similar warning (23:15–16).

The covenantal punishment formerly threatened against the whole people is now about to come upon the northern kingdom. The Mosaic threat of complete destruction must be understood, in context, as a hyperbole typical of ancient Near Eastern literature. The point is that they will be completely removed from the land and destroyed as a kingdom. But in the same breath (Deut. 4:30–31) the Lord declares that he will have compassion: "When you are in distress and all these things have happened to you, then in later days you will return to the LORD your God and obey him. For the LORD your God is a merciful God; he will not abandon or destroy you or forget the covenant with your forefathers, which he confirmed to them by oath" (NIV). In Deuteronomy, the threat of destruction is followed by a clear indication that not all will be destroyed; so now, the Lord promises, "I will not completely destroy the house of Jacob." And, just as in Deuteronomy there is a promise of restoration, so at last in Amos (vv. 11–15).

anger of the LORD your God would be kindled against you and he would destroy you from the face of the earth" (Deut. 6:15). אֶפֶס כִּי (except that) is a collocation that qualifies a previous statement. Here, it is a merciful proviso—Yahweh will not destroy the nation completely. אֶת־בֵּית יַעֲקֹב לֹא הַשְׁמֵיד אַשְׁמִיד (I will not completely destroy the house of Jacob): In a similar phrase (using niphal) in Deuteronomy 4:26, Yahweh threatens, in case of disobedience, complete removal from the land he has given them. The infinitive absolute with the finite verb, הַשְׁמֵיד אַשְׁמִיד (I will not completely destroy), is intensive or emphatic, strengthening the verbal idea in some way (GKC §113n). Here, the sense is I will not *utterly* destroy. בֵּית יַעֲקֹב (the house of Jacob): See the Exegesis of 3:13. נְאֻם־יהוה (oracle of Yahweh): See the Exegesis of 2:11.

9. כִּי (for) sustains a broad causal relationship to the foregoing statement, which may be paraphrased: I will not completely destroy this kingdom because I intend to preserve a remnant (as the metaphor of the sieve indicates). אָנֹכִי מְצַוֶּה (I am commanding): For this phrase as a prelude to judgment, see the Exegesis of 6:11, where the wording is identical except that the subject is Yahweh (i.e., third person), rather than I (first person). אָנֹכִי (I): For the deictic use of this pronoun, see the Exegesis of 2:9. וַהֲנִעוֹתִי (and I will shake up) is used once of shaking or disturbing the bones of the dead (2 Kings 23:18), but most frequently of shaking or "wagging" the head (e.g., 2 Kings 19:21; Pss. 22:8 [7]; 109:25). Only here is it used of shaking in a sieve. הַגּוֹיִם (the nations): See the Exegesis of 6:1. The term indicates those around Israel. Many nations were "shaken" by Assyrian power in the eighth century B.C., Israel among

them. Israel's "shaking" included exile and dispersal among nations that were subordinate to Assyria. This practice, typical of Assyria, assured the effective disintegration of the people group and made rebellion virtually impossible. בֵּית יִשְׂרָאֵל (the house of Israel): See the Exegesis of 5:1. בַּכְּבָרָה (with a sieve) may be related to Arabic *kirbal* (sieve). צְרוֹר (a pebble) is so interpreted by Aquila (ψηφίον), the Targum (אבן), and the Vulgate (*lapillus*). Otherwise in the Old Testament the word signifies a bundle, parcel, or pouch (e.g., Gen. 42:35; Prov. 7:20). אָרֶץ (to the ground) is an adverbial accusative and is translated "ground" rather than "earth," as in 3:5. The idea of the comparison seems to be this: The Lord will shake Israel among the nations, as one might shake grain in a sieve. If the metaphor involves grain, worthless rubbish remains in the sieve, but the good grain falls through to the ground. Thus, the good will make it through, the wicked will not. If, however, the material in the sieve is sand or gravel, then the compact material (צְרוֹר, anything that is compact, as in 2 Sam. 17:13) is preserved. In this view, God affirms that he will preserve a remnant throughout the devastation, for he intends to rebuild the "house of David," not let it terminate with the exile.

10. בַּחֶרֶב (by the sword): In 7:11 the same thing is said of the house of Jeroboam. For the sword as a judgment instrument, see the Exegesis of 7:9. כֹּל חַטָּאֵי עַמִּי (all the sinners of my people): Similar phrases occur in Isaiah 13:9 ("the sinners within it [i.e., the land]," NIV) and 33:14 ("the sinners in Zion are afraid"). הָאֹמְרִים (those who say) is applied to the "cows of Bashan" in 4:1, to those who rejoice in their own strength in 6:13, and to Ama-

---

9. The Lord himself is commanding judgment, as emphasized by the use of the personal pronoun. He is commanding it even now and, if he commands it, none can resist. Perhaps he compares himself to a harvester, who takes grain into a sieve and shakes it. The worthless bits of stone and rubbish remain in the sieve; the good grain falls to the earth. So the Lord will put his people through the sieve. He will bind the wicked, destroying them (v. 10), but he will save the righteous. This principle of God's justice is eternal: the judgment of the wicked and the salvation of the righteous go together. What we see articulated on the historical plane in Amos will also appear at the end of history (Matt. 13:24–30; 25:31–46).

10. The Lord makes it clear that all the sinners among his people shall die by the sword, just as

their king shall die by the sword. The same covenantal punishment shall befall all, without recognition of rank. These same people have been saying, "You shall never approach or confront us with evil" (2:12; 7:13). But the fact that they are oblivious to the "evil" of divine punishment will not keep it away. So it was in the days of Noah, when the world was oblivious to the coming judgment, when "they were eating and drinking, marrying and giving in marriage, until the day Noah entered the ark, and they knew nothing until the flood came and swept them all away." And, we are told, "So too will be the coming of the Son of Man" (Matt. 24:38–39).

ziah, who says, "You shall never prophesy against Israel," in 7:16. In all these cases, the participle is used scornfully to picture the sinful attitude of the speaker. לֹא־תַגִּישׁ (you shall never approach) is an emphatic command (such commands occur elsewhere in 2:12 and 7:13). The verb נָגַשׁ (hiphil) is elsewhere transitive, and so it should be translated here. Alternative emendations are possible, for example, תַּשִּׂיג (overtake, a hiphil from נשׂג; thus understood by the AV and the NRSV) or תִּגַּשׁ (a qal from נגשׁ; so Driver, *Joel and Amos*, p. 226, n. 1); but an emendation to תִּגַּשׁ (a niphal of נגשׁ; so Wolff,

Joel and Amos, p. 344, n. g; and Stuart, *Hosea–Jonah*, p. 390, n. 10a) is precluded by the orthography (the niphal of נגשׁ would have to be תִּנָּגֵשׁ; see GKC, p. 520). וְתַקְדִּים בַּעֲדֵינוּ (or confront us): The verb (hiphil) means "to confront or anticipate" (BDB, p. 870). There is no need to emend it to the piel, as Stuart does (*Hosea–Jonah*, p. 390, n. 10b; nor is it true, as he claims, that the hiphil of the verb is "unattested otherwise," for it also occurs in Job 41:3 [11]). הָרָעָה (evil) is an adverbial accusative. For evil in the sense of impending judgment, see 5:13; 6:3; and 9:4.

III. Prophetic Visions (7:1–9:15)
D. Restoration and Blessing (9:11–15)

11 "On that day, I will raise up
    the collapsing hut of David,
and I will repair their broken walls,
    and his ruins I will raise up,
    and I will rebuild it as in the old days,
12 so that they may possess
    the remnant of Edom,
    and all the nations
over whom my name is pronounced"—
    oracle of Yahweh, who performs this.
13 "Even now, days are coming"—
    oracle of Yahweh—
    when the plowman shall overtake the
      harvester,
    and the grape-treader the seed-sower,
and the mountains shall trickle new
      wine,
    and all the hills shall flow with it.
14 And I will restore my people Israel from
      captivity,
    and they shall rebuild the devastated
      cities and inhabit them,
    and they shall plant vineyards and drink
      their wine,
    and they shall make gardens and eat
      their fruit.
15 "And I will plant them upon their land,
and they shall never again be uprooted from
their land, which I have given to them," says
Yahweh, your God.

11 On that day I will raise up
    the booth of David that is fallen,
and repair its breaches,
    and raise up its ruins,
    and rebuild it as in the days of old;
12 in order that they may possess the remnant of Edom
    and all the nations who are called by
      my name,
    says the Lord who does this.
13 The time is surely coming, says the
    Lord,
    when the one who plows shall overtake the one who reaps,
    and the treader of grapes the one who
      sows the seed;
the mountains shall drip sweet wine,
    and all the hills shall flow with it.
14 I will restore the fortunes of my people
    Israel,
    and they shall rebuild the ruined cities and inhabit them;
they shall plant vineyards and drink
    their wine,
    and they shall make gardens and eat
    their fruit.
15 I will plant them upon their land,
    and they shall never again be plucked
      up
    out of the land that I have given
      them,
        says the Lord your God.

11. הַהוּא בַּיּוֹם (on that day): See the Exegesis of 2:16. The day in view is not the day of Israel's collapse, however, but the day which that collapse initiates and makes possible: the day of restoration. אָקִים (I will raise up): See the Exegesis of 2:11. The verb has here, no doubt, some of the flavor of its covenantal usage: The Lord will *establish* the hut of David as he restores royal sway to the Davidic line. הַנֹּפֶלֶת דָּוִיד סֻכַּת אֶת (the collapsing hut of David): We retain the Masoretic Text and read "hut," rather than plural סֻכּוֹת (Succoth). The booth or hut *is* collapsing (qal active participle). The participle may also be rendered as a perfect, "fallen," and perhaps both nuances—collapsing and collapsed—are to be understood in an intentional ambiguity. The booth is collapsing and, by prophetic anticipation, has already fallen. It falls because royal power is about to depart from Israel—and, implicitly, from Judah (see the Exegesis of 2:4–5), for the hut or booth of David must include the Davidic dynasty in Jerusalem (because of Jerusalem's sin, Isaiah likens her to "a booth in a vineyard," 1:8). There is no inconsistency, however, between the idea of a booth or hut and the idea of royal restoration. Rather, as Keil suggests, the "miserable fallen hut" indicates that "regal sway must have come to an end" (*Twelve Minor Prophets*, p. 330). סֻכָּה (hut) does not necessarily denote "a very humble structure" (Driver, *Joel and Amos*, p. 226), for it is used of the Lord's heavenly pavilion (Pss. 18:12 [11]; 31:21 [20]) and of the canopy that will cover his glory when he comes to dwell on Zion (Isa. 4:5–6). דָּוִיד (David): In biblical-theological terms, the restoration of the hut of David may anticipate the messianic David, as in Ezekiel 37:24 and Hosea 3:5. פִּרְצֵיהֶן אֶת וְגָדַרְתִּי (and I will repair their broken walls): The verb occurs often with the cognate accusative גָּדֵר (wall) (Ezek. 13:5; 22:30; Hos. 2:8 [6]), but elsewhere also with the same direct object, as here, for example: "You shall be called the repairer of

the breech" (Isa. 58:12). The walls here are not, however, the walls of the hut (unless the hut be considered emblematic of Jerusalem, as in Isa. 1:8, or other cities under Davidic sway), for the Old Testament never speaks of repairing the broken walls of huts. Rather, the broken walls referred to are, implicitly, city walls in general (hence the feminine plural pronominal suffix, as, e.g., in Josh. 15:32: "In all, twenty-nine towns, with their villages [חַצְרֵיהֶן]"). The Septuagint's feminine singular suffix is a typical emendation to accomplish consistency with סֻכָּה (feminine singular); but such shifts between singular and plural are well known in ancient Near Eastern literature, especially in Old Testament poetry. For breaches in city walls elsewhere in the Old Testament, see 1 Kings 11:27 and Job 30:14. Significantly, such breaches are sometimes associated with exile or captivity, for example, Psalm 144:14 and Amos 4:3. So here, Amos speaks of Yahweh's restoration of their former security. הֲרִסֹתָיו (his ruins) is a *hapax legomenon*. The cognate verb, however, is used of tearing down cities (e.g., 2 Sam. 11:25; 2 Kings 3:25; Isa. 14:17) and walls (e.g., Prov. 24:31; Jer. 50:15, both niphal). So, here, the ruins of cities are implied. The Septuagint's feminine plural suffix is another emendation for consistency with סֻכָּה, the imagined antecedent. The masculine singular pronoun ending, however, has David as its antecedent, so that, by metonomy of the adjunct, David's ruined cities stand for the fallen dominion of the Davidic dynasty. The Lord will raise up or establish both cities and dynasty "on that day." וּבְנִיתִיהָ (and I will rebuild it): The verb means "rebuild," as in Isaiah 44:28 (niphal). The feminine singular suffix has סֻכָּה as its antecedent. The Lord will rebuild the hut—that is, restore the dynasty—of David. For the general tone and intent of this verse, see Isaiah 44:26: "[The LORD] says of Jerusalem, 'It shall be inhabited,' / and of the cities of Judah, 'They shall be rebuilt, / and I

---

11. This verse introduces the conclusion of Amos's prophecy, which takes the form of an oracle of promise and restoration. The oracle includes promises of reconstruction (v. 11), reconquest (v. 12), fruitful abundance (v. 13), restoration (with rebuilding and planting, v. 14), and lasting security (v. 15). Such concluding promises are typical in Old Testament prophecy (e.g., the final chapters of Isaiah and Ezekiel; Hosea 14; Joel 4:17–21 [3:17–21]).

The Lord is a compassionate God and does not desire the destruction of his people. His holiness

will not countenance sin, but will eradicate it so that a remnant may be saved. This has been the pattern of his saving acts from the days of Noah onward, and so it will be at the end, when the final remnant are saved out of the last judgment. The redeemed of Israel will again inherit the land (just as the redeemed of the world will inherit the earth). The Lord's promise of restoration forms the subject of the last five verses of Amos. As is often the case, the temporal promise has eternal overtones. In this verse, the restoration of the Davidic dynasty looks forward to the installation

will raise up their ruins.'" כִּימֵי עוֹלָם (as in the old days): The old days—one might almost say "the good old days"—were the days of David and Solomon, when the kingdom was whole. The phrase can denote any period more or less remote, for example, preexilic times (Mal. 3:4), the days of Moses (Isa. 63:9, 11; Mic. 7:14), or even the origin of the messianic shepherd (Mic. 5:1 [2]).

12. לְמַעַן (so that) introduces the purpose for which the Lord will restore the collapsing hut of David. It is not primarily for his people's sake, nor even for David's sake, but for his own sake and the sake of his kingdom, as we shall see. יִירְשׁוּ (they may possess) requires a modal translation. The Lord will restore them so that they *may* possess. For the verb, see the Exegesis of 2:10. Against the background of the patriarchal promises and the conquest, the use of the verb here encourages hope, as virtually a new promise of a new conquest. The Septuagint's ἐκζητήσωσιν (they will seek) implies יִדְרְשׁוּ (they will seek) as its Hebrew *Vorlage*. The mistaking of a *dalet* for the second *yod* would have been an easy scribal error. Codex A adds τὸν κύριον (the Lord) as direct object. The addition is natural, since the Lord is often the object of human seeking in the Old Testament

(e.g., Pss. 34:5 [4]; 77:3 [2]; 119:10); he even commands us to seek him (e.g., Ps. 105:4; Isa. 55:6; Amos 5:4, 6). This addition is picked up in James' speech in Acts 15:17, where he quotes these verses to illustrate the truth that the Gentiles will turn to the Lord, exactly according to prophecy. אֶת־שְׁאֵרִית אֱדוֹם (the remnant of Edom): After the reduction of Edom (1:11–12), at some future date Israel will possess what is left of it (Obad. 18–19). Edom is singled out for mention because of his hatred for his brother, and the long-standing enmity that that hatred produced (1:11). The Septuagint has τῶν ἀνθρώπων (of men), obviously reading אָדָם (Adam or humankind) for אֱדוֹם (Edom). This, too, was picked up in Acts 15:17. The reading is a natural one, since אֱדוֹם is paralleled by כָּל־הַגּוֹיִם (all the nations). The nations alluded to are, in the first instance, those conquered long before by David—Philistia, Moab, Ammon, Aram of Zobah, Damascus, Edom, Amalek (2 Sam. 8:1–14). Implicitly, however, there is also a promise here that the whole world ("all the nations") will come under the rule of Yahweh. אֲשֶׁר־נִקְרָא שְׁמִי עֲלֵיהֶם (over whom my name is pronounced; i.e., whom I possess): The phrase expresses ownership and appears in the context of

---

of the eternal David as king (Ezek. 37:24; Hos. 3:5). The promise to Israel is made in terms of more proximate events: the captives will return to enjoy a united and prosperous kingdom, just like it was in the good old days.

12. The Lord, through Amos, uses language reminiscent of the promises to Abraham and to his people at the conquest. They will possess their enemies—even their ancient fraternal foe, Edom, who so earnestly sought their destruction (1:11; Obad. 10–14). The conquest involved would not be bloody, although this would not have been apparent to Amos's audience. Rather, it would be a divine conquest of saving grace, by which a remnant of Edom and all the nations would become people of God. James, after hearing the report of Barnabas and Paul, understood this and announced it in the Jerusalem council: "My brothers, listen to me. Simeon has related how God first looked favorably on the Gentiles, to take from among them a people for his name. This agrees with the words of the prophets, as it is written,

'After this I will return,
and I will rebuild the dwelling of David,
which has fallen;

from its ruins I will rebuild it,
and I will set it up,
so that all other peoples may seek the
Lord—
even all the Gentiles over whom my
name has been called.
Thus says the Lord, who has been
making these things known from long
ago.'" (Acts 15:16–17)

James spoke under the inspiration of the Spirit and used the Scripture, indeed the very translation, that the Spirit desired. This is not infrequently done in the New Testament. We need not hesitate to accept his statement as prophetic, just because the Masoretic Text has a slightly different vocalization. The Masoretic Text is a good reflection of the original; what it says is true and had specific meaning for its people in its time. The Spirit, in his function as interpreter of the Old Testament, made use of a variant translation. And what he has said through James in fact only expands what appeared in the original words of Amos. Thus, Edom is a metonymy for Adam—for it is not only a remnant of Edom who will be saved, but a remnant of all humankind. The prophet said that a remnant would have the Lord's

a military conquest in 2 Samuel 12:28: Joab, upon capturing the royal citadel of Rabbah of the Ammonites, sends to David and implores, "Now, then, gather the rest of the people together, and encamp against the city, and take it; or I myself will take the city, and it will be called by my name [lit. my name will be pronounced over it]." The phrase normally appears, however, in the context of covenant and covenant lawsuit and is used to denote Yahweh's ownership of his covenant people (e.g., Deut. 28:10; Jer. 14:9; of Jeremiah himself in 15:16), of Jerusalem (Jer. 25:29; Dan. 9:18), and of the temple (e.g., 1 Kings 8:43; Jer. 7:10–11, 14, 30). The implication of the present statement is that the nations will not simply come under Israelite hegemony (as before), but that they will actually become one with God's people. We see this intention realized in James' declaration in Acts 15:17. נְאֻם־יְהוָה (oracle of Yahweh): See the Exegesis of 2:11. עֹשֶׂה זֹּאת (who performs this): The participle also occurs in 4:13 and 5:8; as before, the participial phrase is a divine title or epithet. Its purpose is to confirm that Yahweh is able to perform and is in the process of performing what he has promised.

13. הִנֵּה יָמִים בָּאִים (even now, days are coming): See the Exegesis of 4:2. נְאֻם יְהוָה (oracle of Yah-

weh): See the Exegesis of 2:11. וְנִגַּשׁ (shall overtake) does double duty, with both plowman and grape-treader as subjects. חוֹרֵשׁ (the plowman) occurs also in Isaiah 28:24. קֹצֵר (the harvester) occurs also in Ruth 2:3–7; 2 Kings 4:18; Jeremiah 9:21 [22]. עֲנָבִים וְדֹרֵךְ (the grape-treader) is a *hapax legomenon*, the more common expression being "to tread the wine press(es)" (Neh. 13:15; Job 24:11; Isa. 63:2; see also "to tread wine" in Isa. 16:10 and Judg. 9:27, direct object omitted). מֹשֵׁךְ הַזָּרַע (the seed-sower; lit. the drawer-out of seed) is a *hapax legomenon* (but compare the almost identical מֶשֶׁךְ־הַזָּרַע, the seed for sowing; lit. a drawing out of seed, in Ps. 126:6). The verb is used elsewhere of drawing the bow (e.g., 1 Kings 22:34; Isa. 66:19) or of drawing someone from one place to another (e.g., Ps. 10:9; Song of Sol. 1:4; Jer. 31:3). Here, it describes the sower who draws seed out of his seed bag, to scatter it abroad. The promise is one of superabundance, and echoes the original covenant promise that Yahweh made to his people: "Your threshing shall overtake the vintage, and the vintage shall overtake the sowing" (Lev. 26:5). Amos substitutes planters, harvesters, and treaders for the planting, harvesting, and (implicit) treading. הִטִּיפוּ (shall trickle; lit. drip): The verb נָטַף (hiphil) is normally used in a figurative sense for

---

name pronounced over them. And indeed we have, for since the days of Paul's stay at Antioch, those who belong to the Lord Christ have been called Christians (Acts 11:26; cf. 26:28; 1 Pet. 4:16).

But the accomplishment of our salvation is not the end of the story. We long and work for the day when every knee shall bow and every tongue confess that Jesus Christ is Lord, to the glory of God the Father. We desire and pray for the day of his appearing, when he will separate the wheat from the chaff, the sheep from the goats. And as we long for these things, let us long also to be like Jesus—and this will mean also doing those same "signs and wonders" that confirmed the word of salvation to those Gentiles. For Jesus said, "The one who believes in me will also do the works that I do" (John 14:12).

13. The Lord had made strong and lovely promises of prosperity in his original covenant with his people: "If you follow my statutes and keep my commandments and observe them faithfully, I will give you your rains in their season, and the land shall yield its produce, and the trees of the field shall yield their fruit. Your threshing shall overtake the vintage, and the vintage shall over-

take the sowing; you shall eat your bread to the full, and live securely in your land" (Lev. 26:3–5). Such prosperity, however, depended upon their obedience to his commands. Because of disobedience, Israel would experience futility with her crops and vineyards:

> And they will call the farm laborer to
> mourning,
> and [they will call], "Wailing!" to the
> professional mourners.
> And in all the vineyards there will be wail-
> ing,
> for I will pass through your midst,
> says the LORD. (Amos 5:16–17)

But in compassion the Lord would turn and have mercy on the righteous remnant of his people. In hyperbolic language, he expresses the abundance that would overtake them when he returned them to their land. The plower would overtake the reaper—so quickly would the crops sprout up! The grape-treader would overtake the sower, in a cycle of never-ending fecundity.

But even this language is inadequate to express the antitype of which this is only the type, for

prophetic utterance, as in 7:16; only here is it used in a literal sense (i.e., dripping). In the qal it also signifies dripping, either literal ("the clouds indeed poured water," Judg. 5:4) or figurative ("the lips of a loose woman drip honey," Prov. 5:3). It appears in the same figure as here in Joel 4:18 [3:18] (qal): "In that day, / the mountains shall drip sweet wine, / the hills shall flow with milk." The mention of milk in Joel probably harks back to the promise of a land "flowing with milk and honey" in the original covenant documents (e.g., Exod. 3:8). עָסִיס (new wine) also occurs in Isaiah 49:26. The Septuagint has οἶνος νέος in the Isaiah passage, but γλυκασμός here and in the parallel Joel 4:18 [3:18]. New or sweet wine was apparently a sort of grape juice pressed out (cf. the root עָסַס, to press or crush) from the grapes, but not allowed fully to ferment. תִּתְמוֹגַגְנָה (shall flow; lit. melt): The verb מוּג (hithpoel) is used of mountains melting before the Lord (Nah. 1:5), or of people's souls (NIV courage) melting in terror (Ps. 107:26; see also Josh. 2:9, 24, niphal). Here, it is used hyperbolically of the hills dissolving under the flow of new wine down their sides.

14. וְשַׁבְתִּי אֶת־שְׁבוּת (and I will restore [my people Israel] from captivity; lit. restore, return, or turn the captivity): This is a stock phrase in covenant-lawsuit literature (e.g., Jer. 29:14; 30:3; Ezek. 16:53; Hos. 6:11; Joel 4:1 [3:1]; Zeph. 3:20), rooted in the original covenant material (Deut. 30:3). Some have argued for a translation of "turn the fortune," "turn the turning," or "reverse the reversal" (see the discussion in Driver, *Joel and Amos*, p. 230), which is sometimes no doubt

appropriate (e.g., Job 42:10). But the idiom as used in the covenant-lawsuit tradition normally denotes a return from exile. Nor does the sequence in which the verse stands argue against this interpretation, as Keil maintains ("for Israel cannot be brought back out of captivity *after* it has already taken possession of the Gentiles [ver. 12]"; *Twelve Minor Prophets*, p. 335). Time sequence was not strictly observed in Israelite or other ancient Near Eastern documents. עַמִּי יִשְׂרָאֵל (my people Israel) also occurs in 7:8. וְשָׁמֹות וְיָשָׁבוּ וּבָנוּ עָרִים (and they shall rebuild the devastated cities and inhabit them): Compare Isaiah 54:3 ("your descendants . . . will settle the desolate towns") and Ezekiel 36:35 ("the waste and desolate and ruined towns are now inhabited and fortified"). This promise represents a reversal of the earlier judgment: "Houses of dressed stone you have built, / but you will not live in them" (5:11), which in turn harks back to the original curse of Deuteronomy 28:30. Sadly and ironically, Yahweh had commanded the exiles in Babylon to "build houses and live in them, and plant gardens and eat what they produce" (Jer. 29:5, 28) because the exile would be lengthy. וְנָטְעוּ כְרָמִים וְשָׁתוּ אֶת־יֵינָם (and you shall plant vineyards and drink their wine): Compare Isaiah 65:21 ("they shall plant vineyards and eat their fruit"), Jeremiah 31:5 ("again you shall plant vineyards on the mountains of Samaria; / the planters shall plant, and shall enjoy the fruit"), and Ezekiel 28:26 ("they shall live in safety in it, and shall build houses and plant vineyards"). This promise also constitutes a reversal of the earlier judgment, "pleasant vine-

---

there will be a messianic banquet (Isa. 25:6–9; Matt. 8:11; 22:4) with a fruitfulness and peace that we cannot imagine, but that is included in the prophecy:

What no eye has seen, nor ear heard,
    nor the human heart conceived,
what God has prepared for those who love
    him. (1 Cor. 2:9)

14. This verse begins with a promise of restoration from exile and continues with three blessings of the form, "They shall do so-and-so . . . and enjoy the results." This is, therefore, the opposite of the futility curse. These promises herald a complete reversal of the people's fortunes. Formerly, they had suffered futility curses as a result of their transgressions: They built cities, but others destroyed them; they planted vineyards, but oth-

ers drank their wine; they planted gardens, but others ate their fruit. Now, however, the Lord would have compassion on his people and bless them: They would rebuild the desolate cities, and inhabit them; they would plant vineyards, and drink their wine; they would make gardens, and eat their fruit.

This manifold blessing, so similar to others that we find in the prophets (e.g., Isa. 65:21–22; Jer. 29:5, 28; Ezek. 28:26), not only expresses the Lord's desire to restore his people. It also anticipates the ultimate restoration, when the plantation in the city of God will bear fruit monthly for the healing of the nations and there will be no more curse (Rev. 22:1–3). Our citizenship is in this city, and we look forward to it with joy. But let God's people rejoice this very day in the Lord who has compassion on our weaknesses and forgives

yards you have planted, / but you will not drink their wine" (5:11), which also echoes the original covenantal curse (Deut. 28:30, 39). וְאָכְלוּ אֶת־פְּרִיהֶם וְעָשׂוּ גַנּוֹת (and they shall make gardens and eat their fruit): Compare again, ironically, Jeremiah 29:5, 28. The promise here is a reversal of the earlier judgment: "The multitude of your gardens and vineyards / and fig trees and olive trees the locust would devour" (4:9).

15. וּנְטַעְתִּים עַל־אַדְמָתָם וְלֹא יִנָּתְשׁוּ עוֹד מֵעַל אַדְמָתָם (and I will plant them upon their land, and they shall never again be uprooted from their land): The original form of the promise is in 2 Samuel 7:10 ("and I will appoint a place for my people Israel and will plant them, so that they may live in their own place, and be disturbed no more"); also compare Jeremiah 24:6 ("I will plant them, and not pluck them up"); 32:41 ("I will rejoice in doing good to them, and I will plant them in this land [בָּאָרֶץ הַזֹּאת] in faithfulness, with all my heart and all my soul); 42:10 ("I will plant you, and not pluck you up"). אֲשֶׁר נָתַתִּי לָהֶם (which I have given to them): The phrase harks back to original covenantal terminology: "The land [הָאָרֶץ] that I have given them" (Num. 20:12; also in 20:24; 27:12). It reappears in the history of prophecy: "I will cut Israel off from the land that I have given them" (1 Kings 9:7) and "I will send sword, famine, and pestilence upon them, until they are utterly destroyed from the land that I gave to them and their ancestors" (Jer. 24:10; see also Ezek. 28:25). אָמַר יְהוָה (says Yahweh): See the Exegesis of 1:5. אֱלֹהֶיךָ (your God) also occurs at 4:12 and, ironically, at 8:14). יְהוָה אֱלֹהֶיךָ (variously with the singular or plural suffix) appears first in Genesis 27:20 and then, subsequently, often in the covenantal documents (e.g., Exod. 8:24; Lev. 11:44; Num. 10:9; Deut. 1:10). Against the covenantal background it is reassuring: the same Yahweh who graciously married them in covenant will now restore them after they have been disciplined for their adultery.

---

our sins, who has come to bind up the brokenhearted and to set the captives free.

15. Not only will a restored Israel plant vineyards, but the Lord will himself plant the people upon their land and will never uproot them again. The phraseology echoes the original covenantal documents. The land that he gave them in the days of Moses and Joshua, he will now give them again. And this time it will not be taken away, or rather, they will not be taken away from it. He uses the ancient covenantal title to redouble the reassurance: he is "the LORD your God," the same one who entered into covenant with Abraham and with the children of Abraham. He is the mighty one, and he will do it.

This promise was not fulfilled after the exile, however, since the Jewish rejection of Christ brought about yet another exile, which has only recently been ended by the creation of the modern Israeli state. But even the present form of the nation Israel does not fulfill the prophecy, although it anticipates its fulfilment. Israel is still in spiritual exile from her Lord and will be until its blindness is removed (2 Cor. 3:13–15). We eagerly anticipate that removal. For, as Paul says, "If their rejection is the reconciliation of the world, what will their acceptance be but life from the dead!" (Rom. 11:15). The dry bones have been revived and given flesh. We now await the inbreathing of the Spirit. Even so, come, Lord Jesus!

Scripture Index

Genesis

1:1—480
1:11—451
2:7—123, 372, 465
2:7-8—407
2:8—343
2:10—267, 312
2:17—95
2:20—20
2:19—407
2:21-22—463
2:24—366
2:25—373
3:1-6—361
3:5—233
3:10—275
3:14—40, 338
3:17—157
3:18—170
3:19—461
4:1—375
4:3-5—431
4:4—133
4:9—375
4:10—313
4:17—20
4:19—13
4:23—254
5:8—40
5:24—463
6:4—372
6:5—66
6:8—205
6:13—181, 447
6:18—369, 411
7:11—454
8:1—286
8:13—289, 457
8:20—431
9:6—340, 354
9:9—95
9:11—411
9:15—101, 322
10:6—486
10:8-10—372
10:10—436
10:23—343
11:9—97
12:1-7—192
12:3—29, 48, 375
12:7—195
13:3-4—414
13:15—29
14:5—447

14:8—275
14:16—166
14:20—191
14:23—472
15:7—322, 369
15:12—474
15:16—368
15:17—275, 474
16:5—189
16:13—201
17:7—369, 411
17:7-8—27, 29, 150
17:8—120
17:9-14—345
17:13—29
17:19—29
17:21—369
17:22—137
18:3—205
18:6—108
18:12—392
18:17—327, 380
18:25—326, 359
19:2—91
19:24—342
19:25—191, 402
19:30-38—354, 358
20:3—13, 145, 261
20:5—125
20:6—76
20:7—327, 370, 380
21:1—20
21:21—14
21:27—95
21:31-33—414
21:32—95
22:1—447
22:16—380
22:5—53
22:7—447
22:8—150
22:10—105
22:11—447
22:12—161
22:17—29, 30
22:17-18—29
22:20-24—343
22:22-23—254
24:15-50—254
24:67—13
25:22—414
25:22-23—351
25:23—351
25:23-26—345
25:26—201

25:27—425
26:3—411
26:18—192, 269
26:22—32
26:23-25—415
26:28-29—95
27:15—452
27:20—322, 494
27:36—201
27:39-40—351
27:41—145, 348, 351
27:42—452
27:43—210, 461
27:44—53
27:46—428
28:10-22—202, 414
28:12—202
28:14—57, 375, 465
28:18—53
28:22—53
29:13—111
29:18—210
29:19—53
29:20—210
29:21—261
29:30—154
29:31—154
30:28—436
30:30—57
30:31—202, 210
30:37—66
30:41—174
31:13—414
31:20—128
31:40-41—210
31:44-54—341
31:45—160
32:8—166
32:8-12—351
32:13 [12]—29
32:14-16 [13-15]—431
32:22-32—201
32:23-29 [22-28]—409
32:29 [28]—201
34:2—13
34:3—42
34:9—13
34:13—197
34:19—92
35:1—202
35:1-14—414
35:6—202
35:7—202
35:9-12—388
35:15—202

35:20—160
36:9—351
36:11—351
36:15—351
36:33—352
36:43—351
37:34—261
38:2—13
38:9—451
38:24—464
38:25—460
38:29—57
40:10—309
41:28—450
41:50—343
41:52—226
41:56—322, 470
42:15-16—477
42:18—414
42:21—201
43:11—129, 431
43:14—152
43:30—191
44:21—481
45:9—172
45:26—191
46:1-5—415
46:20—343
46:27—388
46:29—50
46:33—184
47:18—465
47:19—174
47:20—465
47:22-23—465
47:26—465
47:30—444
48:4—29
48:5—226
48:14—105
48:15-16—226
48:16—226
48:19—226
49:1—54
49:3—201
49:9—259
49:23—145
50:11—342
50:13—444
50:15—145
50:24—322
50:24-25—20
50:25—444

Scripture Index